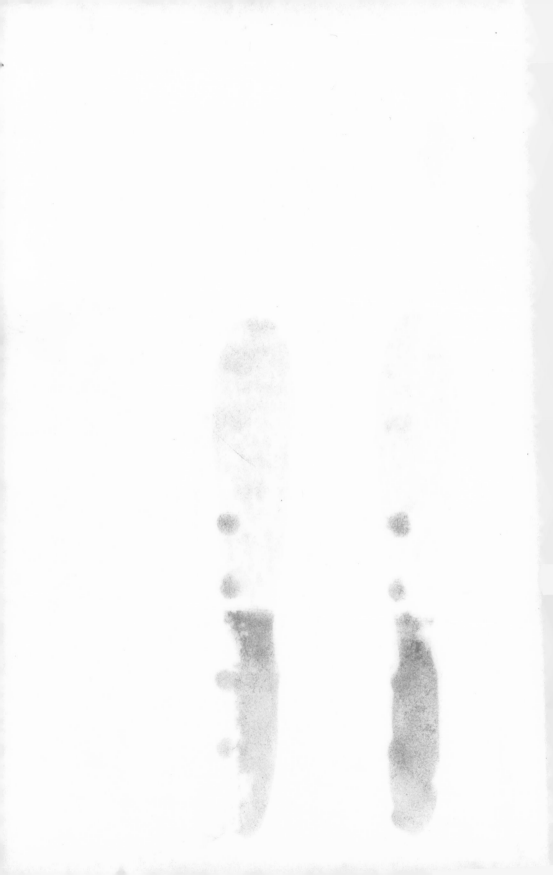

BRITANNICA
BOOK OF
ENGLISH USAGE

Britannica Books

executive editor   Benjamin Hadley

Encyclopædia Britannica, Inc.

chairman of the board   Robert P. Gwinn
president   Charles E. Swanson

Britannica Books

BRITANNICA BOOK OF ENGLISH USAGE

edited by
Christine Timmons
and
Frank Gibney

DOUBLEDAY/BRITANNICA BOOKS
DOUBLEDAY & COMPANY, INC.
GARDEN CITY, NEW YORK
1980

Library of Congress Cataloging in Publication Data
Main entry under title:

Britannica book of English usage.

 (Britannica books)
 Articles reprinted from the Encyclopaedia Britannica,
with additional contributions by various authors.
 Bibliography: p.
 Includes index
 1. English language—Collected work. I. Timmons,
Christine. II. Gibney, Frank, 1924–   III. Encyclopaedia
Britannica. IV. Title: Book of English usage.
PE25.B7   428.2

ISBN: 0-385-14193-9
Library of Congress Catalog Card Number 79-7706

staff for *Britannica Book of English Usage*

editors	Christine Timmons
	Frank Gibney
assistant editor	John Morse
contributing editor	Barbara Shwom
editorial assistant	Mary Hunt
copy editors	Cynthia Susan Ashby
	Mary Peterson Berry
	Shantha Channabasappa
	Karl Keller
	Coleen Withgott
index	Frances E. Latham

Contributors

JOHN ALGEO. Editor, *American Speech,* Journal of the American Dialect Society. Professor of English, University of Georgia, Athens. Author of *Exercises in Contemporary English; Problems in the Origins and Development of the English Language;* and others.

JACQUES BARZUN. Member of the Board of Editors, *Encyclopædia Britannica.* Historian, educator, and author of *Of Human Freedom; On Writing, Editing, and Publishing; Simple & Direct;* and others.

LOIS DE BAKEY. Professor of Scientific Communication, Baylor College of Medicine, Houston, Texas; and Tulane University School of Medicine, New Orleans, Louisiana. Editor, author of *The Scientific Journal: Editorial Policies and Practices,* and contributor to numerous publications of articles on language and communication.

CLIFTON FADIMAN. Member of the Board of Editors, *Encyclopædia Britannica.* Member of the Selecting Committee, Book-of-the-Month Club. Editorial Advisory Board, *Cricket Magazine.* Essayist and author of *Empty Pages: A Search for Writing Competency in School and Society* (with James Howard); *The Lifetime Reading Plan;* and others.

FRANK GIBNEY. Vice-Chairman of the Board of Editors, *Encyclopædia Britannica.* Author of *Five Gentlemen of Japan; Japan: The Fragile Superpower; The Operators;* and others.

RAVEN I. MC DAVID, JR. Professor Emeritus of English and Linguistics, University of Chicago. Director, Linguistic Atlas of the U.S. and Canada. Editor, H. L. Mencken's *The American Language,* one-volume abridged edition, and author of *Dialects in Culture; Varieties of American English;* and others.

ARTHUR PLOTNIK. Editor, *American Libraries,* Journal of the American Library Association.

BRUCE THOMAS. Writer, editor, and founding-director of the Center for Illinois Studies.

Contents

Contents

Preface

Despite the *Britannica*'s reputation as a repository of heavy scholarship
(or partly because of it), our editors have given a considerable portion
of their waking hours to producing clear and understandable English
prose and encouraging the tendency in others. Some of *Britannica*'s
finest articles over the years have been devoted to explaining how and
why the language works. From the first 18th-century article on the
involutions of "Philosophic Grammar"—through classics in the 11th
edition like Sir James Murray's discussion of English language origins—
to notes on the new linguistics in the 15th edition, we have tried to
explain the reason and the rubrics governing the use of our English
tongue. Now in the *Britannica Book of English Usage* we have taken
the more obvious role of teacher. We offer here what we hope will be an
authoritative, accessible, and usable one-volume handbook on how
any consenting American adult can live with his language and enjoy it
with style.

Only a portion of this book consists of *Britannica* excerpts. These
have been heavily cut and trimmed to fit a one-volume work. The
greater part comprises advice and information over the spectrum of
English language subjects, from good style to good spelling. Fittingly,
since this has often been a subject at periodic deliberations of the Britannica Board of Editors, several board members have made contributions. Other writings include those of contributors to the *Britannica* and
scholars who have gained wide recognition in their fields. The impulse
behind them all is the desire to encourage the wide use of good English.
It is a commodity all too often lacking in our daily lives, or at least in
scant supply.

Whether they begin at the beginning, the middle, or the end—or use
the book only as a reference—we feel that most readers will either learn
something they did not know or confirm knowledge of which they were

uncertain. Although written largely by scholars, this is not a scholar's book. It is, by design, a comprehensive, how-to-do-it exercise in how to achieve clarity, style, and forcefulness in contemporary communication.

Frank Gibney, Vice-Chairman
Board of Editors
Encyclopædia Britannica

BRITANNICA
BOOK OF
ENGLISH USAGE

PART I

ENGLISH TODAY
AND HOW IT EVOLVED

CONTEMPORARY ENGLISH

English for the Eighties
English Today: Are We Speaking in Tongues?
Slang
Aspects of Linguistic Change

English for the Eighties

At a time when technology almost daily intensifies the flooding of words and images on an already well-inundated public, it is ironic that one of our most pressing national concerns is how to speak, read, and write English. The greatest problem in the schools, we are told, is that students do not learn how to communicate their own thoughts clearly or to understand what others are saying to them. Congress appropriates funds for back-to-basics programs in the high schools, and college deans cringe at the number of students who must master the rudiments of sentence construction before they can hope to move on to a critical study of Hemingway, not to mention Chaucer or Milton. Children's television programs are widely praised today for teaching basic reading and writing skills, but we easily forget that only two generations ago their radio counterparts, confident of their young audience's basic literacy, were recommending good books to read. Businesses advertise wistfully for employees—and executives—who can write and think clearly. One suspects that the long-extinct professional scribe may yet again appear in offices and factories. In government the turgid prose of bureaucrats has become ground cover for ineptness of expression and foggy thinking. In the arts the contemporary tendency is toward oversimplification of expression in an effort to reach the widest possible audience.

How many of us today are grounded confidently enough in our own language to enjoy the works of Shakespeare? To read Fitzgerald or Lawrence, Melville or Thoreau without impatience? To grasp fully the turns of phrase in Churchill's speeches? The current use of poor English transcends age, race, social position, and education. A commonplace of our time, in fact, is the college graduate who enters the professional world unable to write a coherent paragraph.

The irony is doubled when we realize that English has now become an international language. It is estimated that 75 percent of all the technical and scientific literature in the world is written, or at least circulated, in English. Already the native tongue of 185 million Americans; 14 million Canadians; 55 million English, Irish, Welsh, and Scots; and 13.5 million Australians and New Zealanders, English has become the second language of tens of millions more throughout the world. The *Encyclopædia Britannica*'s latest article on the English language notes that one-seventh of the world's population now speaks English, whether as a native, second, or indispensable professional language. The only comparable cases in history of such wide linguistic domination were the spread of Greek under Alexander, the Latinization of Europe and the Mediterranean in Roman times, and the Sinicization of the Far East under T'ang Dynasty China. Thus the editors of the first edition of the *Britannica* were more prophetic than they realized when they wrote in 1770 that English had become "the most copious, significant, fluent, courteous, and masculine language in Europe, if not in the world."

How paradoxical it is that at the center of this worldwide linguistic realm stands the inarticulate American, his speech a mix of canned phrases and slang, awash with breathless parentheses punctuated by repetitions and obscenities. The ability to use language well threatens to become a memory among us. Yet to speak gracefully but with force, persuasively but with dignity, precisely but with wit is as desirable and necessary in the world of the '80s as it was in past decades. Now, however, developing skill with the language demands a greater effort than before. In an era flash-lit by the television screen, it has become progressively easier to see and hear, harder to read and speak. With our language now dominated by the advertising slogan, the bureaucratic memo, and the political cliché, we are increasingly seduced into mimicking the packaged expressions of others rather than tackling the difficult task of thinking something through and articulating what we think.

In this book the editors of the *Britannica* have sought to address this problem and to help redress some of our current national failings in English. The *Britannica Book of English Usage* is a guide to English in the '80s. It is not, however, a textbook. Nor was it planned as a primer for schools, although we hope that English scholars in high school and college will find it a useful supplement to their studies. We have nonetheless included much of what are called "basics," precisely because these basics are so often forgotten or never learned. It is by mastery of these basics that we avail ourselves of the richness and variety of the language.

Among the basics included in this book are the fundamentals of English grammar. Language usage can change with deceptive rapidity, but certain basic rubrics continue to hold true. We have therefore provided contemporary guidelines on the language but have not been reluctant to point out, where appropriate, the prescribed usages of modern American English. We have been latitudinarian about such prescriptions, acknowledging that usage is often an arbitrary matter and that language is in large part change canonized by custom. Boundaries in English are difficult to define.

In this volume we have also dealt with matters of style as well as substance, since the form of expression is sometimes as important as the content. If style, grace, and forcefulness did not matter, we might already be talking solely by computer with little need for human mediation. Nor have we neglected, among other concerns, such helpful matters as how to use the library to best advantage and compose a good letter. We have also included some of the *Britannica*'s classic writings on language, ranging from that on the early history of English to articles on slang and rhetoric. These selections have been edited, where necessary, to fit the confines of a single volume.

If our exhortations to the reader could be summarized in a phrase, it would be, with apologies to St. Paul: "and of all these, the greatest is clarity." Clarity is language's most obvious and elusive virtue. Without clarity of expression, all attempts at style, persuasion, or humor fail. Generally, thoughts are said best and most clearly when said simply. The ornate and complex have their place in language but must be used with care if they are to be effective. Our literature, for example, may be elevated by the emotional power of Keats or Hopkins, the dark profundities of Eliot or Pound, the complicated intellectual imageries of Crashaw or Herbert. But no poetry strikes the heart so quickly as the simple vocabulary and plain speech of Blake's *Songs of Innocence* and *Songs of Experience;* Lincoln's farewell speech in Springfield before assuming the presidency; or, for that matter, Edward R. Murrow's descriptions of the London blitz. If we learn the art of simple expression well, the complex will follow naturally. But even the most complicated syntax will collapse of its own weight if its meaning is unclear.

In seeking to promote clarity in language, we face the formidable opposition provided by the circumlocution, euphemism, and jargon that are so prevalent in our language today. We confront the modern legalist burying the simplest information in complex codification; we struggle to comprehend the elaborate, arcane terminologies of the various professions; and we seem increasingly driven to sugarcoat unpleasant thoughts and realities with euphemistic expression. In his book *Enemies of Society,* Paul Johnson refers to the "linguistics of happiness" in which, for example, old people have become *senior citizens,* the poor *underprivileged* or *disadvantaged,* and jail a *correctional facility.* In short, language now often serves less to convey thought than to conceal or manipulate it.

To a degree this has always been true. Yet modern society seems oddly vulnerable to the wiles or confusions of language. Not only are we more exposed than ever to the devices of organized persuasion, but we are perhaps less schooled than earlier generations in language's basic disciplines. Nonetheless, in the arts, in business, in education, and in our ordinary social life, the ability to use language well remains the best index of how clearly we think. Clarity in one can hardly be developed without clarity in the other.

FRANK GIBNEY

English Today: Are We Speaking in Tongues?

Are you speaking more and saying less? Hearing more and understanding less? If so, you are not alone. Most of us are immersed in a sea of words, often wanting in substance and clarity. Our eyes and ears are constantly assaulted by a barrage of information—much of which we neither need nor want—from newspapers, magazines, books, letters, memoranda, reports, billboards, signs, radio, television, telephones, and conversations. Undoubtedly encouraged by the verbal incontinence of the "freedom of expression" movement of the 1960s and '70s, we seem inclined now more than ever to loosen our tongues without engaging our minds.

Much contemporary language is inflated, but the "educated" seem to have a special affinity for verbal intemperance. This intemperance, known variously as *doublespeak, newspeak, educationese, journalese, medicalese, legalese, governmentese, Pentagonese,* or more generally as *gobbledygook,* is manifested in a welter of words whose meaning is absent, sparse, or virtually inextricable. At its worst gobbledygook is an impenetrable language characterized by big words, serpentine phrases, prefabricated expressions, grammatical infractions, convoluted syntax, and plain illogic. In short—fuzzy thought expressed in fuzzy language. Because we are largely mimics in our use of language, the affliction is highly contagious, passing freely from teacher to student, speaker to listener, and writer to reader.

The models for abusage abound—often emanating from well-known and influential sources. Because of its prevalence, trite, clumsy, tentative, and evasive language molds our daily speech more than the occasional eloquence we may hear or read. Shortly after the President declares that "regulations should be as simple and clear as possible," he signs this arcane order: "Expedited adjustment assistance would be ineffective in helping the [CB] industry cope with current problems of severe inventory overhang, low prices and financial losses." The same President also praises our legislators effusively for having "a high degree

9

of concentrated experience" and on another occasion solemnly exhorts Congress not to *Balkanize* the nation, but to *retrofit* and *weatherize* with *geothermal* energy and to use *peak-load pricing, cogeneration, wellhead* and *sliding-scale taxes,* and *intangible tax credits,* but no *fast-breeder reactors* (all italics mine). A House majority leader has this to say about further investigations of the Kennedy assassinations: "I think there has to be a demonstration that this isn't going to be a broad, free-wheeling, headline-grabbing attempt to splurge and send investigators willy-nilly like the headless horseman in all directions, like a fishing expedition costing $6.5 million."

Although politicians and bureaucrats are among the worst offenders, they are certainly not alone in their verbal ineptitude. During an interview the author of a book on cloning says: "Medical science stands on the verge of a huge gap they're about to fall into." A television personality reminisces: "Having been born and raised in Houston as well as Bellaire, I know the city well." A highly popular television actor displays this enigmatic reasoning when accepting an honorary degree from his alma mater: "The fact is . . . that I'm a somebody because millions of nobodies like what I do; ergo, the logic follows, I don't exist. . . ." In a television discussion of a "marriage encounter weekend," a lady explains that "George and I having been *encountered* for two years, our children are more sensitive." A college administrator issues this inanity: "For a physician to maintain a depth of knowledge of his intellectual base, it requires at the present time a commitment on the part of the individual and a nonexistent commitment on the part of the medical educational system. . . ." And a psychologist equivocates: "You have to give children the will and the desire to achieve— to be a full person, more or less, in a manner of speaking."

Nor are those who report the news always paragons of reason and rhetoric. A network television anchorman responds thus to an interviewer: "I enjoy the C. S. Forester *kind of stuff* . . . and there are 10,000 imitators of Horatio Hornblower who *kind of keep me going.* . . . I like sitting in the cockpit of my boat, . . . gazing at the stars, thinking of the *enormity,* the universality of it all." A television news reporter, describing a Lutheran church in a small German-speaking community, says: "Although this is not the same church that was built in 1852, the congregation is the same." Reporting the rescue of a cat, a newscaster philosophizes: "Some people consider any *life* to be important, no matter how *small.*" A weatherman notes: "The *weather* associated with this storm has *diminished.*" *The New York Times* refers to a "lifelong native of New York" and to a victim who had been "shot fatally three times." And another newspaper article states that a controversial legal issue before the U.S. Supreme Court "generated six separate opinions from the nine *badly divided justices.*"

Even those who do not listen to politicians or talk shows and do not read the newspapers are still exposed daily to much faulty language in advertisements and in popular songs broadcast on radio and television. Although we may not consciously pay attention to either advertising copy or song lyrics, their subtle power is evident in our easy recall of certain advertising slogans (the nonstandard "Winston tastes good *like* a cigarette should") and song lyrics (the substandard "It ain't necessarily so," "I can't get no satisfaction," or "That ain't no way to treat a lady"). Much advertising is verbally reckless ("We offer a new way to kill bugs in two convenient sizes"; "I have been favorably impressed with the validity of the car"). And many popular song lyrics are not only inane ("That's the way, uh-huh, uh-huh, I like it, uh-huh, uh-huh . . ."), but plainly solecistic ("You never done it like that," "I am so into you, I can't think of nothing else").

Diagnosing the linguistic ills

Now that we have seen some examples of ineffectual use of language, let us try to identify the causes. Why do educated people sometimes speak and write in a swollen, virtually incomprehensible tongue? Some do so to appear learned, others to mask vapidity, and still others to avoid being challenged. If a speaker utters a succession of long, obscure words, few will risk exposing their "ignorance" by asking the speaker what those words mean. Still others may have no real desire to deceive but, in emulating their mentors and peers, innocently fall into pretentious language.

Much convoluted speech results from our failure to think about what we are saying. Murky words are usually rooted in murky thinking. If we want to speak clearly, we must discipline ourselves first to think clearly and then to translate our thoughts into precise language. Toward that end, keeping our minds in gear and steering our thoughts on a straight course will help.

MALAPROPISMS   When we are not as familiar as we should be with the words and phrases we use, we may utter a malapropism*—a word that sounds somewhat like the intended word but is far afield in meaning. Many people, for example, say *noisome* when they mean noisy, *fulsome* when they mean full, and *restive* when they mean restless. A United Nations communication refers to "support for the *depraved* people" of a certain territory. A movie aficionado thinks a mystery show was a real *cliff-dweller*. An educator speaks of the dangers of a *scattering* of

---

*The word is derived from the famous Mrs. Malaprop, the verbal blunderer of Richard Brinsley Sheridan's 18th-century play *The Rivals*.

knowledge; another refers to the *heart-rendering* experience of failing; and still another tells new junior high school students on orientation day: "You are entering one of the most important *phrases* of your lives."

With the proliferation of talk shows on radio and television, malapropisms are multiplying. A few examples culled from talk-show conversations: Don't *get your gander up*. Our *study* is now *under foot*. Off the *top of my hat*, I'd say yes. It's time to *fish and cut bait*. He's off on a *sour foot*. It's worse than the *blue bonnet plague*. That's like taking *colds* to Newcastle. It's a *mute* question. That is my *candied opinion*. I got up at the *crank of dawn*. That's a *pigment* of your imagination. Obviously those verbal offenders had only heard the expressions and had never seen the words in print. The remedy is to use not only the ear but also the brain and a good, modern dictionary. We should look up unfamiliar words and understand their meanings in context before using them ourselves.

INEPT METAPHORS   Closely related to the malapropism is the mixed metaphor, a figure of speech comprising incongruous images, as in: "When they lower the *ax,* it makes you *gun-shy*." A candidate for a municipal office accuses his opponent of *drinking like a fish out of water*. An official, commenting on suspected arson, says: "The *fire* was *cold-blooded* murder." Such inept metaphors ensue from failure to coordinate tongue and brain.

VERBIAGE   One way of improving our speech and writing is to learn to spot, and then promptly reject, certain expressions that occupy space or produce noise without contributing much to meaning: jargon, clichés, euphemisms, vogue words, redundancies, circumlocution, and similar verbiage. Such language, by its overuse and imprecision, is not only inelegant but also perilous, leading as it often does to ambiguity, confusion, or misinterpretation. Because the language to which we are daily exposed is filled with these expressions, they come unbidden to mind, and purging them from our vocabularies requires special effort.

JARGON   The pseudo-educated often flaunt their "erudition" by using pretentious words for simple ideas. Certain phrases seem designed more to conceal than to reveal: *compatible incremental reciprocal capability, synchronized logistical options, systematized third-generation contingency*. Bureaucrats do not start a project; they *operationalize*. They *requisition,* rather than buy or order. In bureaucratese planting trees is *institutionally motivated reforestation*. In the sociologist's lexicon the family is a *microcluster of structured role expectations* or a *bounded plurality of role-playing individuals*.

Each profession has its specialized vocabulary that excludes and awes the uninitiated. Physicians, lawyers, sociologists, economists, politicians, bureaucrats, and others establish for themselves a safe distance from challenge by the ponderous trappings of jargon—high-flown, obscure terms. Indoctrinated in the drab, platitudinous style of their mentors, most professional people are reluctant not to conform. For the fledgling, learning to use the formidable expressions heard and read in professional school means fraternity with an elite group. Jargon, while providing an illusion of wisdom and bolstering the speaker's sense of importance, may also assuage his conscience for not having conveyed his thoughts cogently.

REDUNDANCY Because English has considerable built-in redundancy, we can understand the essence of a message despite extraneous noises and distractions. The sentence "We are all children of God," for example, contains not one, but four signals of plurality—in the subject, the verb, the adjective, and the complement. When we impose further redundancy, we unduly stretch our language and thus use it inefficiently. *The New York Times,* regarded by many as a paragon of journalistic prose, prints such redundancies as *alleged suspect* and *falsely padded expense accounts.* A former President proclaims that inflation is "the *universal* enemy of *100 percent* of the American people." A politician announces that voting for a certain piece of legislation would amount to *self-inflicted political suicide.* And the purpose of one social agency, according to its director, is *to prevent suicides before they happen.* Other redundancies have now become clichés: *abruptly and suddenly, audible to the ears, basic fundamental essentials, circular in shape, combine together, completely unanimous, consensus of opinion, each and every, entirely perfect, exactly the same, few in number, final conclusion, free gifts, green in color, human volunteers, new innovations, obviate the necessity of, one and only, reason was because, reiterate again, small in size, surrounded on all sides, true fact, very unique.*

Advertisements are often deliberately, and outrageously, redundant. The woman on the television screen, for example, tells us that her insecticide "kills bugs dead." Other advertisements are simply repetitive, to ensure that even simpletons get the message. "Iron is important to me," confides the housewife promoting a health tonic, "and what's important to me is really important to me." Repetition can be effective, but only when used with discretion.

CLICHÉS AND CIRCUMLOCUTION Clichés, a major component of inflated language, lull us into inattention. These overly familiar expressions engage the mind of neither the user nor his audience but merely force the listener or reader to traverse unnecessary words. Because so many ideas are constantly vying for our attention, the slightest tedium may divert our minds from the conversation or print at hand. It is, of course, neither possible nor necessary to avoid clichés entirely, but when immoderately used, they deaden our writing and speech. We would do well to delete from our active vocabularies such threadbare expressions as: *all in all, belabor the point, between a rock and a hard place, bite the bullet, the bottom line, conspicuous by its absence, cutting edge, each and every, easier said than done, eyeball to eyeball, fact of life, few and far between, first and foremost, for all intents and purposes, goes without saying, gut feeling, in the final analysis, in terms of, last but not least, sadder but wiser, safe to say, tip of the iceberg, venture the opinion, whole ball of wax.* In language familiarity breeds, if not contempt, at least boredom.

Like clichés, circumlocutory phrases are often fillers—to give the speaker time to think of something to say. Certain prefatory phrases, for example, are semantically inert and merely allow the speaker to temporize or to shore up whatever follows: *It has been demonstrated that, It is generally recognized that, It is interesting* (or *important*) *to note that, It should also be stated that.* Deadwood may also appear in the middle of a sentence. When someone says *appears to be suggestive of the possibility that,* he means only *suggests* but has used seven unnecessary words to say it. *In close proximity to* means *near; in view of the fact that* means *since; has the capability of* means *can; produce an inhibitory effect on* means *inhibit; in short supply* means *scarce; it is the opinion of the author* means *I believe; present a picture similar to* means *resemble; in the majority of cases* means *usually; give consideration to* means *consider;* and *serves the function of being* means *is*—nothing more. In language, as in mathematics, the shortest distance between two points is a straight line; remembering that principle will make our speech and writing not only more direct but more forceful as well.

EUPHEMISMS   Another source of "terminological ponderosity" (to use the jargon in which this abominable phrase is fashioned) is the euphemism—the substitution of a more agreeable, and often more complex, expression for a simpler, more direct word or phrase. Euphemisms have been proliferating wildly since the 1950s. We no longer converse or discuss; we have *substantive, meaningful, viable dialogues.* A recent *New York Times* headline asked, fully seriously: "Will Paris Talks Produce Dialogue?" On the highway a sign announces a low bridge as *impaired vertical clearance.* Our permissive society sometimes uses euphemisms to make past taboos acceptable; *adult movie,* for example, refers to a pornographic film. A common-law marriage is sometimes called a *nonbinding (*or *growth-oriented* or *self-actualizing) relationship.* People used to be lonely; now they *suffer from stimulus impoverishment.* Politicians do not take vacations; they have *nonlegislative* or *district* *work periods.* Criminology and sociology are special provinces of euphemists. Murder may result from an *escalated interpersonal altercation;* jails are *law enforcement centers* or *correctional facilities;* and parole is now known as *community release.* All these euphemisms are longer, and less precise, than the words or terms they replace.

The language of government and of national security agencies is also highly euphemistic. To *terminate with extreme prejudice* means to kill; a *radiation enhancement weapon* is a neutron bomb; *pacification of the enemy infrastructure* means blasting the enemy out of a village; and *impaired combatant personnel* refers to wounded soldiers. A military retreat may be called a *strategic withdrawal,* the result of taking *retrograde action.* A *zero-defect system* ensures success. The State Department attributes its revised body count in the People's Temple tragedy in Guyana to "an administrative undercount." Calling a spade a spade is passé today. Government officials do not lie; they make *inoperative* statements. Wiretapping is *intelligence gathering,* and a burglary is a *surreptitious entry.* The State Department does not fire its employees; rather, they are *selected out.* When a government office purges its files of records that could prove embarrassing, it *de-datafies* the files.

Under the pretext of protecting or enhancing *human rights,* various loose, ambiguous labels have appeared, such as *undocumented worker* (for illegal alien), *disadvantaged* (for poor), *social deprivation* (for juvenile delinquency), and *human resources* (for welfare). Slums have become *substandard housing,* and the elderly live in *senior citizen communities.*

Euphemisms have been applied to certain vocations to enhance their dignity. Today's rat exterminators are *rodent operatives;* garbage collectors are *solid-waste ecologists;* janitors are *custodians;* bus boys are *waiters' assistants;* building superintendents are *maintenance engineers;* hospital maids are *room-care specialists;* window cleaners are *transparent wall maintenance engineers;* and undertakers are *grief therapists.* (When you die, your body may be placed in a *slumber robe* before it is laid to rest in a *memorial park.*) Some euphemisms are designed to make employees feel more important. Instead of desks today's clerical workers have *individual work stations,* and uniforms are now known as *career apparel.* At intervals during the day executives sometimes take time out for *attitude adjustment.*

The language of education is also replete with euphemisms. Students are no longer sent to detention hall; they go to *reality therapy.* They do not attend class but participate in a *classroom learning experience,* where they may see a film on *responsible personhood* (sex education) or be presented with a *media method module* or a *learning activity package.* Students who fail to progress satisfactorily are *underachievers;*

they contribute to the *retention rate* and may be assigned to classes for the *exceptional*. If a student lies, the faculty is instructed to report that he *has difficulty distinguishing between imaginary and factual information;* if he cheats, he *needs help in learning to adhere to rules and standards of fair play*. If he is noisy, he *needs to develop quieter habits of communication*, whereas if he is a bully, he *needs help in learning to use his leadership qualities democratically*. Regardless of the problem, his teacher is expected to practice *mainstreaming* on him.

Since the realities of business are often more palatable when sugar-coated, euphemisms flourish in the world of commerce. Thus, loan firms advertise *convenient terms*, even though a 30 percent annual rate of interest is anything but convenient for those who need the money most. Loans of this kind appeal to *negative savers*, previously known as overspenders. Such extravagant people may be forced to purchase *pre-owned* (secondhand) items. Budget departments, formerly situated in basements, are now housed in *cellars* or the *lower level*. Shops that used to cater to stout women now appeal to *custom-sized* shoppers. Giving pretentious names to mundane items spurs sales: razors in elaborate boxes become *shaving systems*. When products become scarce, they have a *low availability factor*. The result is usually an *upward price readjustment*, which, when extended to enough commodities, may be followed by a *downward economic readjustment* (depression).

Because euphemisms are subject to different interpretations, they may merely appear to convey information. Although euphemisms may make an idea more palatable, they also inflate language, reduce precision, and often tamper with the truth.

VOGUE WORDS AND SLANG   A close relative of euphemisms and clichés is the vogue word, which by definition is short-lived, inevitably giving way to yet a newer word or phrase. We used to observe or follow an event; now we *track the continuum*. Agents used to promote their products; now they *hype* or *tubthump* them for *megabucks*. No longer do we see or view; we *perceive*.

The host on a television show, interviewing a "junk artist," comments: "Most people don't want to *interface* with junk art." I should think not! Our ideas, even when unexceptional, are immodestly called *seminal*, and we often introduce them with gratuitous adverbs like *clearly* or *basically*. *Clout* has given way to *juice*, *abrasive* to *controversial*, and *jet setters* to *glitterati*. Educators gave us *heuristic* and *holistic*, and lawyers contributed *quid pro quo*. Some vogue words have become clichés, thanks largely to the frequency with which the press uses them: *ambience, ballpark figure, cache, clone, dialogue, dichotomize, guesstimate, hard-core, high-profile posture, impact* (as a verb), *in-depth, innovative, mandate* (as a verb), *multidimensional, nadir, overview, parameter, phased out, reprise* (as a verb), *scenario, thrust, time frame, vis-à-vis, watershed.*

Like vogue words slang is evanescent—and contagious. Some slang enriches language; some impoverishes it. The emergence of ethnic pride contributed such slang terms as *kitsch, shtick,* and *chutzpah* and such vivid expressions as *rip-off.* Much current slang is not only inelegant but suggests mental sloppiness and verbal imprecision: "She's a *very together* person, very *laid back;* she just *goes with the flow.*" "Let it *all hang out.*" "I know *where you're coming from—what feeling you're going with.*" "That's not *my bag*—I'm not *into that.*" "I can't *relate to* Shakespeare." "*Where's his head at?*" "Do *your own thing,* man!" "Hey, what's *going down?*"

The drug culture has generated considerable slang, including *freaked out, spaced out,* and *strung out.* To *crash* is to sleep, and *OD*'d no longer refers solely to a fatal drug overdose. A *narc,* formerly a narcotics investigator, is now any tattletale, and yesterdays jerk or yo-yo is today's *turkey* or *wonk.* Whatever is pleasant is a *turn-on,* whatever unpleasant a *bad trip* or *bummer.* Either experience may *blow your mind.* If you're *with it,* you're *plugged in;* if you're not, you're *out of it.*

Anyone who listens to the radio or watches television knows that the broadcast media do their part in spreading slang. A budding pop composer confesses that she's "*heavy into* collecting records—everything from the '20s to *what's happening* now. And right now I'm looking for Ella Fitzgerald, *like* when she was *like* 16 years old." A disc jockey, praising a singer, predicts: "This lady's *gonna happen.*" Another asserts: "Anyone confronted with a *great big badism* is going to deny it." A network television host announces that the weather forecaster is about to *lay the weather on us.* And a newly elected U.S. representative explains that he had gone to Washington early to *get a leg up* on other new congressmen. When used in appropriate context and circumstances, slang adds color and vigor to language. It is not durable, however, and should not saturate our conversation.

PROFANITY Language conveys not only information but also attitudes and feelings. Two kinds of language used expressly for this purpose are profanity and obscenity. Both are almost devoid of lexical meaning and largely express emotion—fear, anxiety, contempt, anger, or rage. The era of social permissiveness has moved profane and obscene language from truck stops, back streets, and riverfront barrooms to drawing rooms, airwaves—and the mouths of women and children. Few Americans today are surprised or shocked by the profanities lacing ordinary conversation. Athletes no longer confine their scurrilities to the locker room. Complaining that a pitcher tried too hard to break a baseball star's hitting streak, the star tells reporters: "I feel p _ _ _ _ _ off!" And whereas much was made of the "expletives deleted" in the Watergate tapes, many public figures no longer bother to expurgate their expletives before issuing statements for the public record. A state comptroller whose political phrasemaking earned him reporters' labels of "colorful," "controversial," and "unpredictable," calls the state attorney general a "s _ _ of a b _ _ _ _." A national weekly magazine prints a White House aide's profane paraphrase of the president's instructions to an American ambassador who had made several politically indiscreet remarks: "Shut his g _ _ _ _ _ mouth permanently."

The lyrics of many pop songs that contain highly suggestive, smutty, and even obscene words are heard over the radio despite a federal ban against "obscene, profane, or indecent broadcasting." "Take This Job and Shove It" was a great hit, and at least one rock star "specializes" in lewd lyrics. In wide, sustained coverage of the Supreme Court's upholding of the Federal Communications Commission's ban on the airing of seven "filthy words" in a recording by a comic, the actual words, interestingly enough, were never mentioned, even though the list of profanities and obscenities censored by the press has progressively shrunk.

Profanity is part of contemporary America. Some of it is so commonplace as to be inconspicuous, but, depending especially on the time and place, it can be extremely offensive. The increase in street and gutter language reflects not only man's declining civility but also his dwindling vocabulary. Scatological terms, which usually come in stock phrases, issue from an unimaginative mind. Even their intended shock effect is mitigated by repetitive use. A plethora of such terms debases both language and the speaker or writer who uses them.

Grammar "good and bad"

It is not simply the misuse or abuse of words, but ignorance, or disregard, of basic grammatical principles that corrupts language. A newsman comments: "Laws are made by congressmen who are elected *by* you and *I*." An athletic manager says: "I *had went* around the world, and it has given me an opportunity to *put my input in.*" A government consultant employed to evaluate a federal reading program produces this totally ungrammatical prose: "There is no realistically promises that addresses the needs identified in the proposed program. . . . The objectivities did not specify to the quantifiable of the success of the proposed program." Sheer nonsense!

Grammatical flaws that result in unintended absurdities are especially conspicuous. A sign in a restaurant decrees: "Shirts, socks and shoes must be worn to be served." After interviewing a veteran clown, a news reporter remarks: "He's talking about retiring more every day." His misplacement of "more" violates English grammatical word order, on which meaning is heavily dependent. The omission of a simple comma can lead to unintended humor like this: "[Their] marriage has withstood 49 years, a disease that has eroded her mind and body and the financial problems the affliction caused."

English grammar is not a set of unnecessary rules some misanthrope dreamed up to torture schoolchildren; it comprises a set of conventions and principles that govern effective use of the language. Grammar keeps words straight to deliver their intended meaning, and a violation of grammatical principles often invites ambiguity and confusion. If, therefore, we are to communicate clearly, we need to make our subjects agree with their verbs and our pronouns agree with their antecedents, to use parallel grammatical structures for parallel ideas, to observe sequence of tenses, to avoid illogical shifts and dangling constructions, and to apply the proper punctuation to aid comprehension.

Since words are the medium we use not only to convey but also to formulate thought, faulty language is often due to faulty reasoning. The relation between language and thought is intimate and reciprocal: words are more likely to be clear if the underlying thoughts are clear. Only as thought is clarified, in fact, is the most precise language possible. (For specific problems that occur with grammar and syntax, *see* All You Need to Know About Grammar. The article entitled Some Hints About Writing is also useful.)

The advantages of clear communication

Concern with language abuse is not, as some believe, a foolish obsession of pedants. The purpose of language is to communicate, and when verbal ineptitude or duplicity prevents clear communication, language fails its function. For an idea to be understood, the words used to convey it must have a common meaning for both speaker and listener. The speaker who wants to deliver his message undistorted will therefore avoid obscure, imprecise, or overly wordy language.

When most eloquently used, language is not only lucid but is also aesthetically appealing and considerate. Inflated language, for example, is discourteous as well as inefficient: it forces the listener to expend inordinate time and effort wading through a torrent of words to extract the meaning. The listener will, of course, usually turn a deaf ear to a long-winded bore. Profane, obscene, or otherwise insulting language is also offensive. By arousing the emotions rather than stimulating the intellect, such terms may hamper communication. Decent, restrained language therefore communicates better.

Memorizing rules of traditional grammar without understanding their basis, using synonym books without recognizing nuances of meaning, and applying readability formulas or similar mechanical indexes to language are tedious and ineffective ways to improve verbal skills. These skills ensue instead from the translation of clear, well-ordered thoughts into carefully selected and strategically arranged words. Such a feat requires hard work, good sense, and good taste. Toward that end, reading good writing will not only provide models for us to emulate but will also painlessly increase our vocabularies. By paying habitual attention to words, we can learn to appreciate clear, eloquent expression and to reject frozen forms and tangled syntax. With experience we will find a middle course between undisciplined gibberish and tyrannical purism.

Language is a precious possession; it has, in fact, been called the door to knowledge. Knowing how to use language effectively allows us to communicate more clearly, listen more critically, and read more efficiently. Beyond those practical benefits, an interest in words and their mastery provides a lifelong source of pleasure.

LOIS DEBAKEY

Slang

Slang is a label used by dictionary makers, linguists, critics, and teachers to indicate the social acceptance of a word on a specific but non-rigid usage scale. The scale used to indicate a word's status in any language, in decreasing order of its social acceptance, is: (1) standard; (2) informal or colloquial; (3) slang; (4) cant; (5) jargon; (6) argot; (7) dialect; (8) nonstandard; and (9) taboo or vulgar. This list of the nine basic usage labels can be used to describe the social status of any word in any language at any given time. It goes from the preferred, completely acceptable standard words to the socially unacceptable ones. Each level is less acceptable than the one above it; contains fewer words than the one above it; and generally contains words used less frequently (less common or popular words) than the one above it.

Although this list categorizes words on a decreasing basis, the words in each category are socially acceptable or unacceptable, many or few, popular or unpopular for different reasons. Thus, cant, jargon, and argot are less accepted and less common than standard, informal, and slang because only certain social subgroups (specific occupational, age, ethnic, hobby, and special-interest groups, etc.) know and use them. Nonstandard words are not popular because they are considered uneducated; so people are taught not to use them by parents and teachers. Although taboo words have become increasingly common in the speech and writing of certain people in most industrialized and developing nations since the 1920s, they are still the least acceptable and are still not popular with many people because of their sexual, antireligious, or otherwise offensive nature. Dialect words are less acceptable and less popular than most other groups simply because fewer people (only those from specific regions) understand and use them. It should be emphasized also that dialect differs from the other categories in being a regional rather than a social category. Hence, many scholars and teachers would consider it more acceptable than cant or even consider it as acceptable as informal. However, because dialect (all dialects) seemed to be losing its importance in the last half of the 20th century and because it seemed to be shrinking rather than growing in both the size of its vocabulary and in its popularity, it was merely placed above nonstandard speech in the list of language usage labels given above.

Note that in the second half of the 20th century slang ranked third among all language levels in the size of its vocabulary, in social acceptance, and in popularity. This was especially true of the slang of the major languages of the countries with the most rapidly changing cultural, social, and economic ways of life: English, French, Italian, Spanish, Portuguese, German, Swedish, Norwegian, Danish, Dutch, Finnish, Russian, Polish, Czech, Bulgarian, Rumanian, Japanese, etc. Slang may not have been as important in some of the more isolated languages, such as Icelandic and Catalan, in some of the Indic, Iranian, and South Slavic languages, and in many of the major non-Indo-European languages (the African, Malaysian, and Oriental languages) of the less rapidly developing and changing countries.

To understand the place slang fills in a language, it is necessary to define each of the nine language levels.

Standard speech consists of all the words and expressions that are or can be readily understood and completely accepted by a majority of the people who use a language. It is employed under any circumstances, regardless of the degree of social formality that is required. These most acceptable, preferred words number several hundred thousand in most major languages, and include the most common words. All the words in this paragraph are standard.

Informal speech is less acceptable than standard but more acceptable than slang. It consists of the words and expressions that are understood and accepted by a majority of the people who use a language, but it is generally not used in the most formal circumstances, such as in formal gatherings, business correspondence, etc. Informal speech includes the second largest number of words in any language (probably somewhere between one-twentieth and one-tenth of the number of standard words and expressions) and the second most common or popular group of words. "Colloquial" is a label that has been used loosely with the same meaning as *informal,* but this label was disappearing in favor of the latter term, although some scholars used it to refer to slightly less formal speech than informal. Colloquial is also often loosely used to refer to speech lacking in education or social polish, to speech associated with small-town or rural usage, or to informal phrases, idioms, clichés, and aphorisms.

Slang is the words and expressions that have escaped from the cant, jargon, and argot (and to a lesser extent, from dialect, nonstandard, and taboo speech) of specific subgroups of society so that they are known and used by an appreciable percentage of the general population, even though the words and expressions often retain some associations with the subgroups that originally used and popularized them. Thus, slang is a middle ground for words and expressions that have become too popular to be any longer considered as part of the more restricted categories, but that are not yet (and may never become) acceptable or popular enough to be considered informal or standard. (Compare the slang "hooker" and the standard "prostitute.")

Cant is the restricted, nontechnical words and expressions of any particular group, as an occupational, age, ethnic, hobby, or special-interest group. (*Cool, uptight, do your thing* were youth cant of the late 1960s before they became slang.)

Jargon is the restricted, technical, or shop-talk words and expressions of any particular group, as an occupational, trade, scientific, artistic, criminal, or other group. (*Finals* used by printers and by students; *Fannie Mae* by money men; *preemie* by obstetricians were jargon before they became slang.)

Argot is merely the combined cant and jargon of thieves, criminals, or any other underworld group. (*Hit* used by armed robbers; *scam* by corporate con men.)

Dialect is the words (and pronunciations) restricted in use to a particular geographical region or regions of a nation's language (*e.g.,* U.S. Midland *jaybird* for "blue jay").

Nonstandard speech is words, expressions, and usages considered to be uneducated, uninformed, or sloppy, such as words whose use is avoided by educated people because they are considered redundant, useless, or traditionally unacceptable (*e.g., ain't* or *irregardless* in English).

Taboo or *vulgar speech* includes words and expressions considered by many people as unfit for almost all uses because of their direct references to sex, excrement, parts of the body concerned with sex and excretion, or because they are considered blasphemous. Of course, what is considered as thus being obscene, crude, rude, or otherwise offensive differs from one period to another. For example, the Victorians considered *stomach, thigh,* and words relating to many other parts of the body, as well as most words and expressions relating directly to pregnancy, as taboo or vulgar.

This last category of the language scale includes the least acceptable words in any language, the smallest number of words (probably 50 to 250 each in most major languages), and generally the least popular words in the speech of the majority of its native speakers and writers.

Slang fills a necessary niche in all languages, occupying a middle ground between the standard and informal words accepted by the general public and the special words and expressions known only to comparatively small social subgroups. It can serve as a bridge or a barrier, either helping both old and new words that have been used as "insiders" terms by a specific group of people to enter the language of the general public or, on the other hand, preventing them from doing so. Thus, for many words, slang is a testing ground that finally proves them to be generally useful, appealing, and acceptable enough to become standard or informal. For many other words, slang is a testing ground that shows them to be too restricted in use, not as appealing as standard synonyms, or unnecessary, frivolous, faddish, or unacceptable for standard or informal speech. For still a third group of words and expressions, slang becomes not a final testing ground that either accepts or rejects them for general use but becomes a vast limbo, a permanent holding ground, an area of speech that a word never leaves. Thus, during various times in history, American slang has provided *cowboy, blizzard, O.K., racketeer, phone, gas,* and *movie* for standard or informal speech. It has tried and finally rejected *conbobberation* (disturbance), *krib* (room or apartment), *lucifer* (match), *tomato* (girl), and *fab* (fabulous) from standard or informal speech. It has held other words such as *bones* (dice), used since the 14th century, and *beat it* (go away), used since the 16th century, in a permanent grasp, neither passing them on to standard or informal speech nor rejecting them from popular, long-term use.

The criteria used by scholars in classifying or labeling a word as slang are obvious from the definition of the category. In order to classify words, modern dictionary makers and other scholars keep large citation files, containing quotations and actual uses of words as found in books, newspapers, magazines, movies, radio and television programs, and recorded conversations. From such sources it can be determined if a word's use is restricted to just one or a few social and regional subgroups or if it is used fairly consistently throughout the entire population of a country, in all regions, economic and social groups, etc. From such citation files, as well as from experienced and educated judgment, dictionary makers and other scholars are able to label a word as slang or any of the other eight major language levels. (From recording and observing the actual use of words in speech and writing, they are also able to define words and pinpoint their most common and also their variant spellings, pronunciations, etc.)

Modern language scholars are almost universally descriptive linguists. They are reporters, not judges. (In earlier periods, and in some countries still, language scholars were prescribers of language, practicing prescriptive linguistics. They acted as judges, deciding on what was "right" and "wrong.") Thus, in modern times a word is classified as slang (or as a member of the other eight categories) because that is the way it is actually used and accepted by the speakers and writers of a language, because that is its actual social status as established by analyzing current use of the word.

Slang words cannot be distinguished from other words by sound or meaning. Indeed, all slang words were once cant, jargon, argot, dialect, nonstandard, or taboo. For example, the American slang *to neck* (to kiss and caress) was originally student cant; *flattop* (an aircraft carrier) was originally navy jargon; and *pineapple* (a bomb or hand grenade) was originally criminal argot. Such words did not, of course, change their sound or meaning when they became slang. Many slang words, such as *blizzard, mob, movie, phone, gas,* and others, have become informal or standard and, of course, did not change in sound or meaning when they did so. In fact, most slang words are homonyms of standard words, spelled and pronounced just like their standard counterparts, as for example (American slang), *cabbage* (money), *cool* (relaxed), and *pot* (marijuana). Of course, the words *cabbage, cool,* and *pot* sound alike in their ordinary standard use and in their slang use. Each word sounds just as appealing or unappealing, dull or colorful in its standard as in its slang use. Also, the meanings of *cabbage* and *money, cool* and *relaxed, pot* and *marijuana* are the same, so it cannot be said that the connotations of slang words are any more colorful or racy than the meanings of standard words.

All languages, countries, and periods of history have slang. This is true because they all have had words with varying degrees of social acceptance and popularity.

All segments of society use some slang, including the most educated, cultivated speakers and writers. In fact, this is part of the definition of slang. For example, George Washington used *redcoat* (British soldier); Winston Churchill used *booze* (liquor); and Lyndon B. Johnson used *cool it* (calm down, shut up).

The same linguistic processes are used to create and popularize slang as are used to create and popularize all other words. That is, all words are created and popularized in the same general ways; they are labeled slang only according to their current social acceptance, long after creation and popularization.

Slang is not the language of the underworld (such language is called argot), nor does most of it necessarily come from the underworld. The main sources of slang change from period to period. Thus, in one period of American slang, frontiersmen, cowboys, hunters, and trappers may have been the main source; during some parts of the 1920s and 1930s the speech of baseball players and criminals may have been the main source; at other times, the vocabulary of jazz musicians, soldiers, Negroes, or college students may have been the main source.

Slang is not vulgar, obscene, derogatory, or offensive. Such words are properly put in the separate category of taboo or vulgar. True, some slang words have come from the taboo or vulgar level (*jazz*, perhaps), just one of slang's many sources. Such words, however, have to lose some of their taboo nature and become at least somewhat generally acceptable before they can properly be classified as slang.

For a full understanding of slang, it must also be remembered that a word's use, popularity, and acceptability can change. Words can change in social level, going from any one of the nine levels to any other level. Thus, some standard words of Shakespeare's day are found only in certain modern-day British dialects or in the dialect of the southern United States. Taboo words of yesterday (*stomach, thigh,* etc.) can be the accepted, standard words of today. The status of any word is fluid and at any one time hundreds, and perhaps thousands, of words and expressions are in the process of changing from one level to another, of becoming more acceptable or less acceptable, of becoming more popular or less popular.

History of the word "slang"

The etymology of the word *slang* is obscure. There are, however, three main theories of origin. Some authorities, including Ernest Weekley in his *Etymological Dictionary of Modern English* (1921, reprinted 1967), have speculated that the English word *slang* is related to our verb to *sling*, because the Scandinavian origin and cognate of *sling* (which is *slenge* or *slengje*) is also the root of two Scandinavian terms that are akin to *slang* (*slengjeord*, "a neologism or newly created word," and *slengjenamn*, "a nickname"). This etymology appeared in some dictionaries and other language reference books, especially during the 1920s and 1930s. Since that time, etymologists have found that the development of meanings and uses of the English word *slang* is probably older than related stages of the development of the Scandinavian words. Other scholars have speculated that *slang* may come from the French *langue* ("language") by the easy introduction of an initial gliding *s* sound. Still other linguists have suggested that the source for *slang* may be the English word *language*. This could have come about by a combined process of blending and shortening, *e.g.*, the phrases *thieve*(s' lang)*uage"* or *beggar*(s' lang)*uage*. This combined method of word formation has several precedents. The word *tawdry,* for example, was created by blending and shortening *Sain*(t Audrey) *lace*." British pronunciation and speech rhythm, however, are much more apt to form *tawdry* from *Saint Audrey lace* than to produce *slang* from *thieves' language* or *beggars' language*.

The word *slang* first entered the English language before the mid-18th century. It was originally used loosely as a synonym for *cant, jargon,* and *argot,* and to refer to low, vulgar language. *The Oxford English Dictionary*'s earliest citation for the word *slang* in writing is from 1756, which equates slang with cant in its quotation "Cant . . . commonly called the slang patter." In 1758 there was a printed reference to slang as "street language"; in 1774, a reference to slang as including the cant of bailiffs. A 1798 citation uses *slang* as a synonym for *dialect;* an 1800 citation refers to "lawyer's slang" (that is, cant or jargon); an 1809 citation equates *slang* to oaths and vulgar words; and one in 1810 refers to *slang* as underworld argot.

Slang generally retained these various meanings for the next 60 years. William Thackeray seems to have been the first major writer to use *slang* in a more general, modern meaning. In 1848, he wrote in *Vanity Fair,* "He was too old to listen to . . . the slang of the youngsters." In 1824, however, Sir Walter Scott was still equating *slang* with argot when he wrote in *Redgauntlet,* "What did actually reach his ears was disguised . . . completely by the use of cant words and the thieves-Latin called slang." In 1872, George Eliot was still using *slang* to mean cant or jargon in *Middlemarch* in a passage critical of writers and "correct usage" rules: "Correct English is the slang of prigs who write history and essays. And the strongest slang of all is the slang of poets."

The original, nonspecialized meaning of the word *slang* is still used by some people and given as a second or third definition of *slang* in some dictionaries. This meaning, however, is not the one lexicographers, linguists, most aware critics, and teachers use. The specialized meaning of *slang* as a separate language label is the one professionals use and the most common meaning today. By 1890, *slang* had already come to have a meaning all its own, and was no longer a mere synonym for other language categories. Slowly it came to mean a separate language level and vocabulary derived largely from various cant, jargon, argot, dialect, nonstandard, and taboo or vulgar vocabularies, but independent of them and more common or popular than any of them. *Slang* thus slowly achieved an independent meaning to lexicographers and, later, to sociologists, though with some laymen it still retains a secondary sense. During the more than 200 years that *slang* has been a word in the English language, its meaning has changed and enlarged to include a large, less restricted, more popular group of words. As vocabulary and society grew, so did the number and sources of slang words.

The history of slang

Theoretically, it takes only two people to create and use a language. At first, all words of such a language would be standard because all of the two person "population" would use, understand, and accept them equally. If the two people developed rituals, they might decide that only certain words were formal enough to use during special occasions and thus begin to divide their private language into standard and informal usage levels. If they felt that certain other words displeased the gods or brought bad luck, they might avoid using them, only whisper them, or use them only to call down the wrath of the gods or bad luck on each other or on animals and objects. Thus, two people could also develop the taboo level of language. A third person, however, would be necessary before cant, jargon, argot, slang, dialect, and nonstandard levels of speech would develop.

Only if a third person (in both the mathematical and grammatical sense) were involved could two of the three people develop and use a slightly different vocabulary when together, creating cant and jargon if they shared an experience, endeavor, or interest and developed a vocabulary for it that the third person did not fully share. If two of the people planned or committed a crime against the third and used special words to discuss it that they kept secret from him, then argot would exist. If two of the people had lived together until a third person came along who then learned, used, or pronounced their words with a slightly different meaning or sound (or added some of his own words which the other two did not fully accept), then dialect would develop. If two of the people felt that some words the third person used were stupid, uneducated, or not explicit enough, then nonstandard would have been added to the levels of speech. As any of the cant, jargon, argot, dialect, or nonstandard words that only one or two of these people used began to be used by the other person or persons, slang would develop. In the most primitive sense, then, cant, jargon, argot, dialect, nonstandard, and slang come into existence when there is a third person present, an outsider who uses a somewhat special vocabulary or who can form a social subgroup with another.

Thus, in a very true sense, the history of slang is the history of third persons, of social subgroups, how they develop and meet and communicate with the general population, and how the general population accepts and absorbs them or part of their special vocabularies. The three things underlying the development of all slang are: (1) the presence of third persons, of social subgroups with their own occupational, age, ethnic, and other special-interest words; (2) free and frequent mingling and communication of these groups with the general public, so that the special words of each group spread to society as a whole (such mingling and communication may be in face-to-face conversation or through stories, songs, written and printed words, radio, television, etc.); (3) a receptive, nonrestrictive, general society willing to accept and use the in-group words of the social subgroups.

All societies have had slang—wandering European nomads and settled agricultural tribes, North and South American Indian tribes, Eskimos, African tribes, Semitic tribes, Australian aborigines, Chinese, Japanese, and Malaysian islanders. There was slang in ancient Greece and Crete and in the Roman Empire, and slang was also used by the Picts and Jutes, Angles, Saxons, Celts, and Norsemen in what was to become the British Isles. Both Plato and Aristotle mention specialized subgroup vocabularies in their writings, and Plato also noted that some of these in-group words had crept into the language of the ruling classes. In a similar manner, when Anglo-Saxons retained a useful but not completely acceptable word from the Picts or Jutes, when a wandering Saxon bard first used a Viking seafaring term, when a king in Cornwall introduced a word from the specialized vocabulary of a magician, an imported cook, or a warrior from the Northern border, slang was being created and spread. When the Normans invaded England in 1066 and certain French words became the standard speech, many of the older Anglo-Saxon words lost their social acceptance and became slang.

Throughout the Middle Ages, and all periods of history, slang continued to grow. In *The Canterbury Tales* Chaucer used it consciously and fittingly to show the different vocabulary levels and speech habits of his pilgrims who represented a sampling of the occupational, social, and interest groups of the 14th century.

It was not until the Renaissance and the growth of cosmopolitan cities that slang truly blossomed. Since many different occupational, ethnic, age, economic, educational, and special-interest groups must exist, mingle, and communicate before a rich and varied slang vocabulary can be created and spread, the modern concept of cities is slang's most fertile ground. Cities create and attract specialists and throw them into close proximity with other subgroups and the general public. Before modern cities, people from one group usually met others only while traveling, as in *The Canterbury Tales*, and few people traveled very far or very often. Before modern cities, the soldier and sailor, the fairly rare wandering minstrel, the traveling scholar or monk, the pilgrim, the slave, the wandering homeless, the professional jester, magician, cook, or blacksmith who changed positions from one court to another, and the traveling king and his retinue were the only ones who met people, speakers, and words outside their own native areas, the only ones to spread the words of their own groups and to learn and broadcast the words of other groups.

With the growth of cities and city states in Europe during the Renaissance, for the first time thousands of different people from a wide variety of social subgroups were brought together to exchange goods, ideas, and words. For the first time on a large scale people could make their living as specialists, and these specialists and people of all occupations met daily in the marketplace, the fairs, the inns and pubs, on the streets, and in each other's homes and shops. All the intellectual interests, the travel, the creativity, and all the wide variety of occupational and interest groups that formed the Renaissance created and spread much slang, and this growth and spread was intensified by the mingling of peoples in the large diverse cities that grew during this period. The Renaissance was the first period in which all three conditions that help create and spread slang came together: many subgroups, free and frequent mingling, and interest in and acceptance of the subgroups and their words.

It is no surprise that many of the Elizabethan playwrights used much slang in their plays, especially Shakespeare, Ben Jonson, and Thomas Dekker. These playwrights knew and wrote about both high life and low life, were socially mobile in the London of their day, and mingled with and knew and used the words of royalty, officials, gentlemen, students, tradesmen, artisans, soldiers, sailors, thieves, and prostitutes.

The 15th-century invention of movable type and the spread and development of ever more rapid typesetting machines and printing presses, which gave rise to increased literacy, penny papers, magazines, etc., were also milestones in the history of slang. The printed word reinforced and complemented the face-to-face spread of slang in the cities, so that all people could see words from all social subgroups on the printed page, so that all words, including slang, saw wider, more general use.

After the Renaissance, no more important date exists in the history of the English language, or in the history of English slang, than 1620, when the Pilgrims landed at Plymouth Rock. The language of most of the colonists was English and so was the slang. French and Spanish explorers, soldiers, trappers, and priests had come and brought their native words, some of which were adopted as American words, including some which were adopted as slang. The new settlers also met the native Indian tribes and adopted some of their words, a few of which also became slang. The American colonies, however, were primarily English, and American slang was primarily English slang from the landing of the Pilgrims in 1620 to after the War of 1812.

Though the United States in the second half of the 20th century probably produces and absorbs more slang than any other nation in the world, from its founding as a separate nation in 1776 until after the War of 1812 most American slang was still borrowed from the British. After 1815, however, Americans began to produce a steady stream of new words, including many new slang words of their own, many of them bearing the earmarks of neologisms. According to many scholars (*see* G. P. Krapp, "Is American English Archaic?" *Southwest Review* [summer 1927]), this new American slang was the child of the new nationalism, reflecting the new spirit of freedom, adventure, and exuberance that entered American life after the close of the War of 1812, when there seemed to be unlimited opportunities for personal freedom, westward movement, and for seeking new occupations, fortunes, politics, and ways of life. Some of these early American slang terms were wildly extravagant and have disappeared, including *conbobberation, ripsniptiously, to exflunctify,* and to *obflisticate* (*see* M. M. Mathews, *The Beginnings of American English* [1931]). Other of the early frontier and rustic slang expressions of this period still have a place in modern American speech on various language levels, including *blizzard, rambunctious, to cut one's eye-teeth,* and *to go the whole hog.*

From the War of 1812 to the Civil War, the most obvious slang was produced on the frontier and sent back eastward to shock or titillate the older, established culture. In the two decades preceding the Civil War, a multitude of slang terms were popularized, including many slang words for drunk, such as *boiled, fried, oiled, ossified, pie-eyed, plastered,* and *stewed* (*see* M. Prenner, "Slang Synonyms for Drunk," *American Speech* [December 1928]). A few African words were also being added from the slaves, though generations of slaves were born and died without ever mingling with or being accepted by the dominant society, and it would be a hundred years before Southern black and big-city ghetto black terms entered the general language with any frequency.

The Civil War, like all wars, created and popularized much slang, as the obvious *bluebelly, Johnny Reb,* and names for new weapons, tactics, and regions. It brought together farmers and city boys, frontiersmen and school teachers, men of every occupation, background, region, and interest. As with all civilian armies, both the Union and Confederate forces mixed together all social subgroups in close daily proximity and in a strange world of new objects, thoughts, feelings, and moods, serving as true melting pots of the specialized or regional vocabularies of all.

After the war, westward expansion continued with more mingling, more new slang words for wagons, horses, types of terrain, fish, trees, clothing, food, drink, women, money, etc. Some words were absorbed from the Indians, some from the Mexicans, some from old-time trappers, hunters, cowboys, Western cavalry men, etc.

Slang was also becoming increasingly important to poets, novelists, and other writers. It had become the subject of a considerable amount of speculation and writing, both in the United States and England. Ralph Waldo Emerson had praised the forceful imagery of some slang in his *Journals* (1840): "What can describe the folly and emptiness of scolding like the word *jawing?*" In 1853 Charles Dickens, who used slang in some of his novels of London street life, was interested enough to publish an article on slang, one of the first by a major fiction writer. In 1885 Walt Whitman, in his "Slang in America," defined slang approvingly as "the wholesome fermentation or eructation of those processes eternally active in language, by which the froth and specks are thrown up, mostly to pass away, though occasionally to settle and permanently crystallize." Victor Hugo, however, in France still thought of slang in its pejorative sense, as "a dressing-room in which language, having an evil deed to prepare, puts on a disguise."

The late 19th and early 20th centuries saw the beginning of a steady stream of German, Irish, Italian, Polish, and other immigrants, each of whom added and continue to add some of their native words to American English, often as standard words, some times as slang. This immigration of diverse people and words continued with the later addition of a few Chinese and Japanese words, and with French, Greek, Russian, Puerto Rican, and Cuban words as various large and small waves of immigrants continued to arrive.

World War I also created or popularized much new slang, such as *doughboy, Big Bertha, frog* (Frenchman), and again threw men of every social subgroup together. This overseas war found American soldiers bringing home new foreign words they had learned in the trenches or while on leave. This war, as all major wars, was followed by a period of intellectual, cultural, moral, and social questioning, a loosening of certain attitudes and restraints. It led to the jazz era and the Roaring Twenties, the first modern fad period with an accent on youth, rebellion, and style, resulting in such slang words as *flapper, lounge lizard, white shoes* (Ivy League college student), a resurgence of the word *pet* (to kiss and caress), and scores of other slang words for clothing items and styles, popular music, personality types, and interests.

The 1920s and early 1930s also saw the mingling of criminals with noncriminals in speakeasies and the mass adulation of sports figures, especially baseball personalities, so that argot and sports words became a main source of the slang of the period. In the 1930s, too, the growth of labor slang began, the growth of new words for the increasing number of new manufactured items and new occupations continued, and there were new slang words of the depression, "dust bowl" migrants, and of hoboes and tramps. The 1920s and 1930s also saw the first truly widespread use of the phonograph, radio, telephone, and "talking" pictures, all major conveyors as far as slang was concerned since all new forms of communications helped popularize and spread words.

The 1940s saw World War II with its many slang words: *jeep, flattop* (aircraft carrier), *G.I., sweater girl, Dear John* (a letter rejecting or dismissing a boyfriend or girlfriend, fiancé or fiancée). In the 1950s, another language milestone was passed with the first truly widespread sale of home television sets, bringing further speech and words from all groups into the living rooms of the general public. In that decade and in the 1960s, the Korean and Vietnam wars kept up the tradition of wars creating obvious new slang words such as *hard hat* (uniformed soldier), *bird farm* (aircraft carrier in the Vietnam War), and an increasing number of political slang words such as *hawk* (one who favours a warlike stand), originally used before the War of 1812, and *dove* (one who favors a peaceful stand).

The 1960s also saw the beginning of the trend toward ever increasing new subgroups caused by the growth of electronics, new sciences, new commercial packaging and marketing methods, the increased leisure time for sports and fads, and a renewed search for human individuality and social freedom by various older subgroups, including youth, women, and various ethnic groups. Thus, there were new and expanded occupational groups, *e.g.,* commercial jet pilots, astronauts, tax lawyers, transplant surgeons, computer technicians, car thieves, uranium miners, professional football players, workers in the frozen-food industry, supermarket employees, welfare workers, and new types of chemists, physicists, geologists, etc. There were new and greatly expanded hobby and interest groups making use of more leisure time and financial affluence, such as golfers, scuba divers, surfers, skiers, hot rodders, skydivers, hi-fi enthusiasts, home-movie makers. There were newly vocal ethnic groups, such as urban blacks, Puerto Ricans, Cuban refugees, and even newly identifiable age groups, ranging from a greatly increased number of college students acting and treated neither as teenagers nor as adults to the newly created class of senior citizens. Each new or expanded group had its own specialized vocabulary, any word of which could become slang.

At the same time, mass communications and transportation continued to develop with color television, worldwide communication satellite hookups, computerized typesetting machines, faster printing presses, large jet planes, increased ownership and use of cars, extensive summer and business travel, etc., so that people from each group continued to see and hear each other more quickly and easily, continued to meet and intermingle with a wider variety of other groups and the general public. Meanwhile, urbanization and suburbanization continued, so that more and more people from all regions, races, occupations, and interests were brought together in the cities or their environs.

Thus, all the conditions necessary for a large, varied slang vocabulary existed in the Renaissance and have continued to exist throughout history to the present time. From primitive times to the present, slang has always been with us as a natural part of any language. Slang, however, was not given the status of being included in early glossaries and dictionaries. Most early dictionaries were written to teach hard words or to teach the less educated classes the "king's English." Indeed, the rise of the great dictionary makers coincided with the rise of the middle class, and early dictionaries were often written and used as verbal etiquette books, showing how the more educated classes spoke and wrote and what was considered acceptable.

Samuel Johnson even hoped to freeze the English language in his great 18th-century dictionary, though in the course of writing it he learned that language was and had always been a living, changing thing. The great 19th-century dictionary maker Noah Webster also came to realize that new words, modern spellings, and slang had a large place in the language. Neither Johnson nor Webster, however, included much slang in their books. Thus, the great dictionaries of the 18th, 19th, and first half of the 20th centuries were mainly of standard words.

Meantime, a few special glossaries and dictionaries of slang began to appear in the late 18th century and others have been produced to the present. Such books have supplemented the standard dictionaries and often served as source material for them. The first major slang dictionary was Francis Grose's personal compilation, *A Classical Dictionary of the Vulgar Tongue* (1785). The major collection of 19th-century slang was J. S. Farmer and W. E. Henley's long and scholarly *Slang and Its Analogues* (1890–1904). Major 20th-century collections include M. H. Weseen's *Dictionary of American Slang* (1934), E. Partridge's *Dictionary of Slang and Unconventional English* (1937), and Harold Wentworth and Stuart B. Flexner's *Dictionary of American Slang* (1960, 1967).

Since the early 1960s, however, standard dictionaries have included an appreciable amount of slang, recognizing its importance and popularity and helping to give it status. Thus, although little slang was found in general dictionaries until the early 1960s, general dictionaries since then have included many slang words. This was partly the result of the keeping of large citation files by dictionary makers, the growth of descriptive lexicography, and the wide acceptance and use of slang in the last half of the 20th century.

In any event, by the last half of the 20th century, slang had achieved an acceptance, a large vocabulary, and popularity ranking it as third behind standard and informal speech and ranking it as important enough for at least representative inclusion in major dictionaries both in the United States and England, as well as in the newer dictionaries of many other languages and countries where descriptive rather than official or prescriptive linguistics ruled.

The history of slang is actually (1) the history of the specialization or fragmentation of society into occupational, age, ethnic, and other special-interest groups; (2) the history of communications, transportation, and urbanization that permit free and frequent mingling and communication; and (3) cultural and political history that determines how free and receptive a society is to accepting and using new words created by its subgroups. The history of the slang of all countries and languages depends on these three items. Thus, the history of the slang of Australia, Canada, Russia, France, Israel, Peru, Japan, and any other country can be told only in terms of its own cultural, industrial, and political history.

ENCYCLOPÆDIA BRITANNICA

Aspects of Linguistic Change

Every living language can readily be adapted to meet changes occurring in the life and culture of its speakers, and the main weight of such changes falls on vocabulary. Grammatical and phonological structures are relatively stable and change noticeably over centuries rather than decades; but vocabularies can change very quickly both in word stock and in word meanings. Consider as an example the changes wrought by modern technology in the vocabularies of all European languages since 1945. Before that date "transistor" and "cosmonaut" did not exist, and "nuclear disarmament" would scarcely have had any clear meaning.

Every language can alter its vocabulary very easily, which means that every speaker can without effort adopt new words, accept or invent new meanings for existing words, and of course, cease to use some words or cease to use them in certain meanings. Dictionaries list some words and some meanings as "obsolete" or "obsolescent" to indicate this process. No two speakers share precisely the same vocabulary of words readily used and readily understood, though they may speak the same dialect. They will, however, naturally have the great majority of words in their vocabularies in common.

Languages have various resources for effecting changes in vocabulary. Meanings of existing words may change. With the virtual disappearance of falconry as a sport in England, "lure" has lost its original meaning of a bunch of feathers on a string by which hawks were recalled to their handler and is used now mainly in its metaphorical sense of enticement. The additional meaning of "nuclear" has already been mentioned; one may list it with words such as computer and jet, which acquired new ranges of meaning in the mid-20th century.

All languages have the means of creating new words to bear new meanings. These can be new creations; "Kodak" is one such, invented at the end of the 19th century by George Eastman; "chortle," new in general use, was a jocular creation of the English writer and mathematician Lewis Carroll (creator of *Alice in Wonderland*); and "gas" was formed

36

in the 17th century by the Belgian chemist and physician Jan Baptist van Helmont as a technical term in chemistry, loosely modeled on the Greek *chaos* ("formless void"). But mostly languages follow definite patterns in their innovations. Words can be made up without limit from existing words or from parts of words; the sources of "railroad," "railway," and "aircraft" are obvious, and so are the sources of "disestablishment," first cited in 1806 and thereafter used with particular reference to the status of the Church of England. The controversy over the relations between church and state in the 19th and early 20th centuries gave rise to a chain of new words as the debate proceeded: "disestablishmentarian," "antidisestablishmentarian," "antidisestablishmentarianism." Usually, the bits and pieces of words used in this way are those found in other such combinations, but this is not always so. The technical term "permafrost" (terrain that never thaws, as in the Arctic) contains a bit of "permanent" probably not hitherto found in any other word.

A particular source of technical neologisms in European languages has been the words and word elements of Latin and Greek. This is part of the cultural history of western Europe, in so many ways the continuation of Greco-Roman civilization. "Microbiology" and "dolichocephalic" are words well formed according to the rules of Greek as they would be taken over into English, but no records survive of *mikrobiologia* and *dolichokephalikos* ever having been used in Ancient Greek. The same is true of Latinate creations such as "reinvestment" and "longiverbosity." The long tradition of looking to Latin and, since the Renaissance, to Greek also, as the languages of European civilization, keeps alive the continuing formation of learned and scientific vocabulary in English and other European languages from these sources. The dependence on the classical languages in Europe is matched by a similar use of Sanskrit words for certain parts of learned vocabulary in some modern Indian languages (Sanskrit being the classical language of India). Such phenomena are examples of loanwords, one of the readiest sources for vocabulary extension.

Loanwords are words taken into a language from another language (the term "borrowing" is used for the process). Most obviously, this occurs when new things come into speakers' experiences as the result of contacts with speakers of other languages. This is part of the history of every language, except for one spoken by an impossibly isolated community. "Tea" from Chinese, "coffee" from Arabic, and "tomato," "potato," and "tobacco" from American Indian languages are familiar examples of loanwords designating new products that have been added to the vocabulary of English. In more abstract areas, several modern languages of India and Pakistan contain many words that relate to government, industry, and current technology taken in from English. This is the result of British rule in these countries up to independence and the worldwide use of English as a language of international science since then.

In general, loanwords are rapidly and completely assimilated to the prevailing grammatical and phonological patterns of the borrowing language. The German word *Kindergarten,* literally "children's garden," was borrowed into English in the middle of the 19th century to designate an informal school for young children. It is now regularly pronounced as an English word, and the plural is kindergartens (not *Kindergärten,* as in German). Occasionally, however, some loanwords retain marks of their foreign origin: examples include Latin plurals such as cacti and narcissi (as contrasted with native patterns such as cactuses and narcissuses).

Languages differ in their acceptance of loanwords. An alternative way of extending vocabulary to cope with new products is to create a descriptive compound from within one's own language. English "aircraft" and "aeroplane" are, respectively, examples of a native compound and a Greek loan creation for the same thing. English "potato" is a loan; French *pomme de terre* (literally, "apple of the earth") is a descriptive compound. Chinese is particularly resistant to loans; "aircraft," "railway," and "telephone" are translated by newly formed compounds meaning literally "fly machine," "fire vehicle," and "lightning (electricity) language."

The origins of slang in language

Slang emanates from conflicts in values, sometimes superficial, often fundamental. When an individual applies language in a new way to express hostility, ridicule, or contempt, often with sharp wit, he may be creating slang, but the new expression will perish unless it is picked up by others. If the speaker is a member of a group that finds that his creation projects the emotional reaction of its members toward an idea, person, or social institution, the expression will gain currency according to the unanimity of attitude within the group. A new slang term is usually widely used in a subculture before it appears in the dominant culture. Thus slang—*e.g.,* "sucker," "honkey," "shavetail," "jerk"— expresses the attitudes, not always derogatory, of one group or class toward the values of another. Slang sometimes stems from within the group, satirizing or burlesquing its own values, behavior, and attitudes; *e.g.,* "shotgun wedding," "cake eater," "greasy spoon." Slang, then, is produced largely by social forces rather than by an individual speaker or writer who, single-handed (like Horace Walpole, who coined "seren-dipity" more than 200 years ago), creates and establishes a word in the language. This is one reason why it is difficult to determine the origin of slang terms.

Civilized society tends to divide into a dominant culture and various subcultures that flourish within the dominant framework. The subcul-tures show specialized linguistic phenomena, varying widely in form and content, that depend on the nature of the groups and their relation to each other and to the dominant culture. The shock value of slang stems largely from the verbal transfer of the values of a subculture to dia-metrically opposed values in the dominant culture. Names such as fuzz, pig, fink, bull, and dick for policemen were not created by officers of the law. (The humorous "dickless tracy," however, meaning a policewoman, *was* coined by male policemen.)

Occupational groups are legion, and while in most respects they identify with the dominant culture, there is just enough social and lin-guistic hostility to maintain group solidarity. Terms such as scab, strike-breaker, company-man, and goon were highly charged words in the era in which labor began to organize in the United States; they are not used lightly even today, though they have been taken into the standard language.

In addition to occupational and professional groups, there are many other types of subcultures that supply slang. These include sexual de-viants, narcotic addicts, ghetto groups, institutional populations, agri-cultural subsocieties, political organizations, the armed forces, Gypsies, and sports groups of many varieties. Some of the most fruitful sources of slang are the subcultures of professional criminals who have migrated to the New World since the 16th century. Old-time thieves still humor-ously refer to themselves as FFV—First Families of Virginia.

In criminal subcultures, pressure applied by the dominant culture intensifies the internal forces already at work, and the argot forming there emphasizes the values, attitudes, and techniques of the subculture. Criminal groups seem to evolve about this specialized argot, and both the subculture and its slang expressions proliferate in response to in-ternal and external pressures.

Most subcultures tend to draw words and phrases from the con-tiguous language (rather than creating many new words) and to give these established terms new and special meanings; some borrowings from foreign languages, including the American Indian tongues, are traditional. The more learned occupations or professions like medicine, law, psychology, sociology, engineering, and electronics tend to create true neologisms, often based on Greek or Latin roots, but these are not major sources for slang, though nurses and medical students adapt some medical terminology to their slang, and air force personnel and some other branches of the armed services borrow freely from engineering and electronics.

The processes by which words become slang are the same as those by which other words in the language change their form or meaning or both. Some of these are the employment of metaphor, simile, folk etymology, distortion of sounds in words, generalization, specialization, clipping, the use of acronyms, elevation and degeneration, metonymy, synecdoche, hyperbole, borrowings from foreign languages, and the play of euphemism against taboo. The English word trip is an example of a term that has undergone both specialization and generalization. It first became specialized to mean a psychedelic experience resulting from the drug LSD. Subsequently, it generalized again to mean any experience on any drug, and beyond that to any type of "kicks" from anything. Clipping is exemplified by the use of "grass" from "laughing grass," a term for marijuana. "Funky," once a very low term for body odour, has undergone elevation among jazz buffs to signify "the best"; "fanny," on the other hand, once simply a girl's name, is currently a degenerated term that refers to the buttocks (in England, it has further degenerated into a taboo word for the female genitalia). There is also some actual coinage of slang terms.

The spread and uses of slang

Slang invades the dominant culture as it seeps out of various subcultures. Some words fall dead or lie dormant in the dominant culture for long periods. Others vividly express an idea already latent in the dominant culture and these are immediately picked up and used. Before the advent of mass media, such terms invaded the dominant culture slowly and were transmitted largely by word of mouth. Thus a term like snafu, its shocking power softened with the explanation "situation normal, all fouled up," worked its way gradually from the military in World War II by word of mouth (because the media largely shunned it) into respectable circles. Today, however, a sportscaster, news reporter, or comedian may introduce a lively new word already used by an ingroup into millions of homes simultaneously, giving it almost instant currency. For example, the term uptight was first used largely by criminal narcotic addicts to indicate the onset of withdrawal distress when drugs are denied. Later, because of intense journalistic interest in the drug scene, it became widely used in the dominant culture to mean anxiety or tension unrelated to drug use. It kept its form but changed its meaning slightly.

Other terms may change their form or both form and meaning, like "one for the book" (anything unsual or unbelievable). Sportswriters in the U.S. borrowed this term around 1920 from the occupational language of then legal bookmakers, who lined up at racetracks in the morning ("the morning line" is still figuratively used on every sports page) to take bets on the afternoon races. Newly arrived bookmakers went to the end of the line, and any bettor requesting unusually long odds was motioned down the line with the phrase, "That's one for the end book." The general public dropped the "end" as meaningless, but old-time gamblers still retain it. Slang spreads through many other channels, such as popular songs, which, for the initiate, are often rich in double entendre.

When subcultures are structurally tight, little of their language leaks out. Thus the Mafia, in more than a half-century of powerful criminal activity in America, has contributed little slang. When subcultures weaken, contacts with the dominant culture multiply, diffusion occurs, and their language appears widely as slang. Criminal narcotic addicts, for example, had a tight subculture and a highly secret argot in the 1940s; now their terms are used freely by middle class teen-agers, even those with no real knowledge of drugs.

Slang is used for many purposes, but generally it expresses a certain emotional attitude; the same term may express diametrically opposed attitudes when used by different people. Many slang terms are primarily derogatory, though they may also be ambivalent when used in intimacy or affection. Some crystallize or bolster the self-image or promote identification with a class or ingroup. Others flatter objects, institutions, or persons but may be used by different people for the opposite effect. "Jesus freak," originally used as ridicule, was adopted as a title by certain street evangelists. Slang sometimes insults or shocks when used directly; some terms euphemize a sensitive concept, though obvious or excessive euphemism may break the taboo more effectively than a less decorous term. Some slang words are essential because there are no words in the standard language expressing exactly the same meaning; *e.g.,* "freakout," "barn-storm" "rubberneck," and the noun "creep." At the other extreme, multitudes of words, vague in meaning, are used simply as fads.

There are many other uses to which slang is put, according to the individual and his place in society. Since most slang is used on the spoken level, by persons who probably are unaware that it is slang, the choice of terms naturally follows a multiplicity of unconscious thought patterns. When used by writers, slang is much more consciously and carefully chosen to achieve a specific effect. Writers, however, seldom invent slang.

It has been claimed that slang is created by ingenious individuals to freshen the language, to vitalize it, to make the language more pungent and picturesque, to increase the store of terse and striking words, or to provide a vocabulary for new shades of meaning. Most of the originators and purveyors of slang, however, are probably not conscious of these noble purposes and do not seem overly concerned about what happens to their language.

ENCYCLOPÆDIA BRITANNICA

ORIGINS

The History of Writing
The History of the Alphabet
The History of Punctuation
The Origins and Characteristics of the English Language
A Brief History of American English
The History of British English
Etymology
The History of the Dictionary
Spelling and the English Language

The History of Writing

Writing, in the widest sense, is a system of human intercommunication by means of visible conventional markings. The earliest and most universal means of communication available to human beings is speech and gesture. These have two features in common: (1) They are of momentary duration and are therefore restricted as to time; as soon as the word is uttered, or the gesture made, it is gone and cannot be revived except by repetition. (2) They can be used only in communication between persons more or less in proximity to each other and are therefore restricted as to space.

The need for finding a way to convey thoughts and feelings in a form not limited by time or space led to the development of methods of communication by means of (1) objects and (2) markings on objects.

Systems of mnemonic signs to keep accounts are known throughout the world. The simplest, commonest ways of keeping records of cattle are with so-called counting sticks—simple wooden sticks with carved notches corresponding to the number of cattle in the custody of a shepherd—and with pebbles in a sack. More complicated is the use, among the Peruvian Incas, of quipu writing, in which accounts concerning objects and beings were recorded by means of strings and knots of various length and colour. Reports of the use of the quipu for recording chronicles and historical events are fantasy. Neither the Peruvian nor the modern knot writings in South America and on the Ryukyu Islands near Japan have any other aim than to record simple statistical facts. Similar is the use of wampum by North American Indians; strings of shell beads, frequently tied together in belts, served as money, ornaments and also as a means of communication. The impracticability of using objects prevented the development of any full system, and such primitive devices are restricted to small geographical areas.

Writing is expressed not by objects themselves but by markings on objects. Writing began when man learned how to communicate his thoughts and feelings by means of visible signs, understandable not only to himself but also to all other persons initiated into the particular system. The relationship between writing and speech was at first very loose, inasmuch as the written message did not correspond to an exact utterance. A message had one meaning and presumably could be interpreted by the reader in only one way, but it could be read, that is, put into words, in several different ways and even in several different languages.

In every great human achievement one important and decisive step can be observed that entirely revolutionizes its further progress. Such a critically important step is the phonetization of script by way of the so-called rebus principle (see the subsection below on word-syllabic writings), which enabled man to express his ideas in a form that corresponded to exact categories of language. From then on, writing gradually lost its function as an independent mode of communication and became a tool of language, a vehicle through which exact categories of language were recorded in a permanent form.

The differences between the earlier and later stages of writing are so crucial and far-reaching that some scholars have defined writing as a device for recording language, dismissing all the early stages, in which visual markings on objects do not serve this purpose, as feeble attempts in the direction of writing, not worthy of study. This may be true of the linguistic science that deals with linguistic elements and with the stage of writing in which writing became a secondary transfer of language and signs of writing can be identified with signs of language. Where these scholars err, however, is in taking for granted the complete identity of language and writing and in assuming that, just as a linguist can operate only with language elements, so a historian of writing should relegate to the wastebasket visual images not having full correspondence with language. But writing in all its stages cannot be identified with language, and a student of writing does not necessarily have to be a linguist. The symbolism of visual images in the early stages of writing, like that of gesture signs, can express meaning without the necessity of a linguistic intermediary, and both can profitably be investigated by a nonlinguist. It is only after writing has developed into a full phonetic system, reproducing elements of language, that one can speak of full correspondence between language and writing and of the study of the latter as being a subdivision of linguistics.

The restriction of the definition of writing to the stage in which writing represents language does not take into account the fact that both stages, earlier and later, have an identical aim: human intercommunication by means of visible marks used conventionally. Furthermore, it is impossible to lump together all the early or primitive stages and consider them all on the same level of development in their loose relation to language. Even though all the early types of writing were quite inefficient in expressing language, some of them, like the Maya and Aztec writings, reached a relatively high level of convention and systematization in the use of their signs.

Pictures, the point of departure

If full writing is defined as a device for expressing linguistic elements by means of conventional visible marks, then writing is no more than 5,000 years old. But in much earlier times, tens of thousands of years ago, man felt the urge to draw or paint pictures on the walls of his primitive dwelling or on the rocks in his surroundings. Primitive man was similar in this respect to a child, who no sooner learns to crawl than he begins to scribble on the wallpaper or to draw pictures in the sand.

The fact that in the table pictures are listed under the first stage, called "No writing," implies (1) that what are normally understood as

Stages of the Development of Writing

No Writing: Pictures				

Forerunners of Writing: Semasiography
  1. Descriptive-representational device
  2. Identifying-mnemonic device				

Full Writing:
  Phonography
    1. Word-syllabic
	Sumerian
	(Akkadian)
	|
		Egyptian
		
		|
			Cretan
			
			|
				Hittite	Chinese
					
					|

2. Syllabic.	Elamite Hurrian	West Semitic (Phoeni- cian) (Hebrew) (Aramaic) |	Linear A Linear B Cypro- Minoan Cypriote Phaistos? Byblos?		Japanese
3. Alphabetic		Greek Aramaic (vocalized) Hebrew (vocalized) Latin Indic			Korean

pictures—that is, creations resulting from an artistic-aesthetic urge—do not fall under the category of writing, and (2) that writing had its origin in simple pictures. The case could be paralleled, for example, by calling steam the first stage in a chart showing the development of the steam engine. Steam, as it issues from a geyser or a tea kettle, is in itself not a steam engine, but it is the element around which the successive stages had to build in order to reach the ultimate development.

In most cases it is, of course, difficult or impossible to ascertain the purpose or the urge that stimulated man to draw or incise a picture, since the circumstances that led to its execution are unknown. Is the picture a manifestation of magic, religious, or aesthetic expression? Was it drawn for the purpose of securing good hunting or was it the result of the artistic impulse? Several causes may have been instrumental at the same time in the origin of a drawing. Such pictures do not represent writing because they do not form part of a conventional system of signs and can be understood only by the man who drew them or by his family and close friends who had heard of the event.

Semasiography

Under Forerunners of Writing in the table are included the various devices by which man first attempted to convey his thoughts and feelings. An all-inclusive term which may be coined for these devices is "semasiography" (Gr. sēmasía, "signification," and graphé, "writing"). This is the stage in which pictures convey the general meaning intended by the writer. In this stage, visible drawn forms—somewhat like gesture language—express meaning directly without an intervening linguistic form. In place of the term semasiography used here, most scholars prefer the terms pictography or ideography. However, the term pictography can be applied not only to such primitive devices as those of the American Indians but also to such fully developed systems as the Egyptian or Hittite hieroglyphic. For that reason, the terms pictography and pictographic are avoided altogether in this treatment.

Primitive communication with visible symbols was achieved by descriptive-representational and identifying-mnemonic devices. As the two devices frequently overlap, it is difficult to assign some primitive writings rigorously to one or the other category.

Descriptive-representational devices are similar to drawings but differ in that they contain only what is important for communication and lack aesthetic embellishment. In the identifying-mnemonic device a symbol is used to depict a person, an animal or an object for the purpose of identifying it individually, or of recording articulate utterances such as proverbs or songs. An illustration of the identifying device is a drawing of a white hawk, to represent a man named White Hawk. Mnemonic devices are exemplified by the symbols used to record proverbs among the Ewe Negroes of Togoland, such as a picture of a threaded needle and of a piece of cloth, representing the proverb, "The needle sews great cloth," meaning that small things can achieve greatness. The descriptive-representational device may seem the more developed because it seems to communicate better than identifying-mnemonic devices. A drawing depicting a battle by the descriptive-representational device, for instance, tells the story better than one or two identifying-mnemonic signs. It is not the descriptive-representational device, however, which leads to fully developed writing. Pictures drawn for this purpose are bound by the conventions of art, which limit and hinder them as vehicles of human intercommunication.

Identifying-mnemonic devices are also drawn; their aim, however, is not to describe but to help the reader remember and identify an event, object, or being. Thus, a complete correspondence is established and gradually conventionalized between certain symbols and certain objects or beings. Since these objects and beings have names in the oral language, the correspondence is further established between the written symbols and their spoken counterparts. Once it was discovered that words could be expressed in written symbols, a new and much better method of human visual communication was established. It was no longer necessary to record an event such as a man killing a lion by drawing the man, spear in hand, killing the lion. Instead, the spoken sentence, "man killed the lion," could be recorded by three conventional symbols representing the words "man," "killed" and "lion." Accordingly, "five sheep" could be expressed by two symbols corresponding to two words instead of by the five separate pictures of sheep required in the descriptive-representational device. The introduction in the identifying device of strict order in the signs, following the order of the spoken words, is in direct contrast to the method of the descriptive device and of the picture, in which the meaning is conveyed by the totality of little drawings wihout any convention as to the beginning of the message or the order in which it should be interpreted.

To a superficial observer the descriptive-representational device may appear to be better adapted to convey communication than the device using symbols of an identifying and mnemonic nature. It is clear, for instance, that a drawing depicting a battle tells the story better than a sign or two intended merely to recall the battle. Similar conclusions might be drawn in comparing, for example, early specimens of Egyptian writing, drawn chiefly by the descriptive-representational device, with Old Sumerian ledger tablets, drawn by the identifying-mnemonic device.

It is not the descriptive-representational device, however, that lies on the direct road toward a fully developed writing. Pictures drawn by this device follow the conventions of art, with all of their drawbacks and limitations as a vehicle of human intercommunication. The binding traditions of art, established thousands of years before man first attempted communication by means of conventional marks, were too strong to allow for the development of the descriptive-representational device in the right direction.

Phonography

WORD-SYLLABIC SYSTEMS   In the process of using pictures to identify and recall objects or beings, a complete correspondence is established and gradually conventionalized between certain written signs, on the one hand, and certain objects and beings, on the other. Since these objects and beings have names in the oral language, the correspondence is further established between the written signs and their spoken counterparts. Once it is discovered that words can be expressed in written signs, a new and much better method of human intercommunication is firmly established. It is no longer necessary to express a sentence such as "man killed lion" by means of a drawing of a man, spear or bow in hand, in the process of killing a lion. The three words can now be written by means of three conventional signs representing man, spear or bow (killing), and lion, respectively. Accordingly, "five sheep" can be expressed by means of two signs corresponding to two words in the language, instead of by five separate pictures of sheep, which would have to be drawn in an artistic picture or in the descriptive-representational device. The introduction in the identifying device of a strict order of the signs that corresponds to the order of the spoken words is in direct contrast to the methods of the descriptive device and of the artistic picture, in which the meaning is conveyed by the totality of separate drawings without any convention as to the beginning of the message or the order in which it should be interpreted.

A device in which individual signs can express individual words should naturally lead toward the development of a complete system of word signs; that is, a word writing or logography. Such a fully developed system probably never existed either in antiquity or in modern times. To create and memorize thousands of signs for the thousands of words and names existing in a language and to invent new signs for newly acquired words and names is so impracticable that logographic writing either can be used only as a very limited system, or it must be adapted in some new way in order to develop into a useful system. Experience with the earliest Alaska and Cherokee writing systems, which employed only word signs, is indicative of the impracticability of such limited systems. Even Chinese, the most logographic of all writings, is not a pure logographic system, because from the earliest times it has used word signs functioning as syllabic signs. And what is true of the Chinese system is even more true of other ancient Oriental systems such as Sumerian, Egyptian, and Hittite.

A primitive logographic writing can develop into a full system only if it succeeds in attaching to a sign a phonetic value independent of the meaning that this sign has as a word. This is phonetization, the most important single step in the history of writing. In modern usage the device is called rebus writing, as exemplified in the drawing of an eye and of a saw to express the sentence "I saw," or in that of a man and a date to express the word "mandate." With the introduction of phonetization and its subsequent systematization, complete systems of writing were established, which made possible the expression of all linguistic elements by means of signs with conventional syllabic values. Thus full writing originated, in contrast to the feeble attempts comprising semasiography, which can only be classified as forerunners of writing.

Word-syllabic, or logo-syllabic, writing—that is, writing in which signs express words and syllables—is found in the Orient, the vast belt of Asia extending from the eastern shores of the Mediterranean Sea to the western shores of the Pacific Ocean. For historical as well as practical reasons, Egypt and, at least in the pre-Hellenic period, the area of the Aegean Sea are included within the orbit of Oriental civilizations.

In this large area are found seven original and fully developed logo-syllabic systems of writing. Sumerian in Mesopotamia, 3100 B.C. to A.D. 75; Proto-Elamite in Elam, 3000 B.C. to 2200 B.C., Proto-Indic in the Indus Valley, around 2200 B.C., Chinese in China, 1300 B.C. to the present; Egyptian in Egypt, 3000 B.C. to A.D. 400; Cretan in Crete and Greece, 2000 to 1200 B.C., and Hittite in Anatolia and Syria, 1500 to 700 B.C. Other logo-syllabic systems may at some time come to light, but at the present there are no likely candidates to be added to the above list of seven. The Proto-Armenian inscriptions discovered within the last few decades are too short and too little known to allow any safe conclusions. The mysterious Easter Island inscriptions, on which so much effort has been wasted by so many imaginative minds, are not writing even in the broadest sense of the word, as they probably represent nothing else but pictorial concoctions for magical purposes. Finally, the systems of the Mayas and the Aztecs do not represent a full logo-syllabic writing; even in their most advanced stages they never attained the level of phonographic development of the earliest stages of the Oriental systems.

Of the seven systems, three—namely, Proto-Elamite, Proto-Indic, and Cretan—are as yet undeciphered. Consequently, modern understanding of the logo-syllabic systems is limited to the remaining four systems—Sumerian, Egyptian, Hittite, and Chinese.

The unifying characteristic of the four systems is that they are all phonographic (with established correspondence between sign and sound) almost from the very beginning of their development and that they all contain word signs or logograms, syllabic signs, and what are often called "auxiliary" signs or marks. The formation of word signs is identical or very similar in all four systems. Also, the general principles of using the auxiliary signs such as punctuation marks and "unpronounced" determinatives, elements that are added to the main signs and in some way specify their meaning, are identical, although the various systems differ formally. Only in the use of syllabic signs are the differences so pronounced as to permit the formation of exact subdivisions by types.

SYLLABIC SYSTEMS   Out of the four logo-syllabic systems listed in the preceding section, four syllabaries, showing various degrees of simplification, were developed in the course of time. An interesting conclusion that can be drawn about these syllabic writings is that they were all created by heterogeneous peoples. Thus, although the Mesopotamian Babylonians and Asyrians accepted almost without change the Sumerian system of writing, the foreign Elamites, Hurrians, and Urartians found the task of mastering the complicated Mesopotamian system too heavy a burden; they merely took over a simplified syllabary and eliminated almost entirely the ponderous logographic apparatus. The Semites of Palestine and Syria went even further in their aim toward simplification and accepted from the Egyptians only the principle of writing monosyllables without indicating differences in vowels. Similarly, while the Linear A and B systems of the Aegean area retained a number of word signs from the earlier writing, other descendants of the Aegean systems, the Cypro-Minoan, the Cypriot, and the Phaistos and Proto-Byblian systems, used only syllabic signs, omitting word signs entirely. The Japanese were not so radical. They too developed a simple syllabary similar in principle to that of the Cyprians, even though it distinguishes by separate marks the voiced from the voiceless consonants; but side by side with the syllabary (kana) they use word signs (kanji) taken over from the Chinese writing.

The term "West Semitic syllabary," given to the various forms of writing used by the Ugaritans, Phoenicians, Hebrews, and other Semites from the middle of the 2nd millennium B.C. on, expresses clearly the contention that these writings are syllabaries and not alphabets, as is often assumed. These Semitic writings follow exactly the pattern of their

Egyptian prototype, and the latter cannot be anything else but a syllabary from the point of view of the structure and typology of writing.

ALPHABETIC SYSTEMS   The question may now be legitimately asked: If these early Semitic writings are not alphabets, what, then, is the alphabet? The answer is clear. If by the word "alphabet" is understood a writing that expresses the single sounds (*i.e.*, phonemes) of a language, then the first alphabet was formed by the Greeks. Although throughout the 2nd millennium B.C. several attempts were made to find a way to indicate vowels in syllabaries of the Egyptian-Semitic type, none of them succeeded in developing into a full vocalic system. The usual way was to add phonetic indicators as help in reading the vowels that were left unindicated in the Semitic systems of writing, as in the case of m^a-l^a-$k^{(a)}$-t^i-y^i for *malaktī* "I reigned," in which y^i was added to establish the reading of t^i in *malaktī*, or in the case of m^a-$l^{(a)}$-k^u-w^u, in which w^u was added to establish the reading of k^u in *malkū*. But while the Semites made sporadic use of these indicators, called *matres lectionis,* the Greeks used them systematically after each syllabic sign. Thus, following the principle of reduction, they were soon able to reach the conclusion that, since in the writing $t^i y^i$ the second sign does not stand for the syllable y^i but for the vowel *i*, the first sign must stand for the consonant *t* and not for the syllable t^i.

It was therefore the Greeks who, having accepted in full the forms of the West Semitic syllabary, evolved a system of vowel signs that, attached to the syllabic signs, reduced the value of these syllabic signs to simple consonantal signs, and thus for the first time created a full alphabetic system of writing. And it was from the Greeks that the Semites in turn learned the use of vowel marks.

In the past 2,800 years the conquests of the alphabet have encompassed the whole of civilization, but during all this period no reforms have taken place in the principles of writing. Hundreds of alphabets throughout the world, different as they may be in outer form, all use the principles first established in the Greek writing.

ENCYCLOPÆDIA BRITANNICA

The History of the Alphabet

Alphabet, strictly defined, indicates by written symbols a set of speech sounds. The alphabet was a Greek invention based upon North Semitic writing which indicated only consonants, a procedure suitable enough for a Semitic language but not for an Indo-European one. The word itself is derived from the names (of Semitic origin) of the first two letters of the Greek alphabet, alpha and beta, and the definition is of quite a general character, as is easily seen in the case of the first letter of the English alphabet, which represents different sounds in the words "father," "man" and "take." Even when a letter represents a single sound, it does so roughly, taking no account of intonation, stress or pronunciation, which vary not only between speakers but also within the speech of an individual according to the position of the sound in a word or phrase and the nature of the phrase.

In most alphabets the symbols are arranged in a definite order, or sequence (*e.g., A, B, C, etc.*). Each of the characters usually represents either a consonant or a vowel, rather than a syllable or group of consonants and vowels. As a result, the number of characters required can be held to a minimum. A language that has 30 consonant sounds and five vowels, for example, needs only 35 separate letters. In a syllabary, on the other hand, the same language would require 30 times five symbols to represent each syllable (*e.g.,* separate forms for *ba, be, bi, bo, bu; da, de, di,* and so on), and an additional five symbols for the vowels, thereby making a total of 155 individual characters.

An alphabet is a highly developed, artificial form of writing. The connection between sound and character is conventional and not essential. This is not the case with all forms of writing. Pictographs, ideographs and hieroglyphs bear an essential relationship to what they represent. Such methods constitute an earlier stage of writing than syllabaries and alphabets. Both syllabaries and alphabets are phonetic symbolizations; that is, they are symbols to record the sounds of words rather than to represent objects or ideas being expressed. (With the passage of

54

time some languages, notably English, failed to synchronize spelling changes with changes in pronunciation, so that these languages can no longer be said to have totally phonetic spelling.)

Pictography, or picture writing, was the first step toward true writing. Ideography, or ideographic writing, extended the possibilities of pictography. The earliest fully developed systems of writing, those of the ancient Near East (Mesopotamia and Egypt), China, and pre-Columbian Central America and Mexico, along with others, were not, however, purely pictographic, ideographic, or phonetic. The oldest of these developed scripts was the cuneiform; the second oldest was the Egyptian hieroglyphic style.

Alphabetic writing is the most convenient and adaptable form of writing. It is learned in childhood with ease, which is not the case with the Chinese script, for instance. The alphabet may also be passed from

modern European	Latin	rúnes	Greek	Cyrillic	Glagolitic
A	A		A	Ꙁ	᛭
B	B	ß	ß	Б(v) Б(b)	Ꙋ Ⴊ
C	Ɔ	ᛱᛌᛏᛲ	ᛱᛌ	Г	℀
D	D	ᛞᛈᛈᛈ(th) ᛥᛘᛘ	DΔ⊙	Ꙃ	℔
E	Ɛ	ᛔᛂᛯᛉ	Ⴆ	E	Ɜ
F	F	ᚠᚥᛩᛇ	φ F	Ψ	⊕
G	G	ᚷ φ			
H	ᛗ	ᚾᛁᚺᚼᚻ	H	H(i)	Ⴟ Ⴒ
I	I	I	I	I(i)	Ꙁ ℳ(g)
J					
K	Ҡ	Ψ	k	К	ҍ
L	Ⴑ	↑	↑	Λ	ℬ
M	₩	Ꙧ	M	M	ℛ
N	N	ᛏᛐᛐᛚ	N	H	℘
O	O	ᛒ℟℟	○ ◇	O	℈
P	ℸ	Πᛘ(e)	Γ	П	Ⴌ
Q	Ọ		Ọ		
R	ᛩ	R R	ᚱ	Ọ	ҍ
S	ᛋ	ᛋ	ᛋ	С	Ⴔ
T	T	↑	T	T	ℳ
U	V	Λᴨ	V		
V					
W		ᛈ ᛈ			
X	X	X(g)	X	X(h)	ҍ
Y	Y	ᛉᛊᛣᛋ		Y(ü)	Ⴍ
Z	Z	Ꙁᛋ(ih,oo)	⊥	Ж(Ȥ)S(dz)3(h)	Ꙃ ♅ ℗
NG		ᚥ ᛇ(ng)		Ⴒ ＋	

value	o sht ts ch sh ŭ	y	i̇ ě yu ya ye	g(ye) g ye ya kh ps θ(th,f)	
Cyrillic	Ш Ѱ Ц Ч Ш Ꙁ	Ꙑ Ꙃ	Ь Ѣ Ю Ие Ѧ Ѧ Ѧ Ж Ҥ Ѯ Ꙃ Ѵ Ѳ		
Glagolitic	O Ꙋ V Ⴕ Ш-Ꙗ ℈Ⴕ-℻℈ Ꙃ-ℬℬ-℈ℬ Ꙃ Ꙗ Ⴔ		Ɇ ℋℋℋ	Ѳ	

one language to another without difficulty. It has changed surprisingly little in nearly 3,000 years, despite the introduction of printing and the typewriter.

Origins of the alphabet

Evidence for the original alphabet is scarce, but such as it is, it comes exclusively from the lands bordering the eastern shores of the Mediterranean, including ancient Canaan and Phoenicia, and belongs to the period between 1700 and 1500 B.C. This alphabet is known as the North Semitic.

Over the centuries, various theories have been advanced to explain the origin of alphabetic writing, and, since classical times, the problem has been a matter of serious study. The Greeks and Romans considered five different peoples as the possible inventors of the alphabet—the Phoenicians, Egyptians, Assyrians, Cretans, and Hebrews. Modern theories include some that are not very different from those of ancient days. Every country situated in or more or less near to the east Mediterranean has been singled out for the honour. Egyptian writing, cuneiform, Cretan, Hieroglyphic Hittite, the Cypriot syllabary, and other scripts have all been called prototypes of the alphabet. The Egyptian theory actually subdivides into three separate theories, according to whether the Egyptian hieroglyphic, the hieratic, or the demotic script is regarded as the true parent of alphabetic writing. Similarly, the idea that cuneiform was the precursor of the alphabet may also be subdivided into Sumerian, Babylonian, and Assyrian cuneiform.

Among the various other theories concerning the alphabet are the hypotheses that the alphabet was brought by the Philistines from Crete to Palestine, that the various ancient scripts of the Mediterranean countries developed from prehistoric geometric symbols employed throughout the Mediterranean area from the earliest times, and that the Proto-Sinaitic inscriptions (discovered since 1905 in the Sinai Peninsula) represent a stage of writing intermediate between the Egyptian hieroglyphics and the North Semitic alphabet. Another hypothesis, the Ugaritic theory, evolved after an epoch-making discovery in 1929 (and the years following) at the site of the ancient Ugarit, on the Syrian coast opposite the most easterly cape of Cyprus. Thousands of clay tablets were found there, documents of inestimable value in many fields of research (including epigraphy, philology, and the history of religion). Dating from the 15th and 14th centuries B.C., they were written in a cuneiform alphabet of 30 letters.

The Early Canaanite theory was based on several undeciphered inscriptions also discovered since 1929 at various Palestinian sites; the writings belong in part to *c.* 1700 B.C. and are thus the earliest preserved documents in an alphabetic writing.

Despite the conflict in theories, leading scholars are generally agreed that for about 200 years before the middle of the 2nd millennium B.C., alphabet making was in the air in the Syro-Palestinian region. It is idle to speculate on the meaning of the various discoveries referred to. That they manifest closely related efforts is certain; what the exact relationship between these efforts was, and what their relationship with the North Semitic alphabet was, cannot as yet be said with certainty.

It can, however, be ascertained that the period from 1730 to 1580 B.C. in Syria, Palestine, and Egypt, during which there was an uprooting of established cultural and ethnic patterns in the Fertile Crescent, provided conditions favourable to the conception of an alphabetic script, a kind of writing that would be more accessible to larger groups of people, in contrast to the scripts of the old states of Mesopotamia and Egypt, which were confined largely to the priestly class. In default of other direct evidence, it is reasonable to suppose that the actual prototype of the alphabet was not very different from the writing of the earliest North Semitic inscriptions now extant, which belong to the last two or three centuries of the 2nd millennium B.C. The North Semitic alphabet was so constant for many centuries that it is impossible to think that there had been any material changes in the preceding two or three centuries. Moreover, the North Semitic languages, based as they are on a consonantal root (*i.e.,* a system in which the vowels serve mainly to indicate grammatical or similar changes), were clearly suitable for the creation of a consonantal alphabet.

The inventor or inventors of the alphabet were, no doubt, influenced by Egyptian writing—perhaps also by other scripts. Indeed, it is probable that the man or men who invented the alphabet were acquainted with most of the scripts current in the eastern Mediterranean lands at the time. Though the nationality of the inventor or inventors of the alphabet is unknown, it is now generally agreed that he or they belonged to the Northwest Semitic linguistic group, which includes the ancient Canaanites, Phoenicians, and Hebrews.

It seems probable that the original letters were conventional signs and not, as is still held by some, pictures used as ideograms (*e.g.,* the letter 'alef representing an ox, bet a house, gimmel a camel, and so on). Indeed, the great achievement in the creation of the alphabet was not the invention of signs but the inner working principle; that is, the production of a system in which each sound is represented by one symbol and each symbol generally represents one sound. The principle governing the conventional names of the letters is known as acrophony—that is, the value of each consonant is the value of the first letter of its name: *b* of "bet," *g* of "gimmel," *d* of "dalet," and so on. These names were not derived from pictographic representations of the letters but were an artificial, mnemonic device similar to those used in modern ABC books for children.

Early development

At the end of the 2nd millennium B.C., with the political decay of the great nations of the Bronze Age—*i.e.*, the Egyptians, Babylonians, Assyrians, Hittites, and Cretans—a new historical world began. In Syria and Palestine, the geographical centre of the Fertile Crescent, three nations—Israel, Phoenicia, and Aram—played an increasingly important political role. To the south of the Fertile Crescent, the Sabaeans, a South Arabian people (also Semites, though South Semites), attained a position of wealth and importance as commercial intermediaries between the East and the Mediterranean. To the west, seeds were sown among the peoples who later constituted the nation of Hellas—the Greeks. As a result, an alphabet developed with four main branches: (1) the so-called Canaanite, or main branch, subdivided into Early Hebrew and Phoenician varieties; (2) the Aramaic branch; (3) the South Semitic or Sabaean branch; and (4) the Greek alphabet, which became the progenitor of the Western alphabets, including the Etruscan and the Latin.

It is difficult to overestimate the importance of the Phoenician alphabet in the history of writing. The earliest definitely readable inscription in the North Semitic alphabet is the so-called Ahiram inscription found at Byblos in Phoenicia (now Lebanon), which probably dates from the 11th century B.C. There is, however, no doubt that the Phoenician use of the North Semitic alphabet went further back. By being adopted and then adapted by the Greeks, the North Semitic, or Phoenician, alphabet became the direct ancestor of all Western alphabets. Only very few inscriptions have been found in Phoenicia proper. This rarity of indigenous documents is in contrast to the numbers of Phoenician inscriptions found elsewhere—on Cyprus, Malta, Sicily, and Sardinia, and in Greece, North Africa, Marseille, Spain, and other places.

The dominant Greek alphabet

As with so many other things, the importance of the ancient Greeks in the history of the alphabet is paramount. All of the alphabets in use in Europe today are directly or indirectly related to the Greek. Although the Greek alphabet was an adaptation rather than an invention, it was such an improvement that it has remained for 3,000 years—with only

slight modifications—an unparalleled vehicle of expression and communication for men of the most diverse nationalities and languages. The
Greek alphabet, created early in the 1st millennium B.C., spread in various directions in Asia Minor, Egypt, Italy, and other places, but far and
away the most important developments of it were the Etruscan-Latin
and the Cyrillic alphabets.

The Greek alphabet derived from the North Semitic script between *c.*
1000 B.C. and the 9th century B.C. The direction of writing in the oldest
Greek inscriptions—as in the Semitic scripts—is from right to left, a
style that was superseded by the boustrophedon (meaning, in Greek,
"as the ox draws the plow"), in which lines run alternately from right to
left and left to right. This change occurred approximately in the 6th
century B.C. There are, however, some early Greek inscriptions written
from left to right, and after 500 B.C., Greek writing invariably proceeded
from left to right.

The letters for *b, g, d, z, k, l, m, n, p, r,* and *t,* which are sounds
common to the Semitic and Greek languages, were taken over without
change. The principal Greek changes were the introduction of vowel
representation, the re-arrangement of the sibilant or fricative sounds
(of which the Semitic alphabets had a considerable variety), the adoption of some Semitic letters for slightly different Greek sounds, and the
invention of symbols for Greek sounds not expressed by any of the
Semitic letters. The different ways in which these adaptations were carried out allow the two main branches of the early Greek alphabet—the
eastern and the western—to be distinguished. These again subdivide,
each into secondary branches. Within this general grouping there were
many local peculiarities, but the differences between all of these local
alphabets involved variations in detail rather than essential structure.
The eastern and western subdivisions were the two principal branches
of the early Greek alphabet.

After the 4th century B.C., the development of the Greek alphabet
was almost wholly external, in the direction of greater utility, convenience, and, above all, beauty. The classical style was retained as a monumental script at the same time that more cursive forms grew up for
writing on such surfaces as parchment, papyrus, and wax. The classical
letters were also retained as the capital letters in the modern print
(though some of the capitals in modern Greek handwriting are borrowed from the Latin alphabet). On the other hand, the classical Greek
alphabet also evolved into the Greek uncials, the cursive, and the minuscule script. (Uncial letters were somewhat rounded and separated versions of capital letters or cursive forms; minuscule letters developed
from cursive writing and have simplified, small forms.) Up until about
809 A.D. the uncials were used as a book hand; later, the minuscule

script was employed for the same purpose. The cursive scripts evolved into the modern Greek minuscule.

In the middle of the 3rd century B.C., the Greek scholar Aristophanes of Byzantium introduced the three accents—acute, grave, and circumflex—that were thereafter used to assist students, particularly foreigners, in the correct pronunciation of Greek words; these continue to be used in most Greek texts printed today. Originally, these marks indicated tone or pitch, not stress.

Countless inscriptions have been discovered all over the Hellenic and Hellenistic world and beyond. They include official decrees, annals, codes of law, lists of citizens, civic rolls, temple accounts, votive offerings, ostraca (fragments of pottery), sepulchral inscriptions, coins, lettering on vases, and so forth. These, along with many thousands of Greek manuscripts, both ancient and medieval, serve as sources for the studies known as Greek epigraphy and Greek paleography and are of untold importance for all branches of ancient history, philology, philosophy, and other disciplines.

Offshoots of the Greek alphabet

The most direct offshoots from the Greek alphabet were those adapted to the languages of the non-Hellenic peoples of western Asia Minor in the 1st millenium B.C.: the scripts of the Lycians, Phrygians, Pamphylians, Lydians, and Carians. The Coptic alphabet was the other non-European offshoot from the Greek and the only one used in Africa. Twenty-four of its 31 letters were borrowed from the Greek uncial writing, and seven were taken over from a particularly cursive variety of the Egyptian demotic writing, the demotic letters were used to express Coptic sounds not existing in the Greek language.

More significant, however, were the European offshoots. In Italy, two alphabets derived directly from the Greek: the Etruscan and the Messapian. The Messapii were an ancient tribe who inhabited the present Apulia (in southern Italy) in pre-Roman times; their language is presumed to belong to the Illyrian group. Over 200 Messapic (or Messapian) inscriptions have been discovered. In southeastern Europe, there were three offshoots from the Greek alphabet—the Gothic, the Cyrillic, and the Glagolitic alphabets.

The Etruscan alphabet

The Etruscans, a highly civilized people who were the ancestors of the modern Tuscans and the predecessors of the Romans, inhabited what is now modern Tuscany in central Italy; their language, still mainly undeciphered, has come down in over 11,000 inscriptions, the earliest being the 8th-century-B.C. Marsiliana Tablet, preserved in the Museo Archeologico in Florence. This is also the earliest preserved record of a Western alphabet. The early Etruscan alphabet, unlike any early Greek alphabet found in the Greek inscriptions, contains the original—the prototype—Greek alphabet, consisting of the 22 North Semitic letters, with the phonetic values given to them by the Greeks, and the four additional Greek letters at the end of the alphabet. The Etruscans introduced various changes in their script, and several features in the modern alphabets can be attributed to the influence of the ancient Etruscans. An example is the phonetic value of "k" for the letters *c, k,* and *q*. Like the Semitic and the early Greek alphabets, Etruscan writing nearly always reads from right to left, though a few inscriptions are in boustrophedon style. The probable date of the origin of the Etruscan alphabet is the late 9th or early 8th century B.C.

About 400 B.C., the "classical" Etruscan alphabet took its final form of 20 letters—four vowels and 16 consonants. Because the voiced and voiceless sounds *b* and *p, d* and *t, g* and *k* were not differentiated in the Etruscan language, letters *b* and *d* never appear in pure Etruscan inscriptions, and after the disappearance of *k* and *q,* the letter *C* was employed for *g* and *k*.

The Etruscan alphabet had many varieties and several offshoots. Among the offshoots, apart from the Latin, were many alphabets used by Italic populations of pre-Roman Italy and by non-Italic tribes (*e.g.,* the Piceni).

The Latin alphabet

The adaptation of the Etruscan alphabet to the Latin language probably took place at some time in the 7th century B.C. From this century, there is a gold brooch known as the Praeneste Fibula. The inscription, written in an early form of Latin, runs from right to left and reads clearly: *manios: med:fhefhaked:numasioi,* which in classical Latin is *Manius me fecit Numerio* "Manius made me for Numerius."

Dating from the end of the 7th or the beginning of the 6th century B.C. is a famous cippus (small pillar) from the Roman Forum; it is inscribed vertically on its four faces, in boustrophedon style. Another inscription, probably of the 6th century B.C., is known as that of the Duenos Vase and was found in Rome, near the Quirinal Hill. It is also written from right to left. Some Sabine inscriptions belong to the 5th or the 4th century B.C. There are also a few inscriptions belonging to the 3rd and 2nd centuries B.C.

The Roman capital letters, a form of writing that was used under the empire with unparalleled effectiveness for monumental purposes, became a byword for precision and grandeur, despite a very unprepossessing beginning. Indeed, for the first six centuries of its existence, Roman writing was relatively unimpressive. Only with the advent of the 1st century B.C. were there signs of magnificence to come.

An opinion that used to be commonly held, and still is held by many, is that the Latin alphabet was derived directly from the Greek in a form used by Greek colonists in Italy. The theory rested on an assertion that the Latin alphabet corresponds to the Chalcidian variety of the western group of Greek scripts employed at Cumae in Campania, southern Italy. This theory is unlikely; indeed, as already mentioned, the Etruscan alphabet was the link between the Greek and the Latin. For instance, the most interesting feature in the inscription of the Praeneste Fibula is the device of combining the letters *f* and *h* to represent the Latin sound of *f*. This was one of the Etruscan ways of representing the same sound. Also, most of the Latin letter names, such as a, be, ce, de for the Greek alpha, beta, gamma, delta, and so on, were taken over from the Etruscans.

As already mentioned, the original Etruscan alphabet consisted of 26 letters, of which the Romans adopted only 21. They did not retain the three Greek aspirate letters, theta, phi, and chi, in the alphabet because there were no corresponding Latin sounds but did employ them to represent the numbers 100, 1,000, and 50. Of the three Etruscan *s* sounds, the Romans kept what had been the Greek sigma. The symbol that represented the aspirate later received the shape *H* as it did in Etruscan. *I* was the sign both of the vowel *i* and the consonant *j*. *X* was added later to represent the sound *x* and was placed at the end of the alphabet. At a later stage, after 250 B.C., the seventh letter, the Greek zeta, was dropped because Latin did not require it, and a new letter, *G*, made by adding a bar to the lower end of *C*, was placed in its position.

After the conquest of Greece in the 1st century B.C., a large number of Greek words were borrowed by the Latin language. At that time the symbols *Y* and *Z* were adopted from the contemporary Greek alphabet, but only to transliterate Greek words; hence, they do not appear in normal Latin inscriptions. They were placed at the end of the alphabet, and the Latin script thus became one of 23 symbols.

A few permanent additions, or, rather, differentiations from existing letters, occurred during the Middle Ages, when the signs for *u* and *v*, and *i* and *j*, previously written interchangeably for either the vowel or the consonant sound, became conventionalized as *u* and *i* for vowels *v* and *j* for consonants. *W* was introduced by Norman scribes to represent the English sound *w* (a semivowel) and to differentiate it from the *v* sound.

The connection of the capital letters of modern writing with the ancient Semitic-Greek-Etruscan-Latin letters is evident even to a layman. The connection of the minuscules (*i.e.*, the small letters) with the ancient Latin letters is not as evident, but in fact both the majuscules and the minuscules descended from the same ancient Latin alphabet. The different shapes of the small letters are the result of a transformation of the ancient letters by the elimination of a part of the letter—as, for insance, *h* from *H* or *b* from *B*—or by lengthening a part of it—for instance, *d* from *D*. Moreover, the change of the Latin writing into the modern script was caused by technical bearings of the tool, primarily the pen, and the material of writing, mainly papyrus and parchment, and, from the 14th century onward, also paper. It was the pen, with its preference for curves, that eliminated the angular forms; it was the papyrus, and still more the parchment or vellum, and, in modern times, paper, that made these curves possible.

In ancient times, the minuscule did not exist, but there were several varieties of the capital and the cursive scripts. There were three varieties of the capitals: the lapidary capitals (used mainly on stone monuments); the elegant book capitals, somewhat rounded in shape; and the rustic capitals, which were less carefully elaborated than the lapidary script and not as round as the book capitals, but more easily and quickly written. In everyday life, the cursive script—*i.e.*, the current hand—was developed with continuous modifications for greater speed. Between the monumental and the cursive scripts, there was a whole series of types that had some of the peculiarities of each group. There were lapidary mixed scripts and book semicursive scripts, and there was the early uncial or, rather semiuncial script of the 3rd century A.D. which seems to have developed into the beautiful uncial script.

When the various European countries had shaken off the political authority of Rome and the learned communities had been dissolved and their members scattered, a marked change took place in the development of the Latin literary, or book hand. Several national hands, styles of the Latin cursive, assumed different features. There thus developed on the European continent and in the British Isles the five basic national hands, each giving rise to several varieties: Italian, Merovingian in France, Visigothic in Spain, Germanic, and Insular or Anglo-Irish hands. At the end of the 8th century, the Carolingian (Caroline) hand developed and, after becoming the official script and literary hand of the Frankish Empire, developed as the main book hand of western Europe in the following two centuries. The combination of the majuscules, or capital letters, and minuscules, or small letters, can be attributed mainly to the Carolingian script.

In the course of the next centuries, various book hands or chart hands and other cursive scripts developed from the Carolingian style. In the late 12th century, and during the next two centuries, the letters gradually became angular in shape; this resulted from the pen being held in a position that made a slanting stroke. The new hand, termed black letter, or Gothic, was employed mainly in northwestern Europe, including England, until the 16th century. It is still used, though rarely, in Germany, where it is called Fraktur script.

In Italy, the black letter was also used, but the Italians preferred a rounder type, called *littera antiqua* "old letter." During the 15th century, the round, neat, humanistic or Renaissance hand was introduced in Florence and was employed for literary productions, while the needs of everyday life were met by an equally beautiful, though not as clearly legible, cursive hand. The two styles developed into two main varieties: (1) the Venetian minuscule, nowadays known as italics, traditionally (though wrongly) considered to be an imitation of Petrarch's handwriting; and (2) the Roman type, preferred in northern Italy, chiefly in Venice, where it was used in the printing presses at about the end of the 15th and the beginning of the 16th centuries; from Italy it spread to Holland, England (about 1518), Germany, France, and Spain. The classical Roman character was adopted for the majuscules. This majuscule writing, along with the Roman type minuscule and the italics, spread all over the world. In England, they were adopted from Italy in the 16th century.

The survival of the black letter (Gothic) in Germany is attributed to the fact that it was the current style at the time of the invention of printing in Germany—it was employed by Gutenberg; in Italy the *littera antiqua* was used by the German printers Konrad Sweynheym and Arnold Pannartz, as well as by Nicolas Jenson, the great Venetian printer who perfected the Roman type.

The modern national alphabets of the western European nations are, strictly speaking, adaptations of the Latin alphabet to Germanic (English, German, Swedish, Dutch, Danish, etc.), Romance (Italian, French, Spanish, Portuguese, etc.), Slavic (Polish, Czech, Slovak, etc.), Baltic (Lithuanian, Latvian), Finno-Ugric (Finnish, Hungarian, etc.), and other languages. The adaptation of a script to a language is not easy, especially when the language contains sounds that do not occur in the speech from which the script has been borrowed. There arises, therefore, the difficulty of representing the new sounds. This difficulty was met quite differently in various alphabets. For instance, the sound *shch* as in English "Ashchurch" is represented in Czech by two signs (šč), in

Polish by four (*szcz*), in English likewise by four, though different ones, and in German by as many as seven (*schtsch*). Thus, in these instances, combinations of two or more letters were introduced to represent the new sounds.

In other cases, new signs were invented; *e.g.*, in the early Greek alphabet, and in the Anglo-Saxon adoption of the Latin alphabet. In more recent times, the most common way of representing sounds that cannot be represented by letters of the borrowed alphabet has been to add diacritical marks, either above or under the letters, to their right or left or inside. To this group belong the German vowels *ü, ä, ö;* the Portuguese and French cedilla in *ç;* the tilde on Spanish and Portuguese *ñ;* the Italian *à, é, è, ì, ù,* etc.; the great number of marks in the Latin-Slavic alphabets (Polish, Czech, Croatian, etc.)—*ą, ę, č, ć, š, ś, ž, ż, ź,* and so on. The Latin-Turkish alphabet, introduced in 1928, became general throughout Turkey in 1930. It contains 29 letters, of which two vowels (*ö* and *ü*) and three consonants (*ç, g,* and *ş*) are distinguished by diacritical marks; in one instance there is a distinction in reverse—the dot from *i* is eliminated (*ı*) to represent a new sound.

Alphabet diffusion

There is no complete agreement as to how or why certain alphabets have come to dominate the world. Some scholars believe that the alphabet follows the flag; that is, that the diffusion of the alphabet results from political and military conquests. Others hold that the alphabet follows trade. More accurate, perhaps, is the theory that the alphabet follows religion. A few examples may illustrate the point: (1) The Latin language and script were carried by Roman legionaires and Imperial officers to all parts of the vast Roman Empire, particularly to the regions that were not Hellenized. In later centuries, however, churchmen and missionaries carried the Latin language and script still further afield. The ascendancy of Latin led to the adoption of the Latin (Roman) alphabet by a large majority of nations; it became used for tongues of the most diverse linguistic groups, not only in Europe but in all other parts of the world as well. (2) Two alphabets, the Cyrillic and the Latin, are used for writing Slavic languages. Cyrillic is used by those Slavic peoples who accepted their religion from Byzantium, whereas Roman Christianity brought the use of the Latin alphabet to the Poles, Lusatians, Wends, Czechs, Slovaks, Slovenes, and Croats. Particularly interesting is the case of Yugoslavia, in which a single language is written differently by the Catholic Croats and the Greek Orthodox Serbs. (3) The Arabic alphabet is, after Latin, the most generally used in

Asia and Africa. The rise of Islām in the 7th century A.D. and the tremendous Islāmic expansion and conquest carried the Islāmic holy book,
the Qur'ān, written in the Arabic alphabet, over a vast area: the Near
and Middle East, North and Central Africa, South and Southeast Asia,
and even southern Europe. The Arabic alphabet was, therefore, adapted
to Semitic and Indo-European forms of speech, to Tatar-Turkish, Iranian, and Austronesian (Malayo-Polynesian) tongues, and to several
African languages. (4) The movement eastward from India of the Indian Brāhmī-Buddhist alphabets was much more peaceful than that of
the Arabic alphabet. These offshoots, which took root in Ceylon, Burma,
Thailand, Cambodia, Laos, Vietnam, Indonesia, and the Philippines,
were again the result of the spreading of a religion—Buddhism, but by
missionaries and not by armies.

Artificial "ideal alphabets"

In a perfect alphabet each sound would be represented by a single symbol, and no more than one sound would be represented by any symbol.
But there are no completely perfect alphabets. All alphabets omit symbols for some sounds, and all contain redundant letters. Indeed, living
speech hardly conforms to the written word. There are, however, languages, such as Italian, Spanish, Portuguese, German, and even Bantu,
that are relatively accurately represented in graphic form. In English,
the spelling in many words is almost an arbitrary symbolism, which
gives rise to interest in phonetic spelling and spelling reform. The I.T.A.,
Initial Teaching Alphabet, invented by Sir James Pitman, is an attempt
to regularize English orthography.

The International Phonetic Alphabet (IPA) is a system of writing
designed to overcome the inconsistencies and redundancies in regular
alphabets. Developed at the end of the 19th century by members of the
International Phonetic Association, this alphabet has been used by
linguists and others who must record with a greater degree of phonetic
accuracy than can be achieved with ordinary alphabets. There are many
additional types of phonetic alphabets.

With all of its deficiencies, the alphabet has been the only, or at least
the best, means of international communication until the present day. Its
privileged position can be attributed to a natural development lasting
many centuries and accompanied by many other elements. The external
development of the individual letters, strongly influenced by cal-
ligraphers and great graphic experts, is mainly the result of aesthetic
considerations.

ENCYCLOPÆDIA BRITANNICA

The History of Punctuation

Punctuation, the system of inserting spaces and standardized signs into printed or written matter to clarify the text, is derived ultimately from the punctuation used with Greek and Latin during the Classical period. From the Latin *punctus,* meaning "point," punctuation was referred to in English until the early 1700s as pointing.

Much work remains to be done on the history of the subject, but the outlines are clear enough. Greek inscriptions were normally written continuously, with no divisions between words or sentences; but in a few inscriptions earlier than the 5th century B.C., phrases were sometimes separated by a vertical row of two or three points. In the oldest Greek literary texts, written on papyrus during the 4th century B.C., a horizontal line called the *paragraphos* was placed under the beginning of a line in which a new topic was introduced. This is the only form of punctuation mentioned by Aristotle. Aristophanes of Byzantium, who became librarian of the museum at Alexandria about 200 B.C., is usually credited with the invention of the critical signs, marks of quantity, accents, breathings, and so on, still employed in Greek texts, and with the beginnings of the Greek system of punctuation. Rhetorical theory divided discourse into sections of different lengths. Aristophanes marked the end of the short section (called a *comma*) by a point after the middle of its last letter, that of the longer section (*colon*) by a point after the bottom of the letter, and that of the longest section (*periodos*) by a point after the top of the letter. Since books were still being written in tall majuscule letters, like those used in inscriptions and like modern capital letters, the three positions were easily distinguishable. Aristophanes' system was seldom actually used, except in a degenerated version involving only two points. In the 8th or 9th century it was supplemented by the Greek form of question mark (;). The modern system of punctuating Greek texts was established by the Italian and French printers of the Renaissance, whose practice was incorporated in the Greek types cut by Claude Garamond for Francis I of France between

1541 and 1550. The colon is not used in Greek, and the semicolon is represented by a high point. Quotation marks and the exclamation mark were added more recently.

In almost all Roman inscriptions points were used to separate words. In the oldest Latin documents and books, dating from the end of the 1st century B.C. to the beginning of the 2nd century A.D., words were divided by points, and a change of topic was sometimes indicated by paragraphing: the first letter or two of the new paragraph projected into the margin instead of being indented, as they have been since the 17th century. Roman scholars, including the 4th-century grammarian Donatus and the 6th-century patron of monastic learning Cassiodorus, recommended the three-point system of Aristophanes, which was perfectly workable with the majuscule Latin scripts then in use. In practice, however, Latin books in their period were written continuously—the point between words had been abandoned. The ends of sentences were marked, if at all, only by a gap (which might be followed by an enlarged letter) or by an occasional point. The only books that were well punctuated at that time were copies of the Vulgate Bible, for which its translator, St. Jerome (died 419/420), devised punctuation *per cola et commata* ("by phrases"), a rhetorical system, based on manuscripts of Demosthenes and Cicero, which was especially designed to assist reading aloud. Each phrase began with a letter projecting into the margin and was in fact treated as a minute paragraph, before which the reader was expected to take a new breath.

During the 7th and 8th centuries, which saw the transition from majuscule to minuscule handwriting (minuscule scripts were usually smaller than majuscule and had projections above and below the body of the letters, as in modern lowercase letters), scribes to whom the Latin language was no longer as well-known as it had been, especially Irish, Anglo-Saxon, and German scribes, to whom it was a foreign language, began to separate words. It was only in the 13th century that monosyllables, especially prepositions, were finally detached from the word following them. To mark sentences, a space at the end became the rule; and an enlarged letter, often a majuscule, generally stood at the beginning of sentences and paragraphs alike. The use of points was somewhat confused by St. Isidore of Seville (died 636), whose encyclopædia recommended an aberrant version of the three-point system; but a point, high or low, was still used within or after sentences. The ends of sentences were often marked by a group of two or three marks, one of which might be a comma and not a simple point.

St. Jerome's concern for the punctuation of sacred texts was shared by Charlemagne, king of the Franks and Holy Roman emperor, and his Anglo-Saxon adviser Alcuin, who directed the palace school at Aachen from 782 to 796. An important element in the educational revival over which they presided was the improvement of spelling and punctuation in biblical and liturgical manuscripts. It is in the earliest specimens of the new Caroline minuscule script, written at Corbie and Aachen (now in northern France and West Germay, respectively), about 780–800, that the first evidence for a new system of punctuation appears. It soon spread, with the script itself, throughout Europe, reaching its perfection in the 12th century. Single interior stops in the form of points or commas and final groups of stops continued in use; but they were joined by the mark later known as *punctus elevatus* (⸫) and by the question mark (*punctus interrogativus*), of much the same shape as the modern one but inclined to the right. The source of these two new marks was apparently the system of musical notation, called neums, which is known to have been used for Gregorian chant from at least the beginning of the 9th century. *Punctus elevatus* and *punctus interrogativus* indicated not only a pause and a syntactical break but also an appropriate inflection of the voice. By the 12th century another mark, *punctus circumflexus* (⸮), had been added to *elevatus* to indicate a rising inflection at the end of a subordinate clause, especially when the grammatical sense of the sentence was still not complete. Liturgical manuscripts in particular, between the 10th and the 13th century, made full use of this inflectional system: it is the origin of the "colon" still used to divide verses of the Psalms in breviaries and prayer books. In the later Middle Ages it was especially the Cistercian, Dominican, and Carthusian orders and the members of religious communities such as the Brethen of the Common Life who troubled to preserve a mode of punctuation admirably adapted to the constant reading aloud, in church and refectory, that characterized the religious life. The hyphen, to mark words divided at the ends of lines, appears late in the 10th century; single at first, it was often doubled in the period between the 14th and 18th centuries.

Most late medieval punctuation was haphazard by comparison with 12th-century work—notably in the university textbooks produced at Paris, Bologna, and Oxford in the 13th and 14th centuries. In them, as elsewhere, a form of paragraph mark representing *c* for *capitulum* ("chapter") is freely used at the beginning of sentences. Within the same period the plain point and *punctus elevatus* are joined by the virgule (/), as an alternative form of light stop. Vernacular literature followed the less formal types of Latin literature; and the printers, as usual, followed the scribes. The first printed texts of the Bible and the liturgy are, as a rule, carefully punctuated on the inflectional principle. The profusion of points and virgules in the English books of the printer William Caxton pays remarkably little attention to syntax. Parentheses, used in the same way as now, appear by about 1500. During the 15th century some English legal documents were already being written without punctuation; and British and American lawyers still use extremely light punctuation in the hope of avoiding possible ambiguities.

The beginnings of postmedieval punctuation can be traced to the excellent manuscripts of classical and contemporary Latin texts copied in the new humanistic scripts by Italian scribes of the 15th century. To about 1450 the point and the *punctus elevatus* seem to have been preferred for minor pauses; after that date they are often replaced by the virgule and what is now called the colon (:). The virgule, originally placed high, sank to the base line and developed a curve—turned, in fact, into a modern comma. The Venetian editor and printer Aldus Manutius (Aldo Manuzio; died 1515) made improvements in the humanistic system, and in 1566 his grandson of the same name expounded a similar system in his *Orthographiae ratio* ("System of Orthography"); it included, under different names, the modern comma, semicolon, colon, and full point, or period. Most importantly, the younger Aldo stated plainly for the first time the view that clarification of syntax is the main object of punctuation. By the end of the 17th century the various marks had received their modern names, and the exclamation mark, quotation marks, and the dash had been added to the system.

By the end of the 16th century writers of English were using most of the marks described by the younger Aldo in 1566; but their purpose was elocutionary, not syntactical. When George Puttenham, in his treatise *The Arte of English Poesie* (1589), and Simon Daines, in *Orthoepia Anglicana* (1640), specified a pause of one unit for a comma, of two units for a semicolon, and of three for a colon, they were no doubt trying to bring some sort of order into a basically confused and unsatisfactory situation. The punctuation of Elizabethan drama, of the devotional prose of John Donne or of Richard Hooker, and indeed of Bunyan's *Pilgrim's Progress* (1678) was almost wholly elocutionary; and it lacked the inflectional element that had been the making of 12th-century punctuation. It was Ben Jonson, in his *English Grammar,* a work composed about 1617 and published posthumously in 1640, who first recommended syntactical punctuation in England. An early example is the 1625 edition of Francis Bacon's *Essayes;* and from the Restoration onward syntactical punctuation was in general use. Influential treatises on syntactical punctuation were published by Robert Montieth in 1704 and Joseph Robertson in 1795. Excessive punctuation was common in the 18th century: at its worst it used commas with every subordinate clause and separable phrase. Vestiges of this attitude are found in a handbook published in London as late as 1880. It was the lexicographers Henry Watson Fowler and Francis George Fowler, in *The King's English,* published in 1906, who established the current

British practice of light punctuation. Punctuation in the United States has followed much the same path as in Britain, but the rules laid down by American authorities have in general been more rigid than the British rules.

The system of punctuation now used by writers of English has been complete since the 17th century. Three of its most important components are the space left blank between words; the indentation of the first line of a new paragraph; and the uppercase, or capital, letter written at the beginning of a sentence and at the beginning of a proper name or a title. The marks of puctuation, also known as points or stops, and the chief parts that they play in the system are as follows.

The end of a grammatically complete sentence is marked by a full point, full stop, or period. The period may also be used to mark abbreviations. The colon (:), which was once used like a full point and was followed by an uppercase letter, now serves mainly to indicate the beginning of a list, summary, or quotation. The semicolon (;) ranks halfway between a comma and a full point. It may be substituted for a period between two grammatically complete sentences that are closely connected in sense; in a long or complicated sentence, it may precede a coordinate conjunction (such as "or," "and," or "but"). A comma (,) is the "lightest" of the four basic stops. As the most usual means of indicating the syntactical turning points in a sentence, it is exposed to abuse. It may be used to separate the elements of a series, before a relative clause that does not limit or define its antecedent, in pairs to set off or isolate words or phrases, or in combination with coordinating conjunctions.

Other punctuation marks used in modern English include parentheses, which serve, like a pair of commas, to isolate a word or phrase; question, exclamation, and quotation marks; the hyphen; and the apostrophe.

Since the late 16th century the theory and practice of punctuation have varied between two main schools of thought: the elocutionary school, following late medieval practice, treated points or stops as indications of the pauses of various lengths that might be observed by a reader, particularly when he was reading aloud to an audience; the syntactical school, which had won the argument by the end of the 17th century, saw them as something less arbitrary, namely, as guides to the grammatical construction of sentences. Pauses in speech and breaks in syntax tend in any case to coincide; and although English-speaking writers are now agreed that the main purpose of punctuation is to clarify the grammar of a text, they also require it to take account of the speed and rhythm of actual speech.

Syntactical punctuation is, by definition, bad when it obscures rather than clarifies the construction of sentences. Good punctuation, however, may be of many kinds: to take two extreme examples—Henry James would be unintelligible without his numerous commas, but Ernest Hemingway seldom needs any stop but the full point. In poetry, in which the elocutionary aspect of punctuation is still important, and to a lesser degree in fiction, especially when the style is close to actual speech, punctuation is much at the author's discretion. In nonfictional writing there is less room for experiment. Stimulating variant models for general use might be the light punctuation of George Bernard Shaw's prefaces to his plays and the heavier punctuation of T.S. Eliot's literary and political essays.

ENCYCLOPÆDIA BRITANNICA

The Origins and Characteristics of the English Language

I. Origins and characteristics

English belongs to the Indo-European family of languages and therefore is related, nearly or distantly, to most of the other languages of Europe and western Asia from Iceland to India. The parent language, usually called Proto-Indo-European, was spoken 5,000 years ago by nomads roaming over the plains of what is now, geographically, the Ukraine and southern Russia, between the Baltic and the Black seas. From this ancestral language descend the groups of which the modern names are Indo-Iranian, Armenian, Tocharian (Tokharian), Hellenic, Romance, Albanian, Celtic, Germanic, and Balto-Slavonic. Germanic later split into three regional groups: East Germanic (Burgundian, Vandal, and Gothic, all extinct); North Germanic (Norwegian, Icelandic, Faeroese, Swedish, and Danish); and West Germanic (German, Plattdeutsch, Dutch, Flemish—*i.e.*, Netherlandic—Frisian, and English). Among the world's great languages, therefore, Modern German is nearest to Modern English; but Modern German is more conservative, both in its retention of inflections and in the homogeneity of its lexis, or vocabulary. Frisian, spoken by people inhabiting the Dutch province of Friesland and the islands off the west coast of Schleswig, is the language most nearly related to Modern English. Icelandic, a language that has changed little during 1,000 years, is the modern language most closely resembling Old English.

Modern English is analytic (*i.e.*, relatively uninflected), whereas Proto-Indo-European, the ancestral tongue of most of the modern European languages (*e.g.*, German, French, Russian, Greek), was synthetic, or inflected. During the course of thousands of years, English words have been slowly simplified from the inflected variable forms found in Sanskrit, Greek, Latin, Russian, and German, toward invariable forms, as in Chinese and Vietnamese. The German and Chinese words for "man" are exemplary. German has five forms: *Mann, Mannes,*

Manne, Männer, Männern. Chinese has one form: *ven.* English stands in between, with four forms: man, man's, men, men's. In English only nouns, pronouns, and verbs are inflected. Adjectives have no inflections aside from the determiners "this, these" and "that, those." (The endings *-er, -est,* denoting degrees of comparison, are better regarded as noninflectional suffixes.) English is the only European language to employ uninflected adjectives; *e.g.,* "the tall man," "the tall woman," compared to Spanish *el hombre alto* and *la mujer alta.* As for verbs, if the Modern English word ride is compared with the corresponding words in Old English and Modern German, it will be found that English now has only five forms (ride, rides, rode, riding, ridden), whereas Old English *ridan* had 13, and Modern German *reiten* has 16 forms.

In addition to this simplicity of inflections, English has two other basic characteristics: flexibility of function and openness of vocabulary.

Flexibility of function has grown over the last five centuries as a consequence of the loss of inflections. Words formerly distinguished as nouns or verbs by differences in their forms are now often used as both nouns and verbs. One can speak, for example, of "planning a table" or "tabling a plan," "booking a place" or "placing a book," "lifting a thumb" or "thumbing a lift." In the other Indo-European languages, apart from rare exceptions in Scandinavian, nouns and verbs are never identical because of the necessity of separate noun and verb endings. In English, forms for traditional pronouns, adjectives, and adverbs can also function as nouns; adjectives and adverbs as verbs; and nouns, pronouns, and adverbs as adjectives. One speaks in English of the Frankfurt Book Fair, but in German one must add the suffix *-er* to the place-name and put attributive and noun together as a compound, Frankfurter Buchmesse. In French one has no choice but to construct a phrase involving the use of two prepositions: Foire du Livre de Francfort. In English it is now possible to employ a plural noun as adjunct (modifier), as in "wages board" and "sports editor"; or even a conjunctional group, as in "prices and incomes policy" and "parks and gardens committee."

Openness of vocabulary implies both free admission of words from other languages and the ready creation of compounds and derivatives. English adopts (without change) or adapts (with slight change) any word really needed to name some new object or to denote some new process. Like French, Spanish, and Russian, English frequently forms scientific terms from Classical Greek word elements.

English possesses a system of orthography that does not always accurately reflect the pronunciation of words. English spelling, it is true, is nothing like so irregular as that of Irish Gaelic (to take an example from within the British Isles, the first "cradle" of English). Among the great languages, French closely rivals English in perversity. But whereas French spelling is systematically unphonetic, English is unsystematically unphonetic.

II. Modern English

PHONOLOGY British Received Pronunciation (RP), by definition, the usual speech of educated people living in London and southeastern England, is one of the many forms of standard speech. Other pronunciations, although not standard, are entirely acceptable in their own right on conversational levels.

The chief differences between British Received Pronunciation, as defined above, and a variety of American English, such as Inland Northern (the speech form of western New England and its derivatives, often popularly referred to as General American), are in the pronunciation of certain individual vowels and diphthongs. Inland Northern American vowels sometimes have semiconsonantal final glides (*i.e.*, sounds resembling initial *w*, for example, or initial *y*). Aside from the final glides, this American dialect shows four divergences from British English: (1) the words cod, box, dock, hot, and not are pronounced with a short (or half-long) low front sound as in British "bard" shortened (the terms front, back, low, and high refer to the position of the tongue); (2) words such as bud, but, cut, and rung are pronounced with a central vowel as in the unstressed final syllable of "sofa"; (3) before the fricative sounds *s, f,* and *θ* (the last of these is the *th* sound in "thin") the long low back vowel *a,* as in British "bath," is pronounced as a short front vowel *a,* as in British "bad"; (4) high back vowels following the alveolar sounds *t* and *d* and the nasal sound *n* in words such as tulips, dew, and news are pronounced without a glide as in British English; indeed, the words sound like the British "two lips," "do," and "nooze" in "snooze." (In several American dialects, however, these glides do occur.)

The 24 consonant sounds comprise six stops (plosives): *p, b, t, d, k, g;* the fricatives *f, v, θ* (as in "thin"), *ð* (as in "then"), *s, z, ʃ* (as in "ship"), *ʒ* (as in "pleasure"), and *h;* two affricatives: *tʃ* (as in "church") and *dʒ* (as the *j* in "jam"); the nasals *m, n, ŋ* (the sound that occurs at the end of words such as "young"); the lateral *l;* the vibrant or retroflex *r;* and the semivowels *j* (often spelled *y*) and *w.* These remain fairly stable, but Inland Northern American differs from British English in two respects: (1) *r* following vowels is preserved in words such as "door," "flower," and "harmony," whereas it is lost in British; (2) *t* between vowels is voiced, so that "metal" and "matter" sound very much like British "medal" and "madder," although the pronunciation of this *t* is softer and less aspirated, or breathy, than the *d* of British English.

Like Russian, English is a strongly stressed language. Four degrees of stress may be differentiated: primary, secondary, tertiary, and weak, which may be indicated, respectively, by acute ('), circumflex (^), and grave (`) accent marks and by the breve (˘). Thus, "Têll mé thĕ trûth" (the whole truth, and nothing but the truth) may be contrasted with "Têll mé thĕ trûth" (whatever you may tell other people); "bláck bîrd" (any bird black in colour) may be contrasted with "bláckbìrd" (that particular bird *Turdus merula*). The verbs "permít" and "recórd" (henceforth only primary stresses are marked) may be contrasted with their corresponding nouns "pérmit" and "récord." A feeling for antepenultimate (third syllable from the end) primary stress, revealed in such five-syllable words as equanímity, longitúdinal, notoríety, opportúnity, parsimónious, pertinácity, and vegetárian, causes stress to shift when extra syllables are added, as in "histórical," a derivative of "hístory" and "theatricálity," a derivative of "theátrical." Vowel qualities are also changed here and in such word groups as périod, periódical, periodícity; phótograph, photógraphy, photográphical. French stress may be sustained in many borrowed words; *e.g.,* bizárre, critíque, duréss, hotél, prestíge, and techníque.

Pitch, or musical tone, determined by the rate of vibration of the vocal cords, may be level, falling, rising, or falling–rising. In counting "one," "two," "three," "four," one naturally gives level pitch to each of these cardinal numerals. But if a person says "I want two," not one," he naturally gives "two" falling pitch and "one" falling–rising. In the question "One?" rising pitch is used. Word tone is called pitch, and sentence tone is referred to as intonation. The end-of-sentence cadence is important for meaning, and it therefore varies least. Three main end-of-sentence intonations can be distinguished: falling, rising, and falling–rising. Falling intonation is used in completed statements, direct commands, and sometimes in general questions unanswerable by "yes" or "no"; *e.g.,* "I have nothing to add." "Keep to the right." "Who told you that?" Rising intonation is frequently used in open-ended statements made with some reservation, in polite requests, and in particular questions answerable by "yes" or "no": "I have nothing more to say at the moment." "Let me know how you get on." "Are you sure?" The third type of end-of-sentence intonation, first falling and then rising pitch, is used in sentences that imply concessions or contrasts: "Some people do like them" (but others do not). "Don't say I didn't warn you" (because that is just what I'm now doing). Intonation is on the whole less sing-song in American than in British England, and there is a narrower range of pitch. American speech may seem more monotonous but at the same time may sometimes be clearer and more readily intelligible. Everywhere English is spoken, regional dialects display distinctive patterns of intonation.

MORPHOLOGY *Inflection.* Modern English nouns, pronouns, and verbs are inflected. Adjectives, adverbs, prepositions, conjunctions, and interjections are invariable. Most English nouns have plural inflection in (-*e*)*s*, but this form shows variations in pronunciation in the words cats (with a final *s* sound), dogs (with a final *z* sound), and horses (with a final *iz* sound), as also in the 3rd person singular present-tense forms of verbs: cuts (*s*), jogs (*z*), and forces (*iz*). Seven nouns have mutated (umlauted) plurals: man, men; woman, women; tooth, teeth; foot, feet; goose, geese; mouse, mice; louse, lice. Three have plurals in -*en:* ox, oxen; child, children; brother, brethren. Some remain unchanged; *e.g.*, deer, sheep, moose, grouse. Five of the seven personal pronouns have distinctive forms for subject and object.

The forms of verbs are not complex. Only the substantive verb ("to be") has eight forms: be, am, is, are, was, were, being, been. Strong verbs have five forms: ride, rides, rode, riding, ridden. Regular or weak verbs customarily have four: walk, walks, walked, walking. Some that end in a *t* or *d* have three forms only: cut, cuts, cutting. Of these three-forms verbs, 16 are in frequent use.

In addition to the above inflections, English employs two other main morphological (structural) processes—affixation and composition—and two subsidiary ones—back-formation and blend.

Affixation. Affixes, word elements attached to words, may either precede, as prefixes (do, undo; way, subway), or follow, as suffixes (do, doer; way, wayward). They may be native (*over*do, wayward*ness*), Greek (*hyper*bole, the*sis*), or Latin (*super*sede, pedi*ment*). Modern technologists greatly favour the neo-Hellenic prefixes *macro*- "long, large," *micro*- "small," *para*- "alongside," *poly*- "many," and the Latin *mini*-, with its antonym *maxi*- Greek and Latin affixes have become so fully acclimatized that they can occur together in one and the same word, as, indeed, in "ac-climat-ize-d," just used, consisting of a Latin prefix plus a Greek stem plus a Greek suffix plus an English inflection. Suffixes are bound more closely than prefixes to the stems or root elements of words. Consider, for instance, the wide variety of agent suffixes in the nouns act*or*, arti*san*, do*tard*, engin*eer*, financi*er*, hire*ling*, magis*trate*, merch*ant*, scient*ist*, secret*ary*, song*ster*, stud*ent*, and work*er*. Suffixes may come to be attached to stems quite fortuitously, but, once attached, they are likely to be permanent. At the same time, one suffix can perform many functions. The suffix -*er* denotes the doer of the action in the words worker, driver, and hunter; the instrument in chopper, harvester, and roller; and the dweller in Icelander, Londoner, and Tobriander. It refers to things or actions associated with the basic concept in the words breather, "pause to take breath"; diner, "dining car on a train"; and fiver, "five-pound note." In the terms disclaimer, misnomer, and rejoinder (all from French) the suffix denotes one single instance of the action expressed by the verb. Usage may prove capricious. Whereas a writer is a person, a typewriter is a machine. For some time a computer was both, but now, with the invention and extensive use of electronic apparatus, the word is no longer used of persons.

Composition. Composition, or compounding, is concerned with free forms. The primary compounds "already," "cloverleaf," and "gentleman" show the collocation of two free forms. They differ from word groups or phrases in phonology, stress, or juncture or by a combination of two or more of these. Thus, "already" differs from "all ready" in stress and juncture, "cloverleaf" from "clover leaf" in stress, and "gentleman" from "gentle man" in phonology, stress, and juncture. In describing the structure of compound words it is necessary to take into account the relation of components to each other and the relation of the whole compound to its components. These relations diverge widely in, for example, the words cloverleaf, icebreaker, breakwater, blackbird, peace-loving, and paperback. In "cloverleaf" the first component noun is attributive and modifies the second, as also in the terms aircraft, beehive, landmark, lifeline, network, and vineyard. "Icebreaker," however, is a compound made up of noun object plus agent noun, itself consisting of verb plus agent suffix, as also in the words bridgebuilder, landowner, metalworker, minelayer, and timekeeper. The next type consists of verb plus object. It is rare in English, Dutch, and German but frequent in French, Spanish, and Italian. The English "pastime" may be compared, for example, with French *passe-temps,* the Spanish *pasatiempo,* and the Italian *passatempo.* From French comes "passport," meaning "pass (*i.e.,* enter) harbour." From Italian comes "portfolio," meaning "carry leaf." Other words of this type are daredevil, scapegrace, and scarecrow. As for the "blackbird" type, consisting of attributive adjective plus noun, it occurs frequently, as in the terms bluebell, grandson, shorthand, and wildfire. The next type, composed of object noun and a present participle, as in the terms fact-finding, heartrending (German *herzzerreissend*), life-giving (German *lebenspendend*), painstaking, and time-consuming, occurs rarely. The last type is seen in barefoot, bluebeard, hunchback, leatherneck, redbreast, and scatterbrain.

Back-formations and blends. Back-formations and blends are becoming increasingly popular. Back-formation is the reverse of affixation, being the analogical creation of a new word from an existing word falsely assumed to be its derivative. For example, the verb "to edit" has been formed from the noun "editor" on the reverse analogy of the noun "actor" from "to act," and similarly the verbs automate, bulldoze, commute, escalate, liaise, loaf, sightsee, and televise are backformed from the nouns automation, bulldozer, commuter, escalation, liaison, loafer, sightseer, and television. From the single noun "procession" are backformed two verbs with different stresses and meanings: procéss, "to walk in procession," and prócess, "to subject food (and other material) to a special operation."

Blends fall into two groups: (1) coalescences, such as "bash" from "bang" and "smash"; and (2) telescoped forms, called portmanteau words, such as "motorcade" from "motor cavalcade." In the first group are the words clash, from clack and crash, and geep, offspring of goat and sheep. To the second group belong dormobiles, or dormitory automobiles, and slurbs, or slum suburbs. A travel monologue becomes a travelogue and a telegram sent by cable a cablegram. Aviation electronics becomes avionics; biology electronics, bionics; and nuclear electronics, nucleonics. In cablese a question mark is a quark; in computerese a binary unit is a bit. In astrophysics a quasistellar source of radio energy becomes a quasar, and a pulsating star becomes a pulsar.

Simple shortenings, such as "ad" for "advertisement," have risen in status. They are listed in dictionaries side by side with their full forms. Among such fashionable abbreviations are exam, gym, lab, lib, op, spec, sub, tech, veg, and vet. Compound shortenings, after the pattern of Russian *agitprop* for *agitatsiya propaganda,* are also becoming fashionable. Initial syllables are joined as in the words Fortran, for formula (computer) translation; mascon, for massive (lunar) concentration; and Tacomsat, for Tactical Communications Satellite.

SYNTAX Sentences can be classified as (1) simple, containing one clause and predication: "John knows this country"; (2) multiple or compound, containing two or more coordinate clauses: "John has been here before, and he knows this country"; and (3) complex, containing one or more main clauses and one or more subordinate clauses: "John, who has been here before, knows this country" or "Because he has been here before, John knows this country." Simple, declarative, affirmative sentences have two main patterns with five subsidiary patterns within each. Verb and complement together form the predicate. "Complement" is here used to cover both the complement and the object of traditional grammarians (see Table 1).

Table 1: Simple Sentences—First Pattern

subject	verb	complement
1. John	knows	this country
2. Science	is	organized knowledge
3. Elizabeth	becomes	queen
4. The captain	falls	sick
5. Nothing	passes	unobserved

In (1) the complement is the direct object of a transitive verb; in (2) it is a predicative nominal group forming the second component of an equation linked to the first part by the meaningless copula *is*; in (3) it is a predicative noun linked with the subject by the meaningful copula *becomes*; in (4) it is a predicative adjective; and in (5) it is a predicative past participle.

Table 2: Simple Sentences—Second Pattern

subject	verb	inner complement	outer complement
6. John	gives	Mary	a ring
7. The sailors	make	John	captain
8. You	have kept	your record	clean
9. The driver	finds	the road	flooded
10. We	want	you	to know

In Table 2 each sentence contains four components: subject, verb, and two complements, first and second, or inner and outer. In (6) inner and outer complements consist of indirect object (without preposition) followed by direct object; in (7) these complements are direct object and appositive noun; in (8) direct object and predicative adjective; in (9) direct object and predicative past participle; in (10) direct object and predicative infinitive.

One can seldom change the word order in these 10 sentences without doing something else—adding or subtracting a word, changing the meaning. There is no better way of appreciating the importance of word position than by scrutinizing the 10 frames illustrated. If, for instance, in (6) one reverses inner and outer complements, one adds "to" and says, "John gives a ring to Mary"; one does not say "John gives a ring Mary." Some verbs, such as "explain" and "say," never omit the preposition "to" before the indirect object: "Johns father explained the details to his son." "He said many things to him." If, in (10), the inner and outer complements are reversed (*e.g.*, "We want to know you"), the meaning is changed as well as the structure.

Apart from these fundamental rules of word order, the principles governing the positions of adjectives, adverbs, and prepositions call for brief comment. For attributive adjectives the rule is simple: single words regularly precede the noun, and word groups follow—*e.g.*, "an unforgettable experience" but "an experience never to be forgotten." There is a growing tendency, however, to abandon this principle, to switch groups to front position, and to say "a never to be forgotten experience." In the ordering of multiple epithets, on the other hand, some new principles are seen to be slowly emerging. Attributes denoting permanent qualities stand nearest their head nouns: "long, white beard," "six-lane elevated freeway." The order in multiple attribution tends to be as follows: determiner; quantifier; adjective of quality; adjective of size, shape, or texture; adjective of colour or material; noun adjunct (if any); head noun. Examples include: "that one solid, round, oak dining table," "these many fine, large, black race horses," "those countless memorable, long, bright summer evenings."

Adverbs are more mobile than adjectives. Nevertheless, some tentative principles seem to be at work. Adverbs of frequency tend to come immediately after the substantive verb ("You are often late"), before other verbs ("You never know"), and between auxiliaries and full verbs ("You can never tell"). In this last instance, however, American differs from British usage. Most Americans would place the adverb before the auxiliary and say "You never can tell." (In the title of his play of that name, first performed in 1899, George Bernard Shaw avowedly followed American usage.) Adverbs of time usually occur at the beginning or end of a sentence, seldom in the middle. Particular expressions normally precede more general ones: "Neil Armstrong set foot on the Moon at 4 o'clock in the morning on July 21, 1969." An adverb of place or direction follows a verb with which it is semantically bound: "We arrived home after dark." Other adverbs normally take end positions in the order of manner, place, and time: "Senator Smith summed it all up most adroitly [manner] in Congress [place] last night [time]."

In spite of its etymology (Latin *prae-positio* "before placing"), a preposition may sometimes follow the noun it governs, as in "all the world over," "the clock round," and "the whole place through." "This seems a good place to live in" seems more natural to most speakers than "This seems a good place in which to live." "Have you anything to open this can with?" is now more common than "Have you anything with which to open this can?"

The above are principles rather than rules, and in the end it must be agreed that English syntax lacks regimentation. Its structural laxity makes English an easy language to speak badly. It also makes English prone to ambiguity. "When walking snipe always approach up wind," a shooting manual directs. The writer intends the reader to understand, "When you are walking to flush snipe always approach them up against the wind." "John kept the car in the garage" can mean either (1) "John retained that car you see in the garage, and sold his other one" or (2) "John housed the car in the garage, and not elsewhere." "Flying planes can be dangerous" is ambiguous because it may mean either (1) "Planes that fly can be dangerous" or (2) "It is dangerous to fly planes."

Two ways in which "John gives Mary a ring" can be stated in the passive are: (1) "A ring is given to Mary by John" and (2) "Mary is given a ring by John." Concerning this same action, four types of questions can be formulated: (1) "Who gives Mary a ring?" The information sought is the identity of the giver. (2) "Does John give Mary a ring?" The question may be answered by "yes" or "no." (3) "John gives Mary a ring, doesn't he?" Confirmation is sought of the questioner's belief that John does in fact give Mary a ring, doesn't he?" Confirmation is sought of the questioner's belief that John does in fact give Mary a ring. (4) "John gives Mary a ring?" This form, differing from the declarative statement only by the question mark in writing, or by rising intonation in speech, calls, like sentences (2) and (3), for a "yes" or "no" answer but suggests doubt on the part of the questioner that the action is taking place.

VOCABULARY   The vocabulary of Modern English is approximately half Germanic (Old English and Scandinavian) and half Italic or Romance (French and Latin), with copious and increasing importations from Greek in science and technology and with considerable borrowings from Dutch, Low German, Italian, Spanish, German, Arabic, and many other languages. Names of basic concepts and things come from Old English or Anglo-Saxon: heaven and earth, love and hate, life and death, beginning and end, day and night, month and year, heat and cold, way and path, meadow and stream. Cardinal numerals come from Old English, as do all the ordinal numerals except "second" (Old English *other,* which still retains its older meaning in "every other day"). "Second" comes from Latin *secundus* "following," through French *second,* related to Latin *sequi* "to follow," as in English "sequence." From Old English come all the personal pronouns (except "they," "their," and "them," which are from Scandinavian), the auxiliary verbs (except the marginal "used," which is from French), most simple prepositions, and all conjunctions.

Numerous nouns would be identical whether they came from Old English or Scandinavian: father, mother, brother (but not sister); man, wife; ground, land, tree, grass; summer, winter; cliff, dale. Many verbs would also be identical, especially monosyllabic verbs—bring, come, get, hear, meet, see, set, sit, spin, stand, think. The same is true of the adjectives full and wise; the colour names gray, green, and white; the disjunctive possessives mine and thine (but not ours and yours); the terms north and west (but not south and east); and the prepositions over and under. Just a few English and Scandinavian doublets coexist in current speech: no and nay, yea and ay, from and fro, rear (*i.e.*, to bring up) and raise, shirt and skirt (both related to the adjective short), less and loose. From Scandinavian, "law" was borrowed early, whence "by-law," meaning "village law," and "outlaw," meaning "man outside the law." "Husband" (*hus-bondi*) meant "householder," whether single or married, whereas "fellow" (*fe-lagi*) meant one who "lays fee" or shares property with another, and so "partner, shareholder." From Scandinavian come the common nouns axle (tree), band, birth, bloom, crook, dirt, egg, gait, gap, girth, knife, loan, race, rift, root, score, seat, skill, sky, snare, thrift, and window; the adjectives awkward, flat, happy, ill, loose, rotten, rugged, sly, tight, ugly, weak, and wrong; and many verbs, including call, cast, clasp, clip, crave, die, droop, drown, flit, gape, gasp, glitter, lift, rake, rid, scare, scowl, skulk, snub, sprint, thrive, thrust, and want.

The debt of the English language to France is large. The terms president, representative, legislature, congress, constitution, and parliament are all French. So, too, are duke, marquis, viscount, and baron; but king, queen, lord, lady, earl, and knight are English. City, village, court, palace, manor, mansion, residence, and domicile are French; but town, borough, hall, house, bower, room, and home are English. Comparison between English and French synonyms shows that the former are more human and concrete, the latter more intellectual and abstract; *e.g.*, the terms freedom and liberty, friendship and amity, hatred and enmity, love and affection, likelihood and probability, truth and veracity, lying and mendacity. The superiority of French cooking is duly recognized by the adoption of such culinary terms as boil, broil, fry, grill, roast, souse, and toast. "Breakfast" is English, but "dinner" and "supper" are French. "Hunt" is English, but "chase," "quarry," "scent," and "track" are French. Craftsmen bear names of English origin: baker, builder, fisher (man), hedger, miller, shepherd, shoemaker, wainwright, and weaver, or webber. Names of skilled artisans, however, are French: carpenter, draper, haberdasher, joiner, mason, painter, plumber, and tailor. Many terms relating to dress and fashion, cuisine and viniculture, politics and diplomacy, drama and literature, art and ballet come from France.

In the spheres of science and technology many terms come from Classical Greek through French or directly from Greek. Pioneers in research and development now regard Greek as a kind of inexhaustible quarry from which they can draw linguistic material at will. By prefixing the Greek adverb *tēle* "far away, distant" to the existing compound photography, "light writing," they create the precise term "telephotography" to denote the photographing of distant objects by means of a special lens. By inserting the prefix *micro-* "small" into this same compound, they make the new term "photomicrography," denoting the electronic photographing of bacteria and viruses. Such neo-Hellenic derivatives would probably have been unintelligible to Plato and Aristotle. Many Greek compounds and derivatives have Latin equivalents with slight or considerable differentiations in meaning.

Ever since the 12th century, when merchants from the Netherlands made homes in East Anglia, Dutch words have infiltrated into Midland speech. For centuries a form of Low German was used by seafaring men in North Sea ports. Old nautical terms still in use include buoy, deck, dock, freebooter, hoist, leak, pump, skipper, and yacht. The Dutch in New Amsterdam (later New York) and adjacent settlements gave the words boss, cookie, dope, snoop, and waffle to American speech. The Dutch in Cape Province gave the terms apartheid, commandeer, commando, spoor, and trek to South African speech.

The contribution of High German has been on a different level. In the 18th and 19th centuries it lay in technicalities of geology and mineralogy and in abstractions relating to literature, philosophy, and psychology. In the 20th century this contribution has sometimes been indirect. "Unclear" and "meaningful" echoed German *unklar* and *bedeutungsvoll,* or *sinnvoll.* "Ring road" (a British term applied to roads encircling cities or parts of cities) translated *Ringstrasse;* "round trip," *Rundfahrt;* and "the turn of the century," *die Jahrhundertwende.* The term "classless society," "inferiority complex," and "wishful thinking" echoed *die klassenlöse Gesellschaft, der Minderwertigkeitskomplex,* and *das Wunschdenken.*

Along with the rest of the Western world, English has accepted Italian as the language of music. The names of voices, parts, performers, instruments, forms of composition, and technical directions are all Italian. Many of the latter—allegro, andante, cantabile, crescendo, diminuendo, legato, maestoso, obbligato, pizzicato, staccato, and vibrato—are also used metaphorically. In architecture, the terms belvedere, corridor, cupola, grotto, pedestal, pergola, piazza, pilaster, and rotunda are accepted; in literature, burlesque, canto, extravaganza, stanza, and many more are used.

From Spanish, English has acquired the words armada, cannibal, cigar, galleon, guerrilla, matador, mosquito, quadroon, tornado, and vanilla, some of these loanwords going back to the 16th century, when sea dogs encountered hidalgos on the high seas. Many names of animals and plants have entered English from indigenous languages through Spanish: "potato" through Spanish *patata* from Taino *batata,* and "tomato" through Spanish *tomate* from Nahuatl *tomatl.* Other words have entered from Latin America by way of Texas, New Mexico, Arizona, and California; *e.g.,* such words as canyon, cigar, estancia, lasso, mustang, pueblo, and rodeo. Some have gathered new connotations: bonanza, originally denoting "goodness," came through miners' slang to mean "spectacular windfall, prosperity"; mañana, "tomorrow," acquired an undertone of mysterious unpredictability.

From Arabic through European Spanish, through French from Spanish, through Latin, or occasionally through Greek, English has obtained the terms alchemy, alcohol, alembic, algebra, alkali, almanac, arsenal, assassin, attar, azimuth, cipher, elixir, mosque, nadir, naphtha, sugar, syrup, zenith, and zero. From Egyptian Arabic, English has recently borrowed the term loofah (also spelled luffa). From Hebrew, directly or by way of Vulgate Latin, come the terms amen, cherub, hallelujah, manna, messiah, pharisee, rabbi, sabbath, and seraph; jubilee, leviathan, and shibboleth; and, more recently, kosher, and kibbutz.

English has freely adopted and adapted words from many other languages, acquiring them sometimes directly and sometimes by devious routes. Each word has its own history. The following lists indicate the origins of a number of English words: Welsh—flannel, coracle, cromlech, eisteddfod; Cornish—gull, brill, dolmen; Gaelic and Irish—shamrock, brogue, leprechaun, ogham, Tory, galore, blarney, hooligan, clan, claymore, bog, plaid, slogan, sporran, cairn, whisky, pibroch; Breton—menhir, penguin; Norwegian—ski, ombudsman; Finnish—sauna; Russian—kvass, ruble, tsar, verst, mammoth, ukase, astrakhan, vodka, samovar, tundra (from Lapp), troika, pogrom, duma, soviet, bolshevik, intelligentsia (from Latin through Polish), borscht, balalaika, sputnik, soyuz, salyut, lunokhod; Polish—mazurka; Czech—robot; Hungarian—goulash, paprika; Portuguese—marmalade, flamingo, molasses, veranda, port (wine), dodo; Basque—bizarre; Turkish—janissary, turban, coffee, kiosk, caviar, pasha, odalisque, fez, bosh; Hindi—nabob, guru, sahib, maharajah, mahatma, pundit, punch (drink), juggernaut, cushy, jungle, thug, cheetah, shampoo, chit, dungaree, pucka, gymkhana, mantra, loot, pajamas, dinghy, polo; Persian—paradise, divan, purdah, lilac, bazaar, shah, caravan, chess, salamander, taffeta, shawl, khaki; Tamil—pariah, curry, catamaran, mulligatawny; Chinese—tea (Amoy), sampan; Japanese—shogun, kimono, mikado, tycoon, hara-kiri, gobang, judo, jujitsu, bushido, samurai, banzai, tsunami, satsuma. No (the dance drama), karate, Kabuki; Malay—ketchup, sago, bamboo, junk, amuck, orangutan, compound (fenced area), raffia; Polynesian—taboo, tattoo; Hawaiian—ukulele; African languages—chimpanzee, goober, mumbo jumbo, voodoo; Eskimo—kayak, igloo, anorak, mukluk; Algonkian—totem; Nahuatl—mescal; languages of the Caribbean—hammock, hurricane, tobacco, maize, iguana; Aboriginal Australian—kangaroo, corroboree, wallaby, wombat, boomerang, paramatta, budgerigar.

ENCYCLOPÆDIA BRITANNICA

A Brief History of American English

Observers frequently wonder whether the British and American varieties of English are drifting apart or coming closer together. In the first edition of *The American Language* (1919), H. L. Mencken proclaimed that the two streams were diverging to such an extent that they would soon be mutually unintelligible. In the fourth edition (1936), however, Mencken altered his judgment on the grounds that, with the growing importance of the United States in world affairs, American usage was coming to influence British English so greatly that at some future date English might be recognized as simply a dialect of American.

Since Mencken's fourth edition, a second world war and a number of lesser convulsions have continued to alter the relative position of these nations. England is no longer the seat of a globe-encompassing empire but merely the eldest sister in a loosely knit Commonwealth family. Nor has the United States established an imperium of its own; rather it is one of two or three great powers, each of which might devastate the others but not escape crippling retaliation. In the continuing shift of power all the major nations have become better acquainted with one another and with their respective cultures and languages. Most important for Americans is increased familiarity with Britain, beginning with the U.S. participation in World War II, when millions of GI's were stationed overseas. Speakers of British and American English know far more than before about each other's usage—not only through books, movies, radio, and television but through personal contact.

Yet the questions about the relationship of the two streams of English are still raised. Robert Burchfield, editor of *A Supplement to the Oxford English Dictionary,* believes that the American Revolution accelerated, if it did not initiate, a process of irreversible separation. On the other hand, Randolph Quirk, director of the London survey of English usage, is convinced that the national varieties are in a period of convergence that is likely to last for some time. I give a qualified endorsement of Quirk's position—qualified in the sense that the convergence reflects a general centripetal tendency throughout the English-speaking world by which mutual abrasion is making local, regional, and national forms of English more and more alike. However, this tendency depends upon the kind of communication that has developed in the 20th century. Should communication break down for whatever reason—a catastrophic nuclear war, a prolonged oil embargo by the producing states—new differences among the varieties of English would arise just as in Western Europe the Romance vernaculars arose from the wreckage of the Roman Empire. I do not prophesy doom but neither can I forget history.

American English today has diversity within unity: a number of acceptable varieties of educated speech, all mutually intelligible. As well, speakers of American English can converse with speakers of other varieties of English throughout the world. (The English language, encompassing all its varieties, is second only to Chinese in the actual number of native speakers but is far more widely disseminated and understood.) Originating in a modest series of scattered settlements along the Atlantic coast, American English is now spoken throughout a vast territory, generally as the primary tongue. Despite the diffusion of speakers of Spanish, Yiddish, and other languages in many areas, the United States is in effect a monolingual country; and despite Quebec nationalism and official policy, so too is most of Canada. As the idiom in which these two powerful nations transact their business, American English holds a position of undisputed importance among languages.

The forces that produced American English

Among the forces that produced American English, most important was the nature of the original settlements. The 13 states that won their independence from Britain and merged their interests by the Constitution of 1787 represented nearly 20 official colonial foundations, excepting the culturally autonomous smaller settlements: Plymouth Colony was separate from Massachusetts Bay, Rhode Island from Providence; East and West Jersey had separate groups of proprietors. Communication among the colonies, especially by land, was difficult. All of the colonies, whatever their official status—royal, proprietary, or charter—had stubbornly independent legislatures. Yet each of them maintained commercial, cultural, and political ties with the homeland, and a small but important group in each colony was responsive to the growing uniformity in the Standard English of London.

THE SETTLERS THEMSELVES   The 17th-century English-speaking settlers in the New World were a diverse group. New England drew its people primarily from East Anglia and the Home Counties, Pennsylvania from the north of England, the Appalachian areas from northern Ireland, and the plantation areas of the southern coast from the western counties. However, there is no evidence of a massive transfer of the characteristics of any regional variety of British English to any single regional variety of American English. For example, although the pronunciation of *greasy* with a /z/ and the loss of the /r/ in *barn* are both characteristic of East Anglia, these patterns were not uniformly adopted when transferred to America: eastern New England uses the latter but not the former.

The social origins of the English-speaking colonists were varied but did not represent a full cross section of the 17th-century British society. Although many Americans speak of illustrious ancestors in Britain, the facts speak otherwise. Among the settlers there were almost no members of the British peerage (Lord Fairfax, George Washington's patron, was an exception) and very few of the gentry; the great colonial families in Virginia and elsewhere generally came from modest stock and owed their status to the profit from land sales and crops on the frontier. Ordinarily there was little incentive for members of the established orders to go overseas.

At the other end of the social spectrum, the peasantry were also poorly represented among the earliest settlers. A crossing cost money, which peasants did not have; and, like the nobility and gentry, the peasantry had a stable and assured place in the society of their time. Migration was left, as always, to the social misfits (somewhere in the middle), the restless, and the inquiring, who saw the potential gains as far outweighing the certain risks.

The English-speaking colonists were not the only settlers in the New World. The Dutch settled New York, East and West Jersey, and, with the Swedes, the western bank of the Delaware until that entire territory came under the English Crown. German settlements were found in every colony outside New England. In Georgia, intended as a refuge for English debtors down on their luck, the ranks of settlers were swelled by more than 1,200 Germans, chiefly Protestant Salzburgers fleeing religious persecution; their passage had been paid by the colony's British trustees, ironic in light of the fact that the trustees had paid the passage for fewer than a dozen English debtors and their families. French Huguenots and Sephardic Jews were likewise numerous in the various colonies. In 1643 the Jesuit priest Isaac Jogues reported 18 languages or dialects spoken among the 500 men of New Amsterdam, later New York; similar diversity was found in Philadelphia and Charleston.

MIGRATION WITHIN THE NEW WORLD   A land of opportunity—that was the implication, if not the express statement, of those who promoted European immigration from the earliest settlement of the New World. Behind the glittering dreams of mountains of gold were the solid realities of rich land, teeming with game and virtually uninhabited, land to be had for the taking. As the coastal areas filled, beyond lay the Piedmont, the Mississippi Valley, and the Pacific slopes. Hardly had a colony become established when it sent out offshoots: lone hunters and trappers, then scattered settlers, then new organized communities. And while the original colonies were working their way inland toward the Appalachians, there was other migration and mixture of the settlers. New England groups moved south to East Jersey, the Chesapeake Bay, the Carolinas, and Georgia. The Ulster Scots of Pennsylvania, deflected by the French and Indians as they moved toward the Ohio Valley, established themselves along the foothills from Pennsylvania to the Carolinas and eventually broke through the gaps into Kentucky and the Great Lakes area. New Englanders came west later, through upstate New York, leaving the north central states with a belt of Yankees to the north and one of upland Southerners along the Ohio River, commingled in the center with still another overland migration from central Pennsylvania. About three percent of the American population have changed their state of residence every year since the first census of 1790. With each move the process of commingling was reinforced, and the mixture of the various regional speech forms in the seaboard communities was repeated. The different varieties of American English, already diluted by the settlers' migration, were further leavened with the establishment of new foreign language settlements—from Scandinavians in the Dakotas to Poles and Czechs in Texas.

Mobility in the New World was not an entirely geographical phenomenon. The opportunity that America offered the settler was a succession of New Deals. The landless younger son, the dissatisfied yeoman or craftsman, the indentured servant, and the transported criminal —all saw chances of gain over the horizon. After two generations a sort of self-made aristocracy had developed in the Chesapeake Bay area, and the process was repeated with every westward movement. If we look at the presidency, we discover that only three of those who have held the office since 1860 have come from families of longtime wealth and social position—Taft, and the two Roosevelts. The others have been the descendants, if not the children, of day laborers, small farmers, railroad men, and shopkeepers. Society in New York City has accepted alongside the descendants of the Dutch Patroons a succession of representatives of new money—the Morrises, Vanderbilts, Astors, Goulds, Rockefellers, Fords, and Kennedys. That many have moved upward and that many limbs have rotted on old family trees are but the Darwinian corollaries to the growth of new stock.

INDUSTRIALIZATION AND THE GROWTH OF CITIES   From the beginning of settlement America has had a shortage of skilled workmen and has always felt a push toward industrialization, toward the substitution of better tools and more effective machinery for human hands. The development of the American curved ax handle, for example, made tree felling vastly more efficient on a continent covered with timber. From the creation of this tool it was but a few steps to the interchangeable parts of Eli Whitney's gun factory, then to Henry Ford's assembly line, and to such modern developments as the computerized blast furnace.

Since industrialization needed concentrations of labor near the mills and foundries, it accelerated the process of urbanization that had begun almost with the first settlements. Those settlements had always been accessible to the wharves through which the colonies received goods from Europe or the West Indies and in turn exported the products of the land. The wharf, the warehouse, and the marketplace with its factor, or planter's agent, were the basic components of the colonial cities. Boston, Newport, New York, Philadelphia, Annapolis, Charleston, and Savannah arose as ports; and the importance of Albany came from its location on a navigable river. Paradoxically, although Virginia was the earliest settlement and the first to develop a profitable export commodity in tobacco, it was slow to develop urban centers. The Chesapeake Bay had provided every tidewater planter with his own deepwater port; it was not until the exhaustion of the first tobacco lands drove the plantations inland that Virginia cities such as Richmond, Norfolk, and Alexandria developed as commercial centers.

The fact that the colonies were independent entities—each with its own governor, council, and legislature—also contributed to the development of an urban society with a provincial elite, even where commerce lagged. The combination of administrative power and trade meant that, by the time of the Revolution, Philadelphia and Boston were more important than any other cities under the British Crown except London.

Moreover, the colonists all shared a strong commitment to education. This commitment sprang in part from the social origins of the settlers, who, as we have seen, disproportionately represented the middle classes, the yeomanry, and the artisans—the groups already most interested in learning. This interest in education was also partly due to the Renaissance and the Reformation, to the general intellectual curiosity of the times, and to the religious belief that access to the text of Holy Writ was essential to salvation. The compact organization of the New England townships made it easier to provide schools in these areas than in the plantations and the scattered settlements inland. Yet every religious body fostered education, and in every colony there was an interest in providing both elementary schools and, for the elite, academies, some of which grew into colleges. The respect for learning is shown by the fact that nine institutions of higher learning had been established before the Revolution.

These social forces indicated the direction that American English was going to take. The scanty representation of both ends of the British social spectrum meant that neither peasant speech nor that of the aristocracy would contribute much to the American idiom. The colonial ports and capitals would be places through which the standard speech of London might filter into the New World. The mixture of settlers—both English- and non-English-speaking—meant that the provincial dialects of Britain would not be imported intact. Geographic and social mobility further reduced the differences between regional and class varieties of speech. Ultimately industrialization meant that local terms, such as those of home butchering, would give way to national ones. Urbanization eroded the most divergent types of pronunciation, and education caused the most distinctive nonstandard grammatical features to atrophy.

By the time of the Revolution the consensus of English travelers to the New World was that there were three general characteristics of American speech: (1) Every community had a great deal of linguistic diversity. (2) Yet there were no striking provincial varieties as in British English, so that a pronounced Yorkshire accent, for example, would stand out by contrast. (3) There was a feeling that the average speech of the colonials was in some ways "better" than that in the homeland, less removed from what had come to be considered standard usage. We will turn next to a summary of the language features of that London Standard English that the first colonists brought with them to America.

The history of American English reflects familiar processes of linguistic change that take place between two different stages in the history of a language. Basically there are four principal types of linguistic change:

1. *External borrowing,* or *cultural borrowing.* This usually involves adopting words—called loanwords, or loans—from the vocabulary of another language, such as the terms that arise in the learned professions, from *algebra* to *zoology.* It may also involve borrowing words from another variety of the same language that is thought more prestigious; for example, American use of the British term *luggage* for *baggage.* These borrowings usually come through reading and have been common since the Renaissance.

2. *Intimate borrowing,* or *dialect borrowing.* This usually involves borrowing words from another variety of one's own language, such as the spread of the Southern terms *snap beans* and *snack* to national use. It may also involve adopting words from another language spoken in the same community. For example, in the Hudson Valley and in eastern Pennsylvania, Dutch and German spoken alongside English have given us such words as *spook* for *ghost, stoop* for *porch,* and *Santa Claus* from a Dutch pronunciation of *St. Nicholas* for the gift bearer whom the British call Father Christmas.

In the Middle Ages, when French was widely spoken among the better educated in England, English acquired from French such everyday words as *face* and *jaw.* Although cultural borrowing and intimate borrowing chiefly affect vocabulary, there are exceptions: the pronoun forms *they, their,* and *them* came into the language of London from the Scandinavians who had occupied northern England for several centuries.

3. *Phonetic change* operates within a language (or within a single variety of a language) at a given time, affecting all words of a given type. For example, every long *a* in Old English—the *a* we have today in *father*—has changed to a long *o* in the standard varieties of British and American English; hence, such words as *home, bone,* and *stone* were pronounced until the middle of the 12th century as *hām, bān,* and *stān.* This change affected only Old English words, not words that later came into Middle English.

4. *Analogy* is a process of simplifying the language by extending a common grammatical pattern to new and irregular words. Nouns in English normally form their plurals by adding the sounds /-s, -z, or -əs/ (spelled -s or -es), as in *cats, dogs, horses.* New nouns in the language, even foreign imports like *sputnik,* are treated according to the regular pattern (*sputniks*), and efforts are made to make many older nouns with irregular plurals conform. For example, in Shakespeare's day, the 16th century, *horse* could be singular or plural; two centuries earlier in Chaucer's day the plural of *toe* could be formed with -s, or with -n. The seven *dwarfs* of the Walt Disney movie have made most Americans forget the *dwarves* of the older fairy tale.

As people use the language these types of change are often mixed up. From Greek, English has borrowed so many verbs ending in -*ize* that it is common to produce verbs by adding this suffix to nouns and adjectives that are not of Greek origin: a man-about-town may be said to *womanize;* a business office may *finalize* plans; and cultural borrowing makes it easy to *analogize.*

Linguistic change in English from the time of Shakespeare to the present has involved a good deal of cultural borrowing and intimate borrowing, a fair amount of analogy, and very little phonetic change. But phonetic change has created a poorer fit between language and spelling than existed in the past. Let us look at the base line from which American English evolved.

English since Shakespeare's day

The English settled at Jamestown near the end of a period of drastic social change and corresponding linguistic change. The medieval social order had been overthrown: the Wars of the Roses had destroyed most of the older nobility, and the break of the Church of England with Rome had been accompanied by the confiscation of most church property. Latin was gone from the village church, and the French of knights and squires was becoming a memory. A wealthy middle class had come to dominate society. The vernacular had been established as the language of the law courts, and under the influence of the Westminster Chancery the forms of written usage had become stabilized. Uniformity of standard spelling was still to come, its establishment coinciding with the growth of the printing trade. Nor had an economical and straightforward prose style yet developed.

The Renaissance had brought the classics to England, and translation had become an important business, a route by which hordes of words from Greek, Latin, Italian, and French came into English. Not all of these imports were welcome, and the tendency of some writers to overload their works with such borrowings triggered attempts to establish a "purer" English, untainted by Latinisms. It was an age of experimentation, often unsuccessful but serving nonetheless to enrich the vocabulary. The vernacular was not yet fully established for all kinds of written communication. It was generally felt that the vernacular was not only an impermanent idiom but also that it was neither copious nor subtle enough to convey the shades of meaning possible in Latin. Nonetheless, the vernacular was on its way. The first monolingual English dictionary, Robert Cawdrey's *A Table Alphabeticall,* had just appeared (1604); but already there were bilingual dictionaries and the beginnings of pedagogical grammars.

In describing the Standard English of Shakespeare's London and comparing it with present-day American usage, we will resort to two fictions. We know that educated American English, especially its pronunciation, is far from uniform, but for purposes of this discussion we will stick to the speech of the northern Middle West. We must also remember that in reality only about five percent of the English populace spoke London Standard. (The proportion is about the same today, but the differences between London Standard and other varieties of British English have decreased.) Educated Londoners, however, were very familiar with other varieties of English.

The consonants of Shakespeare's English were very much like those of American midwesterners today. The /r/ was at least as strong as, possibly stronger than, that in *barn, beard,* and like words. The short vowels of *bit, bet, bat* were similar to our short vowels today; the vowel of *bat* was probably heard in such words as *father* and *want,* now pronounced with quite different vowels by American midwesterners. The vowel of *pot* was a little like our vowel of *caught;* what we have in *wood* was also heard in words like *cut, nut.* Among longer vowels, those of *moon, whole, law* are what we are accustomed to. However, while the vowel of *see* was what it is today, that of *sea* was different—like what we have in *say;* and the vowels of *day* and *dale* were modifications of the vowel of *bat.* The vowel we have in *but* did not appear, nor the vowel of *curt.* In fact, the words *bird, herd, heard, word, curd* originally had different vowel sounds, as their spellings remind us.

All in all the pronunciation that Shakespeare used would be understood today but would sound a little strange. Recorded reconstructions of the speech of Shakespeare's day sound a bit like the present-day rural English of Ireland. This is not surprising since the changes in London Standard speech would have been slow in reaching the Irish countryside, and the changes that have taken place in America would not have penetrated there at all.

A CHANGING GRAMMAR   The grammar of Standard English in 1600 is even less difficult for us to understand than its pronunciation. Perhaps the various modern versions of the Bible have made the language of the King James Bible of 1611 and the Book of Common Prayer of 1549 less familiar than it used to be, but the influence is still with us. And authors from Shakespeare to John Milton (1608–1674) provide ample evidence of both familiar and exalted styles of the period.

What few grammatical innovations have occurred since 1600 have generally been shared by British and Americans alike. One such innovation is the present passive participial phrase, as in *my new house is being built,* where older usage would have employed *is building.* We have now established a rather orderly system of extremely complex verb phrases, as shown, for example, in *By this weekend our living room will have been being redecorated for a whole month.* Informal spoken usage also provides such complexities as *used to didn't, might could, hadn't ought to, might ought, used to could,* which are seldom written except as dialog in fiction. But even these forms appear in the informal writing of the Elizabethan period.

NOUNS The inflections of nouns were pretty well stabilized by Shakespeare's time. The plural was generally formed by that time, as it is today, by adding the sounds /-s, -z, əz/ (spelled -s or -es) to the noun, and new loans automatically take on this plural pattern, as in *dachas* and *kamikazes*. Many older Latinate plurals, such as *data, agenda,* and *media,* are being accepted as singulars upon which to form an Anglicized plural (*an agenda, many agendas*). Not everyone accepts these changes, but the pressure for simplification is difficult to resist.

The genitive, or possessive, form of nouns has become even more rigorously generalized. As late as Milton's *Paradise Lost* (1667), a noun with a final -*f* might have a genitive with -*v*, even reflected in the spelling; Milton wrote about Adam's *"wives* first fall." Today we would think it strange to say anything other than my *wife's* uncle. The apostrophe is now recognized as the written sign of the genitive for nouns, and a common confusion, even among the educated, is to extend the use of this sign to pronouns where it has never been recognized, as in " a dog will have *it's* day" or "that book is *your's.*" By Shakespeare's time about 80 percent of the genitive relationships were signaled not by the inflection (the addition of *'s*) but by the use of the preposition *of;* the proportion of usage has generally stayed the same.

Two developments of the genitive were just coming into use in the 16th century, and both survived the objections of 17th-century critics. One of them is the "double genitive," which permits us to say *a friend of my father's,* which is slightly different in meaning from *a friend of my father.* The other is the "group genitive," *the King of England's crown,* where the possession applies to the whole phrase *King of England.* For some time purists insisted that good English demanded *the King's crown of England;* but the sense of the phrase prevailed, and we do not hesitate to say—though we would not write—*the girl who lives next door's new boy friend.*

PRONOUNS The system of pronouns has undergone more changes than that of nouns and remains still fairly complicated. Nonetheless, we have now stabilized the genitive pronouns into two groups: the "attributive," or adjective, forms (*my, our, your, his, her, its,* and *their*); and the "absolute," or subject and object, forms (*mine, ours, yours, his, hers, its,* and *theirs*). In 1600, however, this distinction was not entirely clear. In the King James Bible the attributive *mine* was used before a word beginning with a vowel or the consonant *h,* and *my* before a word beginning with another consonant. Hence the reader consistently finds, for example, *my friend* but *mine enemy.* Shakespeare, closer to the popular idiom, wrote *mine* rarely, and *my,* the prevalent usage in rapid speech, soon prevailed in all positions. The same kind of alternation was found for *thy* and *thine; no* and *none (no man, none other); a* and *an (a pear, an apple, a minute, an hour).* Only the last distinction survives in written English; in speech it is not always observed, even by the best educated.

The pronoun *its,* the genitive of *it,* crept into English in the 1590s—probably by analogy with the genitive of nouns—and after two generations was fully established in place of the older *his.* The King James Bible, Matthew 5:13, asks "if the salt have lost *his* savor," but no examples are found after 1675 in England or in the colonies.

The greatest changes have taken place in the pronouns of the second person. Historically, as evidenced in the King James Bible, *thou, thee, thy,* and *thine* were used when addressing one person; *ye, you, your,* and later *yours* when addressing more than one. In the Middle Ages, as with other European languages, the singular *thou* (subject form) became generally restricted to familiar speech or to addressing inferiors; the plural *ye* and *you* (subject and object forms, respectively) became the normal pronouns of everyday address, especially in formal situations. Despite the protests of certain religious groups, such as the Quakers, the newer practice prevailed and was extended to every situation. Meanwhile, since pronouns were (and still are) often weakly stressed in speech, rendering *you* and *ye* indistinguishable, the practice developed of writing *you* in all positions, with the pronunciation depending on the rhythm of the sentence. Thus *you,* in Middle English a plural object form, became the second-person singular and plural form for subject and object.

Yet on many occasions it is important to distinguish between addressing a single person and a larger group. As *you* became established for the singular, new forms developed for the plural. The Book of Common Prayer, in the Communion Service, recognizes this distinction in "drink ye all of this" (paraphrased in recent versions as *"all of you,* drink . . ."), which gave rise to the widely recognized Southern *you-all.* Alongside *you-all* there are other American regional usages: upland Southern *you-uns, mongst-ye* on the eastern shore of Chesapeake Bay, *youse* in several metropolitan areas as well as in scattered communities in Pennsylvania, and *oona* among the Gullah Negroes of the Carolina and Georgia coast. Of these only *you-all* has any claim to standard usage, and it is restricted to relatively informal speech.

Relative pronouns have likewise undergone considerable change. By the 14th century the relative pronoun *that* had replaced a variety of earlier usages. Also around that time the first efforts were made to formally distinguish between the two types of relative clauses: the purely descriptive, *nonrestrictive* relative clause, introduced by the relative pronoun *which* and set off by commas (The Michigan Avenue bus, *which I often take,* goes downtown) and the defining, *restrictive* relative clause, introduced by *that* and not set off by commas (The bus *that goes downtown* is the Michigan Avenue bus). The pronoun *which* was first used to refer to both persons and things. Think back to the Lord's Prayer in the King James Bible: "Our Father, *which* art in Heaven." Gradually, however, *who* was introduced—first in the object form *whom*—when referring to persons. But neither the distinction between restrictive and nonrestrictive clauses, nor that between personal and impersonal antecedents, has ever been consistently observed. Further confusion among the pronouns was added by other variants in speech: *the man what owns the orchard, the man as owns,* and simply *he's the man owns the orchard.* For *the boy whose father* such alternates have appeared as *the boy his father* and *the boy that his father.*

ADJECTIVES   The comparison of adjectives had been established by adding inflectional endings: *long, longer, longest.* During the late Middle Ages, however, the practice developed of indicating comparison with *more* and *most,* a practice that became almost universal with longer adjectives and with participles used as adjectives: *a more beautiful daughter, the most experienced players, a more loving child.* For words of these kinds the comparison with *-er, -est* is highly informal and often not standard; for shorter adjectives like *uneasy, fine, red,* the older comparison is still usual.

During Shakespeare's lifetime a form of double comparison was introduced in Standard English—perhaps for emphasis—using both the qualifying markers *more/most* and the inflectional endings *-er/-est,* giving such forms as *more livelier* and *most happiest.* By far the best-known example of this type of construction is Mark Antony's characterization of the dagger wound which Brutus gave Caesar as "the *most unkindest* cut of all." The construction, never very common, faded from standard usage but is still found in old-fashioned speech among the less educated (and among children still struggling to learn the language). A dress may be described as *more prettier* than another, or a boys' gang as the *most fiercest* of them all. But these constructions are not Standard English.

VERBS   As with the other parts of speech, the general direction of change in verbs has been toward the simplification and regularization of forms. The present tense forms have incurred, with a few exceptions, little change since Shakespeare's day. Elsewhere verb forms have been subject to considerable confusion.

In the present tense the old *-th* form for the third-person singular verb (*walketh*) was consistently retained in the King James Bible, but Shakespeare alternated between the *-th* form and the newer *-s* form (*walks*). As a general rule the *-th* was kept most often in the very common forms like *doth* and *hath,* with *-s* used elsewhere. Except in formal church usage the *-th* ending was never established in America.

With the passing from use of the second-person singular subject pronoun, *thou,* so departed all the Shakespearean second-person singular forms of the verb: *thou art, wast, wilt, hast, givest,* and the like. The only relics of the former distinction between the singular and plural past tense forms are *was* and *were.* Elsewhere, even among irregular verbs, we now have only one past tense form, sometimes the old singular, sometimes the old plural. In the verb *ride,* for example, the past singular form *rode (I rode)* predominated over the plural form *rid (we rid),* though in his diary George Washington regularly wrote *I rid.* However, with the verb *hide,* originally of the same conjugation, just the opposite is true: *I hode* gave way to the plural form *we hid.* The form that survived was simply an accident of history.

The basic change in the principal parts of the verb has been toward the regular formation of both the past tense and past participle by adding the sounds */-t, -d,* or *-ə̄d/* (spelled *-d* or *-ed*): *sliced, raged, added.* The verb *climb* originally formed its past tense and past participle with various vowel changes, which would give us such legitimate historical forms as *clam, clom, clum, clome,* and *cloom,* depending on the region. Later the regular pattern was adopted, and *climbed* now serves as past tense and past participle. New verbs, whatever their origin, follow the regular pattern: *cystoscoped, interviewed.*

Sometimes, however, historically "regular" forms have given way to "irregular" ones. The irregular past tense and past participle forms *stuck* and *dug* have replaced the regular 16th-century forms *sticked* and *digged.* In the northern part of the United States the past tense *dived* has given way to *dove* (rhyming with *stove*). A further innovation, at least in standard usage, has been the recent emergence of *snuck* as the past tense and past participle of *sneak.*

Even where the principal parts are irregular, there has been a tendency to simplify the verb and to make past tense and past participle the same. For example, the participle *stood* and its compounds (*understood,* etc.) have replaced the 16th-century forms *standed* and *standen;* and, except in adjectival use and a few formal contexts, the participle *stricken* has been replaced by the past form *struck.* Recently, in many parts of the United States, *have drank* has been accepted in standard speech—perhaps to avoid the connotations of the participle *drunk* used adjectivally to mean "intoxicated." The simplification of principal parts might have gone much further but for the intervention of grammarians in the 17th and 18th centuries, who thought it desirable to preserve the maximum number of distinctions wherever possible.

The verb *to be,* drawing on several Indo-European stems, is irregular in every language of the family. In English it has nonetheless been subject to the same pressure for regularization that affected other verbs. As late as the 16th century it was acceptable to use either the older uninflected *be* in a statement—especially with a plural subject, as in *we be all good Englishmen*—or the newer inflected form *we are.* Today, while *be* is still used frequently in the rural speech of western England, it has dropped out of standard use except in the subjunctive mood. In America it has been associated until recently with the speech of rural New England and is now noted chiefly among some inner-city blacks.

The subjunctive verb forms are moribund in present-day American English. The only form used with any frequency is that in the hypothetical clauses *if I were you, if she were I,* etc. Unfortunately, this use seems to have encouraged such hypercorrections as *If he were at the ball game, I didn't see him,* where the matter-of-fact nature of the events demands *if he was at the ball game.*

Of the complicated system of verb phrases in present-day English, two points deserve mention. The first point reflects a change in English away from the patterns of other European languages. In English we now use the auxiliary verb *have* with all past participles to indicate recently completed action: *I have come, the train has arrived.* When speakers of English learn other European languages, they find it troublesome that the equivalent of the verb *to be* must be used as an auxiliary with past participles of verbs indicating motion or state of being; for example, *il est arrivé* (literally translated from French, "he is arrived"). Until recently English was like its continental kin, allowing Shakespeare to write *I am come, you are arrived, he is ascended.* Today, however, Standard English demands a form of the auxiliary verb *have* with past participles.

The second point has been a problem for teacher and student for more than three and a half centuries: the use of the auxiliary verbs *shall* and *will* to indicate future time. Originally these auxiliaries were meaningful verbs in their own right, although they were often followed by infinitives. *Shall* indicated necessity (*Thou shalt not steal,* meaning in 20th-century terms not the feeble *you shall not* but the stronger *you must not* or *you had better not*); and *will* indicated volition and determination. By 1600 both auxiliaries had come to signify future time, albeit with slightly different meanings. From 1622 to 1765 several generations of grammarians attempted to define and refine the rules governing their use, and schoolmasters and school texts have subsequently tried to impose those rules on their captive audiences. It is only in the last 50 years that students of English have taken a serious look at the evidence on which the rules were based. This period of reappraisal has shown that the school book rules have never fully represented the actual usage of educated writers in any part of the English-speaking world, and in recent years these rules have received far less attention than before.

Another development in the verb system has been the use of *do* as an auxiliary in phrases of interrogation or negation. The King James Bible again furnishes us with models of 16th-century practice: in questions the subject and verb were simply inverted (*What say ye?*), and in negations *not* immediately followed the verb (*They have mouths, but they speak not . . .*). In the early 17th century authors began to use the constructions we are accustomed to, such as *What do you say?* and *They do not speak,* and the negative-interrogative *Don't you know?* The acceptance of these new forms was uneven; an author might use *do* in questions and avoid it in negation, or vice versa. But by the end of the century its practices in standard modern English were established.

A final detail to be noted on the development of verbs is that of the infinitive of purpose used for emphasis. As an infinitive marker *to* was first used only in emphatic situations; when *to* became a general marker something stronger was needed. Chaucer (1340?–1400) used *for to,* as in "the holy blisful martir *for to* seke." This use continued, but Standard English now uses *in order to* and *so as to,* with *for to* now associated with uneducated usage.

These developments in English grammar from Shakespeare's time to the present do not represent any great changes in the structure of the language. Probably most important in a structural sense are the changes in the second-person pronouns and the introduction of the *do* forms of interrogation and negation. What has happened to English grammar has been a rearrangement and a codification of details; in general the same changes have taken place on both sides of the Atlantic. The nature of the settlement of North America meant that some of the more old-fashioned British usages never migrated, like the old second-person singular pronouns, or arrived in a very weakened form, like *be* as a form with a subject. But few forms are unequivocally associated with one side of the Atlantic or the other. The fact is that the standard varieties of British and American English have never lost touch with each other. To this continuing contact is due much of the status that English enjoys in areas where some other language is spoken.

Enriching the vocabulary

CULTURAL AND DIALECT BORROWING   All languages have ways in which they can enlarge their vocabulary to take care of new situations. Chi-

nese often invents descriptive word combinations out of its own resources; for example, a train is literally a "fire-wagon" and a match,
"foreign fire." Japanese, on the other hand, takes over entire words from
other languages that may be useful; *baseball*, even more a national sport
in Japan than in the United States, is simply naturalized as *bei-su-bo-ru*.
Elevator comes out as *e-rei-bei-tah*.

English, like Japanese, is noted for its ability to borrow words from
other languages, and the habit of borrowing has grown stronger with
time. In the Old English period (450–1100) both borrowing and loan
translation of the Chinese type enriched the English vocabulary. Subsequently the great stream of Latin borrowings in the period 950–1100,
and the inundation with Latin and French between 1066 and 1350,
when French dynasties ruled England, made borrowing more common
than loan translation. The process that restricted *swine, deer, sheep, ox,*
and *calf* to the living animal and designated their flesh respectively as
pork, venison, mutton, beef, and *veal* made it easier to accept a neo-
Latin *omnibus* for a public passenger conveyance and reject *folkwain*
(whose elements are from the same Germanic source as *Volkswagen*),
which was advocated by those concerned with the purity of the language. And those who deplored *seaplane* as a barbarous hybrid of a
native and a Romance element were dealing with the word-forming
habits of a language that had long domesticated *beautiful* and *gentle-
woman.*

At the time of the first permanent English settlements in the New
World, British English was freely borrowing words from Greek, Latin,
French, Italian, and Spanish as the need arose. The transplated Englishmen simply continued the tradition that was well established in the
homeland. Their descendants have kept the habit.

As we look at the history of American borrowings from other languages, a few things are apparent. Most of the borrowings are nouns,
though borrowed nouns are sometimes later changed into verbs; for
example, *tomahawk, lasso,* and *stampede.* Borrowed words are used
most often to describe objects or institutions that were new to the
colonial Englishman. The amount of borrowing in a language does not
depend on the size of the group from which the words are borrowed but
rather on the relative size and importance of the two speech communities
at the time they came in contact. The colonial Dutch population was
minute in comparison with the Polish and Italian immigration to the
United States in the last 80 years or so; but it was of the same order,
though smaller, as the population of Massachusetts and Connecticut
with which the Dutch came in contact, and the groups interacted as
equals. In contrast the Poles and Italians came into a long-settled country where English was already the established language; for them, learn-

ing English was a necessity—and as factory workers, largely unskilled, they offered few words that the English-speaking population wanted.

Einar Haugen, the most distinguished student of bilingualism in the Americas, classifies the languages with which the English settlers in America came into contact thus: aboriginal languages of the American Indians; the colonial languages introduced before the War for Independence; the early immigrant languages introduced before 1870; and the later immigrant languages, introduced after 1870, primarily in urban areas. But there is no distinct way of separating languages by periods of contact. Loans from German, for example, have been entering English, though from different groups of speakers, for nearly three centuries.

Most of the aboriginal loanwords came from the various eastern and central Algonkian languages, spoken along the Atlantic seaboard from Canada's Maritime Provinces to North Carolina, and westward beyond the Great Lakes. These were the first Indians the colonists met; they introduced the colonists to foods, farming practices, and woodcraft. The loans are diverse: *possum, coon, moose, caribou, hickory, hominy, terrapin, woodchuck, tomahawk, powwow, sachem, Tammany, squash, succotash, squaw, papoose,* and *wigwam.* In addition, the aboriginal languages produced through loan translation such compounds as *fire-water, warpath,* and *peace pipe* and inspired a large number of compound words with *Indian,* ranging from *Indian corn* to *Indian summer.* From the Western Indians the borrowings were fewer; by the time of the westward expansion the settlers were established and needed fewer new words. Yet we do have such borrowed terms as the *teepee* of the Plains Indians; the *hogan* and *kachina* of the Navajo; and the *cayuse, chinook,* and *hooch* of the Northwest. Twenty-seven states and many of our rivers also have American Indian names, with *Indiana* commemorating their prior residence.

BORROWING FROM OTHER COLONIAL LANGUAGES   The first colonial language the English colonists came in contact with was French, with major settlements of the French in Quebec and Louisiana and French Huguenot immigrants to the English colonies all along the coast. Like the American Indian loans, most of these represent intimate borrowing: *chowder, sault, portage, cache, rapids,* and *shanty* in the North; *bayou, pirogue, levee, crevasse, jambalaya, lagniappe,* and *picayune* along the Gulf; and *gopher, coulee, crappie,* and *prairie,* which owe something to both frontiers. As New Orleans developed into a symbol of luxurious if not decadent living, it added the *praline,* possibly the *cocktail,* certainly a variant in the *Sazerac,* and likely *craps* as a game of chance. *Bateau,* a flat-bottomed boat, was probably introduced by the Huguenot rice planters of South Carolina. The American coins *cent* and *dime* are also from the French, though the once-almighty *dollar* is of German origin. Unlike the American Indian loans, which tapered off after the early days of settlement, the French loans, including those from Canada, continue even today to enrich our vocabulary.

Although the Spanish preceded the English settlers to the New World by more than a century and the settlement (1565) of St. Augustine, Florida, preceded Jamestown by 42 years, there were few close Anglo-Spanish contacts on the Continent before the 19th century. The Louisiana Purchase of 1803 thrust the United States into territory with prior Spanish claims, from the Gulf to the Canadian boundary; the annexation of Texas (1845) and the further southwestern migration brought contact with the Spanish-American culture of mines, missions, and ranches. The Spanish-speaking population in these and many new urban areas has been steadily reinforced over the years by immigration from Mexico, Puerto Rico, and Cuba, among other nations. At present there are more speakers of Spanish in the United States than of any other language except English.

Spanish contributions to English are many and varied. The most widely known are those dealing with ranch life: *ranch* itself, *corral, buckaroo, lariat, poncho, serape, sombrero, lasso, rodeo,* and *stampede*. Others reflect the food and drink and the flora and fauna of the Southwest: *chile con carne, taco, tequila, tortilla, alfalfa, mesquite, marijuana, bronco, cockroach, coyote,* and *mustang*. Mining gave us *bonanza* and *placer;* the legal problems of the frontier yielded *calaboose, desperado, hoosegow,* and *vigilante*. American topography could not be effectively described without *key* (one of the few terms from the Caribbean), *arroyo, canyon, mesa,* and *sierra*.

Most of these loans came from the Southwest, where the first ranchers were Latins who participated as eagerly as the newly arrived Anglos in the revolt against the distant, inefficient, and often capricious administration in Mexico City. In contrast the loans from the large urban Spanish settlements are few and not generally familiar—*barrio* (Spanish-American neighborhood) and *bodega* (neighborhood grocery–liquor store) are perhaps the best known of the recent loans. An earlier urban loan was the self-service *cafeteria,* which appeared in Chicago in the 1890s. Not only are the word and the institution known everywhere, but they have numerous progeny, such as *groceteria, bookateria, snacketeria,* and, lately, such establishments as the *valeteria (i.e.,* a dry cleaner), where the coined word has lost touch with its "root" since there is no self-service.

Considering the relatively small size of their settlements, the Holland Dutch have been remarkably important contributors to American English. Although their settlements were sprinkled from Albany to

Delaware, they were never very numerous; their population was diluted with Swedes and Finns, with French-speaking Walloons, and with English-speaking refugees from New England theocracy. It is difficult to recognize Dutch loans: many of them resemble English words, such as *bush* (back country) and *hook* (point of land); others could have come into English via German, such as *sawbuck, spook,* and *dumb* (stupid). Nonetheless, Dutch loans have contributed a number of familiar terms, most of them adopted not later than the colonial and early national periods: *coleslaw, cookie, waffle, caboose, sleigh, dope,* and *snoop.* American politics would be inconceivable without *boodle* to reward services rendered or a *boss* to distribute it. *Boss,* "master," spread in the northern states as a euphemism, more acceptable to free labor than its English synonym. Then when a *labor boss* (overseer) at the Brooklyn Navy Yard went into the political machine, his title followed him to the top and spread to other leaders, including those without working-class origins, like the Main Line aristocrats who ran the Republican machine in Philadelphia.

The Germans represented a significant portion of the early settlers, and their contributions to American life and language have been of long duration and great influence. No group has been more widely distributed, both regionally and socially, in this country. Of the non-native English speakers in the United States, the Germans are still second in number only to the Spanish.

The German community is a complex composite of at least four groups of German-speaking settlers who have come to the United States over the past three centuries. The earliest German settlers were the religious dissenters, among them the Mennonites and Amish, who arrived in Pennsylvania in 1683 and subsequently migrated in the early 18th century into Maryland, the Shenandoah Valley, and the uplands of the Carolinas and Georgia. Meanwhile, other groups of Germans and German-Swiss established themselves in the Hudson and Schoharie Valleys in New York, in eastern North Carolina, in the South Carolina Low Country, and in the Savannah Valley in Georgia. In the 19th century new rural German settlements appeared, chiefly in the Middle West but also in Texas. Most of these communities were settled by new immigrants, but some were expansions of the older communities in Pennsylvania. Urban Germans, often middle-class and intellectuals, joined the new immigrants, especially after the failure of the revolutions in Europe of 1830 and 1848. Their colonies in Cincinnati, St. Louis, and Milwaukee are best known, but every important American city outside New England, including Charleston, New Orleans, and San Francisco, developed its own German community.

The last group of German-speaking settlers in the New World were the Ashkenazic Jews from Eastern Europe. Their community language was Yiddish, originally a Rhineland German dialect of the 11th century that had been heavily interlarded with Hebrew and Slavic words. Although a declining language that has suffered from the slaughter of European Jews under Hitler, new persecution in the Soviet Union, the resurrection of Hebrew as the official language of Israel, and assimilation of American Jews to the dominant culture, Yiddish is still a rich source of loans.

The loans from German fall into three chief groups. First are those from the rural settlements in Pennsylvania and elsewhere: *fossnocks* (doughnuts), *liverwurst, snits* (dried sliced fruit). From urban life we get such terms as *delicatessen, beer garden, saengerfest, schuetzenfest, rathskeller,* and *pinochle;* such academic terms as *festschrift, semester,* and *seminar* were taken from the German universities when graduate education was developed in America. Finally from Yiddish come a number of terms in social life and retail trade: *schlock, gefilte fish, schnook, schmaltz, borscht,* and *blintz,* as well as a varitey of religious terms, of which *kosher* is best known.

The last of the colonial languages—in this case a language group—is in a special category since its speakers, the African blacks, were for the most part unwilling immigrants, slaves imported to work the fields along the southern Atlantic coast and in Louisiana. Except for the Ulster Scots and the smaller body of Huguenots, no group of Americans can claim as large a proportion of early settlers: of the 400,000 slaves imported to what is now the United States and Canada, seven-eighths arrived before 1800. Their greatest influence was left on the vocabulary of the South Carolina and Georgia coast, which gained such words as *benne* (sesame), *pojo* (a kind of heron), *pinder* and *goober* (both meaning peanut), *cooter* (turtle), and *tabby* (originally from Arabic, the language of the African slavers, meaning a kind of masonry).

LOANS FROM IMMIGRANT LANGUAGES   In contrast with the colonial languages the immigrant languages have added relatively little to the American English vocabulary. Although the Scandinavian languages, Chinese, Japanese, the Slavic languages, and Italian have given us a number of words, most of them have entered the language through cultural borrowing rather than through dialect borrowing that results from neighborhood contacts. Nonetheless, the Little Italys of urban America gave us a number of food terms, such as *pizza* and *espresso,* as well as various words related to the *mafia.* To *cook coffee,* a midwestern variant of *make coffee,* is probably a loan translation from the Scandinavian. *Kielbasa,* a kind of Polish sausage, and *kolach,* a Czech pastry, have been disseminated from Slavic colonies. *Chop suey* and *chow mein,* unknown in China, became familiar terms when the Cantonese restaurant appeared in American cities. *Issei* (first generation) and *Nisei* second generation) were significant words not only to Japanese-Americans but to their west coast neighbors before the agony of World War II made them nationally known terms, and *kamikaze* and *brainwash* (a loan translation) were learned from all too intimate contact with suicide pilots off Japan and "reeducational" experts in Chinese prison camps.

Intimate contacts also yielded *honcho* (big shot, man in charge) from the Japanese word (*hancho*) for squad leader, and the Tagalog (Philippine) word for mountain gave us *boondocks* (the sticks, back country), now often shortened to *boonies*.

A final note on borrowing should be made. We have pointed out that when a number of compounded words are borrowed from another language the elements of the compounds become available to the "adoptive" language to make additional words. We have mentioned this with reference to the words modeled on *cafeteria*. Similarly, in imitation of *frankfurter* and *hamburger,* literally meaning "in the fashion of *Frankfurt* and *Hamburg*" respectively, we have used the elements *-furter* and *-burger* to designate a sausage in a casing and a sandwich in a bun; hence we have *turkeyfurters, cheeseburgers, clamburgers, oysterburgers,* and *burgers* of various eponymous origins—the most notorious being the *Trumanburger* of mashed baked beans, so named in protest against the continuing meat rationing after World War II.

The practice of borrowing technical terms from Greek and Latin has likewise provided English with a ready supply of word-forming elements, and hence our words *anaesthesia* and *anaesthetic, appendicitis* and *appendectomy,* etc. Recognizing the process of word coining from familiar elements, corporations have been known to feed familiar elements into a computer to produce a supply of names that can be registered as trade names in anticipation of products to which they may be applied.

FURTHER EXPANSION OF THE VOCABULARY   The above-mentioned formation of new words based on borrowed elements brings us to another important way in which American English has expanded its vocabulary: the manipulation of familiar English linguistic forms.

There are several ways in which a language may adapt its resources to new situations. It may change the meanings of words; it may make new compounds; it may add prefixes and suffixes to existing words; it may transfer words to different parts of speech; and it may shorten words or create blends and acronyms.

Changes of meaning are of four principal types: *generalization,* in which the word takes on a wider range of meaning; *specialization,* in which it takes on a narrower range; *pejoration*, in which it takes on less favorable associations; and *melioration*, in which it takes on more favorable connotations.

The American use of *freight* is a good example of generalization of meaning. In Britain it was restricted to heavy loads moved by water; in America it refers to any kind of merchandise transported in any fashion. Railroads distinguish between *passenger trains* and *freight trains*, the latter made up of various special kinds of *freight cars*. The development of modern highways and motor trucks made possible *motor freight*, though the term is not as widely used as it once was; and large cargo planes now carry *air freight*.

In contrast the word *fraternity* has acquired a narrower, more specialized meaning in the United States than in Britain. In British usage it can mean brotherhood as an abstract virtue, as in "Liberty, Equality, Fraternity," the motto of the French Revolution; it also means a group organized for religious purposes, otherwise known as a *confraternity*. When an American speaks of *fraternity*, he normally thinks of a socially oriented and generally restrictive association of college men. *Tariff*, which in England means various rate schedules, in the United States is almost entirely restricted to customs duties.

Bug is a rather innocuous term in America, describing any kind of insect life or bacteria as well as electronic devices planted for eavesdropping. In England *bug* is now restricted to the *bedbug*, a pejorative term not used in polite society. A second example of this type of change is found in the word *saloon*, with the setting of the pejoration this time America. In England *saloon*, a variant of *salon*, suggested elegance, as in the *dining saloon* of an ocean liner, and was adopted in America as a fashionable name for a barroom. It soon, however, acquired such overtones of drunkenness and rowdiness that the *Anti-Saloon League* was founded to drive it out of existence and presumably lead the nation to sobriety. It was a generation after the repeal of national prohibition before establishments for slaking the American thirst dared use the title again, and even now a *saloon* is likely to suggest a decor with the atmosphere of the frontier or the turn of the century.

The word *lumber* illustrates the contrasting change of melioration. It once meant heavy, useless articles, or simply junk; the old meaning survives in some Atlantic seaboard communities in *lumber room* to identify a room where discarded furniture and implements are put away. No doubt the piles of cut timber awaiting shipment were so much *lumber* to those who wished to use the wharves for less bulky cargo. But as the shipment of cut timber became profitable, the term lost its ill favor, and a *lumber yard* is now a valuable asset to a community.

The most frequent process for making new American words is compounding. Compounded words are usually nouns but may also be verbs, as in *to chip in, to stand pat, to babysit*. And they may represent any field of activity: *favorite son, grassroots, ward heeler, lame duck* in politics; *bluegrass, water gap, badlands* in terrain; *garter snake, flying squirrel, alligator cooter* in animal life; *worm fence, tobacco barn, milk gap, hog crawl* in farming; *popover, liver pudding, sivvy beans, acorn squash* among foods. In colonial days compounding produced an astronomical number of additions to the vocabulary but is just as common in more recent times as well. Air travel has brought the *wide-body jet, jet lag, sonic booms* from *supersonic planes*, and *noise pollution* around airports. And modern living would be unthinkable without *air conditioners, deep freeze(r)s, travel alarms,* and *convenience foods.*

While compounding is the favorite means of extending the vocabulary, prefixing and suffixing are still common. Perhaps the most interesting prefix in American use is *anti-*. An inventory of its use would give a capsule history of American politics, from *anti-Federalist* to *anti-busing* and *anti-desegregationist*. The suffix *-ite* has two general meanings, residence and allegiance, and has produced innumerable progeny. Used in the first sense, it is the general means of designating an inhabitant of a city, such as *Camdenite,* or of a general type of community, such as *suburbanite*. In its second sense *-ite* may suggest allegiance in a sport, such as the loyal *bleacherites* who attend baseball games, or, more commonly, it involves an ideological identity with a leader, such as the *Hicksites* and *Campbellites* in religion, or the *Tillmanites, Bleasites,* and *Reaganites* in politics. Such political countergroups as the *anti-McGovernites* display a compound utilizing both prefix and suffix.

Functional change, or a change in the part of speech represented by a given word, has been common in English since the late Middle Ages because there is nothing in an English word to indicate its part of speech (noun, verb, adjective, etc.). Nouns have been made into verbs—and vice versa—since the earliest days of American English: before the end of the 18th century, houses had been *clapboarded* (*weatherboarded* in the South), settlers had been *tomahawked* and *scalped*. By the Jacksonian era miscreants had been *lynched* and were later *kukluxed*. When *lumber* ceased to mean rubbish and came to signify cut timber, it soon became a verb and *lumbering* a respectable occupation. Not all of these functional changes were welcome; to *deed* a piece of land, that is to convey by deed, was long denounced as a barbarous Americanism.

Another frequent change is the shortening of many lengthy, familiar terms. *Moving picture* naturally became *movie;* a *gymnasium,* a *gym;* and a *fraternity,* a *frat*. But it is not necessarily the first syllable that survives: *telephone* became *phone; Conestoga* cigars became *stogies; raccoon* (already condensed from its Algonkian origin) became *coon.* Occasionally the shortening process from a noun creates an apparent underlying verb where none had existed before; thus from *donation* Americans devised *donate,* patterned after such verbs as *interrogate* and *accommodate,* and providing another example of alleged American barbarism. The blending of parts of words, making what Lewis Carroll called "portmanteau words," was originally a type of wordplay but is now often used seriously in business. A famous early example is *gerrymander,* after Elbridge Gerry, governor of Massachusetts, whose legislature obediently crowded opposition voters into a serpentine district. Similarly *cablegram* and *radiogram* are blends for messages sent by cable or radio and *motel* for *motor hotel.* By the same process we get *Nabisco* from National Biscuit Company. From there is but a step to the acronym, making a word out of the initial letters of the components. The term is strictly correct only when the letters yield a pronounceable word, like *NATO* for North Atlantic Treaty Organization, but it is often extended to cases where the letters must be read separately, whether a drug like *ACTH* or the most popular Americanism of them all, *OK.* (Various romantic theories of *OK*'s origin still appear, but it almost certainly originated in 1839 in Boston as a mock abbreviation of "all correct.")

Finally a subtle but familiar form of linguistic manipulation is found in slang and argot. Originally both terms referred to the same type of language, the usage of the professional criminal, but they are now distinguished. Slang refers to popular vogue expressions, rapidly disseminated and rapidly lost; argot refers to the specialized language by which members of a subculture identify themselves with the group. Neither slang nor argot is a 20th-century creation; both have been used since colonial days. The slang words *booze, gam* (legs), and *bamboozle* have been part of the English vocabulary for three centuries.

Some current slang expressions originated long ago and have acquired new and different connotations as time passed. The derogatory slang term *pig* for policeman, for example, can be traced in America at least as far back as 1857, when it was in common use in Richmond. The local police wore the initials *P.G.* on their helmets for "Public Guard," and Richmonders commonly called a policeman a *blind pig* (a pig without an *i*). *Pig* for policeman is even older in Australia and probably goes back to earlier use in England.

Euphemy, the reverse of slang and argot, perhaps the mark of an insecure society, has produced many delicate synonyms for taboo terms —some of them becoming taboo in ther turn. *Privy* and *toilet,* once marks of delicacy, have yielded to such newer terms as *washroom* and *powder room.* Nor is an adolescent criminal less troubled or trouble-some for being called a *juvenile delinquent.* (For further discussion of euphemy and slang, *see* English Today earlier in this volume.)

The current state of American English

Finally we come to the question of the standard of English. Today many extremists insist that there is no such thing as Standard English and argue that the teaching of such a standard serves the oppressive ends of society. Surprisingly even some organizations of English teachers have denounced the concept of a standard. But, whether we like it or not, we do have a clear standard for written English. It began when the official clerks of chancery set out to standardize the language of official com-munication in order to avoid error; it was strengthened by the invention of printing and subsequent efforts of printers to standardize spelling. The multiplication of public records through tax returns, draft registration, and social security has meant further standardization, and computer storage of data for ready retrieval will take us yet a step further. As communication grows easier among various parts of our society, the written language will have further influence on the spoken. Where fault lines exist in society, it may be difficult for some groups to master the written standard, but it is important to master if we wish to communi-cate.

In spoken usage we have not attained the uniformity of our written standard. Given the size of the United States, it is unlikely that we ever will have uniform speech, nor is it necessary that we should. Standard English is written effectively by people who speak in various fashions, including those who speak Indian, Pakistani, Filipino, Nigerian, West Indian, and other varieties of English remote from anything used by speakers in the United States. They have mastered the standard written skills through observation and diligent practice. Competent writing is a skill that almost anyone can acquire, given incentive and training.

This brings us to the question frequently raised as to whether the American English language has been deteriorating in recent years. There is nothing wrong with the language itself; it is used widely, and it is increasingly taught as a second language. But there is truth to the fact that our average mastery of English, particularly our written skills, is not as good as it used to be. There are several reasons for this. Our schools are now graduating far more students than in the past, and, un-fortunately, many with high school diplomas read only at fifth-grade level and are unable to write a coherent paragraph. Perhaps an impor-tant reason for this is that schools, including prestigious graduate departments of English, have turned away from the teaching of basic writing. Each higher level expects the job to be done lower down; each lower level hopes that somehow its botched job will be repaired higher up. On all levels the pedestrian task of teaching writing is rejected in favor of the pleasanter work of encouraging self-expression or interpreting literature.

In our society there is now more written communication than ever before, whether for business reports or for customer complaint letters. Inevitably some of this writing is poor, but the wide distribution of such writing in various ways nonetheless elevates it as an influential model for others to follow.

Some of these problems are appropriately beyond the reach of the teacher of English: no one wants to deprive a child of the opportunity to get an education; and for all the jokes about inundations of paper, we are happy to have semipermanent records of written and printed communication. It is entirely possible, however, and desirable for the English instructor to teach, and expect that students learn, basic skills for clear written expression. Yet, if war is too serious a business to be left to the generals, perhaps the writing of American English is too important an assignment to be entrusted entirely to the English teacher. It is something that we all must be concerned with. We must all share in the vital task of teaching and learning how to use well and enjoy our rich American English language.

RAVEN I. McDAVID, JR.

The History of British English

Among highlights in the history of the English language the following stand out most clearly: the settlement in Britain of Jutes, Saxons, and Angles in the 5th and 6th centuries; the landing at Thanet of St. Augustine in 597 and the subsequent conversion of England to Latin Christianity; the Viking invasions of the 8th and 9th centuries; the Norman Conquest of 1066; the passing of the Statute of Pleading in 1362 (*see* below); the establishment of William Caxton's printing press at Westminister in 1476; the full flowering of the Renaissance in the 16th century; the publishing of the King James Bible (Authorized Version) in 1611; the completion of Samuel Johnson's *Dictionary* in 1755; the expansion to North America and South Africa in the 17th century; and to India, Australia, and New Zealand in the 18th.

The beginnings: Old English

The Jutes, Angles, and Saxons lived in Jutland, Schleswig, and Holstein respectively, before migrating across the North Sea and settling in Britain (still an outlying province of the Roman Empire, though the Romans had withdrawn in the 4th and 5th centuries A.D.). According to Bede (A.D. 672 or 673–735; first historian of the English people), the first Jutes, Hengist and Horsa, landed at Ebbsfleet in the Isle of Thanet in 449; and the Jutes later settled in Kent, south Hampshire, and the Isle of Wight. The Saxons occupied the rest of England south of the Thames as well as modern Middlesex and Essex. The Angles eventually took the rest of England as far north as the Firth of Forth, bringing the future Edinburgh and the eastern Scottish Lowlands within their domain. They were called Angles because they inhabited that angle or corner of land fronting on the southern Baltic between Schleswig and Flensburg. In both Latin and Common Germanic their name was *Angli,* later mutated to *Engle* (nominative) *Engla* (genitive) in Old English.

113

Before A.D. 1000 the name *Angel-cyn* "Angle race," and after that date *Engla-land* "land of the Angles," designated collectively all the Germanic tribes in Britain. From the beginning the language was called only Englisc, never "Anglo-Saxon," a name given to it later, but now generally replaced by Old English.

Jutes, Angles, and Saxons had their distinctive dialects. Because the River Humber formed an important geographical and linguistic boundary, the Anglian-speaking region was subdivided into Northumbrian and Southumbrian, or Mercian. There were thus four dialects: Northumbrian, Mercian, West Saxon, and Kentish. In the 8th century, Northumbria assumed preeminence in literature and culture. Hild (Hilda), abbess of Streoneshalh (Whitby), was of royal descent. At some time during her abbacy (*c.* 658–680) the herdsman Cædmon (Celtic Catumanus?) sang that nine-line hymn which marks the beginning of English literature. Benedict Biscop, founder of the Wear-mouth-Jarrow monastery (674–682), brought manuscripts direct from Rome. Bede, his pupil, thus had access to all the main sources of knowledge in the West. The light of learning shone more brightly in Northumbria than anywhere else in England, but unfortunately that light was extinguished by the Viking invaders who sacked Lindisfarne in 793 and Iona in 802. They landed in strength in 865. They comprised both Danes and Norwegians, and their speech was closely related to that of the Jutes, Angles, and Saxons who had landed in Britain before them. The Danes subdued all England north and east of the Roman Watling Street which crossed the country obliquely from London to Chester, but the nucleus of their territory, called the Danelaw, lay between the rivers Tees and Welland. It included the kingdom of York and the five boroughs of Derby, Nottingham, Lincoln, Leicester, and Stamford. The first raiders were Danes. Later they were joined by Norwegians from Ireland and the Western Isles who settled in the areas covered by the modern Cumberland, Westmorland, Lancashire, Cheshire, and the western dales of Yorkshire. When Eric Bloodaxe, last king of York, was slain on Stainmore in 954, England first became one under Eadred (Edred).

King Alfred saved Wessex. During his reign (871–899) learning shifted to the south, and especially to Winchester, his capital, and, in a sense, capital of all England in the period of its domination by Wessex. There the Parker Chronicle (the A manuscript of the Anglo-Saxon Chronicle) was written, there the Latin works of Orosius, Augustine, Gregory, and Bede were translated, and there the native poetry of Northumbria and Mercia was transcribed into the West Saxon dialect. This meant that West Saxon became standard Old English, and later, when Abbot Aelfric (*c.* 955–*c.* 1025) wrote his lucid and mature prose, this preeminence of Wessex was confirmed. Three short sentences from one of Aelfric's homilies may serve to show some of the feature of his language:

> Thā heofonlican æhta sind ūs eallum gemæne. Nacode wē wæron ācennede, and nacode wē gewītath. Thære sunnan beorhtnes and thæs mōnan lēoht and ealra tungla sind gemæne thām rīcan and thām hēanan.
>
> ("Heavenly possessions are to us all common. Naked we were born, and naked we depart. The sun's brightness and the moon's light and [that of] all stars are common to [shared by] the rich and the poor.")

Adjectives are inflected, both strong *gemæne*, *nacode* (nominative plural masculine and feminine), *eallum* (dative plural masculine), *ealra* (genitive plural neuter); and weak *heofonlican* (nominative plural feminine), *rīcan*, *hēanan* (dative plural masculine). The past participle is also inflected, *ācennede* (nominative plural masculine). The determiner or demonstrative pronoun, by then almost, but not quite, a definite article, appears here in four forms: *thā* (nominative plural feminine), *thære* (genitive singular feminine) *thæs* (genitive singular masculine), *thām* (dative plural masculine). The verb present tense ending *-ath* in *gewītath*, historically third person, is shared by all three persons in the plural. Nouns retain their grammatical genders: *sun* is feminine, *moon* masculine, and *star* neuter. All the words are of native Germanic origin, and all except six—*æhta, sind, ācennede, gewītath, tungla,* and *hēanan* —survive in present-day English. Related to *owe* (in its old sense of "possess") and *ought*, *æhta* survives in Scottish *aucht; sind,* cognate with Latin *sunt,* has been superseded by northern *aron* "are"; the base *cen* in *ācennede* is a gradational variant of *cyn* "kin"; *gewītath* lives on into Middle English in the form *wit,* but later falls into disuse through homonymic clash with *wit* "to know"; *tungla,* of obscure etymology, had cognates in the other Germanic languages, but nowhere survives; the adjective *hean* or *hene* "abject, humble, lowly" is last recorded in the 14th century.

The Middle Ages: Middle English

For the first century and a half after the Norman Conquest the main foreign influences naturally came from Normandy and Picardy, but with the extension south to the Pyrenees of the Angevin Empire of Henry II (reigned 1154–89), other dialects, notably Central French or Francien, influenced the speech of court and aristocracy. So Modern English has *catch, warden, warrant, wage,* and *reward* from Norman French side by side with *chase, guardian, guarantee, gage,* and *regard* from Francien.

King John lost Normandy in 1204. With the growing power of the Capetian kings of Paris, Francien predominated. Meantime, Latin—the international language of the Church—remained strong as the language of learning. For three centuries the literature of England was trilingual. *Ancrene Riwle* (*c.* 1200), a manual (rule, *riwle*) for recluses (anchorites), was disseminated in all three tongues. "Pop" songs, too, were gaily macaronic:

> Ma tresduce et tresamé
> Night and day for love of thee
> Suspiro

The first line ("My very sweet and dearly loved") is Norman French, the second English, and the last ("I sigh"), Latin.

One effect of the Conquest was to place all the Old English dialects more or less on a level. Mainly as a result of Scandinavian incursions, the old Mercian dialect had been split into East and West Mercian. All the resultant five dialects (Northern, West Midland, East Midland, South Western, and Kentish) then went their ways independently. The so-called Katherine Group of writings (taking their name from one of them, a life of St. Katherine), associated with the city of Hereford in the early 13th century, adhered most closely to native traditions. It is therefore justifiable to regard the West Midland dialect, remote from both French and Scandinavian influences, as a kind of Standard English in the High Middle Ages.

Then and later, all the kings of England spoke French. Until Edward IV (reigned 1461–83) none of them sought a wife in England. Henry Bolingbroke (reigned, as Henry IV, 1399–1413) was the first king after the Norman Conquest whose mother tongue was English. In 1362, however, Parliament had been formally opened in English for the first time. This was just three centuries less four years after the Battle of Hastings. By the Statute of Pleading, passed in 1362, all court proceedings were henceforth to be conducted in English, though still "enrolled in Latin." Chaucer was then a young man in his 20s. Although well able both to read and write French, he chose English. Nevertheless, half of the 8,000 or so words he used were of Romance origin. Chaucer was born in London and died there. His dialect was that variety of London English that was basically East Midland but that had assimilated a few Kentish and South Western peculiarities.

William Caxton (*c.* 1422–91) was fully aware of the uncertain state of the English language in his day. "What shall a man write?" he asked. In the 15th century, sentence patterns were sorting themselves out. For the first time nonprofessional scribes, including women, were beginning to write for themselves. It was this century of linguistic transition that produced the letters of Margaret Paston (1440–70) and the Cely Papers (1473–88), the letters and documents of a famous and prosperous family of London merchants.

The Renaissance: early modern English

That blossoming of art and letters, that spiritual rebirth or renaissance, had meantime occurred in Italy, and had gradually spread westward to France and England. It evoked, among other things, a revival of Greek learning by men like William Grocyn and Thomas Linacre, Sir Thomas More and Erasmus. John Colet, dean of St. Paul's (1504–19), startled his hearers by expounding the Pauline Epistles as living letters. His decanal predecessors had known no Greek, since they had found in Latin all they required. Only one or two exceptional churchmen such as Robert Grosseteste, bishop of Lincoln (1235–53), and his yet greater pupil, Roger Bacon (*c.* 1200–*c.* 1292), later known as *Doctor Mirabilis,* could read Greek with ease. The names of the seven liberal arts in the trivium and quadrivium of the medieval universities had all, it is true, been taken from Greek: *grammar, logic,* and *rhetoric; arithmetic, geometry, astronomy,* and *music.* (The word *grammar*—showing Greek base *gram*(*m*) + Latin suffix *-ar*(*ius*)—*joined* Greek and Latin components in one form.) Renaissance scholars adopted a liberal attitude to language. They freely borrowed Latin words through French, or Latin words direct; Greek words through Latin, or Greek words direct. Latin was no longer confined to the Church Latin of the Middle Ages: it embraced also all classical Latin. For a time the whole vocabulary of Latin became potentially English. Some words, like *consolation* and *infidel,* could have come from either French or Latin. Many others, like *abacus, arbitrator, explicit, finis, gratis, imprimis, item, memento, memorandum, neuter, simile,* and *videlicet* (abbreviated as *viz*) came direct from Latin. Love of Latin led men to re-borrow words that had already entered the language by way of French. Thus numerous doublets arose: *benison* and *benediction; blame* and *blaspheme; chance* and *cadence; count* and *compute; dainty* and *dignity; fealty* and *fidelity; frail* and *fragile; poor* and *pauper; purvey* and *provide; ray* and *radius; sever* and *separate; spice* and *species; strait* and *strict; sure* and *secure.* It goes without saying that few of these pairs remain synonymous. The Latin adjectives for "kingly" and "lawful" have even produced triplets. In the forms *real, royal,* and *regal*—*leal, loyal,* and *legal,* they were imported first from Anglo-Norman, then from Old French, and last from Latin direct.

After the dawn of the 16th century the movement of English prose toward modernity was swift and vigorous. The year 1525 saw the completion of the translation by Lord Berners of Jean Froissart's *Chronicle* and William Tyndale's translation of the New Testament, both surprisingly modern in syntax and style. With Berners and Tyndale modern English prose begins. One-third of the King James (Authorized) Version of 1611, it has been computed, is worded exactly as Tyndale left it; and between 1525 and 1611 lay the Tudor Golden Age with its majestic culmination in Shakespeare's dramas. Too many writers, it is true, used "ink-horn terms" and composed with memories of Latin rhythms and cadences in their heads. Too many vacillated in their choice of language. Even Roger Ascham (1516–68) remarked casually that he could have written his *Toxophilus* in Latin. Sir Thomas More actually did write his *Utopia* (1516) in Latin. It was translated into French during his lifetime, but not into English until 1551, some years after his death. Francis Bacon published *De Augmentis* in Latin in 1623. William Harvey announced his epoch-making discovery (1628) of the circulation of the blood in Latin—until the 20th century an international language of scholarship. Milton composed polemical treatises in the language of Cicero and, as Oliver Cromwell's secretary, corresponded in Latin with foreign states. Milton's younger contemporary, Sir Isaac Newton (1642–1727), lived long enough to bridge the gap. He wrote his *Principia* (1687) in Latin, but his *Opticks* (1704) in English.

The Restoration

With the restoration of the monarchy in 1660, men again looked to France. Many writers, including John Dryden (1631–1700), admired the Académie Française, founded by Cardinal Richelieu in 1635 and fostered by the Grand Monarch himself, Louis Quatorze (Louis XIV). After the heated emotional upsurges of the English Civil War this was an age of cool scientific rationalism. In 1662 the Royal Society of London for Improving Natural Knowledge received its charter, and its first members were much concerned with language. They appointed a committee of 22 "to improve the English tongue particularly for philosophic purposes." It included Dryden, the diarist John Evelyn, Bishop Thomas Sprat, and the poet Edmund Waller. Dryden deplored that the people had not "so much as a tolerable dictionary, or a grammar; so that our language is in a manner barbarous." Sprat pleaded for "a close, naked, natural way of speaking; positive expressions; clear senses; a native easiness; bringing all things as near the mathematical plainness" as possible. Alas, in the event the committee achieved very little. Its main aim—the foundation of an authoritative academy—proved abortive. A second attempt was made in 1712 when Jonathan Swift addressed an open letter to the earl of Oxford, then lord treasurer, entitled *A Proposal for Correcting, Improving, and Ascertaining* [*i.e.,* stabilizing] *the English Tongue.* This expressed current opinions unequivocally, but completely failed to attain its goal. Queen Anne died in 1714. The earl of Oxford and his fellow Tories (including Swift) lost power. No organized effort to establish an academy on French lines has ever again been made in England.

With Dryden and Swift the English language reached full maturity. In some ways their intention of founding an academy was partially fulfilled by Samuel Johnson in his *Dictionary* (1755) and by Joseph Priestley and Robert Lowth in their *Grammars* (1761 and 1762).

The age of Johnson

"Every language," said Johnson in the Preface to his *Dictionary,* "has its anomalies, which, though inconvenient, and in themselves once unnecessary, must be tolerated among the imperfections of human things, and which require only to be registered, that they may not be increased, and ascertained [*i.e.,* made certain fixed] that they may not be confounded: but every language has likewise its improprieties [incorrectnesses] and absurdities [logical contradictions], which it is the duty of the lexicographer to correct or proscribe." In other words, idiomatic usages may be tolerated and kept within reasonable bounds, but solecisms must be condemned. In practice, however, Johnson showed sound common sense. He took the best conversation of contemporary London and the normal usage of respected writers since Sir Philip Sidney (1554–86) as his criteria; and he elucidated the meanings of words by illustrative quotations. Johnson later conceded that "he had flattered himself for a while" with "the prospect of fixing our language," but that thereby "he had indulged expectation which neither reason nor experience could justify." The two-folio work of 1755 was followed in 1756 by an abbreviated one-volume version, widely used far into the 20th century.

It was unfortunate that Priestley, Lowth, and other grammarians took a narrower view of linguistic growth and development. They spent too much time pillorying such current "improprieties" as *I had rather not, you better go, between you and I, it is me, who is this for? between four walls, the largest of the two,* and *more perfect.* They condemned *you was* outright, without explanation, although it was in widespread general use. (On that ground it was later defended by Noah Webster.) It had, in fact, taken the place of *thou wast* as the singular counterpart of the regular plural *you were.*

As the century wore on, grammarians increased in number. They set themselves up as arbiters of right usage. They wrote manuals that were not only descriptive (stating what people really *do* say) and prescriptive (stating what they *should* say) but also proscriptive (stating what they *should not* say). Too many clung tenaciously to the conviction that Latin was a superior language to English or any other "modern" language and that somehow Latin grammar embodied universally valid canons of logic. This view was well maintained by Lindley Murray, whose *English Grammar* appeared in 1795, became immensely popular, and went into numerous editions. A native of Pennsylvania, Murray settled in England in 1784. He followed his *Grammar* with an *English Reader* (1799) and an *English Spelling Book* (1804), long favourite textbooks in both Old and New England.

The 19th and 20th centuries

Revised and enlarged editions of Johnson's *Dictionary* were made by Archdeacon Henry John Todd in 1818 and by Robert Gordon Latham in 1866. Meantime, in autumn 1857 Richard Chenevix Trench, then dean of Westminster, had read two papers to the Philological Society *On some deficiencies in our English Dictionaries*. Trench already was well known for books on *English, Past and Present* (1855) and *The Study of Words* (1851). His proposals for an entirely new dictionary were implemented two years later when Samuel Taylor Coleridge's great-nephew, Herbert Coleridge (1830–61), began work as first general editor. He continued until his untimely death when he was succeeded by Frederick James Furnivall (1825–1910), a lawyer, who founded the Early English Text Society (1864) with a view to making all the earlier literature available to historical lexicographers in competent editions. Furnivall was succeeded as editor by James A. H. Murray (1837–1915), who published the first fascicle of *A New English Dictionary on Historical Principles* (1884), later titled *The Oxford English Dictionary* (see *Bibliography*). Later Murray was joined by three successive editors who also enjoyed length of days: Henry Bradley (1845–1923), William Alexander Craigie (1867–1957), and Charles Talbut Onions (1873–1965). Their average age exceeded 84 years and their combined span extended over a century and a quarter. Aside from its *Supplements*, the dictionary itself fills 12 volumes, has over 15,000 pages, and contains 414,825 words illustrated by 1,827,306 citations. It is the dictionary of the British Commonwealth and the United States, a fact symbolized by the presentation of the first copies in spring 1928 to King George V and Pres. Calvin Coolidge. It exhibits the histories and meanings of all words known to have been in use since 1150. From 1150 to 1500 all five dialects of Middle English, as has been seen, were of equal status. They are therefore all included. After 1500, however, British and American dialectal expressions are not admitted, nor are scientific and technical terms not in general use. Otherwise the vocabulary is comprehensive. It even embraces denizens (*aide-de-camp, carte-de-visite, table d'hôte,* and *à la carte*); aliens (*back-sheesh, cicerone, geyser, sepoy, shah,* and *targum*); and casuals (Italian *sbirro* and *podestà*) found in travel books.

With the expansion of English to many parts of the world, concepts of what constitutes Standard English inevitably changed. The question of a standard language is indeed not single but tripartite since it concerns: (1) pronunciation or phonology; whether you say "glăss" or "glāss"; (2) vocabulary or lexis; whether you call a *brook* a "burn" or a "beck"; (3) idiom or syntax; whether you say "The sick he is" or "He isn't well." Clearly by the mid-20th century the time had come to recognize more standards than one in all these three spheres, but especially in the first. It is surely a point of major importance that in both lexis and syntax one worldwide standard for all-purpose expository prose was slowly emerging in the later 20th century; helped by the fact that the best modern critical journals share contributors from both sides of the Atlantic.

ENCYCLOPÆDIA BRITANNICA

Etymology

Etymology is that part of linguistics which is concerned with the origin or derivation of words (Gr. *etymos,* "true," and *logos,* "account"). Primitive peoples consider that the name of a person or of a thing is intimately connected, even if not actually identified, with that person or thing: *nomen est omen.* The tymologizing of proper names, which is so conspicuous in the Old Testament, to some degree reflects this primitive concern with names (*cf.* Gen. xvii, 5 and xvii, 15 for the changing of the name Abram to Abraham and that of Sarai to Sarah). Among the ancient Greeks, also, the earliest attempts at etymology assumed that the name by which a thing was called stood in some simple and explicable relationship to the thing itself. To etymologize a name was merely to give a "true account" of its meaning, not to provide a scientific explanation of it in the modern sense. Plato, in his *Cratylus* (with its significant subtitle, *On the Propriety of Names*), pokes fun at the fanciful etymologies of the day; at the claim of Socrates, for example, that *hero* (*hērōs*) is derived "with a slight change of form" from *erōs,* "love," because "the heroes owed their birth to love." But even Plato, like the Stoics, who paid great attention to etymology, had little sense of historical development and little acquaintance with other languages. The Romans, under Greek influence, continued to regard etymology as an arbitrary pastime. Marcus Terentius Varro knew that *meridiēs* ("noon") stood for a nonclassical *medi-diēs* (*i.e.,* "midday") and adduced older forms where he could; but his etymologies, if not self-evident, are largely wordplay.

Scientific etymology had to wait until the 19th century, when the groundwork of comparative linguistics was laid down. The founders of the science, from Franz Bopp to Karl Brugmann, emphasized the so-called "sound laws"; *i.e.,* regular patterns of phonetic correspondence detected over a given period between related languages or between successive historical phases of the same language. These laws, first used to reconstruct a hypothetical Indo-European parent language from which the historically attested Indo-European languages have been derived, were subsequently applied with signal success to the separate Indo-European languages and to other languages not related to Indo-European. To summarize the general principles involved:

1. The earliest form must be ascertained as well as all parallel and related forms.

2. Every sound of a given form must be compared with that of the form from which it is derived (often called its etymon).

3. Should there be a deviation in the previously established phonetic correspondences, a rational explanation must be provided; *e.g.,* Eng. *feeble* via O.F. *feble, foible* (now *faible*) comes from Lat. *flēbilis,* "lamentable," but with the first *l* lost through simple dissimilation.

4. Shift in meaning (semantic change) must also be explained; *e.g.,* Eng. *stink* from O.E. *stincan,* "have a smell" (whether good or bad), has acquired a pejorative sense.

5. Words which are isolated in the language ("boycott," "hooligan"), which present nonnative sounds or combinations of sounds ("loch," "axolotl"), or which, more commonly, show marked deviation from the usual phonetic correspondences (*e.g.,* "root," "nay," which betray Scandinavian origin as opposed to "wort," "no") are probably borrowed rather than inherited.

Subsequent investigators have greatly increased the exactitude of etymological methods. Thus, Rudolf Meringer stressed the connection between the history of a word and the history of the thing it represents: the etymology of fencing "foil" (from Fr. *feuille,* "sword blade"), for instance, presumes the special knowledge that this weapon was originally a rough sword blade used for hacking rather than for thrusting. Jules Gilliéron, whose magnificent *Atlas linguistique de la France* (with E. Edmont, 1902–10) founded the technique of linguistic geography, drew attention to the vast diversity of dialect and substandard forms upon which a standard language draws, as well as to the often complex factors which determine the choice of rival words. A complete etymology must take into account the full history of a word as well as its position with regard to other items of vocabulary; *e.g.,* "female" via O.F. *femelle* from Lat. *femella,* diminutive of *femina,* "woman," has been influenced by "male."

The term popular etymology or folk etymology is sometimes used for the alteration of a word through a mistaken idea of its true etymology; *e.g.,* O.E. *brýd-guma,* literally "bride man" (*guma* is cognate with Lat. *homo,* "man") yielded Eng. *bridegroom* under the influence of "groom."

ENCYCLOPÆDIA BRITANNICA

The History of the Dictionary

The history of dictionaries is part of the history of culture and of ideas, for dictionaries reflect not only the evolution and growth of the languages they record but the development of the linguistic communities they serve. Dictionaries of English thus have their roots in medieval European culture and its international language, Latin. The very term *dictionary,* in its Latin form *dictionarius,* "collection of words," was used about 1225 by the Englishman John Garland as a title for a list of Latin words to be learned by students. The words in Garland's manuscript were arranged not alphabetically but by topic; only a few English glosses occur between the Latin items. The earliest wordbooks of Anglo-Saxon times are similar lists of relatively hard Latin words, often biblical in reference, glossed in easier Latin or in Old English (Anglo-Saxon); examples are the *Erfurt Glossary* (*Glossae Amplonianae*) and the *Corpus Glossary,* found in an 8th-century manuscript. Of the *Corpus Glossary,* its editor says that it is "England's oldest dictionary." More precisely, it is England's oldest-known bilingual dictionary.

Isolated glosses were gathered into a *glossarium,* or glossary. From the 8th century to the 16th such bilingual glosses and collections of glosses continued to be made. One of these glossaries, the *Promptorium Parvulorum sive clericorum* (1499), is among the earliest printed books in English; in it the English words are placed before their Latin equivalents. The first two words of its title, meaning "storehouse for little ones," were borrowed from the title of a preceding Latin wordbook of about 1440, compiled by a Dominican friar named Galfridus Grammaticus (Geoffrey the Grammarian). Wynkyn de Worde, an assistant to the first English printer, William Caxton, published the *Promptorium* and also published in 1500 a "garden of words," *Ortus* [*i.e., Hortus*] *Vocabulorum,* in which Latin terms are translated by English ones. Alongside such alphabetized compilations there were published collections of words arranged logically in categories by subject, often beginning with parts of the human body; these were produced from the

Anglo-Saxon period to the 19th century. They include a 10th-century Latin–Old English vocabulary attributed to Aelfric, abbott of Eynsham, an illustrated 15th-century vocabulary, and other interesting examples. All these works were intended to help learners of other languages, chiefly Latin. Similar works were being published on the Continent, together with bilingual and polyglot manuals that had some influence on the English lexicographical tradition; a typical example is *Janua Linguarum* (1611)—"gates of languages"—a Latin–Spanish manual prepared by the rector of the Jesuit Irish college at Salamanca. This work appeared in England a few years later with the Spanish translated into English, and was published in London in 1617, revised and augmented as a four-language manual under the title *Janua Linguarum Quadrilinguis, or a Messe of Tongues: Latine, English, French, and Spanish Neatly Served up together, for a wholesome repast, to the worthy curiositie of the studious.* The *Janua* comprised about 5,000 words, classified into 12 centuries, with the words exemplified in 1,200 sentences. Each such set of sentences is concerned with some generally defined subject, such as temperance, justice, fortitude, and other virtues, various human activities, things with and without life, and the arts and crafts. This combination of moral uplift with linguistic edification was to distinguish English lexcography for a long time. A further influential combination of elements was provided in the quasi-encyclopaedic works of the Moravian educational reformer Comenius, *Janua linguarum reserata* (1631) and *Orbis sensualium pictus* (1658); the latter work is notable for its association of word, what the word refers to, and illustration, a typical feature of the American encyclopaedic dictionary of the 19th century.

The popularity of these bilingual and polyglot manuals in Renaissance England was matched by that of bilingual dictionaries. In the 16th century French–English, Welsh–English, English–Spanish, and Italian–English lexicons were published, along with the first great classical dictionary, Thomas Cooper's *Thesaurus* (1565). These works clearly reflect the growing interest in and traffic with continental cultures and the Renaissance zeal for classical literature, which led to the influx into English of large numbers of Greek- and Latin-derived terms, including the polysyllabic "ink-horn" words that gave rise to the "hard-word" dictionary characteristic of the 17th century.

The distinction of being the first dictionary of English proper has been claimed for two works: Richard Huloet's *Abcedarium Anglico-Latinum pro Tyrunculis* (1552) and Robert Cawdrey's *Table Alphabeticall* (1604). Huloet's book, "for young beginners," offers first English translations, then Latin, of the terms it comprises—*e.g.*, "Bachiler, or one unmarried, or havyng no wife, *Agamus, mi.*" The gloss for *wench,* which in Huloet's time meant simply "girl, young woman," is "Trymme wench gorgiously decked, *Phalerata foemina.*" The *Abcedarium* contained 26,000 words.

Cawdrey's book, comprising some 2,500 hard English words with very short English definitions, often scarcely more than synonyms, is clearly the work of a schoolmaster and is distinguished by the alphabetic ordering of its entries. The title page describes it as "conteyning and teaching the true writing, and understanding of hard usuall English wordes, borrowed from the Hebrew, Greeke, Latine, or French etc./ With the interpretation thereof by plaine English words, gathered for the benefit and helpe of Ladies, Gentlewomen, or any other unskilfull persons./ Whereby they may the more easilie and better understand many hard English wordes, which they shall heare or read in Scriptures, Sermons, or elsewhere, and also be made able to use the same aptly themselves."

The dictionary in the 17th and 18th centuries

Cawdrey's was only the first of a series of 17th- and 18th-century English dictionaries. It was soon followed by John Bullokar's *English Expositor* (1616) and Henry Cockeram's *English Dictionarie* (1623), the latter notable as the first English wordbook having in its title the word *dictionary*. Between these three small pioneering works and the publication in 1721 of Nathan Bailey's important *Universal Etymological English Dictionary* there appeared no fewer than nine more English lexicons; before the publication in London in 1755 of the famous Scott-Bailey and Johnson dictionaries, there were still more.

The history of the English dictionary in the 17th and 18th centuries is a record of gradual accretion, ramification, experiment, change, and development; it is characterized by constant borrowing and adaptation, occasional brilliant invention. The cross influences are sometimes complex. But the sources and main lines of development have been traced; the most significant contributions have been identified. We can accredit every innovation and advance; the introduction of legal and medical terms (Bullokar, 1616, and Cockeram, 1623); that of cant and dialect terms (Coles, 1676); the first stressing of etymology (Blount, 1656); the first inclusion of a history of the language (Phillips, 1658); the first balanced gathering of "hard" and common locutions and up-to-date scientific expressions in one word list (Kersey-Phillips, 1706); the first abridged English dictionary (Kersey's *Dictionarium Anglo-Britannicum,* 1708); the first carefully planned arrangement of logically divided and classified definitions (Martin, 1749). By the time Samuel Johnson began his work, many features of the English dictionary had become established. Four lexicographical traditions mingled in the 17th century: the pedagogical, the "hard"-word, the general reference book, and the etymological.

The popular Scott-Bailey of 1755, *A New Universal Etymological English Dictionary*, was based on Johnson's work and on the most popular English dictionary of the early 18th century, Bailey's, first published in 1721 and often reprinted. Published in 1731 with some illustrations, Bailey's work appealed because it gave attention to current usage, provided some etymologies, and indicated primary stress in pronunciation; moreover, its price was relatively low. But Johnson's famous book was more powerful, more distinguished, and far more influential. Just as Bailey's preceding dictionary had been the working foundation for Johnson (who used an interleaved copy of the second edition of the 1731 work [1736]), so Johnson's became the basis for later English lexicography.

The strength of Johnson's *Dictionary* lay in two features: original, carefully divided and ordered, elegantly formulated definitions of the main word-stock of the language; and the citation of copious (if occasionally erring) quotations from literature in support and illustration of these. The arrangement of definitions was not an innovation. Benjamin Martin in his remarkable *Lingua Britannica Reformata* (1749) had in this respect anticipated Johnson and begun a new era in English lexicography by outlining and sedulously following an intelligent plan for divided, classified definitions, such as the bilingual and European dictionaries had made use of for years, notably Robert Ainsworth's *Thesaurus linguae Latinae compendiarius* (1736) and Abel Boyer's *Dictionaire [sic] Royal, François-Anglois et Anglois-François* (1699). As for Johnson's use of illustrative quotations, it had been anticipated in previous lexicons of Greek, Latin, Italian, French, and Portuguese. So too the attempt to "fix" the language in its presumed pristine purity and thus save it from "corruption"—*i.e.*, inevitable change—had been anticipated in the lexicographical labours of the European academies, notably the French and the Italian. Johnson himself at last saw the futility of this seductive notion. His accomplishment was to provide for English a dictionary that incorporated with skill and intellectual power the prevailing ideals, the resources, and the best available techniques of European lexicography. His book was intended to be for its time a standard and standardizing work. It included a history of the language, a grammar, and an extensive list of words representing the basic general vocabulary, explained by divided and classified definitions and illustrated with quotations. Johnson gave no pronunciations though he did show primary stress; his etymologies, taken from such then-standard sources as Franciscus Junius and Stephen Skinner, were no better than they could be before the advent of Indo-European studies; his definitions, like Noah Webster's, were sometimes marred by personal animus or eccentricity. But in two of the fundamentals of lexicography he provided for all his successors a large part of the capital that made possible the success of their enterprise.

The dictionary in modern times

Between Johnson's *Dictionary* and Webster's magnum opus in two quarto volumes, *An American Dictionary of the English Language* (1828), which had been preceded by his small *Compendious Dictionary* of 1806 and a few other, largely imitative, American dictionaries, a number of further advances were made. Synonymy had only been begun, introduced by James Barclay in 1774, and the phonetic treatment of pronunciation had not even appeared by 1755. Etymology sorely needed revision, definitions were not always satisfactory, and grammatical notations were needed for irregular verb forms, plurals, and comparisons. All these improvements were introduced in some form by the beginning of the 19th century. Contributions were made by glossarists of obsolete locutions, cant terms, and the like, by dialectologists, grammarians, synonymists, and orthoepists. Much of this work needed further refinement. The establishment of synonymy as a regular part of the English dictionary did not occur until the middle of the 19th century, when Webster's successors and his rival, Joseph Worcester, gradually worked it out.

In the department of orthoepy more immediate success was attained, chiefly by Thomas Sheridan and John Walker, who used Johnson's *Dictionary* as a working base for their influential English pronouncing dictionaries, published in 1780 and 1791, respectively. But the prevailing attitude toward pronunciation was normative, prescriptive, and reformist; formal platform speech was preferred to colloquial by Walker, the most influential of the orthoepists, himself both elocutionist and actor. And the phonetic symbology left much to be desired. The recording of colloquial pronunciation in an accurate, economical set of symbols is not a characteristic of English dictionaries until well into the 20th century. It had to be preceded by the work of phoneticians such as Henry Sweet, Daniel Jones, and Henry C. Wyld in England, John Kenyon, Thomas A. Knott, Charles K. Thomas, and Hans Kurath in the United States. American commercial lexicography remained conservative in this department for a long time, as a comparison of Webster's *Second New International* (1934) with the *Third* (1961) shows. The first commer-

cial dictionaries to show signs of catching up with contemporary phonetics were the American desk dictionaries of the 1940s and 1950s—
Thorndike-Barnhart's *Comprehensive Desk Dictionary,* the *American
College Dictionary,* and the *New World.* The Merriam firm, which had
published Kenyon and Knott's pioneering *Pronouncing Dictionary of
American English* in 1944, finally introduced a new phonetic notation
in 1961 in the *Third;* the preference of the *Second* for eastern platform-
speech pronunciation was abandoned.

George Philip Krapp in 1925 found that Webster's 1828 dictionary
was "the most significant contribution to the growth of English lexicography between Dr. Johnson and the appearance of the first volume of the
New English Dictionary." This remains the accepted view. Webster's
work has serious flaws—fantastic etymologies, a clumsy method of
showing pronunciation, some eccentric spellings, provincialism, prudish-
ness, didacticism, and occasional bias. But Webster was right in claiming
that his chief strength lay in the copiousness of his vocabulary and the
accuracy and comprehensiveness of his definitions. He leaned heavily
on Johnson for basic definitions, but he departed from Johnson in gloss-
ing many scientific and technical terms and in giving much additional
information taken from various reference books and textbooks. By insisting on the inclusion of a number of Americanisms—words either
originated in this country or used in senses peculiar to it—he gave
impetus to an important trend in lexicography, and he influenced American spelling by preferring *honor, labor* to *honour, labour, center* to
centre, and the like. The scope and precision of many of his definitions
were unexcelled before the publication of *A New English Dictionary on
Historical Principles* (NED) in ten volumes (1884–1928), later revised,
updated, and reprinted as *The Oxford English Dictionary.* Together with
Worcester, who contributed much to the tradition by his work between
1830 (*A Comprehensive Pronouncing and Explanatory Dictionary of
the English Language*) and 1860 (*A Quarto Dictionary of the English
Language*), Webster gave to the American commercial dictionary its
characteristic shape and tone. The fine Webster-Mahn dictionary published by the Merriams in 1864, with which they won the commercial
battle with Worcester's publishers, shows how skilfully the Webster
editors gradually overcame Webster's faults by applying the ever increasing linguistic knowledge of the time, and by adapting Worcester's
virtues—the neatness, precision, caution, moderation, and elegance of
his definitions, his able treatment of discriminative synonymy, of divided usage, and of idiomatic phrases. Later Merriam-Websters in the
19th and early 20th centuries, including Webster's *First New International* (1909), the predecessor of *W-2,* show a continuation of this intelligent eclecticism while maintaining their characteristic features: a

greatly expanded vocabulary list containing obsolete, technical, and scientific words; encyclopædically full definitions, often technically phrased and arranged in historical order; adequate scholarly etymologies; notation of irregularities of word form; synonymy; use of labels and abbreviations to indicate technical senses and usage levels; generally conservative treatment of pronunciation, slang, taboo locutions, divided usage, controversial terms, and so on; treatment in appendices of biographical and geographical names, abbreviations, and some other reference materials.

The undertaking of the great *NED* and the publication of *The Century Dictionary* (1889–91), a six-volume work edited by William Dwight Whitney that has been hailed as one of the best English dictionaries ever compiled, are the chief features of English lexicography between 1864 and the end of the century. The latter half of the 19th century also saw the beginnings of large-scale lexicographical projects in French, German, and some other languages. As linguistic knowledge, particularly of the Indo-European languages, grew in consequence of the work of scholars such as Franz Bopp, Rasmus Christian Rask, the brothers Grimm, Henry Sweet, and many others, new insights and methods became available to dictionary-makers. The growth of industrial-technological culture, the ever widening spread of public education in many Western countries, and the increasing demand for reference wordbooks by the general public were other significant factors contributing to the proliferation of dictionaries. Commercial publishers as well as scholars were naturally influenced by these circumstances. In the United States especially, where the dictionary came to occupy a place beside the family Bible because of the importance of "correct English" in an open, status-seeking society, competition for the growing market became sometimes unscrupulous, as the "dictionary wars" between commercial publishers testify. Publishers' claims were often extravagant; advertising campaigns to establish the "supreme" authoritativeness of one or another wordbook were the order of the day.

Twentieth-century lexicography has seen a continuation of some of these trends. Great scholarly works have been published, undertaken, or projected, among them, *The Oxford English Dictionary* in 12 volumes (1928) and Supplement (1933); *A Dictionary of American English on Historical Principles* in four volumes (1938–44); *A Dictionary of Americanisms on Historical Principles* (1951); and the *Middle English Dictionary* (1956–   ). Commercial general-purpose dictionaries, particularly American desk-size and "college editions," have become more numerous and improved in comprehensiveness and reliability. Lexicography is no longer a one-man enterprise as in preceding centuries; reputable dictionaries today are produced by large staffs of trained, specialized editors, linguists, researchers, and other skilled workers, increasingly with the aid of extensive files of citations, electronic computers, and other available devices.

But in essence the making of dictionaries remains what it has been, a human activity involving knowledge, training, judgment, skill, and intuition. The ideal lexicographer, far from being the "harmless drudge" of Johnson's bitter ironic joke, combines attributes of scientist and artist. He must know well the language(s) with which he deals, in both speech and writing, and in historical, regional, social, and stylistic varieties. He must know and effectively put to use the principles and techniques of linguistics. He must be skilled at inferring the precise meanings of locutions in context, at distinguishing nuances of usage and grammar that are often subtle, at judging the relative probability of disputed derivations, at organizing the many-faceted materials with which he deals, and at writing definitions that are accurate, comprehensive, clear, and economical. No machine can do these things.

The OED and other scholarly dictionaries

Of the historical-scholarly dictionaries of English, the most famous is the great *Oxford English Dictionary* (the *OED*). This work, three-quarters of a century in the making, was published in England (Oxford, 1933); it consists of 12 volumes and Supplement. The *OED* is a corrected, updated revision of the *NED,* ten volumes (Oxford, 1884–1928). Edited by James A. H. Murray, Henry Bradley, William A. Craigie, and C. T. Onions, with the assistance of hundreds of readers and contributors over several decades, this huge dictionary (some 15,000 quarto pages, almost 500,000 entries, over 1,500,000 illustrative quotations) was intended to provide an inventory of words alive in English from the middle of the 12th century, in some instances even earlier. The definitions are arranged in historical order and illustrated with dated quotations from English literature and records. Although in the light of later findings it inevitably contains some errors and omissions, although neither the entire scientific-technical vocabulary nor words of recent origin nor many Americanisms are included, and although the pronunciations recorded—with a somewhat cumbersome and old-fashioned apparatus—are exclusively British, the *OED* is an invaluable monument of English linguistic scholarship. Comparable to the *OED* in scope and intention are the *Deutsches Wörterbuch,* begun in 1852 by Jacob and Wilhelm Grimm and completed decades later by others, and Littré's *Dictionnaire de la langue française* (1863–72; new edition, 1956–58). A few similar lexicons exist in some other languages.

Two scholarly dictionaries of American English somewhat resemble the *OED* though on a smaller scale. The earlier, *A Dictionary of American English on Historical Principles* (the *DAE*), edited by Sir William A. Craigie, one of the *OED* editors, and by James Hulbert, was published by the University of Chicago Press in 1938–44 (2nd edition, 1960). Its four large volumes contain approximately 26,000 terms, including not only some of American origin but many which, though previously attested in English, either have taken on new meanings in the United States, have come into wider use in the United States than in England, or have survived in the United States though obsolete in England. The *DAE* provides dated illustrative quotations for most entries. But it omits some interesting and pertinent matter; like the *OED*, it avoids locutions regarded as too vulgar to record, and it leaves out most American slang after 1875 and Americanisms in general after 1900, along with most etymologies and usage labels. To remedy these deficiencies, Mitford M. Mathews edited *A Dictionary of Americanisms on Historical Principles* (the *DA*), published by the University of Chicago Press in 1951 (2nd edition, 1956). These two works provide a valuable lexical record of American English to the middle of the 20th century, a record supplemented by the ambitious but unfinished dialect study known as the Linguistic Atlas of the United States and Canada, begun in 1931 under the editorship of Hans Kurath, and by several other dictionaries both general and specialized.

Of scholarly period dictionaries of English the great example is the *Middle English Dictionary* (the *MED*), an American work edited by Kurath and Sherman M. Kuhn. This work, only part of which has been published (University of Michigan Press, Ann Arbor, 1956–   ), provides an exhaustive lexicon of Middle English from surviving literature and other records, more complete than that of the *OED*. Other scholarly period dictionaries of English have been proposed, notably one of Early Modern English, but none had appeared by the late 1960s. The same is true of a projected *Dictionary of Canadian English on Historical Principles* sponsored by the Canadian Linguistic Association and a comprehensive *Dictionary of American Regional English* envisaged by the American Dialect Society. Of the latter, Harold Wentworth's *American Dialect Dictionary* (1944) is a useful if not comprehensive harbinger, not comparable in scope to the proposed large work or to Joseph Wright's *English Dialect Dictionary*, six volumes (Oxford, 1898–1905). Other notable dialect dictionaries are *A Dictionary of the Older Scottish Tongue,* left unfinished by Sir William A. Craigie at his death in 1957, and Frederic G. Cassidy and R. B. Le Page's historical *Dictionary of*

Jamaican English (1967), covering the period 1655–1962. There are also dialect dictionaries of German, French, and some other tongues.

Specialized dictionaries

Specialized dictionaries are overwhelming in their variety and their diversity. Each area of lexical study, such as etymology, pronunciation, and usage, can have a dictionary of its own. The earliest important dictionary of etymology for English was Stephen Skinner's *Etymologicon Linguae Anglicanae* of 1671, in Latin, with a strong bias for finding a classical origin for every English word. In the 18th century, a number of dictionaries were published that traced most English words to Celtic sources, because the authors did not realize that the words had been borrowed into Celtic rather than the other way around. With the rise of a soundly based philology by the middle of the 19th century, a scientific etymological dictionary could be compiled, and this was provided in 1879 by Walter William Skeat. It has been kept in print in re-editions ever since but was superseded in 1966 by *The Oxford Dictionary of English Etymology,* by Charles Talbut Onions, who had worked many decades on it until his death. Valuable in its particular restricted area is J. F. Bense's *Dictionary of the Low-Dutch Element in the English Vocabulary* (1926–39).

Two works are especially useful in showing the relation between languages descended from the ancestral Indo-European language—Carl Darling Buck's *Dictionary of Selected Synonyms in the Principal Indo-European Languages* (1949) and Julius Pokorny's *Indogermanisches etymologisches Wörterbuch* (1959). The Indo-European roots are well displayed in the summary by Calvert Watkins, published as an appendix to *The American Heritage Dictionary* mentioned earlier. Interrelations are also dealt with by Eric Partridge in his *Origins* (1958).

The pronouncing dictionary, a type handed down from the 18th century, is best known in the present day by two examples, one in England and one in America. That of Daniel Jones, *An English Pronouncing Dictionary,* represents what is "most usually heard in everyday speech in the families of Southern English persons whose men-folk have been educated at the great public boarding-schools." Although he called this the Received Pronunciation (RP), he had no intention of imposing it on the English-speaking world. It originally appeared in 1917 and was repeatedly revised during the author's long life. Also strictly descriptive was a similar U.S. work by John S. Kenyon and Thomas A. Knott, *A Pronouncing Dictionary of American English,* published in 1944 and never revised but still valuable for its record of the practices of its time.

The "conceptual dictionary," in which words are arranged in groups by their meaning, had its first important exponent in Bishop John Wilkins, whose *Essay towards a Real Character and a Philosophical Language* was published in 1668. A plan of this sort was carried out by Peter Marc Roget with his *Thesaurus,* published in 1852 and many times reprinted and re-edited. Although philosophically oriented, Roget's work has served the practical purpose of another genre, the dictionary of synonyms.

The dictionaries of usage record information about the choices that a speaker must make among rival forms. In origin, they developed from the lists of errors that were popular in the 18th century. Many of them are still strongly puristic in tendency, supporting the urge for "standardizing" the language. The work with the most loyal following is Henry Watson Fowler's *Dictionary of Modern English Usage* (1926), ably re-edited in 1965 by Sir Ernest Gowers. It represents the good taste of a sensitive, urbane litterateur. It has many devotees in the U.S. and also a number of competitors. Among the latter, the most competently done is *A Dictionary of Contemporary American Usage* (1957), by Bergen Evans and Cornelia Evans. Usually the dictionaries of usage have reflected the idiosyncrasies of the compilers; but, from the 1920s to the 1960s, a body of studies by scholars emphasized an objective survey of what is in actual use, and these were drawn upon by Margaret M. Bryant for her book *Current American Usage* (1962). A small corner of the field of usage is dealt with by Eric Partridge in *A Dictionary of Clichés* (1940).

The regional variation of language has yielded dialect dictionaries in all the major languages of the world. In England, after John Ray's issuance of his first glossary of dialect words in 1674, much collecting was done, especially in the 19th century under the auspices of the English Dialect Society. This collecting culminated in the splendid *English Dialect Dictionary* of Joseph Wright in six volumes (1898–1905). American regional speech was collected from 1774 onward; John Pickering first put a glossary of Americanisms into a separate book in 1816. The American Dialect Society, founded in 1889, made extensive collections, with plans for a dictionary, but this came to fruition only in 1965, when Frederic G. Cassidy embarked on *A Dictionary of American Regional English* (known as *DARE*).

The many "functional varieties" of English also have their dictionaries. Slang and cant in particular have been collected in England since 1565, but the first important work was published in 1785, by Capt. Francis Grose, *A Classical Dictionary of the Vulgar Tongue,* reflecting well the low life of the 18th century. In 1859 John Camden Hotten published the 19th-century material, but a full historical, scholarly survey was presented by John Stephen Farmer and W.E. Henley in their *Slang and Its Analogues,* in seven volumes, 1890–1904, with a revised first volume in 1909 (all reprinted in 1971). For the present century, the dictionaries of Eric Partridge are valuable. Slang in the United States is so rich and varied that collectors have as yet only scratched the surface, but the work by Harold Wentworth and Stuart B. Flexner, *Dictionary of American Slang* (1960), can be consulted. The argot of the underworld has been treated in many studies by David W. Maurer.

Of all specialized dictionaries, the bilingual group are the most serviceable and frequently used. With the rise of the vernacular languages during the Renaissance, translating to and from Latin had great importance. The Welshman in England was provided with a bilingual dictionary as early as 1547, by William Salesbury. Scholars in their analyses of language, as well as practical people for everyday needs, are anxious to have bilingual dictionaries. Even the most exotic and remote languages have been tackled, often by religious missionaries with the motive of translating the Bible. The finding of exact equivalents is more difficult than is commonly realized, because every language slices up the world in its own particular way.

Dictionaries dealing with special areas of vocabulary are so overwhelming in number that they can merely be alluded to here. In English, the earliest was a glossary of law terms published in 1527 by John Rastell. His purpose, he said, was "to expown certeyn obscure & derke termys concernynge the lawes of thys realme." The dictionaries of technical terms in many fields often have the purpose of standardizing the terminology; this normative aim is especially important in newly developing countries where the language has not yet become accommodated to modern technological needs. In some fields, such as philosophy, religion, or linguistics, the terminology is closely tied to a particular school of thought or the individual system of one writer, and, consequently, a lexicographer is obliged to say, "according to Kant," "in the usage of Christian Science," "as used by Bloomfield," and so on.

ENCYCLOPÆDIA BRITANNICA

Spelling and the English Language

The Latin alphabet originally had 20 letters, the present English alphabet minus *J, K, V, W, Y,* and *Z.* The Romans themselves added *K* for use in abbreviations and *Y* and *Z* in words transcribed from Greek. After its adoption by the English, this 23-letter alphabet developed *W* as a ligatured doubling of *U* and later *J* and *V* as consonantal variants of *I* and *U.* The resultant alphabet of 26 letters has both uppercase, or capital, and lowercase, or small, letters.

English spelling is based for the most part on that of the 15th century, but pronunciation has changed considerably since then, especially that of long vowels and dipththongs. The extensive change in the pronunciation of vowels, known as the Great Vowel Shift, affected all of Geoffrey Chaucer's seven long vowels, and for centuries spelling remained untidy. If the meaning of the message was clear, the spelling of individual words seemed unimportant. In the 17th century during the English Civil War, compositors adopted fixed spellings for practical reasons, and in the order-loving 18th century uniformity became more and more fashionable. Since Samuel Johnson's *Dictionary of the English Language* (1755), orthography has remained fairly stable. Numerous tacit changes, such as "music" for "musick" (*c.* 1880) and "fantasy" for "phantasy" (*c.* 1920), have been accepted, but spelling has nevertheless continued to be in part unphonetic. Attempts have been made at reform. Indeed, every century has had its reformers since the 13th, when an Augustinian canon named Orm devised his own method of differentiating short vowels from long by doubling the succeeding consonants or, when this was not feasible, by marking short vowels with a superimposed breve mark (˘). William Caxton, who set up his wooden printing press at Westminster in 1476, was much concerned with spelling problems throughout his working life. Noah Webster produced his *Spelling Book,* in 1783, as a precursor to the first edition (1828) of his *American Dictionary of the English Language.* The 20th century has produced many zealous reformers. Three systems, supplementary to

136

traditional spelling, are actually in use for different purposes: (1) the Initial Teaching (Augmented Roman) Alphabet (ITA) of 44 letters used by educationists in the teaching of children under seven; (2) the Shaw alphabet of 48 letters, designed in implementation of the will of George Bernard Shaw; and (3) the International Phonetic Alphabet (IPA), constructed on the basis of one symbol for one individual sound and used by many trained linguists. Countless other systems have been worked out from time to time, of which R.E. Zachrisson's "Anglic" (1930) and Axel Wijk's *Regularized English* (1959) may be the best.

Meanwhile, the great publishing houses continue unperturbed because drastic reform remains impracticable, undesirable, and unlikely. This is because there is no longer one criterion of correct pronunciation but several standards throughout the world; regional standards are themselves not static, but changing with each new generation; and, if spelling were changed drastically, all the books in English in the world's public and private libraries would become inaccessible to readers without special study.

ENCYCLOPÆDIA BRITANNICA

PART TWO

THE BASIC TOOLS

ALL YOU NEED TO KNOW ABOUT GRAMMAR

Introduction

A language is not static. It is a human enterprise, created by a community of people to provide access to their thoughts and the thoughts of others. Because language is a medium of communication, it will develop and change, adapting to the evolving needs of its users and their unfolding perceptions of the world. Expressions once fashionable become obsolete; words once limited in meaning expand to encompass a greater range of meaning; words that earlier performed several functions become specialized; and new words come into existence. In such ways a language changes.

Our evolving language is an extremely complex and sophisticated one, capable of subtle nuance if used precisely and of mind-boggling ambiguity if not. For most people reared in an English-speaking community, a knowledge of the language is inbred and generally suffices for speaking. As pointed out in Some Hints About Writing later in this volume, speakers of the language have at their disposal a wide range of resources for oral communication, among them facial expression, tone of voice, pauses, and gestures. These additional resources often allow a speaker to clarify and emphasize his ideas. A writer, however, must rely on the language alone to articulate his thoughts unambiguously. And, unlike the speaker who can rephrase what may be misunderstood, the writer must make his thoughts clear before presenting them to an audience. For the writer, the first and most important step in gaining control over the language is gaining control over its grammar. It is a knowledge of grammar that yields access to the rich possibilities of the language and the means to use them.

In this three-part chapter we describe both the constant and the changing features of our language. We have not been reluctant to point out, where appropriate, those usages that are more acceptable than others and to prescribe which should be adopted. Nor have we failed to note where usage is an arbitrary matter, governed in the end by personal choice. Since a real understanding of the language provides

143

the appropriate context for that choice, the reader is encouraged not only to consult this chapter for answers to specific questions about grammar but also to read through it for clearer sense of the language's structure.

A Review of English Grammar is divided into five sections. The first two companion sections—The Sentence and Its Elements, and Parts of Speech—work together to describe the grammatical resources of our language and are constructed to be read consecutively. The remaining three sections explain how the language is conventionally used. Section III, Usage, presents the accepted principles for clear expression, including basic guidelines for sentence construction. Sections IV and V, Punctuation and Sundry Conventions, treat the established practices governing punctuation and other conventions such as capitalization and abbreviation. Together these five sections cover the basic principles of English grammar.

A Glossary of Grammatical Terms, which defines the terms central to the study of grammar, serves as reference both for A Review of English Grammar and for Verbal Quandaries from A to Z. When the definitions in the glossary can be supplemented by material in the preceding or following section, appropriate cross-references are provided.*

Verbal Quandaries from A to Z addresses specific problems that writers often confront. These quandaries include words whose meanings are frequently misunderstood as well as some important problems of usage. Some of the entries in this section treat a particular problem in detail and, where appropriate, cross-refer to the grammar review for discussion of the general principle governing the issue. The rest of the entries provide direct access to the grammar review through convenient cross-references.

All You Need to Know About Grammar answers most of the problems and queries that writers encounter. When the question is no longer one of grammar but rather one of style, the writer should consult Some Hints About Writing in Part III or any of the books listed in the Bibliography (Section II, Aids to Writing).

---

*Within each of the last two sections of this chapter, A Glossary of Grammatical Terms and Verbal Quandaries from A to Z, internal cross-references are set in **boldface** type. Cross-references from one section to another in this chapter—or to another chapter in the book—are set in lightface type like this, as are all the remaining cross-references in this book.

Outline

A REVIEW OF ENGLISH GRAMMAR

   I. The Sentence and Its Elements
      A. Subject
      B. Verb
      C. Object and object complement
      D. Subject complement
      E. Modifier
      F. Appositive
      G. Connective
      H. Absolute
  II. Parts of Speech
      A. Noun
      B. Pronoun
      C. Verb
      D. Adjective
      E. Adverb
      F. Preposition
      G. Conjunction
      H. Interjection
      I. Verbal
      J. Phrase
      K. Clause
 III. Usage
      A. Writing complete sentences
      B. Using subjects and verbs
      C. Using pronouns
      D. Using modifiers
      E. Balancing sentences
  IV. Punctuation
      A. Period

A GLOSSARY OF GRAMMATICAL TERMS

VERBAL QUANDARIES FROM A TO Z

ABBREVIATIONS USED IN ALL YOU NEED TO KNOW ABOUT GRAMMAR

abs.	absolute	m.	modifier
adj.	adjective	obj.	object
adv.	adverb	o.c.	object complement
ant.	antecedent	p.a.	predicate adjective
app.	appositive	part.	participle
art.	article	phr.	phrase
cl.	clause	p.n.	predicate noun
comp.	complement	poss.	possessive
conj.	conjunction	prep.	preposition(al)
d.; dem.	demonstrative	pres.	present
dep. cl.	dependent clause	pron.	pronoun
d.o.	direct object	r.o.	retained object
ger.	gerund	r. pron.	relative pronoun
ind. cl.	independent clause	s.	subject
infin.	infinitive	sub.	subordinating conjunction
i.o.	indirect object	t.v.	transitive verb
i.v.	intransitive verb	v.	verb
l.v.	linking verb		

A Review of English Grammar

I. The Sentence and Its Elements

Like any other language English is composed of individual words—for example, *faded, that, is,* and *shirt*—that writers and speakers put together into groups that have meaning: *That shirt is faded.* The SENTENCE* is the most important of these meaningful groups because it is more than just a few words that make sense together like *that I forgot* or *this overdue bill.* A sentence is a combination of words that can stand alone and communicate a complete thought: *I found this overdue bill that I forgot to pay.*

Sentences communicate these complete thoughts in four ways. DECLARATIVE SENTENCES make statements: *Wood burns.* INTERROGATIVE SENTENCES ask questions: *Where did you go?* IMPERATIVE SENTENCES make commands or request actions: *Look at this.* And EXCLAMATORY SENTENCES simply express emotions: *What a day we had!*

A grammatically complete thought may be communicated in as little as one word (*No.*) or in a group of words lacking the traditional elements that characterize a complete sentence (*And now for dessert!*). However, such constructions, called INDEPENDENT SENTENCE FRAGMENTS, usually occur in the context of another sentence (*Dinner was wonderful. And now for dessert!*) and in that context are easily understood. To express a complete thought by itself, a sentence normally needs at least one INDEPENDENT CLAUSE. An independent clause is a group of words that contains at least a subject and a verb and can stand alone, requiring no external information to make sense:

s.   v.   s.   v.   s.   v.

we remarked; John returned; sheep are herded.

---

*Throughout A Review of English Grammar grammatical terms important to the discussion are set off in SMALL CAPITAL LETTERS. These terms are defined either at that point or later in text as well as in A Glossary of Grammatical Terms that follows A Review of English Grammar.

148

In addition to the SUBJECT and VERB, however, most sentences contain other elements, including some or all of the following: OBJECTS, SUBJECT COMPLEMENTS, MODIFIERS, APPOSITIVES, CONNECTIVES, or ABSOLUTES. Each of the words in a sentence functions as one of these elements or as part of an element. Often a single word functions alone as a sentence element. For example, in *Mangoes are exotic,* the single word *mangoes* is the subject of the sentence. But sentence elements are not necessarily composed of single words. Sometimes words combine into groups—either as dependent clauses or as phrases—to function together as a single sentence element.

In contrast to an independent clause, a DEPENDENT CLAUSE (often called a SUBORDINATE CLAUSE) is a group of words that contains a subject and a verb but cannot stand alone and express a complete thought: *when I call; what you see.* Within the dependent clause, individual words have specific functions—they can be subjects, verbs, modifiers, etc.—but, within the sentence, the entire dependent clause is a unit, working as a single sentence element. For example, in *What you see is not for sale,* the dependent clause *what you see* is the sentence's subject.

A PHRASE may be any group of related words that does not contain a subject-verb combination. However, the term is generally used to refer to a group of words not containing a subject-verb combination and functioning as a single sentence element. For example, in *Studying ancient history is my favorite pastime, studying ancient history* is a phrase (a group of words without a subject and verb) that functions as the subject of the entire sentence.

Section I of this grammar reviews all of the basic elements of a sentence. Section II takes up the units that function as these sentence elements—that is, words, phrases, and dependent clauses. These two sections together provide a description of the grammatical resources of the language.

A. Subject

The subject of a sentence is what the sentence is about. The sentence *The cow jumped over the moon* says something about the cow; hence the word *cow* is its subject. Except for simple exclamations like *Oh boy!* or *Never again!,* every sentence has a subject. Even sentences like *Look out!* or *Forgive me* that do not appear to have a subject do in fact have a subject (*you*), which is implied rather than explicitly stated. In sentences with explicit subjects, the majority of sentences, NOUNS or other

NOMINALS (that is, words or groups of words that act like nouns) can fill this function.

> s.
> Cows *chew their cud.*   (noun)
>
> s.
> He *peeled some potatoes.*   (pronoun)
>
> s.
> Living a good life *is the American dream.*   (gerund phrase)
>
> s.
> To be honest *is a virtue.*   (infinitive phrase)
>
> s.
> What I want *is peace and quiet.*   (noun clause)

The noun or nominal alone is called the SIMPLE SUBJECT of the sentence. The noun with its modifiers is called the COMPLETE SUBJECT. In *The first page of this book is torn, page* is the simple subject, and *the first page of this book* is the complete subject.

B. Verb

The remainder of a sentence is the PREDICATE—that is, the part that says something about the subject. In *The cow jumped over the moon,* the predicate *jumped over the moon* says something about the subject *cow.* A predicate in itself is not a sentence element; rather it is made up of one or more sentence elements. At the least, a predicate consists of a verb. Hence the essential elements of every sentence are a subject

s.   v.

and a verb: *Everybody laughed.* To these basic sentence elements others can, of course, be added.

C. Object and object complement

1. DIRECT OBJECT   In sentences with transitive verbs—that is, verbs that need direct objects to complete their meanings—the predicate must include this direct object. Like subjects, direct objects can be either nouns, pronouns, noun phrases, or noun clauses:

> s.   v.   d.o.
> He *hailed a taxi.*   (noun)
>
> s.   v.   d.o.
> The crowd *cheered him.*   (pronoun)
>
> s.   v.   d.o.
> I *resent his ignoring me.*   (phrase)
>
> s.   v.   d.o.
> I *will do whatever you say.*   (clause)

The direct object identifies who or what receives the action of the verb: He hailed what? A *taxi*. The crowd cheered whom? *Him*.

2. INDIRECT OBJECT   Many sentences with direct objects also have an indirect object. The indirect object, which always precedes the direct object, tells to whom or what, or for whom or what, the action of the verb is executed:

s.   v.   i.o.   d.o.
He hailed me a taxi.

s.   v.   i.o.   d.o.
I will give the candidate a donation.

s.   v.   i.o.   d.o.
The boss offered John a promotion.

The meaning of the indirect object can alternatively be expressed by a prepositional phrase beginning with *to* or *for* that follows the direct object:

s.   v.   d.o. prep. phr.
He hailed a taxi for me.

s.   v.   d.o.   prep. phr.
I will give a donation to the candidate.

s.   v.   d.o.   prep. phr.
The boss offered a promotion to John.

3. OBJECT COMPLEMENT   In some sentences with direct objects the predicate may also include what is called an object complement; that is, a noun or adjective following the direct object and renaming or describing it. Object complements are often found in sentences using such verbs as *appoint, call, choose, consider, elect, judge, label,* and *make:*

s.   v.   d.o.   o.c.
They judged Benedict Arnold a traitor.

s.   v.   d.o.   o.c.
The villagers called the dwarf Rumpelstiltskin.

s.   v.   d.o.   o.c.
A phone call would make your parents happy.

s.   v.   d.o.   o.c.
We labeled the cans poisonous.

Object complements (sometimes called OBJECTIVE COMPLEMENTS or COMPLEMENTARY OBJECTS) are hybrids, sharing some characteristics with complements and some with objects. As complements they refer back to and complete the meaning of the direct object by defining or describing it. But since the object complement, like the direct object, is necessary to complete the meaning of the verb, it can be considered an object.

4. RETAINED OBJECT   When a sentence in the passive voice (that is, a sentence whose subject is the receiver rather than the performer of the verb's action) has an object following the verb—and not all do—that object is called a retained object:

s.   v.   r.o.
The prisoner was denied his civil rights

s.   v.   r.o.
Astronauts are considered national heroes.

(For a more complete discussion of retained objects, *see* A Glossary of Grammatical Terms: retained object.)

D. Subject complement

PREDICATE NOUN and PREDICATE ADJECTIVE   When the verb of a sentence is a linking verb—like *be, become, appear, seem,* or any verb pertaining to the senses such as *look, smell, sound, taste,* or *feel*—the predicate may include a subject complement, either a predicate noun (also called a PREDICATE NOMINATIVE) or a predicate adjective:

s.   v.   p.n.   s. v. p.a.
Your dog may be a champion, but he is nasty.

These complements refer back to the subject of the sentence, unlike the object complement that refers back, as its name suggests, to the direct object of the sentence. Predicate nouns help to identify the subject (*dog = champion*); predicate adjectives describe the subject (*dog = nasty*).

E. Modifier

Although the basic elements of a sentence are those just reviewed—subject, verb, objects, and complements—sentences rarely consist of these elements alone. Most contain modifiers; that is, words, phrases, or clauses that describe or limit other elements in the sentence and sometimes the whole sentence itself. The most common modifiers are ADJECTIVES and ADVERBS. Adjectives, including articles and possessive pronouns, modify nouns and pronouns. Adverbs modify verbs, adjectives, other adverbs, and clauses.

      m.   s.   v.   m.   d.o.
Angry words have caused lengthy wars.   (adjectives)

    m.   s.   v.   m. d.o.
The gang robbed a bank.   (articles)

    m.   s.   v. m.   p.n.
Your loss is my gain.   (possessive pronouns)

    s.   v.   m.   m.
He ran silently and swiftly.   (adverbs modifying verb)

    s. v.   m.
Leon is thoroughly charming.   (*Thoroughly* is an adverb
      modifying the predicate adjective *charming.*)

    s.   v.   d.o.   m.   m.
We finished lunch very quickly.   (*Quickly* is an adverb
      modifying the verb *finished; very* is an adverb modify-
      ing *quickly.*)

Phrases and clauses that function as adjectives and adverbs can also modify sentence elements:

    s.   v.   m.
He came to find me.   (Infinitive phrase *to find me*
      modifies verb *came.*)

    s.   m.   v.   m.
People crossing the street should watch for cars.   (Par-
      ticipial phrase *crossing the street* modifies the subject
      people; prepositional phrase *for cars* modifies the verb
      should watch.)

    m.   s.   v.
When I saw him, I screamed.   (Adverbial clause *when I
      saw him* modifies the verb *screamed.*)

    m.   s.   m.   v. m.
The scarf that I bought is blue.   (Adjectival clause *that
      I bought* modifies the subject *scarf.*)

Not all phrases, however, need be connected to a particular sentence element. Some phrases, called ABSOLUTE PHRASES, are grammatically independent of any single sentence element and act like adverbs modifying the entire sentence:

> *The fire having burned out, we went to sleep.*
> *We will meet again, God willing.*

These absolute phrases function like condensed clauses indicating time, cause, or circumstance and can always be replaced by an adverbial clause:

> *Since the fire burned out, we went to sleep.*
> *We will meet again if God is willing.*

F. Appositive

Appositives are nouns or nominals that follow other nouns or nominals in order to identify or explain them:

>   s.   app.   v.   m. d.o.
> *Mr. Jones the butcher delivered my order.*   (The appositive, the phrase *the butcher,* identifies which Mr. Jones the sentence is about.)
>
> m. m.   m.   s.   app.
> *The first constitutional amendment, the right to free speech,*
>   v.   m.   d.o.
>   *ensures journalistic freedom.*   (The appositive, *the right to free speech,* explains the nature of the amendment.)

Since appositives give additional information about the words they follow, they look deceptively like modifiers. But modifiers—adjectives and adverbs—describe or limit the words they modify; appositives are equivalent, or substitutable, terms for the nouns or nominals they follow.

G. Connective

As the name suggests, connectives join elements in a sentence. COORDINATING CONJUNCTIONS and CORRELATIVE CONJUNCTIONS (the latter a form of coordinating conjunction used in pairs) join together grammatically similar sentence elements or entire clauses:

>   conj. s. conj. s.   v.   d.o.
> *Either Bob or Bill will wash the car.*
> s.   v. d.o.   m.   conj. s.   v.   d.o. m.
> *I washed it last week, and Sue washed it earlier.*

The correlative conjunction *either . . . or* connects the two subjects *Bob* and *Bill* to make a compound subject; the coordinating conjunction *and* connects the two independent clauses *I washed it last week* and *Sue washed it earlier* to make a compound sentence.

The remaining connectives are PREPOSITIONS and SUBORDINATING CONJUNCTIONS. A preposition introduces a prepositional phrase, which consists of the preposition, a noun or nominal called the OBJECT OF THE PREPOSITION, and sometimes modifiers. The entire prepositional phrase functions as a modifier, with the preposition connecting its object to the word modified and indicating the relation between the two:

> s.   v.   d.o.   prep. phr.
> *I don't need the calories in sugar.*   (The preposition *in* introduces the prepositional phrase *in sugar* and links it to the direct object *calories,* which the phrase modifies.)

A subordinating conjunction introduces a dependent clause, which usually functions as a modifier. The conjunction connects the dependent clause to the independent clause of the sentence, indicating the relationship between the two:

> s.   v.   m.   sub.
> *I will come home when I am ready.*   (The subordinating conjunction *when* introduces the dependent clause *when I am ready* and connects it to the independent clause. In this sentence the dependent clause modifies the verb *will come.*)

H. Absolute

Occasionally sentences will include an element that has no specific grammatical connection to the rest of the sentence yet is clearly a part of the sentence; these elements are called absolutes. Unlike the absolute phrases discussed earlier that actually modify the entire sentence to
> abs. phr.
which they are joined (*That being the case, I will reconsider your offer*), absolutes have no modifying function in the sentence:

> abs.
> *Yes, I have lost weight.*
> abs.
> *Nonsense, no one will believe you.*
>   abs.
> *Your new hair style, I must say, is certainly becoming.*

II. Parts of Speech

The basic sentence elements—subject, verb, object, complement, modifier, connective, appositive, and absolute—are the working components of sentences. When a word is used in a sentence, it functions as one of these elements, and grammarians have traditionally classified words into PARTS OF SPEECH according to the particular role they play in a sentence. NOUNS and PRONOUNS are words that can serve as subjects, objects, complements, and appositives. Words are classified as VERBS when they indicate action performed by the subject, action performed on the subject, or the subject's state of being. ADJECTIVES and ADVERBS function as modifiers. PREPOSITIONS and CONJUNCTIONS serve as connectives. And INTERJECTIONS, because they have no clear grammatical relation to the rest of the sentence, function as absolutes.

Phrases and dependent clauses are also classified into parts of speech according to their role in a sentence. A phrase may function as an adjective (it is then called an ADJECTIVAL PHRASE), an adverb (then called an ADVERBIAL PHRASE), or a noun (then called a NOUN PHRASE). A dependent clause may function as an adjective (then called a RELATIVE CLAUSE), an adverb (then called an ADVERBIAL CLAUSE), or a noun (then called a NOUN CLAUSE).

Because a word's part of speech depends upon its use in a sentence, there is little practical value in knowing whether a particular word out of context is a noun, preposition, adverb, or another part of speech. Many words are able to serve as different parts of speech, depending on their different uses in various sentences. The word *close,* for example, has a different function, and so becomes a different part of speech, in each of these five sentences:

> *I close the door.*   (verb)
> *That was a close call.*   (adjective)
> *The semester came to a close in June.*   (noun)
> *He walked close to the river.*   (preposition)
> *The thunder claps came close together.*   (adverb)

There is intrinsic value, however, in understanding the various characteristics of the different parts of speech. Beyond serving similar functions in sentences, those words, phrases, and dependent clauses that are used as the same part of speech are subject to similar grammatical rules. The following discussion of the parts of speech focuses first on how these parts of speech function in sentences and on the rules governing their use. Next it deals with the ways in which phrases and clauses function as parts of speech. For definition and discussion of each of the sentence elements mentioned below, *see* Section I of this chapter, The Sentence and Its Elements.

A. Noun

Simply stated, a noun is a word that names something: a person (*writer*), place (*library*), thing (*egg*), action (*departure*), quality (*goodness*), or concept (*success*). If the noun names a specific person or place (*Mary, Ohio*), it is a PROPER NOUN; all other nouns (*dog, courage,* etc.) are COMMON NOUNS.

Within clauses nouns can function as the following sentence elements:

Subject of a verb: *The cat meowed.*

Direct object: *The drought ruined the crops.*

Subject complement (in this case, a PREDICATE NOUN): *My performance was a success.*

Object complement: *The will named Harold heir to the estate.*

Appositive: *My favorite city, Chicago, has wonderful restaurants.*

Absolute (in this case, a noun of DIRECT ADDRESS): *I will see you later, Tom.*

Within phrases nouns can function as:

Appositive: *He is from Chicago, my hometown.*

Object of preposition: *The bakery is in town.*

Subject of an infinitive: *We waited for the rain to stop.*

Object of an infinitive: *I want to earn money.*

Complement of an infinitive: *Billy wants to be president.*

Object of a participle: *Someone owning a business must be astute.*

Subject of a gerund: *I stopped the baby's crying.*

Object of a gerund: *Picking weeds is backbreaking work.*

Sometimes words or groups of words that are not normally considered nouns nonetheless function like nouns; these are called NOMINALS. For example, in the sentence *The good die young, good,* normally an adjective, functions as a noun since it serves as subject of the sentence and so is a nominal. Gerunds (*Seeing is believing*), some infinitive phrases (*To see is to believe*), and noun clauses (*What I see is what I believe*) all serve noun functions and hence are nominals.

Conversely, words that are normally nouns may function as other parts of speech. For example, in *John works nights, nights,* which is usually a noun, functions as an adverb describing when John works. Any noun can function as an adjective, either by being made possessive (*Elaine's garden, book's title, child's play*) or simply by being used as an ATTRIBUTIVE to modify another noun (*hat rack, record player, lamp shade, Eisenhower era*).

One of the characteristic features of nouns is that most of them are inflected—that is, they change their form—to become plural or possessive. Usually, they add -*s* or -*es* to form a plural—for example, *day, days; box, boxes.* But many nouns form their plurals irregularly—for example, *mouse, mice; knife, knives; ox, oxen; tooth, teeth; series, series.* Still other nouns (like *friendliness,* which names a quality, or *California,* which names a particular place) do not usually have plurals at all. (For further discussion of the formation of plurals, *see* The Spelling Maze.)

Singular nouns usually form their possessive by adding '*s*—for example, *egg, egg's; caucus, caucus's;* plural nouns, by adding only an apostrophe—for example, *eggs, eggs'; caucuses, caucuses'.* (For details about forming possessives, *see* The Spelling Maze.)

B. Pronoun

Pronouns serve all the same functions as nouns, with the traditional definition of a pronoun being: a word that is used in place of a noun. (The particular noun or nominal that a pronoun stands in place of is called its ANTECEDENT.) That traditional definition, however, is not entirely precise. Although many pronouns—such as *he, she, myself, who,* and *this*—are used to take the place of and refer to particular nouns, other pronouns like *whoever* or *nothing* refer to an unspecifiable person or thing and thus can have no antecedent. The pronoun *it,* when used in sentences like *It is nice to hear from you,* does not refer to any person or thing at all.

Pronouns are divided into the eight categories discussed below, each of which has its own characteristic functions and grammatical features. Some pronouns, however, like *who, that,* and *myself,* can belong to more than one category, depending on how they are used in the sentence. As these pronouns change function and category, they are subject to different rules:

> All the children who finished their projects went home.
>   (Here *who* is a relative pronoun and must refer back
>   to an antecedent, *children.*)
>
> Who goes there?   (Here *who* is an interrogative pronoun
>   . and can have no antecedent.)

1. PERSONAL PRONOUN   The personal pronouns are *I, you, he, she, it, we, they,* and all of their various forms (*me, mine, yours,* etc.). These pronouns always have antecedents, and the antecedents must be known before the meaning of the pronoun can be understood. Out of context, the meaning of *He wants it* is unclear because we do not know to whom *he* refers or to what *it* refers. But when the antecedents of the pronouns are given, *Bob has not yet bought my car, but he wants it,* the meanings of the pronouns become clear.

The most distinctive feature of personal pronouns is that they are inflected, or change their form, to indicate:

    NUMBER (whether they are singular or plural);

    GENDER (whether they refer to a male, female,
       or neuter antecedent); and

    CASE (what their function is in the sentence).

The pronoun's number and gender are determined by its antecedent. For example, if the antecedent is singular and feminine, like *girl* or *Mary,* the pronoun must agree and hence, depending on its case, be *she, her,* or *hers.* The case of a pronoun is determined by its function in a sentence. Pronouns that function as subjects take the SUBJECTIVE (frequently called NOMINATIVE) CASE: *She went home.* Pronouns functioning as objects take the OBJECTIVE CASE: *The falling brick missed her.* And pronouns indicating possession take the POSSESSIVE CASE: *This seat is hers.*

The personal pronouns, listed according to person, case, and number, are:

	SUBJECTIVE	OBJECTIVE	POSSESSIVE
Singular			
First person	I	me	my, mine
Second person	you	you	your, yours
Third person	he, she, it	him, her, it	his, her, hers, its
	(one)	(one)	(one's)
Plural			
First person	we	us	our, ours
Second person	you	you	your, yours
Third person	they	them	their, theirs

As noted in the table above, most possessive pronouns have two possessive forms. The first, called simply the POSSESSIVE PRONOUN (or equally correctly the POSSESSIVE ADJECTIVE), serves as an adjective preceding a noun (*my pleasure, your cake, their responsibility*); the second form, sometimes called the SECOND POSSESSIVE or the INDE-

PENDENT POSSESSIVE, stands alone as a subject or object complement or as an appositive (*The pleasure was* mine. *We made the responsibility* theirs. *These books,* yours *and* mine, *are overdue*).

The pronoun *it*, often a personal pronoun, has so many different uses that it warrants a separate discussion. As a personal pronoun, *it* refers to inanimate things (*Jim gave Ruth a ring, but she did not want* it), living things that are thought of without reference to gender (*Whose puppy is* it?), and entire phrases or clauses (*I have heard that bussing will solve the school integration problem, but I don't believe* it). As a personal pronoun, *it* needs an antecedent. However, *it* has other uses that do not require it to have an antecedent; for example, *it* may be used as an impersonal pronoun referring to "things or a situation in general":

> *Isn't* it *nice out today?*
> *Darn* it, *I stubbed my toe.*
> It *has been three months since you called.*

Additionally, *it* often functions as the "dummy" subject of an expletive sentence, allowing the meaningful subject of the sentence to assume a more emphatic position:

> It *is true that Dale hates jogging but loves lifting weights.*
> It *is Sidney who wears the pants in this family.*

In the same way, *it* may function as a "dummy" object:

> *Rosemary took* it *for granted that she would be hired.*

2. REFLEXIVE PRONOUN and INTENSIVE PRONOUN The pronouns *myself, yourself, himself, herself, itself, oneself, ourselves, yourselves,* and *themselves* may be either reflexive or intensive. They are reflexive pronouns when they function as direct or indirect objects or objects of a preposition and refer back to the subject of the clause:

> *I hurt* myself.　　(direct object)
> *He bought* himself *a new suit.*　　(indirect object)
> *You saw it for* yourself.　　(object of preposition)

They are intensive pronouns if they serve to emphasize a noun or another pronoun:

> *We awarded the prize to the author* herself.
> *They* themselves *are responsible.*

3. RECIPROCAL PRONOUN   Reciprocal pronouns are used to show mutual relation between two or more nouns or pronouns. *Each other* and *each other's* express mutuality between two people or things:

> *Mr. Jones and Mr. Smith respect* each other, *and therefore they respect* each other's *privacy.*

One another and *one another's* express mutual relation among more than two people or things:

> *The three of us like* one another, *so we try to remember* one another's *birthday.*

4. RELATIVE PRONOUN   *Who, whom, whose, which, that, what, whoever, whomever, whichever,* and *whatever* are relative pronouns when they introduce a dependent clause—that is, a clause that serves as an element within a sentence—and when they function as a noun in that clause:

> ant.   r. pron.
> *The electorate voted for the candidates* who *made the biggest promises.*

In this example *who* is a relative pronoun because it (1) introduces the dependent clause *who made the biggest promises* and (2) functions as a noun in that clause, being the subject of the verb *made.* When the relatives function as an adjective in their clause, they are relative adjectives. (*See* II.D.F.)

Only a few relative pronouns can be inflected (change their form) for case:

SUBJECTIVE	POSSESSIVE	OBJECTIVE
who	whose	whom
whoever	(whosever)	whomever
which	whose	which

The case of these pronouns is determined by their function in the clause:

> *He knows* who *broke the window.* (*Who,* the subject of the verb *broke,* is in the subjective case.)
>
> *I enjoyed the people* whom *Tom invited to his party.* (*Whom,* the object of the verb *invited,* is in the objective case.)
>
> *This is the man* whose *picture was in the paper.* (*Whose,* a possessive modifying *picture,* is in the possessive case.)

Usually relative pronouns need antecedents. If they introduce a RELATIVE CLAUSE that functions as an adjective, modifying some other sentence element, the relative pronoun refers back to that element as its antecedent. In the sentence *Charles, who owns a candy store, visits his dentist regularly,* the relative clause *who owns a candy store* functions as an adjective describing *Charles.* The introductory relative pronoun *who* is the subject of this clause and relates the clause back to the antecedent *Charles.* The relative pronouns that most often introduce adjectival clauses are *who, whom, whose, which,* and *that:*

> ant.   r. pron.
> *Foreigners who enter the U.S. must have visas.*
> ant.   r. pron.
> *The committee, which met last night, discussed your report.*
> ant. r. pron.
> *I read the book that you gave me.*

The relative pronoun *that* is used to refer to people or things; *which* is used to refer only to things; and *who,* only to people.

In addition to the relative pronouns listed above, *as* is sometimes used as a relative pronoun referring back to and modifying the words *the same* and *such:*

> *I do not hold the same opinion as you hold.*
> *It was such a day as we had never seen.*

Sometimes relative pronouns introduce INDEFINITE RELATIVE CLAUSES —that is, relative clauses that function as nouns or adverbs rather than as adjectives. These INDEFINITE RELATIVE PRONOUNS—including *what, whoever, whomever, whatever, whichever,* and sometimes even *who, whose, whom,* and *which*—refer to something general or indefinite and so can have no antecedent. For example:

> r. pron.
> *I know what I like.*
> r. pron.
> *Whoever answers the most questions will win the prize.*
> r. pron.
> *I do not remember with whom I danced.*
> r. pron.
> *Ronald told Joan which of the rings he preferred.*
> r. pron.
> *Whatever you do, don't be late.*   (Here the indefinite relative clause functions as an adverb.)

Relative pronouns are troublesome both because their cases and antecedents (if they have them) must be clear and because the same words that function as relative pronouns can also serve other functions. For example, in *The dog that bit me was impounded, that* is a relative pronoun introducing the relative clause *that bit me* and functioning as the subject of that clause. However, in *I found that out, that* is a demonstrative pronoun; it introduces no relative clause. In *Who goes there?,* *who* is an interrogative pronoun since it introduces a question rather than a dependent relative clause. And in *He saw which man stole the car, which* is an indefinite relative adjective modifying *man*, not a pronoun at all. (For a discussion of the use of *that* and *which* in restrictive and nonrestrictive relative clauses, *see* II.K.2.)

5. DEMONSTRATIVE PRONOUN   *This, that, these,* and *those* are demonstrative pronouns when they function as nouns and "demonstrate," or point out, the things or ideas they refer to:

> *This is a disaster.*
> *I ran out of those.*

When the same words *this, that, these,* and *those* are used adjectivally, modifying nouns, they are called DEMONSTRATIVE ADJECTIVES:

> *This soufflé is a disaster.*
> *I ran out of those index cards.*

Demonstrative pronouns should refer to unambiguous antecedents rather than general or vaguely stated ideas. For example, in *I did not know this was your seat, this* clearly refers to a particular seat in question. Consider, however, the sentence *The road Mr. James took home was flooded by the storm; this caused his fatal accident.* In this example *this* has no clear antecedent and hence should not be used. A clearer, more specific subject is needed: *The road Mr. James took home was flooded by the storm; his losing control of the car caused his fatal accident.* (*See also* III.C.2.)

6. INTERROGATIVE PRONOUN   *Who, whose, whom, which,* and *what* are interrogative pronouns when they are used to ask either direct or indirect questions and serve as a noun in the question.

> Direct question: *Whose is this mitten?*
> *Which of the cats ran away?*
> Indirect question: *I asked who would be at the party.*

If the words *whose, which,* or *what* introduce a question but function as an adjective followed by a noun, they are INTERROGATIVE ADJECTIVES:

> *Whose mitten is it?*
> *Which cat ran away?*
> *I asked him what car I should buy.*

7. INDEFINITE PRONOUN   Indefinite pronouns refer to an unspecified antecedent. Among indefinite pronouns are the following:

all	both	everything	nobody	several
another	each	few	none	some
any	each one	many	no one	somebody
anybody	either	most	nothing	someone
anyone	everybody	much	one	something
anything	everyone	neither	other	such

Of course, these words are pronouns only when serving noun functions:

> *Neither of the books is worth reading.*   (subject)
> *I took all of them.*   (direct object)

When these words act as modifiers, they are INDEFINITE ADJECTIVES:

> *Neither book is worth reading.*
> *All cars will be towed.*

The pronouns *one, you, they,* and *we* are often used as indefinite, or IMPERSONAL, pronouns to refer to "people in general." When used this way, *one, you,* and *we* are generally interchangeable, with *one* being the more formal term:

> *One* (or *You* or *We*) *would expect the fish to swim.*
> *Before the fuel shortage,* one (or *you* or *we*) *could get gas any time.*

They occurs in a variety of contexts without a specified antecedent:

> *What do they want from me?*
> *They knew how to have a good time in the Roaring Twenties.*
> *They say that all that glitters is not gold.*

(For special rules about using indefinite pronouns, *see* III.C.2.)

C. Verb

As the heart of the predicate—that part of the sentence that says something about the subject—the verb is really the center of any sentence. The verb indicates either what the subject does (*The witness testified*), what is happening to the subject (*The alarm was activated*), or what the condition of the subject is (*This car is expensive. Your forehead feels warm*).

Depending on what it needs to complete its meaning, a verb is TRANSITIVE, INTRANSITIVE, or LINKING. A transitive verb is one that needs an object to complete its meaning. In effect the transitive verb transmits or passes along its action to the object:

> s.   t.v.   d.o.
> *The farmer milked his cow.*
> s.   t.v.   d.o.
> *Who closed the window?*

An intransitive verb expresses a state or an action of the subject without needing an object to complete its meaning:

> s.   i.v.
> *We were chatting incessantly.*
> s.   i.v.
> *The fire sputtered.*

The linking verb, sometimes called a COPULA, is a special kind of intransitive verb. Its function is to link the subject of a clause with a complement, either a noun in the predicate referring to the subject (PREDICATE NOUN) or an adjective in the predicate modifying the subject (PREDICATE ADJECTIVE):

> s.   l.v.   p.n.
> *Joan of Arc is now a saint.*
> s.   l.v.   p.a.
> *His burden grew heavy.*

The most common linking verbs are *be, become, feel, grow, look, seem, smell, sound,* and *taste.* Many other verbs, however, can function as linking verbs; for example:

> *The weather turned foul.*
> *He acted disturbed.*
> *His grades remain low.*

All verbs, whether transitive, intransitive, or linking, are characterized by various features that are termed NUMBER, PERSON, TENSE, VOICE, and MOOD. Verbs change form (that is, they are inflected) to indicate changes in these features.

1. PERSON and NUMBER   Person is the characteristic of verbs that indicates whether the subject of the verb is speaking (first person: *I am*), being spoken to (second person: *you are*), or being spoken about (third person: *he is*). Number is the characteristic that indicates whether the verb and its subject are singular (*I am; he is*) or plural (*we are; they are*).

English verbs—in contrast, for example, to German or French verbs —are no longer heavily inflected. That is to say, except for the verb *be,* they change very little to indicate person and number. In general they change form only in the third person singular of the present tense. The changes in *be,* however, are more extensive:

	PRESENT	PAST	PRESENT	PAST
	(Verb: *to change*)		(Verb: *to be*)	
I	change	changed	am	was
you	change	changed	are	were
he, she, it	changes	changed	is	was
we	change	changed	are	were
you	change	changed	are	were
they	change	changed	are	were

2. TENSE   Verbs change form to express different times, or tenses. In English 12 tenses are commonly used:

Present   (expressing an action that is current or habitual):

> *I change my mind daily.*

Present progressive   (expressing an action that continues on in the present):

> *I am changing the linens now.*

Present perfect   (expressing an action completed in the indefinite past):

> *I have changed the recipe three times.*

Present perfect progressive   (expressing an action that was begun in the past and continues into the present):

I have been changing jobs yearly since I moved to town.

Past   (expressing an action that is completed):

I changed the time of our meeting.

Past progressive   (expressing an action that was ongoing in the past):

I was changing my clothes when you rang the doorbell.

Past perfect   (expressing a past action that was completed before another past time or event):

I had changed my name before I met you.

Past perfect progressive   (expressing an ongoing action that was completed before another past time or event):

I had been changing my hairstyle monthly before I found a style that I liked.

Future   (expressing an action that will take place later):

I will change my plans if it rains.

Future progressive   (expressing an ongoing action that will take place later):

I will be changing diapers for many more years.

Future perfect   (expressing an action that will be completed at a later time):

I will have changed hundreds of bandages by the time I leave the clinic.

Future perfect progressive   (expressing an ongoing action that will be completed at a later time):

I will have been changing tires for 30 years when I retire from the garage.

a. Most of the verb tenses are derived from three distinctive forms of the verb called its PRINCIPAL PARTS: the PRESENT STEM, the PAST, and the PAST PARTICIPLE. The principal parts of the verb *change*, for example, are *change, changed, changed;* those of the verb *go* are *go, went, gone.* The present stem (the infinitive without *to*) is used in the present and future tenses (*I change; you will go*). The past is used in the past tense (*I changed; you went*). The past participle is used in the perfect tenses (*I have changed; you had not gone*).

On the basis of these forms, verbs are classified as REGULAR or IRREGULAR. The majority of verbs are regular and form their past and past participle by adding *-d* or *-ed* to the present stem: *change, changed; walk, walked.* Irregular verbs, as their name suggests, have entirely irregular principal parts and so must be memorized, for example:

PRESENT	PAST	PAST PARTICIPLE
be	was	been
begin	began	begun
choose	chose	chosen
eat	ate	eaten
go	went	gone
know	knew	known
lay	laid	laid
lie	lay	lain
see	saw	seen
tear	tore	torn

A complete list of irregular verbs is far too long to include here, but a good dictionary provides the principal parts of all irregular verbs.

A fourth distinctive verb form, the PRESENT PARTICIPLE, is formed in the same way by both regular and irregular verbs—by adding *-ing* to the present stem: *changing, going, being, eating,* etc. The present participle is the basis of all the progressive tenses.

b. To form certain of the tenses listed above, the main verb must be combined with an AUXILIARY VERB. In English the most common auxiliaries are *will* and forms of the verbs *to be, to do,* and *to have:*

> *we will change; I am changing; they have changed; did you change?*

Another kind of auxiliary, called a MODAL AUXILIARY, does not change the tense of the verb but changes its emphasis or meaning. The most common modal auxiliaries—*can, could, do, may, might, must, ought, should, will,* and *would*—are used to express possibility, ability, obligation, permission, or changes in emphasis:

> *we might come; he can cook; they should meditate; you*
> *may begin; he does know; we absolutely will succeed*

It is important to know the difference between regular auxiliaries and modal auxiliaries since they differ in more than meaning. They differ both (1) in their own form and (2) in the verb that follows them:

1. The regular auxiliaries *be* and *have,* used to indicate tense, are inflected (change their form) to agree with their subjects:

> *I am crying, you are crying; they have tried, he has tried*

By contrast modal auxiliaries are not inflected:

> *I could believe, you could believe; he might go, we might go;*
> *I may cook, she may cook*

The two auxiliaries, *do* and *will,* that are used both to indicate tense and to show emphasis are a special case. *Do* is always inflected; *will* is never inflected:

> *do you change? does he change? I do believe, she does*
> *believe; I will change, she will go, will he stay?*

2. The regular auxiliaries *be* and *have* are followed by present or past participles:

> *they are staring; we have gotten*

Modal auxiliaries and *do* are followed by the present stem (*i.e.,* the infinitive stem without *to*):

> *they might stare; we should get; they did not go*

Will is followed by the present stem unless combined with other auxiliaries:

> *we will cry; we will be crying; we will have cried*

(For a discussion of the distinction between *shall* and *will, see* Verbal Quandaries from A to Z: shall.)

3. VOICE   Voice is the characteristic of verbs that indicates whether the subject of the clause is the doer or receiver of the action. Any transitive verb can have two voices: the ACTIVE VOICE, indicating that the subject of the sentence is active and performs the action of the verb (*John drove the truck*); or the PASSIVE VOICE, indicating that the sentence's subject is passive and receives the action of the verb (*The truck was driven by John*). Intransitive verbs—that is, verbs that do not pass their action on to any receiver—are always in the active voice: *John laughed; The children played outdoors*. Since linking verbs indicate a state of being rather than an action, the term *voice* does not apply to them.

Note that all forms of the passive voice are based on the past participle:

	ACTIVE VOICE	PASSIVE VOICE
Present	I change	I am changed
Present progressive	I am changing	I am being changed
Present perfect	I have changed	I have been changed
Present perfect progressive	I have been changing	I have been being changed
Past	I changed	I was changed
Past progressive	I was changing	I was being changed
Past perfect	I had changed	I had been changed
Past perfect progressive	I had been changing	I had been being changed
Future	I will change	I will be changed
Future progressive	I will be changing	I will be being changed
Future perfect	I will have changed	I will have been changed
Future perfect progressive	I will have been changing	I will have been being changed

4. MOOD   Mood is the most elusive feature of verbs; it refers to a writer's or speaker's attitude toward what he or she is saying. Verbs change mood to indicate whether one is speaking of factual matters (INDICATIVE MOOD); giving a command (IMPERATIVE MOOD); or speaking of desired, conjectural, probable, or suggested matters (SUBJUNCTIVE MOOD). (The optative mood, once taught in classical grammar, expressed hoping or wishing and is now included in the subjunctive.)

a. The indicative is the most common and familiar mood. It is used for statements of fact or questions about fact:

> *He cooks for the entire family.*
> *Did you spend my money?*

b. The imperative mood is used for commands and directions, whether or not the subject is explicitly stated:

> *Take the train.*
> *Let us eat dinner.*
> *Everybody be quiet.*
> *Do not leave this room.*

For all verbs except *be,* the imperative is identical to the second-person indicative form:

> Indicative: *You play the cello beautifully.*
> Imperative: *Play it again, Sam.*

The imperative of *be* is *be:*

> Indicative: *You are mischievous.*
> Imperative: *Be good.*

A negative imperative is formed by placing *do not* before the imperative itself:

> *Do not play in the street.*
> *Don't be silly.*

In addition to the second-person imperative, English has another imperative form that includes the speaker along with the person addressed:

> *Let us say grace.*
> *Let's play cards.*
> *Let's be friends.*

c. The subjunctive mood, the least common of the three, has almost disappeared from English. Its most frequent use is in certain formulaic sayings that are set in the language, like *as it were, be that as it may, come what may, God bless you, God be with you, Heaven forbid,* and *long live the king.* Otherwise, the subjunctive is used to discuss what is desirable, conceivable, hypothetical, or contrary to fact as opposed to what is factual. (The indicative mood expresses that which is factual.) Verbs have three subjunctive forms: present subjunctive, past subjunctive, and past perfect subjunctive. For all verbs except *be,* the subjunctive is formed in the same way:

	INDICATIVE	IMPERATIVE	SUBJUNCTIVE		
	PRESENT		PRESENT	PAST	PAST PERFECT
I	change		change	changed	had changed
you	change	change	change	changed	had changed
he, she, it	changes		change	changed	had changed
we	change	let's change	change	changed	had changed
you	change	change	change	changed	had changed
they	change		change	changed	had changed

The verb *be,* irregular throughout, is partially conjugated as follows:

	INDICATIVE		IMPERATIVE	SUBJUNCTIVE		
	PRESENT	PAST		PRESENT	PAST	PAST PERFECT
I	am	was		be	were	had been
you	are	were	be	be	were	had been
he, she, it	is	was		be	were	had been
we	are	were	let's be	be	were	had been
you	are	were	be	be	were	had been
they	are	were		be	were	had been

The terms *present subjunctive* and *past subjunctive* are rather confusing since these forms are not used to express different times; instead, they indicate different kinds of uncertainty in the present or in the future. The past perfect subjunctive alone refers to time and always to the past.

1. The present subjunctive is used to indicate that the sentence is about an idea—something conceivable or desired—rather than about something that has actually happened. Thus, it is used in *that*-clauses expressing commands, recommendations, requests, suggestions, or requirements:

> *The sergeant ordered that the troops* be *ready to move out.*
> *I recommend that everyone* see *this movie.*
> *She asked that John* change *his seat.*
> *I suggested that he* follow *directions.*
> *It is necessary that you* be *on time.*

The present subjunctive is also used in *lest*-clauses expressing conceivable fears:

> *I will return lest he* forget *me.*

The contrast between indicative statements expressing fact and present subjunctive statements expressing ideas is as follows:

Indicative: *He leaves at 8 A.M. every day.*
Subjunctive: *I suggested that he leave earlier.*
Indicative: *We eat dinner early.*
Subjunctive: *It is important that we eat dinner early tonight.*
Indicative: *I am always late.*
Subjunctive: *She asked that I be on time.*

2. The past subjunctive is also used to talk about an idea rather than an actual happening. However, in contrast to the present subjunctive, which focuses on something conceivable or desired, the past subjunctive focuses on something unlikely, impossible, or contrary to present fact. Thus the past subjunctive is used in *if*-clauses that express such conditions:

If I believed you, I would be foolish.   (unlikely)

If Prince Charming walked through Anne's door, she would gladly run away with him.   (impossible)

If Paula were here, she would know what to do.   (contrary to present fact)

The past subjunctive is also used in *that*-clauses following the verb *wish*, implying that the wish is hypothetical, unlikely, or doubtful:

I wish that this day were over.
I wish that I knew what was on your mind.

3. The past perfect subjunctive refers to past time and implies that the past condition being discussed is contrary to fact:

I wish that Larry had come to my party.   (The use of the subjunctive implies that Larry did not come.)

If Tim had recognized me, he would have said hello. (The subjunctive implies that Tim did not recognize me.)

Had he discovered your mistake, he would have corrected it.   (The subjunctive implies that he did not discover your mistake.)

The subjunctive mood may be expressed not only by the subjunctive forms of verbs but also by certain auxiliary verbs with subjunctive meaning. Such auxiliaries as *ought, must, may, might, should, could,* and *would* may be used to express conceivable, unlikely, or contrary-to-fact conditions:

> *You ought to have listened to me.*
> *You must have known the truth.*
> *The suspect may be guilty.*
> *She might have tried to warn me.*
> *If he should forget his medicine, he will faint.*
> *Should he forget his medicine, he will faint.*
> *I could have been a great movie star.*
> *I would have been happy to feed your cat.*

D. Adjective

An adjective is a word used to modify a noun (*fine day*), pronoun (*he is arrogant*), or other nominal (*the constant complaining*). Frequently phrases and clauses as well as words normally used as other parts of speech function as adjectives:

> *The man managing this newspaper believes in equal opportunity.* (Participial phrase modifies noun *man.*)
> *We attended a reading of William Stafford's poetry.* (Prepositional phrase modifies nominal *reading.*)
> *He who finishes first wins.* (Relative clause modifies pronoun *he.*)
> *What is the dictionary definition of "yahoo"?* (Noun, called an ATTRIBUTIVE, modifies another noun, *definition.*)

Often adjectives are located immediately before or after the words they modify (*the black tower; an ogre tall and terrible*); these are called ATTRIBUTIVE ADJECTIVES. But some adjectives, called PREDICATE ADJECTIVES, are separated from the words they modify and are located in the predicate after a linking verb (*the tower is black; the ogre looked tall and terrible*).

Adjectives modify nouns or nominals in one of two ways: either by describing them or by limiting them.

1. DESCRIPTIVE ADJECTIVE   Descriptive adjectives indicate a characteristic or quality of the word they modify:

> *the* translucent *window, a* blue *book, the* running *water,*
> *a* good *child, a* blatant *lie, an impish grin*

a. One feature of many descriptive adjectives is that they can be compared —that is, they change their form to describe different degrees of the quality they name; for example, *tall, taller, tallest.* The first of the three degrees of comparison is the base form, called the POSITIVE DEGREE; it indicates no comparison:

> *This tea is* weak.
> *Saul Bellow's novels are* realistic.

The COMPARATIVE DEGREE, used in comparing two persons or things, indicates that one of them has a greater (or lesser) degree of that quality than the other:

> *John is* weaker *than Roger is.*
> *My expectations are* less *realistic than yours are.*

Finally the SUPERLATIVE DEGREE, used in comparing more than two persons or things, indicates that one of them has the greatest (or smallest) degree of that quality:

> *Marilyn's excuse is the* weakest *of all.*
> *Of all your harebrained schemes, this is the* least *realistic.*

Comparative and superlative degrees of adjectives are formed according to the following rules:

1. One-syllable adjectives add the comparative and superlative suffixes *-er* and *-est* to the root of the positive form: *gray, grayer, grayest; old, older, oldest.*
    a. If the positive form ends in *-y* preceded by a consonant, the *-y* changes to *-i* before adding the suffixes: *dry, drier, driest; sly, slier, sliest.*
    b. If the positive form has a short vowel and ends with a single consonant, the last consonant is doubled before adding the suffixes: *big, bigger, biggest; glum, glummer, glummest; hot, hotter, hottest; sad, sadder, saddest; wet, wetter, wettest.*

2. Most two-syllable adjectives form the comparative and superlative degree by using the adverbs *more* and *most,* or *less and least,* before the positive form: *forthright, more forthright, most forthright; gallant, less gallant, least gallant.*

However, many two-syllable adjectives, especially those ending in a consonant followed by *-y,* form their comparative and superlative by adding *-er* and *-est* to the positive form, following the same rules as one-syllable adjectives do: *empty, emptier, emptiest; pretty, prettier, prettiest; quiet, quieter, quietest.*

3. Adjectives of more than two syllables use the adverbs *more* and *most,* or *less* and *least,* before the positive form: *characteristic, more characteristic, most characteristic; flexible, less flexible, least flexible.*

4. Some common adjectives have irregular comparative and superlative forms, which can be found in a good dictionary. For example:

POSITIVE	COMPARATIVE	SUPERLATIVE
bad	worse	worst
far	farther	farthest
good	better	best
little	littler, less	littlest, least
many, much	more	most

b. Not all descriptive adjectives can be compared, however. Some refer to characteristics that cannot exist to a greater or lesser degree. Among these characteristics are the actions described by some PRESENT PARTICIPLES (that is, adjectives formed by adding *-ing* to the present stem of a verb): *running water, fainting woman, falling star, traveling salesman.* These present participles cannot be compared. Other present participles denote qualities, however, and may be compared: *most perplexing puzzle, less entertaining show, more retiring person.*

Some grammarians insist that adjectives naming qualities thought of as absolute (ABSOLUTE ADJECTIVES) cannot be compared. Such adjectives include: *circular, complete, dead, empty, excellent, fatal, final, horizontal, impossible, mutual, perfect, perpendicular, round, square, triangular, unique,* and *vertical.* According to purists, different degrees of these qualities should be indicated by *almost* or *nearly:*

> *One soldier was dead, and the other was almost dead.*
> *This line is more nearly perpendicular than the other.*

In common use, however, these adjectives are rarely used in their absolute sense; they are frequently and acceptably compared:

> *Cleaning the Augean stables was Hercules' most impossible
> task.*
> *The framers of the Constitution wanted to "form a more
> perfect union."*

2. LIMITING ADJECTIVE   Limiting adjectives modify nouns and nominals by making them more specific (*this ear, an ear, his ear, two ears,
either* ear). Since limiting adjectives do not name qualities, they cannot
have degrees and so cannot be compared. Adjectives with this limiting
function are described below.

a. DEMONSTRATIVE ADJECTIVES take the same form as demonstrative
pronouns: *this* and *that,* used to modify singular nouns; *these* and *those,*
used to modify plural nouns. Their purpose is to point to what they
modify: *this chair, these children, that bicycle, those protestors.*

b. The adjectives *a, an,* and *the* are called ARTICLES. *The* is called the
DEFINITE ARTICLE because it modifies singular or plural nouns that refer
to something or someone specific or definite: *The dog bit me.* (Here
the dog refers to a specific dog.)
   A and *an* are called INDEFINITE ARTICLES because they modify nouns
referring to general categories or to something not yet specifically identified:

> *Investing in a dog may be profitable.*   (Here *a dog*
> refers not to a specific dog but to dogs in general.)
> *I found a dog, but it was not the dog you lost.*   (Here
> *a dog* refers to a dog not specifically identified, but
> *the dog* refers to the one specific dog that was lost.)

A is used before words beginning with consonant sounds (*a dog,
a cat, a hotel, a one-sided argument*) or with a long *u* vowel sound
(*a union, a European town*). *An* is used before vowel sounds, except
the long *u* mentioned above (*an elf, an albatross*), and before words
beginning with a silent *h* (*an hour, an heir, an honest man*).

c. Although the POSSESSIVES *my, your, his, her, its, our,* and *their* are
forms of the personal pronouns, they actually function as adjectives,
limiting a noun by indicating to whom or what it belongs: *my book,
your collar, his best interest, its title.* Nouns in the possessive case simi-

larly limit the nouns they modify: *Roland's car, New York's garment district, the coat's sleeve.*

d. Cardinal numbers (*one, two, three, four,* etc.) limit the nouns they modify by indicating how many objects or people are being referred to: *one camera, twenty dollars, four and one-half yards.*

Ordinal numbers (*first, second, third, fourth,* etc.) limit the nouns they modify by indicating their position in a series; *the seventh commandment, the fifteenth phone call, her twenty-eighth birthday.*

e. INDEFINITE ADJECTIVES *do* limit the nouns they modify but do not completely define them: *some books, either car, enough money.* Indefinite adjectives include:

a little	either	many	numerous
all	enough	more	other
another	every	most	several
any	few	much	some
both	innumerable	neither	such
certain	less	no	sufficient
countless	little	not a	various

f. *Which, what, whichever,* and *whatever* function as RELATIVE ADJECTIVES. *Which* often refers back to a definite antecedent:

> ant.
> *I will return this afternoon, by which time I expect to see
> the dishes washed.*

More often, however, relative adjectives have an indefinite reference.

> *Joan told John which ring she preferred.*
> *I do not have much, but I will share what little I have.*
> *The enemy attacked us whichever way we turned.*
> *She objects to whatever suggestions I make.*

Like relative pronouns, these relative adjectives have a connective function, joining their dependent clause to the independent clause.

g. *Which* and *what* function as INTERROGATIVE ADJECTIVES introducing direct or indirect questions. Of the two, *which* is the more definite adjective:

> *Which job did you accept?*
> *What job will give me the most mobility?*
> *I asked him which brother was getting married.*
> *He asked the crowd what honest citizen would refuse to*
>   *defend his country.*

In indirect questions, interrogative adjectives have a connective function, joining their clause to the introductory proposition.

3. PROPER ADJECTIVE Proper adjectives, that is, adjectival forms of proper nouns, as in French *pastry,* Buddhist *priest,* or Christmas *story,* can be either descriptive or limiting, depending on their function. If they name a quality of the noun they modify, they are descriptive and can be compared: *This novel is* more Dickensian *than the other. "America the Beautiful" is the* most American *song I have ever heard.* If, however, their purpose is to limit or identify what they modify, they cannot be compared: *the* German *city, a* Princeton *student, the* United States *flag.*

E. Adverb

An adverb is a word used to modify a verb (*breathe* deeply), an adjective (almost *ready*), another adverb (very *simply*), or even a whole sentence (Fortunately *he arrived just in time*); in fact, an adverb modifies anything but a noun or nominal. Typically adverbs express:

Manner: *happily, thoroughly*
Degree: *less, more, very*
Time: *now, when, yesterday*
Direction and place: *upward, there*
Affirmation and negation: *certainly, not*
Cause and result: *consequently, hence, therefore, thus*
Qualification and doubt: *however, probably*

In addition to being modifiers, two special kinds of adverbs perform additional functions:

1. The adverbs *how, when, where, why, whenever,* and *wherever* may be RELATIVE ADVERBS whose function is to introduce relative clauses:

> *This is the place* where Abraham Lincoln was born.
> *That was the reason* why he stayed home.

In these examples *where* and *why* are adverbs respectively modifying the verbs *was born* and *stayed*. As well, these adverbs introduce relative clauses (that is, clauses that function as adjectives): *where Abraham Lincoln was born* modifies the noun *place*, and *why he stayed home* modifies the noun *reason*.

Relative adverbs can also introduce indefinite relative clauses functioning as nouns or adverbs:

d.o.
I don't know how you do it.
adv.
Whatever happens, I will remain faithful.

2. Certain adverbs, called CONJUNCTIVE ADVERBS, have a special connective function. Not only do they modify the clause to which they are attached, but they also connect that clause to another, forming a compound sentence. Adverbs that can function as conjunctive adverbs include:

accordingly	hence	likewise	otherwise
besides	however	meanwhile	therefore
consequently	indeed	nevertheless	thus
furthermore	instead	nonetheless	too

> *Talking about baseball is boring;* instead, let's talk about food.
>
> *Ann decided she wanted to become a doctor;* consequently, she majored in biology.

Adverbs have no single characteristic form. Although innumerable adverbs end in *-ly* (*quickly, happily, vaguely*), many do not (*better, close, near, slow, straight, upstairs*). Each of these latter example
adv.
words can function as either an adverb or adjective (*go upstairs slowly;*
adj.
upstairs bedroom). Moreover, many words ending in *-ly* are adjectives rather than adverbs (*the cowardly lion, a friendly man, a lonely child*). Hence the only sure sign of an adverb is not its form but its function.

F. Preposition

A preposition always introduces a PREPOSITIONAL PHRASE. Although the entire phrase modifies some element in a sentence, the preposition itself is essentially a connector. It links a noun (*in love*), pronoun (*after you*), noun phrase (*without seeing its ending*), or noun clause (*because of what I said*) to the part of the sentence modified by the whole prepositional phrase, and it shows the relation between the two:

> *His deck of cards was marked.*   (The preposition *of* introduces the prepositional phrase *of cards,* which functions as an adjective modifying *deck.*)
>
> *They were pleased with what I did.*   (The preposition *with* introduces the phrase *with what I did,* which functions as an adverb modifying *were pleased.*)

The noun, pronoun, noun phrase, or noun clause following the preposition is the OBJECT OF THE PREPOSITION. Like other objects, pronouns serving as objects of prepositions must take the objective case:

> *I was upset because of him.*
> *My life passed before me.*

The English language has many prepositions, including some composed of more than one word. Among the most common prepositions are:

about	behind	in front of	since
above	below	in regard to	through
according to	between	into	to
across	by	like	toward
after	by means of	near	under
against	down	of	until
among	due to	off	up
around	during	on	with
at	for	on account of	with respect to
because of	from	out	without
before	in	out of	

One of the problems in identifying prepositions is that several of the words that function as prepositions can also function as adverbs or conjunctions; for example, *after, before, near,* and *since.* These words are prepositions only if they introduce a prepositional phrase and hence have an object:

>   prep.   obj.
> *Ladies go before gentlemen.*
>
>   adv.
> *I have seen you before.*
>
>   conj.
> *Look before you leap.*

G. Conjunction

Like prepositions, conjunctions are connectors; they join together words, phrases, or entire clauses:

> *The players win all or nothing.*
> <small>word conj. word</small>

> *Falling in love and playing in traffic are both dangerous.*
> <small>┌—phr.—┐ conj. ┌—phr.—┐</small>

> *I sneeze whenever I smell pepper.*
> <small>┌—cl.—┐ conj. ┌—cl.—┐</small>

There are two general classes of conjunctions: coordinating and subordinating. COORDINATING CONJUNCTIONS join grammatically equivalent elements—words to words, phrases to phrases, independent clauses to independent clauses, and dependent clauses to dependent clauses. The most common coordinating conjunctions are: *and, but, for, or, so, yet.*

> *Jules and Jim are friends.*
> <small>n.   n.</small>

> *To be or not to be, that is the question.*
> <small>┌phr.┐   ┌—phr.—┐</small>

> *We saw it, yet we did not believe it.*
> <small>┌—ind. cl.—┐   ┌——ind. cl.——┐</small>

> *Twilight is the time after the sun sets but before the sky turns dark.*
> <small>┌—dep. cl.—┐   ┌——dep. cl.——┐</small>

A special form of coordinating conjunction, the CORRELATIVE CONJUNCTION, also joins grammatically equivalent elements; but correlative conjunctions always work in pairs: *both . . . and, either . . . or, neither . . . nor, not only . . . but also, whether . . . or.*

> *I do not care whether Roberta comes or she doesn't.*
> <small>┌—cl.—┐   ┌—cl.—┐</small>

> *It is not only attractive but also economical.*
> <small>adj.   adj.</small>

By contrast, SUBORDINATING CONJUNCTIONS connect unequivalent sentence elements; they introduce grammatically DEPENDENT CLAUSES (sometimes called SUBORDINATE CLAUSES) and connect them with INDEPENDENT CLAUSES. Some of the most common subordinating conjunctions are:

after	because	so that	whenever
although	before	than	where
as	even though	that	wherever
as if	how	though	while
as long as	if	unless	
as soon as	in order that	until	
as though	since	when	

┌────dep. cl.────┐ ┌────ind. cl.────┐
Although *we saw it,* *we did not believe it.*

┌────dep. cl.────┐ ┌────ind. cl.────┐
As soon as *we saw it,* *we did not believe it.*

┌────dep. cl.────┐ ┌────ind. cl.────┐
Until *we saw it,* *we did not believe it..*

┌────ind. cl.────┐ ┌────dep. cl.────┐
We will not believe it unless *we see it.*

Many of the words that function as conjunctions can also function as prepositions, adverbs, adjectives, or even pronouns. Consider, for example, *before, since, until,* and *that.* These words are conjunctions only if they serve as connectors but do not take an object:

conj.
I did not call, for *I knew you were busy.*

prep. obj.
I have a present for *you.*

conj.
Look before *you leap.*

prep.　　　obj.
I need the money before *next week.*

adv.
We have been introduced before.

conj.
I know that *you believe me.*

adj.
That *dog bit me.*

pron.
That *is what I said.*

Coordinating, correlative, and subordinating conjunctions are the only words actually called conjunctions; but certain other words also function as connectors. For example, a relative pronoun functions both as a pronoun and as a connector. It functions as a noun within its own dependent clause and connects this clause to an independent clause: *This salad is full of avocados, which give me hives.* (For a further discussion of relative pronouns, *see* II.B.4.; II.K.2.)

Similarly a conjunctive adverb—like *consequently, furthermore, however,* or *therefore*—functions as both an adverb and a connector. It modifies its clause and connects it to another clause, forming a compound sentence:

> *The physician said John was healthy;* nevertheless, *John felt ill.*
>
> *Karl hated college; he planned,* consequently, *to leave at the end of the term.*

(For a further discussion of conjunctive adverbs, *see* II.E.2.) Other words as well can function as connectors; among them, prepositions, relative adjectives, and relative adverbs.

H. Interjection

Interjections are words or short phrases used to express strong feeling. Familiar interjections include: *oh, alas, oh no, ah,* and *ssh.*

> *Oh no! I forgot my wallet.*
> *Oh. Did you ask for me?*
> *Oh? I had not heard you were sick.*
> *Ah, I remember.*
> *Darn, I ripped my shirt.*
> *Hurray! I finally finished.*

As these examples illustrate, an interjection is always separated from the rest of the sentence by a period, comma, question mark, or exclamation point.

I. Verbal

The three types of verbals—PARTICIPLES, GERUNDS, and INFINITIVES— are hybrid forms. They are derived from verbs and share some characteristics with verbs. Like verbs some verbals have tense and voice; some may have subjects or complements; and some may be modified by adverbs. But, even though these forms are derived from verbs, verbals *never* function as verbs. Rather, participles function as adjectives; gerunds function as nouns; and infinitives can function as nouns, adjectives, or adverbs.

1. PARTICIPLE All verbs have three participial forms indicating three different tenses:

> Present participle (present stem + *-ing*): *changing, falling, being*
> Past participle (a principal part of the verb): *changed, fallen, been*
> Perfect participle (*having* + past participle): *having changed, having fallen, having been*

Present and past participles are in fact used in the formation of some verb tenses (*was changing, has changed, had changed,* etc.; *see* II.C.).

It is only when they function as adjectives, however, that participles become verbals.

> *The startled burglar dropped the jewelry.*   (The past participle *startled* modifies the noun *burglar*.)
>
> *Tiptoeing, she left the room.*   (The present participle *tiptoeing* modifies the pronoun *she*.)
>
> *Having begun, they determined to finish.*   (The perfect participle *having begun* modifies the pronoun *they*.)

Despite their function as adjectives, participles retain many characteristics of verbs. For example, they are inflected, or change form, to indicate not only tense but also voice:

TENSE	ACTIVE VOICE	PASSIVE VOICE
Present participle	changing	being changed
Past participle		changed
Perfect participle	having changed	having been changed

Also, participles may take an object or complement:

> *Having sent him a letter, Mary waited for a reply.*   (The perfect participle *having sent* modifies *Mary; letter* is the direct object and *him* the indirect object of *having sent.*)
>
> *Being a physician, John quickly interpreted my symptoms.*   (The present participle *being* modifies *John; physician* is the complement of *being.*)

And like both verbs and adjectives, participles can be modified by adverbs:

adv.   part.
The conversation was thoroughly fascinating.

adv.   part.   adv.   part.
Finally having won his appeal, Frank felt completely vindicated.

2. GERUND   Gerunds look like present and perfect participles in that gerunds too end in *-ing:*

TENSE	ACTIVE VOICE	PASSIVE VOICE
Present	changing	being changed
Perfect	having changed	having been changed

Gerunds are distinguished from participles, however, by their use. Participles are used as adjectives, while gerunds are used only as nouns.

> Participle: *Changing my mind, I asked for chocolate rather than strawberry ice cream.*   (*Changing* modifies *I.*)
>
> Gerund: *She is notorious for changing her mind often.* (*Changing* is the object of the preposition *for.*)

Since gerunds are used as nouns, they can function in a sentence just as nouns do.

> Subject: *Drinking and driving do not mix.*
>
> Direct object: *The petulant child began crying.*
>
> Predicate noun: *My hobby is collecting maps.*
>
> Object of a preposition: *The teacher failed David for having cheated.*

Like any other nouns, gerunds can be modified by articles, possessives, and other limiting adjectives:

> art.   ger.
> *We watched the running of the Boston Marathon.*
> poss.   ger.   poss. ger.
> *I resent Ellen's insinuating that my crying was insincere.*
> d. adj.   ger.
> *This screaming must stop.*

And sometimes gerunds may be modified by descriptive adjectives:

> adj.   ger.
> *We watched the annual running of the Boston Marathon.*
> adj.   ger.
> *This angry screaming must stop.*

But, since gerunds retain some characteristics of verbs, they may also be modified by adverbs:

> ger.   adv.
> *I prefer running quickly.*

And, like verbs, gerunds can take subjects and objects:

> *Do you mind my asking you a question?*   (The entire gerund phrase *my asking you a question* is the direct object of the verb *do mind*. Within the phrase, *my*, a possessive pronoun, is the subject of the gerund *asking; question* is the direct object and *you* the indirect object of *asking*.

The only difficulty in using the gerund lies in deciding whether the subject of the gerund should be in the possessive case (*We ignored the child's whining*) or in the common, or objective, case (*I have no patience with children whining*). As a general rule, the possessive case is used, but there are exceptions.

a. Usually if the subject is a personal pronoun or a singular noun, it takes the possessive case:

> Our fighting *is destructive.*
> I understand Karen's needing *to take a vacation.*
> The dog's barking *woke me up.*

b. If the subject is plural, it may take the possessive or the common case:

> The firemen's agreeing *to strike surprised me.*
> The firemen agreeing *to strike surprised me.*

c. When the subject of the gerund is modified by other words, however, it usually takes the common case:

> In spite of the money from his inheritance running out,
> *John bought a new Mercedes-Benz.*
> The car's battery running down *made the lights dim.*

3. INFINITIVE   Infinitives are the base forms of verbs, usually preceded by the infinitive marker *to: to change, to drive, to be.* Infinitives can function as nouns, adjectives, or adverbs:

> Noun: To err *is human;* to forgive *divine.*
> Remember to call *me.*
> *Having promised* to help, *Robert arrived early.*

Adjective: *Willard's desire* to manipulate people *has cost him his friends.*   (The infinitive phrase *to manipulate people* modifies the noun *desire.*)

Adverb: *I am pleased* to meet *you.*   (The infinitive phrase *to meet you* modifies the predicate adjective *pleased.*)

After certain verbs such as *watch, help, hear, let,* and *see,* the infinitive appears without its marker *to,* making the infinitive harder to identify. Despite their elliptical form, however, these words are still infinitives:

> *I saw your kite fall.*   (The infinitive *fall* is an adjective
>   modifying *kite.*)
> *Everyone heard your dog bark.*   (The infinitive *bark*
>   is an adjective modifying *dog.*)

Although infinitives function as nouns, adjectives, or adverbs, they share some characteristics with verbs. They can have subjects, objects, and complements:

>   s.   infin.
> *George asked Helen to elope.*
>   infin.   obj.
> *He waited to hear Helen's reply.*
>   s.   infin.   comp.
> *She asked him to remain patient.*
>   infin.
> *If Helen and George get married, I wouldn't want to be*
>   comp.   comp.
>   *him or her!*

(Note that both the subject and the complement of an infinitive take the objective case. For a discussion of the reason for this, *see* III.C.1.b.)

And, like verbs, infinitives change form to indicate tense and voice:

TENSE	ACTIVE VOICE	PASSIVE VOICE
Present	to wash	to be washed
Present progressive	to be washing	———————
Perfect	to have washed	to have been washed
Past progressive	to have been washing	———————

J. Phrase

As the previous discussions have suggested, single words often function as sentence elements. But the job of a sentence element is not always performed by one word alone. Quite often words join together, and the group as a whole functions as a single part of speech and thus as a single sentence element. These groups of words functioning as single sentence elements are either PHRASES or CLAUSES.

Unlike a clause, which contains a subject and a verb, a phrase is any group of words that does not contain a subject-verb combination and that functions in a unit as a single part of speech. Phrases are often named according to the role they play. Hence a verb and all its auxiliaries is called a VERB PHRASE (*is forgotten, could be trying, should have been relaxing*). A noun and its cluster of modifiers that together perform noun functions is a NOUN PHRASE (for example, in *That very old man is my grandfather, that very old man* is a noun phrase functioning as the complete subject of the sentence). Phrases that function as adjectives are ADJECTIVAL PHRASES *(the man in the blue suit);* phrases that function as adverbs are ADVERBIAL PHRASES *(We are sorry to see you go);* and phrases that function as adverbs modifying an entire clause are ABSOLUTE PHRASES *(Their house being a national landmark, we thought they would welcome sightseers).* (For a discussion of absolute phrases, *see* I.E.)

More often, however, phrases are named not according to their function but according to the kind of word that introduces them: PREPOSITIONAL PHRASE, PARTICIPIAL PHRASE, GERUND PHRASE, and INFINITIVE PHRASE.

1. PREPOSITIONAL PHRASE   A prepositional phrase consists of a preposition, its object, and any modifiers of the object (*beside myself, in the way, under the bridge, without a friend in the world*). Prepositional phrases function usually as adjectives or adverbs and on rare occasions as nouns:

> *He is the man of my dreams.*   (used as an adjectival phrase modifying the noun *man*)
> *I was lost in my thoughts.*   (used as an adverbial phrase modifying the verb *lost*)
> *She looks radiant in the morning.*   (used as an adverbial phrase modifying the adjective *radiant*)
> *We talked late into the night.*   (used as an adverbial phrase modifying the adverb *late*)
> *After lunch is the best time for a nap.*   (used as a noun phrase serving as the subject of the sentence)

2. PARTICIPIAL PHRASE   A participial phrase consists of a present, past, or perfect participle and any of its objects, complements, or modifiers (*falling suddenly from the cliff, lifted in the air, having lent him my* *tuxedo*). Participial phrases most often function as adjectives and in that role should stand next to and clearly modify a noun or other nominal in the sentence:

> *Believing himself to be responsible, Jerry apologized.*
> *The door, locked from the inside, had to be broken down.*
> *I gave all my change to the man playing guitar on the street corner.*
> *Having been prepared for the worst, I was pleasantly surprised by the quality of the performance.*

When a participial phrase is placed next to a word that it does not modify, it is called a DANGLING (or MISRELATED) MODIFIER: *While washing the dishes, the doorbell rang.* (*See* III.D.1.)

Although most often used as adjectives, participial phrases sometimes serve as adverbs expressing manner or circumstance:

> *Provided that we have enough room, you are welcome to join us.*
> *Judging from my experience, you should have no difficulty passing the test.*
> *Looking at the problem from all sides, there seems to be no clear solution.*

Such participial phrases modify the entire clause rather than a particular noun or pronoun.

3. GERUND PHRASE   A gerund phrase consists of a gerund; its subject, if any; and all of its objects, complements, or modifiers. Gerund phrases always function as nouns (*i.e.*, they are noun phrases) and thus serve as subjects, objects, complements, or appositives:

> *Our campaigning for Smith helped her win the election.* (subject)
> *I enjoy shopping for antiques.*   (direct object)
> *He was offended by my interrupting him.*   (object of preposition)
> *The craft that I find the most rewarding is weaving rugs.* (predicate noun)
> *My dog's favorite pastime, chasing his tail, tires him out.* (appositive)

4. INFINITIVE PHRASE   An infinitive phrase includes an infinitive and any of its objects, complements, or modifiers. Infinitive phrases can function as nouns, adjectives, or adverbs:

> *I would like to finish my coffee.*   (noun functioning as
>   direct object)
> *I believed you to be my friend.*   (noun functioning as
>   object complement)
> *The book to be discussed is by Mark Twain.*   (adjective
>   modifying *book*)
> *I am ready to see you now.*   (adverb modifying *ready*)

Because there are so many different kinds of phrases, each able to function in many different ways, phrases are often found contained within other phrases. Consider, for example, the sentence *The man running down the street just missed the last bus. The man running down the street* is a noun phrase, functioning as the complete subject of the sentence. Within that noun phrase, however, are several other phrases. *Running down the street* is a participial phrase functioning as an adjective modifying *man. Down the street* is a prepositional phrase functioning as an adverb modifying *running.* And *the street* is a noun phrase functioning as the complete object of the preposition *down.*

K. Clause

In contrast to phrases, clauses are groups of words that *do* contain a subject-verb combination (*I went; if I believe; who understood; that Carol fell*). An INDEPENDENT CLAUSE can stand alone, forming a complete sentence: *Joan searched; she was gone; I have been downtown.* But a DEPENDENT CLAUSE, like a phrase, works as a part of speech, functioning within a sentence as a single sentence element, and is unable to stand alone. Like phrases, dependent clauses are named according to their function in a sentence: NOUN CLAUSE, ADJECTIVAL CLAUSE, and ADVERBIAL CLAUSE.

1. NOUN CLAUSE   Noun clauses can perform any noun function in a sentence. For example:

> *What he said is not worth repeating.*   (subject)
> *I will give what he said very little thought.*   (indirect
>   object)

I took what he said lightly.   (direct object)

He took responsibility for what he said.   (object of preposition)

Believing what he said would be a mistake.   (object of gerund)

Hearing what he said, I changed my opinion of him. (object of participle)

Many noun clauses, like those in the examples above, are introduced by indefinite relative pronouns and thus are sometimes called IN-DEFINITIVE RELATIVE CLAUSES (*see also* II.B.4.). Other noun clauses, however, are introduced by interrogative pronouns and adjectives, indefinite relative adjectives, relative adverbs, or the subordinating conjunction *whether:*

d.o.
He asked whom you were visiting.   (*Whom* is an interrogative pronoun introducing a noun clause in an indirect question. The whole noun clause is the direct object of the verb *asked.*)

d.o.
He asked which road leads to Rome.   (*Which* is an interrogative adjective introducing a noun clause in an indirect question. The whole noun clause is the direct object of the verb *asked.*)

d.o.
I know which road leads to Rome . . . , but I'm not going to tell him.   (In this case *which* is an indefinite relative adjective introducing the noun clause, which functions as the direct object of *know*. The sole difference between the previous example and this is that the former is an indirect question and this a declarative statement.)

s.
How Houdini performed his magic is still a secret.   (*How* is a relative adverb introducing the noun clause, which is the subject of the sentence.)

obj. of prep.
We argued about whether we should see a movie or a play.   (The conjunction *whether* introduces the noun clause, which is the object of the preposition *about.*)

Still other noun clauses are introduced by the subordinating conjunction *that:*

> s.
> *That you are very wealthy is a well-known fact.*
> d.o.
> *He knew that we were in town.*
>
> p.n.
> *Dan's reason for accepting the job was that he needed money.*

Sometimes, however, this subordinating conjunction is omitted, and the noun clause is elliptical:

> *He knew we were in town.*
> *Dan's reason for accepting the job was he needed money.*

2. ADJECTIVAL CLAUSE　Clauses that function as adjectives are also known as RELATIVE CLAUSES. They are usually introduced by a relative pronoun and modify the antecedent of the pronoun:

> ant.　pron.
> *The person who knocked on the door was the exterminator.*
> ant.　pron.
> *My mother, who lives in Cincinnati, is visiting me.*
> ant.　pron.
> *The book that I read last night was a thriller.*
> ant.　pron.
> *Lloyd is the man whom I was telling you about.*
> ant.　pron.
> *Your apple cake recipe, which I tried last night, is superb.*

The relative pronoun, however, may sometimes be omitted if it functions as a direct object or an object of a preposition in its own clause:

> *The book I read last night was a thriller.*
> *Lloyd is the man I was telling you about.*

Besides being introduced by relative pronouns, adjectival clauses may also be introduced by the relative adverbs *how, when, where, why, whenever,* and *wherever:*

> *This is the time when I need you the most.*
> *The city is tearing down the hospital where I was born.*

Adjectival clauses may be either RESTRICTIVE or NONRESTRICTIVE. If the clause is essential to identify or restrict the noun it modifies, it is restrictive:

> *The team that wins this game wins the series.*   (The clause *that wins this game* identifies which team wins the series.)
>
> *Anne introduced me to the woman whom I married.* (The clause *whom I married* identifies which woman Anne introduced me to.)
>
> *I will be staying with my cousin who lives in Miami.* (The clause *who lives in Miami* identifies which cousin I will be staying with.)
>
> *Men who dislike children do not make good fathers.* (The clause *who dislike children* restricts the group of all men, identifying which do not make good fathers.)

Nonrestrictive clauses do not identify the nouns they modify; rather, they provide additional information that is not essential to the sense of the sentence:

> *The Los Angeles Dodgers, who won this game, won the World Series.*
>
> *Anne introduced me to her friend, whom I later married.*
>
> *I will be staying with my cousin Sam, who lives in Miami.*
>
> *Tom, who dislikes children, is not a good father.*

Some grammarians insist upon the distinctive use of *that* to introduce restrictive clauses (*The man that I hired is an experienced painter*) and *which, who,* or *whom* to introduce purely descriptive nonrestrictive clauses (Mr. Jones, *whom I hired to redecorate the house, is an experienced painter*). In common practice, however, *that* is used only to introduce restrictive clauses, and *which* and *who* (or *whom*) may be used to introduce either type of clause. It is the sense of the sentence or the author's intent as signaled by the presence or absence of commas that determines whether the clause is restrictive or nonrestrictive. Whatever the introductory relative pronoun, nonrestrictive clauses are always set off from the main clause by commas, and restrictive clauses are never set off by commas:

> *The flowers that* (or *which*) *grow in my garden are roses.*
>
> *Roses, which grow in my garden, are my favorite flower.*

3. ADVERBIAL CLAUSE   Adverbial clauses function like adverbs to modify verbs, adjectives, other adverbs, or the entire sentence. Most often adverbial clauses are introduced by subordinating conjunctions (*see* II.G.):

> *When he finished eating, he sat gazing at the garden.*
>   (The clause modifies the verb *sat.*)
>
> *Leslie looked happy until he heard the news.*   (The clause modifies the adjective *happy.*)
>
> *The keys are upstairs where you left them.*   (The clause modifies the adverb *upstairs.*)

Sometimes, however, clauses that function as adverbs are introduced by indefinite relative pronouns, including *whatever, however, whichever,* and *whenever.* Such clauses modify the entire sentence.

> *Whatever Frank says, don't believe him.*
>
> *Whichever shirt you choose, make sure you have a tie to match.*
>
> *However much you wanted those flowers, you should not have picked them.*

4. The number of independent and dependent clauses in a sentence determines whether the sentence is simple, compound, complex, or compound-complex.

A SIMPLE SENTENCE has only one independent clause and no dependent clauses: *The sky became ominous.* Even if the subject or the predicate, or both, are compound, the sentence remains simple:

> *The sky and sea became ominous.*
>
> *The sky turned black and became ominous.*
>
> *The sky and sea became ominous and threatened to bring a storm.*

And even if the sentence contains many modifiers other than dependent clauses, the sentence still remains a simple one:

> *Seeing the sky and sea turn black and become ominous, we ran for shelter to protect ourselves from the upcoming storm.*

A COMPOUND SENTENCE contains two or more independent clauses and no dependent clauses:

> *Becky wanted to celebrate the anniversary by going out to dinner, but Jim preferred to watch the baseball game.*
>
> *At the restaurant the food was well prepared, the service was impeccable, and the atmosphere was romantic.*

A COMPLEX SENTENCE contains only one independent clause and one (or more) dependent clause:

> *Whenever I see Sir Laurence Olivier, I think of you.*
>
> *Because I thought that you would enjoy spending the evening out, and because I also thought that you would enjoy seeing Sir Laurence Olivier, who is your favorite actor, I reserved two tickets for tomorrow night's performance.*

A COMPOUND-COMPLEX sentence has two or more independent clauses and at least one dependent clause:

> *I looked, and, although I saw the elephant running down the street, I did not believe my eyes.*
>
> *When Archie comes home from a hard day at work, he wants a cold beer and a hot meal; and he expects that Edith will be there to wait on him.*

III. USAGE

One of a writer's primary goals is to compose sentences that convey meaning effectively. Success in this effort requires mastery of English usage—that is, the ability to put words together into patterns that are not only understandable but also generally acceptable. Sentences marred by ambiguous or otherwise inappropriate use of the language are considered ungrammatical and often elude comprehension. For example, a sentence like "The first robin of spring was sighted by Lorraine Lee, while walking along the branch of a tree, singing and in good view" is ambiguous to the point of being comical—is it the bird that is the tree-walking singer, or is it Lorraine? By contrast, a sentence like "I don't want no more carrots" may not be particularly difficult to understand, but it is equally unacceptable. Not only does the use of a double negative defy logic (if you "don't want no more carrots," then by implication you must want *some* more carrots—certainly not the meaning the writer intended); but it also violates the accepted conventions of good English usage and brands its writer as uneducated. Both sentences, imprecise and ungrammatical in their use of language, are ultimately ineffective.

The first two sections of this grammar review have described the formal features of modern English grammar—the ways words relate to one another in sentences and the ways words change to indicate these relationships. This section presents some of the most important ground rules in English grammar for using words precisely, effectively, and acceptably. Mastering these ground rules will help one write effectively and avoid the risk of losing, misleading, or alienating the reader.

A. Writing complete sentences

1. Sentence fragments should be avoided.

The sentence is the basic unit of communication in English, and, with a few exceptions, writing complete sentences is the standard practice. To be a complete sentence, a group of words must be able to stand alone as an independent unit, communicating a complete thought, and must have as its core a subject and a verb: *Charles works. They are. Marie loafed.* This subject-verb unit serves as the foundation supporting other dependent sentence elements—objects, complements, modifiers, etc.—which add depth and complexity to the basic thought: *Charles works long days and long nights, trying to make money for college. They are thoroughly satisfied with the work you completed. Before she got a job, Marie loafed at home every day.* When any one of these dependent elements is disconnected from the subject-verb unit and punctuated as a sentence, it is a SENTENCE FRAGMENT and is usually unacceptable in writing:

> *Charles works long days and long nights.* Trying to save money for college.
>
> *They are thoroughly satisfied.* With the work you completed.
>
> Before she got a job. *Marie loafed at home every day.*

In speech, where vocal intonations, facial expressions, and hand movements contribute to the meaning of an utterance, incomplete sentences are common and accepted. In writing, only certain sentence fragments are acceptable. INDEPENDENT SENTENCE FRAGMENTS, groups of words that function as independent units even though they do not have a subject-verb combination, are often used effectively in the following ways.

In dialogue:

> *"Who, me?" he asked.*
> *"No," I answered, "the other guy."*

As questions and exclamations:

> *Why the grumbling? Another loss on the stock market?*
> *What rotten luck!*

For special emphasis:

> *We were doomed. No food. No water. No way to escape.*

As transitions:

> *We have already discussed the strong points of the plan.*
> *Now for a discussion of the weak points.*

Independent sentence fragments may be used with discretion where they serve a real purpose. The sentence fragment that must always be avoided, however, is one that is logically or grammatically a part of the sentence that precedes or follows it. The word groups most commonly written as such sentence fragments are modifying phrases and clauses. These incorrect fragments can be remedied either by joining them to their related sentence, rewriting them as complete sentences or revising the entire passage.

Prepositional phrases:

> Fragment—*He left his family. With the bills unpaid and the electricity turned off.*
> Revision—*He left his family with the bills unpaid and the electricity turned off.*

Participial and absolute phrases:

> Fragment—*Joe displayed his gluttony. Eating an entire pizza.*
> Revision—*Joe displayed his gluttony, eating an entire pizza.*

Fragment—*Small European cars have become very popular. The reason being their low gas mileage.*

Revision—*Small European cars have become very popular. The reason for the popularity is their low gas mileage* OR *Small European cars have become very popular because of their low gas mileage.*

Adverbial clauses:

Fragment—*Violent thunderstorms occur occasionally. In fact, whenever a warm air mass and a cold air mass collide.*

Revision—*Violent thunderstorms occur whenever a warm air mass and a cold air mass collide.*

Fragment—*I will be pleased when you apologize. And when you begin to treat me with respect.*

Revision—*I will be pleased when you apologize and when you begin to treat me with respect.*

Adjectival clauses:

Fragment—*The children began to fight again. Which was the fourth time they fought today.*

Revision—*The children began to fight for the fourth time today.*

Phrases and clauses beginning with such words as *except, especially, for example, including, instead of, namely, such as,* or *thereby:*

Fragment—*The test will be easy for everyone. Especially for those who have studied.*

Revision—*The test will be easy, especially for those who have studied.*

Fragment—*There are a number of exercises that will flatten your stomach. Such as sit-ups and leg lifts.*

Revision—*There are a number of exercises, such as sit-ups and leg lifts, that will flatten your stomach.*

2. Run-on sentences should be avoided.

Independent clauses, if they are connected by coordinating conjunctions or properly punctuated, can be joined together to form compound sentences. Independent clauses may be connected simply with a coordinating conjunction (*and, but, or, for, yet, so*) if they are short (*She sang and I danced*); or with a comma and coordinating conjunction if the clauses are longer (*She sang several songs from the 1950s, and I accompanied her on the piano*). Independent clauses may also be joined by a semicolon alone (*She sang songs from the 1950s; I accompanied her on the piano*); or by a semicolon and a coordinating conjunction (*She sang songs from the 1950s, including the top hits of Teresa Brewer; but I did not recognize any of them*). Independent clauses in a series are joined, like other elements in a series, by commas or semicolons with a coordinating conjunction before the final element (*She sang songs from the 1950s, I played the piano, and Herb played the banjo*).

If, however, two or more independent clauses are punctuated as if they were one sentence, without an appropriate connector, they form a RUN-ON SENTENCE. There are two types of run-on sentences. COMMA SPLICES are formed when independent clauses are connected only with a comma:

> "I had no cash when I went to buy gas, luckily I had my credit card."

> "My brother gave me a hard time, however, he finally paid me the money he owed me."   (Conjunctive adverbs, like *however,* are not sufficient to join independent clauses. They must be preceded by a semicolon.)

In FUSED SENTENCES the independent clauses are fused together with no punctuation at all:

> "The Yankees won both games of the doubleheader the fans went home happy."

> "We will not hire him he does not seem responsible."

Comma splices and fused sentences are corrected in the same ways. Each of the following methods of revision will render the sentences grammatically correct. The decision about how to revise depends upon the sentence's context.

The independent clauses may be made into separate sentences:

> *I had no cash when I went to buy gas. Luckily I had my credit card.*

The independent clauses may be joined with a semicolon:

> *My brother gave me a hard time; however, he finally paid me the money he owed me.*

The independent clauses may be joined by a comma and a coordinating conjunction:

> *The Yankees won both games of the doubleheader, and the fans went home happy.*

The clauses may be joined by a subordinating conjunction, making the sentence a complex sentence:

> *We will not hire him because he does not seem responsible.*

B. Using subjects and verbs   *Agreement of Subjects and Verbs.*

1. Whenever possible, one subject should be used consistently throughout a sentence.

Changing the subject of a sentence in midstream often weakens the unity of a sentence and confuses a reader. Shifts from the impersonal pronoun *one* to the personal pronoun *you* are the most common: "Although one should be honest, you should also be discreet." This sentence can be corrected in a number of ways:

> *Although one should be honest, one should also be discreet.*
> *Although you should be honest, you should also be discreet.*
> *Although one should be honest, he should also be discreet.*

While the shift from *one* to *he* has generally gained acceptance in English, the use of the masculine pronoun *he* to refer to "people in general" has more recently fallen into disfavor in many circles. (*See* III.C.2.)

A more problematic shift in subject occurs in the sentence *"He* understood what he was supposed to do, but there was little *understanding* of why he was supposed to do it, and the possible *effects* of his actions were unforeseen by him." The subject of this sentence has been changed unnecessarily three times, making the sentence awkward and difficult to understand. Since the subject of all three clauses could easily be *he*, the sentence should be revised:

> *He understood what he was supposed to do, but he did*
> *not understand why he was supposed to do it, nor*
> *was he aware of the possible effects of his actions.*

2. A verb must agree with its subject in number.

In every clause a singular verb should be used with a singular subject and a plural verb with a plural subject: *He believes that you are innocent. They believe that you are guilty.* Matching subjects and verbs poses few problems as long as the subject and verb stand close to each other and the number of the subject is clear. For more problematic situations, however, there are some guidelines to follow.

a. Words and phrases intervening between the subject and verb do not affect the number of the subject:

> *The* behavior *of those six boys* was *deplorable.*
> *One of the lessons we learned* was *to be more careful.*
> *Terry, no less than Mary, Sue, and Jo,* was *responsible.*
> No one *besides members of the theater staff* belongs back *stage.*
> My watch, *in addition to my television and stereo,* was *stolen.*

The words *each, either,* and *neither,* when used as pronouns, are always singular, even when followed by a plural construction:

> *Each of the plans* has *some merit.*
> *Either of the alternatives* is *acceptable.*
> *Neither of my cakes* deserves *a blue ribbon.*

b. When the subject of a verb is a collective noun (*i.e.*, a noun like *couple, majority, number,* or *group* that is singular in form but may be plural in meaning), the question arises of whether to treat it as singular or plural. Some collective nouns are consistently treated as singular (*milk, sunlight, dust, news*) and take singular verbs and modifiers. Others are always treated as plural (*riches, people, police, clothes*). For still others, the intended meaning of the noun determines whether it is singular or plural. That is to say, if the group is being spoken of as a unit, the noun is singular; if the emphasis is on the individual members, the noun is plural: *The couple was married. A couple of women were there. The number of people present was overwhelming. A number of options were available.*

Similarly, when the subject of a verb is a quantity, such as *thirty children*, it is singular if it refers to a unit and plural if it refers to the individual members of a group: *Thirty children is the number we expected to enroll. Thirty children require a great deal of attention.*

The indefinite pronouns *every, everybody, everyone, anyone, nobody,* and *none* (which are also collectives) have traditionally been treated as singular in every instance, but usage is changing: *None of us is ready for seconds. None of us are willing to support your candidacy.*

It is especially important to be consistent when using collective nouns. Once a collective noun is determined to be singular or plural, all verbs and modifiers relating to it must consistently be singular or plural. Mixes such as the following should be avoided: "After the city *council is* elected tomorrow, *they* will take *their* seats" or "The *group* of delegates *have* arrived with *its* report."

c. When a compound subject is connected by *and*, it takes a plural verb: *Corn and lettuce have been the most successful crops in my garden. John and Eliot are going to help me.* But when the subjects are connected by *or, either . . . or, neither . . . nor,* or *not only . . . but also,* the verb agrees with the subject nearest the verb:

> *Neither corn nor lettuce has grown well in my garden.*
>
> *John or Eliot is going to help me.*
>
> *Either candy or flowers are an appropriate gift.*
>
> *Not only candlelight dinners but also soft music makes me feel romantic.*   (A writer who finds this construction awkward should recast the sentence entirely: *Soft music as well as candlelight dinners make me feel romantic* OR *Candlelight dinners make me feel romantic, and so does soft music.*)

d. When a predicate noun differs in number from a subject, the verb always agrees with the subject:

> *The bane of my existence is my three younger sisters.*
>
> *The object of his attention was the three horses in the center ring.*

This rule holds true even with the introductory (or expletive) construction *it is*. In this construction *it* serves as grammatical subject of the verb, with the real subject—what the sentence is about—following the verb:

> It is *the oil-producing nations that are responsible for the fuel shortage.*

e. When the subject is a clause, phrase, title, or quotation, it takes a singular verb:

> What I want to know is *why you came and when you are leaving.*
>
> Going to museums and theaters is *my favorite way to spend vacations.*
>
> "Some Girls" is *one of the Rolling Stones' most controversial songs.*
>
> "To have and to hold" is *part of the marriage vow.*

f. When the sentence begins with the introductory (or expletive) construction *there*, the number of the verb is determined by the delayed subject (*i.e.*, the noun or other nominal that follows the verb):

> *There* is *too much to do.*
>
> *There* are *too many* people *at this meeting.*

g. When the sentence begins with the pronoun *what,* the number of the verb depends upon whether the writer intends *what* to be singular or plural. Once *what* is identified as singular or plural, it must be treated consistently throughout the sentence:

> *What is needed is* (not "are") *some answers.*
>
> *What was annoying was* (not "were") *his insulting remarks.*
>
> *What are left are* (not "is") *a few odds and ends.*
>
> *What were lost were* (not "was") *three important letters.*

h. When the syntax of a sentence is inverted so that the verb precedes the subject, it is especially important that the verb agree with the real subject of the sentence rather than any earlier noun:

> *In the combination of democracy and individual freedoms lies* (not "lie") *the strength of the American political system.*
>
> *After we have compared the players' performances is* (not "are") *the time to pass judgment.*

i. A verb following a relative pronoun should agree with the pronoun's antecedent:

> *She is the only* one *who is old enough to join.*
> *They are the* ones *who have volunteered to help.*

Although this rule sounds clear, it is sometimes difficult to determine the actual antecedent of a pronoun, and thus it is difficult to determine the appropriate number for the verb. Consider, for example, the sentence *She is one of those women who is/are always on time.* Whether the verb should be singular or plural depends upon whether the antecedent of the pronoun is considered to be *one* or *women.*

Common usage leans toward regarding *one* as the subject, thus making the verb singular (*one of those women who is*). In formal English, however, *women* is considered to be the antecedent of the pronoun *who,* thus requiring the use of a plural verb (*one of those women who are*). Those who insist upon the singular *one* as the antecedent of *who* and choose to ignore the prepositional phrase *of the women* might resolve the dilemma by reducing *one of the women who* to *one woman who,* which clearly takes a singular verb: *She is one woman who is always on time.*

3. The subject and predicate of a clause must agree, or be compatible, in meaning.

Not every subject will logically make sense with every possible predicate. For example, one would never be tempted to say "A rainy day is a cat" or "My persistence got a job." But as sentences become more complex in meaning or in length, the likelihood of such faulty predication increases:

> "Johnson's article on Vietnam *is* an insight into war strategy."   (An article cannot *be* an insight, though it might *provide* an insight.)
> "My persistence paid off by *getting a job.*"   (Persistence itself cannot *get a job,* though it may help a *person* get a job.)

In order to make sense these sentences must be revised:

> *Johnson's article on Vietnam provides an insight into war strategy.*
> *My persistence paid off when I got a job.*

4. The sequence of tense of verbs and verbals should be consistent throughout a passage.

The first verb in a sentence or a paragraph controls the tense in that passage:

> *Because he had endurance, he won the dance marathon.*
>   (past tense)
> *Every day my father wakes me up and brings me the*
>   *morning paper.*   (present tense)

A writer switching to a different tense without having good reason runs the risk of confusing the reader: "Because he *had* endurance, he *wins* the dance marathon." "Every day my father *wakes* me and *will bring* me the morning paper."

Of course there is often good reason to switch tenses. If the verbs are actually intended to refer to different times, then different verb tenses must be used. For example:

>   pres. time   past time
> *I believe that in 1932 you were the prettiest girl in Amarillo.*
> pres. time   future time
> *I am sure that I will finish tomorrow.*
>   past time   pres. time
> *I forgot that you are the best cook in Peoria.*
>   past time   earlier past time
> *John told Marie that he had believed her to be dead.*
>   pres. time   future time
> *Mr. Jones canceled our appointment because he will be*
>   *out of town next Friday.*

For a complete list of verb tenses used to express different times, *see* II.C.2. The general guideline concerning tense is that in passages where all the verbs refer to the same time, the verb tenses should be the same:

> *He walked into my room, sat down in the chair, pounded*
> *his fist on the table, and said, "Aha!"*

And in passages where the verbs refer to different times, the tense of the first verb should control the tenses of all the verbs that follow:

> *I know that my friends have betrayed me and that I will*
> *have to proceed on my own.*
> *I knew that my friends had betrayed me and that I would*
> *have to proceed on my own.*

Verbals (infinitives, participles, and gerunds) also have tenses that are controlled by the tense of the main verb in the sentence. A *present* infinitive, *present* participle, or *present* gerund is used to show action at the same time as, or at a later time than, the time of the controlling verb:

> pres. pres. infiin.
> *I want to believe you.*
> past   pres. infin.
> *I began to mistrust you.*
> pres.   pres. infin.
> *I hope to be able to see you again.*
> pres. part.   past tense
> *Analyzing his comments, I decided he was insulting me.*
> pres. ger.   past perfect
> *Falling into debt had never been Ronald's intention.*

Past infinitives, *past* participles, and *past* gerunds are used to refer to a time earlier than that of the controlling verb:

> past   past infin.
> *The police believed the suspect to have robbed the bank.*
>   future   past infin.
> *When everyone else is studying, you will be glad to have
> finished early.*
> past part.   past
> *Having exhausted all her ideas, she began to consult her
> friends.*
> past ger.
> *Having gained membership at the country club did not
> past
> improve Leon's social standing.*

(For a discussion of the historical present tense often used in discussing a literary work, *see* A Glossary of Grammatical Terms: historical present.)

C. Using pronouns

1. A pronoun should always be in its proper case.

The personal pronouns (*he, she, it,* etc.) and the relative and interrogative pronoun *who* change form to indicate case. Choosing among the objective, subjective, or possessive cases for these pronouns is sometimes difficult, but the general rule to follow is that the case form of a pronoun is always determined by the pronoun's function in a clause.

a. SUBJECTIVE CASE   Whenever the pronoun is the subject of a verb, the pronoun takes the subjective case:

> *He enjoys watching basketball very much.*
> *They have no idea how intricate grammar is.*
> *Who goes there?*

Traditionally the subjective case has also been used when the pronoun is a subject complement: *It is I. That is he.* Some people disdain this usage as excessively fussy and formal, and in conversation the use of the objective case is generally accepted: "It's me." "That's him." In writing, however, it is best to follow standard usage:

> *It is we who must pay for your mistakes.*
> *The ushers were Robert and I.*

b. OBJECTIVE CASE   Whenever a pronoun functions as the direct or indirect object of a verb or verbal, or as the object of a preposition, the pronoun takes the objective case:

> *Herman told her to be careful.*   (direct object)
> *John gave him the benefit of the doubt.*   (indirect object)
> *Peter was determined to like them.*   (object of infinitive)
> *Seeing him in the distance, Sue began to jog in the other direction.*   (object of participle)
> *To whom were you speaking?*   (object of preposition)
> *Taunting us was Joseph's favorite pastime.*   (object of gerund)

Additionally, if a pronoun functions as the subject or complement of an infinitive, it, too, takes the objective case. The reason for this apparent anomaly is that the subject of an infinitive always plays two roles in a sentence: it functions simultaneously as subject of the infinitive and as either a direct object of the main verb, object of a preposition, or object of a verbal:

> *No one told us to attend Thursday's meeting.*   (subject of infinitive and direct object of the main verb *told*)

> *It would take a lifetime for* me *to understand particle*
> *physics.*   (subject of infinitive and object of prep-
> osition)

> *Wanting* them *to like him, Jerome became obsequious.*
> (subject of infinitive and object of the gerund *want-*
> *ing*)

Since the complement of an infinitive must agree with the subject—even
if the subject is not explicit but only implied—the complement, too,
must be in the objective case:

s.   comp.
You thought me *to be* whom?

comp.
I would not like to be him *when the IRS audits his tax return.*

c. POSSESSIVE CASE   Whenever a pronoun indicates possession, it takes
the possessive case. The first possessive form (the possessive adjective)
is used when the pronoun is a modifier standing next to a noun: *my hat,*
your scarf, our *mittens.* The second possessive form is used when the
pronoun stands after or apart from the noun: *this hat is* mine; *this scarf*
is yours; *these books,* yours and hers, *are long overdue.*

A gerund's subject (which is actually a possessive modifying the
gerund) also takes the possessive case:

> Their complaining *has done little to alleviate the problem.*
> Our production manager will accept no excuses for our
> failing *to meet the production schedule.*
> *Mona did not understand* my forgetting our *date.*

(For a more complete discussion of the subjects of gerunds, *see* II.I.2.)

The following, more specific guidelines offer help in determining
pronoun case in some particularly problematic situations.

d. Even if a pronoun is followed by an appositive, the case of the pronoun
is determined by the pronoun's function.

> app.
> We *teachers must organize a union to bargain with the*
> *recalcitrant administration.*   (subject takes the
> subjective case)

> app.
> *There is no other alternative for us* teachers *but to orga-*
> *nize a union.*   (object of preposition takes objec-
> tive case)

e. If the pronoun is part of a compound object, the pronoun remains in the objective case:

> *Herman told Jerry and me* (not "I") *to be careful.* (compound direct object)
>
> *My father bought my sister and me* (not "I") *wonderful Christmas presents.* (compound indirect object)

Similarly, if the pronoun is part of a compound subject or subject complement, it remains in the subjective case:

> *You and I* (not "me") *are going.* (compound subject)
>
> *The finalists are John and I* (not "me"). (compound subject complement)

f. The same rules used to determine case for the personal pronouns are used for the relative and interrogative pronouns *who, whom,* and *whose. Who* is the subjective case pronoun, *whom* the objective case pronoun, and *whose* the possessive case pronoun.

> *Who was at the door?* (subject)
>
> *For whom was your cutting remark intended?* (object of preposition)
>
> *Lina is the woman whose clothes I always borrow.* (possessive)

Deciding when to use *whose,* the possessive relative pronoun, usually poses little problem. In complex sentences, however, or in sentences that vary from the normal subject-verb-object pattern, difficulty often arises in choosing between *who* and *whom.* The key to solving the dilemma is to determine the exact function of the pronoun within its own clause.

> *Rockford worried all night about who was threatening his client.*
>
> (Here the entire clause *who was threatening his client* is the object of the preposition *about.* But the relative pronoun takes the subjective case because within its own clause it functions as the subject of the verb *was threatening.* The function of the clause does not affect the case of the pronoun; rather, the case is determined by the pronoun's function within the clause.)

He whom we believed actually lied to us.

(Here the relative pronoun takes the objective case because it is the object of the verb *believed*. Note that here the case of the relative pronoun's antecedent, *he*, does not affect the case of the relative pronoun itself; again the pronoun's case is determined by the pronoun's function within its own clause.)

Whom can we depend upon if not ourselves?

(Here the interrogative pronoun *whom* takes the objective case because it is the object of the preposition *upon:* "we can depend upon *whom*.")

The man who I think will win has great determination.

(This sentence is more complicated than those above because it has two dependent clauses embedded within the main clause, making it more difficult to figure out the pronoun's function and hence its appropriate case. *Who I think will win* is a relative clause modifying *man*. Within that relative clause, however, the noun clause "who . . . will win" is the direct object of the verb *think*. The relative pronoun *who* takes the subjective case because it functions as the subject of the verb *will win* ["I think *who* will win"].)

Whoever and *whomever* are generally governed by the same rules that govern *who* and *whom: whoever* is used as a subject within its own clause; *whomever* as an object:

> *Whoever finishes first is the winner.*
> *I asked whoever was in the room.*
> *Whomever he meets likes him.*
> *Send this to whomever you want.*

g. Choosing the correct case for a pronoun in a comparison often poses problems:

> *Jim is more conscientious than* we (not "us").
> *Tom is as strong as* I (not "me").
> *Andrew treated Susan better than* me (not "I").

The choice of case is simplified, however, when one remembers that *than* and *as* are not prepositions taking objects but are subordinating

conjunctions introducing clauses. Comparisons like those above are
actually elliptical, or incomplete, clauses:

> *Jim is more conscientious than we* [are].
>
> *Tom is as strong as I* [am].
>
> *Andrew treated Susan better than* [he treated] *me.*

The pronoun in such comparisons takes the subjective case if it is the
subject of the implied verb, and the objective case if it is the object.

Making the appropriate choice between the subjective and objective
case in comparisons often proves crucial to the meaning of the sentence.
Note the difference in meaning between these two sentences:

> *Louise loves bowling more than* [she loves] *me.*
>
> *Louise loves bowling more than I* [love bowling].

2. A pronoun referring to a specific person or thing should have a clear
antecedent and should agree with that antecedent in number, gender, and
person.

An antecedent is the word or group of words to which a pronoun refers.
In the sentence *Anne bought herself a hat, Anne* is the antecedent of
the pronoun *herself.* Most pronouns—particularly personal, relative,
and demonstrative pronouns—substitute for specific nouns or nominals
to avoid the tiresome repetition of nouns. However, some pronouns,
particularly indefinite and interrogative pronouns, cannot have antecedents because what they refer to is unspecified or unknown.

a. If a pronoun does need an antecedent, that antecedent must be explicitly and unambiguously stated. The antecedents of the pronouns in
the following sentences are vague, and as a result the sentences themselves become vague:

> "Whenever they argue, *it* turns into a full-fledged fight."
>   (Although *it* seems to refer to the argument, the
>   noun *argument* does not appear in the sentence,
>   leaving *it* without a clear antecedent.)
>
> "He protested against police brutality, saying that not
>   even *they* have the right to break the law."   (The
>   pronoun *they* apparently refers to the police, but
>   *police* appears in the sentence only as an attributive

noun [*i.e.,* an adjective] modifying *brutality.* Thus *police* cannot be an antecedent.)

These sentences should be revised and made more precise:

ant.   pron.
Whenever they have an argument, it turns into a full-

fledged fight.

ant.
He protested against the brutality practiced by some police,

pron.
saying that not even they have the right to break the

law.

In the next sentences the pronouns' antecedents are explicitly stated but are nonetheless ambiguous:

"James rented the apartment with the terrace because *it* was beautiful."   (Does *it* refer to the apartment or the terrace?)

"Ever since Ralph talked to Sam, *he* has been more agreeable."   (Who has been more agreeable, Ralph or Sam?)

These sentences too should be revised:

ant.   pron.
James rented the apartment because it had a beautiful terrace.

pron.   ant.
Ever since he talked to Sam, Ralph has been more agreeable.

Sometimes the demonstrative pronouns *this* and *that* have an antecedent that is not a single noun or other nominal but rather an entire phrase or clause. Provided no ambiguity results, this construction is acceptable:

Only a select audience patronizes the ballet. That is why ballet needs federal subsidies to survive.   (The antecedent of *that* is the entire previous sentence.)

Jerry denied the charges, but this only antagonized the arresting officer.   (*This* refers to Jerry's actions, which are described in the first clause.)

But pronouns without specific antecedents should be used carefully since they run the risk of being misunderstood:

> "Tony admitted to the judge that he had lied under oath.
> *This* surprised the entire courtroom."   (*This* has no specific antecedent. Was the courtroom surprised that Tony had lied or that he admitted his crime to the judge?)
> "Brad continued to apply for credit cards even though he was on the verge of filing for bankruptcy—*which* was certainly not a prudent financial maneuver." (Does *which* refer to the entire statement or *filing for bankruptcy?*)

To be safe it is always best to have a specific antecedent for every pronoun. If it seems impossible to supply an antecedent, the sentence should be revised:

> *Tony admitted to the judge that he had lied under oath.*
> *This confession surprised the entire courtroom.*
>
> *Even though Brad was on the verge of filing for bankruptcy,*
> *he imprudently continued to apply for credit cards.*

b. A pronoun must agree with its antecedent in number, gender, and person. For example, if the antecedent is singular and feminine, the pronoun must be singular and feminine; if the antecedent is plural, the pronoun must be plural:

> *Although the minister felt ill, he delivered his sermon.*
> *I was offered three jobs, but I did not want any of them.*
> *The elm tree has been a victim of a disease peculiar to its*
> (not "their") *species.*

A pronoun may have as its antecedent another pronoun rather than a noun. Confusion about agreement sometimes arises when certain indefinite pronouns—*anybody, anyone, each, everybody, everyone, nobody, no one, none, somebody,* and *someone*—serve as antecedents. These particular pronouns are usually considered singular and thus must be followed by singular pronouns:

> *Everyone must follow his* (not "their") *own conscience.*
> *I do not blame anyone for protecting his* (not "their") *own interests.*

However, if the indefinite pronoun is used to refer to the individual members of a group, a plural pronoun may follow it:

> None *of us are ready to abandon* our *material possessions.*
> Nobody *was afraid at first, but one by one they began to heed the warnings.*

Recently controversy has arisen over the use of *he, his,* and *him* following singular indefinite pronouns and other antecedents that have no specific gender (*A devoted coin* collector *should check* his *pennies daily*). One alternative to this construction is to use *he or she, his or her,* or *him or her:*

> Everyone *must follow* his or her *own conscience.*
> *A devoted coin* collector *should check* his or her *pennies daily.*

If such wordiness seems cumbersome, however, it can often be replaced by plural constructions:

> All people *must follow* their *own consciences.*
> *Devoted coin* collectors *should check* their *pennies daily.*

Similar confusion plagues agreement with collective nouns. Many collective nouns may be either singular or plural, depending upon whether they refer to a group as a whole or to the individual members of that group:

> *The defense lawyer selected the jury but was not pleased with it.*
> *The lawyer asked the jury to search their hearts before making a decision.*

Once a collective noun has been identified as singular or plural, it should be treated as such throughout the sentence. Shifts like those in the following sentences should be avoided: "The couple *is* celebrating *their* tenth wedding anniversary." "When the team *arrives, they* should be escorted to *their* hotel."

c. Pronouns that refer to "people in general" follow special rules. The pronouns *you, they, we,* and *one,* as well as the nouns *person* and *people,* are often used as indefinites to refer to "people in general" rather than to someone specific and thus do not have antecedents:

> *They say that all is fair in love and war.*
> *If we believe everything we are told, we will be disappointed.*
> *When one has doubts, one should not act rashly.*
> *People who deceive others usually deceive themselves.*
> *A person who asks for trouble should expect to get it.*

It often makes little difference which indefinite term is used in a sentence; but once an indefinite is introduced, it should be used consistently:

> *When one asks a silly question, one will get a silly answer.*
> *When you ask a silly question, you will get a silly answer.*
>   (Not "When *one* asks a silly question, *you* will get a silly answer.")

Alternatively, the indefinite term may be followed by the appropriate personal pronoun:

> *When one believes he is right, he should say so.*
> *When a person believes he is right, he should say so.*
> *When people believe they are right, they should say so.*

D. Using modifiers

1. A modifier should be clearly related to what it modifies.

A modifier changes the meaning of the word or group of words that it modifies. Thus it is crucial that a modifying word, phrase, or clause be clearly attached to what it is intended to describe or limit. Even slight differences in the placement of a modifier may affect the meaning of a sentence. Consider, for example, the changes caused by shifting the modifier *first* in the sentence *First the art critic raved about my painting:*

> *The first art critic raved about my painting.*
> *The art critic first raved about my painting.*
> *The art critic raved first about my painting.*
> *The art critic raved about my first painting.*

Each of these sentences has a different emphasis and hence a different meaning.

When care is not taken to keep related words together in a sentence, DANGLING, MISRELATED, or SQUINTING MODIFIERS may result. All three types of misplaced modifiers introduce confusion into a sentence and should be avoided.

a. Dangling modifiers dangle from the beginning or end of a sentence because they have no term in the sentence to modify. Participial phrases that introduce a sentence are often left dangling:

> "*Rising to the spirit of the occasion,* a toast was pro-
> posed."

Because the term following an introductory participial phrase should be the term modified, the sentence as it stands illogically suggests that a toast rose to the spirit of the occasion.

A careless writer may also leave an infinitive phrase dangling:

> "*To make such advances in research,* massive amounts of
> federal funding are needed."

This sentence too is illogical. It states that massive amounts of federal funding make advances in research, when in fact people or organizations make these advances.

In the two examples above, as in many sentences suffering from dangling modifiers, the dangling phrase precedes a clause in the passive voice—that is, a clause without an active subject. The easiest way to revise these sentences is to revise the main clause, providing an active subject for the introductory modifier to describe:

> *Rising to the spirit of the occasion,* Robert proposed a
> toast.
>
> *To make such advances in research,* our organization
> needs massive amounts of federal funding.

Other modifiers dangle because the word they are intended to modify is a possessive pronoun or the possessive form of a noun. Possessives, although formed from nouns and pronouns, always function as adjectives and hence cannot themselves be modified as adjectives:

> "This dilapidated Thunderbird is Sidney's, *who doesn't
> believe in maintenance.*"
>
> "*Under the instructor's supervision,* their talent devel-
> oped."

One way to eliminate the dangling modifier in these sentences is to sup-ply the noun or pronoun to be modified:

> This dilapidated Thunderbird belongs to Sidney, *who doesn't believe in maintenance.*
>
> *Under the instructor's supervision,* they developed their talent.

Sometimes the best way to eliminate a dangling modifier is to recon-struct the modifier itself. Transforming the modifier into an adverbial clause often solves the problem:

> "Being contrite, Harry's mistake was forgiven."
> *Since he was contrite, Harry's mistake was forgiven.*

b. A misrelated modifier does in fact modify a term in the sentence but does not stand next to that term. Thus it seems to modify an incorrect or inappropriate word. In the sentence "Running under the baseboard, I swatted at the elusive cockroach and missed it," the participial phrase *running under the baseboard* seems to refer to *I* rather than the term it should modify, *the elusive cockroach.* Placing the modifier directly adjacent to the term it modifies eliminates the confusion and uninten-tional humor:

> *I swatted at the elusive cockroach running under the baseboard and missed it.*

The principle here is simple. When related words in a sentence are separated, confusion ensues:

> "Pete will get his chance to run the 10-mile race in 10 minutes."   (This sentence suggests that Pete will sprint 10 miles in 10 minutes!)
> *In 10 minutes Pete will get his chance to run the 10-mile race.*
>
> "This information is from the article in the encyclopedia that Mary read."   (This sentence suggests that Mary read the entire encyclopedia.)
> *This information is from the article that Mary read in the encyclopedia.*
>
> "It is the responsibility of the young to change the future, not their parents."   (This sentence suggests that

the young are not supposed to change their parents—
certainly not the intended meaning.)

*It is the responsibility of the young, not their parents, to
change the future.*

c. A squinting modifier appears to modify two different terms simultaneously. In the sentence "Few readers can understand *thoroughly* ambiguous sentences," it is unclear whether the adverb *thoroughly* modifies
the verb *understand* or the adjective *ambiguous.* Is it that the sentences
in question are thoroughly ambiguous or that ambiguous sentences cannot be thoroughly understood? To eliminate the confusion, the modifier
should be clearly attached to one term or the other:

*Few readers can thoroughly understand ambiguous sen-
tences.*

*Few readers can understand sentences that are thoroughly
ambiguous.*

Here is another example that generates the same kind of confusion:
"Employees *only* may use this lounge." Does *only* modify *employees,*
saying that only they may use the lounge? Or does the sentence say that
this is the only lounge that employees may use? Judicious placement of
the modifier clarifies the problem:

Only employees may use this lounge.
Employees may use this lounge only.

2. The demonstrative adjectives *this, that, these,* and *those* must agree
with the terms they modify.

The singular adjectives *this* and *that* modify singular nouns; the plural
adjectives *these* and *those* modify plural nouns: *this flower, that plant;
these buds, those stems.* Problems in agreement sometimes occur when
these adjectives modify such words as *kind, sort, style,* or *type,* which
are often followed by prepositional phrases. The demonstrative adjective
must agree with the word modified—*kind, sort, type,* or *style*—and not
with the object of the preposition: *this kind of jeans* (not "these kind
of jeans"); *this style of shoes* (not "these style of shoes"); *these brands
of milk; these types of bread.*

3. A double possessive should be used only when needed to clarify
the meaning of a sentence.

Possessive relations can be indicated by an *'s,* or an apostrophe alone
if the noun is plural (*the plane's direction, the boys' behavior*), or by a

prepositional phrase beginning with *of* (*the direction of the plane, the behavior of the boys*). When the two possessive indicators are used together, the construction is called a DOUBLE POSSESSIVE.

Many authorities disapprove of the double possessive, and often the construction does prove to be superfluous. The sentence "I am borrowing a blouse of Mary's" can easily be revised to contain only one possessive: *I am borrowing Mary's blouse.* There are times, however, when both the *of*-phrase and the *'s* or apostrophe alone are needed to clarify the meaning of the sentence. Consider, for example, these two sentences:

> *I agree with this interpretation of Galbraith but not with that one.*
>
> *I agree with this interpretation of Galbraith's but not with that one.*

The first sentence refers to an analyst's interpretation of Galbraith. The double possessive in the second sentence is necessary to indicate that the sentence is about an interpretation *by* Galbraith, not one *of* Galbraith.

4. Double negatives should be avoided.

At one time the double negative was acceptable in English, as can be seen in the works of Chaucer, Shakespeare, and innumerable other noted writers. However, today in Standard English the use of two negative terms in one sentence brands the writer as uneducated. Thus one would write *I do not want any company* (not "I do not want no company") or *Nobody believed anything I said* (not "Nobody believed nothing I said").

Since the terms *hardly* and *scarcely* imply negation, using these words with other negative terms results in a double negative. Thus one would say *He will hardly be able to finish the race* rather than "He won't. hardly be able to finish the race." And such sentences as "He can't scarcely find none," which contains three negatives, need two negatives removed: *He can scarcely find any.*

E. Balancing sentences

1. Sentence elements that are parallel in meaning should be parallel in grammatical form.

Parallelism is one of the most fundamental principles of good writing. Simply stated, parallelism means that elements similar in function should also be similar in form. What follows is a list of the situations that most commonly call for parallelism:

a. Sentence elements linked in a series must be parallel.

> Faulty: "He *got* up from his chair, *strolls* into the kitchen, and *headed* straight for the refrigerator."   (Here the verb tenses are unparallel.)

> Revised: *He got up from his chair, strolled into the kitchen, and headed straight for the refrigerator.* (parallel past tense)

> Faulty: "*Sit-ups, lifting* weights, and *dancing* are good ways to build muscles."   (Here nouns and gerunds are mixed.)

> Revised: *Doing sit-ups, lifting weights, and dancing are good ways to build muscles.*   (parallel gerunds)

> Faulty: "In a momentous decision, the prime minister decided *to sever* diplomatic relations with a neighboring country, *declare* war, *to mobilize* his nation's army, and *sent* his troops across the border." (Here the infinitive structure is not maintained and verb tenses are mixed. The infinitive marker *to* must of course be used with the first in a series of infinitives; thereafter its use in the series is optional. But if used after the first infinitive, it must be used throughout.)

> Revised: *In a momentous decision, the prime minister decided to sever diplomatic relations with a neighboring country, declare war, mobilize his nation's army, and send his troops across the border.*   (parallel infinitives)

> *In a momentous decision, the prime minister decided to sever diplomatic relations with a neighboring country, to declare war, to mobilize his army, and to send troops across the border.*   (parallel infinitives)

b. Sentence elements joined by a coordinating conjunction must be parallel.

> Faulty: "My teacher is concerned *with good writing* and *that I think as clearly as possible.*"   (This sentence mixes a prepositional phrase and a clause. To

be parallel, the sentence must have two prepositional phrases, two clauses, or a preposition with a compound object.)

Revised: *My teacher is concerned with good writing and with clear thinking.*   (parallel prepositional phrases)

My teacher is concerned that I write well and that I think as clearly as possible.   (parallel clauses)

My teacher is concerned with good writing and clear thinking.   (parallel objects of the preposition)

c. Sentence elements joined by correlative conjunctions must be parallel.

Faulty: "According to James, Andrea's troubles are either *her own fault* or *her mother is to blame*."   (Each conjunction in the *either-or* pair should introduce the same grammatical construction. In this sentence *either* introduces a noun phrase, *her own fault*, while *or* introduces a clause, *her mother is to blame*.)

Revised: *According to James, Andrea's troubles are either her own fault or her mother's fault.*   (parallel noun phrases)

Faulty: "Jeremy not only *began talking when he was two years old* but also *reading when he was three*." (The second half of the construction needs a verb to serve as a counterpart to *began* in the first half.)

Revised: *Jeremy not only began talking when he was two years old but also started reading when he was three.* (parallel verb forms)

d. Sentence elements compared using constructions like *more than* or *as much as* must be parallel.

Faulty: "I like *swimming* more than *to skate*."   (Here a gerund is compared with an infinitive.)

Revised: *I like swimming more than skating.*   (parallel gerunds)

Faulty: *"Canoeing down the Mississippi* was even more exciting than *the Ohio*."   (Here a complete gerund phrase is being compared with an elliptical and hence unparallel gerund phrase.)

Revised: Canoeing down the Mississippi *was even more exciting than* canoeing down the Ohio.   (parallel gerund phrases)

e. Elements repeated in a sentence should be parallel.

Faulty: "Although my first objective was *getting my degree,* my second was *to get a job.*"   (Here first a gerund phrase and then an infinitive phrase serve as predicate nouns.)

Revised: *Although my first objective was* to get my degree, *my second was* to get a job.   (parallel infinitive phrases)

Faulty: "Last year *many people rode bicycles* while this year *few are ridden.*"   (Here an active verb construction is paired with a passive verb construction.)

Revised: *Last year* many people rode bicycles, *while this year* few people are riding them.   (parallel active verb constructions)

While parallelism is one of the most basic principles of good writing, it may also be the source of considerable confusion. Sometimes faulty parallelism is difficult to spot. Consider, for example, the sentence "Bruce's talent in playing the stock market made him *an authority on investments and a fortune.*" The phrase "an authority on investments and a fortune" appears to be perfectly balanced—two nouns that complement the verb *made* are joined by a coordinating conjunction. The apparent parallelism here is misleading, however, since the functions of the two terms joined by *and* are different. "An authority on investments" is an object complement referring back to the direct object *him:*

d.o.   obj. comp.

Bruce's talent . . . made him an authority on investments.

By contrast, "a fortune" is the direct object of the verb *made:*

i.o.   d.o.

Bruce's talent . . . made him a fortune.

Because the terms have different functions, they should not be presented as parallels: *Bruce's talent in playing the stock market made him an authority on investments and earned him a fortune.*

To add to the confusion, some constructions that appear to violate the rules of parallelism are actually acceptable. For example, *and which, but which, and who,* and *but who* are often acceptably used in sentences without a preceding *who-* or *which*-clause:

> *I gave away the dress I loved but which no longer fits.*
> *These stories, published in his early years and which deal chiefly with politics, are now anthologized.*
> *These are women working outside the home but who still enjoy their traditional domestic roles.*

These sentences appear to violate the rules of parallelism since the coordinating conjunctions seem to connect elements of dissimilar structure: ". . . I loved *but* which no longer fits"; ". . . published in his early years *and* which deal chiefly with politics"; ". . . working outside the home *but* who still enjoy their traditional domestic roles." In each case, however, the element preceding the conjunction is an elliptical clause and the element following the conjunction a full clause: *(which) I loved but which no longer fits; (which were) published in his early years and which deal chiefly with politics; (who are) working outside the home but who still enjoy their traditional domestic roles.* Thus the elements on either side of the conjunction are of equal grammatical status and are in fact parallel.

Constructions like *and which* do not always ensure parallel structure though and hence should not be used indiscriminately. In the following sentences *but which* and *and which* are both awkward and illogical:

> "I didn't like *her party* but *which you seemed to enjoy.*"
> "The cookies and flowers, *arriving in the morning* and *which were eaten by night,* were very welcome."

In these sentences the elements joined by coordinating conjunctions cannot possibly be construed as equal. In the first sentence *but* connects an independent clause (*I did not like her party*) with a dependent relative clause (*which you seemed to enjoy*). And in the second sentence *and* connects a participial phrase (*arriving in the morning*) with a relative clause (*which were eaten by night*). In these sentences the use of *and which* and *but which* does indeed violate the rules of parallel structure.

2. All words, phrases, and clauses necessary to the meaning of a sentence must be present in that sentence.

When words, phrases, or clauses necessary to the meaning of a sentence are omitted, awkwardness and ambiguity often result. The following sentences illustrate some common incomplete constructions that should be avoided:

a. "The physician tried to resuscitate the victim, but no success." Although the meaning of the sentence is clear, the grammatical structure is incorrect. There should be a verb after *but* to balance the sentence:

> *The physician tried to resuscitate the victim but had no success.*

b. "The bishops expressed belief and support of the pope's appeal." The nouns *belief* and *support* are not able to share the same preposition. *Belief* is generally followed by *in* and *support* by *of:*

> *The bishops expressed belief in and support of the pope's appeal.*

c. "Even the best writers have, and indeed will, construct faulty sentences." The auxiliaries *have* and *will* are followed by different principal parts of the verb. While *will* is completed by the present stem (*construct*), *have* needs to be completed by the past participle (*constructed*):

> *Even the best writers have constructed, and indeed will construct, faulty sentences.*

d. "The *Tribune* critic thought less of the movie than the *Sun-Times* critic." Here an essential verb, *did,* is missing in the second half of the comparison. Without this verb the sentence might be interpreted to mean that the *Tribune* critic thought less of the movie than he thought of the *Sun-Times* critic:

> *The* Tribune *critic thought less of the movie than the* Sun-Times *critic did.*

e. "The President believed the energy crisis the more pressing problem." To clarify the meaning of this sentence, the comparison must be completed: the energy crisis is more pressing than what?

> *The President believed the energy crisis to be a more pressing problem than the issue of tax reform.*

f. "No home-run hitter was as good or better than Hank Aaron." Here the first comparison, *as good as,* has not been completed before beginning the second comparison, *better than:*

> *No home-run hitter was as good as or better than Hank Aaron.*

g. "I believe your testimony is misleading and irrelevant." Without the essential subordinating conjunction *that* after the verb *believe,* the reader may momentarily misread the sentence as "I believe your testimony. . . ." With the conjunction *that* in its proper place, however, the possible ambiguity is eliminated:

> *I believe that your testimony is misleading and irrelevant.*

For a discussion of acceptable omissions in a sentence, *see* A Glossary of Grammatical Terms: elliptical construction.

IV. PUNCTUATION

Punctuation marks have three basic grammatical uses. They signal the end of sentences; they show the relationships between words and groups of words within sentences; and they set off direct quotations. By indicating which words in a piece of writing are grouped together, which are separated, and what emphasis should be put on words or groups of words, punctuation marks indicate a writer's intentions. Thus they clarify a writer's meaning in a sentence.

Beyond their grammatical uses (*i.e.,* those which help clarify the meaning of a sentence), punctuation marks also have certain conventional uses—that is, uses that occur regularly, even outside the context of a sentence. For example, the use of a period in *Jr.* or the punctuation in a date (*Jan. 13, 1979*) does not depend upon a writer's intention. Rather it follows a conventionally established group of rules accepted by most readers and writers. Within certain limits—fundamentally that the writing be clear—the rules of punctuation offer considerable flexibility, allowing individual writers to select a punctuation style that best conveys the ideas and tone of their work. While the *Britannica Book of English Usage,* for example, is in general lightly punctuated, the essays throughout the book display a range of styles characteristic of the individual authors.

A. Period   .

1. A period indicates a complete stop. Thus it is used at the end of every complete sentence that is not a direct question or an exclamation:

> *Ralph, who is obsessed with cleanliness, washes his car*
> *every Saturday.*
> *He is a very intelligent man.*
> *He asked if I wanted my car washed.*

The examples above—even the indirect question—are declarative sentences, that is, sentences that make statements. A period is also used at the end of many imperative requests:

> *Do your homework.*
> *Take a look at that beautiful sunset.*

Because an independent sentence fragment functions as a complete thought even though it lacks the traditional elements that constitute a sentence, it too can end with a period:

> *Do you think I'm responsible for this chaos?* Certainly not.
> *Our analysis of profits is complete.* Now for a look at costs.

When a sentence ends with a quotation, a period is always placed within the quotation marks, even if the quotation is not a complete sentence (*see also* **IV.N.**):

> *"No one will help you," my father said, emphasizing the*
> *words "no one."*

2. Other uses of the period are purely conventional.

a. A period is used with many abbreviations, indicating the omission of letters:

> *Mr. Carter*   *R.N.*   *Dr. Brothers*
> *Mlle. Leclerc*   *Ph.D.*   *Sept.*

In much current usage, however, periods are not used with acronyms (*i.e.*, abbreviations formed from the beginning letters of words in a name):

> *IRA* (Irish Republican Army)
> *NATO* (North Atlantic Treaty Organization)
> *NOW* (National Organization for Women)

If an abbreviation falls at the end of a sentence, one period suffices to end both the abbreviation and the sentence:

The U.S. just signed a peace agreement with the U.S.S.R.

b. A period is used after Roman or Arabic numerals as well as letters when they are used in enumerations:

   I. Core Curriculum
     A. English
       1. One course in composition
       2. One course in literature
     B. History
     C. Science
   II. Electives

In some enumerations, however, single parentheses are used after Arabic numerals and uncapitalized letters (*see* **IV.H.3.**).

c. A period is used between dollars and cents:

      $5.95   *$0.89*

d. A period is used in decimal numbers:

     3.1417   *.025*   *$5.6 million*

B. Question mark   ?

1. A question mark is primarily used at the end of a direct question:

     Do you know what time it is?
     How often do you attend baseball games?

This rule holds true even if the direct question is contained within a sentence:

     "Why is your life so confusing?" Jane asked Marco.
     He tried to convince everyone—did I hear him correctly?
     —that the world will end tomorrow.

More than one question mark may be used in a sentence that contains a series of direct questions:

     Did you enjoy your trip? meet interesting people? see the
     sights?

2. A question mark can also be used to transform a declarative sentence into a direct question in order to express surprise, hesitation, uncertainty, or incredulity:

> *You want me to rob a bank?*
> *He believes the world will end tomorrow?*
> *He hit four home runs in one game?*

3. A question mark, usually enclosed in parentheses, is used to indicate uncertainty about a person's birth date or death date:

> *Geoffrey Chaucer, 1340(?)–1400*

Parentheses around the question marks are not always necessary. For example, when a date is given in the context of a sentence, the entire date is enclosed in parentheses and the question mark needs no additional punctuation:

> *Geoffrey Chaucer (1340?–1400) was a civil servant as*
> *well as a poet.*

C. Exclamation point   !

An exclamation point indicates that a word, phrase, clause, or sentence is strongly stressed. Thus it is used after an emphatic interjection or at the end of an exclamatory phrase, clause, or sentence requiring special emphasis:

> *Ouch!*
> *No way!*
> *How painful it must be!*
> *Damn the torpedoes!*
> *He did it again!*

An exclamation point can also be used to add special emphasis to an imperative or a direct address:

> *Get out of here!*
> *Don't you act that way!*
> *Bill! Run for help!*

Because an exclamation point adds special emphasis, it should be used sparingly, and only to indicate genuine emotion. Overuse of the exclamation point deadens its effectiveness.

D. Comma   ,

The comma is the most frequently used—and misused—mark of punctuation. Its primary use is to separate words and groups of words from one another when such a separation helps clarify a sentence. By separating certain elements of a sentence, commas show the relationship between them. Commas indicate which words work together as complete phrases and clauses and which words are grammatically independent of each other, functioning as separate units.

1. A comma is used to separate independent clauses joined by the coordinating conjunctions *and, but, or, nor, for, so,* and *yet:*

> *The apartment was vacated by the old tenants, and new tenants moved in.*
> *Don't spend too much time on this project, but make sure you do a thorough job.*
> *Princess Grace is the mother of three children, yet she has never changed a diaper.*

If the independent clauses are short, the comma may be omitted:

> *Nixon resigned and Ford became President.*
> *I telephoned her but she was out.*

The comma should not be omitted, however, if the sentence could, even momentarily, be misread without it:

> *Mary cried, for the money was gone.*   (Not "Mary cried for the money. . . .")
> *I wanted nothing, but you wanted it all.*   (Not "I wanted nothing but you. . . .")

2. Commas are used either singly or in pairs to separate modifying clauses and phrases and other parenthetical elements from main (or independent) clauses:

a. TO SEPARATE MODIFIERS PRECEDING THE MAIN CLAUSE   A comma is used in writing much as a pause is used in speaking to indicate when an introductory modifier ends and the main clause begins:

If you decide to swim, watch out for the undertow. (introductory dependent clause)

Taunted by his friends, the young boy ran home crying. (introductory participial phrase)

To be honest, I never liked that tie. (introductory infinitive phrase)

Because of the dent in the hood of the car, the used car salesman deducted $100 from his price. (introductory prepositional phrase)

It is especially important to set off introductory modifiers with a comma if, without the comma, the sentence becomes even momentarily ambiguous:

Although the weather improved, our garden still refused to grow. (Without the comma the sentence may be misread as "Although the weather improved our garden. . . .")

Before long, workdays will average seven hours. (Without the comma the sentence may be misread as "Before long workdays. . . .")

Having been lied to before, he expected to be lied to again. (Without the comma the sentence may be misread as "Having been lied to before he expected to be lied to. . . .")

When no such confusion is possible and when the introductory modifier is clearly distinct from the main clause without a comma, the comma may be omitted. Thus the comma is often omitted after short introductory clauses and prepositional phrases:

When he travels he carries only one suitcase.
After dinner last night we went to the movies.

Finally, a comma is used after introductory transitional elements if the writer wishes to emphasize the transition:

Above all, he tried to do his best.
In addition, they endured hunger and privation.
John did not support the war; nevertheless, he answered his draft call without protest.

b. TO SEPARATE MODIFIERS FOLLOWING THE MAIN CLAUSE   A comma is used to separate a modifier following a main clause only if the modifier is not essential to the meaning of the sentence:

> *My boss gave me three weeks' vacation, for which I am grateful.*
>
> *He wrote until four in the morning, when he collapsed from exhaustion.*
>
> *I hate cats in general, although I like yours.*

If the modifier is necessary to complete the meaning of the sentence, no comma is used:

> *Bruce becomes shy whenever Elaine enters the room.*
>
> *Elaine follows Bruce everywhere to try to get his attention.*
>
> *I hate cats although I have three of them.*

c. TO SET OFF CERTAIN MODIFIERS AND PARENTHETICAL ELEMENTS WITHIN A SENTENCE   If a modifier or an appositive is restrictive—that is, if it is necessary for identifying to what or to whom it refers—that modifier or appositive is not set off by commas:

> *The Secretary of State Cyrus Vance spent the following two weeks in Cairo.*
>
> *The airplane crash that took 273 lives was the worst in U.S. aviation history.*
>
> *The job to be done requires great patience and fortitude.*

But if a modifier or appositive is nonrestrictive—that is, not essential for identifying to what or to whom it refers—it is set off from the rest of the sentence by a pair of commas:

> *Cyrus Vance, the Secretary of State, spent the following two weeks in Cairo.*
>
> *Yesterday's airplane crash, which was the worst in U.S. aviation history, took 273 lives.*
>
> *The job, to be done adequately, requires patience and fortitude.*

Pairs of commas are also used to separate other parenthetical elements (*i.e.,* words or groups of words that interrupt the main structure of the sentence) from the rest of the sentence. Many different grammatical structures can be parenthetical. Among the most common are those described below.

Independent clauses:

> *Marco and Jane,* it appears, *are on the verge of a brawl.*
> *Marco and Jane,* I believe, *will inevitably hurt each other.*

Transitional elements such as *moreover, however,* and *nevertheless:*

> *Conrad's later novels,* however, *are not as artistically successful as his earlier fiction.*
> *The new commander,* moreover, *has established an excellent rapport with his men.*

Direct addresses:

> *The time has come,* Lee, *for you and Bill to make peace.*
> *It is impossible,* my friend, *for me to help you.*

Contrasting or alternative words and phrases:

> *Steve Ovett,* not Sebastian Coe, *holds the world's record for the one-mile race.*
> *The gray,* or timber, *wolf is classified as an endangered species.*

Certain modifying phrases and clauses:

> *Professor Higginbottom is,* without a doubt, *the most boring lecturer in the university.*
> *Karl and Charles,* oddly enough, *were raised in the same neighborhood.*
> *The cost of living,* to be sure, *has risen dramatically.*
> *These instructions,* where they are applicable, *must be strictly followed.*
> *All* ready, meaning "entirely prepared," *is written as two words;* already, meaning "previously," *is written as one word.*

In all of the above examples, the parenthetical elements could be removed from the sentence without destroying the sentence's meaning. Of course, not all modifying phrases and clauses are parenthetical. Many are necessary to define or explain the term they modify. For example:

> Counsel *meaning "advice" is a noun;* counsel *meaning "to advise" is a verb.*
> *The place where we are supposed to meet is at the intersection of State and Randolph Streets.*

3. A comma is used to separate words, phrases, or clauses in a series:

> *The attic was stuffy, dusty, and dark.*
> *Julius Erving grabbed the rebound, dribbled the length of the floor, leaped into the air, and stuffed the ball into the basket.*
> *She is beautiful, she is intelligent, and she even cooks.*

Some writers omit the comma before the final coordinating conjunction in a series (*a house, a boat and a car*). Omission of the final comma, however, often causes ambiguity:

> *In the abandoned house we found broken furniture, an old refrigerator containing spoiled food and a stray cat.*

A comma before the final item in the series would make clear that the cat was not in the refrigerator. Thus consistent use of the comma ensures against the possibility of ambiguity.

A comma is also used to separate adjectives or adverbs modifying the same word if they are not separated by a coordinating conjunction:

> *The biography revealed a cold, withdrawn personality.*
> *The area was divided into two-mile-long, one-mile-wide tracts.*
> *He looked thoroughly, completely satisfied.*

4. A comma is used to separate an introductory or explanatory clause from a quotation:

> *When General McAuliffe received the German demand for the surrender of Bastogne, he replied, "Nuts!"*

A comma is also used to separate an explanatory clause following a quotation, provided the quotation is neither a direct question nor an exclamation:

> *"Man is the only animal that blushes. Or needs to," wrote Mark Twain.*

If, however, the quotation is an integral element in the clause, it is not set off by commas:

> *You must do more than simply say "I'm sorry."*

5. Because a comma separates words, it should never be placed between the main sentence elements that function together as a unit—subjects, verbs, and objects or complements. (Pairs of commas may, of course, set off parenthetical expressions that interrupt the flow of a clause.) While few people would be tempted to put a comma between a short subject and verb ("The dog, barked"), a long subject sometimes poses problems:

> *What Grace and I say to each other in the privacy of our own home is no concern of yours.*

Despite the length of the subject, it should not be separated from its verb with a comma.

Similarly no comma should come between a verb and its complements or objects: *Melissa considered Rhonda to be her best friend.* (Not "Melissa considered Rhonda, to be her best friend.") However, in the few cases in which the direct object precedes the subject and verb, the direct object should be followed by a comma to show that it is not the sentence's subject:

> *That Willie Mays was also a great defensive outfielder, few fans would dispute.*

6. Commas are used conventionally in certain contexts.

a. A comma is used to separate every three digits in a number of more than four digits: *45,450; 600,420; 5,479,323.* The comma is optional in four-digit numbers: *5,235* or *5235.* Some exceptions to this rule include: digits of years *(1979)*, telephone numbers *(555-1212)*, ZIP codes *(19149)*, serial numbers *(A1347962E)*, and numbers following a decimal point *(3.141593)*.

b. A comma is used in dates to separate the day of the month from the year: *July 4, 1776.* When just the month and year are given, a comma is optional: *July 1776* or *July, 1776.* In the context of a sentence, if a comma precedes the year, a comma should also be used to separate the year from the rest of the sentence: *The Declaration of Independence was adopted on July 4, 1776, in Philadelphia* BUT *The Declaration of Independence was adopted in July 1776 in Philadelphia.*

c. Commas are used to separate items in an address:

> *279 Kingsley Road, Evanston, Illinois*
> *Madison, Wisconsin*
> *Department of Miscellany, Omnium University*

In the context of a sentence commas are used to separate city and state, when both are used, from the rest of the sentence: *The Declaration of Independence was adopted in Philadelphia, Pa., on July 4, 1776.*

d. Commas are also used to separate titles following names:

> *John Law, J.D.*
> *Mortimer Feeny, Jr.*
> *William Pullin, Ph.D.*

E. Semicolon ;

1. The most common use of the semicolon is to join two independent statements that are closely related. The semicolon is especially appropriate as a connector if the second statement explains the first, providing additional, specific information:

> *My father greeted us warmly; we had not seen him for over a year.*
>
> *Calico fabrics are almost invariably woven in the "gray" state; that is, they retain the natural color of the raw cotton staple.*

But a semicolon is also the appropriate punctuation before a conjunctive adverb (such as *moreover, however, therefore,* or *indeed*) that shows the relation between the two clauses:

> *Vladimir Nabokov was not a native speaker of English; nevertheless, he wrote brilliant novels in that language.*

A semicolon may also be used before a coordinating conjunction to connect two related independent clauses if the clauses are long and complex or contain commas within them:

> *His paintings, which reflected a view of the world not generally shared by other artists of his time, seemed remote and strange to the casual viewer; and the influence of the newly discovered African primitives tended to startle a public brought up in the well-ordered world of neoclassicism.*

In a sentence this long the semicolon indicates more clearly where the second independent clause begins.

2. The second common use of the semicolon is to separate items in a series if the items themselves contain commas. Semicolons help prevent ambiguity, indicating clearly where each of the items ends:

> *The firm founded branches in Sydney, Australia; Ibadan, Nigeria; and New Delhi, India.*
>
> *The work is divided into an introduction; a historical survey, covering the period from approximately 1500 to the present; an analysis of current problems, with special emphasis on the United States; and a plan for the future.*

F. Colon :

Beyond its conventional uses, listed in IV.F.5. immediately below, the colon is basically an introducer. It can introduce quotations, figures, statements, or series of illustrative or amplifying terms.

1. Most commonly, a colon is used to introduce quotations, extracts, or speeches. Such quotations can also be introduced by a comma, but a colon makes the introduction more formal:

> *The Senator from Massachusetts firmly stated his position: "I will not run for President in 1980."*

2. A colon is used to introduce figures:

> *The rate of inflation varied from country to country: 94 percent in Brazil, 23 percent in Colombia.*

3. A colon is ordinarily used in place of "namely" or "for instance" to introduce series of words, phrases, or clauses. It also is used after such formal introductory phrases as "as follows" and "including the following":

> *The following types of bread are produced: rye, white, and whole wheat flavored with honey.*
>
> *Of particular value are the accounts of Greek travelers and historians: the geographer Strabo, Hecataeus of Miletus, and Herodotus.*
>
> *The struggling young author had only one objective: to write the great American novel.*
>
> *The recipe is as follows: Take two cups of flour. . . .*

When such informal introductory terms as *namely, for instance, like,* or *such as* are actually used in the statement, a colon is not required:

> *The trains ran in two directions, namely, north and south.*
>
> *Anthony Trollope is not as well known today as other Victorian authors such as Charles Dickens, George Eliot, and Thomas Hardy.*

Similarly a colon is not used if there is no genuine stop in the sentence before a list: *I asked the grocer to send me five pounds of flour, a pound of butter, and three cans of cat food.* A colon after *to send me* would separate the infinitive from its object.

Capitalizing elements following colons is sometimes problematic. A general rule to follow is that if items following a colon include complete sentences or if they are enumerated in a series, each item should be capitalized. Otherwise no capitalization is needed:

> *The conditions agreed upon were: (1) Hostilities would cease forthwith. . . . (2) An exchange of prisoners would take place. . . .*
>
> *The specifications are as follows:*
> *1. Height of not less than 25 feet*
> *2. Weight of not less than 50 pounds*

4. Much like a semicolon, a colon can be used between two independent clauses if the first clause introduces the second:

> *Slavery tended to persist in the Middle Eastern countries: in Saudi Arabia it was not abolished until well into the 20th century.*
>
> *The sailor had only two alternatives: he could either swim three miles to shore or be thrown in the brig.*

In such situations the second clause is not usually capitalized, but a capital may be used after a colon to lend special emphasis:

> *The truth of his statement was undeniable: We cannot trust others until we trust ourselves.*

5. Other uses of the colon are conventional.

a. A colon is used between hours and minutes in expressing time:

> *3:45* A.M.   *11:00* P.M.

b. A colon is used after the salutation of a business letter:

> *Dear Mr. Sagan:*   *Dear Sir:*

c. A colon is used between the title and subtitle of books:

> *Lad: A Dog*

d. A colon is used in ratios:

> *3:1*   *100:1*

G. Dash —

A dash is used—singly at the beginning or end of a sentence and in pairs in the midst of a sentence—to set off a word or group of words from the main structure of a sentence.

1. At the beginning or end of a sentence, a single dash is often used to emphasize the dramatic, ironic, or humorous qualities of the words it sets off:

> *Freedom of speech, freedom of worship, freedom from want, freedom from fear—these are the fundamentals of moral world order.*
>
> *The mayor knew the ward committeeman could be counted on to deliver the votes—for a price.*

2. A dash can also substitute as a less formal equivalent for a colon. Like a colon it can set off groups of words that summarize or provide additional details:

> *Another characteristic is their lack of differentiation of personality—i.e., one god can easily be equated with another.*
>
> *Maurice would settle for only the best—Gucci shoes on his feet, filet mignon on his table, and a Rolls-Royce in his garage.*

And like a colon, a dash can be used between two independent clauses, especially when the second clause develops, expands, or makes a surprising contrast with the first:

> *There were few pleasures for Gregory in his tiny hometown—he had lived too long in Chicago.*
>
> *James was reluctant to let go of his dream—but it was too late for someone his age to become a major league baseball player.*

3. A pair of dashes can be used to enclose parenthetical elements— that is, a word or group of words that interrupts the main flow of a sentence. In this function a dash provides a separation stronger than that of a comma:

> *The cook—not the caretaker—will assist you.*
>
> *No matter what the season—spring, summer, winter, or fall—the temperature in San Diego is virtually always 70 degrees.*
>
> *The general shuddered at the terrible toll—he never did get used to it—that the battle took in men's lives.*

4. A dash is a strong mark of punctuation and therefore supplants other punctuation that would ordinarily be appropriate in a given sentence. Because dashes, commas, colons, and semicolons are all used to separate, using a dash along with any of these other punctuation marks would be redundant.

> *I ate the following for dinner: soup, chicken, and salad* (not ". . . the following:—soup, chicken, and salad").

If we arrive late—after ten o'clock—we won't be seated
(not ". . . late—after ten o'clock—, we won't be
seated").

H. Parentheses ( )

Like the comma and the dash, parentheses primarily serve to set off
parenthetical information—words or groups of words that interrupt the
main structure of the sentence. The separation provided by the parentheses is less dramatic than that provided by the dash. Parentheses often
have the effect of removing the material from the main thrust of the
sentence, making it seem incidental or digressive.

1. Parentheses are used to set off words and groups of words that add
examples, definitions, or facts to the sentence without placing undue
emphasis on these additions:

> *A few tabloids (like the Chicago* Sun-Times*) are for the
> most part well written and well edited.*
>
> *The Peter Principle (that a person rises to his level of
> incompetence) has operated in this corporation for
> too long.*
>
> *Marco became extremely nervous (as he always does)
> when Jane entered the room.*

2. Parentheses are used to enclose incidental information, such as numbers, dates, references, and digressions from the main idea of the sentence:

> *You must vacate your apartment in thirty (30) days.*
>
> *The Eisenhower years (1952–60) are now generally con-
> sidered a period of apathy and conservatism.*
>
> *Naturally grown foods are good for your health (soy
> products are especially nutritious), but they are some-
> times difficult to find.*

3. Parentheses are also used to enclose numbers or letters that mark an
enumeration within a sentence:

> *Ralph had four major ambitions: (1) to make a lot of
> money, (2) to spend a lot of money, (3) to invest a
> lot of money, (4) to enjoy all his money.*

When the enumeration is presented in outline form, the period, or sometimes the single parenthesis, is used instead of the parentheses:

> 1. *History courses*
>   *a) Ancient History*
>   *b) World History*
> 2. *English courses*
>   *a) Medieval Poetry*
>   *b) Restoration Drama*

(*See also* IV.A.2.b.)

4. Parentheses may enclose complete statements that do not stand within other sentences. In such cases the final punctuation mark should remain inside the parentheses:

> *I am afraid Marco and Jane are not getting along. (Some things never change.)*
> *He grew up in rural Ireland. (This fact, omitted from many of his biographies, goes far toward explaining much of his later career.)*

When a complete sentence in parentheses occurs within another sentence, it needs neither capitalization nor a final period:

> *Although his speciality is Baroque music (he plays Handel especially well), he is best loved for his jazz interpretations.*

A question mark or exclamation point may, however, be placed within the parentheses:

> *After he lectured me for an hour (you would think I had purposely disobeyed him!), my boss fired me.*

As these two examples illustrate, marks of punctuation in the main sentence always follow the parentheses.

I. Brackets [ ]

Brackets are rarely used in most writing, but when they are used they have two very specific functions.

1. Brackets are primarily used to enclose a writer's own words when they are inserted in quoted material. A bracketed insertion is usually explanatory:

> *"There was nothing Ralph [Nader] and his safety-minded cohorts could have done to prevent the tragic air disaster."*

In this example the name enclosed within the brackets is not part of the original quotation but is necessary to clarify the reference.

The bracketed, italicized word *sic* (from Latin, meaning "thus it is") is interpolated into a quotation to indicate that an error or peculiarity in the quotation is being reproduced exactly as it was said or written:

> *"This is a worthful* [sic] *enterprise," said the inarticulate senator.*
> *According to the mayor's press release, the looters "did not create disorder; they perserved* [sic] *disorder."*

Alternatively, brackets can be used to insert a correction into the quotation:

> *"The bride's gown, decorated with handmade lace, was made of silk chiffon [actually it was crepe de chine]."*

2. Brackets are also used to enclose parenthetical material within parentheses:

> *(Later Lydia M. Child published* An appeal in Favor of That Class of Americans called Africans *[1833], the first antislavery volume published in the United States.)*

J. Ellipsis . . .

1. The ellipsis, which consists of three equally spaced points, is used to indicate that one or more words has been omitted from a quotation:

> *The Federal Communications Commission declared today that station licenses "would be renewed . . . using the ordinary procedures" and that "no outside political pressure . . . would be tolerated."*

2. Ellipsis points are used at the beginning of a formal quotation (*i.e.*, one introduced by a colon) to indicate that the quoted material does not begin with the beginning of a sentence:

> *The Hickenlooper amendment provided that: ". . . not-
> withstanding any other provision of law, no court in
> the United States shall decline . . . to make a determi-
> nation on the merits."*

3. At the beginning or end of short, informal quotations (*i.e.*, those preceded or followed by clauses or phrases set off by commas), it is not necessary to use ellipsis points even when the quoted material is incomplete. Such informal quotations should stand on their own as syntactically complete sentences and will begin with a capital letter, even if they were not capitalized in the original:

> *According to the Hickenlooper amendment, "Notwith-
> standing any other provision of law, no court in the
> United States shall decline . . . to make a determina-
> tion on the merits."*
>
> *As the signers of the Declaration of Independence decreed,
> "All men are created equal."*

4. If the quoted material is not syntactically complete, it should be made an integral part of the sentence that introduces it:

> *Unfortunately the Declaration of Independence did not
> stipulate that all women "are created equal."*

Any time a quotation—even a syntactically complete quotation—is made an integral part of the sentence introducing it, ellipses are not needed and capitalization is needed only to reproduce capitals in the original quotation:

> *The Hickenlooper amendment provided that "notwith-
> standing any other provision of law, no court in the
> United States shall decline . . . to make a determination
> on the merits."*
>
> *In Tennyson's poem, Ulysses desired "To strive, to seek,
> to find, and not to yield."*   (The capital used here
> reproduces that found in Tennyson's poem).

5. Punctuation accompanying an ellipsis sometimes poses problems to writers, but there are guidelines governing its use.

a. When an ellipsis occurs within the sentence, the three points alone are used:

> *"Surely goodness and mercy shall follow me . . . and I will dwell in the house of the Lord forever."*

b. Other punctuation may be used on either side of the ellipsis, however, to clarify the sense of the quotation or to help indicate what has been omitted:

> *"This statute applies to police, firemen, teachers, . . . and all other city employees."*
>
> *"Mayor Fields addressed his statement to teachers, policemen, firemen . . . : all city employees must reside in the city."*

c. If words are omitted between sentences in a quotation, the end punctuation of the first sentence should be retained, followed by three points:

> *Marco was in a rage over Jane's behavior: "She is constantly screaming at me! . . . I won't put up with it any more."*

d. If the last words of a quoted sentence are omitted, the final period precedes the ellipsis:

> *"In the absence of sufficient proof of guilt, we find the defendant to be innocent. . . ."*

e. Often, however, when the end punctuation is other than a period, the final punctuation may need to follow the ellipsis to help clarify the quotation:

> *"What is the end of Shylock's speech 'Hath not a Jew . . . ?' "*

6. When a whole line or more of verse, or a whole paragraph or more of prose, is omitted, a complete line of spaced points signals the omission:

> *He wandered through the summer's heat, the winter's cold,*
> *He was determined and restless, but daring and bold,*
> . . . .
> *Ralph, the traveling salesman, would not be outsold.*

7. An ellipsis is sometimes used in dialogue to indicate an interruption in thought or a dramatic falling off in speech:

"Do you think this is . . . ?" Mary whispered.

8. Outside of quotations, ellipses are sometimes used as the final punctuation of a sentence that is allowed to trail off and remain unfinished. Because in this instance the ellipsis itself serves as the final punctuation mark, no final period is needed:

The truth is sometimes hard to bear, but nevertheless . . .

K. Apostrophe '

Most of the uses of the apostrophe are conventional—that is, accepted practice, whether in or out of the context of a sentence.

1. The most common use of apostrophes is to signal the possessive case of nouns (*the book's cover, Janet's room*) and indefinite pronouns (*anyone's dream, nobody's fault*). (For a more complete discussion of the formation of possessives, *see* The Spelling Maze.)

2. The apostrophe is used to indicate the omission of one or more letters in common contractions: *didn't, don't, wouldn't, I'm, he'll.*

3. The apostrophe is also used to indicate the omission of one or more digits in a number, especially in dates:

We barely made it through the blizzard of '72.

When the date expresses a span of years, however, no apostrophe is needed:

World War II was fought during the years 1939–45.

4. An apostrophe is often used to form the plural of numbers, letters of the alphabet, and words being discussed as words:

*The 1950's are often considered years of apathy and con-
servatism.
Is your name spelled with three e's or four?
Your essay contains too many which's.*

Although many writers omit the apostrophe with such plurals—especially with numbers; *e.g.*, 1920s—it is especially important to use the apostrophe if confusion would otherwise result:

p's and q's (not "ps and qs")
Avoid using I's. (not "Is")

5. To convey the authenticity of dialectical speech, an apostrophe can be used, indicating that certain sounds and syllables of ordinary speech have been eliminated:

> *Then Pa said to Ma: "I'll be down at the south 40 choppin'*
> *wood, buildin' fences, and chewin' tabacky."*

The apostrophe should be used sparingly in this fashion.

L. Hyphen -

Hyphens are chiefly used to divide words that are incomplete at the end of a line of text, to separate prefixes in certain words, and to connect the parts of some compound words and phrases. (For a discussion of the use of hyphens, *see* The Spelling Maze.)

M. Slash /

1. The slash (sometimes called *virgule, slant,* or *solidus*) is used to separate two alternatives. It is used most often in the expression *and/or,* but it may be used in other circumstances:

> *Judge Sirica could have sentenced the burglar to five years*
> *in jail and/or a $50,000 fine but instead gave him*
> *immunity in return for testimony against his accom-*
> *plices.*
> *It disturbs me that you think this is an either/or situation.*
> *Why can't we compromise?*
> *His book is about the church/state controversy.*

(For a discussion of the problems with the expression *and/or, see* Verbal Quandaries from A to Z: and/or.)

2. The slash is also used to indicate the line divisions in a brief verse quotation that is integrated into the body of a paragraph:

> *When the poet Doggerel writes that the traveling salesman suffers "the heat and the cold/Because he is brave and restless, daring and bold," he defines modern man's existential situation.*

3. The slash may be used to express the word *per* in constructions like *feet per second squared (ft/sec²)*. It can also be used to express fractions *(3/4)* or dates written as figures *(6/28/79)*.

N. Quotation marks   " "

Quotation marks are among the most widely used marks of punctuation and have a number of specialized functions. They are used to: signal direct speech in dialogue; set off material quoted from other texts; mark particular titles, definitions, and translations; and call attention to words with special meanings or emphasis.

1. Quotation marks are used to set off direct speech in dialogue:

> *Before he spoke, Marco scratched his head. He then said,*
> *"I wish I knew why Jane despised me so."*
> *"Why don't you forget about her?" I asked.*
> *"Never!" Marco replied.*

In written dialogue each character's speech is placed in a separate paragraph. Whenever a speech extends more than one paragraph, quotation marks are used at the beginning of each paragraph, but the end quotes (*i.e.*, the last pair of quotation marks) occur only at the end of the final paragraph of the quotation:

> *Arthur bemoaned, "Ever since I was a young child, people have disliked me. The kids in the neighborhood wouldn't play with me. When I hid in hide and seek, my sisters wouldn't come seek me. . . .*
> *"As I grew older, the problem got worse. . . ."*

2. Quotation marks are used to set off material quoted verbatim. Such a quotation may be separated from the rest of the sentence by a colon or a comma, or it may be integrated into the writer's own sentence:

> *The Red Cross pamphlet states: "Please give blood today. You may save a life."*

"The Mongol hordes were particularly vicious," writes Professor Foulchild in his famous study of the invaders.

Senator Percy Flowers brought the Senate to a halt Monday by calling his colleague Jason Bumble "a devious fiend."

If a quotation is particularly long (some 100 words or more), it is set off from the text not by quotation marks but by indentation (on a double-spaced typed page, these quotations, sometimes called BLOCK QUOTATIONS, are usually single-spaced, unless on a typescript for publication, where *all* text is double-spaced.):

Professor Foulchild's moral revulsion at the Mongols' behavior is obvious:

> *They murdered, they pillaged, they plundered, they raped. Everywhere they went, everywhere they rode, there came destruction and terror. . . . Human life seemed worthless to them, and the glee they took in extinguishing life . . . points to an appalling lack of ordinary morality.*

When material is quoted (set either in quotation marks or as a block quotation), the quotation should be reproduced exactly. Any changes in the quotation should be enclosed in brackets, and omissions should be indicated by ellipsis points. (For a complete discussion of the use of brackets and ellipses within quotations, *see* IV.I. and IV.J., Brackets and Ellipsis. For a discussion of how to capitalize quotations, *see* V.A., Capitals.)

If a quotation contains another quotation within it, the internal quotation is set off by single quotation marks:

According to the article, "When Jones was asked about his involvement in the tax fraud scheme, he replied, 'No comment.' "

With a block quotation, however, double quotation marks signal the internal quote:

The newspaper article did not inspire confidence in Jones:

> *Jones has always been a reticent politician. Even in televised press conferences, he generally answers questions with a monosyllabic "yes" or "no." Thus it was not surprising that when Jones was asked about his involvement in the tax fraud scheme, he replied, "No comment."*

Short verse quotations (up to three lines) should be placed in quotation marks and integrated into the body of the text:

> *Poe's most famous line of verse is undoubtedly "Quoth the Raven, 'Nevermore.' "*

Longer verse quotations, like long prose quotations, are indented and single-spaced:

> *The poet Doggerel demonstrates the traveling salesman's dedication to his profession:*
>
> > *He wandered through the summer's heat, the winter's cold,*
> > *He was determined and restless, but daring and bold,*
> > . . . .
> > *Ralph, the traveling salesman, would not be outsold.*

Omissions, changes, and quotations within quotations are handled in verse quotations much as they are in prose quotations.

3. Quotation marks are used to set off titles of written works shorter than one volume and titles of other short works of art. For example, the titles of short poems, articles, essays, short stories, songs, book chapters, and also paintings are enclosed within quotation marks:

> *We spent one week of the semester studying Doggerel's great poem "Ralph, the Traveling Salesman."*
>
> *His new novel has 50 chapters, the last of which is called "The Chapter to End All Chapters" and is accompanied by an etching entitled "Terminus."*
>
> *Professor Foulchild's article "The Mongols and Their Saddles" is a fine study of an important but neglected area of Eurasian history.*

In most current usage the titles of long works, such as books, magazines, journals, operas, and symphonies, as well as the titles of poems that occupy an entire volume, are not set off by quotation marks; rather they are italicized. (Newspapers and magazines generally avoid italics in their text and use instead quotation marks for all titles.)

4. Quotation marks are used to emphasize or call attention to certain words or phrases. For example, quotation marks enclose unusual nicknames, appellations, or coinages:

Elroy "Crazylegs" Hirsch was one of the great running backs in football history.

Senator Joseph McCarthy's fear of the "red menace" is now considered the product of a troubled mind.

Using quotation marks in this fashion is a matter of discretion. Many words or phrases that once seemed unusual enough to merit quotation marks have now become a standard part of the language. For example, the phrase *third world countries* is now so commonly used that quotation marks around it would be superfluous.

Quotation marks are also used to emphasize that a word or group of words is being used as terminology and not to stand for a particular thing or concept:

Certain phrases like "third world countries" are not enclosed within quotation marks unless they are being discussed as words or phrases.

In his essay "Politics and the English Language," George Orwell bemoans the use of certain military euphemisms like "pacification" and "transfer of the civilian populace."

(Italics are equally acceptable to emphasize words used as terminology. In the case of definitions embedded in sentences, the word defined is usually italicized and the definition set off in quotation marks. *See* IV.N.5., below.)

Quotation marks may also be used to indicate that a writer is using a term derisively or finds a term inappropriate:

My "faithful" friend has just betrayed me.

The Nazi solution to the "Jewish Problem" was horrible beyond comprehension.

Finally, quotation marks call attention to words or phrases whose conventional meaning is insufficient or unacceptable in a particular context:

To ask whether a 10,000-line epic poem is a "better" kind of poem than a 14-line sonnet is to ask an irrelevant question.

5. Quotation marks are often used to enclose definitions or translations of words:

> *The German word* Gemütlichkeit *is difficult to translate,*
> *but it suggests something akin to "the quiet pleasures*
> *of hospitality" combined with "the enjoyment of*
> *conviviality."*
>
> *When used as an adjective,* intimate *means "in close*
> *physical or spiritual contact," but when used as a*
> *verb, it means "to suggest or to imply."*

6. Quotation marks present special problems when used in conjunction with other marks of punctuation. For the sake of clarity, the following conventions should be followed:

a. When quotations are preceded by such expressions as *he said, they asked, Bob replied,* or *someone suggested,* these expressions are usually separated from the quotation by a comma outside of the quotation marks:

> *Polonius said to Laertes, "To thine own self be true."*
> *Laertes should have replied, "Are you true to yourself?"*

If, however, the quotation is an integral element in the sentence, the comma is omitted:

> *The advice that Polonius gave Laertes was "to thine own*
> *self be true."*
> *This pretentious advice caused one critic to call Polonius*
> *"a fatuous man."*

(For rules of capitalization with quotations, *see* V.A.1.d.)

When the *he said*-construction follows the quotation, the quotation is usually separated from that construction by a comma within the quotation marks:

> *"To thine own self be true," Polonius advised Laertes.*

Similarly when the *he said*-construction occurs in the middle of a quotation, it is usually preceded by a comma within the quotation marks and also followed by a comma:

> *"I don't understand," said one Shakespeare critic, "why*
> *Laertes' father gave him such terrible advice."*

When the interrupted or completed quotation is a question or exclamation, it should be followed by a question mark or an exclamation point within the quotation marks:

> *"Why did my father give me that advice?" Laertes must have wondered.*
>
> *"To thine own self be true!" should have been Laertes' response.*

b. As a general rule commas and periods following the quoted material are placed inside the quotation marks, even if the quotation itself had no punctuation:

> *Polonius told Laertes, "To thine own self be true," but it is clear that this is pretentious advice from what one critic has called a "fatuous man."*

Colons and semicolons are always placed outside the quotation marks:

> *Polonius advised Laertes, "To thine own self be true"; and like much of what Polonius advised, this was hypocritical.*
>
> *"To thine own self be true": is this helpful advice?*

Question marks and exclamation points may be placed either inside or outside the quotation marks, depending upon the context of the sentence. If the quotation is itself a question or an exclamation, the question mark or exclamation point is included inside the quotation marks:

> *The prosecutor asked the accused, "With whom were you conspiring?"*
>
> *The irate defense attorney exclaimed, "I object!"*

However, when the question mark or exclamation point is not a part of the quotation, the end punctuation mark is placed after the quotation marks:

> *Do you believe that the prosecutor did not know why the defense attorney yelled "I object"?*
>
> *I am stunned that he did not know why the defense attorney yelled "I object"!*

When these marks of punctuation are placed outside the quotation marks, the reader assumes that the question or exclamation is posed by the writer of the entire sentence and not by the person or text being quoted.

Whether the end punctuation is inside or outside the quotation marks, this single mark of punctuation suffices to end the sentence.

V. SUNDRY CONVENTIONS

In addition to punctuation, various other points of grammar are governed by convention. It is generally accepted that the first letter of sentences and proper names be capitalized; that book titles be italicized; that *Mr.* and *Mrs.*, for example, be written as abbreviations; and that numbers rather than words generally be used to represent sums of money (*$5.36*). By following these accepted practices, a writer avoids confusing readers and calling undue attention to relatively unimportant points.

This section discusses the accepted conventions for using capitals, italics, abbreviations, and numbers and figures. The established practices governing punctuation are covered in Part IV, Punctuation; other matters of convention—spelling, formation of possessives and plurals, and hyphenation—are discussed in The Spelling Maze.

A. Capitals

Capital letters have a number of different uses. Some of these uses are fully accepted conventions, followed at all times; others are more flexible and may be used as a matter of choice.

1. Capitalizing the first letter of a sentence:

a. The first letter of every English sentence is always capitalized, whether the sentence is an independent clause or an independent sentence fragment:

> *I hope you can come to my party. You can? Wonderful!*

b. The first letter of a sentence contained within parentheses is capitalized if that sentence does not occur in the midst of another sentence.

> *Marco was loath to see Jane at Phil's house. (The last time they met there, Jane threw a carving fork at him.) But Marco agreed to go because of his affection for Phil.*

A parenthetical sentence occurring in the midst of another sentence, however, does not begin with a capital:

> *The police knew that the kidnaper would have to be taken by force (three days of negotiations were unsuccessful), so they prepared for the final violent confrontation.*

c. The first letter of a direct question contained within a sentence is capitalized:

> *My first thought was, What can I do to help my fellow man?*

d. The first letter of a direct quotation contained within a sentence is capitalized when the quotation begins the sentence or is set off from the sentence by an introductory phrase or clause:

> *"What can I do?" Bernice complained.*
> *According to my father, "What's good for the goose is good for the gander."*
> *The prime minister made an announcement: "This nation is at war."*

As in the examples above, quotations set off from the sentence introducing or concluding them should be able to stand alone as syntactically complete sentences.

If a quotation is not a complete sentence, it should be integrated into the sentence containing it:

> *"What's good for the goose" was the beginning of my father's favorite quotation.*

Whenever an integrated quotation—whether syntactically complete or not—occurs in mid-sentence, the first word of the quotation is not capitalized—unless, of course, that word is a proper noun or adjective or was capitalized in the original text:

> *The President declared today that this treaty is "essential to our national interests."*
> *My father always told me that "what's good for the goose is good for the gander."*

> *The faculty council recommended that "English composi-*
> *tion be required for all freshmen."*
> *What did Rossetti mean when he said that "A sonnet is a*
> *moment's monument"?*   (The capital letter is
> found in Rossetti's poem.)

The rules that apply for capitalizing short quotations also apply for capitalizing long block quotations.

e. If a quotation is interrupted in mid-sentence, the second part of that quotation does not begin with a capital:

> *"I want the nation to know," said the President, "that this*
> *treaty is essential to our national interests."*

f. The first letter of a sentence following a colon is not usually capitalized, but a capital may be used to lend special emphasis:

> *His idea was full of bravado: he would cross the Atlantic*
> *Ocean in a rowboat.*
> *The mandate was clear: All nations shall work for peace.*

2. Capitalizing the titles of books, poems, paintings, etc.:

The established practice for writing titles is to capitalize the first and last words of the title, the first word following a colon, and all other major words. Articles (*a, an, the*), conjunctions, and short prepositions, unless any are in key positions, are left in the lower case:

> *"Watching the Rhine: An Ecological Study of the River-*
> *bank"*
> What Makes Sammy Run?
> The Excursion

3. Capitalizing the words *I* and *O:*

The pronoun *I* is always capitalized. Likewise, the exclamation *O* is always capitalized:

> *O dear, what can I do!*
> *I have given you my life, O my country!*

The expression "oh" is not capitalized unless it is used at the beginning of a sentence.

4. Capitalizing proper names:

a. All proper names—those of people, places, business organizations, colleges, most ethnic groups, nations, cities, states, religious denominations, languages, ships, etc.—are capitalized. For example:

Evanston, Illinois	*Soviet Union*
Cummins Engine	*Bible*
DuPont	*Boy Scouts of America*
Sanyo	*Coors Beer*
U.S.S. Enterprise	*University of Pennsylvania*
Lutheran Church in America	*Lithuanians*

b. The names of specific institutions and their formal divisions are also capitalized. For example:

> *The Art Institute of Chicago*
> *Simmons College, Department of English*
> *Sullivan High School*
> *Scripps Oceanographic Institute*

Terms for institutions used in a general sense, however, are not capitalized: *university, high school, hospital.*

c. The names of many formally organized groups are capitalized, but terms for groups not formally organized are uncapitalized. For example: *Democratic Party, National Organization for Women, United Farm Workers, Daughters of the American Revolution;* BUT *the middle class, the women's liberation movement, the antinuclear power movement.*

d. Sacred names—*Yahweh, God, Virgin Mary, Allah, the Lamb of God,* etc.—are always capitalized. The pronouns referring to the deity and his manifestations are now often uncapitalized unless the meaning becomes unclear: *Let the Lord's work be done and his name praised* BUT *God created man in His image.*

e. Most adjectives derived from proper names are capitalized:

Greek city-states	*Shakespearean sonnets*
Flaubertian craftsmanship	*Einsteinian paradoxes*
Comtian ethics	*Roman numerals*

But many are not: *biblical verse, french fries, roman type, venetian blinds.*

f. When common nouns and adjectives are used as proper nouns and adjectives, they are capitalized: *the South, Spring semester, Northwest*

Passage; BUT *go south for the winter, spring cleaning, northwest New England.*

5. Capitalizing historical terms:

The names of historical events, periods, and concepts are often capitalized:

French Revolution	*Industrial Revolution*
Six-Day War	*Manifest Destiny*
Third Battle of Kharkov	*Russo-Japanese War*

6. Capitalizing dates and holidays:

The days of the week, months of the year, and names of holidays are capitalized: *Tuesday, January 12, 1979; June 6, 1944; Easter; Mother's Day.* (For capitalization of seasons, *see* V.A.4.f., above.)

7. Capitalizing titles, positions, names of relatives:

Titles used before proper names are generally capitalized:

Senator Proxmire	*General Dwight D. Eisenhower*
Professor Galbraith	*Aunt Bessie*

Apart from use with proper names, however, titles are not consistently capitalized. Certain full titles, such as *President of the United States* and *Chief Justice of the United States* are always capitalized; but when these titles are shortened (*the president, the chief justice*), they are often not capitalized. Others, like *colonel, senator,* or *father,* are often capitalized when they refer to a specific individual:

> *The Senator has missed only one roll-call vote in his entire six-year term. It takes determination, talent, hard work—and money—to become a senator.*
> *I call my father Father and my father-in-law Dad.*

Abbreviations, such as *M.D., Ph.D., J.D.,* or *M.S.W.,* that follow names are usually capitalized. (For further information about titles and forms of address, *see* A List of Honorifics that accompanies Preserving the Art of Letter Writing.)

B. Italics

Italic typeface is thin and slanting *like this type;* it is used in certain conventional situations to set words off from ordinary roman type like the type used in this sentence. In typed or handwritten matter, italics are indicated by underlining. Sometimes an entire text is printed in italics; for instance, most of the examples in this book. When a word or phrase within that italicized text needs itself to be italicized (*i.e.*, set off by contrasting type), it must be set in roman type—just the opposite of what is ordinarily done. The examples in Section V.B.2., immediately below, illustrate the different treatment of "italicized" phrases in regular roman type and in text that is itself italicized. The first example sentence in that section is set in roman type and the foreign phrase in italic type. The second example sentence is set entirely in italic, with the foreign phrase, normally italicized, set in roman type. In order to show clearly the ordinary treatment of italics, in this section alone of *All You Need to Know About Grammar* full-sentence examples are set in roman type rather than the italic type used elsewhere.

Italics have a number of standard uses:

1. Italicizing titles:

Italics are used to indicate the titles of books, very lengthy poems, magazines, motion pictures, periodicals, newspapers, and other large works:

The Golden Bowl	*Paradise Lost*
The Iliad	*Chicago Tribune*
The Atlantic Monthly	*The New York Times*

(For the styling of titles of shorter works, *see* IV.N.3.)

2. Italicizing foreign words:

Italics are used to indicate foreign words not assimilated into Standard English:

Good defense is the *sine qua non* of a winning baseball team.

For some the Equal Rights Amendment has become a cause célèbre.

(For an explanation of the different treatment of italic type in these examples, *see* the introductory remarks at the beginning of Section V.)

Scientific and technical terms, especially those in Latin, are also italicized:

Populus tremuloides

Ursus horribilus californicus

As in this book, italics are often used with familiar Latin abbreviations such as *cf., i.e., e.g.,* and *q.v.;* but opinion is divided on this point, and italics are not uniformly required. Whatever the style selected, be consistent about italicizing such abbreviations.

While many foreign words and expressions are italicized, some have become so familiar that they are no longer set off; for example, ad hoc, blasé, blitzkrieg, bourgeoisie, cliché, and tableau. If you cannot find a given foreign word or phrase in a good English dictionary, it is safe to assume that it needs to be italicized.

3. Italicizing words used as words:

Like quotation marks, italics may be used to indicate that words are being discussed as words:

> Some words, like *contingent* and *contiguous,* look similar
> but in fact have different meanings.

In most circumstances it makes little difference whether italics or quotation marks are used to signal that a word is being discussed as a word —provided the punctuation selected is used consistently. In definitions, however, it is best to put the word being defined in italics and to enclose the definition in quotation marks:

> *Stationary,* an adjective meaning "fixed in one place,"
> should not be confused with *stationery,* a noun
> meaning "writing supplies."

4. Italicizing words for emphasis:

Italics may be used to indicate that a word or phrase should be read with emphasis. Excessive use of italics for emphasis, however, weakens a piece of writing and should not substitute for careful explanation ("Wasn't dinner *awful?*"). The best guideline for using italics effectively is to use them to emphasize a word or phrase only when the emphasis helps clarify a sentence:

> De Tocqueville believed that racial disharmony would be
> *the* problem in America's future.

Italics may be used to emphasize words or phrases within a quoted passage, but a writer must make clear that he or she, not the author of the passage, is responsible for the italics:

> Martin Luther King, Jr., did not imply that all oppressed people
> resign themselves to oppression. What he said was that "In every

movement toward freedom *some* of the oppressed prefer to remain oppressed." (italics added)

C. Abbreviations

Abbreviations are primarily used to save space. Their use poses two problems: knowing their meaning and knowing where they are appropriate. Some standard abbreviations, such as *Mr., Dr.,* and *Jr.,* have become so familiar that they are appropriate in all written contexts. Others are appropriate only in informal writing. Still other abbreviations should be reserved for use in footnotes and other citations.

1. Standard abbreviations:

a. Abbreviated courtesy titles, such as *Mr., Mrs., Ms., Mlle., Mme.,* and *Dr.,* are always appropriate before proper names.

b. Academic degrees and certain other designations, such as *M.D., D.D., Ph.D., M.A., LL.D., Jr., Sr.,* and *Esq.,* are appropriate after proper names.

c. The abbreviations B.C. (Before Christ) and A.D. (Anno Domini) are appropriately used with dates when their absence would result in confusion:

> *He lived from 42* B.C. *to* A.D. *10.* (Note that B.C. follows the date while A.D. precedes it.)

d. The abbreviations A.M. and P.M. are appropriately used after time expressed in figures: *8:30* A.M., *10:00* P.M.

e. The acronyms (*i.e.,* abbreviations formed from the initial letters of a name) of certain organizations are acceptable abbreviations: *NATO, FBI, ROTC, HUD.* (Note that these acronyms generally do not have periods after the letters.)

Certain scientific terms can be abbreviated with an acronym. Such acronyms are appropriate after the full term has been identified:

> *Tetrahydrocannabinol (THC) is the active ingredient in marijuana. THC has been found effective in relieving the pressure of glaucoma.*

2. Using abbreviations in formal writing:

Except for the standard abbreviations listed above, it is best to avoid abbreviations in formal writing. The following types of words, often abbreviated in informal writing, are not generally abbreviated in the main body of a text.

> Locations: *Illinois, Cincinnati, United States*
>
> Given names: *Robert, James, Charles*
>
> Days, months, and holidays: *Tuesday, September, Christmas*
>
> Titles: *President, Senator, General*
>
> Units of measure: *feet, hours, pounds, grams* (except in technical texts)

3. Using abbreviations in citations:

Many abbreviations that are not appropriately used in the main text of an essay are commonly used to save space in footnotes, parenthetical references, and bibliographies. These abbreviations refer to examples, illustrations, or works consulted. (For a glossary of these and other abbreviations, *see* Abbreviations: An Abbreviated Guide.)

D. Numbers

The rules governing when to write out numbers as words (*fifty-three*) and when to use figures (*53*) are not universal. Scientific and technical styles generally use figures in every instance. Journalistic style prefers the use of words for numbers up to 10 and figures for large numbers. Many book styles use figures for numbers over 100. The style for this book uses words for one-digit numbers and figures for all numbers that are two or more digits. Another common convention in general writing is to use words for all numbers that can be expressed in one or two words (*six, forty, seven hundred, five million*) and figures for all other numbers (*143; 7569; 54,357*).

Despite the flexible styling of numbers, there are certain circumstances in which figures are called for and other circumstances in which words are required.

1. Writing figures:

Figures are customarily used in the situations described below.

> Dates: *June 6, 1944; 6/6/44*
>
> Addresses: *1905 Carney Place, Apt. 4f, Chicago, Illinois 60699*
>
> Decimals and sums of money: *3.1416; $5.79*

Hours: *5:30* A.M.; *6:00* P.M. (but *six o'clock*)
Page numbers: *pp. 147–153; p. 13; page 6*

When numbers are written in a series, words and figures should not be mixed. Hence, if any one number in the series should be written as a figure, all the numbers should be written as figures:

> *The candidates received, respectively, 3 votes, 25 votes, and 139 votes.*
>
> *We expect that there will be from 90 to 125 people at the reception.*

The plural of a figure is formed using *s* or *'s* (*see* The Spelling Maze).

2. Writing numbers as words:

Numbers at the beginning of the sentence should always be written as words.

> *Twenty thousand dollars a year is a very good starting salary.*

If the number is too cumbersome, however, the entire sentence should be recast so that the number comes later in the sentence.

People's ages are, by convention, always written out, except in newspapers or magazines.

> *Henry was twenty-three when he arrived in Paris.*

3. Writing fractions:

Fractions are customarily set as figures when used in tables, attached to other numbers (*5½*), or written as part of a series of numbers (*½, ⅔, ⅞, ⅓*). In text, fractions are most often written as words, especially if the fraction is simple. Fractions functioning as adjectives or adverbs are always hyphenated.

> *I am two-thirds finished.*
> *This diamond weighs one-half carat.*

Hyphenating fractions that function as nouns is optional.

> *Nine-tenths of the work is finished.*
> *We divided the territory, each taking one half.*

4. Using Roman numerals:

Arabic numerals (*1, 2, 3, 4* . . .) are used in most contexts, but Roman numerals (*I, II, III, IV* . . .) have some conventional uses. Roman numerals are used in outlines and headings. They also are used to designate sections of articles, poems, books, and plays (*Act I, scene ii*). Lowercase Roman numerals are used to designate the pages that precede the main text of a book (*pp. vi–xiv*).

5. Using ordinal numbers:

The primary use of ordinal numbers (*first, second, third; 1st, 2nd, 3rd*) is to designate divisions of time, space, and action: *the first half, second in line, the third mistake, the eleventh hour.*
Ordinal numbers also occur in enumerations. Except in technical enumerations, ordinal numbers are always spelled out.

> *John had three goals in his life: first, he wanted to make a lot of money; second, he wanted to spend a lot of money; and third, he wanted to enjoy all his money.*

While such ordinal forms as *firstly, secondly,* and *thirdly* are not incorrect, most writers prefer the forms *first, second,* and *third* for these ordinal numbers.

A Glossary of Grammatical Terms

absolute As a grammatical term, *absolute* usually means "grammatically independent." The word is used to refer to sentence elements that clearly belong to a sentence but which have no specific grammatical connection with the rest of the sentence (*Your attitude, to be honest, is reprehensible.*) Among the most common absolutes are interjections (*Ssh, you'll disturb the watchdog!*) and direct addresses (*Have you finished your dinner, Mr. Smith?*). *See also* **absolute phrase.**

absolute adjective Absolute adjectives are adjectives like *unique*, *mutual*, and *perfect*, denoting qualities that are considered absolute or complete. Theoretically there are no degrees of uniqueness, perfection, or mutuality; something is either unique, perfect, or mutual, or it is not. In practice, however, people often refer to things as being more or less unique, more or less mutual, and more or less perfect; but some grammarians insist that only the adverbs *almost* and *nearly* are appropriately used with absolute adjectives to indicate degree (*almost perfect*). For a discussion of the problems in forming the comparatives and superlatives of absolute adjectives, *see* Grammar: II.D.1.b.

absolute phrase Absolute phrases are grammatically independent of any particular sentence element and act like adverbs modifying an entire sentence. Most absolute phrases are participial phrases containing the noun that the participal modifies: *This is the wisest decision, all things considered. Jason being a baseball enthusiast, he explained the infield fly rule in great detail.*

abstract noun Abstract nouns name intangible things like ideas, qualities, relationships, and emotions; for example, *equality, perseverance, brotherhood*, and *envy*. By contrast CONCRETE NOUNS* name things that can be touched: *rock, raincoat, mother*. *See also* **noun.**

---

*In this glossary many grammatical terms important to the discussion in a particular entry are set off in SMALL CAPITAL LETTERS. These terms are defined either at that point in the text or in a separate entry in the glossary.

accusative *See* **case.**

active voice *See* **voice.**

adjectival The term *adjectival* means "functioning as an adjective" and is used to refer to clauses and phrases that function as adjectives: adjectival clause and adjectival phrase. As well, nouns functioning as adjectives are often called adjectivals, or ATTRIBUTIVES. *See also* **attributive.**

adjectival clause *See* **clause; relative clause.**

adjective An adjective is a word used to modify a noun or another nominal; that is, a pronoun or a phrase or clause used as a noun. Some adjectives describe nominals, naming a characteristic or a quality (*a blue dress, a perfect way to proceed*); other adjectives limit nominals, making them more specific (*my diary, that book, two books to read*).

As in the examples above, adjectives usually precede the words they modify; such adjectives are called ATTRIBUTIVE ADJECTIVES. But some adjectives, called PREDICATE ADJECTIVES, occur in the predicate of a sentence, following a linking verb like *is, seem, become,* or *appear.* In *The milk is sour,* the predicate adjective *sour* modifies the sentence's subject, *milk.* In *Whatever I say seems wrong,* the predicate adjective *wrong* modifies the entire noun clause *whatever I say,* the subject of the sentence. *See also* Grammar: II.D.

adverb An adverb is a word used to modify a verb (*go quickly*), an adjective (*very difficult*), another adverb (*quite easily*), or even a whole sentence (*Obviously I was mistaken*). Special kinds of adverbs, called CONJUNCTIVE ADVERBS, include *otherwise, thus, however,* and *therefore;* they are used to join two or more independent clauses and show how these clauses are connected to each other: *I have an appointment; otherwise I would meet you. James failed the exam; therefore he withdrew from the course. See also* Grammar: II.E.

adverbial The term *adverbial* means "functioning as a adverb" and is most often used to refer to adverbial clauses.

adverbial clause *See* **clause.**

agreement The principle of agreement refers to the matching in form of words that are grammatically connected. All verbs must agree with their subjects in number and person (*I sing; he sings*). All personal pronouns, like *I, you, he, she,* and *we,* agree with their antecedents in number, person, and gender. For example, in *Rather than flog Captain Bligh, the crew set him adrift in a small boat, him* agrees with its antecedent *Captain Bligh;* both are singular, third person, and masculine. The only other words that must follow the principle of agreement are the demonstrative adjectives *this, that, these,* and *those,* which agree in number with the nouns they modify (*this car,* *these cars; that boy, those boys*). For further discussion of subject-verb agreement, *see* Grammar: III.B.2; for discussion of pronoun agreement, *see* Grammar: III.C.2.b.

antecedent The antecedent of a pronoun is the word or group of words for which the pronoun stands. In *The book which I am reading is from the library, book* is the antecedent of the pronoun *which.* In *After John and George sat down, they began to talk, John and George* is the antecedent of *they. See also* Grammar: III.C.2.

antonym An antonym is a word that means the opposite of another word: *right/wrong; slow/fast. See also* **homonym; synonym.**

appositive An appositive is a noun, or nominal, that immediately follows another nominal and identifies or explains it. In *Dickens's best-known skinflint, Mr. Scrooge, learned a lesson about generosity, Mr. Scrooge* is an appositive identifying the Dickensian skinflint. In *The doctor prescribed codeine, a painkiller, a painkiller* is an appositive explaining the term *codeine. See also* **restrictive and nonrestrictive elements;** Grammar: I.F.

article Only the words *a, an,* and *the* are articles. Strictly speaking, an article is an adjective that limits the noun it modifies. Because *the* always precedes a noun that refers to something specific or definite, it is called the DEFINITE ARTICLE. *In The lie Bill told his mother caused her much pain, the lie* refers to one specific lie. *A* and *an* are called INDEFINITE ARTICLES because they precede either nouns that refer to general categories or singular nouns not previously identified. In *Telling a lie can cause trouble, a lie* refers, not to a specific lie, but to lies in general. And in *Bill told his mother a lie, a lie* refers to a lie which has not yet been specifically identified. *See also* Grammar: II.D.2.b., II.C.3.

attributive The term *attributive,* meaning "to express an attribute," is most often used to refer to an adjective that stands next to the nominal it modifies (*long trip*) as opposed to a predicate adjective that follows a linking verb (*The trip was long*).

Any noun may function attributively, modifying another noun: *race horse, garden party, Carter administration.* Such nouns functioning as adjectives are often called ATTRIBUTIVES or ADJECTIVALS.

auxiliary verb An auxiliary verb (also called a helping verb) is a verb form that combines with a main verb or a participle to make a verb phrase; in *I have gone,* for example, the auxiliary verb *have* combines with the past participle *gone* to form the verb phrase. The most common auxiliaries are *can, may, might, must,* and *ought;* they and their variations in other tenses are used in verb phrases to express possibility, ability, obligation, or permission, as in *she might call, he can swim, I must read this,* and *you may leave.* The verbs *shall* and *will* and their past tenses, *should* and *would*, as well as forms of the verbs *be*, *have*, and *do* also function as auxiliaries to indicate the tense and voice of a verb, as in *I shall return, he will finish, it was stolen, they have gone*, and *he did call. See also* Grammar: II.C.2., II.C.3.

case   Case refers to the forms of a pronoun or noun that change according to the word's function within a sentence. Personal pronouns and the pronoun *who* have three cases: SUBJECTIVE (frequently called NOMINATIVE), POSSESSIVE (or GENITIVE), and OBJECTIVE (or ACCUSATIVE). The subjective forms of the personal pronouns are *I, you, he, she, it, we, you,* and *they;* the subjective form of the pronoun *who* is *who.* When a pronoun functions as a subject or a predicate noun, it takes the subjective case, as in *I ran, Who won?,* or *I am he.*

The possessive forms of these pronouns are *my, mine; your, yours; his; hers; its; our, ours; your, yours; their, theirs;* and *whose.* A pronoun in the possessive case (like a noun in the possessive case— *the girl's books, Mary's cat*) indicates ownership. There are two forms of the possessive pronoun: the first, called the POSSESSIVE PRONOUN or the POSSESSIVE ADJECTIVE, always serves as an adjective (*It is my book. Whose book is this?*); the second possessive form, also called the INDEPENDENT POSSESSIVE, stands after or apart from the noun modified (*This book is mine. This suitcase of yours is heavy*).

The objective forms of the pronouns are *me, you, him, her, it, us, you, them,* and *whom.* When a pronoun functions as an object of a verb, verbal, or preposition, it takes the objective case, as in *Dogs love me, Anne wants to see them,* or *To whom was the package sent?*

All nouns and indefinite pronouns, such as *somebody, nobody,* or *one,* have two case forms. When they function as either subjects or objects, they have the same form, called the COMMON CASE: *Nobody loves a loser, and a loser loves nobody.* But when they function as adjectives indicating ownership, they change to a POSSESSIVE CASE form: *Bill's sister is everybody's friend. The book is on the teacher's desk.*

clause   A clause is a group of words containing a subject and predicate, like *the bell rang* or *although he assured me.* Some clauses make complete statements and thus are able to stand alone: *Cactus thrives in the desert.* These are called INDEPENDENT (or MAIN) CLAUSES and are the basis of all sentences. Other clauses, however, do not make complete statements and so cannot stand alone as sentences. Rather, these DEPENDENT (or SUBORDINATE) CLAUSES function within a sentence as either nouns, adjectives, or adverbs.

A noun clause functions as a noun in a sentence. In *What you do is your business,* the noun clause *what you do* acts as the subject of the sentence. A noun clause may also function as an object, a complement, or an appositive.

An adjectival clause, like any adjective, modifies a noun or other nominal. Adjectival clauses are sometimes called RELATIVE CLAUSES because they are always introduced by a relative pronoun, such as *which, who,* or *that.* In *The man who gave you the book is the author,* the adjectival clause *who gave you the book* modifies the noun *man.*

An adverbial clause functions as an adverb modifying a verb, an adjective, an adverb, or an entire independent clause. Adverbial clauses are usually introduced by subordinating conjunctions like *because, although* or *as soon as.* In *As soon as I feel happy, I sing,* the adverbial clause *As soon as I feel happy* is introduced by the subordinating conjunction *As soon as* and modifies the verb *sing.* Sometimes, however, adverbial clauses are introduced by indefinite relative pronouns (for example, *whoever* or *whatever*), indefinite relative adjectives (*whichever, whatever*), or the relative adverb *however.* In *Whatever you do, don't call after 11:00, whatever you do* is an adverbial clause modifying the entire independent clause. *See also* **conjunction; relative pronoun; restrictive and nonrestrictive elements;** Grammar: II.K.

collective noun   A collective noun is a noun that refers to a group of individuals, such as *majority, jury, flock, team,* or *audience.* If the collective noun refers to the group as a whole, it is treated as a singular noun: *The jury is deliberating. A new city council was elected. The majority wants tax reform.* If the collective noun refers to the individual members of the group, it is treated as a plural noun: *The city council are casting their votes now. The majority of voters want tax reform. See also* **noun;** for problems with collective nouns, *see* Grammar: III.B.2.b.

common case   *See* **case.**

common noun   A common noun is a noun that refers to any member of a group or class, like *woman, book,* or *city.* In contrast, a PROPER NOUN names a particular member of the group or class, like *Ellen, Bible,* or *Chicago. See also* **noun.**

comparison   In grammar the term *comparison* refers to the changes made in the form of adjectives and adverbs to indicate degree— for example, *thick, thicker, thickest.* Most adverbs and descriptive adjectives have three forms which indicate three degrees of comparison: POSITIVE (the root word, or form found in the dictionary), COMPARATIVE (showing a greater degree of that quality), and SUPERLATIVE (showing the greatest degree of that quality).

Like the example above (*thick*), some adjectives and adverbs form their comparative and superlative degrees by adding *-er* and *-est* to the root word (the positive degree); others form their comparative and superlative degrees by modifying the root word with the adverbs *more* and *most*. The comparisons of the adjectives *grand* and *afraid* and the adverbs *friendly* and *fondly* are:

POSITIVE	COMPARATIVE	SUPERLATIVE
grand	grander	grandest
afraid	more afraid	most afraid
friendly	friendlier	friendliest
fondly	more fondly	most fondly

For a discussion of the rules on the formation of comparisons, *see* Grammar: II.D.1.a.

complement   Usually the term *complement* refers to SUBJECT COMPLEMENT, the predicate adjective or predicate noun of a sentence. In its broadest sense, however, COMPLEMENT is a term for any noun or adjective that completes the meaning of a verb, subject, or object. *See also* **direct object; indirect object; object complement; predicate adjective; predicate noun;** Grammar: I.C., I.D.

complementary object   *See* **object complement.**

complex sentence   A complex sentence is a sentence containing one independent clause and at least one subordinate clause: *While he talked, she listened. See also* **clause; sentence.**

compound-complex sentence   A compound-complex sentence consists of at least two independent clauses and at least one subordinate clause: *She listened while he talked, and she did not say a word. See also* **clause; sentence.**

compound sentence   A compound sentence contains at least two independent clauses but no subordinate clause: *He talked and she listened. See also* **clause; sentence.**

concrete noun   *See* **abstract noun; noun.**

conjugation   Conjugation refers to the changes made in the form of a verb to indicate variations in tense, number, person, voice, and mood. The conjugation of the verb *write,* for example, would include *I write, he wrote, it was written. See also* Grammar: II.C.

conjunction   A conjunction is a word used to connect and indicate the relationship between words, phrases, and clauses. The most commonly used conjunctions are *and, but, or, for, yet,* and *so.* They are called COORDINATING CONJUNCTIONS because they connect elements of the same grammatical order—words to words, phrases to phrases, and clauses to clauses. In *Bill and Tom planned the party, and* connects the nouns *Bill* and *Tom.* In *We were told to enter but first to take off our shoes, but* connects the infinitive phrases *to enter* and *to take off our shoes.* In *He must be captain* or *he will not play,* or connects the two independent clauses.

A special kind of coordinating conjunction, always used in pairs to connect grammatically equivalent elements, is the CORRELATIVE CON- JUNCTION, including *either . . . or, neither . . . nor, not only . . . but also, both . . . and,* and *whether . . . or.* In *Neither Robert* nor *Sue knew the answer, neither . . . nor* connects the two nouns *Robert* and *Sue.*

A third group of conjunctions, including such words as *although, whenever, because,* and *until,* is used to connect subordinate, or dependent, clauses with independent clauses and so are called SUB- ORDINATING CONJUNCTIONS: *I went home because I was ill.* For a more complete discussion of conjunctions, *see* Grammar: II.G.

conjunctive adverb *See* **adverb.**

consonant Consonants are sounds that are made with a complete or partial blockage of the vocal channel and that serve as the periphery of a syllable; they are also the letters of the alphabet like *b, c, d, f, g, h,* and *j* that represent such sounds.

contraction A contraction is the shortening into a single word of two or more words, with an apostrophe replacing the omitted letters: *isn't* ("is not"), *wouldn't* ("would not"), *can't* ("cannot").

coordinating conjunction *See* **conjunction.**

copula *See* **verb.**

correlative conjunction *See* **conjunction.**

count noun *See* **mass noun; noun.**

declarative sentence *See* **sentence.**

declension Declension refers to the changes made in the form of a noun or pronoun to indicate variations in person, number, and case. The declension of the pronoun *I*, for example, includes *I, me, mine,* and *myself. See also* **inflection;** Grammar: II.B., III.C.1.

definite article *See* **article.**

demonstrative adjective *See* **demonstrative pronoun.**

demonstrative pronoun The demonstrative pronouns *this, that, these,* and *those* are used to point out that which is being referred to, as in *That is the movie I want to see.* If these words are used as modifiers, as in *I want to see that movie,* they are called DEMONSTRATIVE AD- JECTIVES. *See also* **adjective; pronoun;** Grammar: II.B.5. For a dis- cussion of demonstrative adjectives, *see* Grammar: II.D.2.a.

dependent clause *See* **clause.**

descriptive adjective *See* **adjective.**

direct address Direct address is an ABSOLUTE construction that names the audience to which a sentence is addressed: *Are you in favor of* *tax reductions, Senator Blake? The key to throwing a Frisbee, Michael, lies in the wrist. Our Father who art in Heaven, hallowed be thy name.*

A direct address construction is always separated from the rest of the sentence by commas. *See also* **absolute;** Grammar: I.H.

direct object A direct object is a noun or other nominal following a transitive verb and telling who or what is affected by or receives the action of the verb. For example, in *Priscilla eats only vegetables, vegetables* is a direct object telling what Priscilla eats. In *Lawrence met his father for lunch, father* is the direct object, telling whom Lawrence met. *See also* Grammar: I.C.1.

elliptical construction In an elliptical construction, words are omitted but nonetheless understood because they are parallel to the words in a nearby construction: *Her hair is blonde; her eyes [are] blue. This dress is older than that one [is]. Peter likes candy more than [he likes] cookies. Peter likes candy more than she [does].*

exclamatory sentence *See* **sentence.**

expletive Commonly the term *expletive* refers to a profanity or an exclamatory statement. But in grammar the term refers to a sentence construction beginning with *it is, there is,* or *there are: It is clear that Richard dislikes me. There is nothing to do today. There are several children coming.* In these expletives, *it* and *there* serve as "dummy" subjects, allowing the real subjects (*Richard, nothing, children*) to assume a more emphatic position. *See also* Grammar: II.B.1.

gender Gender refers to the classification of nouns and pronouns as masculine (*body, he*); feminine (*girl, she*); or neuter (*car, it*).

genitive *See* **case.**

gerund *See* **verbal.**

helping verb *See* **auxiliary verb.**

historical present Sometimes the present tense is used to describe or summarize something that is already completed—an incident in history; the plot of a story, poem, or drama; or the contents of an essay or speech. This use of the present tense is called the historical present. (*In this chapter Stephen Daedalus walks the streets of Dublin on his way to school. As he passes the various landmarks along the way he is reminded of writers he admires.*)

A summary or description written in the historical present must observe the appropriate sequence of tenses. The present tense is used for the action under immediate discussion, the past for action previous to that, and the future for action following the present. (*As he*

pres. pres. past
walks down the street he is thinking of writers he has read and is
pres. future
wondering if he will be a writer.)

homonym Homonyms are words that have identical pronunciations but different spellings and meanings: *bore/boar; pair/pear/pare. See also* **antonym; synonym.**

idiom An idiom is a phrase—like *catch a cold, by and large,* or *strike a bargain*—which is an established and correct part of a particular language but which makes little sense, if taken literally.

imperative mood *See* **mood.**

imperative sentence *See* **sentence.**

impersonal pronouns The pronouns *it, one,* and *you* are considered impersonal when they refer to "things, situations, or people in general" rather than to a specific antecedent: *It is hot today. It has been three years since I have seen you, but it seems like it has been only days. One should respect others. You would expect the greyhound to chase the rabbit.*

indefinite pronoun Indefinite pronouns, such as *anyone, someone, either, one,* and *each, refer* to an unspecified antecedent: *Someone stole my money. See also* **pronoun;** Grammar: II.B.7, III.B.2, II.C.2; Verbal Quandaries: anyone, each, either.

indefinite relative adjective *See* **relative pronoun.**

indefinite relative clause *See* **relative clause.**

indefinite relative pronoun *See* **relative pronoun.**

independent clause *See* **clause.**

independent sentence fragment *See* **sentence fragment.**

indicative mood *See* **mood.**

indirect object An indirect object is a noun or other nominal that follows a transitive verb and tells to whom or what, or for whom or what, the action of the verb is executed. (A noun that follows the verb and tells who or what is directly affected by the action of the verb is the DIRECT OBJECT.) In *Steve brought her flowers, her* is the indirect object, indicating to whom Steve brought the flowers, and *flowers* is the direct object, indicating what Steve brought. *See also* Grammar: I.C.2.

infinitive *See* **verbal.**

inflection An inflection is any change in the form of a word. Pronouns are inflected, or change their form, to indicate case (*I, me, mine*), number (*this, these*), and person (*I, you, he*). Nouns are inflected to indicate number (*mouse, mice; horse, horses*) and case (*mouse, mouse's*). Verbs are inflected when conjugated to indicate person and number (*he talks; we talk*) and tense (*I will go; he went*). In contrast to nouns, pronouns, and verbs, adjectives in modern English are now less inflected than they once were. Except for the demonstrative adjectives *this* and *that* (which are inflected to show plurality: *these, those*), modern English adjectives are not inflected to show case, number, or person; but they do change form, often by adding -*er* or -*est,* to indicate degree (*young, younger, youngest*). Some grammarians, however, prefer to consider these endings not as inflections but as noninflectional suffixes.

intensive pronoun   Pronouns like *myself* and *yourselves* are called intensive pronouns when they are used to add emphasis, as in *You yourself must go. See also* **pronoun; reflexive pronoun;** Grammar: II.B.2.

interjection   An interjection is a word used for simple exclamations: *Wow! Aha! Hey! See also* Grammar: II.H.

interrogative adjective   *See* **interrogative pronoun.**

interrogative pronoun   The pronouns *who, whose, whom, which,* and *what* are interrogatives when they function to introduce a question: *Who was she?* If they are used as modifiers that introduce a question, *whose, which,* and *what* are INTERROGATIVE ADJECTIVES: *Which suit did you wear? See also* **adjective; pronoun.**

interrogative sentence   *See* **sentence.**

intransitive verb   *See* **verb.**

limiting adjective   *See* **adjective.**

linking verb   *See* **verb.**

main clause   *See* **clause.**

mass noun   Mass nouns, such as *butter, water, wealth,* and *oxygen,* name masses that can be divided into parts but whose parts cannot be counted as separate units. Mass nouns contrast with COUNT NOUNS, which name things that can be counted: *onions, beverages, cents,* and *couches. See also* **noun.**

modifier   A modifier is a word, phrase, or dependent clause that describes or makes more exact another word or group of words. Adjectives and adjectival phrases or clauses modify nominals; adverbs and adverbial phrases or clauses modify verbs, adjectives, and other adverbs. *See also* **adjective; adverb; clause; phrase;** Grammar: I.E., II.D., II.E.

mood (mode)   Mood refers to the forms of the verb used to indicate whether one is speaking about factual matters, speaking about conjectural or desired matters, or giving a command. In a statement or question about fact, the verb is in the INDICATIVE MOOD: *You passed the house. Are you going home?* In a statement or question that expresses a wish or an unlikely, impossible, or contrary-to-fact condition, the verb is in the SUBJUNCTIVE MOOD: *Bob is a bookkeeper, but he wishes that he* were *an astronaut. Why did Laura act as if she had won? If I* were *a cat, I would sleep all day.* Commands and directions use the IMPERATIVE MOOD: *Go home. Turn at the corner. See also* Grammar: II.C.4.

nominal (substantive) A nominal is a word or group of words that functions as a noun. Nouns themselves, as well as pronouns, noun clauses, gerund phrases, and some infinitive phrases, are nominals. In *I like what you are wearing,* the noun clause *what you are wearing* functions as the object of the sentence. In *Finding a job is dffiicult,* the gerund phrase *finding a job* is the subject of the sentence. *See also* **clause; noun; pronoun; verbal.**

nominative *See* **case.**

nonrestrictive element *See* **restrictive and nonrestrictive elements.**

noun A noun is a word that names a person (*Henry, girl*), place (*Boston, city*), thing (*banana*), action (*arrival*), quality (*beauty*), organization (corporation, or concept (*realism*). Nouns generally function as subjects, objects, and complements of sentences as well as objects of prepositional phrases; but they can serve various other functions. *See also* **abstract noun; collective noun; common noun; mass noun; nominal;** Grammar: II.A.

noun clause *See* **clause.**

noun phrase *See* **phrase.**

number In grammar, number refers to the form of a noun, pronoun, demonstrative adjective, or verb that indicates whether the word is singular or plural. *Girl* is singular in number; *girls,* plural in number. *See also* Grammar: II.C.1., III.B.2.

object complement An object complement is a noun renaming a direct object, or an adjective describing a direct object. In *The committee appointed Julia chairwoman, because they thought her deserving, chairwoman* is an object complement renaming the direct object *her,* and *deserving* is an object complement describing the direct object Julia. The object complement completes the meaning of the direct object and thus the meaning of the sentence. *See also* Grammar: I.C.3.

objective case *See* **case.**

objective complement *See* **object complement.**

object of a preposition The object of a preposition is the noun or other nominal that follows a preposition (*in the car, around the next corner, after midnight*) to form a phrase that modifies some other sentence element. In *Tony parked beside the curb, curb* is the object of the preposition *beside,* and the entire phrase *beside the curb* functions as an adverb telling where he parked.

object of a verb *See* **direct object; indirect object.**

participial phrase *See* **phrase.**

participle *See* **verbal.**

passive voice *See* **voice.**

past participle *See* **verbal.**

person When used as a grammatical term, person refers to the form of a verb or pronoun that indicates that someone is speaking (first person: *I am*), being spoken to (second person: *you are*), or being spoken about (third person: *he is*).

personal pronoun The personal pronouns include *I, you, he, she, it, we, they,* and all the various forms these pronouns can take (*me, mine, yours, his,* etc.). *See also* **case; pronoun;** Grammar: II.B.1.

phrase A phrase is any group of words, like *of the twentieth century, taking his time,* or *to be or not to be,* that does not contain both a verb and its subject. (A group of words that does contain a subject-verb combination is called a CLAUSE.) All phrases function within sentences as single grammatical units—most often as adjectives and adverbs but also as nouns and verbs.

Commonly phrases may be introduced by prepositions: *after the dance, during the winter, with his fist, of the song.* These PREPOSITIONAL PHRASES usually function as either adverbs, adjectives, or occasionally as nominals. In *I found my car keys under the bed, under the bed* acts as an adverb describing where the keys were found. In *George brought a box of candy, of candy* acts as an adjective describing *box.* In *After meals is the best time to brush your teeth, after meals* is a nominal functioning as subject of the sentence.

Other common phrases begin with participles: *trying his luck, staying in bed all day, having come this far.* These PARTICIPIAL PHRASES always function as adjectives. In *Stretching for miles in front of me, the road was hypnotic, stretching for miles in front of me* is a participial phrase, containing three prepositional phrases (*for miles, in front,* and *of me*), which describes the road.

Not every phrase, however, is introduced by a special word. For example, a noun and its cluster of modifiers that together perform noun functions is a NOUN PHRASE. In *The soft and sultry singer winked at the drunken sailor, the soft and sultry singer* is a noun phrase functioning as the sentence's subject; and *the drunken sailor* is a noun phrase functioning as the object of the preposition *at. See also* **verb phrase;** Grammar: II.J.

possessive *See* **case.**

predicate The predicate of a clause or sentence is composed of the verb along with any modifiers, objects, predicate nouns, or predicate adjectives. The predicate may be a single verb (*The wind whistled*), a transitive verb and any object or object complement (*He grew a beard*), or a linking verb and its predicate noun or adjective (*The first time was the best time*). *See also* Grammar: I.B.

predicate adjective A predicate adjective is an adjective that follows a linking verb like *is, seem, become,* or *taste* and modifies the subject of the clause. In *The soprano's voice is* excellent, *excellent* is a predicate adjective describing the subject *voice. See also* **adjective;** Grammar: I.D.

predicate noun (predicate nominative) A predicate noun is a noun or other nominal that follows a linking verb, usually forms of the verbs *to be* or *to become,* and refers back to the subject of the clause. In *That dog is a* terrier, *terrier* is a predicate noun referring back to the subject *dog.* A predicate nominative must be in the nominative case. *That person is he* is a predicate nominative, or predicate pronoun, referring back to the subject *person. See also* Grammar: I.D.

prefix A prefix is one or more letters or syllables added to the beginning of a word that changes the meaning of the word: *re-, regain; in-, inside; pre-, preview. See also* **suffix;** The Spelling Maze.

preposition A preposition is a word generally expressing motion or position like *with, on, in, of, by, across, between,* or *from.* A preposition always introduces a prepositional phrase. *See also* **prepositional phrase.**

prepositional phrase A prepositional phrase is a group of words like *during the night, without me,* or *in a new dress,* consisting of a preposition, the nominal that is its object, and any modifiers. Prepositional phrases function in sentences as either adjectives or adverbs. In *The man* with the carnation *walked* across the room, the prepositional phrase *with the carnation* functions as an adjective describing *man;* the prepositional phrase *across the room* functions as an adverb indicating where the man walked. Occasionally prepositional phrases can function as nominals. In Between 10 a.m. and 2 p.m. *is the best time to get a suntan,* the prepositional phrase serves as the subject of the sentence. *See also* Grammar: II.J.1.

present participle *See* **verbal.**

present stem *See* **principal parts of a verb.**

principal parts of a verb A verb's principal parts are the three basic forms of the verb from which all of its tenses are derived. These parts are the BASE, PRESENT STEM, or INFINITIVE, form (*play, speak*); the PAST TENSE form (*played, spoke*); and the PAST PARTICIPLE form (*played, spoken*). *See also* Grammar: II.C.2.

pronoun A pronoun is a word like *he, myself, her, who, this,* or *somebody* that is used in place of a noun. In *When I saw* Deborah, she *thanked me, she* is a pronoun substituting for the noun *Deborah.* The word that a pronoun stands for is called its ANTECEDENT. In order for most pronouns to be understood, their antecedents must be mentioned. For example, the sentence *I did not take* it makes little sense unless we know the antecedent of *it.* In contrast, the sentence *John* *offered me a cookie, but I did not take it* makes sense because we know that *it* stands for *cookie.*

There are some pronouns, however, whose antecedents need not be mentioned—for example, the personal pronoun *me* or indefinite pronouns like *someone* or *anyone.* And there are some pronouns whose antecedents are unknown and hence cannot be mentioned—for example, interrogative pronouns like *who* or *whom. See also* **antecedent; demonstrative pronoun; indefinite pronoun; intensive pronoun; interrogative pronoun; personal pronoun; reciprocal pronoun; reflexive pronoun; relative pronoun;** Grammar: II.B., III.C.2.

proper noun *See* **common noun.**

reciprocal pronoun The reciprocal pronouns *each other* and *one another* express mutual relation: *We see each other every day.* Reciprocal pronouns are only used as objects of verbs and prepositions. *See also* **pronoun;** Grammar: II.B.3.

reflexive pronoun Reflexive pronouns like *myself* and *yourselves* are used as direct or indirect objects referring back to the subject of the clause (*I blame myself. She gave herself a present*) or as objects of the preposition referring back to a noun or another pronoun in the sentence (*I love you for yourself*). *See also* **intensive pronoun; pronoun;** Grammar: II.B.2.

relative adjective *See* **relative pronoun.**

relative adverb The adverbs *where, when, how, however, why, whenever,* and *wherever* may be used to introduce adjectival clauses and noun clauses and in this capacity are called relative adverbs. In *We visited 17 homes where George Washington slept,* and in *Mr. Short knows why you are late, where* and *why* are relative adverbs, respectively modifying *slept* and *are late.* Additionally, in these sentences, *where* introduces the adjectival clause *where George Washington slept* that modifies the noun *homes;* and *why* introduces the noun clause *why you are late,* which functions as the direct object of the sentence.

relative clause A relative clause, like *that I saw* or *whom we loved,* is a dependent clause introduced by a relative pronoun or relative adverb and functioning as an adjective. In *This begonia, which came from the garden, is now flowering indoors,* the relative clause *which came from the garden* serves as an adjective modifying *begonia.*

An INDEFINITE RELATIVE CLAUSE, introduced by an indefinite relative pronoun or relative adverb, functions as a noun or as an adverb. In *I know what I like,* the indefinite relative clause *what I like* functions as a direct object of the verb *know.* In *Whoever calls, tell them I'm not home, whoever calls* is an adverbial clause modifying the main clause of the sentence. *See also* **clause; restrictive and nonrestrictive elements;** Grammar: II.K.2.

relative pronoun The pronouns *who, whose, whom, which,* and *that* are relative pronouns when they are used to introduce adjectival clauses. In *This is the kind that I like,* the relative pronoun *that* introduces the adjectival clause *that I like,* which describes *kind.* When *who, whose, whom, which, what, whoever, whomever, whatever,* or *whichever* introduce noun clauses or adverbial clauses, they are INDEFINITE RELATIVE PRONOUNS. In *I take what I want,* the indefinite relative pronoun *what* introduces the noun clause *what I want,* which is the direct object of the verb *know.*

Many of the same words that can function as relative and indefinite relative pronouns can also function as adjectives introducing relative and indefinite relative clauses. When they do so, they are either RELATIVE ADJECTIVES (*I am leaving tomorrow, after which time you can reach me in Brazil*) or INDEFINITE RELATIVE ADJECTIVES (*Did John tell you what plans he made?*). *See also* **clause; pronoun;** Grammar: II.B.4.

restrictive and nonrestrictive elements Consider these two sentences:

> *I lost the book that I was reading yesterday.*
> *Carol's favorite book, which she first read when she was ten, is* Treasure Island.

While *that I was reading yesterday* and *which she first read when she was ten* are both relative clauses, they serve different functions in their sentences. In the first sentence the relative clause functions to identify which book was lost out of all the possible books that might have been lost. In the second sentence the relative clause does not function to identify the book in question because Carol can only have one favorite book; rather it gives supplementary information about the book. The first kind of relative clause is RESTRICTIVE because it restricts the term *book* to the one in question in the sentence. The second kind of relative clause is NONRESTRICTIVE because its subject, *Carol's favorite book,* is already restricted or defined; the clause serves instead to describe, or provide additional information about, the noun *book.*

The examples above involve relative clauses, but the distinction between restrictive (defining) and nonrestrictive (descriptive) applies equally to appositives and adjectival phrases. For example, in *John the plumber called this morning,* the appositive *the plumber* is restrictive, identifying which man named John called. By contrast, in *Ralph's wife, Mary, was a pianist,* the appositive *Mary* is nonrestrictive; it describes but is not needed to define the word *wife,* since Ralph had only one wife. If, however, Ralph had been married more than once, then *Mary* would be a restrictive appositive—that is, necessary to define the wife in question—and hence not set off by commas.

Similarly in *Ben borrowed the jacket hanging in the back closet,* the phrase *hanging in the back closet* is restrictive, identifying which coat Ben borrowed. And in *Jesse James, running from the law, fled to Mexico,* the phrase *running from the law* is nonrestrictive because it does not identify Jesse James but rather tells us something about him.

Because restrictive elements are essential for identifying their subjects, they are never enclosed in commas. Nonrestrictive elements, giving only parenthetical information, are always enclosed in commas.

retained object   Retained objects occur only in sentences in the passive voice (that is, sentences whose subject is the receiver rather than the performer of the verb's action). When an active voice sentence with two objects (either a direct object plus an indirect object, or a direct object plus an object complement) is made passive, one of the objects becomes the sentence's subject and the other remains in the predicate as a retained object.

> Active: *The boss gave John a promotion.*
> Passive: *John was given a promotion.*
>
> Active: *They deemed Benedict Arnold a traitor.*
> Passive: *Benedict Arnold was deemed a traitor.*
>
> Active: *We labeled the cans poisonous.*
> Passive: *The cans were labeled poisonous.*

Retained objects that are derived from object complements, like those in the second and third examples above, are considered by some grammarians to be predicate nouns and predicate adjectives rather than retained objects since, like subject complements, they refer back to the sentence's subject.

sentence   A sentence is a complete unit of thought, usually containing a subject and predicate, that makes an assertion, called a DECLARATIVE SENTENCE (*I feel fine*), or exclamation, called an EXCLAMATORY SENTENCE (*Oh no!*); asks a question, called an INTERROGATIVE SENTENCE (*Is Clara here?*); or gives a command, called an IMPERATIVE SENTENCE (*Put down your pens*). *See also* **clause; complex sentence; compound-complex sentence; compound sentence; simple sentence.**

sentence element Sentence elements are the working components of a sentence: subject, verb, objects, complements, modifiers, appositive, connectives, and absolutes. For a complete discussion of sentence elements, *see* Grammar: I.

sentence fragment A sentence fragment is a group of words which is not a complete sentence but which is punctuated as a sentence: *Virginia said she has never been. To the lighthouse.* A sentence fragment such as *to the lighthouse* is actually a sentence element (in this case a modifier) that is disconnected from its sentence; hence this and similar fragments should be avoided.

However, some sentence fragments, called INDEPENDENT SENTENCE FRAGMENTS, can function as independent units, even though they do not contain the usual elements (subject and verb) necessary for a sentence. In context such independent sentence fragments read like an elliptical, or abbreviated, sentence rather than a disconnected sentence element: *The view was perfect. A lonely beach. Jagged cliffs. The sun just setting.* The independent sentence fragment can also be used effectively as an exclamation or for emphasis: *I do not want to see you. Not now, not ever.*

simple sentence A simple sentence contains one independent clause and no subordinate clauses: *He talked. See also* **clause; sentence.**

subject In a sentence the subject of the verb is the noun or other nominal that causes the action of the verb (*Michael rowed the boat*); or it is the person or thing about which the rest of the sentence makes a statement (*The car ran out of gas*) or asks a question (*Isn't that old dress worn out yet?*). In a sentence in the passive voice, the subject is acted upon (*The boat was rented*).

subject complement *See* **complement.**

subjective *See* **case.**

subjunctive mood *See* **mood.**

subordinate clause *See* **clause.**

subordinating conjunction *See* **conjunction.**

substantive *See* **nominal.**

suffix A suffix is one or more letters or syllables added to the end of a root word that changes the meaning of the root: *-ness, happiness; -al, musical; -ize, criticize. See also* The Spelling Maze.

synonym A synonym is a word having nearly the same meaning as another word: *dish/plate; finish/complete. See also* **antonym; homonym.**

syntax The syntax of a sentence is the grammatical arrangement of words, phrases, and clauses that allows the sentence to make sense and be more than a mere string of words. The randomly juxtaposed words *aglow, embers, the,* and *are* make no sense. But when rearranged in syntactical order—in this case, article, subject, verb, and complement—the words make sense: *The embers are aglow.*

tense The tense of a verb is the form of the verb used to indicate time. Although a verb may have approximately 30 tenses, only six of these are basic:

Present: *walk*	Present perfect: *have walked*
Past: *walked*	Past perfect: *had walked*
Future: *will walk*	Future perfect: *will have walked*

See also Grammar: II.C.2.

transitive verb *See* **verb.**

verb A verb is a word that shows action (*dance, open, meditate*) or state of being (*is, seem, become*). In a sentence the verb is the heart of the predicate, the part of the sentence that says something about the subject: *The lightning flashed. This water tastes terrible.*

Some verbs, like *put* and *raise,* need a direct object in the predicate to complete their meaning: *I put the laundry away. The students raised their hands.* These are TRANSITIVE VERBS.

Other verbs, like *go* or *sit,* do not need a direct object in their predicate to complete their meaning: *The dog barked. We sat quietly.* These are INTRANSITIVE VERBS.

LINKING VERBS, sometimes called COPULAS ("connectives"), are a special form of intransitive verb that forms a predicate by linking a subject to a noun or adjective: *John is my brother. The cake seems done.* Common linking verbs are *be, become, appear,* and *seem,* as well as verbs pertaining to the senses like *look, smell, taste, sound,* and *feel.* A number of other verbs can, with a shift in meaning, also be used as copulas (*He runs wild. She keeps busy. Her patience wears thin*).

Some verbs, like *feel* or *grow,* can function in different sentences as any of the three kinds of verbs:

Transitive: *When it rained, Harry felt his arthritis.*

Intransitive: *Having dropped my key in the dark, I felt around for it.*

Linking: *After a good night's sleep, I felt rested.*

See also **auxiliary verb; mood; predicate; tense; verb phrase; voice;** Grammar: II.C.

verbal A verbal is a word derived from a verb but different from a verb in function. Like verbs, verbals may take objects, complements, modifiers, and sometimes subjects; but they cannot stand as the main verb in a clause. Verbals function as nouns, adjectives, or adverbs. There are three kinds of verbals: gerunds, infinitives, and participles.

A GERUND is a verb form ending in -*ing* that functions as a noun: *Swimming is good for your health.*

A PARTICIPLE is a verb form that functions as an adjective. Like a gerund, the PRESENT PARTICIPLE ends in -*ing: the running stream, the babbling brook.* PAST PARTICIPLES regularly end in -*d* or -*ed* (*a tired, old man; a confused explanation*); but many verbs have irregular past participles (*a written apology, a torn page*). Participles, of course, can also function as parts of verb phrases: *The child was crying. We had already eaten dinner.* But when they function as part of the verb phrase and not as adjectives, participles are no longer considered verbals.

An INFINITIVE is the base form of the verb, usually preceded by the word *to.* Infinitives, or infinitive phrases (an infinitive and all of its modifiers or objects), can function as nouns (*To err is human; to forgive, divine*); adjectives (*The meeting to be held in Cleveland was postponed*); or adverbs (*I am happy to know you*). *See also* Grammar: II.I.

verb phrase   A verb phrase is composed of a verb and its auxiliaries: *will seem, should have thought, could not have helped. See also* **auxiliary verb; phrase; verb.**

voice   Transitive verbs have two voices: ACTIVE (*Mary and John cleaned the house*) and PASSIVE (*The house was cleaned by Mary and John*). While it is the verb that changes form to indicate voice, the terms *active* and *passive* actually refer to the subject of the sentence. For example, in the first sentence the verb *cleaned* is in the active voice; the subject *Mary* acts. By contrast, in the second sentence the verb *was cleaned* is in the passive voice; the subject *house* is passive, being acted upon by Mary.

vowel   Vowels are sounds that are made with an open vocal channel and that serve as the center of a syllable when pronounced; they are also the letters *a, e, i, o, u,* and *y* (as in *shy* but not *yours*) representing such sounds.

Verbal Quandaries from A to Z

a / an   *A* and *an,* both forms of the same indefinite article, cause little trouble in speaking but do occasionally cause confusion in writing. Remember that the initial sound of a word, not its initial letter, determines the article that precedes it. Use *a* before words beginning with a consonant sound (*a book, a day, a euphemism, a one-way street, a union, a year*) and before words whose initial *h* is pronounced (*a habit, a handle, a hotel*). Use *an* before words beginning with a vowel sound (*an eye, an idol, an ocean, an* S) and before words beginning with a silent, unpronounced *h* (*an heirloom, an hour, an honorable man*).

Historically an initial *h* was usually pronounced weakly or not at all in words with an unaccented first syllable, and *an* commonly preceded such words (*an historical event, an hotel, an humiliation*). Today, since the initial *h* in such words is pronounced, they are now usually preceded by *a,* though *an* is still common (*a habitual liar, a historical event, a humiliating experience*).

abbreviations   For guidelines on styling abbreviations, *see* Grammar: V.C.; for a list of common abbreviations, *see* Abbreviations: An Abbreviated Guide.

accept / except   The verb *accept* means "to receive" (*He would not accept payment for changing the tire*). As a verb *except* means "to exclude, to omit" (*They excepted George from membership*) and as a preposition, "with the exclusion of" (*I enjoy all vegetables except spinach*).

accompanied by / accompanied with   Use *accompanied by* with persons (*James was accompanied by his mother*) and *accompanied with* with things (*The letter was accompanied with a check*).

advert / avert   *Advert* means "to pay attention (to)" or "to refer (to)" (*The president adverted to the spiraling rate of inflation*); avert, "to turn away" (*She averted her eyes from the body*) and "to prevent" (*The speech was canceled to avert violence*).

284

advice / advise Spell the noun (rhyming with *ice*) with a *c* and the verb (rhyming with *eyes*) with an *s*.

affect / effect *Affect*, almost always a verb (except in its narrow psychological sense of a feeling or emotion), means "to influence generally" (*The gas shortage greatly affects the tourist industry*); "to influence emotionally" (*She was greatly affected by the divorce*); and "to assume, to take up artificially" (*Tom affected a British accent*). *Effect* is either a verb meaning "to cause" (*The new chairman effected many changes*) or a noun meaning "the result of a cause" (*The effect of our protest was a raise in pay*).

afflict / inflict *Afflict* means "to distress with mental or physical pain" (*She is afflicted with severe back pain*); *inflict*, "to impose something distasteful" (*The teacher inflicted an hour's study period on the students*). The victim is *afflicted;* the pain or punishment, *inflicted*.

again *See* **back.**

aggravate / irritate Although *aggravate* and *irritate* are in general used synonymously, careful writers distinguish between *aggravate,* meaning "to worsen an existing situation," and *irritate,* "to annoy" (*My rundown condition was aggravated by a lack of sleep. Her thoughtless remarks irritated me*).

ago / since Use either one word or the other, not both together (*It has been four weeks since they signed the contract. They signed the contract four weeks ago*). *Ago* may also follow a *that*-clause (*It was four weeks ago that they signed the contract*).

agreement of subject and verb *See* Grammar: III.B.2.

ain't Despite its wide use, "ain't" is not Standard English.

alike *See* **both alike.**

all ready / already The adjective phrase *all ready* means "entirely prepared" (*The presents were all ready*); the adverb *already* means "before, previously" (*The gifts are already sent*).

all right *All right* is the accepted form. *Alright* is not acceptable.

all together / altogether *All together* means "in union" (*All together they finished the job in a day*); *altogether,* "completely, entirely" (*The idea was altogether wrong*).

allude / elude *Allude* means "to refer to indirectly" (*The speaker alluded to the issue*); *elude* means "to escape, to avoid" (*The thief eluded capture by the police*).

allusion / illusion *Allusion* means "an indirect reference" (*The allusion to the incident was clear*); *illusion* is a misconception or a misleading image (*The UFO was an optical illusion*).

a lot *A lot* is a colloquialism but, if used in informal writing, is correctly spelled as two words rather than one.

alternate / alternative Most careful writers distinguish between the adjectives *alternate,* meaning "occurring or succeeding by turns," that is, one thing occurring after another; and *alternative,* referring to the choice between one thing or another. (*I have an alternative sugges-tion: let's drive on alternate days*). The distinction is likewise ob-served between the adverbs *alternately* and *alternatively.*

among / between   In general *among* is used to refer to three or more persons or things (*The cake was divided among the people at the party*); *between,* to refer to only two persons or things (*Jim and Anne split the bill between them*). *Among,* however, always refers to a group as a unit (*Let's place the tables among the trees in the garden. Trade negotiations among the exporting nations are under-way*); *between* refers to the individual relationships between mem-bers of a group—even when that group consists of more than two (*We strung the clothesline between the four trees in the garden. Trade negotiations between the three nations are still inconclusive*).

amoral   *See* **immoral.**

amount / number   *Amount* is used with mass nouns (*a large amount of work, equal amounts of milk and sugar*); *number* is used for things that can be counted (*a number of books, a number of students*). The word *number* can take a singular or plural verb, depending on whether the elements making up that number are referred to indi-vidually or as a unit (*A number of the books are lost. The number of workers absent today is 10*). *See also* **few.**

ampersand (&)   This symbol (&) stands for the word *and,* but it should not be used to replace *and* in formal writing unless the ampersand is part of a proper name or a title, as in *G. E. Jones & Sons.*

and / but / or   Many people object to beginning sentences with the coordinating conjunctions *and, but,* and *or* because they usually link grammatically equivalent elements within a sentence. For example, they might link a noun with a noun (*He bought crackers and cheese*), an infinitive with an infinitive (*To be or not to be, that is the ques-tion*), or a clause with a clause (*I invited her, but she cannot come*).

While these conjunctions usually link only parts of a sentence, they may nonetheless be used to link sentences themselves. That is to say, it is acceptable to begin a sentence with *and, but,* or *or* when that sentence could logically have been a continuation of the pre-ceding sentence. Such usage occasionally permits a welcome breaking up of a lengthy, complex sentence into shorter, more readable sen-tences. But these conjunctions should not be overworked as sentence openers.

and / or   While the expression *and/or* has become popular, it often serves only to introduce ambiguity. In the sentence *I am hoping to go to England and/or France,* does the writer mean *I am hoping to* *go to both England and France* or *I have not decided yet whether to go to England or to France?* *And/or* is seldom really required in a sentence and is best avoided unless actually needed to convey this particular set of alternatives: *If convicted, the man faces a jail sentence and/or a stiff fine. He will be tested to determine if he is allergic to pollen and/or certain foods.*

angry at / about / with Use *angry at* or *angry about* with things (*I'm angry at having gotten a parking ticket*) and *angry with* with people (*She's angry with me* [not "at me"] *for my remark*).

antecedent For a general discussion of antecedents, *see* Grammar: II.B.; for problems of usage with antecedents, *see* Grammar: III.C.2.

any one / anyone *Any one*, referring to an individual who is part of a particular group, is written as two words (*Any one of you may attend the meeting*). *Anyone*, referring to people in general or to an unspecific member of a group, is written as one word (*Anyone is welcome to attend the meeting*). Both take singular verbs.

appositive For a general discussion of appositives, *see* Grammar: I.F., IV.D.2.c. For a discussion of the most common problem with appositives, whether to set them off with commas, *see* Glossary of Grammatical Terms: restrictive and nonrestrictive elements.

apt *See* **liable.**

as (meaning *if* or *that*) Avoid using *as* when *if* or *that* is meant (*I do not know if* [or *that*] *I should do it,* not "I do not know as I should do it").

as . . . as / so . . . as Some grammarians insist that the *as . . . as* construction be used only for positive comparison (*This is as good as that*) and that *so . . . as* be used for the negative comparison (*This is not so good as that*). Others, however, prescribe *so . . . as* as an intensifier meaning "to an unusually high degree," as in *Have you ever seen anything so beautiful as this?* Although either is correct in positive or negative comparisons, *as . . . as* is generally preferred for both types of comparisons, with *so . . . as* reserved for its special use as an intensifier.

Remember that *as* is a conjunction meant to introduce a clause. Often in comparisons the clause introduced by *as* is elliptical, that is, some of its words are left out but are understood. *You like him as much as I* means *You like him as much as I* [*like him*]. *You like him as much as me* means *You like him as much as* [*you like*] *me.* If necessary to avoid confusion in such elliptical sentences, the missing words should be supplied. A sentence like "George sees Bill as often as Fred" becomes clear only when the clause is completed: *George sees Bill as often as Fred does* or *George sees Bill as often as he sees Fred.*

When a pronoun is the subject of the elliptical clause, the subjective form of the pronoun is needed after *as* (*She is as tall as I* [*am*], not "She is as tall as me."

as / because / since   Most contemporary writers and grammarians approve the use of the conjunctions *as, because,* and *since* to introduce clauses that show cause or reason (*I have not written him since* [*or as or because*] *I do not have his address*). However, *as* is the least forceful of the three as a causal conjunction and is better reserved for introducing other kinds of clauses (*As I walked in, she left. This is as expensive as the other one. As she explained, there is only one thing to do*).

ascent / assent   *Ascent* means "the act of climbing"; *assent,* "agreement, approval" (*The ascent of the mountain was arduous. The chairman gave his assent to the plan.*)

as if   In formal writing, a past subjunctive verb is used with *as if* (*He acts as if he were crazy*). For a discussion of the subjunctive, *see* Grammar: II.C.4. *See also* **like.**

as / like   *See* **like.**

as . . . than   In using constructions like *as much as, if not more than* (*This is as much as, if not more than, I want. This train is as slow as, if not slower than, the bus*), the first comparison must be completed (*as much as, as slow as*) before beginning the second comparison (*more than, slower than*). Hence avoid using the incomplete construction "as much if not more than."

as to whether   Do not use *as to* with *whether* (*I am not sure whether* [not "as to whether"] *we will go*).

as yet   Except when used at the beginning of a sentence, the phrase *as yet* can usually be shortened to *yet* with no change in meaning (*He has not yet decided,* not "He has not as yet decided").

aural / oral   *Aural* refers to the ear and to that which is heard (*The boy had an aural deficiency and required a hearing aid*); *oral* refers to the mouth and to that which is spoken (*I dislike giving oral presentations before groups*). *See also* **oral.**

avert   *See* **advert.**

avocation / vocation   An *avocation* is one's hobby or secondary occupation; a *vocation* is one's main business or occupation (*Fred's vocation is computer typesetting; his avocation is sailing*).

a while / awhile   *A while* is a noun phrase and should be preceded by a preposition (*after, for, in,* etc.); *awhile* is an adverb and must stand alone (*We stopped for a while. We stopped awhile*).

back / again   Since the prefix *re-* means "again" or "back," do not use words beginning with this prefix (*return, refer, repay,* etc.) with the adverbs *back* and *again.* Using both together is redundant: *He returned* [not "returned again"] *to the scene of the crime.*

bad / badly / ill *See* **feel bad.**

because / on account of *Because* introduces an adverbial clause that gives a reason for the statement in a sentence's main clause (*We came because the movie was free*). To avoid redundancy, do not use the words *because* and *reason* together. Awkward sentences, such as "The reason I left was because I was tired" are better reworded: *I left because I was tired* OR *The reason I left was that I was tired.*

Both *because of* and *on account of* introduce prepositional phrases, not clauses, although a noun clause may, of course, serve as the object of a preposition (*I left because of her. She left because of what I said. They came late on account of car trouble*). *See also* **due to.**

beside / besides *Beside,* a preposition, means "by the side of" (*I sat beside my father*); *besides,* both a preposition and an adverb, means "in addition to" (*Besides basketball, he also plays hockey. The dinner was terrible, and besides there was not any dessert*).

between *See* **among.**

bi- / semi- Words beginning with the prefixes *bi-* and *semi-* are often confused. Remembering that *semi-* means "half" or "occurring halfway through a specified period of time" and that *bi-* means "two" will help to keep straight such troublesome pairs as *semiweekly* ("twice a week") and *biweekly* ("once every two weeks"), *semimonthly* and *bimonthly,* and *semiannual* and *binannual.*

Bible / biblical The noun *Bible* is capitalized; the adjective *biblical,* usually uncapitalized, though this is a matter of preference.

black / Black Names of racial, linguistic, or tribal groups (such as *Caucasian, Indo-European,* or *Negro*) are always capitalized, while designations based on color or local usage (such as *aborigine, black, colored,* or *white*) are lowercased. Since *black* is a racial designation based on color that is also becoming the preferred name of a racial group, there is some confusion regarding its usage. The usage preferred by the *Britannica* is to lowercase *black,* as, for example, in *black English;* but capitalization of the term is equally correct (*Black history*).

bloc / block Use *bloc* in political and ideological senses and *block* in all other senses (*The Communist bloc countries voted together on the issue. The post office is down the block*).

born / borne *Born* and *borne* are both past participles of the verb *bear. Born* is used only in the passive voice to denote "given birth" (*A baby was born*) and as an adjective, *a born liar.* In all other cases use *borne* (*The mother had borne three daughters. The entire bill was borne by the insurance company*).

both alike *Both alike* is redundant; use simply *alike* (*The dresses are alike,* not "both alike").

but *See* **and.**

calendar / calender / colander Do not confuse the spelling of these words. *Calendar* and *calender* are pronounced alike; the former is a noun meaning "a system for reckoning time," and the latter is usually a verb meaning "to glaze paper or textiles." (The noun *calender* denotes "the machine for calendering.") A *colander* (the first syllable rhymes with *doll*) is a utensil with holes in it for draining off liquids from solids.

can hardly Avoid the expression "can't hardly" since the word *hardly* is already a negative. The expression *can hardly* is correct (*She can hardly see*). *See also* **hardly.**

can / may *Can* and *may* are both used to suggest possibility (*This can be done quickly, but it may not be done well*); but only *can* implies physical ability (*He can swim*). *Can* and *may* both suggest circumstantial possibility (*I can arrive early, if necessary. She may be late if the weather is bad*), but *may* is preferred to *can* in such expressions. *May* is also used to request permission (*May I leave early?*).

capital / capitol *Capital* has a variety of meanings, but in speaking of the seat of government it refers to the city serving as that seat (*Madison is the capital of Wisconsin*). *Capitol* refers to the building housing the legislative body.

Catholic / catholic *Catholic,* spelled with a capital *C,* refers in general usage to the Roman Catholic Church or to Roman Catholics; *catholic,* uncapitalized, means "universal" (*an organization with catholic rather than provincial concerns*).

cause due to This expression is redundant; use either *cause* or *due to,* but not both together. Instead of "The cause was due to an explosion," use *The cause was an explosion* or *The fire was due to an explosion. See also* **due to.**

censor / censure / censer As a verb *censor* refers to examining books, plays, movies, etc., with an eye to deleting that which seems objectionable for moral or political reasons (*Much of the movie was censored prior to its release*). As a noun *censor* refers to one who does this examination. To *censure* means "to criticize severely" and is chiefly used with reference to people or groups of people (*He was sternly censured by his colleagues for his behavior*). A *censer* is a receptacle in which incense is burned.

center on / center around The expression to *center on* is entirely correct (*His play centers on crime*), but to *center around* is a physical impossibility and hence is best avoided.

childish / childlike *Childish* and *childlike* are distinctly different in meaning. The former is generally used pejoratively to mean "silly," "weak," or "infantile," referring to behavior suitable only in children; *childlike* refers to the generally admired qualities in children—innocence, freshness, trustfulness (*Her childish whining was maddening. Her childlike trust in the outcome was heartening*).

cite / sight / site   The verb *cite* means "to quote, to refer to" (*She cited Shakespeare but misquoted him*), "to commend for meritorious action" (*Jack was cited for bravery and citizenship*), "to enumerate" (*I can cite all the pros and cons of the issue*), or "to call before a court of law" (*If you don't slow down, you will be cited for speeding*). *Sight,* as a verb, generally means "to catch a glimpse of" or "to take aim at" (*to sight land, to sight a target*); and as a noun, "something seen or worth seeing" (*The sight of the accident was horrifying*). *Site,* both noun and verb, means respectively "a location" and "to locate" (*The site of the disaster is one of the sights of the city*).

climactic / climatic   *Climactic* refers to the climax, or end, of something; and *climatic,* to atmospheric changes and to the weather.

close proximity   *See* **proximity.**

coincidence   *Coincidence* does not refer to an unusual happening nor to a single event; rather it means "the simultaneous happening of two or more events" (*It was sheer coincidence that she arrived when the fight broke out*).

colander   *See* **calendar.**

collective nouns   For discussions of the main problem with collective nouns, whether to treat them as singular or plural, *see* Grammar: III.B.2., III.C.2.

compare / contrast   To *compare* things is to look at them in terms of their similarities and differences; to *contrast* things is to focus on their differences. Use *compare to* to point out similarities (*His voice has been compared to Caruso's*) and to liken two persons or things of different categories (*The poet compared the woman's hair to sunshine*). Use *compare with* to point out similarities or differences of two persons or things of the same category (*Compared with last year's crop, this year's was very small. Compared with the fish we bought last week, this is excellent*).

The verb *contrast* is generally followed by the preposition *with* (*They contrasted my work with yours*), but the noun *contrast,* especially when used in the phrase *in contrast,* is followed by the preposition *to* (*In contrast to what was budgeted, we actually spent very little*).

complement / compliment / supplement   *Complement* means "that which completes something" (*The complement to a meal is dessert; a ship's complement of 50 men*). *Compliment* is an expression of approval or praise (*He complimented her dress*). *Supplement* also refers to that which completes, but it emphasizes the aspect of adding to something rather than making it complete (*He supplemented his income by taking a weekend job*).

compose/ comprise The first meaning of *comprise* ("to include, to be made up of") has largely been supplanted by its second meaning ("to constitute, to compose"). Nonetheless it is still better to say that the whole *is composed of* its parts (not "the whole is comprised of its parts") or that the whole *comprises* its parts (not "the parts comprise the whole"); they would write, for example, *The complex is composed of six buildings* or *The complex comprises six buildings*.

comprehensible / comprehensive *Comprehensible* means "able to be understood" (*Her composition was poorly written but comprehensible*); *comprehensive* means "covering thoroughly" or "including a great deal" (*Her work on the subject was hardly comprehensive*).

concurrent *See* **continual.**

connotation / denotation Both *connotation* and *denotation* refer to the meaning of a word; but while the *denotation* of a word provides its strict definition, the *connotation* of that word provides the additional ideas that have come to be associated with it. For example, childhood *denotes* the period during which a child grows up. To some it may *connote* a pleasant period of innocence and few responsibilities, while to others it may *connote* a period of fear, frustration, and general discomfort.

consecutive *See* **continual.**

consensus Note the spelling of this word—an initial *c* and three *s*'s— and avoid using it in the phrase "consensus of opinion." *Consensus* alone suffices to mean "a combined or aggregate opinion."

consul *See* **council.**

continual / continuous / concurrent / consecutive *Continual* and *continuous* mean "without interruption" (*The woman was in a continual state of panic. The siren sounded continuously for five minutes. We have a continuous view of the ocean from the kitchen window*). Only *continual*, however, means "repeated regularly, often in rapid succession" (*Throughout the speech, there were continual interruptions by hecklers*). *Concurrent* means "happening at the same time" (*The play had concurrent runs in New York City and in Chicago*). *Consecutive* means "happening sequentially, one thing after another without gaps" (*The three symphonies were played on three consecutive evenings*).

contrast *See* **compare.**

corps / corpse *Corps* (both singular and plural) is a body of people, whether military or civilian, working together or bonded by a common direction (*the army signal corps, corps planning team, corps de ballet*); *corpse* is a dead body.

council / counsel / consul Although pronounced alike, *council* and *counsel* are distinct in meaning. *Council* refers to a group of individuals that meets to deliberate or administer (*city council*), while *counsel* refers to an advisor or to an attorney (*the defendant's counsel*). As a noun *counsel* also means "advice" and as a verb, "to advise" (*The minister's counsel to the troubled youth went unheeded*). *Consul* refers to a government representative in a foreign country.

credible / creditable / credulous *Credible* means "believable" (*Her excuse was credible*). *Creditable* means "worthy of belief, praise, or esteem" (*Considering his recent illness, his performance was creditable*) or "capable of being credited to" (*Her dramatic victory of the set was creditable to her strong backhand*). *Credulous* means "ready to believe on slight evidence, believing too easily" (*The old woman was as credulous as a child*).

dangling participle *See* Grammar: III.D.1.

decent / descent / dissent Do not confuse the spelling of this similar-sounding trio. *Decent* means "proper, fitting"; *descent*, "the act of going down, or descending"; and *dissent*, "disagreement."

deduction / induction In general *deduction* means "to arrive at a conclusion by reasoning" (*He admired Sherlock Holmes for his powers of deduction*). However, in contrast with *induction*, *deduction* refers to reasoning from the general to the specific (*Given that all human beings must die and that I am a human being, I can deduce that I, too, will die*). *Induction* refers to reasoning from the specific to the general (*Since I must eat to stay alive and since I am human, I induce that other human beings must also eat to stay alive*). Faulty reasoning, whether *deductive* or *inductive*, has produced many an illogical conclusion; for example, *Based on a sample of 50 elementary school teachers, all of whom were women, one might induce that all elementary school teachers are women.* Think carefully through inductive and deductive statements.

denotation *See* **connotation.**

descent *See* **decent.**

desert / dessert The noun *desert* means either "an arid place" or (usually used in the plural) "deserved reward or punishment" (*just deserts*); the verb *desert* means "to leave." Be careful in writing not to confuse the spelling of these words with the sweet course ending a meal, *dessert*.

device / devise *Device* is a noun meaning "a mechanism or plan by which something is accomplished"; except in a limited legal sense, *devise* is a verb meaning "to invent, to contrive."

die / dye While there is no confusion between the simple verbs *die* ("to expire") and *dye* ("to color"), the spelling of their present participles causes some difficulty: *die/dying, dye/dyeing.*

different from / different than Since *from* is a preposition and thus takes an object, use *different from* before a noun or other nominal (*My hat is different from yours, different from the green one, and different from what I wanted*). Since *than* is a subordinating conjunction that introduces a dependent clause, use *different than* before adverbial clauses, whether they are complete or elliptical (*The result is different than I expected it to be. The outcome is different than planned*).

disassemble / dissemble *Disassemble* means "to break up an assembly of people or an assemblage of parts" (*The group disassembled after presenting the report*). To *dissemble* means "to hide or disguise facts or feelings" (*The worker dissembled his anger with his boss*).

discreet / discrete *Discreet* means "cautious, prudent" or "modest" (*She was not very discreet in telling the tale at dinner*). *Discrete* means "separate, distinct" (*The chapters were discrete essays on the subject*). The respective antonyms of these words are *indiscreet* and *indiscrete.*

disingenuous *See* **ingenious.**

disinterested / uninterested Despite the fact that *disinterested* and *uninterested* have been taken as synonyms, most writers prefer to observe the distinction between these words that has long predominated. In general *disinterested* is used to mean "impartial, unbiased" (*The negotiations were overseen by a disinterested third party*) and *uninterested* to mean "lacking interest in something, indifferent" (*He is completely uninterested in politics*).

dissent *See* **decent.**

distinct / distinctive *Distinct* means "separate," "clear," or "explicit" (*These are two distinct approaches to the problem. He speaks distinctly*). *Distinctive* means "characteristic, that which sets apart or makes distinct" (*Her eyes are her distinctive feature*).

divers / diverse *Divers* (accent on the first syllable) means "various, several"; *diverse* (accent on the second syllable) means "differing one from another, different in kind" (*The divers members of the audience held diverse opinions on the subject*).

double negative *See* Grammar: III.D.4.

due to / because of While the use of *due to* in place of *because of* is prevalent, it is better avoided. Both are prepositions and hence take objects, but *due to* correctly introduces a prepositional phrase used adjectivally (*His death, due to heart trouble, was unexpected. His unexpected death was due to heart trouble*). *Because of* correctly introduces a prepositional phrase used adverbially (*She won the race because of her long legs,* not "She won the race due to her long legs." *We went home early because of my mother's illness,* not "We went home early due to my mother's illness").

dying / dyeing *See* **die.**

each / every Both *each* and *every* take singular verbs (*Each of the men has one chance. Every man has one chance*). Avoid the worn phrase *each and every,* which needlessly expands the sentence; use one or the other (*every student* or *each student,* not "each and every student"). *See also* Grammar: III.B.2.

Earth / earth *Earth* is usually capitalized when speaking of the planet *Earth* and uncapitalized when speaking of the ground.

effect *See* **affect.**

egoism / egotism *Egoism* refers to the philosophical belief that self-interest is the motivating force behind all conscious action; *egotism* refers to excessive talk and concern about self, or an overblown sense of self-importance. An *egoist* may or may not be an *egotist,* but most *egotists* are unlikely to stray far enough from the pronoun *I* to consider philosophy of any kind.

either / neither *Either* means "one or the other of two"; *neither* means "not either of two." Nouns modified by these adjectives take singular verbs (*Either dress is suitable. Neither car runs*).

When used as conjunctions, *either* can only be followed by *or,* and *neither* only by *nor.* Both constructions, *either . . . or* and *neither . . . nor,* are followed by singular verbs unless the element after *or* or *nor* is plural (*Either Eddie or Maria has the money. Neither the two boys nor their sister is willing to babysit. Neither Mr. Smith nor the Howards are free for dinner.*)

elemental / elementary *Elemental* generally refers to the great forces in nature—the four elements: earth, air, fire, and water—and hence means "fundamental" (*winds of elemental violence*). *Elementary* means "simple, rudimentary" (*an elementary problem*).

elicit / illicit The verb *elicit* means "to draw out, to extract" (*We finally elicited a response from him*); the adjective *illicit* means "unlawful" (*illicit gambling*).

ellipsis For a discussion of the correct use of ellipsis, *see* Grammar: IV.J.

elude *See* **allude.**

emigrate / immigrate / migrate To *emigrate* is to leave one's own country to take up residence in another country (*After many years ballet stars Valery and Galina Panov were allowed to emigrate from the Soviet Union to Israel*). To *immigrate* is to come into the new country of residence (*For many years immigrants to the United States* *entered the country through Ellis Island*). To *migrate* is to move from one place to another, usually periodically (*The Browns migrate to Florida for the winter*).

eminent / imminent / immanent *Eminent* means "distinguished, noted, remarkable, conspicuous" (*an eminent author, eminently sensible*); *imminent* means "about to occur" (*The speaker's arrival is imminent*). *Immanent,* usually restricted to theological or psychological usage, means "inherent" (*Some theologians believe a spirit of love to be immanent in the universe*).

ensure / insure Both verbs can be used to mean "to guarantee, to make sure," but only *insure* can be used to mean "to guarantee compensation for loss or damage," as in *insured packages*.

etc. Opinion is divided about the use in writing of *etc.,* short for the Latin *et cetera* ("and other things"). If used, *etc.* should not follow the word *and* nor should it end a series begun with *such as* or similar phrases.

every *See* **each.**

every one / everyone *Every one* refers to each individual in a group (*Every one of the jury had a slightly different opinion about the case*); *everyone,* to everybody or every person in a group, none of whom is being considered individually (*Everyone on the team gets a prize*). Both *every one* and *everyone* use singular verbs and singular possessive pronouns (*Everyone has his or her* [not "their"] *speech ready*).

except *See* **accept.**

exhausting / exhaustive *Exhausting* means "fatiguing, tiring" (*The evening was exhausting*); *exhaustive* means "thorough, complete" (*The report is an exhaustive look at the problem*).

extent / extant *Extent* (accent on the second syllable) means "the limit or degree to which something extends" (*The extent of the damage to the car is not yet known*). *Extant* (accent may be on either syllable) is an adjective, meaning "still in existence" (*This tool is the only extant artifact from that period*).

fact Avoid the tautology a "true fact"; a fact is a fact. Also, the phrase *the fact that,* while popular, is often unnecessary and can usually be eliminated with no ill effects. "Because of the fact that we won" is better and more simply written *because we won.*

farther / further Both are the comparative degree of the adjective *far,* but some careful writers distinguish between *farther* to refer to distance (*farther down the road*) and *further* to figuratively indicate additional degree, extent, or quantity (*further goals ahead, to take the argument a step further*). The same distinction is made with the superlatives *farthest* and *furthest.*

fatal / fateful *Fatal* means "deadly" (*a fatal heart attack*); *fateful* implies momentous, and often ominous, consequences that are, or appear to be, governed by fate (*The fateful argument signaled their downfall*).

feel bad / badly; feel good / well To *feel bad* means "to feel ill" and is not synonymous, despite common usage, with to *feel badly*. The correct meaning of to *feel badly* is "to have a poor sense of feeling (touch)." To *feel badly* also colloquially means "to feel intensely about something" (*I feel badly about her illness*). Nowadays both *feel bad* and *feel badly* are commonly used to mean "to feel ill," but in the interest of correct usage, the writer is encouraged to *feel bad* or *ill* when sick, to *feel bad* when sorry or regretful, and to *feel badly* when numb!

Confusingly, the distinction between *feel good* and *feel well* is not analogous to that between *feel bad* and *feel badly*. To *feel well* means either "to feel healthy" or "to have a good sense of feeling (touch)." To *feel good* means "to be in a good frame of mind" (*I feel good about my new job*).

felicitous *See* **fortuitous.**

few / little; few / less *Few* is used when referring to people or things that can be counted and *little* when referring to quantity in general. Hence, *There are few people who can produce the same results with as little money.* The comparative forms of *few* and *little* are *fewer* and *less*. Again, use *fewer* to refer to that which can be counted: *He has fewer children than I. We have fewer problems this year than last. Fewer than 10 people appeared.* Use *less* to refer to quantity, extent, or the sum total (including figures of money that are spoken of as a sum total, not as individually counted dollars): *She has less trouble with this car than with the previous one. He received less than $75 for the piano. Less than 20 percent of those eligible applied for the benefits. See also* **less.**

figurative *See* **literal.**

flammable / inflammable / inflammatory Contrary to what many believe, *inflammable* does not mean "not combustible"; both *flammable* and *inflammable* mean "combustible, easily ignited," and *inflammable* also means "easily excited or angered." The appropriate term to state that something is not combustible is *nonflammable* or *noncombustible*. *Inflammatory* means "causing inflammation," whether in the medical sense, the incendiary sense, or the figurative sense of exciting, arousing, or angering (*an inflammatory remark*).

forbear / forebear *Forbear* (accent on the second syllable) is a verb meaning "to avoid" or "to refrain from" (*The committee forbore a decision on the matter*). *Forebear* (accent on the first syllable), also variantly spelled *forbear,* is a noun meaning "an ancestor," as in *Her forebears* (not "forebearers") *were Norwegian.*

forceful / forcible *Forceful* means "full of force" (*His argument for the new project was forceful*); *forcible* means "effected by force" (*The policeman's forcible entry left the door in shreds*).

foreword / forward / forwards / froward *Foreword* is the preface, or introduction, to a book. *Forward,* both adjective and adverb, and *forwards,* only an adverb, mean "in a frontward direction"; the former is the preferred adverb (*She moved forward to the edge of her seat*). *Forward,* as an adjective, can also mean "presumptuous," "fresh," or "progressive," (*forward thinking, a forward move*). *Froward* means "inclined to disobedience or opposition" (*a froward child*).

former / latter *Former* and *latter* refer to only two persons or things, the *former* being the first of two and the *latter* the second of two. *Between the beach and the mountains for a vacation, I prefer the former and he prefers the latter.* Do not use *former* or *latter* with three or more persons or things; use instead the *first* or *last.*

fortunate / fortuitous / felicitous *Fotunate* means "lucky" (*He was fortunate to have escaped unharmed*); *fortuitous,* "that which happens by chance" (*The meeting was a fortuitous one*); and *felicitous,* "apt, appropriate" (*Her suggestion offered a felicitous solution to the problem*).

forward / forwards / froward *See* **foreword.**

fulsome *Fulsome* refers predominantly to that which is excessive or overdone, not just full or abundant (*The party was a fulsome affair*).

further *See* **farther.**

good / well *Good* is an adjective and should not be used in place of the adverb *well. She is a good swimmer. She swims well. See also* **feel bad.**

gourmand / gourmet A *gourmand* is one who enjoys eating well and in large quantity, and the term is often pejorative; a *gourmet* is one who enjoys fine food and drink but who may well eat sparingly.

hanged / hung *Hanged* and *hung* are both past tenses and past participles of the verb *hang. Hanged* is used only when referring to death by hanging (*He hanged himself*); *hung* is now used both as a synonym for *hanged* (*She hung herself*) and to mean "suspended" (*We hung the picture on the wall*).

hardly / scarcely / barely The restrictive adverbs *hardly, scarcely,* and *barely* imply negation and should never be used with other negative words, as in "can't hardly" or "barely without" since the double negative produces an unintended positive.

"Hardly . . . than" ("Hardly had the tide come in than the rain began") and its counterparts ("barely . . . than," "scarcely . . .

than") are ill-formed constructions patterned on the perfectly correct adverbial comparison "no sooner . . . than" (*No sooner had she arrived than we left*). *Hardly, barely,* and *scarcely* should correctly be paired with the conjunctions *when* and *before* (*Hardly had the movie begun when the projector broke. The class had scarcely begun before a fire drill interrupted*). *See also* Grammar: III.D.4.

healthy / healthful   While these words are now considered synonyms, it is best in writing to observe the original distinction between them. *Healthy* means "in good physical condition" (*a healthy man*), and *healthful* means "promoting good health" (*a healthful diet*).

historic / historical   The distinction between these words merits remembering. *Historic* means "significant in history" (*The historic Camp David agreement marked a new stage in the Middle East peace negotiations*). *Historical* refers to that which is part of or based on history (*The historical setting of the play was Colonial America*).

hopefully   The word *hopefully* means "in a hopeful manner" or "full of hope" and should not be used to mean "I hope that" or "it is hoped that." While this incorrect usage is daily gaining acceptance among more and more speakers (and writers!), do not be drawn in. If you mean "I hope that . . . ," say it; if you mean "probably" or "maybe," use these adverbs. Sentences like "Hopefully the car will run" are both incorrect and fatuous.

hung   *See* **hanged.**

if you were me   Although often used in speaking, this construction is incorrect and should be avoided in writing. The correct construction is *if you were I,* since the subjective form of the pronoun is required when the pronoun is used as a predicate nominative. Similarly, *if you were he, if I were she, if they were we,* and so forth, are correct. If you find these constructions awkward in writing, consider rewordings such as *if you were in my place* or *if they were like us.*

illegible / unreadable / unintelligible   *Illegible* means "impossible to read or decipher," usually the result of poor handwriting; *unreadable* describes that which is unsuitable for reading because it is dull or poorly written. *Unintelligible* means "that which is obscure or incomprehensible." The respective antonyms of these words are *legible, readable,* and *intelligible.*

illicit   *See* **elicit.**

illusion   *See* **allusion.**

immanent   *See* **eminent.**

immerge / emerge   *Immerge* means "to immerse in a liquid", though the term is now almost obsolete (*The otter immerged into the river and swam off*); *emerge,* "to come forth into view" (*The man emerged from the crowd*).

immigrate   *See* **emigrate.**

imminent *See* **eminent.**

immoral / amoral / unmoral *Immoral* refers to that which conflicts with standards of morality (*Some religious sects consider smoking and drinking immoral*); *amoral* and *unmoral* both refer to that which is outside the code of morality, being neither moral nor immoral (*From a physician's point of view, smoking is an amoral but unhealthy habit*).

imply / infer These terms are often confused though they are distinct in meaning. The speaker or writer *implies* ("indirectly states"), and the listener or reader *infers* ("concludes, reasons") a meaning from what has been stated (*She implied that I was wrong. I inferred from her remarks that she was angry*).

incredible / incredulous *Incredible* means "unbelievable"; *incredulous,* "unbelieving, skeptical" (*His tale was incredible, and I proved an incredulous listener*). *See also* **credible.**

indiscreet / indiscrete *See* **discreet.**

induction *See* **deduction.**

infer *See* **imply.**

infinitives For a general discussion of infinitives, *see* Grammar: II.C., II.I.3., II.J.4. Below is discussed a common concern with the use of infinitives: the split infinitive.

The grammatical taboo against the split infinitive (separating *to* and its verb by another word or words: *to quickly eat, to finally finish*) is still strong, although a total taboo is outdated and frequently the cause of the awkward prose it seeks to clarify. It is obvious to the ear that *to correctly build the porch* is preferable to *to build correctly the porch.* In this case, of course, the adverb could be placed at the end of the infinitive phrase (*to build the porch correctly*), but it then receives greater emphasis than if positioned closer to the verb it modifies. If such emphasis is desired, this phrasing is fine. If not, it is acceptable to split an infinitive and even advisable to do so if confusion or awkwardness otherwise results. Nonetheless the split infinitive should not be overworked in writing. Note also that with compound infinitives it is common to separate the auxiliary and main verbs by an adverb (*to have rightly won, to have been finally vindicated*).

inflammable / inflammatory *See* **flammable.**

inflict *See* **afflict.**

-ing For a discussion of the formation of the present participle and its use in verb tenses, *see* Grammar: II.C.2.; for discussion of participles used adjectivally, *see* Grammar: II.I.1.; for participial phrases, *see* Grammar: II.J.2.; for dangling participles, *see* Grammar: III.D.1.; for a discussion of gerunds, *see* Grammar: II.I.2.

ingenious / ingenuous *Ingenious* means "clever, inventive" (*The child devised an ingenious solution to the problem*); *ingenuous* means "candid" or "innocent" and now connotes almost foolish naiveté (*The ingenuous young girl answered without the slightest hesitation*). The antonym of *ingenuous* is *disingenuous,* meaning "cunning, deceptive."

insure *See* **ensure.**

irregardless *See* **regardless.**

irresponsible / irresponsive *Irresponsible* means "lacking a sense of responsibility" (*He was irresponsible with money*); *irresponsive* means "unresponsive" (*She was irresponsive to treatment*).

irritate *See* **aggravate.**

its / it's *Its* is the possessive pronoun, or possessive adjective, meaning "belonging to it," not to be confused with the contraction *it's,* meaning "it is."

-ize The suffix *-ize* is frequently added to nouns and adjectives to produce such awkward hybrids as "accessorize," "channelize," or "prioritize." Such terms, however, offer no real advantage over the words they seek to replace and are opposed by many writers. In the case of the above examples, use *choose accessories for* for "accessorize"; *put through channels* for "channelize"; and *establish priorities* for "prioritize."

judicial / judicious *Judicial* refers to courts of law, judges, or the process of judgment (*The judicial review will take some time*); *judicious* means "displaying good judgment" (*The decision to drop the issue was a judicious conclusion to the episode*).

latter *See* **former.**

lay / lie In general usage the verb *lay* (*laid, laid*) means "to place, to put down" and is transitive, that is, takes a direct object (*The hen is laying an egg. Lay the book down*). *Lie* (*lay, lain*) means "to rest" or "be at rest" and is always intransitive, that is, unable to take a direct object (*I must lie down. The book lay unopened on the table*). The present participles of these verbs often are confused; that of *lay* is *laying* (*Fred was laying the tile floor*) and that of *lie, lying* (*She is lying on the couch*). The principal parts and present participle of the verb *lie,* meaning "to tell an untruth," are *lie, lied, lied, lying.*

legible *See* **illegible.**

less / least / lesser *Less* is the comparative form, and *least* the superlative form, of the adjective *little.* Use *less* only when speaking of two things; *least,* when speaking of three or more. *Lesser* is an adjective meaning "of less size, quality, or significance" (*The author's lesser works are not well known*). *See also* **few.**

liable / likely / apt In addition to its primary sense of "legally responsible," *liable* also refers to the probability of a troublesome outcome (*Parked here, your car is liable to be towed*). Neither *likely* nor *apt* connotes the inauspicious element associated with *liable*. Very close in meaning, *likely* refers to that which is probable or promising and *apt* to that which is suitable, predisposed, or inclined to be (*Fred is a likely candidate for the post, but he is apt to refuse the job. Her decision was apt in light of the circumstances*).

lie *See* **lay.**

like / as Among its various uses, *like* is a preposition, meaning "similar(ly) to," and takes an object, whether a noun, pronoun, or other nominal (*He eats like a pig. I feel like dancing. My sister looks like me. This meatloaf is like the army's.* (Note that a pronoun used as an object of the preposition *like* must be in the objective case; *e.g., like us, like him.*) Although *like* is also technically classified as a conjunction and as such can theoretically introduce a clause, this usage has long been vehemently opposed by most writers and grammarians. They consider nonstandard such sentences as "Do this like you were taught" and "Anne speaks with a drawl like Henry does." Because of this prevailing opposition, the use of *like* as a conjunction should be avoided.

The conjunction *as* always correctly introduces a clause (*Do this as you were taught. Anne speaks with a drawl as Henry does* [or *as does Henry*]), although this clause may be elliptical (*I am as old as he* [is]. *The meeting started late today, as* [it did] *yesterday*). While most often used as a conjunction, *as* can also serve as a preposition to mean "in the capacity of." In this single instance *as* is followed by a simple object rather than a clause (*While my boss was ill, I acted as supervisor. In makeup Hal Holbrook looks like Mark Twain and appears as him on stage*). A pronoun used as an object of the preposition *as* must be in the objective case.

Like is also often used to mean "as if" ("Act like you are busy." "She looks like she needs help"), but this use of *like* draws opposition too. In formal writing, use *as if* if that is meant and use a past subjunctive verb in the clause (*Act as if you were busy. She looks as if she needed help*). *See also* **as . . . as;** for a discussion of the subjunctive, *see* Grammar: II.C.4.

likely *See* **liable.**

literal / literate *Literal* means "adhering to the words of an original text" or "construing words or ideas in their strictest, denotative sense" (*a literal translation; We literally broke the door down to get in*). By extension *literal* implies that which is unimaginative and matter-of-fact (*literal-minded*). The opposite of *literal* is *figurative*. *Literate* means "educated, cultured" or "the basic ability to read and write" (*Her report was a literate, thoughtful piece of work*). The antonym of *literate* is *illiterate* (*Despite being promoted each year, fifteen-year-old Daniel is still illiterate*).

literally   *Literally* is best restricted to use in its denotative sense (*see* **literal** above) and is not to be confused with its antonym, *figuratively*. Avoid using *literally* merely for emphasis, when the statement is not literally true, as in "she had literally five hundred cats"; find other words or expressions to emphasize the statement.

little   *See* **few.**

mad   The primary meaning of the word *mad* is "insane," and the scrupulous writer avoids using *mad* in formal writing in its secondary sense of "angry."

majority / plurality   In an election a candidate wins by a *majority* if he or she receives more than half of the total number of votes cast (*Of 100 votes cast, Fred won the majority with 65 votes*). If the winner in a field of three or more does not receive a majority, he or she wins by a *plurality,* that is, the number of votes greater than that cast for the first runner-up (*Anne got 10 votes, Jane seven, and Mary five; and thus Anne won the election with a plurality of three votes*).

metaphors, mixed and pure   For a general discussion of metaphors, *see* Figures of Speech in Part III, under The Finer Points of Writing. Below is discussed a common problem in using metaphors: the mixed metaphor.

A metaphor is a figure of speech in which a word or phrase denoting one kind of object or idea is used to describe an entirely different object or idea in order to suggest an analogy between the two, as in *the bloom of life.* A mixed metaphor is one in which several incongruous references are made. "She is a real workhorse, but her feathers are easily ruffled." "Try as he might, he could not cage the mounting tide of resentment within." Be careful to avoid mixed metaphors unless humor is intended.

may   *See* **can.**

migrate   *See* **emigrate.**

moral / morale   *Moral,* as an adjective, refers to the correctness of something or the distinction between right and wrong (*Many felt the violence had a moral justification*); as a noun, it means "the lesson learned from a story or experience." *Morale* generally refers to the mental attitude of an individual or group (*Following his dismissal, his morale was very low*).

negligent / negligible   *Negligent* means "neglectful, lax"; *negligible* means "unimportant, small" (*He was negligent about paying his bills, despite the fact that the money in question was negligible*).

neither *See* **either.**

neither / none Use *neither* to mean "not either of two" and *none* to mean "not one of several" (*Neither of the two boys has returned. None of the class has read the assignment. None of the three cars works*). *Neither* always takes a singular verb; *none* can take either a singular or plural verb, depending on whether the members of the group being talked about are considered collectively as a unit or individually (*None—not one—of the class has failed the exam. None of the towels are clean*). *See also* **neither . . . nor.**

neither . . . nor Always follow *neither* with *nor,* not *or*. Remember too that *neither* takes a singular verb (*Neither Jack nor Anne is here*), unless the element following *nor* is plural (*Neither Jack nor his friends are here*).

nice *Nice* is much overworked to indicate mild approval and now carries almost no semantic weight. Avoid the word in writing unless intending it in the sense of "precise" or "exacting" (*The speaker made a nice distinction between heroism and martyrdom*). If "pleasant" or "agreeable" is intended, use these or other words more expressive than *nice*.

nor / or *See* **either; neither.**

notable / noted / notorious *Notable* means "worthy of note" (*Despite a notable effort, he lost the tennis match*); *noted* means "famous, celebrated." While *notable* and *noted* both connote distinction for positive reasons, one may be *notable* while not being *noted* or, conversely, *noted* without being *notable! Notorious* connotes being well known for negative, and frequently unsavory, reasons (*John is noted for his musical accomplishments and his brother for his notorious gangland connections*).

number *See* **amount.**

numbers and figures For the preferred styling of numbers and figures, *see* Grammar: V.D.

official / officious *Official* refers to an office or position, or that which is formal or authorized (*The mayor's official explanation of the episode was curiously unclear*). *Officious* means "meddlesome, or forward in offering help" (*Much to the host's annoyance, his officious guest busied herself with the details of the party*).

on account of *See* **because.**

one of the For a discussion of the question that arises when this phrase is expanded to a clause, whether to follow it with a singular or plural verb (*one of the women who is/are*), *see* Grammar: III.B.2.

only Be careful to place *only* close to the word it modifies. Note the different meanings that result from the various placements of *only* in the following sentences: *Anne gave me only a birthday gift this* *year. Only Anne gave me a birthday gift this year. Anne gave a birthday gift only to me this year. Anne gave me a birthday gift only this year.* See also Grammar: III.D.1.

or / nor *See* **either; neither.**

oral / verbal *Oral* refers to that which is spoken; *verbal*, in its primary sense, to that which is conveyed by words, whether written or spoken. What is *oral* is also *verbal*, but that which is *verbal* is not necessarily *oral*. Hence, many careful writers insist that the common expression "a verbal agreement" meaning "an unwritten, spoken agreement" is more correctly "an oral agreement." *See also* **aural / oral.**

ordinance / ordnance *Ordinance* refers to an authoritative command, a law (usually municipal), or a prescribed practice (*Dog owners in New York City must comply with the new ordinance*). *Ordnance* refers either to military supplies as a whole or specifically to cannon and artillery (*Even their heavy ordnance was inadequate to combat the enemy's sophisticated weaponry*).

orient / orientate Although both *orient* and *orientate* mean "to position facing the East" and hence "to rearrange or adapt to existing circumstances," *orient* is the preferred word.

ostensible / ostentatious *Ostensible* means "apparent, that which appears or professes to be" (*Having previous plans was his ostensible reason for refusing the invitation, but in fact he does not get along with the hostess*). *Ostentatious* means "showy, pretentious" (*The diamond ring was more ostentatious than attractive*).

ought *Ought*, originally the past subjunctive of the verb *owe* and now always used as an auxiliary verb, implies moral obligation, advisability, or logical expectation or consequence. Since it is an auxiliary verb, its only correct usage is before another verb, usually an infinitive (*He ought to come home. Ought I to make dinner? I ought to have called her*), never after another auxiliary (as in "had ought to," "should ought to," "used to ought"). Negative statements are made by immediately following *ought* with *not* (*I ought not go. She ought not to have left*). Note also that the colloquial expression "ought to of" is an incorrect version of *ought to have.*

out loud This expression is colloquial; *aloud* is more formal.

outside The expression "outside of" is redundant; use *outside* alone (*He lives outside town*).

parallel construction *See* Grammar: III.E.1.

paramount / tantamount *Paramount* means "of superior rank" or "of chief importance" (*His paramount concern was money*); *tantamount* means "virtually equivalent to" (*Her explanation was tantamount to an admission of guilt*).

parentheses In general writing, parentheses are used to enclose new or explanatory material that is separate from the main sentence. Use parentheses sparingly and not at all when simple commas can easily set off the material. Abundant parentheses are distracting to the reader and best avoided by reworking the material into separate sentences. *See also* Grammar: IV.H.

parlay / parley The verb *parlay* refers to betting an original sum and its earnings on another wager or, by extension, to turning a small stake or position to great advantage (*He parlayed a single boat into an entire shipping industry*). *Parley* refers to a debate, discussion, or conference, especially with an enemy to arrive at a settlement (*The Sadat-Begin parleys eventually produced an accord*).

participles For a general discussion of participles, *see* Grammar: II.I.1.; for a discussion of dangling participles, *see* Grammar: III.D.1.a.

penultimate *See* **ultimate.**

perceptible / perceptive *Perceptible* means "able to be perceived, noticeable" (*The spices made a perceptible difference in the taste*); *perceptive* means "able to perceive, observant, sensitive to" (*The teacher was perceptive about the needs of her individual students*).

persecute / prosecute *Persecute* means "to harass" (*She was persecuted for her religious beliefs*); *prosecute*, "to begin legal proceedings against someone for the commission of a crime or violation of the law" (*The state prosecuted the former governor for allegedly misusing state funds*).

plurality *See* **majority.**

prepositions For a general discussion of prepositions, *see* Grammar: II.F.

When the object of a preposition is a pronoun, the objective form of that pronoun (*me, him, her, us, them*) must be used. Do not be confused when the object of the preposition is a combination of nouns and pronouns or a mixture of several pronouns; the objective form of all the pronouns is still required (*between you and him, for Mrs. Smith and me, to her and me*).

With regard to the traditional ban on ending a sentence with a preposition, many good writers consider it an outmoded grammatical taboo. When clarity or verbal grace require it, a prepositional end to a sentence is nowadays a permissible construction (*The contract was one all the parties agreed to*).

prescribe / proscribe These often confused words are very different in meaning. *Prescribe* means "to set down a rule or course of action" or "to order a medical treatment" (*The teacher prescribed hard work. The physician prescribed bed rest*). *Proscribe* means "to forbid or condemn as harmful" (*In some states smoking is proscribed in public places*).

principal / principle   *Principal*, when used as an adjective, means "chief, most important" (*principal parts of a verb, principal ideas*); as a noun, it means "head, leader" (*school principal*) or "a capital sum of money placed at interest" (*The interest on the principal is five percent*). *Principle*, which is solely used as a noun, means "a fundamental truth" (*principle of motion*), "a basic doctrine" (*principle of democracy*), or "a standard of conduct" (*a woman of high principle*).

pronouns   For a general discussion of pronouns, *see* Grammar: II.B.; for a discussion of usage problems with pronouns, *see* Grammar: III.C.

proscribe   *See* **prescribe.**

prosecute   *See* **persecute.**

proximity   The expression "in close proximity" is redundant since *proximity* means, in one sense, "closeness"; use either *close* or *in proximity*, but not both together (*The two houses are in proximity*).

punctuation   For questions about punctuation, *see* Grammar: IV., V.

raise / rise / raze   The verb *raise* (*raised, raised*) always takes an object (*raise the window*); the verb *rise* (*rose, risen*) never takes an object (*The temperature rises every hour*). Do not confuse the spelling of *raise* with its homonym *raze*, meaning "to demolish."

readable   *See* **illegible.**

real / really   *Real* should be used as an adjective; *really*, as an adverb. Avoid using *real* as an adverb to mean "very," as in *This is really* (not "real") *sour*; and avoid overworking *really* itself as an intensifier. Reserve *really* instead to mean "in fact" (*I really did lose your keys*).

recur / reoccur   The two are synonyms. "Recur" is an elision of "reoccur."

regardless / irregardless   "Irregardless" is a corruption of the word *regardless*, perhaps patterned after the words *irrespective* or *irresponsible*. Whatever its origins, it is incorrect and redundant since both the prefix *ir-* and the suffix *-less* indicate negation. Use instead *regardless* (*Regardless of her income, she was seriously in debt*).

reoccur   *See* **recur.**

scarcely   *See* **hardly.**

semi-   *See* **bi-.**

sensuous / sensual   *Sensuous* refers to the senses as opposed to the mind (*Art, music, and good food all give sensuous pleasure*). *Sensual* refers to a preoccupation with the senses and the pleasures of the flesh (*a sensual person*).

sentence construction For a discussion of sentence construction and the various problems of usage, *see* Grammar: III. *See also* Some Hints About Writing.

sequence of tenses *See* Grammar: III.B.4.

set / sit The verb *set* (*set, set*) usually means "to place, to put" and is transitive, that is, takes an object (*Set the bag of groceries on the counter*). Occasionally *set* is used intransitively (*The sun set at 6:00 this evening. Let the custard set overnight in the refrigerator*). The verb *sit* (*sat, sat*) is usually intransitive, or unable to take an object (*My grandfather sat in his rocker all afternoon*), but is sometimes used transitively (*He sat out all the dances. Sit the child in the stroller. She sits her horse well*). The present participles of *set* and *sit* are respectively *setting* and *sitting*.

shall / will *Shall* and *will* are auxiliary verbs used to form the future tenses. For several hundred years grammarians have insisted that simple futurity be expressed by the use of *shall* in the first person and *will* in the second and third persons (*I shall be there this evening. If you come late, you will miss the fireworks*) and that statements of obligation, determination, or prohibition be expressed by respectively reversing these auxiliaries (*I will stay, no matter what happens. You shall not be late. She shall not come here again*). Today, however, except for the standard use of *shall* in first-person questions (*Shall I leave?*), *shall* and *will* are no longer restricted in their use. Both can be used with all persons to express simple futurity as well as obligation, determination, or prohibition. In U.S. usage, however, *will* is today by far the more common auxiliary.

Should and *would*, the past tense forms of *shall* and *will*, are commonly used in indirect discourse (*He said that he would [should] be on time. When asked my reply, I answered that I would [should] have to think about it.*) In this case *should*, like *shall*, is dying out in U.S. usage in favor of *would*, largely because of the connotation of obligation carried by *should*. Elsewhere the distinctive uses of *should* and *would* are still in force. *Should* is used to express obligation (*I should do the dishes*), probability (*If cared for, this car should run another 30,000 miles*), and supposition (*If you should lose the number, it is listed in the telephone book*). *Would* is used to express customary past action (*In the evening my grandfather would always sit in his rocker and smoke his pipe*), volition (*I would buy a car if I didn't have to pay for gas and insurance*), and to form polite requests (*Would you please be quiet*). For a discussion of verb tenses and auxiliary verbs, *see also* Grammar: II.C.2.

should / would *See* **shall.**

since *See* **ago.**

sit *See* **set.**

so . . . as *See* **as . . . as.**

spelling problems For problems with spelling, *see* The Spelling Maze.

split infinitive *See* **infinitives.**

stationary / stationery *Stationary* is the adjective, meaning "fixed in one place, not moving" (*a stationary car*). *Stationery* is a noun referring to writing supplies, such as paper, pens, and ink.

supplement *See* **complement.**

tantamount *See* **paramount.**

tenses, sequence of *See* Grammar: III.B.4.

that / which / who Knowing which of these relative pronouns should introduce various relative clauses is troublesome to many writers. For a discussion of relative pronouns and relative clauses, *see* Grammar: II.B.4., II.K.2.

there is / there are The choice of a singular or plural verb to be used with *there* is determined by the number of the real subject that follows *there* (*There is an answer to every problem. There are two problems I now face*). With a compound subject a singular verb is commonly used if the noun closest to the verb is singular (*There was a girl and three boys in the room*). In such cases, however, inverting these nouns permits use of the plural, and less awkward, verb form (*There were three boys and a girl in the room*). *See also* Grammar: III.B.2.

thus The addition to *thus* of the suffix *-ly* is an incorrect and meaningless expansion of the word; *thus* alone is an effective adverb.

till / until These words are interchangeable, although *until* is preferred at the beginning of a sentence. Note that the single *l* in *until* is doubled in *till*.

titles For styling the titles of books, plays, etc., *see* Grammar: IV.N.3., V.A.2., V.B.1.; for styling titles as forms of address, *see* Grammar: V.A.7. and A List of Honorifics accompanying Preserving the Art of Letter Writing.

tortuous / torturous *Tortuous* means "winding," "crooked, tricky," or "complex" (*tortuous road, tortuous plan, tortuous speech*); *torturous*, derived from *torture*, means "painful" (*torturous exercises*).

try to / try and The use of *try and* in place of *try to* is colloquially acceptable but should be avoided in writing (*He should try to* [not "try and"] *do it*).

ultimate / penultimate / antepenultimate In reference to sequence *ultimate* is last; *penultimate*, the next to last; and *antepenultimate*, the third from last.

unaware / unawares *Unaware*, either an adjective or adverb, is usually followed by a prepositional phrase (*She was unaware of the accident.*

We turned left, unaware of the blockade). *Unawares,* used only as an adverb, generally stands apart from the word it modifies. (*We stumbled onto the scene of the crime, unawares*).

uninterested   *See* **disinterested.**

unmoral   *See* **immoral.**

unreadable   *See* **illegible.**

until   *See* **till.**

urban / urbane   *Urban* means "that which relates to, is characteristic of, or constitutes a city" (*urban residents, urban problems*); *urbane* means "polished, suave" (*an urbane gentleman; a witty, urbane piece of writing*).

use / utilize   *Utilize* is often indiscriminately substituted for the term *use,* perhaps because it sounds more precise. However, *utilize,* meaning "to put to practical use," and *use,* meaning generally "to employ," are not completely interchangeable. For example, while one could either *utilize* or *use* the means at hand to accomplish a goal, one would never *utilize* an egg to make an omelette. *Use,* the more general term, can always be substituted for *utilize;* and since *utilize* offers no real advantage in meaning, *use* is almost always preferable.

venal / venial   Although similar in spelling and in pronunciation (the first syllables rhyme with *me*), these terms are distinct in meaning. Venal means "able to be bribed, open to corrupt influence" (*venal officials*); *venial* means "excusable" or "relatively slight" (*venial sins* as opposed to mortal sins).

verbal   *See* **oral.**

verbs   For a general discussion of verbs, *see* Grammar: I.B., II.C.; for a discussion of usage problems with verbs, including agreement of subject and verb, treatment of collective nouns, and sequence of tenses, *see* Grammar: III.B.; for a discussion of verbals, *see* Grammar: II.I.

vocation   *See* **avocation.**

well   *See* **good.**

what is / what are   The choice of a singular or plural verb following *what* depends on whether the writer intends *what* as a singular or plural pronoun. It can be either, but, having once decided its number, the writer should consistently use the appropriate singular or plural verb: *What is needed is* (not "are") *some flowers. What was annoying was* (not "were") *his insulting remarks. What are left are* (not "is") *a few odds and ends. What were lost were* (not "was") *three important letters.*

whether   It is unnecessary to add the phrase "or not" to *whether;* the alternative is understood (*I wonder whether it will rain*).

which For a discussion of *which* as a relative pronoun, *see* Grammar: II.B.4., II.K.2.

while The first meaning of the conjunction *while* is "during the time that" (*I did the dishes while she cooked dinner*); additionally *while* is often used to mean "although" (*While he is well-coordinated, he is not very athletic*) as well as "but" or "and" (*Jean is from Boston, while John is from New York*). Some grammarians and writers consider these last two substitutions weak, and thus *while* should be used sparingly except in its first meaning.

who *See* **that.**

who(ever) / whom(ever) *See* Grammar: III.C.1.

whose / who's *Whose* is the possessive form of the pronoun *who*, not to be confused with the contraction *who's,* meaning "who is." The relative pronoun *whose* was once used only to refer to persons, with the possessive construction *of which* used to refer to things, as in "the book of which the cover was torn." Now *whose* serves to refer to both people and things (*the woman whose hair is blond, the coat whose sleeve is torn*). The interrogative pronoun *whose* still refers only to people (*Whose is this?*).

will *See* **shall.**

-wise The suffix *-wise* has become an all-purpose tail to pin on any passing word, but this practice often results in bad usage. Although constructions using *-wise* to mean "in the manner or position of" are perfectly acceptable (*clockwise, lengthwise, edgewise*), those using *-wise* to mean "with reference to" are dangerous. Verbal creations such as "furniturewise," "jewelrywise," and "salarywise" are imprecise and awkward. Avoid such words by rephrasing the sentence and making use of other expressions; for example, *in terms of furniture, speaking of jewelry,* or *as regards salary.*

word division *See* The Spelling Maze.

would *See* **shall.**

yet *See* **as yet.**

SPELLING

The Spelling Maze: Keys to Correctness

Call it what you will—complex, unpredictable, intractable—the spelling of English is a difficult matter. If pressed, many of us would admit to being frequently lost in the orthographic maze of the English language. And most of us would readily concede that in writing, whether for personal or professional purposes, correct spelling *does* matter. It contributes to the initial, and sometimes sole, impression a reader has of a writer. Careless spelling may therefore have embarrassing and occasionally more serious consequences when it seriously affects meaning.

Some people have an innate talent for spelling. Once they have seen a word written, they can retain its spelling indefinitely even though that word may serve only infrequently in their writing. For others spelling is a struggle. Words squirm out of their grip, refusing "capture" and forcing endless trips to the dictionary, often to the same well-worn spots. Accounting for the difference between naturally good and naturally bad —or just mediocre—spellers is difficult. Certainly verbal awareness, visual memory, and power of concentration bear on the ability to spell, but none ensures it. Neither does a good education nor a genuine affinity for language; some of our best-known authors have in fact been notoriously bad spellers. But if you are a poor speller, take heart. Improvement is possible, though not easy, and may for many be downright tedious. Yet for those who *really* want to learn to spell better, a bit of effort, concentration, and change in habit can produce significant spelling improvement in a fairly short time.

The confusing nature of English spelling reflects the fact that the evolution of English pronunciation from the Middle Ages to the present was not accompanied by a systematic and coordinated change in spelling. Instead, English spelling and pronunciation evolved largely independently of one another. As a result our legacy is not a concise, tidy set of absolute rules for English spelling but rather an unwieldly body of rules, generously accompanied by exceptions.

Some spelling rules—those set off typographically below—are useful to memorize. Others are useful to study chiefly because they force us to focus our eye and attention on the sequence of letters in a word. And that, after all, is at the heart of learning to spell. The mental image we have of a word, of how it looks when written, is in the end the way we usually remember the spelling of a word. The key to better spelling lies in careful reading, in taking visual and mental note of the arrangement of letters in the words we read, and in consciously committing to memory the correct spelling of both new and familiar but troublesome words.

Finally brief mention should be made of the differences between British and American spelling. The reader will undoubtedly notice some British spellings in the extracts from the *Britannica* that punctuate this book. Originally a Scottish publication, the *Britannica* began its history with British spellings and continues to use some of them today. Among the principal distinctions in British spelling, which the *Britannica* observes, are the following: words that end in *-our* rather than the *-or* of American English (*behaviour, colour, favour, neighbour*); words that end in *-re* rather than *-er* (*centre, fibre, metre, theatre*); and words that double a final consonant, usually *l, t,* or *p,* for a past tense, participial form, or other derivative (*dialled, counselled, combatted, woollen, worshipping*). In American English, the final consonant is sometimes doubled, if stress is on the last syllable (*occur, occurring*). Other notable differences in British spelling include the retention of diphthongs (mainly *-ae* or *-oe*) from Latin and Greek, which American English usually reduces to *-e* (*anaesthetic, foetus, mediaeval,* and the spelling of *Encyclopædia Britannica* itself); the retention of the *-x* in Latinate words, which American English replaces with *-ct* (*connexion, inflexion, reflexion*); and the frequent use of *-ise* or *-se* in verbs and their derivatives where American English prefers *-ize* or *-ze* (*analyse, recognise, paralyse*).

Cultivating the spelling habit

1. *Use your dictionary.*

When you are unsure of the spelling of a word, look it up in the dictionary instead of guessing. And when you meet a new word in conversation or in reading, find it in the dictionary. In both cases note the word's spelling, pronunciation, and various meanings and then put the word to work in your own conversation and writing.

2. *Keep a list of words you frequently misspell.*

Take time to record the words that you consistently misspell and make an effort to use them, correctly spelled, in your writing.

3. *Write with care.*

Many misspellings result from hasty or careless writing. Concentrate when writing, use the dictionary when questions arise, and proofread the final written work.

Be sure to distinguish between homonyms, or similar sounding words that are different in meaning and spelling. The list of Commonly Misspelled Words that ends this chapter includes troublesome homonym pairs.

4. *Pronounce words correctly.*

Some misspelling results from the careless or incorrect pronunciation of words. Syllables omitted, added, or transposed in pronunciation are usually repeated in writing. If unsure about a word you hear or read, look it up in the dictionary and learn to pronounce it correctly. (For a discussion of pronunciation, *see* The Spoken Word.)

5. *Learn some useful spelling rules.*

The spelling rules set off typographically below are helpful to memorize. The other rules warrant study to focus your attention on the nature of the remaining problem areas in English spelling.

6. *Read!*

Perhaps the most important—and pleasantest—route to better spelling is reading, and readers are usually far better spellers than nonreaders. Make reading a habit, cultivating along the way your eye and memory for the "look" of words.

Rules to spell by

A. *ie* **or** *ei*

> I before E, when sounded as E,
> Except after C
> Or when sounded as A
> As in *neighbor* or *weigh*.

The old jingle, with an addendum noted below, applies for most words.

When the sound is a long ē, write ie, except after c.

> *achieve, believe, cashier, chief, field, piece, yield; ceiling, conceive, deceit, perceive, receipt, receive*

When the sound is other than a long ē, not just when it is a long ā, *ei* is usually written.

> *deign, eight, freight, neighbor, reign, sleigh, weigh; counterfeit, foreign, forfeit, heifer, sovereign, surfeit; height, sleight, seismograph*

EXCEPTIONS to both rules include:

> *ancient, either, fancier, fiery, financier, friend, glacier, leisure, mischief, mischievous, seize, sheik, view, weird*

B. Words ending in *-ceed, -cede,* and *-sede*

In English there are only 12 words ending with the sound */-sed/.* Eleven are derived from the Latin root CEDERE (to yield), and all seem to cause confusion for spellers. The difficulties are sorted out by remembering the following rules.

Only one English verb ends in -sede: *supersede.* The *-sede* comes from Latin SEDERE (to sit).

Only three common verbs end in -ceed: *exceed, proceed, succeed.*

The eight other similar-sounding words end in -cede: *accede, antecede, cede, concede, intercede, precede, recede, secede.*

C. Prefixes

A prefix is one or more letters or syllables added to the beginning of a root word. The two together make a new word.

When a prefix is added to a word, the spelling of both the prefix and root remains unchanged.

For the euphonious elision of prefix and root, however, some prefixes have variant spellings (*see* Common Prefixes in English). Otherwise no letters are dropped or added, and thus only when the last letter of the prefix and the first letter of the root are the same will the letter be doubled.

dis + appear = disappear	*dis + satisfy = dissatisfy*
inter + state = interstate	*inter + racial = interracial*
mis + place = misplace	*mis + spell = misspell*
over + work = overwork	*over + run = overrun*
un + stable = unstable	*un + necessary = unnecessary*

Latin, Greek, and Anglo-Saxon have all richly supplied English with prefixes, the most common of which are listed in Common Prefixes in English. In each case the prefix's variant spellings, origin, and meaning are provided along with examples of its use in familiar words. The list repays study.

D. Suffixes

A suffix is one or more letters or syllables added to the end of a root word that is mainly used to change the part of speech. (*See* Common Suffixes in English.) Various spelling changes may occur when a suffix is added to a root word. When the root word ends with

Final silent e:

A final silent e is usually retained before a suffix beginning with a consonant.

> *bone, boneless; late, lateness; resolute, resolutely; state, statewide; taste, tasteful; whole, wholesome*

A final silent e is usually dropped before a suffix beginning with a vowel.

> *bore, boring; compare, comparable; quote, quotation; raise, raising; state, statable; violate, violation*

EXCEPTIONS

- An *e* following a *c* or *g* is retained to keep the sound of the *c* or *g* soft: *change, changeable; courage, courageous; manage, manageable; notice, noticeable; peace, peaceable; salvage, salvageable*

- A final *e* is retained if its absence would cause confusion: *agree, agreeable; dye, dyeing; hoe, hoeing; mile, mileage; shoe, shoeing*

Final y:

A final y preceded by a consonant usually changes to *i* before a suffix, except when the suffix itself begins with *i*.

> *lazy, laziness; cry, crying; duty, dutiful; funny, funnier; happy, happily; mystery, mysterious stately, stateliness*

A final y preceded by a vowel is usually unchanged before a suffix.

> *boy, boyish pay, payable; enjoy, enjoyment; play, playful; stay, staying; toy, toying*

Final c:

Add *k* to words ending in c before a suffix beginning with e, i, or y.

> *frolic, frolicked; mimic, mimicking; panic, panicky; picnic, picnicking; traffic, trafficking*

Final l:

A final *l* is retained before suffixes beginning with *l*.

> *cruel, cruelly; evil, evilly; formal, formally; national, nationally; tail, tailless*

Final consonant:

In one-syllable words or in words accented on the last syllable, a single final consonant is usually doubled before a suffix beginning with a vowel.

> *begin, beginning; commit, committed; drop, dropping; fit, fitting; occur, occurrence; omit, omitted; plan, planned; run, running; slim, slimmer; sad, sadden; stop, stopping; swim, swimmer*

> EXCEPTION If the suffix causes the accent to shift to a preceding syllable, the final consonant is not doubled: *confér, conférring* BUT *cónference; infér, inférring* BUT *ínference; prefér, preférral* BUT *préference; refér, referral* BUT *réference*

In polysyllabic words accented on a syllable other than the last, a single final consonant is usually not doubled before a suffix beginning with a vowel.

> *classic, classical; despot, despotic; develop, developing; graphic, graphically; happen, happening; merit, meriting; pilot, piloting*

E. Formation of plurals

Common nouns:

Regular plurals are formed by adding s to the singular.

> *cake, cakes; girl, girls; tree, trees; tray, trays*

Irregular plurals are variously formed.

> Changing a final y preceded by a consonant to *ie* before adding s:
> *body, bodies; lady, ladies; spy, spies; story, stories*

Adding *es* to nouns ending in *ch, sh, x, s,* or *z:*

buzz, buzzes; dress, dresses; fox, foxes; match, matches; wish, wishes

Changing a final *f* to *v* before adding *es:*

self, selves; leaf, leaves; thief, thieves; wolf, wolves

EXCEPTIONS include:

beliefs, griefs, roofs

Some nouns retain their Old English *en* plural ending (*child, children; man, men; woman, women*); or are otherwise irregularly formed (*foot, feet; goose, geese; mouse, mice; tooth, teeth*). These irregular plural forms must be learned.

Proper nouns:

Add *s* to most singular proper nouns to form the plural.

Nancy, two Nancys; Lee, all the Lees; Mr. Smith, the Smiths

Add *es* to proper nouns ending in *s, sh, ch,* or *z* sounds.

The Atlases, the Churches, the Joneses, the Wazzes

Foreign words:

Of the many foreign words in English, most long ago acquired anglicized plural forms (*circuses, museums, reflexes*). For some, however, their foreign plural is the more acceptable plural form in English (*bases, codices, phenomena, theses*). Still others have retained their foreign plural and have as well acquired a newer English plural form (*memoranda* or *memorandums, tableaux* or *tableaus, thesauri* or *thesauruses, vertebrae* or *vertebras*). It is this last category that proves troublesome in that there are no consistent rules for deciding which form to use. Generally speaking, the *Britannica* prefers the foreign plural for a word with two plural forms, but it should be noted that the anglicized plural form is always acceptable. When in doubt about the acceptable plural form(s) of a word, consult *Webster's Third New International Dictionary* or *Webster's New Collegiate Dictionary.*

Letters, figures, and words used as words:

The plural of figures and numbers, and combinations of figures and letters, is formed by adding either a final *s* or *'s*. Since confusion with plural figures is unlikely, either formation is acceptable.

the 1960s	*three 20s*
the mid-1800's	*B-52s*
with eights and nines	*three A-4's*

In order to avoid confusion in forming the plural of letters, however, an 's should be used, whether the letter is lowercase or capital:

two B's and three C's	*t's or* th's
MIRV's	*all the o's*
SDR's	*A's and I's*

To avoid confusion, the plural of words being discussed as words should be formed by adding 's:

the three how's *in the first line*
All the of course's *in that passage are monotonous.*
None of the precede's *is spelled correctly in the report.*

(For forming the plural of compound nouns, *see* Section G, Compound words, below.)

F. Formation of possessives

Regular formation:

Add 's to singular common and proper nouns.

actress's, girl's, father's; Alan's, Burns's, Dickens's, Keats's, Stevenson's

EXCEPTION   Traditionally multisyllabic classical Greek names ending in *es* and the names *Jesus* and *Moses* add only an apostrophe to show possession: *Achilles', Aristophanes', Jesus', Laertes', Moses', Ulysses'*

N.B. The added 's' is a matter of preference. The above reflects Britannica's style.

Add 's to plural nouns that do not end in s.

children's, everyone's, people's, team's

Add apostrophe (') only to plural common and proper nouns that end in s.

actresses', girls', families'; the Carters', the Johnsons'

Compound nouns and joint possession:

Compound nouns and nouns in joint possession show the possessive in the last word only. But if there is individual or separate possession, each noun takes the possessive form.

my brother-in-law's house; my two brothers-in-law's houses
Hazel and Margaret's piano (joint ownership)
Hazel's and Margaret's pianos (individual ownership)

Possessive pronouns and contractions:

Possessive pronouns and contractions should not be confused. No apostrophe is used with possessive pronouns: *his, hers, its, ours, yours, theirs.* The apostrophe in contractions indicates letters omitted, *not* possession:

> *it's* = *it is* (not "its"); *they're* = *they are* (not "their"); *you're* = *you are* (not "your"); *who's* = *who is* (not "whose")

G. Compound words

Compound words frequently cause confusion because, with a few exceptions, there are no hard-and-fast rules governing their spelling. Compound words can be spelled open (*civil rights, high school*), solid (*bookshelf, pocketbook*), or hyphenated (*self-respect, vice-president*). For numerous compound words listed in *Webster's Third* or in *Webster's Collegiate,* the preferred spelling is established. However, countless other compound words—often temporary or new compounds—are not found in *Webster's* nor in any other dictionary. It is the spelling of these compounds that is often puzzling.

It should be noted that the general trend in recent years has been away from the use of hyphens, toward the solid spelling of compound words accepted as permanent compounds and the open spelling of other compounds. The general exception to the solid or open spelling of any compound remains the use of hyphens to avoid ambiguity or difficulty in reading. For example, "all gold watches" is quite different in meaning from "all-gold watches"; if the writer's intended meaning is the latter, only hyphenation can ensure conveying this meaning. In such words as "tri-city" or "co-winner" the use of hyphens eliminates the possible confusion or mispronunciation that might occur in reading "tricity" or "cowinner."

In general, *Webster's* should be followed for the spelling of compound words. For temporary, new, or other compounds not listed in *Webster's,* use the guidelines below. Compound types not included in these guidelines should be spelled open.

Hyphenate the types of compound words listed below.

1) Two nouns of different but equal function:	*actor-writer, city-state, director-producer, secretary-treasurer*
2) Permanent compound nouns composed of three or more words:	*fly-by-night, good-for-nothing, hand-me-down, hit-and-run, know-it-all, mother-in-law, stick-in-the-mud* BUT *commander*

in chief, editor in chief, justice of the peace

3) Words with the suffixes *-designate, -elect,* or *-odd:*	*chairman-designate, major general-designate; mayor-elect, vice-president-elect; ten-odd, one hundred-odd*
4) Words with the prefixes *all-, great-, half-,* or *self-:*	*all-purpose, all-star; great-aunt, great-grandfather; half-completed, half-wit; self-confidence, self-reliable*
5) Adjectives with the prefix *quasi-:*	*quasi-historical, quasi-official, quasi-original, quasi-respectable*
BUT nouns with the prefix *quasi* are usually spelled open:	*quasi contract, quasi corporation, quasi expert, quasi partner*
6) Proper nouns and adjectives with prefixes:	*post-Bronze Age, pre-World War I, pro-Israeli speech, un-American sentiment*
7) Two or more words joined to form a compound adjective *preceding* a noun, including phrases and clauses used in this way:	*ever-growing fame, music-loving audience, little-discussed issue, long-awaited film, well-known author; hard-to-find brand, on-the-spot report, an I've-got-something-up-my-sleeve look*

EXCEPTIONS

• Such compound adjectives *following* a noun are not hyphenated: *The author is well known. The brand is hard to find.*

• Compound modifiers whose first word is *very* or an adverb ending in *-ly* are not hyphenated: *a very well known author, a heatedly discussed issue, a poorly received film.*

• A foreign phrase used as an adjective before a noun hyphenated only to reproduce hyphenation in the original language: *bona fide agreement, prima facie evidence* BUT *laissez-faire policy, soi-disant singer.*

8) A compound adjective containing a number that *precedes* a noun:	*one-page letter, 10-year-old child, 18-minute gap, 17th-century chair, twentieth-century problems* BUT *The letter is one page. The child is 10 years old. The chair is from the 17th century.*
BUT do not hyphenate a modifier that is a number plus a possessive noun:	*four weeks' vacation, 24 hours' wait*

9) A successive compound adjective:	*short- and long-term loans; pre- and postnatal care; 17th- and 18th-century literature; first-, second-, and third-place winners*
10) A compound adjective composed of two proper adjectives:	*Arab-Israeli agreement, Spanish-American descent*
11) The written numbers from 21 to 99, and numerals with the suffix *-fold:*	*twenty-one, ninety-nine; 30-fold, 100-fold* BUT *thirtyfold, one hundredfold*
12) Fractions used as adjectives, though the hyphenation of fractions used as nouns is optional:	*three-quarter length, two and one-half times, one-fourth cup; one-half* (or *one half*), *two-thirds* (or *two thirds*)
13) Whenever necessary to avoid ambiguity:	*co-op, re-cover* (a chair), *re-create* (to create again), *re-form* (to form again)

In general write solid all compound words wtih prefixes or suffixes, unless confusion or very awkward letter combinations result.

> *antidemonstration, bipartisan, cooperate, ladylike, nonconformist, predetermine, pseudosophisticated, reentry, semisolid, thermonuclear* BUT *anti-inflation, pro-abortion, re-utter, shell-like, thrill-less*

Forming plural compound nouns:

Many compound nouns are treated as simple nouns and form their plural by adding a final *-s:*

> *cure-alls, forget-me-nots, hand-me-downs, mousetraps, poet-musicians, post offices, stick-in-the-muds*

Other compound nouns add an internal *-s* to the most important element of the compound:

> *aides-de-camp, editors in chief, justices of the peace, lookers-on, mayors-elect, mothers-in-law, passersby*

And some compound nouns composed of two nouns pluralize both nouns:

> *gentlemen callers, lords justices, menservants, women singers*

These examples provide models for the plural formation of most types of compound nouns. However, since some compounds have two acceptable plural forms (*e.g., attorneys general, attorney generals; courts-martial, court-martials; cupfuls, cupsful; knights templar, knight templars*), if you are doubtful about a correct plural form, consult *Webster's Second* or *Collegiate*.

H. Division of words

When a word must be divided at the end of a line, the division is made between syllables and indicated by a hyphen added to the first fragment of the word. In most dictionaries the division of words into syllables is marked by centered dots (*syl·la·ble*). Some dictionaries indicate only those syllabic breaks that are acceptable at the end of a line. Other dictionaries use centered dots to mark all syllabic breaks, whether or not each is an appropriate end-of-line division. Use the guidelines below to ensure the correct division of words at the end of a line.

Do not divide.

> One-syllable words:
> *hour, rained, screamed, three*

> So that a one-letter fragment results:
> *amuse* (not "a-muse"), *iris* (not "i-ris"), *speedy* (not "speed-y"), *taxi* (not "tax-i")

> So that a fragment is difficult to pronounce:
> *dirndl* (not "dirn-dl"), *dispos-able* (not "disposa-ble"), *en-titled* (not enti-tled")

> Abbreviations, or figures.

Divide.

> Between double consonants unless they complete a root word:
> *ac-com-mo-date, com-mit-tee, run-ning, stop-ping* BUT *fall-ing, sell-er, small-ish, tall-est*

> Between two consonants separating vowels, unless the consonants represent a single sound (for example, *st, th, wh*):
> *cus-tom, doc-tor, for-get, plun-der* BUT *be-tween, fore-shadow, no-where*

> When a consonant separates two vowels, the division occurs *before* the consonant if the first vowel is long or unstressed: *de-note, infi-nite, re-late*. The division occurs *after* the consonant if the first vowel is short and stressed: *den-im, infin-itive, rel-ative*.

Between two vowels unless they represent a single sound:

ambigu-ous, co-operate, obvi-ate, usu-ally BUT *maneu-ver, persua-sive, pneu-matic, rigor-ous*

After a full prefix, when possible:

anti-capitalist, pseudo-sophisticate, thermo-nuclear

Hyphenated words only at the hyphens:

father-in-law, mayor-elect, quasi-historical, secretary-treasurer, vice-president

Common Prefixes in English

Prefix*	Origin†	Meaning	Examples
a-	A-S	on, at, in, to	afire, afoot, aloft, asleep
a- (an-)	G	not, without	anarchy, asymmetrical, atheism
ab- (a-, abs-)	L	from, away	abnormal, absent, abstain
ad- (a-, ac-, af-, ag-, al-, an-, ap-, ar-, as-, at-)	L	to, toward, addition	adjunct, accept, affirm, allow, abase, aggravate, announce, approximate, arrest, ascend, attune
ambi-	L	both	ambidextrous, ambiguous, ambivalent
amphi-	G	around, on both sides	amphibious, amphitheater
ana-	G	again, back, up	analogy, analysis, anathema
ante-	L	before	antecedent, antedate, anteroom
anti- (ant-)	G	against, opposed	anticlimax, antidote, antonym
arch- (arche-, archi-)	G	chief, primitive (the earliest), preeminent	archbishop, archfool, archetype, architect
auto- (aut-)	G	self	autobiography, autograph, automibile, autism
be-	A-S	over, around, thoroughly, excessively, about, make	because, bedeck, befall, belittle, besiege, beset
bi- (bin-, bis-)	L	two, twice	biceps, bicycle, biennial, bisect, binocular
cata-	G	down, away, against, throughout	cataclysm, catalepsy, catapult, catastrophe
circum-	L	around, about	circumscribe, circumstance, circumvent

---

*Variant spellings for euphonious elision with various roots are given in parentheses.

†A-S = Anglo-Saxon; G = Greek; L = Latin

Prefix	Origin	Meaning	Examples
com- (co-, col-, con-, cor-)	L	with	collaborate, combat, congress, corrupt
contra- (contro-, counter-)	L	against, opposite	contraception, contradict, controvert, countermand
de-	L	from, down, away	debase, decrease, degrade, depose
dis- (di-, dif-)	L	away, opposite	diffuse, disbelief, discourteous, divide
dia-	G	through, between, apart	diagonal, diagram, dialogue, diameter
ec-	G	from, out of	eccentric, ecstatic
epi- (ep-, eph-)	G	upon, beside	epidemic, epilogue, ephemeral, eponymous
equi-	L	equal	equidistant, equilibrium, equivalent
eu-	G	good, well	eulogy, euphonious, euthanasia
ex-	L	former	ex-wife, ex-governor
ex- (e-, ec-, ef-)	L	out, from, away	ecstasy, effervescent, enervate, exit, extant
extra-	L	outside, beyond	extracurricular, extraordinary
for-	A-S	away, off, extremely, wrongly	forbear, forbid, forlorn, forspent
fore-	A-S	before	forebear, foreground, forehead, forewarn
hetero-	G	different	heterodox, heterogeneous, heterosexual
hom- (homo-)	G	the same	homonym, homogenous, homosexual
hyper-	G	excessively, over, above	hyperbole, hyperventilation
hypo-	G	under, beneath, down	hypochondriac, hypodermic, hypothesis
in- (il-, im-, ir-)	L	in, into, on, toward, within (used with verbs and nouns)	induce, illuminate, import, irrigate
in- (ig-, il-, im-, ir-)	L	not (used with adjectives)	ignoble, illegible, impair, indecent, irrational

Prefix	Origin	Meaning	Examples
infra-	L	below, within	infrared, infrastructure
inter-	L	between, among	international, interpersonal, interstate
intra-	L	within	intramural, intrastate, intravenous
mal- (male-)	L	bad	malformed, malpractice, malevolent
meta- (met-)	G	after, beyond	metabolism, metaphor, metaphysics, metonymy
mis-	A-S	error, opposite, wrong	misbehavior, misspell, mistake
mon- (mono-)	G	one	monaural, monogamy, monologue, monotone
multi-	L	much, many	multicolor, multiple, multiply
neo-	G	new	neoclassical, neonatal, neophyte
non-	L	not	nonchalance, nondescript, nonsense
ob- (o-, oc-, of-, op-)	L	against, to, toward, completely	object, omit, occult, offend, oppose
out-	A-S	beyond, completely	outbreak, outrage, outside
over-	A-S	over, in excess, with damaging effect	overlook, overturn, overwork
para-	G	beside, closely related, abnormal, almost	paradox, paragraph, parallel, paranoid
per-	L	through, throughout, thoroughly	perceive, perfect, pervade
peri-	G	around, about	perimeter, periscope
poly-	G	many	polygamy, polyglot, polysyllable
post-	L	after	postdate, postpone, postwar
pre-	L	before (in time & place)	preamble, precede, predict, pretend

Prefix	Origin	Meaning	Examples
pro-	L	forward, in favor of	proceed, produce, project, promote
pro-	G	before	program, prologue, prophet
re-	L	again, back	recall, recapture, reiterate
retro-	L	back, backward	retroactive, retrograde, retrospect
semi-	L	half	semiannual, semisolid, semivowel
sub- (suc-, suf-, sug-, sum-, sup-, sur-, sus-)	L	under, beneath	submerge, subterranean, succinct, suffuse, suggest, summon, supplant, surrogate, suspicion
super- (sur-)	L	above, over	superfluous, supernatural, surfeit
syn- (syl-, sym-)	G	with, together	synonym, syllable, symmetry, sympathy
trans- (tra-)	L	across, over	transparent, transplant, traverse
tri-	L & G	three	triangle, triennial, triumvirate
ultra-	L	beyond, outside, unusual, extreme	ultraconservative, ultramodern, ultraviolet
un-	A-S	not	undo, uninspired, unmanageable
under-	A-S	beneath, less than	underestimate, underground, underrate
uni-	L	one	uniform, unilateral, university
up-	A-S	upward, on high	uplift, upset, upshot
with-	A-S	from, against	withdraw, withhold, within, withstand

Common Suffixes in English

NOUN SUFFIXES:

Suffix*	Origin†	Meaning	Examples
-acy	L & G	Used to form abstract nouns meaning state of, act of, or quality of	accuracy, celibacy, democracy, supremacy
-age	L		bondage, damage, marriage, passage
-ance (-ancy, -ence, -ency)	L		appearance, buoyancy, emergency, hindrance, independence
-ation (-ion, -sion)	L		civilization, creation, dissension
-dom	A-S		boredom, freedom, kingdom, martyrdom, wisdom
-hood	A-S		boyhood, childhood, falsehood
-ism	L & G		barbarism, criticism, communism, plagiarism
-ment	L & G		agreement, government, statement
-ness	A-S		happiness, kindness, sadness
-ship	A-S		fellowship, friendship, kinship
-th	A-S		dearth, warmth, wealth
-ty (-ity)	L		authority, modesty, security
-an (-ant, -ent)	L	Used to form concrete nouns meaning one who does or one who is	artisan, European, vagrant, student
-ard	A-S		drunkard, dullard, wizard
-ee	L		addressee, legatee, lessee
-er (-ier, -ar)	L		trader, writer, clothier, scholar

*Variant spellings for euphonious elision with various roots are given in parentheses.
†A-S = Anglo-Saxon; G = Greek; L = Latin

ADJECTIVE AND ADVERB SUFFIXES:

-ac	G		cardiac, elegiac, hypochondriac, maniac
-ful	A-S		forceful, handful, harmful, spiteful
-ic	L	Used to form	civic, domestic, endemic, public
-ish	A-S	adjectives or adverbs	boyish, childish, foolish, British
-ive	L	meaning resembling, full of,	active, captive, native, secretive
-ly	A-S	pertaining to, or belonging to	closely, evenly, fatherly, queenly
-ory	L		compulsory, illusory, hortatory
-ous	L		glamorous, gracious, poisonous
-y	A-S		bony, funny, greedy, nosy
-able	L	capable of,	breakable, movable, perishable
-ible	L	able to	collectible, irresistible, visible
-ile	L		agile, ductile, fertile, fragile
-fold	A-S	number, quantity	fivefold, manifold, tenfold
-less	A-S	lacking, wanting	careless, harmless, thoughtless
-most	A-S	(indicates superlative degree)	foremost, inmost, outmost
-oid	G	like	anthropoid, humanoid, spheroid
-ward	A-S	in the direction of	downward, inward, southward
-wise	A-S	way, manner	edgewise, lengthwise, otherwise

VERB SUFFIXES:

-ate	L		animate, consecrate, facilitate
-en	A-S	to make, give, or cause to be	deepen, hasten, loosen, strengthen
-fy	L		fortify, liquefy, intensify
-ize (-ise)	G		civilize, criticize, fertilize

Commonly Misspelled Words

absence
abscess
accede
accept (receive)
  except (v., omit;
  prep., excluding)*
access (passage; ability or
  right to make use of)
  excess (surplus)
accommodate
accumulate
accurately
acetic (acid)
  ascetic (one who
  practices self-denial)
achieve
acquaintance
across
adolescent
advantageous
advice (n.)
advise (v.)
affect (v., influence)
  effect (v., cause;
  n., result)
aggravated
aghast
aisle (passageway)
  isle (island)

all ready (adj. phrase,
  entirely prepared)
  already (adv., previously)
all right
allude (refer to)
  elude (avoid)
allusion (reference)
  elusion (escape, evasion)
  illusion (false impression)
already (see all ready)
analysis
analyze
angel (celestial being)
angle (figure formed by
  two meeting lines)
anonymity
anonymous
anxiety
appearance
appropriate
aquatic
arbitrary
arctic
arithmetic
artisan
ascend
ascent (act of rising)
  assent (agreement)
ascetic (see acetic)

*adj. = adjective; adv. = adverb; conj. = conjunction; n. = noun;
part. = participle; prep. = preposition; pron. = pronoun; v. = verb

334

assassin

assent (see ascent)

assess

athlete

athletics

author

authoritative

auxiliary

awkward

baccalaureate

bachelor

baring (uncovering)

barring (excluding)

bearing (carrying,
withstanding)

before

beginning

belligerent

besiege

bestial

biased or biassed

bigoted

bivouac

bookkeeper

bourgeois

bouillon (*see* bullion)

breadth (width)

breath (*n.*)

breathe (*v.*)

bridal (*adj.*, pertaining to
a bride or wedding)

bridle (*n.*, part of a horse's
harness)

brilliant

budget

bullion (gold or silver)
bouillon (broth)

buoy

buoyant

bureau

bureaucracy

camouflage

cannon (weapon)

canon (rule, law,
churchman)

capital (city, letter)

capitol (building)

casualty

category

cede

ceiling

cemetery

champagne

changeable

characteristic

chauffeur

choose (*present tense*)

chose (*past tense*)

cigarette

cinnamon

cite (quote, refer to)
sight (spectacle, vision)
site (location)

clientele

climactic

climatic

colloquial

colonel (military officer)
kernel (seed,
essential part)

column

committee

complement (that which
completes)

compliment (expression
of praise)

concede

conceivable

condemn

condescend

confidentially

connoisseur

connotation

conscience

conscientious

consensus

consul (government
  representative)
council (assembly
  of officials)
counsel (adviser,
  or advice given; *v.*, advise)
continuous
controlled
controversial
convenient
copyright
cordially
correlate
correspondence
council (*see* consul)
counsel (*see* consul)
counterfeit
courageous
courteous
curiosity
daily
dairy (where milk is
  produced or sold)
  diary (journal)
debris
debut
deceased (dead)
  diseased (ill)
deceive
decent (fitting)
  descent (act of coming
    down)
  dissent (difference of
    opinion)
defendant
deficit
deity (a god)
  diet (food)
dependent (always spelled
  thus when used as *adj.*;
  as *n.*, may also be spelled
  dependant)
descent (*see* decent)
despair

desperate
desert (*v.*, leave; *n.*, arid
  place)
dessert (meal's final course)
device (*n.*)
devise (*v.*)
diary (*see* dairy)
die (*v.*, cease living; *n.*, cubed
  gaming piece, or a tool)
  dye (*v.* & *n.*, color)
diet (*see* deity)
dilemma
disappear
disappoint
discriminate
diseased (*see* deceased)
disillusioned
dissatisfied
dissent (*see* decent)
doesn't
dominant
dropped
dual (composed of two)
duel (combat between two)
duly
dye (*see* die)
dyeing (coloring)
dying (near death)
echoes
eclectic
ecstasy
edifice
effect (*see* affect)
efficiency
eight
eighth
elementary
elicit (to call forth)
  illicit (illegal)
eligible
eliminate
elliptical
elude (*see* allude)
elusion (*see* allusion)

embarrass

emigrate (migrate from)
    immigrate (migrate to)

eminent (noted)
    immanent (inherent)
    imminent (about to happen)

endeavor

enthusiasm

entirely

envelop (*v.*)

envelope (*n.*)

etiquette

evenness

evilly

exaggerate

exceed

except (*see* accept)

excerpt

excess (*see* access)

exhilarate

extraordinary

feasible

feign

fiery

foresee

forfeit

formally (in a formal way)

formerly (at an earlier time)

forth (forward)
    fourth (4th)

forty

fulsome

gage (pledge)

gauge (measure)

genealogy

genius

gerrymander

gesture

gnaw

gorilla (*see* guerrilla)

government

gruesome

guarantee

guaranty

guerrilla or guerilla (soldier)
    gorilla (ape)

gypsy

handkerchief

harass

hegemony

height

helm

hemorrhage

heroes

hippopotamus

hoard (hidden supply)
    horde (unruly crowd, army)

holey (with holes)

holy (sacred)
    wholly (totally)

horde (*see* hoard)

human

humane

humor

humorous

hygiene

hypocrisy

hypocrite

idiosyncrasy

idle (unoccupied)

idol (object of worship)

illegible

illicit (*see* elicit)

illusion (*see* allusion)

immanent (*see* eminent)

immediate

immigrate (*see* emigrate)

imminent (*see* eminent)

impetuous

impromptu

independent

influential

ingenious (clever)

ingenuous (frank, naive)

inoculate

intercede

intermittent
interrupt
introvert
irrelevant
irresistible
irritable
isle (*see* aisle)
itinerary
its (*possessive form of* it)
it's (*contraction of* it is)
jeopardy
kaleidoscope
knowledge
laboratory
labyrinth
laid
later
latter
lead (*n.*, metal; *v.*, guide)
led (*past tense of v.*, lead)
legible
legitimate
leisure
length
liaison
lightening (making lighter)
lightning (flashes of light)
likelihood
likely
liquefy
loose (*adj.*, not tight; *v.*, free
    from restraint)
lose (*v.*, be deprived of)
maintain
maintenance
manageable
manual
marshal (*v.*, conduct or
    gather; *n.*, official)
martial (military)
medicine
mediocre
melancholy
millennium

miner (mine worker)
minor (lesser, smaller, or
    underage)
miscellaneous
mischief
mischievous
misspell
mnemonic
muscle (body tissue)
mussel (shellfish)
naive or naïve
nausea
naval (nautical)
navel (belly button)
ninety
ninth
noticeable
notoriety
occasion
occur, occurred, occurrence
omniscient
overrun
paid
pamphlet
parallel
paralysis
paralyze
parenthesis (*plural*,
    parentheses)
parliament
pastime
pavilion
perceive
perennial
permissible
perpendicular
personal (private)
personnel (staff)
physician
picnic, picnicking
plain (*adj.*, simple; *n.*, flat
    area)
plane (*v.*, smooth; *n.*, tool for
    smoothing)

plausible
playwright
pneumonia
poignant
precede
predecessor
prefer, preferred, preference
prejudice
prevalent
principal (*adj.* & *n.*, chief, most important)
principle (*n.*, standard of conduct; fundamental truth)
privilege
procedure
proceed
profit (benefit)
  prophet (one who predicts)
prominent
propaganda
prophet (*see* profit)
psychoanalysis
pumpkin
pursue
putrefy
qualify
quantify
questionnaire
quotation
rain (falling drops of water)
  reign (sovereign's rule)
  rein (strap of harness)
raise (lift up)
  raze (destroy)
rarefy
rarity
raze (*see* raise)
recede
receipt
receive

recipe
recipient
reckless
recommend
reconnaissance
recur, recurrence
refer, referred, reference
reign (*see* rain)
rein (*see* rain)
relief
relieve
religion
rendezvous
renown
repetitious
reservoir
rhetoric
rhyme
rhythm
ridiculous
right (correct)
  rite (ceremony)
  write (record)
sacrilegious
sailer (sailing ship)
sailor (mariner)
sapphire
satellite
schedule
secede
seismograph
seize
separate
sergeant
sheriff
siege
sieve
sight (*see* cite)
silhouette
sincerely
site (*see* cite)
skiing
soliloquy

soothe
sophomore
source
sovereign
spatial
sponsor
spontaneity
squabble
stair (steps)
stare (look at)
stationary (*adj.*, immobile)
stationery (*n.*, writing
    supplies)
straight (uncurved)
strait (narrow, tight)
strength
strictly
stupefy
subterranean
subtle
subtlety
succeed
succinct
succumb
sufficient
superintendent
supersede
suppress
surveillance
syllable
symbol
symmetry
symptom
synonym
tableau
technique
their (*possessive pron.*)
there (*adv.*)
they're (*contraction,*
    they are)
thorough
through
till

tobacco
tortuous (winding)
torturous (painful)
tragedy
tyranny
ukulele
umbrella
unanimous
undoubtedly
unnecessary
until
unwieldy
vacuum
vain (*adj.*, unsuccessful;
    conceited)
vane (*n.*, wind indicator)
vein (*n.*, blood vessel)
vengeance
verbatim
vernacular
victuals
villain
vitamin
warrant
weather (*n.*, atmospheric
    conditions)
    whether (*conj.*)
weird
wholly (*see* holy)
who's (*contraction,* who is)
whose (*adj. & pron.*)
wintry
withhold
woeful
worthwhile
wretched
write (*see* right)
wrought
yacht
yeoman
yield
your (*possessive pron.*)
you're (*contraction,* you are)

PRONUNCIATION

The Spoken Word:
    Varieties of English Pronunciation

How Is It Pronounced?

The Spoken Word:
Varieties of English Pronunciation

The pronunciation of English has undergone some striking changes during its history. Geoffrey Chaucer, who died in 1400, pronounced the word *doom* approximately the way we now say "dome," *loan* like our "lawn," *mouse* like "moose," *mine* like "mean," and *feet* like "fate."*
He pronounced the *gh* in *through,* sounding it like the *ch* in German *ach* or Scottish *loch;* the *k* in *knot;* and the *g* in *gnaw.* He pronounced the *e,* which we now call a "silent *e,*" in *name,* making the word sound something like "nah-muh." And his pronunciation differed from ours in numerous other details as well. If we could resurrect King Alfred the Great or any of his 9th-century fellow English speakers, we would find them completely incomprehensible—so much has English changed in 1100 years.

In our own time it is obvious that we do not all talk alike. The Texan and the Down Easter, the television announcer and the migratory farmhand, the Chicano and the Pennsylvania Dutchman—all speak English in their own distinctive ways. Compared with Europe or even the British Isles, the United States is relatively uniform in speech, and visitors from the earliest times have commented on the lack of sharp dialect differences on these shores. Nevertheless, we do have our variations. How we talk is a result partly of where we come from (regional dialect), partly of our cultural background (ethnic dialect), and partly of our education and social position (social dialect).

Varieties of English pronunciation

There are four main regional dialects in the United States—the Northern, North Midland, South Midland, and Southern dialects—each of

---

*In the interest of readability, impressionistic phonetic spellings are used in this article to indicate pronunciations. In the list of words that follows, more traditional phonetic transcriptions are used.

which has many dialect subregions within it. The Northern region extends from New England and New York State to the northern parts of New Jersey, Pennsylvania, Ohio, and thence westward; it includes among its most distinctive subregions eastern New England and the metropolitan New York area. The North Midland region includes southern Pennsylvania and New Jersey and extends westward through the middle of Ohio, Indiana, and Illinois and onward through northern Missouri and southern Iowa. The South Midland region (or Inland South) covers West Virginia, western Virginia, North Carolina, and South Carolina; northern Georgia and Alabama; most of Tennessee, Kentucky, the Ozarks, Oklahoma, and much of western Texas. The Southern region (or Coastal South) encompasses much of Maryland; eastern Virginia, North Carolina, and South Carolina; southern Georgia and Alabama; northern Florida; Mississippi, Louisiana, and eastern Texas. Charleston is a striking Southern subregion, as is New Orleans, with its Cajun French influence. The farther west one goes, the less clear dialect boundaries are. The fieldwork for the *Dictionary of American Regional English*[†] has shown that in the western half of the United States speech in the cities tends to be Northern dialect and speech in the country, predominantly Midland. Thus in these more recently settled western areas, what were purely regional differences in the East have become urban and rural dialects instead.

Ethnic dialects are associated with cultural groups that have maintained a strong sense of solidarity among their members and often with their antecedents. The Polish community in Chicago, the Italian community in Pittsburgh, the Chicanos in the Southwest, the Puerto Ricans in New York City, the Irish in Boston, and the Swedes in Minnesota are only a few of many such ethnic enclaves in the United States that are recognizable by their cultural traditions and distinctive speechways. But ethnic dialects are not necessarily restricted to a particular location. During the past 100 years black Americans have settled in many northern cities, bringing with them a combination of Southern regional speech and their own ethnic speech fused into a combination often called "black English." Among the characteristics of black English, although by no means exclusive to it, are the loss of consonants from terminal clusters (*e.g.,* "fine" for *find*), including the loss of the verbal ending *-s* ("He talk a lot") and the possessive *'s* ("I got my brother car"); complete

---

[†]The *Dictionary of American Regional English* (*DARE*), under the editorship of Frederic G. Cassidy at the University of Wisconsin, is scheduled for publication in the 1980s. Under preparation since 1965, it will be, when completed, the fullest available record of American dialects.

loss of final *r* ("doe" for *door*); substitution of *f* for *th* in some positions ("bofe" for *both*); a wider pitch range than that used by most whites; the omission of *am, is,* and *are* ("They here now"); use of the invariant form *be* to indicate habitual conditions ("She be around here all the time"); and a rich vocabulary that often spreads to standard use (*e.g., juke box, nitty-gritty, something else* for something extraordinary). The exact origins and historical development of black English are the subject of much dispute among linguists, but its existence today as a distinctive ethnic dialect seems beyond question.‡

Social dialects in the United States are less clearly defined than either regional or ethnic ones. Nevertheless, we all recognize that speech is one clue to social standing. Those who "talk nicely," as it is sometimes put, are likely to be the ones who are elected, promoted, invited, and otherwise honored. To be sure, the correlation is only approximate, and things are not so extreme today as they were in the era depicted in George Bernard Shaw's play *Pygmalion,* later made into the musical *My Fair Lady.* By virtue of her newly learned, upper-class pronunciation, Shaw's street-girl heroine Eliza Doolittle could be passed off as a lady of quality, regardless of her grammar or subject matter. She could talk about anything in any way provided her pronunciation was properly upper-class: "What became of her new straw hat that should have come to me? Somebody pinched it; and what I say is, them as pinched it done her in." In satirizing British preoccupation with the posh accents of his day, Shaw, of course, exaggerated the situation. Even in the England of his time—and certainly in our current-day America—pronunciation alone has never escalated people up the social ladder, but it has always signaled their approximate social standing.

The types of variation mentioned above—regional, ethnic, and social—are interrelated in complex ways. A form of speech that has high social standing in one part of the country may be disdained in another. Regional varieties may be influenced by ethnic ones, as Southern speech around New Orleans has been modified by Cajun French or Northern speech in parts of the upper Midwest has been affected by the Scandinavian settlers of that region. Moreover all such variation is closely related to historical change in the language. Indeed, contemporary variation is historical change caught on the wing. Some forms, such as "hit" for *it,* are the modern survivals of ancient pronunciations that were once universal but now have very little prestige.

---

‡The best guide to the literature on the subject is *A Comprehensive Annotated Bibliography of American Black English* (1974) by Ila W. Brasch and Walter M. Brasch.

Other forms, such as the pronunciation of *knotty* and *naughty* alike, are probably a glimpse into the future. (Although most Americans still distinguish between the italicized words in "They were *caught* on the *cot*," an increasingly large number do not, with the prevalent pronunciation varying from region to region.)

In addition to the dialect differences discussed above—which, for the most part, one is born to—there is also style or functional variation in language, which is learned. One person may use several pronunciations of the same expression, depending on the conversational situation. For example, the question *What is your name?* can be variously pronounced. If the situation is formal, such as a courtroom in which a lawyer is addressing a witness, the words of the question may be given their "full" pronunciation. But if the situation is more relaxed and comfortable, such as an informal party or meeting where people are getting acquainted, the question is likely to sound like "Whacher name?" That spelling looks sloppy or uneducated, but it represents a quite normal, albeit relaxed, pronunciation. Switch the pronunciations and the situations, and the result is ludicrous. Pronunciation must suit the situation to be correct. There is no single right way to talk that will fit all circumstances.

Functional variation is often described as a dichotomy of formal and informal, or as a continuum between those extremes. It is, however, more complex than that. There are styles of speech that are used characteristically in particular situations. For example, in drilling soldiers the drillmaster may use a special pronunciation in which the word *march* comes out "harch," and certain other words, such as the numbers called out to set the marching cadence, are not recognizable at all to the uninitiated. In church services special pronunciations may be used, some of which are archaic, such as *travail* pronounced "travel," and others merely exaggerated, such as *God* pronounced "gawd" in a prolonged and ululating fashion that is presumably an indication of piety. Every well-defined activity, especially if it contains some element of ritual, is likely to evoke a special style of speech. Debating, reciting poetry, and lecturing have their own styles—but so do gossiping, asking for gasoline at a filling station, and talking to a barber or hairdresser.

In addition to dialects, which depend on who we are, and styles, which depend on the circumstances we are in, every person has his or her own individual characteristics of speech. We can identify a person by speech and recognize mimicry when one person imitates another. The idiosyncratic features of an individual's speech (the idiolect) is a personal signature as unique as handwriting. In this respect variation in pronunciation is completely unlimited, for there are as many such variants as there are persons speaking English.

What is Standard English?

Despite all the variation mentioned above, we often talk about Standard English as though it were some simple and well-defined form of the language. Instead it is complex and difficult to characterize adequately. Standard speech has, however, three main characteristics, which were recognized and described as early as the 18th century:

1. currency—that is, it is freely used today, being neither old-fashioned nor a faddish innovation;
2. generality—it is used widely, not limited regionally, ethnically, or functionally;
3. prestige—it is used with respect and is not socially stigmatized.

Because all three characteristics are continuums, every pronunciation is more or less current, general, and prestigious. The pronunciation of the *l* in *calm* is rapidly becoming current so that "cahm" is already somewhat old-fashioned, although not nearly as much so as the pronunciation "cam," which was standard several generations ago but is now archaic. The pronunciation of *sh* before consonants other than *r*, for example, in *shnook, schmaltz,* and *shlock* was once limited ethnically but is now more general, although it is still not universal. Conversely the pronunciation of *s* before *r*, as in "srimp" for *shrimp*, is limited geographically to the Southeast, and its general use seems to be declining even there. "Liberry" has little prestige, but "lib'ry" has a good deal—more for some speakers than the pronunciation that matches the spelling *library*. Standard English is a multidimensional and ever-changing reality that resists all efforts to tie it down by a simple definition.

Some pronunciations, such as *it* versus "hit," are standard all over the English-speaking world. Others vary from country to country. Thus Americans pronounce *garage* as "ga-rodge" stressing the second syllable as in the original French, whereas the British pronounce it "gar-ahge" or even "gar-idge" stressing the first syllable. There is no international standard for this word, only separate national standards. In other cases there may not be even a national standard: people from the northern half of the United States tend to say "greassy," whereas those from the southern half usually say "greazy." For the word *greasy* there are only regional standards. The pronunciation of individual words is standard or nonstandard within geographical limits—universal English, American English, Northern English, eastern New England English, Bostonian English—but there is no single dialect, no one way of talking, that is standard as a whole.

Britain used to have a way of speaking called Received Pronunciation (RP) that came close to being a single standard for England. It was this form of speech that Shaw satirized. However, today RP no longer reigns as the undisputed standard for all Britishers since local accents are heard increasingly on the British Broadcasting Company and in the halls of Parliament. In America there has never been a single standard. Earlier in the 20th century people talked about General American, but what went by that name was a diverse combination of Northern and Midland dialects; it was in fact a term for everything except the speech of the New England and the Coastal South. Today, with more justification, there is some talk of Network Standard—the kind of pronunciation favored by anchoring newscasters, actors delivering commercial messages, and other highly visible and hence influential speakers on television. If American English does develop a single form of standard speech, it will very likely be that used by such prestigious "role models."

Network Standard is sometimes held up as a model of "accentless" speech. The very notion is an illusion; there is no accentless pronunciation any more than there is a flavorless coffee or an odorless perfume. The illusion is fostered, however, by the fact that the word *dialect* is used in two different ways in English. On the one hand, it refers to some regional, ethnic, or social variety of the language (we can call this use *dialect*$_1$); since every way of talking is used somewhere, by some group, on some social level, all ways of talking are dialects$_1$. On the other hand, the term (distinguished as *dialect*$_2$) is sometimes used to mean a nonstandard form of speech. In this second use we might say that English consists of a standard and many dialects$_2$; it is in such a sense that Network Standard is said to be "accentless." However, as already noted, there is no single homogeneous standard of pronunciation for English. Even Network Standard has a good deal of variation within it. Thus when linguists use the term *dialect,* most intend it in the *dialect*$_1$ sense. Persons who like things to be simple and clear-cut have to reconcile themselves to the fact that language is a vast and complex muddle, full of variation in all its parts—including the standard dialect.

Some kinds of variation

One cause of the variation that we find even within Standard English is that a word pronounced one way in isolation may be pronounced quite differently when used in connected speech. In some parts of the country *wasn't* is usually pronounced "wadn't" in ordinary conversation; the the z-sound (represented by the s-spelling) under the influence of the following *n* changes into a *d*. Such change, by which two sounds become more alike (called assimilation), is extremely common in English. In a "careful" pronunciation the *is* of *What is your name?* ends in a *z*-sound. In a more casual pronunciation, however, under the influence of the preceding *t,* it changes to an *s*-sound, as in *What's your name?* In a still more casual pronunciation the *s* is lost altogether, being merged with the *t* of *what* and the *y* of *your* into a single *ch*-sound: "Whacher name?" The unconventional spelling makes a normal, relaxed pronunciation look disreputable. There is, however, nothing wrong with such a pronunciation used in the appropriately relaxed and casual situation.

The sentence just discussed also illustrates another kind of change (vowel gradation). When the word *your* is pronounced without emphasis, it is sounded like "yer," and its vowel is generally reduced to a sound represented by the phonetic symbol [ə] (called *schwa*). The same reduced vowel sound occurs in the last syllable of *policeman* ("-mun") and as the pronunciation of the word *of* in *cup of coffee* ("cuppa"). Anyone who insists on giving full value to every word and syllable in the sentence *The policeman had a cup of coffee* will sound as though he were reading from a first-grade primer. Normal speech requires that unemphasized words and parts of words be reduced in pronunciation. Full pronunciation indicates emphasis, and all words cannot be equally emphatic. Unemphasized parts of the sentence are either reduced, like the vowel of *-man* in *policeman,* or omitted altogether, like the final consonant in *of* as it is pronounced in a normal utterance of *cup of coffee.*

The omission of unstressed vowels inside a word (syncope, pronounced "'sing-ko-pee") is frequent in most types of English. Thus a three-syllable pronunciation of *family* may sound overnice to many speakers, who would say "fam'ly" instead. Similarly, "av'rage," "sep'rate," "cel'ry," "bach'lor," "pris'ner," and "di'mond" are all pronounced in two syllables much of the time. Consonants are also lost: *postpone* is usually pronounced without the *t*; *asked* is often pronounced without the *k* (though "ast" is sometimes thought inelegant); and *tests* is frequently pronounced like "tess." Such loss of sounds is by no means recent. Long ago the *t* was lost in words like *castle* and *soften.* It was also lost in *often* but in this case has been restored rather recently, probably through the efforts of schoolteachers to make their charges pronounce the *t* and thereby avoid the misspelling "offen."

Sounds are added (intrusion) as well as lost in pronunciation. The oldest recorded spelling of *arctic* in English is *artic,* found in Chaucer's *Treatise on the Astrolabe,* written to teach his son how to use a navigational instrument. The record clearly shows how the word was pronounced originally in English—and is still pronounced by persons who use the word unselfconsciously. By the 16th century, however, classical scholars had begun to respell the word to show that it derives ultimately from the Greek *arktikos,* and some of them doubtless pronounced as they spelled. Now many speakers, especially television reporters and meteorologists, carefully sound both *c*'s under the impression that omitting the first is wrong. At present the word can be pronounced either way in Standard English, but if enough of us imitate the spelling-conscious way of saying it, the "ark-tic" pronunciation, which began as a half-educated mistake, will become the correct form of the word.

Sounds sometimes change to become less like neighboring ones (dissimilation). The sequence of *f-* and *th*-sounds in *diphtheria* is hard to articulate, so many English speakers change the first sound to *p.* Perhaps because the resulting misspelling ("diptheria") has been so castigated, the pronunciation with *p* is widely rejected as wrong and should be avoided. On the other hand, the omission of an *r*-sound from a word with several *r*'s ("rese'voir," "gove'nor," "su'prise"), although quite frequent, is seldom noticed and almost never reproved.

The order of sounds can also be changed (metathesis, pronounced "me'tath-e-sis"). *Task* and *tax* are historically the same form, both from one Latin source (*taxare*), and hence were once pronounced alike. But distinct meanings arose along with the change in pronunciation— the reversal of the *ks* sound to *sk*—and thus we now have two words. A similar kind of metathesis changed the earlier *aks* to our current *ask*; far from being a corruption of *ask,* the modern dialectal "aks" or "ax" is actually a preservation of the older form, which died out of Standard English. A frequent sort of metathesis in current usage is in the first syllable of words like *perform* and *pretend,* which may come out as "preform" and "pertend." Such mispronunciation generally escapes notice, unless it leads to a misspelling that calls attention to it; but if enough speakers metathesize *per-* and *pre-,* the new pronunciations will cease to be mistakes and become part of Standard English. There is no sign of that happening yet, but we can never be sure when an error in pronunciation may become the fashionable way of talking.

Some causes of variation

The person who says "diptheria" for *diphtheria* or "grammother" for *grandmother* is using pronunciations that are easier to produce than the more formal ones represented by the spellings of those words. Ease of articulating sounds (sometimes castigated as laziness or sloppiness) is one cause for the existence of variants. Another, and an increasingly powerful one, is the influence of spelling. There is a mistaken though widespread idea that good pronunciation stays close to the spelling and that spelling is more real, permanent, and reliable than pronunciation. Those who are seduced by the appeal of writing into thinking of writing as primary and sound as secondary are likely to change their pronunciations to suit spelling whenever the opportunity arises. The pronunciation of *often* with a *t* has already been mentioned as an example. Similarly many people are giving a "full" pronunciation to *forehead* (instead of "forrid"), pronouncing the last syllables of *educator* and *legislator* like "tore" instead of "ter," and pronuncing *conduit* as "con-doo-it" instead of "condit." The fact that several of these pronunciations are now quite common does not change the fact that they began as mispronunciations, slavishly adhering to what the spelling seemed to indicate. The widespread literacy of our time—on at least a basic level—is having a profound effect on pronunciation.

Educator pronounced with a final "tore" not only follows the spelling but is also a voguish pronunciation that apparently lends a touch of class to what some regard as the otherwise humdrum occupation of teaching. The sound *zh* (as in the middle of *vision* and *pleasure*) is also voguish today, probably because it connotes foreignness and sophistication. Given the choice between "garodge" and "garahzh" for *garage,* many people choose the second as more elegant, though in some areas, that has always been the standard pronunciation. Indeed nowadays the *zh*-sound is often used where it does not belong historically; for example, in *kosher* ("kozher"), *cashmere* ("cazhmere"), and *rajah* ("razhah"). Similarly, at his investiture as Prince of Wales, Prince Charles swore to be his mother's *liege* ("leezh") man, whereas the traditional English pronunciation of that word—part of our language since it was borrowed from French in the 13th century—is "leedge." The pronunciation that the prince used began as a hypercorrection; that is, an effort to be correct that overshoots its mark. Linguistic vogues often lead to such hypercorrection, the effort to be fashionable resulting in excessive and thus erroneous use of the voguish pronunciation. The *a*-sound in *hand,* as it is pronounced in some parts of the country— for example, in New York City—approaches "haind" and is often thought to be inelegant. In an effort to avoid that extreme, some speakers—especially those who read hand lotion commercials on television—go to the other extreme and pronounce *hand* hypercorrectly as though it were "hahnd."

A special kind of hypercorrection is our treatment of foreign words. English speakers have long followed the custom of anglicizing foreign words by pronouncing them as though their spellings represented English sounds. Thus in the 17th century we borrowed *junta* from

Spanish and pronounced the beginning of the word like that of *jump*. Today, however, it is usually given a pseudo-Spanish pronunciation, "hoonta," which has only a remote likeness to the original Spanish. Similarly, borrowed Latin words and phrases were once universally pronounced according to the English tradition—as a few still are; *e.g.*, our national motto: *e pluribus unum* ("ee pluribus yoonum")—but now the so-called classical pronunciation is used, at least in part, even for quite ordinary English words derived from Latin. In the traditional English pronunciation *alumni* ended like "nigh" and *alumnae* like "knee"; now many speakers have reversed the pronunciations, with the result that the two forms are difficult to distinguish in speech.

Deciding among the options

There is more than one way to pronounce most English words, and deciding which pronunciation to use is no simple matter. The standard pronunciation of English is not homogeneous. As noted above, it varies from place to place, among various groups, and from one situation to another. For ordinary everyday words the pronunciations used most frequently by educated or otherwise influential members of the community provide models. For rare, technical, or bookish words the pronunciations used by those who have occasion to employ that special vocabulary are the best models. It is such pronunciations that dictionaries try to record. However, a good dictionary, especially a large one like *Webster's Third New International Dictionary*, will record all of the most frequently used standard pronunciations and thus will provide several options for the reader to choose among. In deciding upon a variant to use, each person must rely on individual taste and sense of fitness. Although most speakers stress the second syllable of *harass* ("huh-rass"), some prefer the older, more conservative pronunciation stressing the first syllable ("harr-us"). Some Americans prefer to pronounce *kilometer* with the continental-sounding stress on the second syllable ("ki-lom-eter"), whereas others prefer to associate the word with *kilo* and *meter* by putting stress on the first and third syllables ("kill-o-meeter"). In such cases there is no disputing taste, a fact that will not stop contentious people from disputing bitterly in favor of the pronunciation they happen to like.

The concern over correct pronunciation, as well as other aspects of correct usage, has become a hot issue in the schools. Some advocate that the school should seek to eradicate all nonstandard usage from the language of its students. Others propose that Standard English should be taught as a second dialect, much like a foreign language, to those whose native speech is nonstandard. Yet others maintain that the schools should recognize the students' right to their own language and not attempt to abridge their right—by implication denying that standard speech should be taught at all. Finally others view the school as an instrument for neither social change nor social repression but rather as the arena in which to help students understand the best that mankind has thought and written. True understanding, they believe, requires the reader to articulate a response through intelligible and sensible speech and writing.

Learning correct pronunciation is a very small part of good education, although it is not to be despised. The clarity and effectiveness of what we say is conditioned in part by how well we say it. But correct or incorrect pronunciation alone rarely ensures or precludes successful communication. Those who pronounce differently from others generally still communicate well—indeed they may communicate more than they intend. Unusual pronunciation seldom destroys a message; rather it reveals something about the speaker's background and attitudes.

In ancient Palestine there were two peoples, the Ephraimites, who had no *sh*-sound in their language, and the Gileadites, who did. When they were at war with one another, the Gileadites used the word *shibboleth,* meaning "stream," as a password. An Ephraimite who tried to say it would utter "sibboleth" instead and was soon dispatched by a Gileadite sword. We still use pronunciation differences as shibboleths; that is, criteria to distinguish who does or does not belong to a particular group. While hardly an admirable use of language, it reflects the human context in which language functions.

In selecting a pronunciation we must necessarily consider several factors in order to make the best choice: What will most effectively communicate the message we want to convey? What is appropriate to the circumstances we are in? What will be the response of those who hear the pronunciation we use? What pronunciation do we prefer, for esthetic, traditional, or other reasons? If in doubt we are likely to consult a dictionary, but in doing so we need to exercise caution. First, dictionaries differ, often surprisingly so, in the information they record; hence it is often useful to look in several dictionaries rather than only one. Second, no dictionary can record all the pronunciations for every word, and a pronunciation that is not listed may still be acceptable. Third, in most dictionaries the order in which pronunciations are listed is not one of "preference"; it may indicate what the editors think is the relative frequency of the various pronunciations. However, if frequency is about the same for all pronunciations listed—or if the editors do not know—the order of pronunciations may indicate nothing at all. The dictionary's introduction is often helpful in explaining such things. A good dictionary is a great help to those who want to use the language precisely, clearly, and gracefully; but even the best dictionary must be used with intelligence and common sense. Above all, the user needs to remember that no dictionary is infallible and that none can do more than report how the language is actually used by our fellows.

There is no magic list of "100 most often mispronounced" words, the learning of which will guarantee success, respect, and self-satisfaction. Any such proposed list is fraudulent. Nevertheless, there are numerous words that cause many people hesitation in pronunciation. Some of them are listed on page 357 with their variant pronunciations and occasional comment.

JOHN ALGEO

How Is It Pronounced?

As in the main body of the article, comments on the pronunciations in this list include impressionistic phonetic spellings. The phonetic transcriptions themselves employ the pronunciation symbols used in *Webster's New Collegiate Dictionary* (1979) and reproduced below. Acceptable variant pronunciations of a word are listed, separated by commas, but their order does not indicate preference of one variant over another. A variant that is chiefly British is so noted. A stress mark set above the line (') is used to show primary, or major, stress on the syllable it precedes; a stress mark set below the line (‚) notes secondary, or minor, stress on the syllable it precedes: **archetype** \ 'är-ki-‚tīp\. Parentheses in a transcription indicate that the parenthetical element is pronounced by some speakers and not pronounced by others: **clothes** \ 'klō(th̲)z\. Partial pronunciations are shown when two or more variants have one or several commonly pronounced elements: **amen** \ (')ā-'men, (')ä-\.

Pronunciation Symbols

ə......banana, collide, abut

ˈə, ˌə......humdrum, abut

ə......immediately preceding \l\, \n\, \m\, \ŋ\, as in battle, mitten, eaten, and sometimes cap and bells \-ᵊm-\, lock and key \-ᵊŋ-\; immediately following \l\, \m\, \r\, as often in French table, prisme, titre

ər......operation, further, urger

ˈər-⎫
         ⎬......as in two different pronunciations
ˈə-r⎭   of hurry \ˈhər-ē, ˈhə-rē\

a......mat, map, mad, gag, snap, patch

ā......day, fade, date, aorta, drape, cape

ä......bother, cot, and, with most American speakers, father, cart

à......father as pronounced by speakers who do not rhyme it with bother

au̇......now, loud, out

b......baby, rib

ch......chin, nature \ˈnā-chər\ (actually, this sound is \t\ + \sh\)

d......did, adder

e......bet, bed, peck

ˈē, ˌē......beat, nosebleed, evenly, easy

ē......easy, mealy

f......fifty, cuff

g......go, big, gift

h......hat, ahead

hw......whale as pronounced by those who do not have the same pronunciation for both *whale* and *wail*

i......tip, banish, active

ī......site, side, buy, tripe (actually, this sound is \ä\ + \i\, or \à\ + \i\)

j......job, gem, edge, join, judge (actually, this sound is \d\ + \zh\)

k......kin, cook, ache

k̲......German ich, Buch

l......lily, pool

m......murmur, dim, nymph

n......no, own

n......indicates that a preceding vowel or diphthong is pronounced with the nasal passages open, as in French un bon vin blanc \œ̜ⁿ-bōⁿ-vaⁿ-bläⁿ\

ŋ......sing \ˈsiŋ\, singer \ˈsiŋ-ər\, finger \ˈfiŋ-gər\, ink \ˈiŋk\

ō......bone, know, beau

ȯ......saw, all, gnaw

œ......French boeuf, German Hölle

œ̄......French feu, German Höhle

ȯi......coin, destroy, sawing

p......pepper, lip

r......red, car, rarity

s......source, less

sh......with nothing between, as in shy, mission, machine, special (actually, this is a single sound, not two); with a hyphen between, two sounds as in death's-head \ˈdeths-ˌhed\

t......tie, attack

th......with nothing between, as in thin, ether (actually, this is a single sound, not two); with a hyphen between, two sounds as in knighthood \ˈnīt-ˌhu̇d\

th̲......then, either, this (actually, this is a single sound, not two)

ü......rule, youth, union \ˈyün-yən\, few \ˈfyü\

u̇......pull, wood, book, curable \ˈkyu̇r-ə-bəl\

ᵫ......German füllen, hübsch

ᵫ̄......French rue, German fühlen

v......vivid, give

w......we, away; in some words having final \(ˌ)ō\ a variant \ə-w\ occurs before vowels, as in \ˈfäl-ə-wiŋ\, covered by the variant \ə(-w)\ at the entry word

y......yard, young, cue \ˈkyü\, union \ˈyün-yən\

y......indicates that during the articulation of the sound represented by the preceding character the front of the tongue has substantially the position it has for the articulation of the first sound of yard, as in French digne \dēnʸ\

yü......youth, union, cue, few, mute

yu̇......curable, fury

z......zone, raise

zh......with nothing between, as in vision, azure \ˈazh-ər\ (actually, this is a single sound, not two); with a hyphen between, two sounds as in gazehound \ˈgāz-ˌhau̇nd\

\......slant line used in pairs to mark the beginning and end of a transcription: \ˈpen\

ˈ......mark preceding a syllable with primary (strongest) stress: \ˈpen-mən-ˌship\

ˌ......mark preceding a syllable with secondary (next-strongest) stress: \ˈpen-mən-ˌship\

-......mark of syllable division

( )......indicate that what is symbolized between is present in some utterances but not in others: factory \ˈfak-t(ə-)rē\

By permission. From Webster's New Collegiate Dictionary © 1979, by G. & C. Merriam Co., Publishers of the Merriam-Webster Dictionaries.

abdomen \\'ab-də-mən, ab-'dō-mən\\ Since both pronunciations have been used for 200 years, you have your choice.

abhor \\əb-'hȯ(ə)r, ab-\\

acetic \\ə-'sēt-ik\\ *See also* **ascetic.**

acorn \\'ā-ˌkȯ(ə)rn, -kərn\\ The most common pronunciation shows a false association with *corn;* the historically regular pronunciation would be "achern," but this survives only in some dialects.

adult \\ə-'dəlt, 'ad-ˌəlt\\

advertisement \\ˌad-vər-'tīz-mənt; əd-'vərt-əz-mənt, -ə-smənt\\ The first pronunciation results from analogy with *advertise.*

aegis \\'ē-jəs\\ This word is sometimes pronounced "ay-gis" but not by those who use it comfortably.

affluent \\'af-ˌlü-ənt, *also* a-'flü-ənt *or* ə-\\

alumnae \\ə-'ləm-(ˌ)nē\\ This traditional pronunciation and that of the next word are often reversed through the influence of school Latin.

alumni \\ə-'ləm-ˌnī\\

always \\'ȯl-wēz, -wəz, -(ˌ)wāz\\ The third variant is a spelling pronunciation that invites confusion with *all ways.*

amateur \\'am-ə-ˌtər, -ət-ər, -ə-ˌt(y)ù(ə)r, -ə-ˌchù(ə)r, -ə-chər\\ There are so many options for the final syllable of this word that it is hard to go wrong.

amen \\(')ā-'men, (')ä-\\ The first pronunciation is traditional; the second was introduced as a sung form and is now often regarded as more stylish.

antithesis \\an-'tith-ə-səs\\

antithetical \\ˌant-ə-'thet-i-kəl\\

apricot \\'ap-rə-ˌkät, 'ā-prə-\\ Both are used in the United States, but the second is typically British.

archetype \\'är-ki-ˌtīp\\ Though historically related to the *arch-* of *archbishop,* the prefix of this word, like that of *archangel,* is pronounced with a *k.*

arctic \\'ärk-tik, 'ärt-ik\\ The second is now a mistake despite the older pronunciation, as the earliest spelling, *artik.*

aristocrat \\ə-'ris-tə-ˌkrat, a-; 'ar-ə-stə-\\ In British English the first syllable is stressed rather than the second, which translates for American speakers as an aristocratic way of saying the word.

arsenic \\'ärs-nik, -ᵊn-ik\\ The first, syncopated (that is, with the unstressed vowel being lost) pronunciation is usual.

asbestos \\as-'bes-təs, az-\\ The pronunciation with *z* results from assimilation; that with *s* is spelling-reinforced.

ascetic \\ə-'set-ik\\ *See also* **acetic.**

Asia \\'ā-zhə, -shə\\ The first pronunciation is more common in the United States, the second in Great Britain.

ate \ 'āt, *chiefly Brit. or substandard* 'et\ *

athlete \ 'ath-₁lēt\ The three-syllable pronunciation "athalete" is favored by sports announcers but is generally regarded as improper.

aunt \ 'ant, 'ȧnt\ The second pronunciation is used in eastern New England; in black English the word typically rhymes with *font.*

avoirdupois \ ₁av-ərd-ə-'pȯiz, 'av-ərd-ə-₁\

balm \ 'bäm, 'bälm\ The Middle English spelling *baume* suggests the traditional pronunciation; the pronunciation of the *l* is prompted by the spelling.

Baptist \ 'bap-təst\ "Babdist" is common among Southern Baptists.

bayou \ 'bī-(₁)(y)ō, -(₁)(y)ü, -(y)ə\

been \ (')bin, *chiefly Brit.* (')bēn\

bestial \ 'bes(h)-chəl, 'bēs(h)-\

boor \ 'bu̇(ə)r\ In some regions the word is identical in sound with *bore.*

bouquet \ bō-'kā, bü-\ The second is the traditional pronunciation from French.

bourbon \ 'bər-bən\ This pronunciation signals the whiskey (or the Kentucky county after which it is named); the French royal house is usually pronounced "Boorbon."

bowdlerize \ 'bōd-lə-₁rīz, 'baud-\ The second is the traditional pronunciation.

breech \ 'brēch, *pl. usu.* 'brich-əz\ The garment, whether spelled *breeches* or *britches,* is pronounced like the latter, although riding trousers may be "breeches."

brooch \ 'brōch, 'brüch\ From the same source as *broach* and traditionally pronounced like it, this word developed its second pronunciation from the spelling.

broom \ 'brüm, 'bru̇m\ These are historical variants with regional distribution in the United States.

cacophony \ ka-'käf-ə-nē\

cadre \ 'kad-rē\

calm \ 'käm, 'kälm\ *See* **balm.**

caramel \ 'kar-ə-məl, -₁mel; 'kär-məl\

caveat \ 'kā-vē-₁at, 'kav-ē-, -ət; 'käv-e-₁ät, -ət\ The second and third variants show in part the influence of school Latin.

Celt \ 'selt, 'kelt\ The first pronunciation is traditional; the second is used by historical linguists.

chaise longue \ 'shāz-'lȯŋ\ "Chase lounge" is a combination of a spelling pronunciation for the first word and folk etymology for the second.

---

*The following abbreviations are used in this list: *Brit.* (British), *Canad.* (Canadian), *esp.* (especially), *pl.* (plural), *pron.* (pronoun), *S.* (Spanish), *usu.* (usually), *var.* (variant).

chamois \ˈsham-ē\

chic \ˈshēk\ "Chick" is a spelling-influenced pronunciation—and usually a tired joke.

chignon \ˈshēn-ˌyän\

chivalry \ˈshiv-əl-rē\ A beginning consonant sound like that of *Chevy Chase* is historically correct but is archaic nowadays, having been replaced by the initial *sh* of the modern French pronunciation.

clapboard \ˈklab-ərd; ˈkla(p)-ˌbō(ə)rd, -ˌbȯ(ə)rd\ The first is traditional; the second pronunciation derives from the spelling.

clique \ˈklēk, ˈklik\

clothes \ˈklō(th̠)z\ The pronunciation without *th* is traditional, but the spelling has been influential.

colloquy \ˈkäl-ə-kwē\

comely \ˈkəm-lē *also* ˈkōm- *or* ˈkäm-\

comparable \ˈkäm-p(ə-)rə-bəl\ *See* **incomparable.**

conduit \ˈkän-ˌd(y)ü-ət, *also* -d(w)ət\ The Middle English spelling *condit* suggests the traditional pronunciation; the other pronunciations are spelling-influenced.

coop \ˈküp, ˈku̇p\ *See* **broom.**

coronal \ˈkȯr-ən-ₑl, ˈkär-; kə-ˈrōn-\

coupon \ˈk(y)ü-ˌpän\ Related to *coup,* meaning "blow, cut," *coupon* ("a piece cut off") traditionally sounded its first syllable like *coup,* but the pronunciation with "kyew" is increasingly common.

covert \ˈkō-(ˌ)vərt, kō-ˈ; ˈkəv-ərt\ The word is related to *cover,* and hence the last pronunciation for the noun is traditional; the first results from analogy with *overt.*

creek \ˈkrēk, ˈkrik\ The difference is regional, the first being Northern.

cuckoo \ˈkük-(ˌ)ü, ˈku̇k-\ *See* **broom.**

dais \ˈdā-əs, ˈdī-\ The second is recent; the traditional pronunciation, rhyming with *face,* is now obsolescent.

data \ˈdāt-ə, ˈdat-, ˈdät-\ The last is a pseudoclassical pronunciation.

decorous \ˈdek-ə-rəs, *also* di-ˈkȯr-əs *or* -ˈkȯr-\ The second results from analogy with *decorum.*

demesne \di-ˈmān, -ˈmēn\

denouement \ˌdā-ˌnü-ˈmäⁿ, dā-nü-ˌ\

derby \ˈdər-bē, *Brit.* ˈdär-\

desperado \ˌdes-pə-ˈräd-(ˌ)ō, -ˈrād-\ The first pronunciation is a remodeling of the word to make it sound more like the original Spanish.

desuetude \ˈdes-wi-ˌt(y)üd, di-ˈsü-ə-ˌt(y)üd\

desultory \ˈdes-əl-ˌtōr-ē, -ˌtȯr-, *also* ˈdez-\

detritus \di-ˈtrīt-əs\

dilettante \ˌdil-ə-ˈtänt(-ē), -ˈtant(-ē)\ This loanword from Italian is traditionally pronounced to rhyme with *panty;* the mistaken idea that it is a French word led to the rhyme with *font.*

dishabille \ ,dis-ə-'bē(ə)l, -'bil,-'bē\

disputable \ dis-'pyüt-ə-bəl, 'dis-pyət-ə-bəl\

doctoral \ 'däk-t(ə-)rəl\ "Doctorial" rhyming with *territorial* is a mispronunciation.

drama \ 'dräm-ə, 'dram-\ The first is now general and the second old-fashioned.

draught \ 'dråft\ A rhyme with *ought* is a mispronunciation that the alternate spelling *draft* prevents.

dynasty \ 'dī-nə-stē, *also* -,nas-tē\ A pronunciation beginning like *dinner* is British or old-fashioned.

economic \ ,ek-ə-'näm-ik, ,ē-kə-\

eczema \ ig-'zē-mə, 'eg-zə-mə, 'ek-sə-\ Many used to regard the first pronunciation as déclassé, and some still do.

either \ 'ē-thər *also* 'ī-\ The second is sometimes thought more sophisticated.

elm \ 'elm\ A two-syllable pronunciation, "elum," is substandard.

empyrean \ ,em-,pī-'rē-ən, -pə-; em-'pir-ē-ən, -'pī-rē-\ Various dictionaries record other equally acceptable pronunciations; it is hard to go wrong.

enclave \ 'en-,klāv; 'än-,klāv, 'äŋ-, -,kläv\ The first is an anglicized pronunciation; the others are confused stabs at sounding French.

en masse \ än(n)-'mas\

ennui \ 'än-'wē\

envelope \ 'en-və-,lōp, 'än-\ The second is an approximation of the original French pronunciation of the word.

epoch \ 'ep-ək, 'ep-,äk\ The second is only half-British since in Great Britain the word is typically pronounced "ee-pock."

era \ 'ir-ə, 'er-ə, 'ē-rə\ The first and third are traditional; the second is pseudoclassical but becoming more common.

err \ 'e(ə)r, 'ər\ The second is traditional; the first, by analogy with *error,* is gaining popularity.

ex libris \ ek-'slē-brəs, -,brēs\ The traditional "ex lie-bris" has been generally replaced by these school Latin pronunciations.

explicable \ ek-'splik-ə-bəl, 'ek-(,)splik-\ The second is traditional, but the first is more common.

extant \ 'ek-stənt; ek-'stant, 'ek-,\

falcon \ 'fal-kən, *also* 'fȯl-, *sometimes* 'fȯ-kən\ Pronunciation of the *l* in the first is due to the spelling; traditionally it is silent as in the second.

fiancé *or* **fiancée** \ ,fē-,än-'sā, fē-'än-,\

fiat \ 'fē-ət, -,at, -,ät; 'fī-ət, -,at\ The last two pronunciations (rhyming with *quiet* and *why at*) are traditional; the first three show the influence of school Latin.

film \ 'film\ The two-syllable pronunciation "filum" is substandard.

finance \ fə-'na(t)s, 'fī-„ fī-'\ Both variants are well established.

flaccid \ 'flak-səd, 'flas-əd\ The first is traditional.

fluorescent \ „flu̇ (-ə)r-'es-ᵊnt, flȯr-, flȯr-\

fluorine \ 'flu̇(-ə)r-„ēn, -ən\ The word is also pronounced with an initial "floor-."

forehead \ 'fȯr-əd, 'fär-; 'fō(ə)r-„hed, 'fȯ(ə)r-\ The first is traditional; the second is a spelling pronunciation that is rapidly taking over.

formidable \ 'fȯr-məd-ə-bəl *also* fȯr-'mid- *or* fər-'mid-\

foyer \ 'fȯi(-ə)r, 'fȯi-„(y)ā *also* 'fwä-„yā\ The first pronunciation is anglicized; the second, half-French; and the third, similar to the original French.

fungi \ 'fən-„jī, 'fəŋ-„gī\ The first is traditional; the second, the plural form of the singular *fungus*. School Latin also produces a pronunciation rhyming with "dun ghee."

fuselage \ 'fyü-sə-„läzh, -zə-\ The word also has pronunciations ending like "lodge."

gaol \ 'jā(ə)l\ This is a British spelling for *jail;* both words are pronounced alike.

garrulous \ 'gar-ə-ləs, *also* 'gar-yə-\

geisha \ 'gā-shə, 'gē-\ The first is closer to the Japanese pronunciation; the second is anglicized.

genealogy \ „jē-nē-'äl-ə-jē, „jen-ē-; -'al-\ The first is by analogy with the many words ending in *-ology,* which sometimes also causes a misspelling of this word.

giblets \ 'jib-ləts, *also* 'gib-\ A pronunciation beginning like that of *gibbon* is regarded by many as unacceptable.

gladiolus \ „glad-ē-'ō-ləs\ There is also a rarer pronunciation "gla-dye-olus."

Gnostic \ 'näs-tik\ There is a regional variant "Gnaw-stic."

government \ 'gəv-ər(n)-mənt, 'gəv-ᵊm-ənt\ The first *n* is rarely pronounced in normal speech.

greasy \ 'grē-sē, -zē\ The first is Northern, the second Southern; the verb *grease* has the same variants.

grovel \ 'gräv-əl, 'grəv-\ The second is traditional; the first is a spelling pronunciation.

gynecology \ „gīn-ə-'käl-ə-jē, „jin-\

hallow \ 'hal-(„)ō, -ə(-w) \ A pronunciation like "hollow" is occasionally heard.

Halloween \ „hal-ə-'wēn, „häl-\

harass \ hə-'ras, 'har-əs\ The second is traditional; the first is influenced by the spelling.

hegemony \ hi-'jem-ə-nē, -'gem-; 'hej-ə-„mō-nē\

herb \\'(h)ərb\\ The pronunciation without an *h* is traditional, but the influence of the spelling is a strong force.

heterogeneous \\ˌhet-(ə)rə-'jē-nē-əs, ˌhe-trə-, -nyəs\\

hiatus \\hī-'āt-əs\\

hiccough \\'hik-(ˌ)əp\\ The earlier spellings *hickop* or *hickup* were changed because of a false association with *cough;* now a pronunciation ending like *cough* is occasionally heard.

homage \\'(h)äm-ij\\ *See* **herb.**

homicide \\'häm-ə-ˌsīd, 'hō-mə-\\ The first is traditional; the second is by analogy with *homo,* showing the influence of school Latin.

hoodlum \\'hüd-ləm, 'hu̇d-\\ The first seems to be the older pronunciation; the second is probably influenced by *hood* ("head covering").

hoop \\'hu̇p, 'hüp\\ *See* **broom.**

hover \\'həv-ər, 'häv-\\

human \\'hyü-mən, 'yü-\\ *See* **herb.**

humble \\'həm-bəl, 'əm-\\ *See* **herb.**

humor \\'(h)yü-mər\\ *See* **herb.**

hundred \\'hən-drəd, -dərd\\ "Hunderd" is an ancient variant that remained in educated use until about a century ago; now it is often wrongly thought a careless mistake.

hygienic \\ˌhī-jē-'en-ik, hī-'jen-, hī-'jēn-\\

ideology \\ˌīd-ē-'äl-ə-jē, ˌid-\\

ignominy \\'ig-nə-ˌmin-ē, -mə-nē; ig-'näm-ə-nē\\

impious \\'im-pē-əs, (')im-'pī-\\ The first is traditional; the second is by analogy with *pious.*

incomparable \\(')in-'käm-p(ə-)rə-bəl\\ A pronunciation of the central part of the word like *compare* occurs but is regarded by many as unacceptable.

indecorous \\(')in-'dek-(ə-)rəs; ˌin-di-'kōr-əs, -'kȯr-\\ *See* **decorous.**

-ing \\iŋ, *in some dialects usu.,* *in other dialects informally,* ən, in, *or (after certain consonants)* ᵊn, ᵊm, ᵊŋ\\ The pronunciation of *baking* like "bacon" or *fishing* like "fission" (popularly, but wrongly, thought of as "dropping one's *g*'s") is used informally almost everywhere, being most common in the South, where such pronunciations are also used formally. The pronunciation of *-ing* as "-in" is an old and honorable variant that used to be upper-class usage on both sides of the Atlantic.

ingenious \\in-'jēn-yəs\\ Sometimes confused in pronunciation with *ingenuous.*

ingenue \\'an-jə-ˌnü, 'än-; 'aⁿ-zhə-, 'äⁿ-\\ The variants result from a mixture of French and anglicized pronunciations.

ingenuous \\in-'jen-yə-wəs\\ Sometimes confused in pronunciation with *ingenious.*

intaglio \in-'tal-(,)yō, -'täl-; -'tag-lē-,ō, -'täg-\

interested \'in-trəs-təd; 'int-ə-rəs-təd, -ə-,res-təd', -ərs-təd; 'in-,tres-təd\

internecine \,int-ər-'nes-,ēn, -'nēs-,īn, -ᵊn; in-'tər-nə-,sēn, -sən; int-ər-nə-'sēn\

irrefutable \,ir-i-'fyüt-ə-bəl, (')ir-'(r)ef-yət-\

isthmus \'is-məs\ The traditional pronunciation is sometimes affected by the spelling so that a *t* is pronounced after the first *s*; few people achieve a "th" in that position, though doubtless some try.

jejune \ji-'jün\

junta \'hùn-tə, 'jənt-ə, 'hən-tə\ The second is traditional; the first and third are partially successful efforts to sound like the original Spanish.

juvenile \'jü-və-,nīl, -vən-ᵊl\

karma \'kär-mə, 'kər-\ The rare pronunciation "kur-ma" better approximates the Sanskrit original.

ketchup, *var. of* **catsup** \'kech-əp, 'kach-; 'kat-səp\ This loanword from Chinese has nothing to do with *catch, up, cat,* or *sup* but is spelled and pronounced in a variety of ways under the influence of these words.

kibitzer \'kib-ət-sər, kə-'bit-\

kiln \'kiln, 'kil\ Traditionally pronounced like "kill," the word has acquired an *n*-sound from the spelling.

kilometer \kil-'äm-ət-ər (*not parallel with other metric-system compounds*), 'kil-ə-,mēt-\

kudos \'k(y)ü-,däs\ This fancy word, more common in print than in speech, sometimes ends like "-doughs."

laissez-faire \,le-,sā-'fa(ə)r, ,lā-, -,zā-, -'fe(ə)r\

lasso \'las-(,)ō, la-'sü\

lava \'läv-ə, 'lav-\

legerdemain \,lej-ərd-ə-'mān\

leisure \'lēzh-ər, 'lezh-, 'lāzh-\

library \'lī-,brer-ē\ Among the several other variants of this word, only "lie-berry" is nonstandard.

lingerie \,län-jə-'rā, ,laⁿ-zhə-, -'rē\ The first is very common but is often disapproved of as departing too greatly from the French.

liqueur \li-'kər\

longitude \'län-jə-,t(y)üd\ This Latin loanword is not derived from English *long.*

long-lived \'lȯŋ-'līvd, -'livd\ The first is traditional, the word being derived from *long life + ed,* with *f* changed to *v* by assimilation; the second pronunciation is from an incorrect association of the word with the verb *live.*

macabre \mə-'käb(-rə), -'käb-ər, -'käbrᵊ\

machete \mə-'shet-ē, -'chet-; -'shet\

majuscule \ 'maj-əs-ˌkyü(ə)l, mə-'jəs-\ The second is traditional (compare *minuscule*).

margarine \ 'märj-(ə-)rən, -ə-ˌrēn\ The pronunciation with a "hard *g*," though suggested by the spelling, is rare.

mauve \ 'mōv, 'mȯv\ The first is traditional; the second is an anglicized spelling pronunciation.

menstruate \ 'men(t)-strə-ˌwāt, 'men-ˌstrāt\ The first is suggested by the spelling, but the second is more common.

mezzo \ 'met-(ˌ)sō, 'med-(ˌ)zō\

mien \ 'mēn\

mimesis \ mə-'mē-səs, mī-\

minuscule \ 'min-əs-ˌkyü(ə)l, min-'əs-, 'min-yəs-, mī-'nəs-\ The second is traditional; the first by analogy with compounds of *mini-* leads to the misspelling "miniscule."

mnemonic \ ni-'män-ik\

mobile \ 'mō-bəl, ˌ-bēl, -ˌbīl\ The first is common for the adjective; the second or third for the noun.

naiveté \ (ˌ)nä-ˌē-və-'tā, nä-'ē-və-ˌ; ˌnä-ˌēv-'tā\

naked \ 'nā-kəd, 'nek-əd\ The second is old-fashioned.

naphtha \ 'naf-thə, 'nap-\ The first is spelling-conscious; the second is traditional.

neither \ 'nē-<u>th</u>ər, *also* 'nī-\ Like **either.**

nephew \ 'nef-(ˌ)yü, *chiefly Brit.* 'nev-\ The first, generally used in the United States, shows influence of the spelling, which was changed from the Middle English *neveu.*

nihilism \ 'nī-(h)ə-ˌliz-əm, 'nē-\ The first, *h*-less pronunciation is traditional; the others show the influence of school Latin.

nuclear \ 'n(y)ü-klē-ər\ "Nucular" is a mispronunciation used even by Presidents.

often \ 'ȯf-(t)ən\ The *t*-less pronunciation is traditional, but pronunciation of the *t* in the spelling is becoming more usual.

pajamas \ pə-'jäm-əz, -'jam-\

palm \ 'päm, 'pälm\ *See* **balm.**

papier-mâché \ ˌpā-pər-mə-'shā, ˌpap-ˌyä-mə-, -(ˌ)ma-\ The first is usual; the others are efforts to match a foreign-looking spelling with an equally foreign-sounding pronunciation.

paradigm \ 'par-ə-ˌdīm, -ˌdim\

parliament \ 'pär-lə-mənt, *also* 'pärl-yə-\ The pronunciation of *ia* as "yuh" or "ee-uh" (in two syllables) is an effort to force the sound of the word to match its spelling; the oldest spelling of the English word, *parlement,* is a better representation of its sound.

patronize \ 'pā-trə-ˌnīz, 'pa-\

pecan \ pi-'kän, -'kan; 'pē-ˌkan\

percolate \pər-kə-,lāt\ There is also a common, though anomalous, pronunciation as though the word were spelled "perculate."

perhaps \pər-'(h)aps, 'praps\ The second is informal but perfectly correct.

pestle \'pes-əl, *also* 'pes-t°l\ The first is traditional; the second is a spelling pronunciation (*see* **often**).

polka \'pōl-kə\ An *l*-less pronunciation also occurs, perhaps by analogy, with words like *folk* and *yolk*.

porte cochere \,pōrt-kō-'she(ə)r, pȯrt-\

program \'prō-,gram, -grəm\

pronunciation \prə-,nən(t)-sē-'ā-shən\ "Pronunciation" is a mispronunciation (and sometimes a misspelling) influenced by *pronounce*.

protein \'prō-,tēn, 'prōt-ē-ən\

psalm \'säm, 'sälm\ See **balm**.

puberty \'pyü-bərt-ē\ "Poo-berty," occasionally heard, is probably the result of school Latin.

pulpit \'pùl-,pit\ A pronunciation beginning like *pulse* is spelling-influenced.

pumpkin \'pəŋ-kən, 'pəm(p)-kən\

qualm \'kwäm, 'kwälm, *also* 'kwȯm\ The variation of vowels after "wa" is also common in a number of other words (*wash, squash, want*); for comment on the *l*, look at **balm.**

quasi \'kwā-,zī, -,sī; 'kwäz-ē, 'kwäs-; 'kwā-zē\ The first two are traditional; the others show the influence of school Latin.

quay \'kē, 'k(w)ā\

quixotic \kwik-'sät-ik\ The pronunciation is based on the traditional English pronunciation of *Don Quixote* as "Don Quick-sit"; the change, especially in America, of the name to "Donkey-hoe-tee" has not yet popularized "key-hoe-tick" for the adjective but in time may do so.

rapprochement \,rap-,rōsh-'mäⁿ, -,rȯsh-; ra-'prōsh-,\ These French-sounding pronunciations are still common.

ration \'rash-ən, 'rā-shən\

renege \ri-'nig, -'neg, -'nēg, -'nāg\ The first is still usual, although the spelling favors some of the others.

reverend \'rev-(ə-)rənd, 'rev-ərnd\ The two-syllable pronunciation is usual as a title for churchmen.

ribald \'rib-əld, *also* 'rib-,ȯld, 'rī-,bȯld\

root \'rüt, 'rùt\ See **broom.**

route \'rüt, 'raùt\ The second, though often criticized, is very common.

sacrilegious \,sak-rə-'lij-əs, -'lē-jəs\ The first pronunciation arises by analogy with the unrelated word *religious*.

sadism \'sā-,diz-əm, 'sad-,iz-\

saga \'säg-ə, *also* 'sag-\

schedule \skej-(ˌ)ü(ə)l, 'skej-əl, *Canad. also* 'shej-, *Brit. usu.* 'shed-(ˌ)yü(ə)l\ "Schedual" is a common over-articulation.

schism \'siz-əm, 'skiz-\ The second, a spelling pronunciation, is rarely used by people who talk much about *schisms*.

secretary \'sek-rə-, ter-ē\ "Sec'etary" has lost the first *r* by dissimilation.

sheik \'shēk, *also* 'shāk\ Neither pronunciation represents the original Arabic very well; the first is the more popular anglicized form.

sherbet \'shər-bət\ "Sherbert" is a pronunciation with an intrusive *r* that is occasionally seen as a misspelling.

sine qua non \ˌsin-i-ˌkwä-'nän, -'nōn, *also* ˌsēn-; *also* ˌsī-ni-ˌkwä-'nän\ The last is the traditional pronunciation but has become less common nowadays.

sobriquet \'sō-bri-ˌkā, -ˌket, ˌsō-bri-'\

soot \'sut, 'sət, 'süt\ *See* **broom.**

sophomore \'säf-ᵊm-ˌō(ə)r, -ˌȯ(ə)r; 'säf-ˌmō(ə)r, -ˌmȯ(ə)r\ The first syllable may also begin like *soft,* especially in the common two-syllable pronunciation.

sovereign \'säv-(ə-)rən, 'säv-ərn, 'səv-\

species \'spē-(ˌ)shēz, -(ˌ)sēz\ The first is traditional, but the second is frequent nowadays.

stationery \'stā-shə-ˌner-ē\ There is also a syncopated three-syllable pronunciation, "station'ry."

status \'stāt-əs, 'stat-\

strata \'strāt-ə, 'strat-\

strength \'streŋ(k)th\ "Strenth," though common, is often criticized.

suave \'swäv\ The traditional pronunciation, rhyming with *wave,* is now rare.

subpoena \sə-'pē-nə, *substand.* -nē\ Efforts to pronounce the *b* are influenced by the spelling.

suggest \sə(g)-'jest\ Pronunciation of the first "hard *g*" probably results from the influence of the spelling; it is more common in the United States than in Great Britain.

suite \'swēt\ In speaking of furniture, "soot" is frequent but often criticized.

superfluous \su̇-'pər-flə-wəs\

sycophant \'sik-ə-fənt, *also* -ˌfant\

syrup \'sər-əp, 'sir-əp, 'sə-rəp\

thence \'then(t)s, *also* 'then(t)s\ The first is traditional, but the second is becoming more common.

thither \'thith-ər, *also* 'thith-\ The traditional pronunciation, beginning like *there,* is now rare.

timbre \'tam-bər, 'tim-\

trauma \\'traủ-mə, 'trȯ-\\ The second is traditional; the first shows the influence of school Latin.

travail \\trə-'vā(ə)l, 'trav-ˌāl\\ The traditional pronunciation, identical with that of *travel* (the two words being historically the same), is now rare.

tryst \\'trist\\

tsetse \\'(t)set-sē, 'tet-, '(t)sēt-, 'tēt-\\ The pronunciation is almost as bothersome as the insect.

turquoise \\'tər-ˌk(w)ȯiz\\

ukase \\yü-'kās, -'kāz, 'yü-ˌ; ü-'käz\\

ultimatum \\ˌəl-tə-'māt-əm, -'mät-\\ The second shows the influence of school Latin.

vacuum \\'vak-yủ-əm, -(ˌ)yüm, -yəm\\

valet \\'val-ət, 'val-(ˌ)ā, va-'lā\\ The first is traditional; the second and third, closer to the French, are more common.

vanilla \\və-'nil-ə, -'nel-\\

vehicle \\'vē-ˌ(h)ik-əl, 'vē-ə-kəl\\

venal \\'vēn-ᵊl\\

venial \\'vē-nē-əl, -nyəl\\

victual \\'vit-ᵊl\\ The variant plural spelling *vittles* better represents the pronunciation.

vita \\'vēt-ə, 'vīt-ə\\ The second is traditional, and "wee-tah" from school Latin is also heard.

waffle \\'wäf-əl, 'wȯf-\\ There is also a common pronunciation rhyming with *awful*.

waistcoat \\'wes-kət, 'wās(t)-ˌkōt\\ The first is a traditional pronunciation revived in the United States as a more elegant term than *vest* for the modern garment.

wash \\'wȯsh, 'wäsh\\ "Warsh" is common but usually disapproved of by those who do not say it—and sometimes by those who do!

with \\(')wit͟h, (')with, wət͟h, wəth\\

wont \\'wȯnt, 'wōnt, *also* 'wənt, 'wänt\\ The traditional pronunciation "wunt" survives in the United States but is rare; the common pronunciations are spelling-influenced.

worsted \\'wủs-təd, 'wər-stəd\\ The first is traditional; the second pronunciation is influenced by the spelling.

wrestle \\'res-əl, 'ras-\\ The second is a variant, used since the 13th century, but now usually regarded as uneducated.

xenophobia \\ˌzen-ə-'fō-bē-ə, ˌzēn-\\

yolk \\'yōk, 'yəlk (*dialect*) *also* 'yōlk, 'yȯlk, 'yälk, 'yəlk\\ Pronunciation of the *l* shows influence from the spelling.

zoology \\zō-'äl-ə-jē, zə-'wäl-\\ "Zoo-ology" is by analogy with *zoo* and is regarded by many as unacceptable.

WORDS AND DICTIONARIES: THE BASIC TOOLS

Fluency with Words
Use of the Dictionary
List of Dictionaries

Fluency with Words

*His words . . . like so many nimble and airy servitors
trip about him at command.*
　　　—John Milton, *Apology for Smectymnuus* (1642)

Words are so basic that we often assume our abilities with them to be complete and settled. We might assume, for example, that practice with words ends on the day we leave school. Or we might assume that ease and skill with words—call it fluency—is a talent that one is born with or that a large vocabulary is synonymous with fluency. Each of these assumptions is a leaky vessel. In fact, practice with words is a lifelong enterprise; the fluency that comes with practice is developed, not inherited; and in itself a large vocabulary has little to do with fluency.

The benefits of fluency are pervasive. It underwrites individual competence, promotes comfort in social situations, and enhances personal choice. Competence with words—the ability to talk convincingly, read widely, and write well—is a fundamental skill. Modern life is often a murky thicket of words. Fluency enables us to penetrate this verbal thicket. It is sometimes a defensive skill, sometimes an offensive one, but always essential.

In our social lives fluency allows us greater ease with all manner of people in a variety of situations. Comfortable in the give-and-take of conversation, fluent speakers are more inclined to confidently exercise that vital conversational skill of asking good questions. Fluency gives us as well a far greater measure of choice in both our professional and personal lives. Fluency makes possible many forms of entry—into schools or colleges, for example, or into training programs or civil service lists—because entry procedures usually involve tests, and tests invariably involve words. The more fluent we are, the easier such tests become—and the more we are able to exercise choice in our work.

In leisure time fluency also fosters choice. Compare, for example, the

371

offerings on television for any given evening with the variety of books on one shelf of the local library. The realm of the printed word is a realm of wide choice. In the electronic media, by contrast, selection is confined to the spectrum of choices made by others.

Fluency begins with a certain confident attitude toward words and their use—like a good carpenter's approach to his workshop. The carpenter owns tools that he knows how to use or intends to learn how to use. He acquires more tools as his skill and ambition increase. He knows when to use simple tools, when to use more elaborate ones. The carpenter's skill results from practice; so it is with words. We all have some measure of skill with words. Fluency comes with the practice of that skill.

Practice with words involves two different kinds of vocabulary—one active, one passive. Our active vocabulary consists of words we know well and use daily. Our passive vocabulary consists of words we recognize and understand but do not use regularly. The distinction between the two is important but not rigid. Some words enter our passive vocabulary and remain there; others stop for a time in the passive list and then move on to the active. The passive vocabulary is no less important than the active, for it is the one that often provides the crucial measure of choice, enabling us to handle words on a test, to read widely, and to be at ease with many different kinds of people.

Practice with words

Fluency is rarely achieved directly. It is rather a by-product of other activities. Setting out to achieve fluency by some rigid regimen of daily word acquisition is neither particularly interesting nor very effective. Successful practice with words, by contrast, is inherently rewarding and interesting. This means discovering words by aggressive reading and listening; using the dictionary to capture new words; and letting curiosity stimulate and guide the exploration into the world of words.

Aggressive and adventurous reading is essential to fluency. We should read articles, books, and newspapers that we might ordinarily pass by. We should occasionally read the dictionary itself rather than only referring to it for a definition. We should make reading a daily habit, an interstitial activity. We all have interstices of time when we can, but often do not, read: while taking public transportation to and from work, waiting for appointments, standing in the supermarket line, or before going to sleep at night.

Aggressive listening is a companion activity to reading. Experiment with radio and television programs that are not part of your regular fare. Attend a lecture that you would ordinarily ignore. Listen more carefully to friends and colleagues. Listen and read not only for unfamiliar words but also for familiar words used in novel ways. The word *earnest,* for example, is familiar as an adjective (*He has an earnest way about him*). It is not so familiar as a noun meaning "a token of what is to come" (*His early poems were an earnest of the talent that was to flower 20 years later*).

Once encountered, new words must be studied and learned. The primary source of knowledge about words remains the dictionary. Look up each new word, note its meaning, and break the word down for closer examination. Determine any prefixes, roots, or suffixes it may have. Note also its synonyms, antonyms, and etymology. Once a word's meaning (or meanings) has been mastered, it must be put to use. Try it out in a sentence or two. Use it in letters or conversations if appropriate. In short, make the word part of your vocabulary.

Etymologies are as useful as they are interesting, and often provide a handle with which to grasp and hold onto meanings. The word *geminate,* for example, is potentially elusive unless we remember from its etymology that it stems from the same root as *Gemini* (Latin *geminus,* meaning "twin"), thus jogging the memory to recall that *geminate* means "to become double or paired."

Even if a word itself is entirely familiar, its etymology may not be. The word *trivial,* for example, derives from the division in medieval schools of the seven liberal arts into two groups of study, the trivium and the quadrivium. The trivium, consisting of grammar, rhetoric, and logic, comprised the elementary sequence of learning and led to the bachelor's degree; it preceded the quadrivium of arithmetic, music, geometry, and astronomy, which led to the master's degree. The trivium was thus the more elementary, though not the lesser of the two groups of study.

Just as every word has a history, every language has a history. Within the history of a language live the explanations for its particular rhythms, patterns, and logic. Unfortunately many schools and colleges do not approach English historically, and we are therefore deprived of a direct avenue to its richness, liveliness, and variety. But the discovery of English in all its dimensions may well be more rewarding for coming later than earlier in life and for being a personal rather than academic enterprise.

The sheer stock of words in English is itself rather awesome. Unabridged general dictionaries of the language contain approximately

500,000 entries, and some experts estimate, depending on the method of word count, that the language contains at least one million words. Their roots are sunk in rich and varied soil. Latin and Greek account for a significant portion of our English vocabulary, particularly if we include words borrowed from other languages, such as French, that derive largely from Latin and Greek. But English has proven hospitable to many tongues, which provide us such familiar terms as *squash, succotash* (American Indian); *jungle, shampoo* (Hindi); *bamboo* (Malay); *flannel* (Welsh); and *amber, syrup,* and *zero* (Arabic).

The Latin and Greek origins of English provided many of the prefixes, suffixes, and roots that recur in our language. A knowledge of them constitutes an investment in vocabulary capital. The investment bears interest in the form of keys to the meaning of literally thousands of words. The word *production* offers a good example. It consists of a prefix, *pro-;* root, *duct-;* and suffix, *-ion. Pro-* means "forward"; *duct-* means "that which leads" (in the interest of easy pronunciation, the root *duc-,* here spelled *duct-,* also appears as *duit-* or *duke-*); *-ion* means an "act or process," the "result of an act or process," or a "state or condition." Once the word *production* has been broken down and its elements mastered, an encounter with a sentence like *He had a ductile mind* will not immediately require a visit to the dictionary. Knowing the root *duct-* and the suffix *-ile* permits an educated guess that *ductile* means "capable of being fashioned into a new form" or "easily led or influenced." (For many of the Latin and Greek roots in English, *see* the table following. For common prefixes and suffixes in English, *see* the tables in the section on Spelling.)

LATIN ROOTS:

Root	*Meaning*	*Examples*
ac-, acr-	sharp	acrid, acumen, exacerbate
agr-	field	agriculture, agronomy
ali-	other	alias, alibi, alien
am-, amic-	love, friend	amatory, amicable, amorous

Root	Meaning	Examples
aud-, audit-	hear	audible, audience, auditorium
capit-	head	capital, capitation, decapitate
ced-, ceed-, cess-	go, yield	antecedent, concession, proceed, secede
cid-, cis-	cut, kill	homicide, incision, incisive, matricide
cogn-	know, be acquainted with	cognizant, incognito, recognize
cur-, curr-, curs-	run, course	concur, currency, cursory, precursor
dic-, dict-	word, say, speak	abdicate, addiction, benediction, contradict
ego-	I, self	egocentric, egoist
gen-	birth, origin, kind	congenial, generate, generic, progeny
greg-	flock	aggregate, congregate, egregious
junct-	join	adjunct, disjunction, injunction
jur-	swear	abjure, conjure, perjury
leg-	law	illegal, legislate, legitimate
locut-, loqu-	talk, speech	colloquy, eloquence, locution
magn-	large	magnanimous, magnify, magnitude
mal-	bad	malady, malevolent, malign
man-, manu-	hand	emancipate, manacle, manicure, manual
mar-	sea	marinade, marine, maritime, submarine
mater-, matr-	mother	maternity, matriarchy, matron, matrix
miss-, mit-	send	missile, remit, submit, transmission

Root	Meaning	Examples
mob-, mot-	move	automobile, emotion, motive, motor
mor-, mort-	die, death	immortal, morbid, moribund
nav-	ship, sail	circumnavigate, naval, nave, navigate
nomen-, nomin-	name	denominate, nomenclature, nominee
nov-	new	innovate, novelty, novitiate
pater-, patr-	father	paternal, patrimony, patrician
ped-	foot	centipede, impede, pedal
pon-, pos-	place, put	component, indisposed, proponent, postpone
port-	carry	import, portage, transport
pot-	power	omnipotent, potence, potential
reg-	rule	regal, regicide, regulation
rupt-	break	abrupt, corruption, rupture
sect-, seg-	cut	dissect, insect, sector, segment
sol-	alone	desolate, soliloquy, solitude
tang-, tact-	touch	tactile, tangible, tangent
ten-, tent-, tin-	hold	continence, detention, tenant, tenure, untenable
vid-, vis-	see	evident, provident, vision
verb-	word	proverb, verbal, verbose
vit-, viv-	life, lively	vital, vitamin, vivacious, vivid
voc-	call	advocate, vocal, vociferous

GREEK ROOTS:

Root	Meaning	Examples
anthrop-	man, mankind	anthropology, misanthrope, philanthropic
aster-, astr-	star	asterisk, astral, astrology
auto-	self	autocratic, automation, autopsy
bio-	life	amphibious, biology
chrom-	color	chromatic, chromosome
chron-	time	chronicle, chronology, synchronize
cosm-	order, world	cosmic, cosmopolitan, microcosm
crac-, crat-	power, rule	autocrat, democracy
dem-	people	demagogue, democracy, pandemic
derm-	skin	epidermis, hypodermic, taxidermy
dox-	belief, teaching	heterodox, orthodox
erg-	work, power	energetic, erg, synergy
gam-	mate, marry	bigamy, gamete, monogamous
gen-	kind, race	eugenics, genealogy, genesis
gon-	corner, angle	diagonal, polygon
graph-	write, writing	graphite, orthography
heli-	sun	heliotropism, helium
hem-	blood	hemoglobin, hemorrhage
hetero-	other, different	heterodox, heterogeneous
hom-	same	homogeneous, homonym
hydr-	water	dehydrate, hydrant, hydrophobia
iso-	same, equal	isosceles, isotope
lith-	stone	monolithic, neolithic
log-	speech, word, study	epilogue, logarithm, theology

Root	Meaning	Examples
micr-	small	microbe, microscope
morph-	form	morpheme, morphology
nom-	rule, law	autonomy, economy, metronome
orth-	straight, correct	orthodontist, orthodox, orthography
paed-, ped-	child	pedagogue, pedant, pediatrician
pan-	all, entire	panacea, pancreas, panorama
phil-, philo-	love, like	anglophile, bibliophile, philanthropy, philosophy
phor-	bear, bearing	euphoria, phosphorus, semaphore
poli-	city	metropolis, police, policy, politician
psych-	mind	psychology, psychotic
pyr-	fire	pyre, pyromaniac
soph-	wise	philosophy, sophomore, theosophy
tele-	far	telepathy, telephone, telescope
therm-	heat	thermal, thermometer
top-	place	topic, topical, topography
typ-	model, impression	archetype, typewriter, typical
zo-	animal	zodiac, zoo, zoology

BRUCE THOMAS

Use of the Dictionary

For virtually any exploration into the world of words, resources are readily available at a library or bookstore. Whatever your interest—the history of English, regional or national dialects, slang, pronunciation, spelling—you will find articles and books to satisfy your inquiries. One exceedingly useful supplemental resource is a thesaurus. Its value lies in the fact that it reverses the sequence of reference used in a dictionary: with a thesaurus, you begin with a meaning and seek out the appropriate word. Most words belong to a family, a kinship network of meaning. Using a thesaurus is the easiest means of becoming acquainted with the entire family. The word *nonsense,* for example, is quite an adequate and expressive word—but it might not always be the most effective word to use in a given context. A thesaurus provides other members of the family: *e.g., poppycock, eyewash, drivel, bunk, rot,* and *claptrap.* Any one of these, under certain circumstances, might work better than *nonsense.*

Whatever additional resources you acquire in your continuing practice with words, the dictionary will remain your single most important backstop. As the critic Albert Jay Nock once noted: "As sheer casual reading matter, I still find the English dictionary the most interesting book in our language."

A few facts about dictionaries

Dictionaries, like any subject or artifact, have a history. An examination of the history of dictionaries reveals some interesting, and in some cases surprising, points:

• We tend to think of dictionaries as thick and heavy with the weight of ancient scholarship. Thick and heavy they may be; ancient they are not. The first purely English dictionary appeared only in 1604.

379

• Lexicography, the process of compiling dictionaries, might be assumed to be the exclusive domain of professional scholars. In fact many of the most notable lexicographers were amateurs. In the 17th and 18th centuries, for example, schoolmasters in England were particularly significant producers of dictionaries. Even full-time lexicographers have required the help of amateurs and volunteers to complete the arduous and time-consuming work of compiling a dictionary. James A. H. Murray, editor of *The Oxford English Dictionary* (*OED*), enlisted the help of his children in sorting out the millions of slips that poured into his office. (And even with his 11 children, Murray still required the help of many volunteers plus a regular, paid staff.)*

• Dictionaries give off an air of calm, unperturbed scholarship. They seem utterly removed from the tumult and controversy, not to say glamour, of rowdier realms like politics; but the making of a dictionary is an intensely human enterprise and so is fraught with all the reverses, mistakes, and misadventures as well as the pleasures of human endeavors. A 16th-century English lexicographer, Thomas Cooper, had the half-completed manuscript for his *Thesaurus Linguae Romanae et Britannicae,* commonly known as *Cooper's Dictionary,* tossed into the fireplace by his irate wife. (Cooper, we must presume, in turn heaved a sigh and went back to work, because he finished it anyway.)

One of the supreme achievements of lexicography, the *OED,* began, after two decades of planning, as a 10-year project in 1879—and was not completed until 1928. In 1933 a one-volume Supplement was issued to accompany the existing 12 volumes. The tale of the *OED*'s design, financing, and execution contains as much dramatic tension, political intrigue, and personal heroics as any best-seller.

• Because dictionaries do not, as a rule, appear on best-seller lists, they may seem quite removed from the fierceness of marketplace competition. But dictionaries are of course market goods; they are made to be sold, and if they do not sell their lexicographers must find other employment. One such fierce competition developed in the United States during the middle decades of the 19th century; it involved Noah Webster and Joseph Worcester, and at stake was domination of the U.S. dictionary market. Webster issued his masterpiece, *An American Dictionary of the English Language,* in 1828. Worcester followed in 1846 with *A Universal and Critical Dictionary of the English Language* and, 14 years later, *A Dictionary of the English Language.* The battle was inconclusive for a number of decades, but in the end the Webster forces prevailed.

---

*A full account of the writing of the *OED* is found in an engaging biography of its editor, *Caught in the Web of Words* (1977), written by Murray's granddaughter K. M. Elisabeth Murray.

For John Palsgrave, a 16th-century tutor of French in London, the relevant market was not that of dictionary sales but of language instruction. Palsgrave published a bilingual dictionary on condition that his consent be obtained for each sale! He was thus able to exclude his tutoring competitors from the benefit of his labors.

In short, dictionaries are human artifacts; they represent the work of a quietly extraordinary assembly of men and women throughout the ages. Any one dictionary is the sum of a collaborative effort that stretches out over centuries, for lexicographers must build upon the work of their predecessors. The amount of work that goes into any dictionary is quite literally incalculable.

How to use a dictionary

Effective use of a dictionary is more a matter of habit than of technique. The only secret is to use it regularly. Even among highly fluent people, the dictionary is consistently underused. Since the editors of any good dictionary always work with the reader in mind and strive to make their dictionary as easy to use as possible, the nuts and bolts of dictionaries are generally simple.

Dictionaries set out entries, whether a word or a phrase, in alphabetical order. If there are special rules for alphabetizing in a particular dictionary, the introduction to the dictionary will provide explanation. Once the word or phrase is located, only familiarity with dictionary notation is needed to unlock the wealth of information provided. Many notations are self-evident (*v.* for verb, *adj.* for adjective, *n.* for noun, etc.), and all are explained in the introduction.

An entry in most dictionaries usually contains the following elements: syllabication, pronunciation, part of speech, meaning, etymology, related words, and synonyms.

SYLLABICATION is the way the word or phrase is broken into syllables. It is often rendered by separating the syllables with centered dots. Thus *serendipity* will be shown as *ser · en · dip · i · ty*.

PRONUNCIATION is indicated by a set of phonetic symbols, some of them self-evident, some not. In any case the key to the phonetic symbols will be provided in the introduction and is usually repeated throughout the dictionary itself. Some of the symbols may initially look strange, such as the *schwa* (ə), but with use of the dictionary these notations will soon become familiar. (For a full discussion of pronunciation, *see* The Spoken Word.)

PART OF SPEECH refers to the grammatical category to which the word belongs, such as noun, adjective, or adverb. The part of speech is usually indicated in abbreviated form (*n.* for noun, *adj.* for adjective), with all the abbreviations explained in the introduction. (For any grammatical questions about the parts of speech, *see* All You Need to Know About Grammar.)

Other grammatical or lexical notations may supplement the basic indication of an entry's part of speech. Certain nouns, for example, are always used in the plural, in which case the notation usually reads: *n., pl.*; verbs are generally classified as transitive (*tr.*) or intransitive (*int.*). Other words may be archaic or obsolete, or their usage restricted to slang or regional dialect; notation of such usage information is commonly provided in the entry.

Another important label designates a specific field of knowledge or endeavor to which a word, or one meaning of that word, applies. A simple word like *base,* for example, has many meanings, some with a special meaning in a given context; *base* denotes one thing in chemistry, another in sports, yet another in linguistics. *The Oxford English Dictionary* lists 28 different meanings for the noun *base,* many of which are specific to a particular realm of knowledge or activity. Here is an excerpt from the entry, showing the use of such lexical notations:

> . . . **6.** In mechanical arts: **a.** in *Printing,* The bottom or footing of letters. **b.** in *Gunnery,* The protuberant rear-portion of a cannon. . . . **7.** *Bot*[any] and *Zool*[ogy] That extremity of a part or organ by which it is attached to the trunk. . . . **8.** *Her*[aldry] The lower part of a shield. . . .

DEFINITION As the example immediately above suggests, a word often has many meanings. If it has only a single meaning, then the definition is provided without a prefacing number. If it has more than one meaning, the definitions are set out in numerical sequence, as in the excerpt above. In *Webster's New Collegiate Dictionary* the word *driver,* to take another example, has at least five meanings:

> one that drives: as **a:** coachman **b:** the operator of a motor vehicle **c:** an implement (as a hammer) for driving **d:** a mechanical piece for imparting motion to another piece **e:** a golf club . . . . used in driving."

These several meanings are grouped together within one entry because, for all their variety, they all share a common root meaning: "the manipulation or application of force."

A second category of multiple meanings requires different treatment. Some words have several distinctly different meanings and function as different parts of speech. In *Webster's Collegiate* the word *drone,* for example, has three separate entries, which are indicated numerically but in a different way from the category above. These numbers look like preceding footnote numbers: [1]**drone,** [2]**drone,** [3]**drone.** The first is a noun that refers to a male bee; to a sluggard or loafer; or to a pilot-less, radio-controlled plane or ship. The second is a verb that refers to making a continuous humming sound. The third is a noun referring to one of the pipes on a bagpipe that sounds the fixed, continuous tone.

ETYMOLOGY   deals with the origin and history of a word. The word *serendipity,* for example, meaning "the faculty of finding valuable or agreeable things not sought for," was coined by the 18th-century English author Horace Walpole. He took the word from the title of the ancient Persian fairy tale *The Three Princes of Serendip,* whose three protagonists were always making unexpected discoveries of pleasant or fortunate things. Some dictionaries use special abbreviated etymological notations whose meanings are explained in the book's introduction.

RELATED WORDS   (called cognates) are usually given at the end of the entry. These are the various forms that the root word can take; for example, a root verb (*extend*) may have noun, adjective, and adverb cognates (*extension, extensive, extensively*). In order to keep dictionaries to reasonably manageable size, editors usually define root words and then simply list their cognates. In the case of the word *ethic,* for instance, a dictionary might list separate entires for *ethic, ethical,* and *ethics,* but not for *ethically, ethicalness,* or *ethicality;* these last three forms of *ethic* will be noted in the entry for *ethical.* The moral of this tale is that, if you cannot find a word listed alphabetically in a dictionary, that word may be found elsewhere in the entry for its root.

SYNONYMS   are words that are approximately the same in meaning. Most good dictionaries provide synonyms for the entry when appropriate; the degree of detail varies with the size and quality of the dictionary. An entry for *hinder,* for instance, might note that it has the synonyms *hamper, retard, obstruct, dam,* and *block.* It might further include a brief sketch of the differing implications of each of the words within the family of synonyms and of the contexts appropriate for each. Some dictionaries also provide antonyms, or words opposite in meaning.

The variety of dictionaries

The distinguishing characteristics of dictionaries is their arrangement of material by alphabetical order. We tend to think of dictionaries in a restrictive sense as containing only definitions of words, but in fact a marvelous spectrum exists within the world of the dictionary. The word *dictionary* is not copyrighted; anyone can use it. Many have. Here is only a very brief subject list of reference works that use a dictionary format and the word *dictionary* in their full title: American regional usage; American slang; Catholic biography; CB "slanguage"; clichés; crossword puzzles; etymology; modern English usage; proper names; pronunciation; the Low-Dutch element in the English language; and thought.

The dictionary format is in fact so elastic that it can be put to many uses. Students at a private eastern secondary school periodically revise and publish a dictionary of terms peculiar to their institution. Their dictionary serves as a device for settling old scores with faculty and administrators as well as for disseminating the peculiarities of usage that serve to distinguish this particular community.

Finally one might mention the U.S. journalist and satirist Ambrose Bierce (1842–1914?) and his *Devil's Dictionary* (1906). For Bierce the dictionary format provided an apt device for social commentary that cut through the pretensions and hypocrisies of his day. His barbs still sting:

Politics, *n.*	A strife of interests masquerading as a contest of principles. The conduct of public affairs for private advantage.
Gunpowder, *n.*	An agency employed by civilized nations for the settlement of disputes which might become troublesome if left unadjusted.
Acquaintance, *n.*	A person whom we know well enough to borrow from, but not well enough to lend to.
Piracy, *n.*	Commerce without its folly-swaddles, just as God made it.
Prejudice, *n.*	A vagrant opinion without visible means of support.
Saint, *n.*	A dead sinner revised and edited.

Choosing a dictionary

Anyone in the market for a dictionary has nearly as much choice as the buyer in search of a new automobile. Indeed many of the same rules apply: you need to have an idea of what you want, how much you are willing to pay, what use you will make of your purchase, and where you will use it. Without having in mind your own needs and specifications, you might well be stumped by the range of choice. At one end of the spectrum are the general-purpose dictionaries found in homes, schools, and libraries. They are usually abridged in length, modest in price, and manageable in size.

At the other end of the spectrum are the scholarly dictionaries. The most famous—and deservedly so—is the *OED*. It is a truly awesome achievement, one that from date of earliest conception to final completion required three-quarters of a century. The time and energy that went into it are reflected in its size: some 16,000 pages and approximately 250,000 entries, with some 2,000,000 illustrative quotations (not to mention the supplements that have been issued since its completion in 1928). Fortunately the publishers decided to put the *OED* within reach (in terms of both size and price) of a more general audience by issuing a two-volume compact edition made possible through the photo-reduction process. The publishers have thoughtfully included with the compact edition a magnifying glass, which is essential for reading the tiny print and is included in the purchase price.

The following overview of what is presently available in the way of dictionaries is not exhaustive but will serve as a useful guide. It lists general dictionaries, abridged and unabridged; specialized dictionaries; dictionaries for the visually handicapped; and dictionaries for children. The shopper is advised to remember that price may be a more definitive indicator of the cover than of the contents. As always, *caveat emptor!* (If you don't know what that means, look it up in the dictionaries you are considering.)

BRUCE THOMAS

List of Dictionaries

General Dictionaries

UNABRIDGED DICTIONARIES

Amortized over a lifetime, the investment in a dictionary is a hard value to beat. Still, the investment of between $50 and $150 is no trifle (and the $500, 13-volume edition of *The Oxford English Dictionary* is probably best consulted in a library). The decision to make such an investment will hinge on a degree of importance you attach to the scope and depth of lexicographical detail provided and to the extra features included in an expensive dictionary.

> *The Compact Edition of the Oxford English Dictionary*, 2 vols. (1971). (with magnifying glass)
> *The Oxford English Dictionary*, 13 vols. (1933).
> *The Random House Dictionary of the English Language* (1973).
> *Webster's Third New International Dictionary of the English Language, Unabridged* (1961).

SUPPLEMENTS

> *6,000 Words: A Supplement to Webster's Third New International Dictionary* (1976).
> *A Supplement to the Oxford English Dictionary*, Vol. I (A-G), 1972; Vol. II (H-N), 1976.

ABRIDGED DICTIONARIES

Dictionaries in this category range from pocket-size to desk-size. Some have limited word lists and few additional features; others will meet most home, school, and work needs. The category includes some remarkable bargains. You can easily spend $15 for a best-seller that

386

is read once and then retired to the bookshelf; for the same investment you can purchase a desk dictionary that you will use for the rest of your life.

The American Heritage Dictionary of the English Language, New College Edition (1976).

The Concise Oxford Dictionary of Current English, 6th ed. (1976). (based on the *OED* and supplements)

The Doubleday Dictionary for Home, School, and Office (1975).

Funk & Wagnalls Standard College Dictionary, rev. ed. (1977).

The Little Oxford Dictionary of Current English, 4th ed. (1969).

The Pocket Oxford Dictionary of Current English, 6th ed. (1978). (abridgment of *The Concise Oxford Dictionary of Current English*)

Random House College Dictionary, rev. ed. (1975). (abridged version of *The Random House Dictionary of the English Language*)

Scribner-Bantam English Dictionary.

Webster's New Collegiate Dictionary†.

Webster's New World Dictionary of the American Language, Modern Desk Edition.

Webster's New World Dictionary of the American Language, Second College Edition (1975).

Webster's New World Handy Pocket Dictionary (1977).

Specialized Dictionaries

Americanisms: A Dictionary of Selected Americanisms on Historical Principles, edited by Mitford M. Mathews (1966).

Bernstein, Theodore M., *Bernstein's Reverse Dictionary* (1975).

Craigie, Sir William A., and James R. Hulbert, eds., *A Dictionary of American English on Historical Principles,* 4 vols. (1940; 7th impression 1968).

Davis, Walter, *et al.,* eds., *A Dictionary of Canadianisms on Historical Principles: Dictionary of Canadian English* (1967).

Evans, Bergen, and Cornelia Evans, *A Dictionary of Contemporary American Usage* (1957).

---

*These starred entries are more comprehensive than the other works listed here and are sometimes referred to as "semi-unabridged."

†The word *Webster* is not copyrighted and appears in the titles of numerous dictionaries. Only the Merriam-Webster dictionaries, published by G. & C. Merriam Company, however, are the direct descendants of Noah Webster's original works.

Farmer, John S., and William E. Henley, eds., *Slang and Its Analogues, Past and Present,* 7 vols. (1890–1904).

Hunsberger, I. Moyer, *The Quintessential Dictionary* (1978).

Kenyon, John S., and Thomas A. Knott, *A Pronouncing Dictionary of American English* (1953).

Klein, Ernest, *A Comprehensive Etymological Dictionary of the English Language,* 2 vols. (1966–67).

The Merriam–Webster Book of Word Histories (1976).

Partridge, Eric, *A Dictionary of Slang and Unconventional English,* 7th ed., rev. and enl. (1970).

———, *Origins: A Short Etymological Dictionary of Modern English,* 4th ed. (1977).

Pei, Mario, ed., *Language of the Specialists: A Communications Guide to Twenty Different Fields* (1966).

Shipley, Joseph T., *Dictionary of Early English* (1955).

The Shorter Oxford English Dictionary on Historical Principles, 3rd ed. (1973).

Skeat, Walter W., *A Concise Etymological Dictionary of the English Language,* new and corrected impression (1911: reprinted 1958).

Urdang, Laurence, ed., *The New York Times Everyday Reader's Dictionary of Misunderstood, Misused, Mispronounced Words* (1972).

Wentworth, Harold, and Stuart B. Flexner, eds., *Dictionary of American Slang,* 2nd supplemented ed. (1975).

Dictionaries for the visually handicapped

Merriam-Webster Dictionary for Large Print Users. (based on *Webster's Third New International Dictionary of the English Language, Unabridged*)

For the blind there are braille dictionaries that can be purchased from the American Printing House for the Blind, 1839 Frankfort Avenue, Louisville, Ky. 40206. Because braille dictionaries are very costly and necessarily bulky, however, it is well to keep in mind that most large libraries should have copies of:

Webster's New World Dictionary of the American Language (72 vols.)

Webster's Student Dictionary (36 vols).

Dictionaries for children

Buying your child a dictionary is both a thoughtful gesture and a sound first step in helping foster the dictionary habit. There are two types of dictionaries for children. Those for very young children (aged roughly four to seven) list about 1500 to 2500 words, use each in several sentences, and sometimes accompany the illustrative sentences with a picture:

The New Golden Dictionary (1972).
The Rainbow Dictionary for Young Readers (1978).
Thorndike–Barnhart Beginning Dictionary, 8th ed. (1974).

The second category of children's dictionaries, for children eight years and older, consists of adult dictionaries that have been adapted to make the word lists shorter, the print often larger, and the explanations simpler. Note that the phrase "For Young Readers" is used in titles in both categories, so look at the dictionary carefully to determine whether it is appropriate for your child.

American Heritage School Dictionary (1972).
Thorndike–Barnhart Advanced Dictionary, 4th ed. (1974).
Thorndike–Barnhart Intermediate Dictionary, 2nd ed. (1974).
Webster's New World Dictionary for Young Readers (1976).

THE LIBRARY

The Open Door: Using the Library

Nineteenth-century English author and philosopher Thomas Carlyle observed that "in books lies the soul of the whole past time." Unfortunately many people think of the library as a mausoleum—a silent place where outmoded ideas, yellowed and brittling, gather dust. On the contrary, the library is a lively, bustling assembly hall where the voices of history's great orators continue to ring, where new ideas thrive, where the language is used to its fullest potential. What better way to improve and enrich one's English than by mingling with the world's greatest writers, teachers, thinkers, and most colorful characters—in short, with the masters of our English tongue! The library is a club of open minds and travelers in time. Each of us is a life member, with curiosity the only dues.

Most ordinary citizens speak of their community library with reverence, but six out of 10 Americans over age 18 almost never use it.* The four out of 10 who do use the library are not only from the wealthier half of society, but many of them get there partly from the enormous, lifelong advantage of knowing how to use a library.

Using a library means more than knowing how to look up a "call number" and pluck a book from the shelves, though that is a convenient skill. It also means knowing how to dig into every research tool—every catalog, index, bibliography, and information source available—and how to obtain the information quickly. The serious library user knows how to get to information in any form—book, magazine, newspaper, sound recording, motion picture, microfilm, videotape, computer display, or whatever it may be—and does not stop when a clerk mumbles, "It's not on the shelf."

But what has become of the local library for people who simply want a good book to read? It's there. Our libraries still contain the best read-

---

*From a Gallup Organization Poll published as *The Role of Libraries in America, 1975.*

ing material of the last 2,500 years, but they also house what is called the "information explosion." In this age of multimedia communication, we are constantly inundated with new information from every source and in every type of packaging. And access to this new information is an important tool for surviving well in today's incredibly complex society.

The secret of most profitably using the library is one of attitude, not of technique. The collections and inner workings of modern libraries are often elaborate and complicated, yet libraries have managed to keep the information they house accessible to all. The rudiments of library use can be learned in 15 minutes; the finer skills will develop as rapidly as needed for a particular project. It has been wisely said that the best library training of all is to spend time using a good library. In a single visit the inexperienced library user can, with a bit of effort, begin to become knowledgeable about the library and comfortable with exploring and using it further.

The intrepid approach to libraries

The approach is simple. March through the doors of the library, walk up to any desk marked "Information" or "Reference," and request help. Far from being a shameful confession, that request only acknowledges that a librarian is a professional who is trained and paid to help people use the library. If your library has no separate reference desk, information may be available at the circulation desk. However, if your library does have a reference desk, begin your search there. It is the duty, and usually the pleasure, of the librarian to make the library's resources equally available to all patrons. And that duty translates into an obligation far greater than pointing to the card catalog and wishing you the best of luck.

Modern professionals working in the library's public service areas (not in the back offices and workrooms) are there to provide reference services—that is, to answer all types of questions from any patron who needs assistance. No matter how trivial these reference questions may seem, every library patron is fully entitled to such assistance. For newcomers or otherwise reluctant patrons, *not* taking advantage of this right to ask questions may be the greatest single obstacle to effective library use.

Librarians generally find that patrons who ask for assistance rarely articulate at the outset exactly what they want. But the librarian is trained to elicit the appropriate information in order to answer each reference question. The exchange, called the "reference interview," might proceed hypothetically like this:

PATRON: Where's your music section, please?

LIBRARIAN: On the third floor. But may I ask if you're looking for sheet music, books and magazines *about* music, recorded music, or information about musicians?

P: About musicians.

L: One in particular?

P: Yes, Ella Fitzgerald.

L: Fine. Was it just a few facts you needed or all the information you can find?

P: Well, I want to know when and where she was born.

L: Then you might look under her name in *Who's Who in America,* which is right here. And if you want something more about her, I'm sure a lot of information can be found through our catalog and indexes.

The reference interview is meant to save the library user hours of searching and to teach the most efficient use of a particular library since every library is different and has its own specialties. In the sample reference interview above, the librarian might also have produced a special collection of clippings on jazz singers in its "vertical file," where brochures and newspaper and magazine cutouts are kept. Suppose the patron were doing a more scholarly study of the U.S. jazz vocalist—for example, of her impact on music abroad. The reference interview might have helped to identify a nearby library that collected and indexed the appropriate foreign publications. Librarians are trained to help patrons reach *all* available reference sources, not just those in their particular library.

On your own

Doing one's own research can be enormously educational and productive. Good librarians gladly teach the use of the library's research tools and encourage people to carry out as much independent research as they care to do. But how does one learn to do independent research? Sometimes through orientation sessions that are periodically scheduled in most college libraries or arranged by request in others. Such orientations are useful for learning the physical layout of the library but are usually too brief to fully acquaint new patrons with the library's resources. Often colleges give class lectures or even credit courses on how to do research in the library. If the opportunity arises, such a course is well worth the effort.

There are a number of publications on using the library, some of which are listed at the end of this chapter, and libraries often produce brief guides of their own. All such aids are best studied in the library, where each concept can be put to work and each title examined in hand. Additionally most reference books contain detailed instructions for their use, which is best learned through practice on sample problems. Oddly the only major library tool without its own introduction or instructions for use is the most important of all: the general catalog to library's collection.

The library's catalog

We traditionally think of the library's catalog as a lengthy row of cabinets whose drawers are stuffed with alphabetically arranged 3 × 5 cards—the card catalog. Basically this is still the research tool that we are talking about. Yet more and more libraries are beginning to use other kinds of general catalogs, which take up less space and work more efficiently.

Whatever its size and format, every catalog performs three services: it organizes the library's collection of books and other materials by 1) author; 2) title; and 3) subject. Thus, when looking for a work by a particular author, you can search in the catalog under that author's name and find a complete record identifying all the books or other materials by that author in the library's collection. (For purposes of

---

ML
102
.J3
C34

Case, Brian.
 The illustrated encyclopedia of jazz / ₍authors, Brian Case and Stan Britt ; consultant, Joseph Abend ; editor, Trisha Palmer₎. — New York : Harmony Books, c1978.
 223 p. : ill. ; 30 cm. — (A Salamander book)
 Includes discographies and index.
 ISBN 0-517-53343-X. ISBN 0-517-53344-8 pbk.

 1. Jazz music—Bio-bibliography. 2. Jazz music—Discography. I. Britt, Stan, joint author. II. Palmer, Trisha. III. Title.

ML102.J3C34   785.4'2'0922   77-27647
            ₍B₎   MARC

Library of Congress   77   MN

this discussion, let us assume that "book" refers to all types of library materials.) The identifying record will include in each case the book's location in the library. If you already have the title of the book that you need, a search in the catalog under that title will produce the author's name and the remainder of the identifying record.

The illustrated encyclopedia of jazz.

ML
102
.J3
C34

Case, Brian.
   The illustrated encyclopedia of jazz / ₍authors, Brian Case and Stan Britt ; consultant, Joseph Abend ; editor, Trisha Palmer₎. — New York : Harmony Books, c1978.
   223 p. : ill. ; 30 cm. — (A Salamander book)
   Includes discographies and index.
   ISBN 0-517-53343-X. ISBN 0-517-53344-8 pbk.

   1. Jazz music—Bio-bibliography. 2. Jazz music—Discography. I. Britt, Stan, joint author. II. Palmer, Trisha. III. Title.

ML102.J3C34   785.4'2'0922   77-27647
                ₍B₎   MARC

Library of Congress   77   MN

Finally materials on a certain subject can be found in the catalog without having specific authors or titles in mind. All that is needed is a subject heading—the name of the subject as it is likely to appear in the catalog. Generally the librarians who decide upon the subject headings to be used try to anticipate the words that people will look for. These librarians, called catalogers, take many of the headings from an enormous list entitled *Library of Congress Subject Headings,* which is ordinarily available for public use near the general catalog or by request. In this list most of the headings likely to be used for a given subject can be quickly found.

The subject heading may be a single word, such as MUSIC, SONG, or VOICE. It may also be a phrase, for example, JAZZ MUSIC; or it may be a word or phrase followed by a subheading—a further refinement of the main subject: JAZZ MUSIC—BIO-BIBLIOGRAPHY or JAZZ MUSIC—DISCOGRAPHY.

A good rule of thumb in researching a particular topic is to seek the subject heading describing it most directly and specifically. If you want a book about COLLIES, start with that heading, not DOGS. To "earn" a subject heading, a book must have abundant information on the subject, not just a mention or two. So the more specific you are in looking for subject headings, the better.

① Subject heading
② Library call number
③ Author
④ Title
⑤ Facts of publication
⑥ Physical description
⑦ Miscellaneous facts about book
⑧ Information for librarians

The catalog also directs you to subject headings that are worth researching in addition to those already consulted. It performs this important service with cross-references. Suppose, for example, you are interested in researching some aspect of the broad topic WATER, but the specific area of interest has not yet been defined. Under the heading WATER, let's imagine, the library's catalog yields only one book: *Water; the Vital Essence*. But this is too broad. Hence, it is necessary to look back at the subject card (the first one with the heading WATER at the top) and consider the *see also* cross-references: *"see also* Dew; Drinking water; Erosion; Feedwater; Floods; Fog; Geysers; Glaciers; Hail; Hydraulic engineering; Hydrotherapy; Ice; Lakes; Mineral waters; Ocean; Rivers (Geology); Snow; Springs; Steam; Waterspouts; Wells and well-boring." However, you may not want to check the *see also* headings, which take you elsewhere in the catalog, until you have seen which headings directly follow the general heading WATER. There will be subheadings under the main heading WATER, for example, WATER—ANALYSIS, as well as headings beginning with the word, such as WATER CONSERVATION. By now the catalog has provided you with a much better grasp of the possible avenues to explore.

Author, title, and subject—these are the three obvious "hooks" with which to search when trolling in the catalog for items on the shelves. When an author or the subject of a book is known by several different names, catalogers ensure that each can be found in the catalog. For example, for works about Muhammad Ali, formerly Cassius Clay, the catalog will have subject entries with appropriate cross-references for both names. Catalogers also ensure that each main subject in the book has an entry in the catalog since many books deal with more than one topic. As for the title, it must be known just as it appears in the front of the book in order to find it in the catalog, but librarians can help even when you are unsure of the wording.

A library's catalog is used to best advantage by exploring all the aids it offers. Many libraries have now split their main catalog into a "divided" catalog: one half of the catalog listing authors and titles, the other half listing the same books but by subject alone.

The author-title half of the catalog is used primarily to look up a specific book or to see what the library has in its collection by a particular author. If you are looking for the title *Zen and the Art of Motorcycle Maintenance* by Robert M. Pirsig in the card catalog, the title will be more easily found in the author-title section than in the subject catalog where it will be buried among all the subject cards labeled ZEN-BUDDHISM. However, if you are looking for books on motorcycle maintenance in general, the subject catalog is the place to start. There, under MOTORCYCLES–MAINTENANCE AND REPAIR, every title will be a book that, unlike Pirsig's, deals primarily with repairing a bike.

In either section the catalog card will provide a call number for each title, that is, the code for the book's exact location on the shelves. That call number might look something like this:

M
1630.18
.J3
G6

In the Chicago Public Library that dull-looking number would lead you to the Rolling Stones' rock songbook "Goats Head Soup."

"Classified" information

In a library with "open stacks," where patrons can wander among the shelves (as opposed to libraries with "closed stacks" that are restricted to library personnel), you benefit from one of the library's most convenient characteristics: the fact that materials are classified, or grouped by subject. The classified grouping is infinitely more useful than the shelf arrangement of a bookstore where titles falling roughly into a broad subject area, such as psychology or cooking, are gathered into sections. A library examines the main subject of each work and gives it a very specific subject code: the classification number.

The famous Dewey Decimal numbers are one type of classification, although more and more libraries are adopting the Library of Congress classification system. While the types of call numbers for these two systems look very different, they function alike. Library of Congress

CORRELATION OF THE DEWEY DECIMAL AND
LIBRARY OF CONGRESS CLASSIFICATION SYSTEMS

Library of Congress	Main Subjects (Simplified)	Dewey Decimal
A	General Works	000
B	Philosophy and Religion	100 (Philosophy) and 200 (Religion)
C	History—Auxiliary Sciences	900
D	History and Topography	930–990
E and F	American History	
G	Geography and Anthropology	910 (Geography) and 570 (Anthropology)
H	Social Sciences	320
J	Political Sciences	320
K	Law	340
L	Education	370
M	Music	780
N	Fine Arts	700
P	Language and Literature	400 (Philology) and 800 (Literature)
Q	Science	500
R	Medicine	610
S	Agriculture	630
T	Technology	600
U	Military Science	355–358
V	Naval Science	359
Z	Bibliography and Library Science	010, 020, 090

call numbers use a combination of letters and numbers; for example, ML102.J3C34 for Brian Case's *The Illustrated Encyclopedia of Jazz,* or BL480.W66 for William Woods's *A History of the Devil.* The Dewey Decimal system uses numbers between 0 and 999.99 and may carry those numbers out to several decimal places, depending on the size of the library and how detailed that library's catalogers wish the subject groupings to be. (Under the Dewey Decimal system, Case's book about jazz would have the number 785.4, 785.42, or even 785.420922. Woods's book about the devil would have either the number 291.2 or 291.216.) Dewey Decimal numbers are also often followed by a letter and a number, together called a Cutter number. This number ensures that within any subject grouping the works are arranged alphabetically by the author's last name. As different as these two systems may look, they function very similarly and accomplish the same goal—grouping together books about similar subjects. Once the specific classifications are assigned to books, these numbers are placed on the spines of the books before distribution on the shelves.

Look at a classified shelf in your library. Knowledge and information are organized in a systematic, accessible, and highly usable fashion. There are few faster educational experiences than browsing through the classified collections of a good library. To get the most out of an open-stack library, do not stop looking when you find the right call number on the spine of a particular book. Browse through the books near the one that you wanted. Not only will you discover how the library shelf reflects the relationship of all human experience, but you may also find related information on the topic you are exploring.

A quick browse through some 10 feet of Dewey-classified stacks can illustrate the point. Entering the 300s (social sciences), the browser comes quickly to the 301s (sociology) and a title of interest at 301.31 (ecology): *Earth Care Manual.* Moving on to 301.32 (demography), he examines *The Population Bomb;* and 301.41 (the sexes and their relations) brings him to another ominous title, *Sexual Suicide,* an anti-women's liberation treatise. Working back and forth, he dips into the past at 301.4 (social structure) with *The Structure of Medieval Society.* At 301.451 (aggregates of special national, racial, or ethnic origins) he looks at *Race and Culture;* at 301.56 (educational institutions) *Children's Rights* catches his attention. Under 301.633 (violence) is a narrower classification 301.6333 (revolutions) and a fascinating book *Autopsy of a Revolution.* But it is in the 301.57 section (recreational institutions) that he finds a book combining several of his interests: *Sports in the Sociocultural Process,* with such timely chapters as "The Revolt of the Black Athlete." In glancing through the book, he

realizes that he has come upon an entirely unexpected book but one
that is still related to his original point of entry: the social sciences.

The reference collection

The books in the reference collection are probably best known as
those with the "R" or "REF" on the spine—the books that cannot be
borrowed. Yet they can certainly be used to find answers and explanations in a hurry. When questions become more complex and time is
more available, reference becomes research; and the researcher needs
to go beyond the "ready reference" collection. At any level, however,
one benefits from asking a reference librarian for clues. There is also
a category of books called reference guides, which describe thousands
of reference tools by subject, from ready-reference handbooks to more
elaborate research volumes. Most U.S. librarians use *Guide to Reference Books* as their basic reference bible, and it is available to patrons
as well. There are many different kinds of books in the reference collection, among them encyclopedias, some dictionaries, *Who's Who*
books, and certain indexes and bibliographies. (*See* Reference Works
to Know: A Quick Dozen at the end of this chapter.) The last two
kinds of references are very important tools for research in the library
and warrant a brief look. (For a selection of frequently consulted reference works related to subjects treated in this book, *see* Sections II
and III of the Bibliography at the end of this book.)

Indexes

It would be wonderful if every piece of published information could
be examined by the library and listed in its one main catalog, but
imagine the work involved, even for a single issue of *Time* magazine.
Someone would need to identify every author in that issue, determine
all the main subjects in each article, and squeeze the entries into the
library catalog while they were still current. Multiply that work by
all the magazines, newspapers, and other media being published; and
it is obvious why the main catalog restricts itself to the books and
pamphlets in the library for its author, title, and subject listings. The
catalog indicates which magazines and newspapers are in the library's
collections but not what is inside each issue. That service is performed
by the library's indexes.

Some indexes are prepared by the library, others by outside publishers, but they all list what is *in* a periodical or other publication.

The New York Times Index, for example, annually records what was in *The New York Times* by arranging all the newspaper articles under subject headings and listing those subjects in alphabetical order. Look up PRESLEY, ELVIS, in the 1977 index or SPACE in a more recent one. You will find informative "headlines" referring to dozens of stories on these subjects. The index will provide date, page, and column for each story listed, enabling you to return to the newspaper itself to read the whole text. If the index reference is for a newspaper that is more than a year old, the newspaper is probably recorded on microfilm. The librarian can direct you to where the rolls of microfilm are stored. You need only select the roll with the correct dates, snap it on the reels of a microfilm reader, and roll through these pages to arrive at the original story.

Perhaps the most famous index of all is the *Readers' Guide to Periodical Literature,* which records what is in more than 180 magazines now being published. Under the heading "AUTOMOBILE driving" in a recent index, one intriguing entry read:

> Shameless joys of self-induced kinesthesia. S.
> Thompson. Car & Dr 23:14 F'78

By consulting the index's introductory explanation of the symbols and abbreviations it uses, the entry can be decoded. That entry, if you are curious, means that S. Thompson's discussion of those mysterious joys can be found in the February 1978 issue (Volume 23, Page 14) of *Car and Driver* magazine.

There are numerous indexes on many different subjects, and they are the real key to serious library use, once the general catalog has been mastered. The catalog is, in fact, the place to look first for indexes dealing with a given subject. There is everything from an *Art Index* to an index called *Zoological Record* to guide you to current and specialized information on a particular topic.

Bibliographies

Under subject headings in the library's general catalog, yet another invaluable research tool can be found: the bibliography. A bibliography is a list of books and other items that are all concerned with a particular topic. If you do not know which books to look for on a given subject, a bibliography can be of great help. Indexes and bibliographies work hand in hand. The index guides you by subject to what is in books and magazines currently being published; the bibliography gives you a listing of many books and articles—most published fairly recently—that treat a particular topic. Often bibliographies include annotations describing each item listed to help you decide if you want to make use of it.

When searching in the catalog, look for the word *bibliography* in the subject headings. For example, under the subject heading MEXICAN AMERICANS IN THE UNITED STATES—BIBLIOGRAPHY, you may find Linda Fowler Shramko's *Chicano Bibliography,* which contains about 1,000 items on Mexican Americans, including the names of periodicals, books, articles, and theses, all of which deal in one way or another with this subject. Once you have selected the items that look promising, you will need to check the card catalog again to determine which of the books listed are included in the library's collection. Many of the individual items on a bibliography will in turn indicate in their own bibliographies still further sources of information on the subject.

These are the essentials in library research. Begin with the librarian; consult the correct catalog; find the specific items that interest you; and check for indexes and bibliographies that will lead to related material, some of which may take you outside to other libraries.

Catalogs, indexes, bibliographies, reference, research—it would seem overwhelming if it all had to be mastered at once. But simple research can usually be accomplished with only one or two tools. As you keep using the library, your research skills will gradually build. Library skills, like language skills, improve with practice, and both richly reward the effort.

ARTHUR PLOTNIK

Reference Works to Know: A Quick Dozen

The following dozen were chosen from dozens of other possibilities in answer to the question "What are the outstanding reference works every library user should get to know well?" The nation's foremost reference-book columnist and four practicing librarians advised in the selections but stressed that several other titles would do just about as well in each category. For full descriptions of each entry, consult *Guide to Reference Books,* published by the American Library Association.

Dictionary: *Webster's Third New International Dictionary of the English Language, Unabridged**. This is the dictionary that you will find first in most U.S. libraries. An especially useful feature is the inclusion of modern quotations to illustrate definitions. There is an important update called *6,000 Words: A Supplement to Webster's Third. . . ,* issued in 1976.

Thesaurus: *Roget's International Thesaurus* (4th ed.). Arranged by categories, rather than dictionary-style by alphabetical word entry, the thesaurus is the most popular available source of synonyms. An invaluable book in which to find the better word you are trying to think of.

Style handbook: *Standard Handbook for Secretaries* (8th ed.) by Lois Irene Hutchinson. This is one of the most widely used guides in libraries for the everyday problems of written communications, whether formal or informal. For formal research papers and professional publication, however, the University of Chicago's *A Manual of Style* must be mentioned as the most successful book of its kind.

Quotations: *Familiar Quotations* (15th ed.) by John Bartlett. One of two classic collections in every library (the other is Burton Egbert Stevenson's *The Home Book of Quotations*), it has been around since 1855, growing fatter with every edition.

---

*When no date is given with the title, the latest printing should be sought.

Biographical identification: *Who's Who in America.* In the 1980–81 edition, there are brief biographical facts—birthdate, parents, schools, jobs, publications, etc.—for nearly 75,000 prominent Americans.

Biographical background: *Current Biography.* With essay-length profiles of people in the news since 1940, it is issued 11 times a year with indexes covering current and past issues. The contents of the monthly issues are gathered together each year in *Current Biography Yearbook.* The prose is lively and accurate and is accompanied by a photograph of each subject.

Quick facts: *The World Almanac and Book of Facts.* Published annually 1868–76 and since 1886, this is the champion among library users. Each year it reassembles the latest information in social, industrial, political, financial, religious, educational, and many other areas. One should get to know the wide range of its statistical offerings.

General knowledge: *The New Encyclopædia Britannica.* This is the title of Britannica's 15th edition, which has more than 102,000 short articles in its 10-volume *Micropædia.* These articles lead, with references, to information in the 19-volume *Macropædia,* whose in-depth essays number more than 4,200. The authority, cross-referencing, and research apparatus of the successive Britannicas have made them a fixture in libraries of almost every type.

Current-events summaries: *Facts on File.* Described as a "weekly world news digest with cumulative index," *Facts on File* summaries arrive at the library just a week or two after the news occurs. They are added to a looseleaf binder, and every two weeks a complete index to the whole file is provided. One reference critic calls it the closest thing to a current-events encyclopedia.

Newspaper index: *The New York Times Index.* A guide to every significant article in what many consider the world's greatest newspaper, this index comes out every two weeks and is bound each year into larger volumes, providing an excellent source for historical research. Discussed briefly in this chapter, it is arranged by subject, and its "headline" synopses are themselves a source of quick information.

Magazine index: *Readers' Guide to Periodical Literature.* The most widely used of any such index, it analyzes the contents of magazines recommended by librarians that are likely to be collected in any sizable library. So when you find the page citation for an item that interests you, there is a good chance the magazine will be available. Concentrating most on general interest magazines in the humanities and social sciences, the *Guide* now has a companion *General Science Index,* launched in 1978, with 89 science periodicals indexed.

Geographical information: Rand McNally *Commercial Atlas and Marketing Guide.* While there are better atlases for details of countries other than the United States (*The Times Atlas of the World* being one), this is the main reference for U.S. commercial facts. The Rand commercial atlas provides considerable information on population, business, manufacturing, agriculture, and other socio-economic areas. The atlas comes out yearly and is supplemented by an airline map and road atlas.

Further Reading on Using the Library

Bell, Marion V., and Eleanor A. Swindon, *Reference Books: A Brief Guide,* 8th ed. (1978). Guide to the use and scope of over 900 popular and scholarly reference books. Revised and greatly expanded from the 7th ed. (1970).

Barzun, Jacques, and Henry F. Graff, *The Modern Researcher,* 3rd ed. (1977). Excellent guide to techniques and processes necessary for good researching and report writing.

Besterman, Theodore, *A World Bibliography of Bibliographies and of Bibliographical Catalogues; Calendars, Abstracts, Digests, Indexes and the Like,* 5 vols., 4th ed., rev. and enl. (1965–66). An authoritative guide to approximately 117,000 volumes of bibliography arranged under 16,000 headings. Supplemented in 1977 by Alice Toomey's *A World Bibliography of Bibliographies* (below).

Bradshaw, Charles I., *Using the Library: The Card Catalog* (1971). A programmed text designed for undergraduates, analyzing every part of the catalog with scores of illustrated examples explaining filing rules, cross references, form of subject headings, etc.

Cleary, Florence D., *Discovering Books and Libraries,* 2nd ed. (1977). Good introduction for those unfamiliar with libraries.

Cook, Margaret G., *The New Library Key,* 3rd ed. (1975). One of the best, most straightforward handbooks available for college students. It clarifies library terms and practices and includes a good bibliography.

Cottam, Keith M., and Robert Pelton, *Writer's Research Handbook: The Research Bible for Freelance Writers* (1977).

Downs, Robert B., and Clara D. Keller, *How to Do Library Research,* 2nd ed. (1975). Update of a classic 1966 work that provides an excellent introduction to the world of libraries and research techniques.

Gates, Jean K., *Guide to the Use of Books and Libraries,* 3rd ed. (1974).

Lolley, John, *Your Library: What's in It for You* (1974). A light-hearted, self-study guide.

McCormick, Mona, *Who—What—When—Where—How—Why—Made Easy* (1971), reprinted under the title *The New York Times Guide to Reference Materials* (1972). A compact guide to reference libraries, card catalogs, and 323 reference sources.

Sheehy, Eugene P., *Guide to Reference Books,* 9th ed. (1976). An excellent guide to research and reference works, published by the American Library Association.

Toomey, Alice F., *A World Bibliography of Bibliographies, 1964–1974* (1977). Intended as a supplement to Besterman's *A World Bibliography of Bibliographies* (above).

ABBREVIATIONS

An Abbreviated Guide

An Abbreviated Guide

The word *abbreviation,* though strictly a shortening or abridgment, commonly refers to a letter or group of letters taken from a single word or phrase and used, for brevity's sake, to represent that word or phrase. The use of abbreviations is not a recent phenomenon. Ancient writings and inscriptions were liberally sown with abbreviations of both single words and phrases. The most elementary abbreviation is the substitution for a word of its initial letter, but often one or more of the other letters are added. To indicate a plural or superlative, letters are frequently doubled. Although not exhaustive, the list below provides a generous selection of commonly encountered abbreviations and their meanings. Geographical names are omitted from this list, as are abbreviations for Christian names, weeks and months, medical terms, points of the compass, most businesses, and those abbreviations which have passed into common usage as ordinary words, such as *Benelux, gestapo,* or *telex.*

There is no universally accepted rule as to the use of periods in abbreviations. In this list periods have been eliminated from the abbreviations for all associations and organizations, including U.S. government agencies and branches of the military service. Abbreviations of foreign words and phrases are italicized, with the exception of the few noted that *Encyclopædia Britannica* always prefers to set in roman type. In cases where an abbreviation has multiple meanings, only the most common are given. Finally it should be noted that in British usage the use of a period is optional for abbreviations that retain the last letter of the word. For example, *hrs* (hours), *Dr* (Doctor), *Mr* (Mister), *pd* (paid), and *wt* (weight) are equally correct with or without a period. For guidelines on the use and conventional styling of abbreviations, *see* All You Need to Know About Grammar: V.C.4.

a.	answer; *ante;* at
A.	absolute (temperature); alto
AA	Alcoholics Anonymous; antiaircraft
AAA	American Automobile Association
AAU	Amateur Athletic Union of the United States
A.B.	(*artium baccalaureus*) Bachelor of Arts
ABA	American Bar Association; American Basketball Association
Abb.	abbot
abbr.; abbrev.	abbreviated; abbreviation
ABC	American Broadcasting Company
ab init.	(*ab initio*) from the beginning
ABM	antiballistic missile
Abp.; Archb.	archbishop
abr.	abridged; abridgment
ac.	acre(s): 4840 square yards
a/c	account; aircraft
A.C.	alternating current; (*ante Christum*) before Christ
acc.	accusative
accel.	(*accelerando*) with increasing speed
acct.	account
ACLU	American Civil Liberties Union
A.D.	(*anno Domini*) in the year of our Lord
ADA	American Dental Association; Americans for Democratic Action
adag.	(*adagio*) slow
ADB	Asian Development Bank
ADC	aide-de-camp; Aid to Dependent Children; Air Defense Command
ad fin.	(*ad finem*) at or to the end
ad inf.	(*ad infinitum*) to infinity
ad init.	(*ad initium*) at the beginning
ad int.	(*ad interim*) in the meantime
adj.	adjective
Adj.; Adjt.	adjutant
ad lib.	(*ad libitum*) at will; to any extent
ad loc.	(*ad locum*) at the place
Adm.	admiral(ty)
ADR	American depository receipt
ad us.	(*ad usum*) according to custom
adv.	adverb
ad val.	(*ad valorem*) according to the value

AEC	Atomic Energy Commission (became NRC and ERDA in 1975)
aet.; aetat.	(*aetatis*) of the age (followed by number of years)
AFB	air force base
AFC	American Football Conference
AFL-CIO	American Federation of Labor—Congress of Industrial Organizations
A.F.P.	Agence France-Presse
AFT	American Federation of Teachers
AFTRA	American Federation of Television and Radio Artists
A.H.	(*anno Hebraico*) in the Hebrew year; (*anno Hegirae*) in the year of the Hegira (Moslem era)
AID	Agency for International Development
a.k.a.	also known as
AL	American League; American Legion
ALA	American Library Association
Ald.	alderman
alleg.	(*allegro*) lively
alt.	alternate; altitude; alto
AM	amplitude modulation
A.M.; a.m.	(*anno mundi*) in the year of the world; (*ante meridiem*) before noon; (*artium magister*) Master of Arts
AMA	American Medical Association
A.M.D.G.	(*ad majorem Dei gloriam*) to the greater glory of God
AME	African Methodist Episcopal (church)
Ameslan	American Sign Language
amp.	ampere(s)
amp.-hr.	ampere-hour(s)
Amtrak	American Track
AMVETS	American Veterans of World War II, Korea, and Vietnam
and.	(*andante*) moderately slow
anon.	anonymous
ans.	answer
ant.	antonym
AP	Associated Press
app.	appendix
approx.	approximate(ly)
A.R.A.	Associate of the Royal Academy
Archbp.; Abp.	archbishop
Archd.	archdeacon; archduke

art.	article; artificial; artist
A.R.V.	American (Standard) Revised Version (Bible)
AS	Anglo-Saxon
ASCAP	American Society of Composers, Authors, and Publishers
ASCII	American Standard Code for Information Interchange (data processing)
asdic; ASDIC	Allied Submarine Detection Investigation Committee
ASE	American Stock Exchange
ASEAN	Association of South East Asian Nations
ASPCA	American Society for the Prevention of Cruelty to Animals
assn.	association
assoc.	associate; association
ASW	antisubmarine warfare
ATC	Air Traffic Control
atm.	atmosphere; atmospheric
atty.	attorney
Atty. Gen.	attorney general
A.U.C.	(*ab urbe condita* or *anno urbis conditae*) from the founding of the city (Rome)
av.	average; avenue
a.v.	(*annos vixit*) he or she lived (a certain number of years)
A.V.; a–v	audiovisual
ave.	avenue
avg.	average
A.W.O.L.	absent without leave
b.	born
B.A.	(*artium baccalaureus*) Bachelor of Arts
Bart.; Bt.	baronet
BASIC	Beginner's All-purpose Symbolic Instruction Code (computer language)
BBC	British Broadcasting Corporation
bbl.	barrel(s)
B.C.	before Christ
BCD	binary-coded decimal
B.C.E.	before the common era
B.C.P.	Book of Common Prayer
B/D; b.d.	brought down (accounting)
bf.; b.f.	boldface (typography); brought forward
Bib.; bibl.	Bible; biblical
bibliog.	bibliographer; bibliography

bk.	book
bldg.	building
blvd.	boulevard
b.m.	bench mark; board measure
bn.	battalion
Bn.	baron
BOQ	bachelor officers' quarters
BOT	board of trade
boul.	boulevard
bp	boiling point
Bp.	bishop
BP	before the present
B.P.O.E.	Benevolent and Protective Order of Elks
Brig.	brigade; brigadier
Brig. Gen.	brigadier general
bros.	brothers
B.S.; B.Sc.	Bachelor of Science
BSA	Boy Scouts of America
Bt.	baronet
BT	board of trade
BTU	board of trade unit(s); British thermal unit(s)
bu.	bushel(s): 4 pecks or 32 quarts
B.V.M.	Blessed Virgin Mary
BW	bacteriological or biological warfare
bx(s).	box(es)
c.	cents; chapter; cup(s): 16 tablespoons
c.; ©	copyright
c.; ca.	(*circa*) about
C.	celsius; centigrade
ca.	centare (1 square meter): about 1.31 cubic yards
CAB	Civil Aeronautics Board
CACM	Central American Common Market
cal.	caliber; calorie(s)
cap(s).	capital(s)
CAP	Civil Air Patrol; Common Agricultural Policy
Capt.	captain
car.	carat(s)
CARE	Cooperative for American Relief Everywhere
CARICOM	Caribbean Community and Common Market
CARIFTA	Caribbean Free Trade Association
CATV	community antenna (*or* cable) television
CB	citizens band
C.B.E.	Commander of the Order of the British Empire

CBS	Columbia Broadcasting System
CBW	chemical and biological warfare
c.c.; C.C.	carbon copy; cubic centimeters): .001 liter
CCTV	closed-circuit television
CD	(*corps diplomatique*) diplomatic corps
Cdr.	commander
C.E.	common era
CEA	Commodity Exchange Authority (became CFTC in 1974)
cent.	centigrade; central; (*centum*) hundred; century
CENTO	Central Treaty Organization
CETA	Comprehensive Employment and Training Act
cf.	(*confer*) compare
C.F.A.	certified financial analyst
c.f.i.	cost, freight, and insurance
CFTC	Commodity Futures Trading Commission
cg.	centigram(s): .01 gram
c.g.	center of gravity
C.G.	coast guard; commanding general; consul general
ch.; chap.	chapter
chg.	charge
CIA	Central Intelligence Agency
cie.	(*compagnie*) company
CINC	commander in chief (*e.g.,* CINCPAC, Commander in Chief, Pacific)
cit.	citation; cited
cl.	centiliter(s): .01 liter
cm.	centimeter(s): .01 meter
CMH	Congressional Medal of Honor
co.	company; county
c.o.; c/o	care of; carried over
C.O.	commanding officer; conscientious objector
COBol; Cobol	common business oriented language (computer language)
COD	cash or collect on delivery
co-ed	coeducational
col(s).	column(s)
Col.	colonel
Comdr.	commander
Comdt.	commandant
Comecon; CMEA	Council for Mutual Economic Assistance
comp.	compiled; compiler

COMSAT	Communications Satellite Corporation
con.	consolidated; consul; (*contra*) against
Conelrad	control of electromagnetic radiation
Cong.	congregation; congress
Conrail	Consolidated Rail Corporation
cont.	contents; continue(d); (*contra*) against
co-op	cooperative
cop.; ©	copyright
CORE	Congress of Racial Equality
corp.	corporation
cp.	compare
C.P.	Communist Party
C.P.A.	certified public accountant
CPI	consumer price index
Cpl.	corporal
C.P.O.	chief petty officer
cps; c.p.s.	cycles per second
cpu	central processing unit
CREEP	Committee to Reelect the President
cres.; cresc.	(*crescendo*) with gradually increasing volume
CRT	cathode-ray tube
CSC	Civil Service Commission
C.S.O.	chief signal officer; chief staff officer
CST	central standard time
ct.	cents; count; court
cu.	cubic
cu. cm.; c.c.	cubic centimeter(s): .000001 cubic meter
cu. ft.	cubic foot (feet): 1728 cubic inches
cu. in.	cubic inch(es): .00058 foot
cu. m.	cubic meter(s) (stere): about 1.31 cubic yards
cu. yd.	cubic yard(s): 27 cubic feet
C.W.O.	chief warrant officer
cwt.	hundredweight(s): 100 pounds
d.	date; daughter; day; dead; died
da	daughter
D.A.	district attorney
dag.; dkg.	dekagram(s): 10 grams
dal.; dkl.	dekaliter(s): 10 liters
dam.; dkm.	dekameter(s): 10 meters
D & C	dilation and curettage
DAR	Daughters of the American Revolution
DAV	Disabled American Veterans
D.B.E.	Dame Commander of the Order of the British Empire

D.C.	(*da capo*) from the beginning; direct current
dcg.	decigram(s): .1 gram
D.D.	(*divinitatis doctor*) Doctor of Divinity
D.D.M.	Doctor of Dental Medicine
D.D.S.	Doctor of Dental Surgery
DDT	dichloro-diphenyl-trichloroethane
dec.	deceased
decresc.	(*decrescendo*) with a gradual decrease in loudness
del.	(*delineavit*) he (or she) drew (it)
Dem.	Democrat; Democratic
dept.	department
DEW	Distant Early Warning (radar line)
DFC	Distinguished Flying Cross
D.F.M.	Distinguished Flying Medal
dg.	decigram(s): .1 gram
D.G.	(*Dei gratia*) by the grace of God
dial.	dialect
diam.	diameter
dim.	diminutive
dim.	(*diminuendo*) with gradually diminishing power
diss.	dissertation
dist.	district
div.	division; divorced
dl.	deciliter(s): .1 liter
D. Lit(t).	(*doctor litterarum*) Doctor of Letters; Doctor of Literature
dm.; decim.	decimeter(s): .1 meter
DMT	dimethyltryptamine
DMZ	demilitarized zone
DNA	deoxyribonucleic acid
DNF	did not finish
D.O.	district officer
DOA	dead on arrival
DOD	Department of Defense
DOE	Department of Energy
Dom	(*dominus*) title used for monks of certain orders in the Roman Catholic Church
DOT	Department of Transportation
doz.	dozen
DP	displaced person
dr.	debtor
Dr.	doctor; drive
DSC	Distinguished Service Cross

DSM	Distinguished Service Medal
D.S.O.	Distinguished Service Order.
DST	daylight saving time
d.t.'s	delirium tremens
D.V.	(*Deo volente*) God willing; Douay Version (Bible)
dwt.; pwt.	pennyweight(s): .05 ounce
ea.	each
EAC	East African Community
ECOWAS	Economic Community of West African States
ed.	edited; edition; editor; education
EDP	electronic data processing
eds.	editions; editors
E.E.	Early English; electrical engineer
E.E. & M.P.	envoy extraordinary and minister plenipotentiary
EEC	European Economic Community
EEOC	Equal Employment Opportunity Commission
EFTA	European Free Trade Association
e.g.	(*exempli gratia*) for example
EKG	electrocardiogram
enc.; encl.	enclosed; enclosure(s)
ency.; encyc.	encyclopedia
Eng.	English
Ens.	ensign
EPA	Environmental Protection Agency
ERA	Equal Rights Amendment
ERDA	Energy Research and Development Administration (replaced by DOE)
ESC	Economic and Social Council
esp.; espec.	especially
ESP	extrasensory perception
Esq.; Esqr.	esquire
est	Erhard Seminar Training
est.	established; estimated; estuary
EST	eastern standard time
e.t.a.	estimated time of arrival
et al.	(*et alia* or *alii*) and others; (*et alibi*) and elsewhere
etc.	(*et cetera*) and so forth
et. seq.	(*et sequens, sequentes,* or *sequentia*) and the following
ETV	educational television
EURATOM	European Atomic Energy Community
ex.	example
Eximbank	Export-Import Bank
ext.	extension; external(ly); extinct

f.	female; feminine; folio; following
f.	(*forte*) loud
F.	Fahrenheit
FAA	Federal Aviation Administration
FAO	Food and Agriculture Organization
F.B.A.	Fellow of the British Academy
FBI	Federal Bureau of Investigation
FCA	Farm Credit Administration
FCC	Federal Communications Commission
FCIC	Federal Crop Insurance Corporation
FDA	Food and Drug Administration
FDIC	Federal Deposit Insurance Corporation
FEA	Federal Energy Administration
fem.	feminine
ff.	folios; following (pages)
ff.	(*fortissimo*) very loud
FHA	Federal Housing Administration
FICA	Federal Insurance Contributions Act
FIFO	first-in, first-out system of inventory accounting
fig.	figure
fl.	(*floruit*) flourished
FLA	Federal Loan Administration
fl. oz.	fluid ounce(s): 8 fluid drams
fm.	fathom(s): 6 feet
FM	frequency modulation
F.M.	field marshal
fn.	footnote
f.o.b.	free on board
fol.	folio; following
FORTRAN; Fortran	formula translation (computer language)
fp	freezing point
FPC	Federal Power Commission
fr.	father; franc(s); from
Fr.	Father (title); French; Friar
FSLIC	Federal Savings and Loan Insurance Corporation
ft.	foot (feet): 12 inches; fort
FTC	Federal Trade Commission
fut.	future
f.v.	(*folio verso*) on the back of the page
fwd.	forward
g.	gram(s); about .035 ounce; acceleration of gravity
gal.	gallon(s): 4 quarts

GAO	General Accounting Office
GATT	General Agreement on Tariffs and Trade
G.B.E.	Knight (or Dame) Grand Cross of the Order of the British Empire
GCA	ground-controlled approach
GCI	ground-controlled interception
GCT	Greenwich civil time
GED	general educational development (tests)
gen.	general; genitive; genus
Gen.	general (rank)
GeV	giga-electron-volts: one billion electron volts
GHQ	general headquarters
GI; G.I.	general issue; government issue
GIGO	garbage in, garbage out (describes computer whose output is suspect because the input is suspect)
gm.; g.	gram(s): .035 ounce
G.M.	general manager
GmbH.	(*Gesellschaft mit beschränkter Haftung*) limited liability company—Germany
GMT	Greenwich mean time
GNP	gross national product
GOP	Grand Old Party (Republican)
Gov.	governor
G.P.	general practitioner
g.p.m.	gallons per minute
GPO	general post office; Government Printing Office
gr.	grain(s); gross
GSA	General Services Administration
ha.	hectare(s): 10,000 square meters
h.c.f.	highest common factor
HCIS	House Committee on Internal Security (formerly HUAC, dissolved in 1975)
HE	high explosive
H.E.	His Eminence; His Excellency
HEW	Department of Health, Education, and Welfare (replaced by HHS and Department of Education)
HF	high frequency
hg.	hectogram(s): 100 grams
H.G.	His (or Her) Grace
H.H.	His (or Her) Highness; His Holiness (the pope)
HHS	Department of Health and Human Services
H.I.H.	His (or Her) Imperial Highness
H.I.M.	His (or Her) Imperial Majesty

H.J.S.	(*hic jacet sepultus*) here lies buried
hl.	hectoliter(s): 100 liters
hm.	hectometer(s): 100 meters
H.M.	His (or Her) Majesty
H.M.S.	His (or Her) Majesty's Ship, or Service
H.M.S.O.	His (or Her) Majesty's Stationary Office
Hon.	honorable; honorary
hp; HP	high pressure; horsepower
HQ; h.q.	headquarters
hr.	hour(s)
H.R.	House of Representatives
H.R.H.	His (or Her) Royal Highness
HSUS	Humane Society of the United States
HUAC	House Un-American Activities Committee (later HCIS)
HUD	Department of Housing and Urban Development
Hz	hertz (unit of frequency)
i.; I.	island
IAAF	International Amateur Athletic Federation
IAEA	International Atomic Energy Agency
IATA	International Air Transport Association
ib.; ibid.	(*ibidem*) in the same place
IBRD	International Bank for Reconstruction and Development (World Bank)
IBT	International Brotherhood of Teamsters
IC4A	Intercollegiate Association of Amateur Athletes of America
ICBM	intercontinental ballistic missile
ICC	Interstate Commerce Commission
id.	(*idem*) the same
ID	identification
IDB	Inter-American Development Bank
i.e.	(*id est*) that is
IFR	instrument flight rules
IGY	International Geophysical Year
IHP	indicated horsepower
IHS	symbol representing IHΣ, the first three letters of the Greek name of Jesus; also *Ieusus Hominum Salvator* (Jesus the Savior of Man)
ILGWU	International Ladies' Garment Workers' Union
ILO	International Labor Organization
ILS	instrument landing system
IMF	International Monetary Fund

imp.	imperative; imperfect (tense); (*imprimatur*) let it be printed
in.	inch(es): .083 foot
Inc.	incorporated
incl.	inclosure; including; inclusive
inf.	(*infra*) below
info.	information
in loc. cit.	(*in loco citato*) in the place cited
in mem.	(*in memoriam*) in memory of
I.N.R.I.	(*Iesus Nazarenus Rex Iudaeorum*) Jesus of Nazareth, King of the Jews
inst.	instant; institute; institution(al); instrument
int.	interest
int. al.	(*inter alia*) among other things
Intelsat	International Telecommunications Satellite Consortium
intr.; intrans.	intransitive
intro.; introd.	introduction
I/O	input/output
IOC	International Olympic Committee
I.O.O.F.	Independent Order of Odd Fellows
IOU	I owe you
IPA	International Phonetic Association (or Alphabet)
i.q.	(*idem quod*) the same as
IQ	intelligence quotient
IRA	Irish Republican Army; individual retirement account
IRBM	intermediate-range ballistic missile
IRC	International Committee of the Red Cross
IRO	International Refugee Organization
irreg.	irregular(ly)
IRS	Internal Revenue Service
ital.	italics
ITF	International Tennis Federation
ITT	International Telephone and Telegraph Corporation
IUD	intrauterine device
jato	jet-assisted take-off
JBS	John Birch Society
J.C.D.	(*juris civilis doctor*) Doctor of Civil Law
J.D.	(*jurum doctor*) Doctor of Laws
jg	junior grade
jp	jet propulsion
J.P.	justice of the peace
jr.; Jr.	junior
k.	carat(s); knot(s)

K.	Kelvin
K.B.E.	Knight Commander of the Order of the British Empire
kc.	kilocycle(s)
KGB	(*Komitet Gosudarstvennoy Bezopasnosti*) (Soviet) Committee of State Security
kHz	kilohertz
KIA	killed in action
kilo(s); kg.	kilogram(s): 1,000 grams
KKK	Ku Klux Klan
kl.	kiloliter(s): 1,000 liters
km.	kilometer(s): 1,000 meters
KO	knockout (boxing)
kt.	carat(s); kiloton; knot(s)
Kt.	knight
kv.	kilovolt(s)
kva.	kilovolt-ampere(s)
kW	kilowatt(s)
kWh	kilowatt-hour(s)
l.	left; length; line(s); liquid; liter(s)
L.	(*liber*) book; (*libra*) pound(s) (money)
LAFTA	Latin American Free Trade Association
lat.	latitude
Lat.	Latin
lb.	(*libra*) pound(s) (weight): 16 ounces
l.c.	lower case (typography)
L/C	letter of credit
l.c.d.	lowest common denominator
LCD's	less developed countries
L.d'H.; L.H.	(*Légion d'honneur*) (French) Legion of Honor
LEAA	Law Enforcement Assistance Administration
LED	light-emitting diode
LEM	lunar excursion module
LF	low frequency
lib.	liberal; librarian; library
Lieut.; Lt.	lieutenant
LIFO	last-in-first-out (system of inventory accounting)
lit.	literal(ly); literature
Lit(t). D.	(*literarum doctor*) Doctor of Literature; (*literarum doctor*) Doctor of Letters
ll.	lines
LL.D.	(*legum doctor*) Doctor of Laws
LL.M.	(*legum magister*) Master of Laws
LM	lunar module

loc. cit.	(*loco citato*) in the place cited
log	logarithm
long.	longitude
LP	liquefied petroleum; long-playing (record)
LPGA	Ladies' Professional Golfers' Association
L.S.	(*locus sigilli*) place of the seal
LSD	lysergic acid diethylamide
l.t.	long ton(s): 2,240 pounds
ltd.; Ltd.	limited
m.	male; married; masculine; meter(s); minim
M.	mark(s); (*meridies*) meridian, noon; (*mille*) thousand(s); monsieur
M.A.	(*magister artium*) Master of Arts
MAC	Military Airlift Command
MAD	mutual assured destruction
Maj.	major
Marq.	marquess (marquis)
masc.	masculine
MATS	Military Air Transport Service (changed to MAC)
max.	maximum
M.B.	(*medicinae baccalaureus*) Bachelor of Medicine
M.B.A.	Master of Business Administration
M.B.E.	Member of the Order of the British Empire
mc.	megacycle(s)
M.C.	master of ceremonies; Member of Congress
MCA's	monetary compensatory amounts
M.D.	(*medicinae doctor*) Doctor of Medicine
ME	Middle English
M.E.	mechanical engineer; Methodist Episcopal (church); mining engineer
med.	median; medical; medieval; medium
Messrs.	messieurs
mf.	(*mezzo forte*) moderately loud
mfg.	manufacture(d); manufacturing
mfr.	manufacture; manufacturer
mg.	milligram(s): .001 gram
Mgr.	manager; monseigneur; monsignor
MH	Medal of Honor
mHz	megahertz
mi.	mile(s): 5,280 feet
MIA	missing in action
min.	minute(s)
MIRV	multiple independently targeted reentry vehicle

misc.	miscellaneous; miscellany
ml.	milliliter(s); .001 liter
Mlle(s).	mademoiselle (mesdemoiselles)
mm.	millimeter(s): .001 meter
m.m.	(*mutatis mutandis*) necessary changes being made
MM.	messieurs
Mme(s).	madame (mesdames)
mo.	month(s)
mod.	moderate; modern; modify
mol.	molecular; molecule(s)
MOL	manned orbiting laboratory
mol. wt.	molecular weight
m.p.	melting point; (*mezzo piano*) moderately soft
M.P.	Member of Parliament; military police
MPAA	Motion Picture Association of America
m.p.g.	miles per gallon
m.p.h.	miles per hour
Mr.	mister
mRNA	messenger RNA
Mrs.	mistress
ms(s).; MS(S).	manuscript(s)
Ms.	alternate form of address for Miss or Mrs. when marital status is unknown or irrelevant
Msgr.	monseigneur; monsignor
M.S.; M.Sc.	Master of Science
MST	mountain standard time
m.t.	metric ton(s): about 1.1 tons
mt(s).	mount(s); mountain(s)
mus.	museum, music
MVP	most valuable player
n.	name; (*natus*) born; neuter; note; noun
NAACP	National Association for the Advancement of Colored People
NASA	National Aeronautics and Space Administration
NASCAR	National Association for Stock Car Auto Racing
NASL	North American Soccer League
nat.	national; native; natural
NATO	North Atlantic Treaty Organization
n.b.; *N.B.*	(*nota bene*) note well
NBA	National Basketball Association
NBC	National Broadcasting Company
NBS	National Bureau of Standards
NCAA	National Collegiate Athletic Association

NCCJ	National Conference of Christians and Jews
N.C.O.	noncommissioned officer
n.d.	no date; no decision (boxing)
NEA	National Education Association
nem. con.	(*nemine contradicente*) no one contradicting; unanimous
neut.	neuter; neutral
New Test.	New Testament
NFL	National Football League
n.g.	no good
NG	National Guard
NHL	National Hockey League
NKVD	(*Narodny Komissariat Vnutrennikh Del*) People's Commissariat of Internal Affairs (former Soviet police agency, dissolved in 1946)
NL	National League of Professional Baseball Clubs
NLF	National Liberation Front
NLRB	National Labor Relations Board
nn.	notes
no(s).	(*numero*) number(s)
NOAA	National Oceanic and Atmospheric Administration
nol. pros.	(*nolle prosequi*) unwilling to prosecute
nom.	nominative
non obst.	(*non obstante*) notwithstanding
non seq.	(*non sequitur*) it does not follow
NORAD	North American Air Defense Command
NOW	National Organization for Women
n.p.	no place; no publisher
N.P.	notary public
n.p.t.	normal (blood) pressure and temperature
NRA	National Recovery Act
NRC	Nuclear Regulatory Commission
NSF	National Science Foundation
N.T.	New Testament
nt. wt.; n. wt.	net weight
NUL	National Urban League
NYSE	New York Stock Exchange
o	ohm
OAPEC	Organization of Arab Petroleum Exporting Countries
OAS	Organization of American States
OASDI	Old-Age and Survivors Disability Insurance
OAU	Organization of African Unity
ob.	(*obiit*) he (or she) died; obstetric

O.B.E.	Officer of the Order of the British Empire
OCD	Office of Civilian Defense
OCS	officer candidate school
OD	overdose
O.D.	overdraft
OE	Old English
OECD	Organization for Economic Cooperation and Development
OEEC	Organization for European Economic Cooperation
OEO	Office of Economic Opportunity
O.F.M.	(*Ordo Fratrum Minorum*) Order of Friars Minor (Franciscans)
OGPU	(*Obyedinyonnoye Gosudarstvennoye Politicheskoye Upravleniye*) former Soviet security police agency, absorbed by the NKVD in 1934
OGU	orbiting geophysical observatory
O.H.M.S.	On His (or Her) Majesty's Service
OMB	Office of Management and Budget
op.	opera; operation; opus
o.p.; OP	out of print
O.P.	Order of Preachers (Dominicans)
OPEC	Organization of Petroleum Exporting Countries
op.cit.	(*opere citato*) in the work cited
opp.	opposite
OSHA	Occupational Safety and Health Administration
OSO	orbiting solar observatory
OSRD	Office of Scientific Research and Development
OSS	Office of Strategic Services
O.T.	Old Testament
otb	off-track betting
OTC	Officers' Training Corps; over the counter
OWI	Office of War Information
oz.	(*onza*) ounce(s): about 28.35 grams
p.	page; past
p.	(*piano*) soft
P	parking
p.a.	per annum
P and L	profit and loss
par.	paragraph; parallel; parenthesis; parish; parochial
parl.	parliamentary
Parl.	Parliament
part.	participle
pass.	(*passim*) throughout

pat.; patd.	patent; patented
PAU	Pan American Union
PBS	Public Broadcasting Service
PCB	polychlorinated biphenyl (industrial chemical and environmental pollutant)
pd.	paid
PD	police department
PCP	phencyclidine pill ("angel dust," a dangerous drug)
PEN	International Association of Poets, Playwrights, Editors, Essayists, and Novelists
p.f.	(*più forte*) a little louder
Pfc	private first class
PGA	Professional Golfers' Association
PH	Purple Heart
PHA	Public Housing Administration
Ph.D.	(*philosophiae doctor*) Doctor of Philosophy
PHS	public health service
pinx.	(*pinxit*) he (or she) painted (it)
pizz.	(*pizzicato*) plucked (music)
pk.	peck(s): 8 quarts
pkg.	package
pkwy.	parkway
pl.	place; plate; plural
PLO	Palestine Liberation Organization
pls.	please
P.M.; p.m.	postmaster; (*post meridiem*) afternoon; post mortem; prime minister
PMF	Presidential Medal of Freedom
P.N.	practical nurse; protonotary apostolic
P.O.	petty officer; postal order; post office
POD	Post Office Department (later USPS)
P.O.E.	port of embarkation or entry
pop.	population
POS	point of sale
POW	prisoner of war
pp.	pages
pp.	(*pianissimo*) very soft
P.P.; p.p.	parcel post; parish priest; past participle; postpaid
p.p.c.	(*pour prendre congé*) to take leave
P.P.S.	(*post postscriptum*) an additional postscript
pr.	pair
P.R.	proportional representation; public relations
pref.	preface; prefatory; preference; preferred; prefix

prep.	preparation; preparatory; preposition
pres.	president; present
proc.	proceedings
Prof.	professor
pron.	pronoun; pronunciation
prop.	property; proposition; proprietor
pro tem.	(*pro tempore*) for the time being
prov.	province; provisional; provost
Prov.	Proverbs (Bible)
prox.	(*proximo* [*mense*]) next month
PS	public school
P.S.	(*postscriptum*) postscript
PSC	Public Service Commission
pseud.	pseudonym(ous)
PST	Pacific standard time
pt(s).	part(s); pint(s): ½ quart or 2 cups; point(s); port(s)
PT	physical training
p.t.	(*pro tempore*) for the time being
PTA	parent-teacher association
P.T.O.	please turn (the page) over
PTV	public television
pub.; publ.	public; publication; published
PUC	Public Utilities Commission
PUSH	People United to Save Humanity
Pvt.	private
PWA	Public Works Administration
pwt.; dwt.	pennyweight(s): .05 ounce
PX	post exchange
pxt.	(*pinxit*) he (or she) painted (it)
q.; qu.	query; question
q.e.	(*quod est*) which is
Q.E.D.	(*quod erat demonstrandum*) which was to be demonstrated
Q.E.F.	(*quod erat faciendum*) which was to be done
q.l.	(*quantum libet*) as much as you please
Q.M.	quartermaster
qq.v.	(*quae vide*) which (things) see
qr.; quar.	quarterly
q.s.; quant suff.	(*quantum sufficit*) as much as is sufficient
qt.	quart(s): 2 pints or 4 cups
q.v.	(*quantum vis*) as much as you will; (*quod vide*) which (thing) see
R.	(*regina; rex*) queen, king; river

Rx.	(*recipe*) take
RADA	Royal Academy of Dramatic Art
RADM	rear admiral
RAF	Royal Air Force
rall.	(*rallentando*) gradually slower
R and D	research and development
R and R	rest and relaxation
RC	Red Cross
R.C.	Roman Catholic
rd.	road
REA	Rural Electrification Administration
Rear Adm.	rear admiral
rel.	relative; religion
REM	rapid eye movement
Rep.	representative; Republican
ret.	retired; return
rev.	reverse(d); review(ed); revise; revision; revolution
Rev.	reverend
RFD	rural free delivery
Rh	Rhesus factor
R.I.P.	(*requiescat in pace*) may he (or she) rest in peace
rit.	(*ritardando*) gradually slower
riv.	river
rm.	room
RN	Royal Navy
R.N.	registered nurse
RNA	ribonucleic acid
ROTC	Reserve Officers Training Corps
r.p.m.	revolutions per minute
r.p.s.	revolutions per second
rpt.	repeat; report
R.R.	railroad
R.S.V.	Revised Standard Version (Bible)
R.S.V.P.	(*répondez s'il vous plaît*) please reply
rte.	route
Rt. Hon.	right honorable
Rt. Rev.	right reverend
RV	recreational vehicle
R.V.	Revised Version (Bible)
Rwy.; Ry.	railway
s.	second(s); series; son; subject
S.	saint; Senate; Senate Bill (with number)
SAC	Strategic Air Command

SAG	Screen Actors' Guild
SALT	Strategic Arms Limitation Talks
SAM	surface-to-air missile
SAR	Sons of the American Revolution
SAT	Scholastic Aptitude Test
sb.	substantive
SBA	Small Business Administration
sc.	scene; (*scilicet*) namely, of course; (*sculpsit*) he (or she) sculptured (it)
sc.	(*scilicet*) namely; (*sculpsit*) he (or she) carved or engraved (it)
SC	Security Council (of the United Nations)
s.c.	small capital letters
S.C.	Sisters of Charity; Supreme Court
SCLC	Southern Christian Leadership Conference
sculp.; sculpt.	(*sculpsit*) he (or she) carved or engraved (it)
s.d.	(*sine die*) without (appointing) a day (on which to assemble again)
SDR's	Special Drawing Rights
SDS	Students for a Democratic Society
SEATO	Southeast Asia Treaty Organization
sec(s).	second(s); secretary; section(s)
sec.	(*secundum*) according to
SEC	Securities and Exchange Commission
semp.	(*sempre*) always; continually
Sen.	senate; senator; senior
seq.; seqq.	(*sequens; sequentia*) the following
ser.	series
Sergt.; Sgt.	sergeant
SHAPE	Supreme Headquarters, Allied Powers Europe
SIDS	sudden infant death syndrome
sing.	singular
S.J.	Society of Jesus (Jesuits)
SNCC	Student National Coordinating Committee
SOP	standard (or standing) operating procedure
sp.	species; specific; spelling; spirit
s.p.	(*sine prole*) without offspring
SP	shore patrol
SPCC	Society for the Prevention of Cruelty to Children
sq.	squadron; square
sq.	(*sequens; sequentia*) the following
sq. ft.	square foot (feet): 144 square inches
sq. in.	square inch(es): .007 square foot

sq. km.	square kilometer(s): about .386 square mile
sq. m.	square mile(s): 640 acres
sq. yd.	square yard(s): 1,296 square inches
Sr.	senior; señor
Sra.	señora
S.R.O.	standing room only
Srta.	señorita
ss.	(*scilicet*) namely
S.S.	steamship
SS.	saints; (*santissimus*) most holy
SSA	Social Security Administration
SST	supersonic transport
st(s).	stanza(s); street(s)
s.t.	short ton(s): 2,000 pounds
St.	saint; statute(s); strait; street
Sta.	(*santa*) saint; station
stacc.	(*staccato*) distinct, separated
stat.	statistics; statute
stat.	(*statim*) immediately
Ste.	(*sainte*) saint
STOL	short take-off and landing
sub.	subject; submarine; subscription; substitute(s)
subj.	subject; subjunctive
sup.	(*supra*) above
supp.; suppl.	supplement
Supt.	superintendent
s.v.	(*sub verbo; sub voce*) under the word (or heading)
S.V.P.	(*s'il vous plaît*) please
SWAPO	South West Africa People's Organization
SWP	Socialists Workers Party
syn.	synonymous
t.	short ton(s): 2,000 pounds; town; transitive
TA	teaching assistant
TAC	tactical air command
TASS	(*Telegraphnoye Agenstvo Sovyetskovo Soyuza*) Soviet News Agency
TB	tuberculosis
tba	to be announced
tbs.; tbsp.	tablespoon(s)
t.d.s.	(*ter die sumendum*) to be taken three times a day
TEFL	teaching English as a foreign language
temp.	temperance; temperature; temporary
terr.	terrace; territory

TESL	teaching English as a second language
TESOL	Teachers of English to Speakers of Other Languages
t.i.d.	(*ter in die*) three times daily (pharmaceutical)
TKO	technical knockout (boxing)
TM	transcendental meditation
TNT	trinitrotoluene (explosive)
tr.	transitive; translated; translator; transpose; trustee
trans.	transaction(s); transferred; transitive; translation; transportation
treas.	treasurer
trem.	(*tremolo*) trembling; fluttering
tsp.	teaspoon
T.S.V.P.	(*tournez s'il vous plaît*) please turn (the page)
TV	television
TVA	Tennessee Valley Authority
twp.	township
UAW	United Automobile Workers (common abbreviated form of full title)
UCMJ	Uniform Code of Military Justice
UDC	United Daughters of the Confederacy
UFO	unidentified flying object
UHF; uhf	ultrahigh frequency
UJA	United Jewish Appeal
ult.	(*ultimo*) last (month)
UMTA	Urban Mass Transportation Administration
UMW	United Mine Workers
UN	United Nations
UNAC	United Nations Appeal for Children
UNCTAD	United Nations Conference on Trade and Development
UNEF	United Nations Emergency Force
UNESCO	United Nations Educational, Scientific, and Cultural Organization
UNICEF	United Nations Children's Fund (formerly United Nations Children's Emergency Fund)
univ.	universal; university
UPI	United Press International
u.s.	(*ubi supra*) in the place above mentioned
USA	United States Army
USAC	United States Auto Club
USAF	United States Air Force
USAFA	United States Air Force Academy
USCG	United States Coast Guard

USDA	United States Department of Agriculture
USIA	United States Information Agency
USIS	United States Information Service
USLTA	United States Lawn Tennis Association (later USTA)
U.S.M.	United States mail
USMA	United States Military Academy
USMC	United States Marine Corps
USN	United States Navy
USNA	United States Naval Academy
USNR	United States Naval Reserve
USO	United Service Organizations
USOC	United States Olympic Committee
USPHS	United States Public Health Service
USPS	United States Postal Service
USS	United States Senate
U.S.S.	United States ship
USSS	United States secret service
USTA	United States Tennis Association
u.s.w.; usw.	(*und so weiter*) and so *forth* (in German language writing)
ut sup.	(*ut supra*) as above
v.	verb; verse; (*versus*) against; very; village; volt(s)
v.	(*vide*) see
V.	viscount
VA	Veterans Administration
VAT	value-added tax
V.C.	vice-chancellor; Victoria Cross; Vietcong
VD	venereal disease
VDT	video display terminal (data processing)
Ven.	venerable
verb. sap.	(*verbum satis sapienti*) a word to the wise suffices
vet.	veteran; veterinarian
VFR	visual-flight rules
VFW	Veterans of Foreign Wars
VHF; vhf	very high frequency
v.i.	verb intransitive
vid.	(*vide*) see
VISTA	Volunteers in Service to America
viz; viz.	(*videlicet*) namely
v.l.	(*varia lectio,* pl. *varia lectiones*) variant reading(s)
vol(s).	volume(s); volunteer(s)
VOLAR	volunteer army
vox pop.	(*vox populi*) voice of the people

V.P.; veep	vice-president; Vice President (of U.S.)
vs.	verse; (*versus*) against
v.s.	(*vide supra*) see above
v.t.	verb transitive
VTO	vertical take-off
Vul.; Vulg.	Vulgate (Bible)
w.	wife
W	watt(s)
WAC	Women's Army Corps
WAF	Women in the Air Force
WASP	white Anglo-Saxon Protestant
WAVES	Women Accepted for Volunteer Emergency Service
WBA	World Boxing Association
WBC	World Boxing Council
WCC	World Council of Churches
W.C.T.U.	Women's Christian Temperance Union
wt.	weight
WHA	World Hockey Association
WHO	World Health Organization
wk.	week; work
w.l.	wave length
W.O.	warrant officer
WPA	Works Projects Administration
WTT	World Team Tennis
X	Christ; Christian
YAF	Young Americans for Freedom
yd.	yard(s): 3 feet, or 36 inches
YMCA	Young Men's Christian Association
YMCathA	Young Men's Catholic Association
YMHA	Young Men's Hebrew Association
yr.	year(s); younger; your
YWCA	Young Women's Christian Association
YWHA	Young Women's Hebrew Association
z.B.	(*zum Beispiel*) for example

PART III

WRITING AND SPEAKING EFFECTIVELY

THE FINER POINTS OF WRITING

Some Hints About Writing
Literary Style
Figures of Speech
Poetic Imagery
Allusions
 Common Allusions from Past and Present
 Proverb and Gnome
 Classical Religion and Mythology
Glossary of Selected Foreign Words and Phrases

Some Hints About Writing

Everybody has laughed at Molière's bourgeois *gentilhomme,* who learned only in middle age that he had been speaking prose all his life. As his grammar teacher put it, "there is only prose and poetry and since you haven't been speaking poetry, you have been speaking prose" —a good joke for the stage. But the more one thinks about the nature of writing, and not even necessarily of good writing, the more one is convinced that old M. Jourdain had a point. He had not been speaking prose; he had been speaking speech.

Speech is made up of short phrases, single words, exclamations, questions, negatives out of order or inconsistent—all these bits and pieces tied together and given force by gestures, tones of voice, facial expressions, and emphatic accents. These somehow fill the gaps of incomplete and incoherent utterance, though even with their aid it is often necessary to repeat or to answer questions because the listener has failed to understand. If anyone disbelieves that speech is this kind of performance, let him record on tape his own impromptu conversation with a friend.

Prose is obviously something else. Prose is a form of writing which, to begin with, replaces all the facial and vocal aids by words and grammatical devices, and which then goes on to make continuous and consistent the spurts and fragments of verbalized thought. It cuts out repetitions and stumblings and connects smoothly each full-formed idea with the next.

One proof that there is nothing natural or spontaneous about prose is that in all the modern languages of Western civilization the earliest samples of prose are awkward, strung out anyhow, and not easy to read at first sight. Here, for example, is the prose of Roger Ascham, a contemporary of Elizabeth I of England who was a scholar and teacher. He declared: "I . . . have written this English matter, in the English tongue, for Englishmen," meaning that he rejected foreign influences; "for surely vain words do work no small thing in vain, ignorant, and young minds, especially if they be given any thing thereunto of their own

443

nature. These books (as I have heard say) were made the most part in abbeys and monasteries—a very likely and fit fruit of such an idle and blind kind of living.

"In our time now, when every man is given to know much rather than to live well, very many do write, but after such a fashion as very many do shoot. Some shooters take in hand stronger bows than they be able to maintain."

All the words in that passage are simple and clear, but the intent is not easy to fathom, because the verbs and objects are vague ("work no small thing"); phrasings repeat with the same or different meanings (given . . . given . . . very many . . .very many . . . in our time/now); and concrete and abstract are hitched together as if equivalent ("take in hand . . . maintain"). The *drift* of the passage, including a few lumps hard to grasp at sight, is not impossible to make out, but the prose falls short of analyzing the thought far enough to make it fluent and un-mistakable.

A hundred years later Thomas Fuller writes prose which is also felt as different from ours, yet analytic and made for sight-reading, as we expect prose to be: "Francis Drake was born nigh South Tavistock in Devonshire, and brought up in Kent; God dividing the honour betwixt two counties, that the one might have his birth, and the other his edu-cation. His father, being a minister, fled into Kent, for fear of the Six Articles, wherein the sting of Popery still remained in England, though the teeth whereof were knocked out, and the Pope's supremacy abol-ished."

Fortunately, from the beginning, talented writers who struggled with others' and their own clumsy prose noticed the shortcomings, dug into the resources of the language, and created new ways of expression to make writing more exact and flexible. Soon a tradition of prose writing develops. Prose improves. Prose, in short, is an invention like the wheelbarrow or the steam engine.

Anyone who starts out to write prose today is thus the beneficiary of a long course of past effort. He does not have to begin from scratch. But that statement is true only if he has done a good deal of reading. For it is the prose of the best earlier writers that contains the models— the devices, forms, idioms, usages, convenient words and turns of phrase —all ready-made to his hand for reducing his thoughts to writing. Just as in dealing with numbers there are tested ways of multiplying, divid-ing, extracting square roots, and solving equations, so in dealing with words there are tested ways of composing, simplifying, making distinc-tions, varying rhythm, and sustaining levels of tone. If one reads from childhood on, while the mind is still at the exploring and noticing stage, all these means of expression are acquired virtually without effort. But if one has read little and has mostly listened to speech, the task of writing is much harder. One is then in a position akin to that of the first inventors of prose, having not simply to use but to forge the instruments of self-expression. Since to do this would be as foolish as hammering out one's own knife and fork, the first piece of advice for better writing is: START READING.

Choose something you have some interest in, but not some breathless story of passion or spywork, because in the excitement of the plot you will overlook the words, and the purpose of reading at this point is to *notice words*. Naturally you cannot "notice" every word indiscriminately and without plan. What you are on the lookout for is the elements that cause you difficulty in writing. It may be that some of these elements— say, transitions or proper words—are lacking; until you read, you are not aware of them; or you are aware but do not use them right; or you use them right up to a point but need to extend and vary them to make them adequate to your full meaning.

In the present chapter some particulars under these heads will be discussed and illustrated—only some, because a complete inventory of faults and predicaments in writing cannot be drawn up. Language is infinitely more complex than any systematic procedure, and the individual thoughts that may call for and find due expression cannot be foretold. But some difficulties recur often enough to be listed and labeled and thus brought to consciousness, together with the ways to avoid or remove them.

Even with such hints clearly in mind, nothing will be accomplished by the writer who does not also make himself acutely conscious of words. Words must stand out and be felt and weighed, not just when you are writing or reading purposefully, but at all times—when you are listening to yourself and others and when you are going about and catch sight of signs, ads, and public notices. For example, you step into an office and see a sign: "Salesmen not received without prior appointment." Clear enough—what's wrong with it? Well, would a salesman be received if he made an appointment *after* he came in? That's absurd; an appointment can only be made before; hence the word *prior* is both foolish and redundant. And the ideal of good writing is: NO UNNECESSARY WORDS.

No doubt it is hard at first to force oneself into the habit of haggling over every word encountered, because the practical use of words in daily life makes their role as instruments disappear beneath their role as meanings. But if one wants to write well, there is no avoiding the continual exercise of word consciousness, which turns practical information back into verbal materials. The musician and the graphic artist have an easier time concentrating on *their* materials, which more readily stand out from the context of utility; yet it is clear that the best performers in those arts are the ones to whom line, color, or sound, wherever met, is invariably important and suggestive in itself.

Words: the point of departure

We began the conscious effort by noticing the failure to think straight in the sign that called for a *prior* appointment. The example illustrates the importance of the single word. It is obvious that if you do not know the meaning *and force* of your words taken one at a time, your writing will mislead and be quite misunderstood or impatiently dismissed. It is true that written words occur in combination and thus affect each other's meaning. But single words nonetheless refer to root ideas or objects in a way that can be disregarded only at the cost of confusion. Make sure, then, that you know what you are saying when you use words which you have often seen and heard but which remain hazy in their denotation; for example, *fortuitous* or *fulsome*. The first does not mean *fortunate;* the second does not mean *complete*. The hint here scarcely needs saying: USE ONLY WORDS THAT YOU UNDERSTAND. Don't trust vague similarities of sound. Keep a dictionary at your elbow and when in doubt, verify.

Above all, don't fall a victim to the false teaching that excuses mistakes in the choice of words by saying that if the drift somehow comes through you have done well enough; the reader ought to help you out by making a little effort of imagination. In the first place no one is obliged to read your prose, and if it proves confusing and irritating its proper resting place is not the bookshelf but the wastebasket. To write carelessly is discourtesy to the reader who is taking pains to follow and who will appreciate, just as you do, the author who makes reading a pleasure instead of a task.

In the second place, note that within the range of simple and familiar words you yourself would not tolerate any switching of meanings. If someone testified to an event that called for the word *whisper,* you would not accept the word *hiss* or *mutter* or *murmur* in its place. Each of these denotes a different kind of sound or loudness, and a faithful report demands the right word. If *wet* and *damp, warm* and *hot, bitter* and *sour* are not interchangeable, neither are *fortunate* and *fortuitous*. Distinctions do not become hairsplitting just because the words have three syllables instead of one. And there is no law requiring anybody to use words of three syllables whose meaning escapes him.

Besides a denotation, many words possess a connotation. The two together correspond to the "meaning and force" mentioned above. The force or connotation of *mutter* differs from that of *murmur* in that the first suggests a rough, harsh, and perhaps incomplete utterance, whereas the second is soft and gentle and can apply to a complete phrase or sentence. The small child who said "This ice cream is defective" was trying out his vocabulary without regard to connotation and had to be told that a defect somehow implies a structure or surface flawed at certain points. The ice cream had turned sour all over; it had *spoiled,* not become *defective.*

Often, pairs of words from the same root have diverged very usefully by acquiring different connotations. *Wordage* connotes the number of words in a piece of writing; *verbiage* applies to words that mean little or nothing. *Masterly* defines the ability of a master (artist); *masterful* refers to a person who leads firmly or dominates. *Elemental* is applied to the great forces of nature or passions of man; *elementary,* to the simplest parts of a subject or substance. *Precipitous* implies a sharp descent or fall; *precipitate,* a hasty move; and so on. Watch for those dangerous pairs!

There is only one way to learn the connotations of words, and that is by reading good writers, to whom connotations are as obvious as the qualities of a diamond are to a jeweler. True, you may find in some dictionaries a clue to connotations given through illustrative comparisons. You will be told: *"famous* is applied to persons or things that have received wide public attention; *renowned* suggests a person named publicly again and again for outstanding achievement; *notorious* suggests a person unfavorably known and talked about; *eminent* stresses the conspicuous superiority of persons or things." The list goes on to *celebrated, distinguished, noted, notable,* and *illustrious,* the dangerous pair being *notable* (good) and *notorious* (bad).

But such examples will not be given for every word you need when writing, and you cannot stop every few minutes to look up and memorize unsuspected connotations. The right word must present itself to you as you compose, and the happy choice is possible only when your stock of words is large and accurate. Only reading will supply these requisites.

Among the words that everybody knows and uses in casual conversation are a good many that professional writers avoid and critics denounce as JARGON. These words are also known as *vogue words,* because they come into fashion and go out of it very fast. This lack of staying power is one reason why they should be avoided; in a few months or years they will no longer be understood—like slang. An even stronger reason for avoidance is that they lack definiteness. Such words as *interface, viable, commitment, motivation, parameter,* and *dimension* show up as jargon because they recur over and over again in many different contexts without telling us exactly what each intends. Thus *dimension* is a maid-of-all-work doing duty for *facet, aspect, feature, trait, characteristic, charm, power, value, merit, novelty,* and many other ideas, of which one and one only is the most apt and true in the given situation. The jargon word conceals that one from our view. *Viable,* like *dimension,* has a strict meaning (capable of living), but that meaning is blurred and lost when the word is used for every variety of the possible: *practical, congenial, convenient, economical, popular, lasting, durable, tested, seasoned, fruitful.* Using jargon is like referring to every object as a thingamajig.

These cautions about single words apply with the same force and for the same reasons to phrases and idioms. A good writer knows that *hard labor* is a term of the criminal law and does not mean *hard work;* that to *have words* with someone is to quarrel, not to engage in small talk; that to *look askance* does not mean show a questioning face but look with suspicion or disapproval—nothing to do with *ask.* Again you cannot guess your way about meanings; and since misconceptions of this sort, picked up from ill-informed speakers and publicists, do not disclose themselves, you must read writers whose diction you can trust because it follows standard usage. Only the shock of discovering that good writers do not use *connive* to mean *plan shady deals,* or *transpire* to mean *happen* will wake you up to the shortcomings of your present vocabulary.

Linking words together

Prose, as we saw earlier, seeks the clearest possible combination of words so as to convey to the reader the very thought in the writer's mind. The act of writing is therefore called com-position, or putting together, and the shortest definition of the art ever given—by Jonathan Swift—is "Proper words in proper places." Having paid our respects to words (quite literally respecting their meanings at the core and at the fringe), we go on to consider the required ways of combining them, which we may call linking.

In most modern languages, English included, LINKING IS ALL-IMPORTANT, because the message depends on the sequence of words. "The boy hit the ball" raises a very different image from "The ball hit the boy." The same five words in a slightly modified order signify opposite facts. Nor does the influence of linking stop at this simple inversion of subject and object. In most of the sentences that a writer finds himself putting together, the placing of the various parts determines, first, whether the author has said what he meant and, second, whether that meaning is plain or hard to see. It is possible to frame a simple sentence that falsifies its own intention and an accurate sentence that is hard to figure out. Both these errors are avoided only by correct linking.

To a native speaker and writer the elementary forms of linking present no difficulty. He writes *I am, we are, they are;* he is never tempted to say *we am, I is*. Yet on the longer stretch he may do just that; he writes: "I who as a born and bred countryman, is used to roughing it . . ." which amounts to *"I who is = I is."* Or again (a very common fault): "She is one of those women who is at her best in an emergency." This says in plain sight *women who is*. Even more common, perhaps, is the false link: "They were fond of people whom they thought were likely to help them" = *people whom were likely*.

The hint here is that vigilance is needed even in the simplest types of linking when its requirements are concealed by the presence of surrounding words. It is fatally easy to write: "The poor quality of the books, pictures, and periodicals *make* us wonder whether the library committee . . ." The plural *make* results from the nearness of *books, pictures, and periodicals*, although the true subject is the singular *poor quality*, which should lead to *makes*.

All these errors show the need for developing that "acute consciouness" of the word watcher. They also show what is meant by the maxim that good writing depends on good thinking. It takes thought to overcome the "attraction" of plural nouns on nearby verbs and logic to catch even more plausible inconsistencies. Darwin wrote: "This archipelago consists of ten principal islands, of which five exceed the others in size." Figure out the confusion here and speculate as to what may have caused it.

One kind of linking fault in particular betrays the amateur. That link is the relative pronoun in its several forms: *who, which, that*. A full display of their typical mismanagement would cover many pages; all that can be said here is that all relative pronouns must be unmistakably attached at both ends—that is the only way they truly link. As to the nearer end there is usually no difficulty. In "the woman I love and who loves me," the relative *who* is clearly tied to *loves* by simple nearness; and the other end is also well attached—to *the woman,* for there is no other noun to cling to. Trouble comes when a relative pronoun is preceded by two or more possible forerunners (antecedents), so that the reader is stopped by doubt and has to choose one antecedent as more probable than the rest. Consider this sentence: "Almost as much as the loud, hoggish people, they disliked the hotel, the view, and the climate, which in the travel brochure had been touted as the main attraction." Name the attraction.

The careless writer, if he thinks about his pronouns at all, seems to rely on a vague trust that the reader will link the pronoun with the last noun, especially if it is the word just preceding. But that is to lean on a nonexistent prop. There is no such rule, and it could not cover all cases if there were. What is the reader to make of this: "The interpretation of the law which says that negligence is not actionable if it is also shared by the victim is not one that can be traced to the beginnings of the law." Not just the relative *which,* but other pronouns in that sentence add to the grand confusion. Start by asking what the *which* refers to. Is there "a law which says" or only "an interpretation which says"? If we suspend judgment and read further, we may work out an answer on the strength of "one that can be traced," which suggests that *interpretation* is the subject throughout; but we are thrown off again by "the beginnings of the law," where *law* suddenly means the whole body of laws and not solely the law of negligence. So much work is too much to ask of a reader.

Notice, too, how one link dropped can endanger what follows. The uncertainty about *which* makes a close reader suspicious at every point, so that when he comes to the clause "if it is shared" he hesitates and asks himself whether *it* goes back to *negligence* or to *interpretation,* for one can "share an interpretation." Such a sentence is beyond patching up. It has to be done over entire, possibly like this: "The law of negligence did not always include the idea of contributory negligence— negligence shared by the victim and thus not actionable. That interpretation came late in the history of the Common Law."

The handling of all pronouns in English is particularly difficult because English nouns have no gender. In other languages noun gender is reflected in the pronoun, forming a visible link across intervening words. But even where English has this advantage, in the *he/she/him/her/his/ her* series that applies to persons, trouble is hard to avoid: "Susan told her sister Mary that she thought she ought to go and see their grandmother." Who is the *she* after *thought,* Susan or Mary? With objects, *it* and *its* can even more easily produce ambiguity. In short, the writer who wants to be read—let alone respected as a good craftsman—must watch his pronouns with a ferociously critical eye; it is fatal for him to assume that what he knows and sees plainly in the thicket of *who*'s, *she*'s, or *its*'s will be clear to his reader.

Linking ideas

We now pass to the linking that occurs without words—by simple closeness. Every sentence achieves meaning by juxtaposing its parts in a certain order. And not merely the clarity of the prose but its chance of being pleasing depends on the good management of these linkings of larger parts. The hint here is: JOIN TOGETHER WHAT BELONGS TO-GETHER in your mind or in the outward facts, KEEP APART THE THINGS THAT ARE SEPARATE. That sounds too obvious to need saying; yet the principle is so often violated that it must be repeated until it is believed in and acted on automatically. In speaking, one may string one's ideas together haphazardly; for instance: "I'll meet you at the bridge to take the bus in plenty of time." In writing, the linking must be: "I'll meet you at the bridge in plenty of time to take the bus," for it is the *meeting* which you promise to make in good time.

When a number of descriptive details must be mentioned, their proper order takes a little thought. "He was found in a ditch with a broken leg dressed in casual attire." A ditch with a broken leg is an unlikely sight, and a leg is not usually dressed independently of the whole body. The true scheme of things is: He was found /with a broken leg/ in a ditch *and* dressed, etc. The *and* prevents a false link and substitutes a parallel: he was found—how? *with* a broken leg *and dressed* . . .

Bad linking on this scale comes from yielding to afterthoughts with-out reorganizing the sentence to express their true relation to each other and to the main subject. For example: "The astronauts will describe what it's like to fly the space shuttle during a press conference at the Chamber of Commerce on Thursday"; "$5,000 reward for information leading to the conviction for burglary of any A.B. Service Station"; "Illinois Man Pulls Needle from Foot He Swallowed 60 Years Ago." One might suppose that these absurd linkings would give themselves away and would be corrected in the course of revising; yet they ap-peared in print like many others that are not funny but only stupid: "Three hours of screening were devoted to each child and given certifi-cates"; "He proceeded to deplore the increase of country-house rob-beries with overtones of social ease"; "He built his house with a heavy mortgage and a two-story porch."

The cure for all such blunders is: THINK!—think either before putting down the nonsense or afterwards, in revising. At that time be also on the watch for faulty links due to the modern habit of piling up modifiers without regard to which word goes with which. In "the report on a thermal ice suppression test was released . . .," one is puzzled by *thermal ice,* which sounds contradictory. Actually the operation was but the diverting of warm (thermal) by-products from power plants to melt or prevent (not *suppress*) ice in the Great Lakes. It is fancy phrasings based on crowded linking that make modern writing so tiresomely bad. One writer complaining in *The New York Times* of the city subways could evidently not come out with "the danger of derailments"; he felt compelled to say "track-and-wheel disengagement possibilities." But perhaps he was satirizing.

To conclude about linking, note some supposed RULES STILL CURRENT WHICH ARE NOT RULES AT ALL. The first is the bugbear of the split infinitive. The link between *to* and its verb, it is said, should never be broken. The truth is that the split is desirable whenever its avoidance would prove awkward or affected or misleading; *e.g.,* "I hesitate suddenly to call off the meeting" is both affected and inaccurate, for it isn't the hesitation that's sudden. "To call off suddenly the meeting" would sound odd because it breaks the proper link between *call off* and *meeting.* "To suddenly call off" is manifestly right. Note further that in compound tenses it is not a split at all to insert an adverb between the auxiliary and the main verb: "To have duly registered an objection," "to have sincerely regretted," "to have been sorely tempted" are the correct forms, and any shifting of the *-ly* inserts to another place shows ignorance of the language.

A second false rule prohibits putting a preposition at the end of a sentence, as if it had dropped its proper link at an earlier spot. Nothing, on the contrary, is more idiomatic in English than this practice of winding up a statement strongly with a preposition. Just think of the familiar lines in Hamlet's soliloquy: "The heartache and the thousand natural shocks that flesh is heir to," and again "Rather bear those ills we have than fly to others that we know not of." Speed and force would be lost, let alone rhythm, if Hamlet said "shocks to which flesh is heir" and "others of which we know not."

Finally, there is a modern superstition, chiefly American, which calls it wrong to use *which* and *that* interchangeably or to use *and which* without a preceding *which.* To discuss these two points would use up scarce space. For a treatment of the pros and cons the reader is referred to All You Need to Know About Grammar (A Review of English Grammar: II.K.2. and III.E.1.e.) in this volume. Here it is enough to say that absolute decrees of this sort rarely help the writer who wants to improve his prose style; rather he must understand the conditions in which some usage is or is not appropriate. But this flexibility does not extend to set phrases or what one rhetorician has called "cast-iron idiom." WHEN YOU USE PHRASES ESTABLISHED BY LONG USE, LEAVE THEM AS THEY ARE. Do not twist, invert, or decorate them. Let the advertiser write of "cake at its tastiest best"; stick to *at its best,* and similarly with *day by day, in the long run, first and foremost,* and the like. Do not dress up *day by beautiful day,* etc. The links have been welded solid by time and repeated use.

Beyond correctness: writing with style

The recommendation of taste just given brings us quite naturally to consider in prose those features which go beyond correctness and elementary clarity and produce good writing in the honorific sense—writing which is agreeable to read. Among these additional features are tone, rhythm, variety, vividness, euphony, and a number of others, most of which cannot be obtained by prescription, like vitamins to supply a deficiency. The virtues of good prose come only by practice coupled with some talent. Yet it is possible to learn about these qualities and how their presence or absence in writing decisively affects the power of the prose and contributes to the ease and pleasure of reading.

It was the perception of this bond between matter and manner that led laborious writers like Benjamin Franklin and Robert Louis Stevenson to read a passage in an admired author and try to reproduce from memory both its sense and its effects. The first two or three attempts gave these students a shocking insight into the truth that when one thinks one knows what one has just read, one has in fact retained but a small portion of it.

This training exercise is not proposed here as one to follow nowadays. Our good models are of too many different kinds. It is better and safer to read the classics and the moderns with an eye to the resources of the language as a whole, rather than with the aim of imitating any one style. A good style is the outgrowth of individual interest and effort, not a deliberate construction, and least of all a copy of another style. The hints in this section will accordingly deal with these main objects of attention: tone, rhythm, variety, and forthrightness. These should be, once again, objects of close attention, of acute consciousness, in both what one writes and what one reads.

To speak of tone in writing implies that not all words and expressions stand on the same level. In this way they correspond to life as we know it. Some matters are trivial, others important; some occasions are solemn, others laughable. Everybody understands the difference between formal and informal and more or less instinctively adapts manners to persons and events along an imagined scale between these pairs of extremes. Language is part of manners and is equally adaptable.

What this social reality requires of the writer is that he decide from the start of a piece of work what audience it is intended for. This decision will determine his tone. Some presidents of the United States have broadcast "fireside chats" which they probably wrote out in advance. The tone differed from that of their messages to Congress on the state of the union. Tone arises from the choice of words, length of sentences, type of allusions, use or avoidance of contractions, and forms of syntax. A good writer who prepares a text to be read aloud will use constructions different from those he would use in an essay on the same subject.

With so many means and effects available, tone can vary widely and its species become difficult to define. Speaking generally, TONE SHOULD BE SUSTAINED AND UNIFORM AND IT SHOULD NEVER BE FORCED. Accordingly, a good many negative hints on the subject will bear repeating. The one intolerable tone is that which talks down to the reader, treats him as a child or an imbecile. No matter how much you know about your topic, your presentation of it should be modest and civil, as from equal to equal—the tone of good instruction or exposition. You may explain what you alone have discovered, and the explanation may start with the rudiments, but the tone should not vary from the level chosen at the outset. An audience of specialists may be addressed more briskly than a mixed one, but the writer's attitude toward both must be that of respect for the reader's intelligence, and that holds true also for writings aimed at children: the vocabulary must be simpler, but the tone remains the same.

Almost as offensive as talking down is the affected tone, whether it employs airs and graces, or jocularity, or the pretended intimacy of "you-and-me, chum," or a supernatural gravity. Any kind of "stance," role, or pretension—make-believe, in short—is bad; it does not fool anybody, and it cannot be kept up without distracting the reader's mind from what is being said (if anything). It must be added that after Hemingway the very simple style, with many repetitions of the same monosyllable, is dangerous to imitate; just as after Kipling the "knowing" style, in which the writer refers continually to things the reader cannot know but keeps hoping to learn, is soon tedious. As for the gutter tone, which has had some success on the stage, its vocabulary seems too restricted for matters to be communicated through print without accompanying action.

In addition to these tones, which might be said to go with certain character traits, real or assumed, there are two other kinds which call for discussion, because they are prevalent and thus influence innumerable writers who never suspect that tone is involved. These two are the abstract and the metaphorical. Though dealt with separately here, they are sometimes combined. Then, like many mergers, they offer the worst features of each.

The abstract style is marked by an excess of nouns, most often nouns in *-tion, -sion, -avity,* and *-ility.* This noun plague, as it has been called, necessitates a matching number of *by, to, with,* and *of* to tie the lot together in long rows. The verbs then fall into the passive voice or swing tirelessly between *is* and *was, has* and *had*. For example, "This memorandum is addressed to the perspective that a self-examination of the probable future status of an institution such as ours might adopt in the eventuality that the decentralization of similar institutions throughout the state is implemented through legislative action after decision of the recently appointed Commission on Charitable and Educational Institutions."

This style, now frequent in business, government, art discussions, and academic life, is derived from science, which properly insists that laboratory results be set down in flat technical prose without personality or emotion. Because the experiments consist in manipulating objects clearly indicated by technical nouns, these and passive verbs suffice to make things clear; and any pain in following the description is soon relieved by the really exciting equations. None of this obtains in the world to which that neutral language has been transferred. The upshot is what you see in the sentence above—total absence of charm and of lucidity. The reason the meaning is hard to grasp is that the terms are indefinite and inappropriate; they raise vague and yet conflicting ideas; they give no handles whereby to hitch them into a continuous train of thought. To *address a perspective,* a *self-examination of future status,* which (again) might *adopt the perspective*—all these are beyond conceiving.

A further ill effect arising from this jam of abstract nouns is that the prose lacks any perceptible rhythm. It goes on and on, could stop anywhere, or proceed without end. Rhythm is not only pleasurable in itself, it helps understanding by forecasting a sequence of beats or a measured space, into which the right phrase falls and gives the ear the satisfaction of fitness.

For this purpose good prose employs many forms of the *parallel construction,* or "matching parts." When expressed in like forms or turns of phrase, a comparison, a contrast, a description, a qualification slips more readily into the mind; the way has been prepared. For example, "Before graduation, he wasted his time; after, he wasted his money." Change the second half to "afterwards he ran through his money like a spendthrift," and you lose both sharpness and rhythmic force.

The device must not be overused—and of course it does not always take the short and quick form of our example. In any case matching parts gives only one kind of balance. Another kind is secured by handling the weight (length, sound, complexity) of the parts so as to avoid feeble endings or abruptness, as in "Although it is unusual for a fledgling navigator, especially in a sailboat with few facilities and in unfamiliar waters, to make his first landfall within half a dozen miles, he did." Even the inattentive reader notices that the long opening clause is top-heavy in relation to the rest. The ear requires at least "he did it."

For the ear participates in silent reading just as it does in following speech; that is why one can discuss prose rhythm. Writers who cram together on the page words that would be difficult to utter are deficient in an important organ of style and should practice reading their works aloud. The reader will be impeded by the vocal obstacle whether he knows the cause or not. In reverse, the mind's ear is exploited by some writers who hope to create continuous excitement through the short, sharp cracks of monosyllables and explosive consonants. The attempt defeats itself. The relentless beat fatigues, and attention wanders as a relief from overstimulation.

The hint to be found in these observations is that in writing, formal or informal, VARIETY IS MORE IMPORTANT THAN ANY OTHER SINGLE FEATURE. Remember that words on the page lack the benefit of vocal shifts of pitch and stress; these must be made up for by changes of form, rhythm, and relations, which together contribute to emphasis. The deplorable noun-plague sentence from which we started drains away without emphasis. It flows in monotone, offers no high point to fix attention and memory. A string of similar sentences—and that is what most reports and papers on serious subjects nowadays consist of—is inescapably narcotic. A conscientious writer who prefers his readers awake can only keep them so by varying the shape, length, and syntax of his sentences. Let him study in a handbook the uses of simple, compound, and complex sentences if he is not already familiar with these forms; and let him GUARD AGAINST THE CLOSE REPETITION OF OPENING PHRASES leading to identical structures: *There is . . ., It is the . . . which . . ., Another factor is . . ., However . . ., Moreover . . ., In addition . . ., On the other hand . . ., Now we turn . . . .*

Having used the abstract noun-plague style as a negative model from which to draw the lessons of rhythm, emphasis, and variety, we have to take account of its apparent opposite in modern writing, the metaphorical style. The abstract is a borrowing from science; the metaphorical from poetry. It goes like this: "Areas of societal needs can be pinpointed in the light of the germinating cells at the bottom of the power hierarchy, whose architecture is not so stable as the picture most people have of it in their day-to-day framework of color-blind assumptions."

A ghost of an idea may be supposed to hover over that mess of images, but that is all. Tone and form resemble those of the noun-ridden sentence. Metaphor has merely replaced abstraction and has achieved the feat of being just as vague. By challenging each image one can see how uncommunicative the metaphorical mode is. How does one pinpoint an area? What are these germinating cells and how do they generate light? What is the architecture of the power hierarchy? What sort of architecture is it that is not so stable as a picture? What is a day-to-day framework and how do assumptions become color-blind? Even if these questions had rational answers, the succession of images defies analysis and shows an entire absence of tenable thought.

The metaphorical evades responsibility through the deliberate or careless *impropriety of terms*. Why *pinpoint* an area when it is just as easy to *find* it or *name* it? Why are small groups of struggling people *germinating cells*? But are we sure we have hit upon the hidden meanings? If as a reader one takes the given words seriously, the meaning is anybody's guess. It is only by a daring translation that a glimmer appears. And for a subject as important and complex as people's needs in society, a glimmer is not enough. Our conclusion must be that the two most usual tones (styles) adopted by our supposedly serious writers, other than novelists, are not only hard to read and hopelessly puzzling, but also wanting in the prime quality of forthrightness.

To put the point more generally, if the thought in the writer's mind is to survive whole—let alone get carried swiftly into another mind— the words for it must be used soberly and exactly. We have come full circle in our set of hints. We began with the meaning of single words, and we end with the sense of words combined. Knowing what each word or phrase means and implies once it is set down next to its fellows is the prerequisite to even the most modest success in writing. After considering denotation, connotation, jargon, linking, tone, rhythm, variety, and straightforwardness, the next-to-last hint offered here can serve as a summary: CHOOSE FOR EVERYTHING YOU SEE OR CONCEIVE THE SHORT, CONCRETE, AND COMMON WORD THAT YOU FULLY UNDERSTAND IN PREFERENCE TO THE LONG, ABSTRACT, UNCOMMON, VOGUISH, OR METAMORPHICAL TERM WHICH NEITHER YOU NOR YOUR READER CAN BE SURE OF.

If that is the next-to-last hint, what is the final one? It is less a hint than an imperative: REVISE, REVISE, REVISE. All good writing means rewriting. In revising your text you must never relax your alertness to language nor forget the artful ways noted in your reading. Writing well demands an unflagging attention to language; and a tireless critical eye must be bent on your diction, your linkings, your tone, before you can be said to have exhausted the means at your disposal, before you can hope *to have written*.

JACQUES BARZUN

Literary Style

Literary style involves the selection and organization of the features of language for expressive effects, and includes all uses of sound patterns, words, figures of speech, images, and syntactic forms. In an absolute sense, the word "style" (Lat. *stilus*, "writing-rod") means a good or distinguished manner with language, as in: "Proust has style," or "Theodore Dreiser lacks style." Prose style only is treated here.

Views on style

Aristotle, Cicero, and Quintilian treated style as the proper adornment of thought. In this view, which prevailed throughout the Renaissance period, devices of style can be catalogued. The essayist or orator is expected to frame his ideas with the help of model sentences and prescribed kinds of "figures" suitable to his mode of discourse.

Jonathan Swift's dictum on style, "Proper Words in Proper Places" (in *A Letter to a Young Gentleman, Lately Enter'd into Holy Orders,* 1721), stands midway between the idea of style as something properly added to thoughts, and the 20th-century ideas that derive from Charles Bally (1865-1947), the Swiss philologist. According to followers of Bally, style in language arises from the possibility of choice among alternative forms of expression, as for example, between "children," "kids," "youngsters," and "youths," each of which has a different evocative value. Any expression may give rise to a variety of effects, and the effect will be more forceful as the expression deviates from normal usage. Thus style depends on choice, evocation, polyvalency, and deviation in language. This theory emphasizes the relation between style and linguistics.

Style is also seen as a mark of character. Buffon's famous epigram, *"Le style est l'homme même"* ("Style is the man himself") in his *Discours sur le style* (1753), and Schopenhauer's definition of style as "the physiognomy of the mind" suggest that, no matter how calculatingly choices may be made, a writer's style will bear the mark of his personality. Style is "the mental picture of the man who writes," to quote Edmund Gosse's article "Style" for the 11th edition of *Encyclopædia Britannica* (1911). This view would account for the underlying consistency of individual styles. An experienced writer is able to rely on the power of his habitual choices of sounds, words, and syntactic patterns to convey his personality or fundamental outlook. Some effects of the possible choices are illustrated below.

Syntax

Different expressive effects arise from every kind of phrase, clause, and sentence; from coordination and subordination, parallelism, word order, grammar, and other sentence features.

LOOSE AND PERIODIC SENTENCES. The distinction between the loose sentence (in which the main clause is completed early and other main clauses or subordinate ones follow) and the periodic (in which the main clause is not completed until the end) is central to style. Tacitus used the loose structure, with curt main clauses, for swift movement and smart concision: *"Quattuor principes ferro interempti: trina bella civilia, plura externa ac plerumque permixta: prosperae in Oriente, adversae in Occidente res: turbatum Illyricum, Galliae nutantes, perdomita Britannia et statim omissa"* ("Four emperors perished by the sword; there were three civil wars; there were more with foreign enemies; there were often wars that had both characters at once. There was success in the East, and disaster in the West. There were disturbances in Illyricum; Gaul wavered in its allegiance; Britain was thoroughly subdued and immediately abandoned"; *Historiae,* I, ii, *c.* A.D. 110). Sir Thomas Malory demonstrates the ease and flow of loose structure; Rabelais shows how flexible and informal it can be. Periodic structure is more apt to increase tension, heighten detail, and command attention, since the meaning is held in suspense. Cicero used a lengthy periodic structure to great emotional effect in the "grand style" (*genus grande*) of his oratory; Macaulay used a short variety, with dramatic twists in meaning, for surprise, as in "To this step, taken in the mere wantonness of tyranny, and in criminal ignorance or more criminal contempt of public feeling, our country owes her freedom" (*History of England,* 1848).

PARALLELISM. Parallelism can be a means of ordering, emphasizing, or pointing out relations in the sentence; to some degree it is a feature of all good prose. In John Lyly's *Euphues* (1578) transverse alliteration is used to draw attention to parallel structure, as in "Ah my Philautus, if the *w*asting of our *m*oney might not *d*ehort us, yet the *w*ounding of our *m*inds should *d*eter us . . ." Such emphasis can cloy; but parallelism lends wit and authority to the antithetic aphorism, as in La Rochefoucauld's *"Nous aimons toujours ceux qui nous admirent, et nous n'aimons pas toujours ceux que nous admirons"* ("We always love those who admire us, but we do not always love those whom we admire"; *Maximes,* 1665). John Henry Newman, in his *Apologia pro vita sua* (1864), used chiasmic or inverted parallel structure for strong emphasis: "I have changed in many things: in this I have not."

WORD ORDER. Expressive effects of word order are most forceful when words are in prominent position (*e.g.,* at the end of the sentence) or out of their usual order. In Thomas Love Peacock's sentence "King Gwythno had feasted joyously, and had sung his new ode to a chosen party of his admiring subjects, admidst their, of course, enthusiastic applause" (*The Misfortunes of Elphin,* 1829), humor results from the placing of the "of course" in a logical, rather than a conventional, position. Flaubert's word order can mirror psychological processes, as in *"Au milieu de cette ombre, par endroits, brillaient des blancheurs de baïonnettes"* (*L'Éducation sentimentale,* 1869). Here the order of the words follows the order of impressions as they occur to the onlooker: *"ombre"* (darkness), *"par endroits"* (here and there), *"brillaient"* (shone), *"blancheurs"* (whiteness), and *"baïonnettes"* (bayonets).

GRAMMAR. Different grammatical forms give rise to different expressive effects. In "Bill kissed Sally" and in "Sally was kissed by Bill" the same event is described; but the passive form focuses attention on Sally (and what happened to her) and the active on Bill (and what he did). In dialogue, and in psychological realism, grammatical conventions are sometimes violated for effect. For example, Dickens put into the mouth of his quick-witted scalawag Mr. Alfred Jingle such staccato asyntactical speeches as "Epic poem,—ten thousand lines—revolution of July—composed it on the spot—Mars by day, Apollo by night,—bang the field-piece, twang the lyre" (*The Pickwick Papers,* 1836–37). In such sentences as "Invent a story for some proverb which?" James Joyce depicted half-thoughts running through Mr. Bloom's mind in *Ulysses* (1922).

OTHER SENTENCE FEATURES. Complication in structure, sentence length, punctuation, and various typographical devices can all be expressive. Thomas Carlyle used heavy punctuation, italics, and many capitals in involuted sentences to underline his role as an original prophet, as in

"All Anarchy, all Evil, Injustice, is, by the nature of it, *dragon's-teeth;* suicidal, and cannot endure" (*The French Revolution,* 1837).

Words

WORD-FORMS. Although word-formation normally allows little scope for expressive choice, since most word-forms are fixed, some styles make effective use of it. Lewis Carroll's portmanteau word "chortle" ("chuckle" + "snort") is a device of comic wit; Gerard Manley Hopkins's "inscape" ("inside" + "landscape") expresses a new vision of reality. James Joyce, in *Ulysses,* freely compounded words (*e.g.,* "softcreak-footed," "husbandwords," and "swiftseen") for various rhythmic and emphatic effects. In *Finnegans Wake* (1939) he developed a system of "polyphonic" terms to delineate the subconscious mind, where meanings (often comically) merge and overlap: *e.g.,* "funnominal," "jinglish janglage," and "tellibly divilcult." Dickens, with such forms as "buzzums," "creetur," " 'umble," and "excuge," vigorously characterized the speakers in his novels; and misspellings, in fictional epistles and dialogue, for example, can be very expressive.

WORD-MEANINGS. The widest scope for style is offered at the level of word-meanings. Phrases such as "the little house," "the diminutive house," and "the petite house" have overlapping or synonymous meanings, but "little" may suggest endearment as well as size; "diminutive," good construction; and "petite," prettiness. Synonymy enables the writer to choose the word that has the evocative value he wants. Samuel Johnson habitually used general, abstract, and nonemotive words: "This quality of looking forward into futurity seems the unavoidable condition of being, whose motions are gradual, and whose life is progressive" (*The Rambler,* no. 2, 1750). Many English essayists have preferred particular, concrete, and emotive words; but great thoughts, Johnson claimed, "are always general." Evocative values are attached also to slang, technical, dialect, colloquial, formal literary, and standard contemporary words, as well as to archaisms and foreign expressions. George Meredith used the archaic "damsel" to suggest the immaturity of a heroine; Ronald Firbank, in "Mrs. Henedge lived in a small house with killing stairs just off Chesham Place" (*Vainglory,* 1915), characterized Mrs. Henedge with a colloquially used "killing," in stark and witty contrast to the standard words around it. Only a mention can be made here of imagery and ambiguity as rich sources of possibility in word style. In general, the gap between the image and the object is smaller in prose than in poetry; farfetched images are a mark of preciosity or inflated style.

Sounds

RHYTHM. Aristotle maintained that while prose should not lack rhythm it should avoid metre; and metrical prose often has achieved only that "flatness" and "disenchantment" that R. L. Stevenson complained of. Lyly used the classical schemes of isocolon (like-length in phrases or clauses) and parison (like-length + like-form) to give close rhythmic order to prose, as in "I will to Athens there to toss my books, no more in Naples to live with fair looks" (*Euphues*), where rhyme is another device of order; and Dickens used isocolon for emphasis, as in "So I called myself Pip, and came to be called Pip" (*Great Expectations*, 1860).

Thomas Mann imitated the musical "leitmotiv" of Wagner by assigning special rhythms (and words) to recurrent characters and symbols, as in *"Die blonde Inge, Ingeborg Holm," "Inge Holm, die lustige Inge,"* and *"Ingeborg, die blonde Inge"* (*Tonio Kröger*, 1903). In general, except in prophetic writing (*e.g.*, Nietzsche, and parts of the Bible) and oratory (*e.g.*, Cicero, and Winston Churchill), good prose avoids insistent or obvious rhythms.

PHONEMIC PATTERN. The expressive effect of any phrase, clause, or sentence is partly determined by the pattern of its speech-sounds or phonemes. Alliteration lends dignity and force to the 14th-century devotional prose of Richard Rolle of Hampole, as in "It wanes in to wrechednes, þe welth of þis worlde." Later writers have also used alliteration to point out and underline relations in meaning, as in Jane Austen's simple "She watched him well" (*Emma*, 1815). Unobtrusive sound repetition is vital to euphony as well as to clarity. In Emily Brontë's sentence "She rang the bell till it broke with a twang; I entered leisurely" (*Wuthering Heights*, 1847), contrasting sounds fit contrasting actions, and euphony—in its fullest sense of "pleasing sound"—is perfectly achieved.

ENCYCLOPÆDIA BRITANNICA

Figures of Speech

Figures of speech are more or less intentional deviations from literal statement or common usage in formal or informal language. The term is strictly a misnomer, since it applies to both spoken and written language; however, most systematic study of figures of speech (as a branch of rhetoric) has been directed toward their use in literature.

This article is concerned primarily with the use of figures of speech in English and, to some extent, in other European languages; their use in languages outside the Western classical tradition is considered in the concluding section, *Usage in Non-European Cultures*.

Introduction

Textbook treatment of figures of speech often leaves the impression that they are ornamental additions, found chiefly in sophisticated literary language; the student may even be invited to pull them out of poems like plums from a pudding. Figures of speech are, however, found in primitive literatures, even in those still in the oral stage. and in non-literary writings, informal conversation, and the talk of children and illiterates. Slang consists mainly of metaphors, metonymies, and synecdoches, as do euphemisms in everyday use; onomatopoeia plays a large part in the speech of young children, especially when they first begin to talk, and in nursery rhymes and nursery stories; and swearing often exemplifies metaphor, metonymy, or hyperbole. Crossword puzzles of the more intellectual kind consist almost entirely of figures of speech, each used as an isolated unit; so do such language pastimes as acrostics and conundrums. Greeting-card rhymes, Christmas and party cracker mottoes, advertising slogans, newspaper headlines, the captions of cartoons, the mottoes of families and institutions also often use figures of speech, generally for humorous, mnemonic, or eye-catching purposes. Their use is also exemplified in such traditional forms as the proverb and riddle.

463

They appear, in fact, to be an integral part of language itself (and, going behind language, of the development of consciousness and sensory perception, and of the earliest thought processes), rather than merely a set of ornamental devices. They are often used unconsciously in everyday conversation and writing; and how far the use of metaphor and some other figures of speech is fully deliberate in even the most finished poetry and oratory is open to question. It has been suggested—by the classical and neoclassical poets and critics, with their theories of inspiration, as well as by prophets, and by some aestheticians and psychologists—that in states of heightened emotion or sensibility some poets, orators, and prose writers may use figurative language without fully conscious intention, to express their profound sense of resemblances. The psychoanalytical approach to dreams assumes that they too are partly metaphorical, symbolic, or allegorical.

In everyday speech and writing and in literature the chief functions of figures of speech are probably to emphasize or to clarify. Other functions include the manifestation of exuberance by verbal play, the giving of tone or atmosphere to discourse, and the stimulation of thought by startling the reader or listener. Through constant use, many metaphors (e.g., "wooden-headed," "he flared up," "he's a wolf," "she's a cat," "their mother has nerves of steel") and similes (e.g., "as warm as toast," "as fierce as a lion," "as white as a sheet") have become clichés and rather than performing their proper function as figures of speech may indicate some poverty of language in the person using them.

Indeed, metaphor is so natural a part of language that much of it is buried in etymology. Even the highly educated speaker is unaware that he is using a fossilized metaphor when, for example, he uses the verb "to bless," which, derived from Old English blóedsian (a word originally connected with the sprinkling of blood in religious ritual), acquired its modern meaning when, with the arrival of Christianity, it was used to translate the Latin benedicere. Similarly, the word "calm" comes, through Latin, from Greek kauma, meaning "the heat of the day," when many people (especially in Mediterranean and Eastern countries) like to rest; and "to rebuke" is derived ultimately from an Old French word meaning "to cut down wood"—so that the slang expression "cut him down to size" has surprisingly respectable antecedents.

Use

IN SPEECH. A few examples of figures of speech used in casual conversation, generally unwittingly, will demonstrate the naturalness of their application in everyday contexts. Thus, to say "This room is a pigsty!" or "That problem is your headache, not mine" is to speak of one thing in terms of another; *i.e.*, to use metaphor. Use of simile (a comparison, usually indicated by "like" or "as") is exemplified in the sentences "His letter was like a slap in the face" and "These buns are as hard as rocks." Personification—speaking of an abstract quality or inanimate object as if it were a person—is exemplified in "Drink has got hold of him"; metonymy—using the name of one thing for another closely related to it—in "The Town Hall may object to the scheme" or "How would the Pentagon react?"; synecdoche—use of a part to imply the whole—in "He spends too much time chasing skirts"; hyperbole—exaggeration for the sake of effect—in "I dropped the jar, and there I was swimming in a sea of honey"; the rhetorical question—asked for effect, with no answer expected—in "Have you made up your mind to break every dish we possess?"; and litotes—an emphasis by negation—in "Then the Gestapo caught me and interrogated me; it wasn't frightfully amusing." Onomatopoeia—imitation of natural sounds by words—is generally used consciously and for effect in narrative or description, even in conversation; *e.g.*, "But the old woman didn't hear the crash and clatter; she still sat there mumbling and chuntering."

IN LITERATURE. Almost all the figures of speech to be found in everyday talk and nonliterary writing may also be found in literature; and practically all those found in literature are at some time exemplified in casual talk. In serious poetry and prose, however, the use of figures of speech is likely to be more fully conscious, more artistic, and much more subtle; it will thus have a stronger intellectual and emotional impact, will be more memorable, and will sometimes contribute a range and depth of association and suggestion far beyond the scope of the casual colloquial use of imagery. The effect of cliché is to deaden language; good imagery vitalizes it.

The following examples will help to clarify the use of imagery in literature:

Metaphor:

> A fiery Soul, which, working out its way,
> Fretted the Pigmy Body to decay:
> And o'er informed the Tenement of Clay.
>
> (Dryden, *Absalom and Achitophel*, 1681;
> description of Achitophel)

Here, the metaphors "Fiery Soul" and "Tenement of Clay" suggest a powerful destructive force within a poor, perhaps contemptible, container,

Simile:

> *Othello:* Never, Iago. Like to the Pontic Sea,
> Whose icy current and compulsive course
> Ne'er feels retiring ebb, but keeps due on
> To the Propontic and the Hellespont;
> Even so my bloody thoughts, with violent pace,
> Shall ne'er look back. . . .
>
>   (Shakespeare, *Othello*)

The simile here does more than merely assert that Othello's urge for vengeance cannot now be turned aside; it suggests huge natural forces. The proper names also suggest an exotic, remote world, with mythological and historical associations, reminding us of Othello's foreign culture and adventurous past.

Personification:

> Death lays his icy hand on kings: . . .
> (James Shirley, "The glories of our blood and state," 1659)

Metonymy:

> Mr. Middleton, from that time, extended his iron sceptre
> without resistance.
>   (From Sheridan's speech on the impeachment
>   of Warren Hastings, 1787)

The sceptre is an attribute of government; an iron sceptre implies harsh government.

Synecdoche:

> He prayeth best who leaves unguessed
> The mystery of another's breast.
> (John Greenleaf Whittier, "The Prayer-Seeker," 1870)

Hyperbole:

> *Lodovico:* O, I could kill you forty times a day,
> And use't four years together, 'twere too little!
>   (John Webster, *The White Devil*, 1612)

Rhetorical question:

> Where wast thou when I laid the foundations of the earth?
>   (Job)

Much of the great oration addressed by God to Job "out of the whirlwind" (Job 38–41) consists of rhetorical questions designed to humble him by reminding him of his ignorance and of God's omniscience, and power to do what he will with men.

Litotes:

And the same time there rose no small stir about that way. For a certain man named Demetrius, a silversmith which made silver shrines for Diana, brought no small gain unto the craftsmen.

(Acts 19:23–24; Authorized Version)

Onomatopoeia:

> I chatter over stony ways,
> In little sharps and trebles,
> I bubble into eddying bays,
> I babble on the pebbles.
>> (Tennyson, "The Brook," 1864)

Classification

Of the many categories into which figures of speech have been classified the following are perhaps the clearest:

1. Figures of resemblance or relationship. These are the most important, interesting, and frequent figures of speech in both everyday and literary use, and also the most relevant to the distinctions between literal and figurative language.

2. Figures of emphasis or understatement.

3. Figures of sound.

4. Verbal games and gymnastics—some of which may be minor tricks and variations rather than emotive devices.

5. Errors. If unintentional, their status as figures of speech is doubtful; however, intentional errors may have an artistic function.

FIGURES OF RESEMBLANCE OR RELATIONSHIP. All the figures in this category are to be found both in everyday use and in literature. Most people are delighted, stimulated, amused, or even disgusted by perceiving unexpected resemblances. Moreover, the pointing out of resemblances and relationships is a centrally important aspect of poetic imagery.

Perhaps the easiest to recognize of all figures of speech is the simile, which, in pointing out a resemblance, introduces it by some acknowledging word, usually "like" or "as," as in the line

> Hyr rode as rede as roose yn may
> (Her complexion as red as rose in May)
>> (From an anonymous, probably 15th-century, lyric)

The Homeric or epic simile (so-called because of its use by Homer and in epic poetry generally) is a simile extended to give a detailed picture:

> ... *Atrides* hastes away.
> So turns the lion from the nightly fold,
> Though high in courage, and with hunger bold,
> Long gall'd by herdsmen, and long vex'd by hounds:
> Stiff with fatigue, and fretted sore with wounds;
> The darts fly round him from an hundred hands,
> And the red terrours of the blazing brands:
> Till late, reluctant, at the dawn of day
> Sour he departs, and quits th'untasted prey,
> So mov'd *Atrides* from his dangerous place
> With weary limbs, but with unwilling pace; ...
>
> (*Iliad*, trans. by Alexander Pope, 1720)

Metaphor, perhaps the most important figure of speech, also points out resemblance but with no acknowledging word. Its function varies from that of clarifying a point by helpful analogy to the forcing of fresh thought by startling; from compliment or euphemism to vilification or debasement; from something that may be described as a linguistic sacrament to a joke; from the mere noting of a likeness to the evocation of a swarm of associations; from the central concept of a poem to a minor beauty.

The following quotations exemplify some of these uses:

> Boys and girls, tumbling in the streets and playing,
>   were moving jewels.
> (Thomas Traherne, *Centuries of Meditations,* written *c.* 1670)

> There are masked words droning and skulking about us
> in Europe just now.
>   (John Ruskin, "Of King's Treasuries," 1865)

> The dog authority slavering at your throat.
>   (Karl Shapiro, "The Conscientious Objector,"
>   in *Trial of a Poet*, Random House, Inc.,
>   New York, 1947)

> The boiling purgatorial tide
> Revolves our dreary shorts and slips
> While Mother coolly bakes beside
> Her little jugged apocalypse.
>   (John Updike, "Bendix," in *Telephone Poles,*
>   Alfred A. Knopf, Inc., New York, 1964)

Falstaff: 'Sblood, you starveling, you elf-skin, you dried
neat's tongue, you bull's pizzle, you stock-fish, O, for
breath to utter what is like thee!—you tailor's yard,
you sheath, you bow-case, you vile standing tuck. . .

(Shakespeare, King Henry IV, Pt. I)

Cleopatra: O see, my women, [Antony dies.]
The crown o' the earth doth melt. My lord!
O, wither'd is the garland of the war,
The soldier's pole is fall'n . . .

(Shakespeare, Antony and Cleopatra)

A mixed metaphor (the linking of two or more disparate elements) is often regarded as a stylistic fault. It may be comic in effect especially if unintentional: ". . . a country squire or rector, on *landing* in Oxford with his *cub* under his *wing*, finds himself at *sea*" (Mark Pattison, *Memoirs*, published 1885; metaphorical words italicized). It may be used with serious intention and power, however, to suggest a state of mental and emotional stress, in which thoughts and images follow one another in confused juxtaposition, as, for example, in Macbeth's speech before the murder of the king:

. . . This Duncan
Hath borne his faculties so meek, hath been
So clear in his great office, that his virtues
Will plead like angels, trumpet-tongued against
The deep damnation of his taking-off;
And pity, like a naked, new-born babe,
Striding the blast, or heaven's cherubin horsed
Upon the sightless couriers of the air,
Shall blow the horrid deed in every eye,
That tears shall drown the wind . . .

(Shakespeare, Macbeth)

A mixed metaphor may also be used to provide that shock of surprise at an unusual juxtaposition: Hamlet's

Whether 'tis nobler in the mind to suffer
The slings and arrows of outrageous fortune
Or to take arms against a sea of troubles . . .

would lose much of its effect were "sea" replaced by "host" (the proper completion of the metaphor).

A kenning (a type of metaphor used much in Germanic, Icelandic, and Old English poetry) is a concise compound; *e.g.,* "gannet's-bath" for "sea."

A conceit is a metaphor or simile, somewhat farfetched, much elaborated, and very much an intrinsic part of the structure of a poem. It was used particularly in English by the prose writers and Metaphysical poets of the late 16th and early 17th centuries (*see* below, *Historical Background*). For example, in the following stanzas from "A Valediction: Forbidding Mourning," John Donne (1572–1631) describes two lovers' souls:

> If they be two, they are two so
> As stiffe twin compasses are two,
> Thy soule the fixt foot, makes no show
> To move, but doth, if th'other doe.
>
> And though it in the center sit,
> Yet when the other far doth rome,
> It leanes, and hearkens after it,
> And grows erect, as that comes home.

The metaphor shades into the symbol, an image which may itself be a metaphor that seeks to express, partly by evocation, something that cannot be expressed otherwise. Even in early literature something of the kind is to be found (perhaps half-conscious), as in the ballad "Fair Margaret and Sweet William":

> I dreamed a dream, Sweet William,
> That seldom comes to good:
> My bower was fill'd with wild-wood swine,
> And our bride-bed full of blood.

A more fully conscious and highly developed example of a symbol is William Blake's "Ah! Sun-Flower":

> Ah, Sun-Flower, weary of time,
> Who countest the steps of the Sun,
> Seeking after that sweet golden clime,
> Where the traveller's journey is done:
>
> Where the Youth pined away with desire,
> And the pale Virgin shrouded in snow
> Arise from their graves, and aspire
> Where my Sun-Flower wishes to go.
>
> (*Songs of Experience,* 1794)

Personification, which attributes some of the characteristics of a person to an inanimate thing or an abstraction, is exemplified in:

> Vertue could see to do what vertue would
> By her own radiant light, though Sun and Moon
> Were in the flat Sea sunk.
>
> (John Milton, *Comus,* 1634)

Closely related are metonymy and synecdoche—(for definitions and examples, *see* above, *Use: In Literature*).

Euphemism—describing something of a distressing or indelicate nature in less offensive terms—may be tactful, amusing, or affected. It is exemplified in the following piece of dialogue:

> *Belinda:* And if he besieged you two years more, he'd be well enough paid, so he had the plundering of you at last.
> *Lady Brute:* That may be so; but I'm afraid the town won't be able to hold out much longer; for, to confess the truth to you, Belinda, the garrison begins to grow mutinous.
> (Sir John Vanbrugh, The Provok'd Wife, 1697)

Antonomasia is reference to a person by a usual epithet, or the use of a proper name generically: "the foam-born" for the goddess Aphrodite; "Morpheus [son of the god of sleep] overcame him" for "sleep overcame him."

To figures of resemblance are related the story forms allegory, fable, and parable.

FIGURES OF EMPHASIS OR UNDERSTATEMENT. The chief function of these is to draw attention to an idea.

Hyperbole is exaggeration for the sake of emphasis. In speech this may be vulgar; in literature it can be impressive, but can also fall into absurdity, as in the seriously intended description, in Richard Crashaw's poem "The Weeper" (*c.* 1634), of St. Mary Magdalene's eyes as

> Two walking baths, two weeping motions,
> Portable and compendious oceans.

The poetic and emotional validity of any hyperbole is very much a matter of subjective response, however. For example, it is a figure much used in love poetry to convey the lover's intense sense of the unique value of the beloved; as in the description of Portia ending:

> Why, if two gods should play some heavenly match,
> And on the wager lay two earthly women,
> And Portia one, there must be something else
> Pawned with the other, for the poor rude world
> Hath not her fellow.
> (Shakespeare, The Merchant of Venice)

In devotional poetry, too, it expresses an intensely personal feeling. To the reader lacking erotic or religious experience similar in kind and degree to that felt by the writer, it may seem merely absurd exaggeration, but someone who has experienced the feeling described will recognize its subjective truth. Even Crashaw's use of hyperbole in the example above was more readily accepted by those who shared his religious outlook and were accustomed to the extravagance of the baroque style than by modern readers.

Litotes is an affirmative expressed by the negative of the contrary: "he is no fool," meaning "he is wise."

A rhetorical question emphasizes an opinion by asking a question, to which, by implication, there can be only one answer. Its use to give force to a statement of fact can be seen in Shylock's speech railing against his treatment by the Christian merchants:

> . . . Hath not a Jew eyes? hath not a Jew hands, organs, dimensions, senses, affections, passions? fed with the same food, hurt with the same weapons, subject to the same diseases . . . warmed and cooled by the same winter and summer, as a Christian is? . . .
> (Shakespeare, *The Merchant of Venice*)

Antithesis emphasizes a contrast by placing the two contrasted ideas in sharp juxtaposition, as in the ballad "Sir Patrick Spens":

> O laith, laith were our gude Scots lords
> To wet their cork-heel'd shoon;
> But lang or a' the play was play'd
> They wat their hats aboon.
>
> ("O loath, loath were our good Scots lords to wet their cork-heeled shoes, but long before the play was over they were wet above their hats"; *i.e.,* "drowned.")

Here, as often in poetry, and especially in the ballad and folk song (and, in prose, in the folktale), the effect of antithesis is one of tragic irony.

A simple form of antithesis is found in many proverbs and proverbial expressions: "A living dog is better than a dead lion" (Eccles. 9:4).

Climax is the listing of things in ascending order of importance:

> All that most maddens and torments; all that stirs up the lees of things; all truth with malice in it; all that cracks the sinews and cakes the brain; all the subtle demonisms of life and thought; all evil, to crazy Ahab, were visibly personified, and made practically assailable in Moby Dick.
> (Herman Melville, *Moby Dick,* 1851)

Anticlimax (or bathos) is the listing of things so that a trivial item comes last, for ludicrous effect:

> Here thou, great Anna, whom three realms obey,
> Dost sometimes counsel take, and sometimes tea.
> (Pope, *The Rape of the Lock,* 1714)

A paradox is an apparently self-contradictory statement, the purpose of which is to provoke fresh thought.

> For thence—a paradox
> Which comforts while it mocks,
> Shall life succeed in that it seems to fail ...
>   (Browning, *Rabbi Ben Ezra*, 1864)

Oxymoron is a paradox compressed into two words:

> Thou pure impiety and impious purity!
>   (Shakespeare, *Much Ado About Nothing*)

Irony, a term that covers a wide field of techniques, always includes some element of saying or implying the reverse of, or more than, the literal meaning of the words used. It includes casual irony—*e.g.*, "That was a smart thing to do!" ("very foolish"); dramatic irony as used notably by Sophocles and Shakespeare; and such minor techniques as ironical juxtaposition and allusions, ironical choice of words, and ironical ambiguities. In literature, it is closely related to satire; it is exemplified briefly in:

> Make plain to them the excellence of killing
> And a field where a thousand corpses lie.
>   (Stephen Crane, *War Is Kind,* 1899)

Apostrophe is the addressing of an absent person or a personified object or abstraction:

> O judgment, thou art fled to brutish beasts,
> And men have lost their reason.
>   (Shakespeare, *Julius Caesar*)

FIGURES OF SOUND. These are most often found in verse, although prose also makes use of them (as it does of the major poetic structural elements, rhythm and rhyme). Rhyme and assonance (a form of near rhyme), which depend on sound, are not regarded as figures of speech but as integral parts of verse stucture.

Of figures of sound that make use of resemblances the most common is probably alliteration. This, the occurrence of the same sound (usually a consonant) at the beginning of neighbouring words, is exemplified in the line "Bring me my Bow of burning gold!" from a lyric by William Blake commonly but erroneously called "Jerusalem."

A similar device is the use of the same, or related, vowel sounds within neighbouring words: a form of assonance, it can vary from the simplicity of "Say nay, say nay, for shame!", the second line of Sir Thomas Wyat's "An Appeal," repeated in part after each verse, to the subtlety of word music in Sir Philip Sidney's "Leave me, O Love which reachest but to Dust."

Repetition, in itself self-explanatory, is also a figure of emphasis with several subdivisions. These include epizeuxis, the simple repetition of a word or phrase; anaphora, repetition of a word or phrase at the beginning of several sentences or lines of verse; symploce, repetition of a word or phrase at the beginning and end of the same sentence or stanza; epistrophe, repetition of a word or phrase at the end of a sentence, or shorter word group, e.g., "O no, he cannot be good that knows not why he is good, but stands so far good, as his fortune may keep him unassailed"; epanodos, repetition of a word or phrase at the beginning and in the middle of, or in the middle and at the end of, a sentence; epanalepsis, repetition of the same word or phrase at the beginning and end of a sentence; polyoptoton, use of one word in several of its grammatical forms, as is exemplified in Sidney's lines:

> Thou art of blood, joy not to make things bleed:
> Thou fearest death, think they are loath to die.

Anadiplosis, repetition of the last words of one sentence or phrase at the beginning of the next, is, like the other kinds of repetition mentioned, particularly frequent in 16th- and early 17th-century English poetry and prose. It is exemplified in "Out of sight, out of mind," a poem to his lady by Barnabe Googe (1540–94), beginning:

> The oftener seen, the more I lust,
> The more I lust, the more I smart,
> The more I smart, the more I trust,
> The more I trust, the heavier heart;
> The heavy heart breeds mine unrest,
> Thy absence therefore, I like best.

Repetition to no purpose is a stylistic fault, and is called tautology.

Onomatopoeia is the use of words that imitate relevant sounds. In poetry it is a device used both to convey simple sense impressions:

> The moan of doves in immemorial elms,
> And murmuring of innumerable bees.
>   (Tennyson, The Princess, lyric added, 1853)

and to evoke more complex emotional atmosphere:

> Dry clash'd his harness in the icy caves
> And barren chasms, and all to left and right
> The bare black cliff clang'd round him, as he based

His feet on juts of slippery crag that rang
Sharp-smitten with the dint of armed heels—
And on a sudden, lo! the level lake,
And the long glories of the winter moon.
(Tennyson, Morte d'Arthur, 1842)

VERBAL GAMES AND GYMNASTICS. Many of these are rare and minor figures: these will be mentioned first, before the commoner ones.

Syllepsis makes one word refer to two items grammatically but incongruously: "She was serving soup with a ladle and a scowl."

Zeugma makes one word refer to two items when it properly refers to only one of them:

> . . . when the Scourge
> Inexorably, and the torturing houre
> Calls us to Penance.

(Milton, Paradise Lost)

Hendiadys is the use of a conjunction instead of a shorter form: "in goblets and gold" for "in golden goblets."

Hypallage reverses the expected order of ideas: "I'll give you to a good steak."

Prolepsis is the anticipation of an event for effect, often of tragic irony:

> So the two brothers and their murdered man
> Rode past fair Florence . . .

(John Keats, Isabella, 1817–18)

The nameless reverse figure is common: "I have washed your dirty stockings."

A transferred epithet is an adjective transferred to a noun to which it is not wholly appropriate: two examples from Pope are "the flying wound" (arrow) and "thy mournful bier."

Far more important and frequent is the group that follows. Perhaps the commonest of verbal games is the pun (paronomasia), a play upon words. Common as jokes and in riddles, puns may be used seriously in poetry, as by Donne in his "A Hymne to God the Father":

> Sweare by the selfe, that at my death thy sonne
> Shall shine as he shines now, and heretofore;
> And, having done that, Thou haste done;
> I feare no more.

Here the play upon the words "son/sun," "done/Donne" is used to express Donne's faith in his Redeemer.

Ambiguity, or *double entendre,* is the use of a word or phrase that has two meanings. This provides numerous jokes, or may amuse when accidental; in poetry or oratory it may have depth and impact:

> When we have run our passion's heat,
> Love hither makes his best retreat.
>> (Andrew Marvell, "The Garden," written 1651–52)

Here "heat" suggests both a stage in a race and animal sexuality (the traditional "flames of love"); and "retreat" both acceptance of defeat (in love) and religious contemplation.

An anagram is a rearrangement of all the letters in one word to produce another: "melon/lemon." Normally a mere pastime (as in crossword puzzles), it is occasionally used seriously. Two examples by the religious Metaphysical poet George Herbert (1593–1633) show how it can be used to express serious thought and feeling. The first, called "Ana- $\frac{(Army)}{(Mary)}$ Gram," is an anagram of "Mary," the name of the mother of Jesus:

> How well her name an ARMY doth present
> In whom the Lord of Hosts did pitch his tent!

The second, "Jesu," is more complex, playing on the sound as well as on the letters of the anagram word:

> Jesu is in my heart, his sacred name
> Is deeply carved there: but the other week
> A great affliction broke the little frame,
> E'en all to pieces; which I went to seek:
> And first I found the corner where was J,
> After, where ES, and next where U was graved.
> When I had got these parcels, instantly
> I sat me down to spell them, and perceived
> That to my broken heart he was I EASE YOU
> And to my whole is JESU.

A portmanteau word is the packing together, usually for humorous intent, of two words: "gorgy" for an orgy of eating.

ERRORS. If intended, these are usually used for comic effect.

A malapropism (from Mrs. Malaprop, a character in Sheridan's play *The Rivals*) is a word used in a wrong sense: "She is having a historical fit" (for "hysterical").

Circumlocution, or periphrasis, is the expression in a roundabout manner of something that could be said simply, and when not used for comic effect—*e.g.,* "He brought his enfolded hand into abrupt juxta-position with his rival's olfactory organ" (for "He punched him on the nose")—is a major stylistic fault.

A spoonerism (from the celebrated Dr. Spooner of Oxford) is the transposing of the initial letters of a word: "I have a half-warmed fish in my mind" (for "half-formed wish"). A source of many jokes, it is not significant in literature, unless in the conversation of a character in a novel or play.

Metathesis is the transposition of letters within a word: "Her hair was decked with robins" (for "ribbons"). Similar to a spoonerism, it is a minor source of jokes, and is sometimes used in imitating children's speech.

Mimesis is the imitation of incorrect spelling, or of dialect. The effect aimed at is usually comic, but pathos may also be intended, as in some of William Barnes's Dorset poems or in Whittier's "Song of the Negro Boatman." Mimesis is used almost throughout James Russell Lowell's *The Biglow Papers* (1848), where it suggests a kind of innocence:

> Ez fer war, I call it murder—
> There you hev it plain an' flat;
> I don't want to go no furder
> Than my Testyment fer that;
> God hez sed so plump an' fairly,
> It's ez long ez it is broad,
> And you've gut to git up airly
> Ef you wan to take in God.

Historical background

The classical writers of Greece and Rome considered figures of speech to be part of the art of rhetoric. The earliest known discussion of them is by Aristotle (384–322 B.C.), who examined them in the *Poetics,* in which he treated the use of metaphor as the greatest skill in figurative writing, and in the *Rhetoric,* the first full textbook on the art of literary style considered as a means of persuasion. The next landmark in the exposition of "rhetorical figures and devices" was the *Institutio oratoria* (c. A.D. 95) by the Roman orator and educational and stylistic theorist Quintilian. This textbook on the training of an orator discusses also the interpretation of literature, and was widely influential when rediscovered at the Renaissance. Also in the 1st century A.D., the Greek treatise *On the Sublime,* attributed to an uncertainly identified author known as Longinus, was written. By sublimity the author means "excellence in language"—the power to express greatness of "spirit" and to evoke

an emotional response; and the work is an exposition of style in literature, illustrated by plentiful quotation, and discussing the use of figures
of thought and language and the effects of well-chosen metaphor particularly.

In the Middle Ages rhetoric was regarded as one of the seven liberal
arts and, with grammar and dialectic (logic), formed the *trivium* (the
three subjects on which the university student spent his first four years
of study). Use and identification of "figures" was an important part of
rhetoric, and in much medieval literature they are used with enjoyment
for their own sake. With the Renaissance, Humanistic scholars brought
the work of the classical rhetoricians into literary practice and criticism
in the vernacular, and the literature of Western Europe was strongly
influenced by classical thought and terminology. Humanist scholarship
spread from Italy, where it had its beginnings, to France, where the
seven poets known as the *Pléiade* aimed at providing France with a
vernacular literature equal to that of Italy. The outstanding poet of the
Pléiade was Pierre de Ronsard (1524–85), who himself used imagery
as an integral part of the expression of profound thought and feeling.
The group's chief theorist—and also an outstanding poet—was Joachim
du Bellay (1522–60), whose sonnets exemplifying his theories of the
enrichment of French by blending classical and vernacular language
and imagery, *Les Antiquitez de Rome,* were translated by Edmund
Spenser as *Ruines of Rome* (published in *Complaints,* 1591). Spenser's
own verse is rich in figurative language, often blending classical mythology with elements from legend, medieval romance, and folklore to produce the highly decorative style that gives perfect expression to his
complex thought.

The use of rhetorical figures by poets of the Elizabethan period was
accompanied by critical interest. Abraham Fraunce (*c.* 1558–1633),
in his *Arcadian Rhetorike* (1588), names and examines 22 figures of
speech (illustrated by quotations from "ancient" and "modern" authors);
and *The Arte of English Poesie* (1589; almost certainly by George
Puttenham, *c.* 1529–90) anglicizes the Greek names for the figures,
assembles plentiful examples from vernacular poetry, and classifies
figures in almost excessive detail. Critical interest in "ornament,"
combined with a tendency to overrate use of figures of speech as a
criterion of literary merit, gave rise to much poetic experiment, and
in prose to the extravagant use of rhetorical devices in the "conceited"
style (*i.e.,* full of conceits; *see* above, *Classification: Figures of Resemblance or Relationship*) called euphuism from the title of the work that
made it famous, *Euphues, the Anatomy of Wit* (1578) by John Lyly.
Although imitated by some Elizabethan novelists, notably Robert

Greene and Thomas Lodge, its vogue was short-lived, and Shakespeare poked fun at current excesses in *Love's Labour's Lost* (*c.* 1590).

Euphuism and the later but related use of imagery and play on words by the early 17th-century English Metaphysical poets had their counterparts in Italy, France, and Spain; how far the movements were connected is a matter of conjecture. In Italy, the style was represented by *marinismo,* which took its name from the work of its chief exponent Giambattista Marino (1569–1625); in France by a movement beginning in a praiseworthy attempt to regenerate poetry by fresh imagery, but declining into *préciosité.* (France also had its Metaphysical poets; *e.g.,* Jean de Sponde, 1557–95). In Spain the corresponding movement was *culteranismo,* which reached its height in the work of Luis de Góngora y Argote (1561–1627), whose elaborate subtlety of language and metaphor was rediscovered in the 19th century and widely known as Gongorism. Closely related to *culteranismo* was *conceptismo,* a style marked by elaboration of the metaphor into the conceit.

The English Metaphysical poets widened the scope of imagery; the work of Milton (1608–74) brought the use of figurative language in English to a climax. Markedly influenced by classical rhetorical theory and practice, Milton used imagery with a grandeur and capacity to express and communicate "sublimity" unequaled in English poetry. In the 18th century, the classical influence was strong (in France as well as in England) but gradually degenerated into the ". . . gaudiness and inane phraseology" condemned by Wordsworth in the Advertisement to the 1798 edition of *Lyrical Ballads.* His own imagery, like his poetic diction, however, was often more exalted than his theory would suggest. His reaction against the debasement of 18th-century classicism was the beginning of a period when, throughout Western Europe, successive and various waves of Romanticism produced much exuberant use of figures of speech in a wide variety of styles, both in poetry and prose.

New approaches were made by the late Victorian poet Gerard Manley Hopkins, most of whose work remained unpublished until 1918; and in France by the Parnassians and Symbolists, groups whose theories were adopted and adapted elsewhere. The outstanding early 20th-century development in English was Imagism. The first half of the century saw much experiment in England and the United States, by such poets as T. S. Eliot, Ezra Pound, W. H. Auden, Hart Crane, e.e. cummings, Edith Sitwell, Wallace Stevens, Dylan Thomas, William Empson, and Allen Tate, to name only some of those who used new figures of speech not yet classified or named and revivified old ones. In prose, though the arts of rhetoric have been brought into some disgrace by their association with unscrupulous techniques in propaganda and advertising, figures of speech still have important uses, and there is a tendency toward those conveying understatement, irony, and a deliberate ambiguity.

Usage in non-European cultures

All languages use figures of speech, but use outside languages that are European in origin is not identical with that described above. Differences of language structure dictate different stylistic criteria. Where a culture is not based on or affected by that of classical Greece and Rome, some figures may be absent; and irony is likely to be confined to fairly sophisticated cultures. In primitive cultures, in the folktale, and in poetry derived from or still part of oral tradition repetition is common, partly because it aids memory and partly because it has the cumulative effect exemplified in the nursery rhymes and fairy tales even of sophisticated countries. Among Oriental literatures, that of Japan exemplifies a difference of stylistic tradition: the brevity and subtlety of most Japanese poetic forms does not allow of the epic simile or the conceit; delicate structures of implication are important; and there is a Japanese vocabulary of aesthetic values almost untranslatable to the West. The nature of each language and culture will affect the use of figures of speech, with other elements of style.

However, some kind of metaphorical language appears to be widely prevalent: metaphor has some relation to myth and a function in ritual; and to note resemblances seems to be a natural part of human observation. Arabic literature, for example, is rich in simile and metaphor, but the constructions used are so different from those familiar in the West that translation requires much adaptation. This is true also of the "oral literatures" of Africa and of the written literatures deriving from them.

One of the most powerful single literary influences upon Western culture, and, through missionary work, on other cultures, has been the Bible. The Old Testament may be taken to represent Hebrew culture, which, through quotation and background influence, forms also an important element in the New Testament. Simile, metaphor, and personification are frequently found in the Bible, and with them the special figure of Hebrew poetry, parallelism, a device of limited popularity in English. Allusions to figurative biblical phraseology abound in European and other literatures, however, and at times make the discerning reader conscious of a faintly Oriental flavour, not wholly congruous with the culture and language structure of which they form a part.

ENCYCLOPÆDIA BRITANNICA

Poetic Imagery

The term "poetic imagery" may be considered as including all possible methods of making the kind of statement by which one thing is perceived as resembling, or in terms of, another. These may be compressed into three broad classifications: simile, metaphor, and symbol. The simile, introduced by "like" or "as," indicates a specific and unequivocal correspondence; its variant, the so-called Homeric or epic simile, is merely a passage of greater or less length introduced by "as" or "like" and bound into the main narrative by "so" or some equivalent. Metaphor also involves such a correspondence, but here the statement is direct, without the introductory "like" or "as"; the reader is invited to infer the poet's intention by an effort of his own imagination and to set up, as it were, a fusion between the object and the image. The symbol carries the method a stage further, calling for a more intense and subtle imagination and often employing a system of correspondences of great complexity.

From classical times the making of images has been recognized as a central poetic activity. Aristotle pointed out that the capacity for making metaphors was the mark of the superior poet, Shelley that the language of poetry was "vitally metaphorical." Longinus devoted 17 chapters of his treatise *On the Sublime* to a consideration of the "figures" of speech. The methods of using them were elaborated and analyzed by the classical rhetoricians, and passed into English criticism with the Renaissance. Such analysis belongs to a method of poetic composition that is only of academic interest to modern critics and writers; and its terms have only a limited critical application. Here an attempt must be made to return to first principles.

The object or experience that the poet is contemplating is perceived by him in a relationship to some second object or event, person or thing, to which he directs attention. By this act he may be thought to transfer from this image certain qualities which are then perceived as attributes of the original object; the poet's intention being to decorate,

481

illuminate, emphasize, or renew by such transferences the original character of that which he contemplates. The making or finding of the image is an activity by which the poet is inviting the reader to establish certain relationships, which in turn involve judgments of value. Image and symbol are, in one sense, the outcome of the poet's impulse to perceive unity in diversity, or to draw together a number of apparently unrelated experiences, or to communicate through their submerged or penumbral statements meanings that are beyond the resources of direct language. Images also differ in the depth or profundity or complexity of the meanings implied, as well as in their purpose and origin; and they may derive additional force and vitality from their contextual relation to other images in the poem, from the tradition in which the poet is working, and from the meanings which he may have established in his other work. All may be modified by the usual methods of poetic technique; they may become charged with special significance or interact one upon another.

In making these comparisons the "gap" between the object and the image will vary; if this gap is small, so that the least possible imaginative effort is needed to bridge it, the image may soon become "dead" or ineffectual, as with much "household" or proverbial imagery; for instance, "black as pitch," "sharp as a needle," "dumb as an ox." If the gap is too wide, the imagination may refuse to bridge it, and the comparison fails in its purpose. Good metaphysical imagery, at its best involves a gap that is wide enough to startle the reader into attention, yet not so wide as to frustrate the imaginative effort. Bad metaphysical imagery, on the other hand, may become ineffective because the comparison is too remote, fantastic, or unduly cerebral in its origins; hence Dr. Johnson's famous stricture on Abraham Cowley: "The most heterogeneous ideas are yoked by violence together." Both good and bad categories are included in the term "conceit," meaning any far-fetched comparison; that it is not necessarily used with pejorative intention can be seen from Dr. Johnson's comment on the metaphysical poets: "If their conceits were far-fetched, they were often worth the carriage."

Examples of unsuccessful metaphysical imagery are to be found in Joseph Addison's "Essay on True and False Wit" (*Spectator*, No. 62):

The passion of love in its nature has been thought to resemble fire; for which reason the words fire and flame are made use of to signify love. The witty poets therefore have taken an advantage from the doubtful meaning of the word fire, to make an infinite number of witticisms. Cowley, observing the cold regard of his mistress's eyes, and at the same time their power of producing love in him, considers them as burning-glasses made of ice; and finding himself able to live in the greatest extremes of love, concludes the Torrid Zone to be habitable. When his mistress has read his letter written in juice of lemon by holding it by the fire, he desires her to read it over a second time by love's flames. . . . Sometimes he is drowned in tears, and burnt in love, like a ship set on fire in the middle of the sea.

The foregoing aspects of poetic imagery may be illustrated by quotations of varying degrees of complexity. The simplest type of simile occurs in the lines:

> Set me as a seal upon your heart, as a seal upon your arm;
> for love is strong as death, jealousy is cruel as the grave.
>
> (Song of Solomon, 8:6)

In the following simile from Bishop Henry King's *Exequy* on the death of his young wife, we are aware of a greater depth:

> But hark! My pulse, like a soft drum,
> Beats my approach, tells *Thee* I come. . . .
> (Bishop Henry King, *The Exequy, c.* 1624)

since the *"soft drum,"* in conjunction with the *"approach,"* suggests both the advance party of the army nearing the billets for the night and the slow, inexorable, and welcome progress to death and reunion. When John Donne uses the metaphor of *"spider love"* in "Twicknam Garden":

> But O selfe-traytor, I do bring
> The *spider love,* which transubstantiates all,
> And can convert Manna to gall . . . .

we can distinguish several differing overtones of meaning: the web or net (and perhaps a hair-image behind that), the destruction of male by female, voraciousness, subtlety, patience, the Elizabethan lore of the poisonous spider, the peculiar force of the theological "transubstantiates" in conjunction with "manna" and "gall," which themselves have a double biblical reference. But there is a wholly different usage or invention of the metaphor in the following passage from "Solomon and the Witch" by W. B. Yeats, in which some of the connotations of *"spider"* mentioned above are joined by the new idea of the spider's *"eye"* with its host of magnifying lenses:

> For though love has a spider's eye
> To find out some appropriate pain—
> Aye, though all passion's in the glance—
> For every nerve, and tests the lover
> With cruelties of Choice and Chance . . .
>
> > (Reprinted with permission of the publisher from
> > *The Collected Poems of W. B. Yeats.* Copyright
> > 1924 by the Macmillan Company. Renewed 1952
> > by Bertha Georgie Yeats.)

Many metaphors are used for the human body, such as "the vessel of clay," "the soul's dark cottage," the dungeon in which the soul is imprisoned. It may also be regarded as something "woven" or "knotted"; thus Donne's

> As our blood labours to beget
> Spirits, as like soules as it can,
> Because such fingers need to knot
> This *subtile knot,* which makes us man . . . .
>
> > (*The Extasie*)

or Cleopatra's

> Come, thou mortal wretch
> With thy sharp teeth this *knot intrinsicate*
> Of life at once untie.
>
> > (Shakespeare, *Antony and Cleopatra*)

Sometimes we have a system of technical reference which (depending on the degree to which we are prepared to consider and accept such technicalities) may succeed as an image or fail as a conceit; as in Shakespeare's *King John:*

> The tackle of my heart is crack'd and burn'd
> And all the shrouds wherewith my life should sail
> Are turned to one thread, one little hair . . .

where the normal image of the voyage of life is "compounded" with the details of seamanship, Elizabethan physiology (the "heartstrings"), and perhaps the familiar image of the "thin-spun thread" of life.

The metaphor shades into the symbol; and if the same image is used consistently throughout a poem it may be appropriate to call it a symbol. It may be thought of also in terms of correspondences; a person, event, object, or myth is perceived by the poet to embody a number of significances, to which he directs the reader's attention. Religious symbols offer the most familiar examples: *e.g.,* cross, cup, lamb, rose, candle. Birds, beasts and reptiles, the heavenly bodies, sea and desert, forest and river, music and dance, artifacts of many kinds are symbols often used in poetry. If we contrast these symbols with metaphor, we may recognize correspondences involving a far more complicated series of meanings. The poet will justify himself by asserting that these meanings can be communicated in this manner and in no other; they are not susceptible to analysis. In this lies a danger; for in the interpretation of many symbols, and of some metaphors, there is an element which is in part subjective. This gives rise to the accusation of impreciseness often leveled against certain types of symbolism, as well as to variations in exegetical findings among critics.

The field of symbolism is one of immense complexity, and here again illustrations must be arbitrary. The tower appears traditionally in many forms; as man's aspiration toward heaven, as a defense or refuge, as an expression of his pride or defiance. We may think of Milton's poet-scholar in the "high lonely tower" of "Il Penseroso" or of Shelley's *Prince Athanase*. The tower may have many ancillary aspects: an upper room lit by night (for the dissemination of wisdom and learning); its battlements may be defensible or in decay; the poet may emphasize aspects of its winding stair. To quote Yeats:

> I declare this tower is my symbol; I declare
> This winding, gyring, spiring treadmill of a stair is my
>   ancestral stair;
> That Goldsmith and the Dean, Berkeley and Burke have
>   travelled there.

("Blood and the Moon," II. Reprinted with permission of the publisher from *The Collected Poems of W. B. Yeats*. Copyright 1933 by The Macmillan Company. Renewed 1961 by Bertha Georgie Yeats.)

Blake offers symbols of profound significance in apparent simplicity; as in "The Sick Rose," to which his own illustration provides subsidiary but complementary symbols in the caterpillar and the thorns on which humanity is as it were crucified:

> O Rose thou art sick.
> The invisible worm,
> That flies in the night
> In the howling storm:
> Has found out thy bed
> Of crimson joy:
> And his dark secret love
> Does thy life destroy.

It is possible to isolate some of these symbols, in their traditional aspects, and so to indicate some points of departure toward the apprehension of their meaning. The rose is traditionally the symbol of womanhood, the worm (or serpent or dragon) the male principle; the storm suggests any conflict, physical or mental. But (as always with the symbol) its peculiar qualities and significance rest in the totality of the statement of which the symbol is a component part.

For a last example of a different kind of complexity, in which the symbol is fused with mythology, we may consider the swan. All birds are likely (for obvious reasons) to become associated with the human soul or spirit. The swan has many associated qualities: whiteness, purity, strength, fidelity in love, its mysterious music of wingbeat or of cry, its song at death; therefore the human associations become more intense. These qualities are stabilized in myth and folklore; they pass through many imaginations and emerge, for instance, in Yeats's poem "Leda and the Swan" in which the symbol has become enriched not only by tradition but also by contextual images and associations in the rest of the poet's work.

It should be stressed again that the correspondences that appear in the symbol do not make use of the arbitrary or precise equivalents such as are found in allegorical or emblematic writing. The symbol is independent in usage and meaning in each work in which it exists (however much it may be rooted in tradition); it appears to renew itself and to radiate fresh significance, when it is handled afresh by genius, in each new context in which it manifests itself.

Certain metaphors and symbols, because they are constant throughout world literature, are often called archetypal. Their continued vitality suggests that they correspond to profound and perennial aspects of the human situation. Among them are many myths, such as the descent into the underworld, the slaying of the dragon, the rescue from the enchanted castle; flowers of all kinds, often symbolizing womanhood or its virtues; tower, tree, cave; the sea voyage; fountain or well; and birds, beasts, and reptiles of many kinds. The investigation of them has brought both anthropology and psychology to the service of literary criticism.

ENCYCLOPÆDIA BRITANNICA

Allusions

Common Allusions from Past and Present

I recently noticed a full-page *Time* magazine advertisement for an Italian liqueur called Patrician. The headline slogan ran: "Nothing gets lost in translation." While it is not essential to know the source of these words in order to understand the slogan, how much more interesting the words suddenly become if we recognize their source—Robert Frost's famous definition of poetry, that which is lost in translation. That slight shock of recognition makes the words come alive.

Allusive words, phrases, and sentences like the example above make up a useful, supplementary vocabulary. A single allusion may consist of a word ("bowdlerize"), a phrase ("to chronicle small beer"), or a sentence ("Something is rotten in the state of Denmark").* If it is a phrase or sentence that puzzles us, we may look up in the dictionary each of its component words—and still find ourselves puzzled. A familiar allusion such as "blood, toil, tears and sweat" consists of five monosyllables with obvious meanings. But the *whole* meaning of the phrase derives from our awareness of the circumstances in which it was first uttered. The five words taken together form, as it were, another word whose meaning encompasses much more than a literal dictionary definition. This composite "word" draws its power from a great historical event and from the personality of its originator, Winston Churchill.

Allusions must be distinguished from slang or argot or vogue phrases (discussed elsewhere in this volume). They must also be distinguished from technical or semitechnical phrases (*e.g.*, "fourth dimension") derived from specialized disciplines. In general what we mean by allusions is references that have a literary, historical, mythological, or

---

*All allusions mentioned but unexplained in this text are defined in the glossary of allusions that follows.

anecdotal source, references that reveal their meanings a little more clearly if we know that source.

It is difficult to say anything about "vogue" allusions because their life expectancy is indeterminate. Fifty years ago the word "Babbitt," the title of Sinclair Lewis's once-famous novel, was in common use to denote a conventional-minded middle-class businessman. Today there are more Babbitts than ever, but no writer would dare to use the word because it would date him. Babbitt will remain in the dictionary but as a verbal fossil. "A Walter Mitty" (from James Thurber's *The Secret Life of Walter Mitty*) is still used to indicate a henpecked man who daydreams of being a hero, but Mitty may soon join Babbitt in the ossuary. The other day I heard "She's a Lolita" and found out that this remains a popular vogue phrase, derived from Vladimir Nabokov's wonderful novel. How long its vogue will last is difficult to say. "A gay Lothario" is an allusion almost 300 years old. Originally a vogue phrase drawn from Nicholas Rowe's tragedy *The Fair Penitent*, it has somehow persisted and is still encountered, thanks largely to the parched imaginations of newspaper copy editors. It is impossible to determine which vogue allusions will in time disappear. Allusions may be drawn from an array of sources—ancient mythology and history; the vast treasury of the arts, especially literature; general history; and folklore, anecdote, or the current scene. Some allusions, those of the disk jockey, for example, may be comprehensible only to a specially trained audience.

Many allusions are direct quotations or parts of quotations, used with or without quotation marks. Many of us have used or read the useful bromide (a word that is itself an allusion) "A little learning is a dangerous thing" without knowing or recalling that it is from Alexander Pope's "An Essay on Criticism." It is not the sort of phrase we would normally look up. But suppose we came across the sentence "He has drunk deep of the Pierian spring." A little research discloses that "Drink deep, or taste not the Pierian spring" is the line that completes the couplet about "a little learning" and that Pierian spring, from Pieria, the region in Thessaly where the muses were worshipped in ancient times, refers to learning or poetry. The first line is fairly familiar; the second is less so and would not these days be often encountered. Most of us would need to look it up.

The ability to use and understand allusions is helpful for those who wish to use our language more efficiently. It both expands our vision and better focuses it. By connoting entire legends, historical events, literary plots, and other concepts in single words or phrases, allusions form a kind of shorthand. If you describe someone as having "kissed the Blarney Stone," you have made your point vividly but economically. In this rich language there are literally tens of thousands of such allusive words and phrases—many familiar, numerous others far less familiar or even obscure.

Fifty or more years ago high school graduates (not to mention college students) were more or less at home within a fairly large frame of references, allusions, quotations. I was graduated in 1920 from a high school in New York City. During my stay there I was required to read and study carefully four plays of Shakespeare, Homer's *Odyssey,* and at least a dozen English and American classics. I had learned the elements of Greek, Roman, and Norse mythology and had had enough English and American history to understand references to, for example, the "Fourth Estate", "the Old Lady of Threadneedle Street", and the "Boy Orator of the Platte."

Today things have changed. We have vastly more high school and college graduates than there were 50 years ago, but their frame of reference has narrowed. The Bible is no longer universally included in our upbringing, having been supplanted by television and movies, which supply their own allusions and references to which we most naturally respond. In calling someone an "Archie Bunker," we assume the characterization will at once be understood by everyone. The media provides us with a world that has to a considerable degree crowded out the alternative worlds of the Bible, Shakespeare, Dickens, Pope, or the Olympian deities.

How can we acquaint ourselves with the vast, vaguely bounded world of allusions if they were not taught to us in school? The best way is to read. If we so desire, we may still educate ourselves. The best public libraries in the world are open to us. Paperbacks, often containing the finest literature available, are within the reach of many. All we need do is to sacrifice some of the several hours a day we spend, on the average, watching television and movies and to make a habit of reading. In time we will have built up a vocabulary of allusions, grasping their meaning more firmly as they are encountered in different contexts. This process must include looking up every unfamiliar allusion in a standard or specialized dictionary. Suppose you come across the phrase "the village Cassandra." You may recognize the reference at once, or you may vaguely associate the phrase with a character in some dusty classic or ancient myth. Or it may mean nothing at all to you. In that case your curiosity is aroused; you would like to know what the writer means. You turn to your dictionary and learn that Cassandra was a daughter of Priam, endowed with the gift of prophecy but fated never to be believed. You might also find yourself looking up Priam and learning that he was the King of Troy during the Trojan War. At any rate you now know exactly what "the village Cassandra" means—a prophet or prophetess who predicts (usually disaster) but is not believed.

EXAMPLES To keep you in touch with the world of allusions, we have listed below a few commonly encountered allusions with brief explanations. The list could be multiplied several hundredfold and so is not intended for study or memorization. The entries are arranged in alphabetical order with ample cross-references signaled by SMALL CAPITALS. Each entry provides the current meaning of the allusive word or phrase as well as the source of that allusion. Mythological allusions are discussed using the character's original Greek names. When a particular character also appears prominently in Roman mythology or in English literature under his or her Roman name, that name has been included in parentheses.

Achilles' heel A point of weakness or vulnerability; from Greek mythology, a reference to the hero Achilles whose only point of vulnerability was his heel. According to the legend his mother dipped him in the River Styx, making him invulnerable except in the heel by which she held him. Later, during the Trojan War, he was killed by Paris, who shot him in the heel with an arrow.

(an) admirable Crichton One distinguished by remarkable versatility; an epithet bestowed on a Scottish poet, athlete, and scholar, James Crichton (1560–1582) by his contemporaries; the epithet was borrowed by J. M. Barrie for his play *The Admirable Crichton* (1902), in which the butler, Crichton, shipwrecked with his aristocratic employers, proves to be better than all of them in the arts of survival.

(an) Adonis A beautiful young man; in classical mythology the handsome youth loved by Aphrodite (Venus).

alpha and omega The first and the last; from the biblical phrase, "I am Alpha and Omega, the beginning and the ending, saith the Lord" (Revelation 1:8). Alpha and omega are names of the first and last letters of the Greek alphabet.

(an) amazon A strong masculine woman; supposedly from a Greek word meaning "without a breast." The Amazons were a mythical race of female warriors who burned off their right breasts to better draw the bow.

ancien régime An antiquated system of society or government, the old order of things; from the political and social system of France before the Revolution of 1789.

angry young man One who is bitterly critical of established social, moral, political, and intellectual values and practices; from the name given to the members of a group of young writers in Great Britain after World War II whose work reflected this bitterness.

Apocalypse *See* FOUR HORSEMEN OF THE APOCALYPSE.

Apollonian Rational, temperate, or restrained in character; from Apollo, the Greek god of music, poetry, archery, prophecy, and healing. The term is often used in contrast to DIONYSIAN.

apple of discord Cause of a dispute; from the Greek myth in which Eris, the goddess of discord and the only deity not invited to the wedding of Thetis and Peleus, threw an apple among the wedding guests that was inscribed "for the fairest." Hera (Juno), Athena (Minerva), and Aphrodite (Venus) all claimed the prize. Zeus (Jupiter) assigned the decision to Paris who awarded it to Aphrodite. This angered Hera and Athena and ultimately brought about the death of Paris and the fall of Troy.

Arden, Enoch *See* ENOCH ARDEN.

Argus-eyed Vigilant, jealously watchful; from the 100-eyed creature of Greek mythology. Hera (Juno) was jealous of Io and assigned Argus to watch her. But at Zeus's (Jupiter's) instruction, Hermes (Mercury) charmed the monster to sleep and slew it, whereupon Hera set the eyes of Argus on the tail of her favorite bird, the peacock.

Armageddon A great or decisive or bloody battle; from the name of the place where, according to the Book of Revelation (16:16), the final, decisive battle takes place between the forces of good and evil when the Day of Judgment comes.

arms of Morpheus *See* MORPHEUS.

artful dodger A young thief, especially one that combines great skill with youthful charm; from the nickname of Jack Dawkins, a boy pickpocket in Charles Dickens's *Oliver Twist* (1838).

Augean stables *To cleanse the Augean stables* To perform a large and unpleasant task that has long called for attention, to clear away corruption; from the stables kept by Augeas, the mythical king of Elis. The stables held 3000 oxen and had not been cleaned for 30 years when Hercules (*see* HERCULEAN) was assigned the job as one of his 12 tasks. Hercules accomplished the task by causing two rivers to run through the stables.

Augustan age The apogee of a national literature; referring to the reign of Caesar Augustus (27 B.C.–A.D. 14), the golden age of Latin literature.

bacchanal A drunken feast or orgy; from Bacchus, the Roman name of the Greek god of wine, Dionysus. *See also* DIONYSIAN.

bang, not with a *See* NOT WITH A BANG BUT A WHIMPER.

Barkis is willin' A phrase indicating that a man is willing and ready to marry or, by extension, willing to undertake some task; from the message that Barkis sent to Clara Peggotty, a young woman in Charles Dickens's *David Copperfield* (1849–50).

basilisk eye   A glance that kills; referring to the legendary reptile basilisk, king of serpents, whose mere look was fatal to those who caught its gaze.

beer, to chronicle small   *See* CHRONICLE SMALL BEER.

(to) bend Ulysses' bow   *See* ULYSSES.

(a) Benjamin   A pet, the youngest; from the youngest and favorite son of Jacob in the Old Testament.

between Scylla and Charybdis   *See* SCYLLA AND CHARYBDIS.

beware the ides of March   *See* IDES OF MARCH.

billingsgate   *To talk billingsgate*   To use abusive or offensive language; from the old fish market in London where the porters and fishwives were known for centuries for their coarse language.

blackboard jungle   Inner-city schools troubled by delinquency and lack of discipline; from the title of a novel by Evan Hunter (1954) and the movie (1955) that was made of it. Set in a New York City high school, the novel criticized the decay of American education.

Black Hole of Calcutta   A place of punishment or great suffering; referring to the small dungeon in Calcutta, India, where in 1756, 123 of 146 British prisoners were said to have suffocated in the heat.

Blarney stone   *To have kissed the Blarney stone*   To possess great skills in smooth talk and flattery; referring to a stone in the wall of Blarney Castle in Ireland. The reputation of the stone derives from the many excuses, protocols, and soft speeches the lord of the castle delivered to the English in 1602 in order to delay endlessly the surrender of the castle.

blood, toil, tears and sweat   A phrase used in a wartime speech to the House of Commons by Winston Churchill upon becoming prime minister on May 13, 1940: "I would say to the House, as I have said to those who have joined this Government, I have nothing to offer but blood, toil, tears and sweat." Variations on this theme appear in the works of John Donne ("Mollifie/It with thy teares, or sweat, or blood") and Lord Byron ("Year after year they voted cent. per cent.,/Blood, sweat, and tear-wrung millions—why? for rent!").

Bloomsbury group   A small intellectual or literary group; from the group, including Virginia Woolf, Lytton Strachey, E. M. Forster, and others, that met in the Bloomsbury section of London in the early 20th century.

bluestocking   A woman with, or pretending to have, intellectual or literary interests; from the 18th-century "conversations," evening events to which men and women of letters and members of the aristocracy were invited. Benjamin Stillingfleet was invited to such an occasion and declined because he lacked appropriate clothing. He was nevertheless told to come in his blue stockings, the ordinary worsted stockings he was wearing.

bowdlerize To expurgate, or remove, passages considered offensive from a book, poem, etc.; after Thomas Bowdler, an English editor who published in 1818 an expurgated Shakespeare.

Boy Orator of the Platte The nickname of William Jennings Bryan (1860–1925), American orator, prosecutor, and political leader. The Platte is the major river in Nebraska, a state in which Bryan lived and worked for part of his life.

(a) Brahmin One who is intellectually and socially cultivated, though often aloof, used especially in the phrase Boston Brahmin to refer to the cultivated Bostonian; from the highest of the Hindu castes.

Briarean Many-handed, or ruthlessly grasping; from Briareus, a monster of Greek mythology with 100 hands and 50 heads.

Bridge of Sighs A bridge in Venice connecting the Doge's Palace with the state prison. Condemned prisoners crossed the bridge on their way from the judgment hall to the place of execution.

brinkmanship A policy or activity that will lead to the verge of war or other disaster; a term attributed to presidential contender Adlai Stevenson in a 1956 reference to the foreign policy of then Secretary of State John Foster Dulles.

brobdingnagian Giant; from the land of the giants in Jonathan Swift's *Gulliver's Travels* (1726).

bromide A trite, hackneyed expression or idea, or a boring person; from the common name of the medicine (potassium bromide) usually taken as a sedative.

Calcutta, Black Hole of *See* BLACK HOLE OF CALCUTTA.

calf, to kill the fatted *See* FATTED CALF.

Camelot An idyllic place; from the location of King Arthur's Court.

(a) case of January and May *See* JANUARY AND MAY.

Cassandra One whose prophecies of misfortune or disaster are disregarded; from the daughter of Priam, king of Troy, in Greek legend. Although Cassandra's prophecies of disaster were invariably correct, they always went unheeded.

Cerberus A watchdog, a guardian; from the three-headed dog of Greek mythology that guarded the entrance to the infernal regions.

Charles's head, King *See* KING CHARLES'S HEAD.

Charon's toll A coin placed in the mouth or hand of the dead; in Greek mythology, the fee paid to the boatman Charon for ferrying the spirits of the dead across the Rivers Styx and Acheron to Elysium.

(to) chronicle small beer To write or speak of trivialities; from a speech in Shakespeare's *Othello* in which Iago cynically describes an ideal woman.

> She was a wight, if ever such wight were, . . .
> To suckle fools and chronicle small beer.

Small beer generally meant a weak brew.

Cimmerian darkness Extreme darkness; from the Cimmerians, a legendary tribe (according to Homer) in a land of never-ending gloom bordering Oceanus just before Hades.

Circe A dangerously fascinating woman; from the sorceress in Greek legend who turned Odysseus' men into swine. Hence Circean, dangerously attractive or misleading.

(to) cleanse the Augean stables *See* AUGEAN STABLES.

(to) cleanse the doors of perception *See* DOORS OF PERCEPTION.

Cleopatra's nose Feminine beauty that alters events; from Blaise Pascal's (1623–62) allusion to Cleopatra's romantic conquests of Julius Caesar and later Mark Antony: "If the nose of Cleopatra had been shorter, the whole face of the earth would have been changed" (*Pensées* viii, 29).

(to) climb Parnassus *See* PARNASSUS.

Cliveden set A group of people favoring appeasement of or compromise with a potential adversary; from the group of British Conservatives who favored appeasement of the Axis powers before World War II. Cliveden is the name of the country estate of Lady Astor, said to be the meeting place of this group.

comstockery Vigorous suppression of plays, books, etc., alleged to be offensive or immoral; a term coined by George Bernard Shaw, referring to Anthony Comstock (1844–1915), leader of the New York Society for the Suppression of Vice.

(a) Cordelia One who remains loyal in devotion even though ill-treated, also one incapable of stylized or overly effusive expressions of affection; from the daughter of Shakespeare's *King Lear* who remained loyal to her father even when rejected by him. Lear disinherited her for refusing to compete with her sisters in making dramatic expression of love for him.

Crichton, James *See* ADMIRABLE CRICHTON.

Croesus *Rich as Croesus* Extremely wealthy; referring to the last king of Lydia (c. 550 B.C.), who was famous for his wealth.

Crystal Night A night of anti-Jewish rioting and terrorism that occurred in Germany on November 9–10, 1938; from the German *Kristallnacht*, meaning "night of the broken glass."

curate's egg *Good in parts, like the curate's egg* A catchphrase used to describe a situation in which someone displays excessive timidity; from an illustration in *Punch* in which a young curate having breakfast with his bishop is asked if his egg is to his liking. Afraid to say that it is bad, he stammers, "Parts of it are excellent."

(a) Daedalus   An inventor or artist; referring to the legendary Athenian artisan who built the Cretan labyrinth and made the wings with which he and ICARUS attempted to fly from Crete.

Damon and Pythias   Two inseparable friends; from a Greek legend in which Pythias, condemned to death, left Damon in his place in order to go home to settle his affairs. When Pythias returned for execution, his accuser was so struck with their friendship that both were released.

(a) Daniel come to judgment   One who shows wisdom beyond his years; reference to the story in the Apocrypha in which the youthful Daniel proved the innocence of Susanna who had been falsely accused. The phrase itself comes from Shakespeare's *Merchant of Venice,* spoken by Shylock in reference to Portia who he thinks will side with him in the dispute over the pound of flesh.

Darby and Joan   A virtuous married couple with an old-fashioned love; from the ballad called "The Happy Old Couple," probably by Henry Woodfall, which first appeared in *Gentleman's Magazine* in 1735.

deer   *And such small deer*   A trifling matter; from Shakespeare's *King Lear.*

> But mice and rats, and such small deer,
> Have been Tom's food for seven long year.

"Deer" here means any sort of animal.

Denmark, something is rotten in the state of   *See* SOMETHING IS ROTTEN IN THE STATE OF DENMARK.

despond   *See* SLOUGH OF DESPOND.

Dionysian   Unbounded, lawless, or irrational; from Dionysus (Bacchus), the Greek god of wine. Friedrich Nietzsche (1844–1900), German philosopher and critic, uses the terms Dionysian and APOLLONIAN to describe two opposing tendencies of the tragic hero, the creative-passionate (Dionysian) and the critical-rational (Apollonian).

discord, apple of   *See* APPLE OF DISCORD.

dismal science   Economics; from a definition of economics by Thomas Carlyle:

> The social science—not a "gay science," but a rueful—which finds the secret of this Universe in "supply and demand" . . . what we might call, by way of eminence, the dismal science. (1849)

In Latter-Day Pamphlets (1850) Carlyle used the phrase to apply to all the social sciences, addressing the political and social scientists as "Respectable Professors of the Dismal Science."

Doctor Jekyll   *See* JEKYLL-HYDE PERSONALITY.

doors of perception   *To cleanse the doors of perception*   To sharpen the senses; from William Blake's prose poem *The Marriage of Heaven and Hell* (1790–93): "If the doors of perception were cleansed everything would appear to man as it is, infinite." The phrase was later used by Aldous Huxley as a title for his book *The Doors of Perception* (1954) in which he described how sensitivity is increased by certain drugs.

draconian   Extremely severe; from Draco (fl. 650 B.C.), the Athenian legislator who drew up a code of laws noted for their severity, which were said to be written in blood rather than ink.

dragon's teeth   *To sow dragon's teeth*   To stir up trouble, especially while trying to pacify; from the Greek legend in which Cadmus killed a dragon and planted its teeth in the ground. Armed men sprang up from the ground and attempted to kill him.

Electra complex   The equivalent of the OEDIPUS COMPLEX when it occurs in a female; from the character in Greek mythology, Electra, who joined her brother in killing their mother, Clytemnestra, to avenge the murder of their father, Agamemnon.

elysian fields   Paradise; from the "happy" land in Greek poetry.

Enoch Arden   A long-lost husband who comes back to find his wife married to another; from Alfred, Lord Tennyson's poem of this name (1864). Arden, finding his wife happy, did not announce his presence and died of a broken heart.

Estate, Fourth   *See* FOURTH ESTATE.

Fabian tactics   Delaying tactics; from Quintus Fabius Maximus (d. 203 B.C.), the Roman general who defeated Hannibal by avoiding decisive contests.

fatted calf   *To kill the fatted calf*   To celebrate with the best of everything; from the New Testament parable (Luke 15:30) of the return of the PRODIGAL SON.

Four Horsemen of the Apocalypse   Agents of destruction; from Revelation (6:2–8) in the New Testament, the personifications of war, famine, pestilence, and death.

Fourth Estate   The public press; reputedly after a speech by Edmund Burke (1729–97) about the estates (political groups or classes) of the British realm. The first three estates were the clergy, the nobility, and the commoners. Burke is supposed to have pointed to the reporters' gallery and said, "Yonder sits the fourth estate, more important than them all."

(a) Frankenstein monster Anything that becomes dangerous to its creator; from Mary Wollstonecraft Shelley's novel, *Frankenstein* (1818), in which a young medical student creates a monster that destroys him.

Friday *A man Friday* A faithful follower or efficient helper; after the devoted servant of Robinson Crusoe in the novel *Robinson Crusoe* (1720) by Daniel Defoe.

Furies *Pursued by the Furies* Pursued relentlessly; referring to the Furies, the Roman name for the Greek Erinyes, the three merciless goddesses who punished all transgressors even after death.

gall and wormwood Something extremely disagreeable and annoying; from the biblical phrase, "Remembering mine affliction and my misery, the wormwood and the gall" (Lamentations 3:19). Gall is the bitter fluid secreted by the liver and associated with grief or rancor. Wormwood is a bitter-tasting, dark-green oil used in making absinthe.

(a) gay Lothario *See* LOTHARIO.

(a) good Samaritan *See* SAMARITAN.

Gordian knot A great and intricate problem; from the legendary knot with which Gordius, king of Phrygia, tied the beam of his wagon to its yoke. The knot was said to be tied so ingeniously that no one could untie it. Alexander the Great, upon being told that whoever could undo the knot would rule all Asia, cut it in two with his sword. Thus *to cut the Gordian knot* is to resolve a difficult situation by force or by decisive or evasive action.

(a) Gradgrind A devoted materialist or ardent seeker of facts, one who gives little credence to human nature, treating men and women as facts; from a character, Thomas Gradgrind, who possessed these qualities in Charles Dickens's *Hard Times* (1854).

Grand Guignol A play or film involving macabre or gruesome incidents; from the Punch-like principal character in a popular 19th-century French puppet show that regularly involved such incidents.

Greeks bearing gifts Givers of treacherous gifts; from the English translation of a line in Virgil's *Aeniad.*

Gresham's law A law of economics that states that when two types of currency with some nominal value are in circulation and one type is intrinsically more valuable than the other, the more valuable will be hoarded and only the less valuable will remain in circulation. The law was wrongly attributed to Sir Thomas Gresham in the court of Elizabeth I in 1558 and is usually summarized as "bad money drives out good."

Guignol, Grand *See* GRAND GUIGNOL.

Heep, Uriah, *See* URIAH HEEP.

herculean Of monumental difficulty; referring to Hercules, the Greek hero of superhuman physical strength. Having slain his wife and children in a fit of madness, he was ordered by Apollo to serve King Eurystheus, who imposed upon him 12 tasks of great difficulty and danger, known as *the 12 tasks of Hercules*.

Herod *To out-herod Herod* To outdo in extravagance or violence; from Herod the Great (d. 4 B.C.), who ordered the massacre of the infants of Bethlehem (Matthew 2:16) and who was depicted as a raging tyrant in medieval mystery plays. The phrase itself comes from the scene in Shakespeare's *Hamlet* in which Hamlet warns a group of actors against overplaying their parts.

> O, it offends me to the soul to see a robustious periwig-pated fellow tear a passion to tatters, to very rags, to split the ears of the groundlings. . . . It out-herods Herod. Pray you, avoid it.

Hobson's choice A choice between taking what is offered or nothing at all, lack of an alternative; from Thomas Hobson (1544?–1631), a livery stable operator in Cambridge, England, who insisted on renting his horses in precisely the order in which they were arranged in his yard.

hoist with his own petard To be defeated by one's own plan, literally to be blown up by a bomb that one has planted; from the lines in Shakespeare's *Hamlet* in which Hamlet explains to his mother that he intends to defeat Rosenkrantz and Guildenstern's plot against him by turning it back on them.

Homer sometimes nods Even the best or most trustworthy of us sometimes err; from *Ars poetica* (19?–18 B.C.), a classic work of literary criticism by Horace.

Horseman of the Apocalypse, Four *See* FOUR HORSEMEN OF THE APOCALYPSE.

(a) hotspur A rash, hotheaded person; from the nickname given Sir Henry Percy (1364–1403), by which he is known in Shakespeare's *Henry IV*, Part I.

Houyhnhnms \ *hü-'ín-əms* or *'hwín-əms*\ A race of horses with reasoning power and human virtues; from Jonathan Swift's *Gulliver's Travels* (1726). The word was coined by Swift to suggest a horse's whinny.

Hyde, Mr. *See* JEKYLL-HYDE PERSONALITY.

hydra-headed A difficulty that increases as it is combated; from Hydra, the many-headed water snake that was to be killed as one of the 12 HERCULEAN tasks. However, each time Hercules severed a head two would grow in its place.

Icarus A recklessly brave person; from Icarus, the son of Daedalus, in

Greek mythology. Daedalus fashioned wings for their escape from imprisonment on Crete, but despite his warning, Icarus flew too close to the sun, causing the wax that fastened his wings to melt and his fall into the sea.

ides of March *Beware the ides of March* A phrase said as a warning of impending danger; from the warning received by Julius Caesar before his assassination (44 B.C.), especially as related by Plutarch and in Shakespeare's *Julius Caesar.*

January and May *A case of January and May* The marriage of an old man to a young girl; from "The Merchant's Tale" in Chaucer's *Canterbury Tales* (*c.* 1387) in which May, a young girl, marries January, a 60-year-old Lombard baron.

Janus-faced Two-faced; from Janus, the ancient Roman deity who kept the gates of heaven and was thus the guardian of doors and gates. He was depicted with two faces looking in opposite directions.

(a) jehu A coachman, especially one who drives furiously; from the Old Testament story of Jehu, who was known as the driver of a swift chariot.

(a) Jekyll-Hyde personality A person possessing two apparently distinct characters, one good and the other evil; from the protagonist with two such personalities in Robert Louis Stevenson's *The Strange Case of Dr. Jekyll and Mr. Hyde* (1886).

(a) Jeremiah A doomsayer; from the Old Testament prophet and author of the Book of Jeremiah. Hence a **jeremiad,** a tale of woe and misfortune.

(a) jezebel *A painted jezebel* A flaunting woman of bold spirit and loose morals; referring to Jezebel, the Old Testament wife of King Ahab, who established the worship of Baal at her husband's court.

Joan and Darby *See* DARBY AND JOAN.

Job *The patience of Job* Extreme patience in the face of adversity; from the Old Testament patriarch Job, who lost his wealth and his children and who was smitten with boils but whose unceasing faith was finally rewarded.

(a) Jonah One whose presence brings misfortune to his companions; after Jonah, the Old Testament prophet who was instructed to preach in the wicked city of Nineveh but instead took flight in a ship going the other direction. A storm arose and the sailors cast him overboard, suspecting that he had offended God. He was swallowed by a large fish which deposited him on dry land, whereupon he went to Nineveh and inspired widespread repentance.

(to) kill the fatted calf *See* FATTED CALF.

King Charles's head An obsession, a fixed fancy; from Mr. Dick, a harmless half-wit in Charles Dickens's *David Copperfield* (1849–50) who, no matter what the subject at hand, always managed to bring up King Charles's head, a topic with which he was obsessed.

kissed the Blarney stone   *See* BLARNEY STONE.

Lady of Threadneedle Street   *See* OLD LADY OF THREADNEEDLE STREET.

(a) Lazarus   A diseased beggar; from the parable of Lazarus and the rich man in the New Testament (Luke 16:20): "And at his gate lay a poor man named Lazarus full of sores, who desired to be fed with what fell from the rich man's table." The name Lazarus is also given to the man raised from the dead by Jesus (John 11:1–44).

legion   *Their name is legion*   An expression of large number, similar to HYDRA-HEADED; from the biblical phrase, "My name is legion; for we are so many" (Mark 5:9).

lilliputian   Of diminutive size, a very small person, also a small-minded person; from Lilliput, the land of tiny people described in Jonathan Swift's *Gulliver's Travels* (1726).

(a) Lolita   A sexually provocative young girl; from the sexually precocious young girl to whom Humbert Humbert is overwhelmingly attracted in Vladimir Nabokov's novel *Lolita* (1955).

Lothario   *A gay Lothario*   A libertine, a seducer of women; after the character of that name in Nicholas Rowe's *The Fair Penitent* (1703). He probably took the name from William Davenant's *The Cruel Brother* (1630), which also has a character by this name.

Lot's wife   One who looks back despite the consequences; from the Old Testament story of Lot and his family. God allowed them to escape from Sodom, which was to be destroyed for the sins of its inhabitants, but prior to its destruction forbade them to look back. Lot's wife disobeyed and was turned into a pillar of salt.

Lucullan   Lavish, especially in reference to a feast; from Lucius Lucullus (*c.* 117–58/56 B.C.), a Roman general and administrator. Reputedly asked who were to be his guests at an elaborate banquet, he replied, "Lucullus will sup tonight with Lucullus."

Maecenas   A generous patron, especially of literature; referring to Gaius Maecenas (d. 8 B.C.), a Roman statesman who during the reign of Augustus subsidized the work of young writers, including Horace and Virgil.

Maginot mentality   Belief in a strategy of defense, especially a defense that employs out-of-date tactics; from the line of fortifications built along France's eastern frontier between 1927 and 1936 and named for André Maginot, a minister of war who sponsored its construction. The French believed that the line made them secure from Germany, but Hitler's troops went around the line and invaded France through Belgium in 1940.

Manchurian candidate   A programmed or brainwashed individual, especially one who is unconscious of his dangerous or violent potential;

from the novel *The Manchurian Candidate* (1959) by Richard Condon and the movie (1962) made of it.

man Friday   *See* FRIDAY.

March, beware the ides of   *See* IDES OF MARCH.

May and January, a case of   *See* JANUARY AND MAY.

Medusa head   Something ugly; referring to Medusa, one of the Gorgons, three monsters in Greek mythology whose hair was a tangle of serpents and whose faces were so ugly that a glance at them turned beholders to stone.

(a) mentor   A wise and faithful counselor; referring to the old man in Greek legend who was made guardian and teacher of Odysseus's son Telemachus when the hero left for the Trojan War.

Methuselah   *As old as Methuselah*   A person of great age; referring to the longest-lived person in the Bible, reported to have lived 969 years.

Midas touch   An uncanny ability to make money; from the story of Midas, legendary king of Phrygia to whom Dionysus granted the power to turn everything he touched to gold. When he found that even his food and drink turned to gold, he prayed to lose his gift. He was told to wash in the River Pactolus, whose sands thereafter were filled with gold dust.

(a) momus   One who complains about everything; from Momus, the Greek god of ridicule, who was driven out of heaven for his constant criticism of the gods.

Morpheus   *The arms of Morpheus*   The land of dreams; from Morpheus, the Greek god of dreams, and the son of Hypnos, the god of sleep.

(the) mountain in labor   A mighty effort producing small result; from the line in Horace's *Ars poetica* (19–18 B.C.) in which he warns writers against grandiosity: "The mountain in labor brought forth a silly mouse."

Muhammad and the mountain   *If the mountain will not come to Muhammad, Muhammad must go to the mountain*   A phrase expressing acceptance of the inevitable, especially when the inevitable necessitates taking some action; from the story of Muhammad's response when Mount Safa failed to come to him after he had prayed that it would.

myrmidons   Subordinates, or those who carry out orders unquestioningly; from the legendary people of Thessaly who followed Achilles to the Siege of Troy and who were known for their fierceness and devotion to their leader. The name, meaning "ant people," derives from Zeus's transformation of ants into men to repopulate the island after a plague.

(their) name is legion   *See* LEGION.

(a) Narcissus One infatuated with himself; from Narcissus, a handsome Greek youth who was untouched by love until he fell in love with his own reflection in a pool. He died, pining for his own reflection, and his body was turned into a flower, the narcissus. Hence also **narcissism,** egocentrism.

nemesis An act of retributive justice or its agent; from Nemesis, the Greek goddess of vengeance who punished all who violated the natural order of things.

newspeak Language marked by ambiguity and deception, especially by government officials seeking to mold public opinion; a word coined by George Orwell in his novel *Nineteen Eighty-four* (1949).

not with a bang but a whimper A phrase used to characterize a situation that ends anticlimactically; from the final lines of T.S. Eliot's "The Hollow Men" (1925).

> This is the way the world ends
> Not with a bang but a whimper.

In Eliot's poem the lines are meant to suggest that our culture may not end cataclysmically but from a loss of vitality.

Odysseus *See* ULYSSES. Ulysses is the Roman name for the Greek hero Odysseus. Ulysses is the name used in most English poetry, including early translations of the Greek poet Homer.

Oedipus complex A son's unrecognized attachment for his mother and jealous hatred of his father; from the Greek myth of Oedipus, the king of Thebes, who unknowingly killed his father and married his mother. *See also* ELECTRA COMPLEX.

(as) old as Methuselah *See* METHUSELAH.

Old Lady of Threadneedle Street The Bank of England; from the street where it stands. "Old Lady" is meant to allude to the bank's conservativeness.

old school tie The loyalties, traditions, and attitudes, usually conservative, of the graduates of exclusive private schools; from the distinctively colored striped neckties of upper-class English schools.

Oliver *See* ROLAND.

omega *See* ALPHA AND OMEGA.

Orator of the Platte *See* BOY ORATOR OF THE PLATTE.

(to) out-herod Herod *See* HEROD.

Pandora's box A source of innumerable troubles; from the Greek myth of Pandora, the first woman. Pandora was given a vessel by Zeus to present to her husband when she married. Against all advice the box was opened (in some versions by Pandora, in others by her husband), and all evils flew out to afflict the world. In a later version the vessel contained not evils, but blessings, which were lost to the world forever when it was opened.

Parnassus *To climb Parnassus* To write poetry; from Mount Parnassus, a peak within sight of Delphi (the seat of a famous oracle) consecrated to Apollo and the Muses and regarded as the seat of poetry and music.

Pegasus Poetic inspiration; referring to Pegasus, the winged horse of Greek mythology that kicked Mount Helicon, causing the fountain of the muses to flow.

(a) Penelope A faithful wife; from Odysseus's wife Penelope who remained faithful to him throughout his 20-year absence.

perception, to cleanse the doors of *See* DOORS OF PERCEPTION.

petard *See* HOIST WITH HIS OWN PETARD.

(a) philipic A tirade; from the speeches Demosthenes, the Athenian orator and statesman, made against Philip II of Macedon to arouse the Athenians to resist the Macedonians.

Pickwickian *In a Pickwickian sense* Not to be taken in a literal or obvious sense, used especially of words that, taken literally, would be insulting; from an incident in Charles Dickens's *Pickwick Papers* (1836–37) in which Pickwick and another character exchange insults, only to decide later that no offense had passed since each had spoken in a Pickwickian sense.

pillar of salt *See* LOT'S WIFE.

Platte, Boy Orator of the *See* BOY ORATOR OF THE PLATTE.

Plutus *Rich as Plutus* Very rich, capable of bestowing lavish gifts; from Plutus, the Greek god of wealth who bestowed riches on mankind, often regardless of merit.

Procrustean bed A forcible method of instituting conformity; from the legendary Greek robber Procrustes (Greek for "stretcher") who placed all of his victims on an iron bed and cut or stretched them to fit.

(the) prodigal son A repentant sinner or reformed pleasure-seeker; from the New Testament parable of the prodigal son who "wasted his substance in riotous living" (Luke 15:13) but then returned to his forgiving father, who killed the FATTED CALF in his honor.

Promethean Creative; from the Greek myth of Prometheus who created man out of earth and water. Later he stole fire from heaven and took it to mankind in the stalk of a fennel plant. As punishment for this theft, Prometheus was chained to a mountain. There, by day, an eagle tore out his liver; by night it grew back again.

protean Variable or versatile, constantly shifting and assuming different forms; from Proteus, the Greek sea god and prophet who had the power to assume different shapes to elude those who sought his knowledge.

pursued by the Furies *See* FURIES.

Pyrrhic victory Victory at too great a price; referring to Pyrrhus, king of Epirus, who defeated the Romans at Ausculum (279 B.C.) but lost all of his best officers and many men. He is said to have exclaimed after the battle, "One more such victory and we are lost."

Pythias   *See* DAMON AND PYTHIAS.

(a) quisling   A traitor or collaborator; after the Norwegian politician Vidkun Quisling who betrayed his country to the Nazis and became its puppet ruler.

quixotic   Idealistic to an impractical degree, especially in a person extravagantly or unrealistically romantic or chivalrous; from the character Don Quixote in Cervantes's novel *Don Quixote de la Mancha* (1605, 1615).

redbrick   Of or relating to British universities founded in modern times (*i.e.*, universities other than Oxford and Cambridge), often connoting social inferiority; from the typical building materials used in these universities, in contrast to the stone used at Oxford and Cambridge.

régime, ancien   *See* ANCIEN RÉGIME.

rich as Croesus   *See* CROESUS.

rich as Plutus   *See* PLUTUS.

Roland   *To give a Roland for an Oliver*   To return just as much as one receives, as in a contest, tit for tat; from the contest between Roland and Oliver, two of Charlemagne's knights whose strength and valor were so evenly matched that in a lengthy battle neither could vanquish the other.

Rosetta stone   A clue to understanding or deciphering a mystery; from the black basalt stone found in 1799 at Rosetta, Egypt, bearing an inscription in Greek, demotic Egyptian, and hieroglyphics that gave a key for the deciphering of ancient Egyptian hieroglyphics.

rotten in the state of Denmark   *See* SOMETHING IS ROTTEN IN THE STATE OF DENMARK.

Rubicon   *To cross the Rubicon*   To take an irrevocable step; from the small stream that separated Cisalpine Gaul from Italy during the later Roman republic. When Julius Caesar led his forces across the Rubicon into Italy in 49 B.C., his act amounted to a declaration of war against the Roman Senate and in fact precipitated a three-year civil war.

Samaritan   *A good Samaritan*   One who helps the poor and needy or one who would help a stranger in need; from the New Testament parable (Luke 10:25-27) of the good Samaritan who, coming upon a man left for dead by robbers, bound up the stranger's wounds and brought him to an inn. There he further attended to the man and the next day left money with the innkeeper to pay for the victim's care.

school tie   *See* OLD SCHOOL TIE.

Scylla and Charybdis *Between Scylla and Charybdis.* Caught between two equal dangers or difficulties; from the two monsters in Greek mythology who endangered shipping in the Strait of Messina between Italy and Sicily. Scylla, a female monster with 12 feet and six heads, each with pointed teeth, barked like a dog from the rocks on the Italian side. Charybdis lived under an immense fig tree on the Sicilian side and caused a whirlpool by swallowing the waters of the sea and throwing them up again.

serendipity Fortunate discovery of things not sought for; a term coined by Horace Walpole (1717–97) after *The Three Princes of Serendip,* a Persian fairy tale in which the princes made such discoveries.

siren song Seductive utterance; from the Greek myth of the sirens, monsters who were half-woman and half-bird. They enticed sailors with songs, so sweet that listeners forgot all and died of hunger.

Sisyphean labors Everlasting fruitless work; from the Greek myth of Sisyphus, king of Corinth. As a punishment for the tricks he played on Death, Sisyphus was condemned to eternally roll a great stone up a hill, only to have it roll back down again.

slough of despond Deep, hopeless dejection or discouragement; from the name of the deep swamp that entrapped the travelers in John Bunyan's *Pilgrim's Progress* (1678).

small beer, to chronicle *See* CHRONICLE SMALL BEER.

small deer, and such *See* DEER.

Socratic irony Leading on an opponent by pretending ignorance; from Socrates (*c.* 470–399 B.C.), the Athenian philosopher, whose "Socratic method" of teaching consisted of asking questions and drawing out answers from his students while claiming to know nothing himself.

something is rotten in the state of Denmark A phrase suggesting that secret and evil doings are afoot; from Marcellus's line in Shakespeare's *Hamlet* after seeing the ghost of Hamlet's father, the old king.

(to) sow dragons' teeth *See* DRAGON'S TEETH.

(a) sphinx Something enigmatic or puzzling; from the Sphinx of Greek mythology, a winged monster with a woman's head and a lion's body, who asked a riddle and devoured those unable to answer it.

stables, to cleanse the Augean *See* AUGEAN STABLES.

star chamber A secret, irresponsible tribunal; after the Star Chamber, a royal English court during the late 15th, 16th, and 17th centuries. The court was notorious for its secret sessions without jury, for its harsh and arbitrary judgments, and for its role in suppressing religious dissent. It is said to have taken its name from the ceiling that was ornamented with stars.

stentorian   *Stentorian voice*   Having a very loud voice; from the name of the Greek herald in the Trojan War who, according to Homer, had a voice as loud as 50 men combined.

Struldbrug   One lacking vigor, strength, or intellect but incapable of dying; from the name of the inhabitants of Luggnagg, an imaginary island described in Jonathan Swift's *Gulliver's Travels* (1726).

such small deer   *See* DEER.

(to) talk billingsgate   *See* BILLINGSGATE.

teeth, to sow dragon's   *See* DRAGON'S TEETH.

terpsichorean   Relating to the dance; from Terpsichore, the Greek muse of dancing and the dramatic chorus.

Threadneedle Street, Old Lady of   *See* OLD LADY OF THREADNEEDLE STREET.

tie   *See* OLD SCHOOL TIE.

(to) tilt at windmills   To battle an illusory foe; from the scene in Cervantes's *Don Quixote de la Mancha* (1605, 1615) in which Don Quixote tries to joust a windmill, thinking it to be a giant. *See also* QUIXOTIC.

Tiresias   A blind phophet; from the character in Greek mythology who was struck blind by Athena for seeing her bathe. The goddess later relented and granted Tiresias the gift of prophecy as a consolation. He is often portrayed as very old as well as blind, as in the story of Oedipus; as changed to a woman, as in Guillaume Apollinaire's play *Les Mamelles de Tirésias* (1917); or as bisexual, as in T.S. Eliot's "The Waste Land" (1922).

torquemada   A cruel and wicked authoritarian; from Tomás de Torquemada, a Spanish Dominican monk, the first grand inquisitor of the Spanish Inquisition.

(a) Trojan horse   Something that undermines from within; from the story of the Trojan War. Odysseus had an enormous horse built, filled it with armed men, and placed it before the gates of Troy as an offering to the gods. Despite the warnings of Laocoön, a priest of Apollo, against GREEKS BEARING GIFTS, the Trojans dragged the horse into the city. In the dark of night the Greek soldiers emerged, slew the guards, opened the city gates, and set fire to Troy.

Turks   *See* YOUNG TURKS.

(the) Two Cultures   The humanities and the sciences; from a controversial speech and pamphlet (1959) by C.P. Snow, English novelist, scientist, and administrator, describing English society as divided into a scientific culture and a literary and humanistic culture. The literary and humanistic culture, in this scheme, was upper-middle class and conservative, while the scientific culture—lower-middle class and unappreciated—was the center of progress.

Ulysses *To bend Ulysses' bow* A test of fitness or authenticity; from the scene in Homer's *Odyssey* in which Ulysses (Greek name, ODYSSEUS) reveals his identity to his wife, PENELOPE. In the story only Ulysses is strong enough to bend the bow and shoot an arrow through 12 rings. By this sign Penelope recognized her husband after his absence of 20 years.

(a) Uriah Heep A base, malignant, or scheming character; from the lowly character in Charles Dickens's *David Copperfield* (1849–50) who, despite constant boasting of his " 'umble" birth, position, and calling, is actually an accomplished forger and thief.

Valhalla A building or place used as a last resting place for famous personages; from the name of the celestial hall in Norse mythology to which the Valkyries (the divine attendants) brought the souls of heroes slain in battle.

Vanity Fair A setting dominated by frivolity or ostentation; from the continuous fair in the town of Vanity in John Bunyan's *The Pilgrim's Progress* (1678).

Wardour Street English English language marked by the affected use of archaic words and phrases; a term used by William Morris in 1888 to describe a translation of the *Odyssey* so archaic in tone, he said, that it reminded him of the pseudo-antique stores found on Wardour Street in London. The street today is better known for its association with the British film industry.

whimper *See* NOT WITH A BANG BUT A WHIMPER.

widow's mite A small offering that represents self-sacrifice; from the New Testament story (Mark 12:42–44) of such a gift. In the Bible the widow's gift is described as greater than other larger gifts, since the latter issued from the donor's abundance while the widow had given everything she had.

windmills *See* TILT AT WINDMILLS.

wormwood *See* GALL AND WORMWOOD.

(a) Xanthippe A woman who is scolding or shrewish; from the proverbially bad-tempered wife of the philosopher Socrates (*see also* SOCRATIC IRONY).

yahoos Uncouth, rowdy, or coarse characters; from the race of brutish creatures in human form with all the vices of man in Jonathan Swift's *Gulliver's Travels* (1726).

Young Turks A young, usually liberal group that seeks to take control of an organization from an entrenched, usually conservative, older group; from a 20th-century revolutionary party in Turkey.

CLIFTON FADIMAN
with the assistance of John Morse

Proverb and Gnome

The Oxford Dictionary's definition of a proverb as "A short pithy saying in common use . . ." emphasizes that proverbs are part of the spoken language. They belong, in origin, to the same stage of racial history as ballad and folksong, and are related to the fable and riddle. Their literary counterparts are the apothegm, aphorism, maxim, epigram, and gnome, although many proverbs show literary refinement. Thus "God tempers the wind to the shorn lamb," found in Sterne's *Sentimental Journey* (1768), is derived from Latin and was translated from French in George Herbert's *Outlandish Proverbs* (1640) as "To a close-shorn sheep God gives wind by measure."

DISTRIBUTION AND COMPARISON   Proverbs are found all over the world, and their comparison provides insight into the effects of cultural conditions, language, and local variations on expression. Thus the biblical "An eye for an eye, a tooth for a tooth," has an equivalent among the Nandi of East Africa: "A goat's hide buys a goat's hide and a gourd a gourd." Both form part of codes of behaviour, and exemplify the proverb's use for transmission of tribal wisdom and rules of conduct. Often, the same proverb may be found in many variants. In Europe this may result from the international currency of Latin proverbs in the Middle Ages. "A bird in the hand is worth two in the bush" originated in the medieval Latin *Plus valet in manibus avis unica fronde duabus,* and is first found in English in the Harleian manuscript (*c.* 1470) as "Betyr ys a byrd in the hond than tweye in the wode." Later English versions are "three" (or "ten") "in the wood," and "One . . . in the net is worth 100 flying." The Rumanian version is "Better a bird in the hand than 1,000 on the house"; the Italian, "Better one in a cage than four in the arbour"; the Portuguese, "Better a sparrow in the hand than two flying"; the Spanish, "A sparrow in the hand is worth a vulture flying"; the German, "A sparrow in the hand is better than a crane on the roof"; and the Icelandic, "Better a hawk in the hand than two in flight."

CONTENT AND STYLE   Attempts have been made to see in proverbs indications of national characteristics. Certain stylistic similarities are shown by proverbs from the same part of the world. Thus, Arabic and other Middle Eastern proverbs use pictorial forms of expression and hyperbole. Some Arabic proverbs are fables in miniature, or refer to fables: so do classical proverbs (*e.g.,* Seneca's "Every cock crows [crouse = is master of] on his own dunghill"). Hyperbole is exemplified in the Egyptian, "Fling him into the Nile, and he will come up with a fish in his mouth" of a lucky man. Dialogue proverbs are popular in Arabic, and in Greek, Ruthenian, Russian, and Polish. Classical proverbs are often terse (*e.g., Praemonitus, praemunitis* = "Forewarned is forearmed"). *Homo proponit, Deus disponit* (derived from the Vulgate version of Prov. 16:9) keeps its style in English and other translations: "Man proposes, God disposes."

Alliteration is found in proverbs of Germanic origin, which also show a liking for personification, as in *"Herr Pfennig geht voran"* ("Mr. Penny heads the procession"). Many languages make use of rhyme and play on words (*e.g.,* the German *"Voll, toll"* = "A drunken man is a mad man"; and the Scots "Many a mickle makes a muckle"; *i.e.,* "Many small things make one big thing").

Proverbs originating among the early Germanic peoples may reflect the heroic spirit. An 8th-century Saxon proverb *"Oft daedlata domae for-eldit gigistha gahwem; swyltit i ana"* ("A coward often misses glory in some high enterprise: therefore he dies alone") illustrates this. Its emergence, by way of the 15th-century "Tarying draweth peril," John Lyly's "Delays breede dangers: nothing so perilous as procrastination" (*Euphues,* 1579) and Shakespeare's "Delays have dangerous ends," as "Delays are dangerous" shows how changing thought and language affect expression.

Folk proverbs use homely imagery—pot and kettle, pig, sheep, horse, cock and hen, cow and bull, dog, the events of everyday life. Some proverbs first found in literary form have been adapted from speech. It is difficult to decide the authorship of a particular proverb. Abraham Lincoln is said to have invented the saying about not changing horses in the middle of the river, but he may only have used a proverb already current. Many biblical proverbs have classical parallels. "A soft answer turneth away wrath" was known to Aeschylus as well as to Soloman. "Physician, heal thyself" (Luke 4:23) is classical in origin, and "It is hard for thee to kick against the pricks [goad]" (Acts 26:14) is used by Aeschylus and Euripides.

Some proverbs refer to historical occasions. "When in Rome do as Rome does" translates St. Ambrose's answer to St. Augustine's mother, who asked whether, when in Milan, she should follow the Roman usage there and keep the Sabbath as a feast day, or that of her home town Tagaste, where it was a fast. Popular usage sometimes creates new proverbs from old ones. Thus some biblical proverbs have acquired new meanings: *e.g.,* "The love of money is the root of all evil" has become "Money is the root of all evil."

Many proverbs are legal in origin, although the laws to which they refer may be obsolete. The allusion in "Possession is nine [or eleven] points of the law" has defied explanation. Some refer to well-known legal principles. "An Englishman's house is his castle" is a reference to the principle by which a man is safe from the bailiffs if he shuts himself up in his own house and denies access.

Proverbs are of interest for their reference to old customs. "Good wine needs no bush" refers to the medieval custom of marking shops by a sign, and "If the cap fits, wear it" to the fool's cap. Proverbs also preserve words in obsolete senses: in "The exception proves the rule," "prove" = "test" (cf. "The proof of the pudding is in the eating"). They also embody superstitions. "Marry in May, repent alway," for example, is recorded by Ovid as a current superstition and refers to the pagan idea that spring, the time of planting, was a critical period when certain tabus should be observed. Weatherlore and medical advice also find their way into proverbs: *e.g.,* "Rain before seven, fine before eleven"; and the early 16th-century "Early to bed, early to rise/Makes a man healthy, wealthy, and wise."

Use of rhyme may show long history. "Who goes a-borrowing, goes a-sorrowing" has its origin in "He that fast spendyth must nede borowe; but whan he schal paye agen, then ys al the sorowe" (*c.* 1470). Sometimes style shows literary origin: *e.g.,* "Faint heart ne'er won fair lady," of which a version is found in John Gower's *Confessio Amantis* (*c.* 1390).

COLLECTIONS AND USES   Proverbs in the biblical Book of Proverbs, traditionally associated with Solomon, include earlier compilations. Ancient Egyptian collections include the "Precepts of Ptah-hotep" (*c.* 2500 B.C.) and the "Teachings of Amen-em-apt" (*c.* 1000 B.C.). Sumerian inscriptions give grammatical rules in proverbial form. Proverbs were used in ancient China for ethical instruction, and the Vedic writings of India use them to expound philosophical ideas; and although these, like the Greek gnomes, are poetic and literary, they may embody popular sayings. Classical proverbs were collected in the 1st century A.D. In 1500, Erasmus published *Adagia,* a collection of 800 Greek and Latin proverbs. A later edition (1536) contained more than 4,000.

Early English proverb collections include the so-called *Proverbs of Alfred* (*c.* 1150–80), containing religious and moral precepts; and the more worldly *Proverbs of Hendyng* (*c.* 1250). Use of proverbs in monasteries to teach novices Latin, in schools of rhetoric, and in sermons, homilies, and didactic works made them widely known and led to their preservation in manuscripts.

The use of proverbs in literature and oratory was at its height in England in the 16th and 17th centuries. John Heywood wrote a dialogue in proverbs (1546, later enlarged) and Drayton a sonnet; and in the 16th century a speech in proverbs was made in the House of Commons. Proverbs were used as titles for plays (*e.g.*, *All's Well That Ends Well*), illustrated in tapestries and paintings, engraved on cutlery, and, from the 16th to the 19th centuries, set as copies for schoolchildren, and for the making of samplers. In North America the best-known use of proverbs is probably in *Poor Richard's Almanac,* published annually between 1732 and 1757 by Benjamin Franklin. Many of "Poor Richard's" sayings were traditional European proverbs reworked by Franklin and given an American context when appropriate. In France proverbs gave rise to the *proverbes dramatiques,* dramatic sketches illustrating a proverb popular in the *salons* in the 17th and 18th centuries, which reached their height with Alfred de Musset. In the 19th century, they were used in the novel to give a colloquial character to speech or to evoke the atmosphere of the past. The study of folklore led to the collection and study of proverbs, and this continued in the 20th century.

GNOME AND GNOMIC POETRY   The Greek word *gnome* means moral aphorism or proverb. Short memorable sentences enshrining traditional wisdom are found in early Greek literature, both poetry and prose, from Home and Hesiod onward. Their form may be either imperative, as in the famous command "know thyself," or indicative, as in the couplet by Theognis of Megara (6th century B.C.): "No mortal who misled a stranger or a suppliant, Polypaides, has gone unheeded by the immortal gods." (The tense of the last verb is the so-called gnomic aorist, often used in Greek to express truths of permanent validity; English usage generally prefers the present tense; *e.g.*, "Too many cooks spoil the broth.") Such aphorisms were collected into anthologies, called *gnomologia,* and used in instructing the young. Aeschines, the 4th-century B.C. Athenian orator, remarks that as children we learn the gnomes of the poet so that as adults we may practise them. One of the best known *gnomologia* was compiled by Joannes Stobaeus in the 5th century A.D., and such collections remained popular in the middle ages.

Gnomes appear frequently in Old English epic and lyric poetry. In *Beowulf* they are often interjected into the narrative, drawing a moral from the hero's actions with such phrases as "Thus a man ought to act" and "Fate often aids a man not doomed to die, when his courage holds good" (the equivalent of the modern saying "God helps those who help themselves"). The main collections of Old English gnomes are to be found in the 10th-century *Exeter Book* and the Cotton Tiberius manuscript (early 11th century), clearly examples of early verse, abrupt and disconnected, yet picturesque and of great power.

ENCYCLOPÆDIA BRITANNICA

Classical Religion and Mythology

GREECE   The religion of the ancient Greeks is no longer absurdly abused nor foolishly idealized, and can be seen clearly for what it was. It contained savage and barbarous elements as well as elements of civilization, although the savagery and barbarism are still sometimes exaggerated. It was creedless, developing without any authoritative writing like the Bible or the Koran, and without any inflexible tradition to hamper or to guide it. It varied from age to age, from place to place and probably also from class to class, being now more backward, now more advanced, but always retaining certain characteristics. It was, first, an anthropomorphic polytheism, the worship of a number (not very large) of gods, thought of as human in form and largely human in mind. These gods were neither passionless nor without characteristics seen by the developed ethics of philosophy as moral faults. But as the history of this worship covers some 2,000 years, it can be seen that ideas, even popular ideas, on these matters were somewhat variable. The gods were normally, though not always, clear-cut figures, made concrete by poetry and art and surrounded by a large mythology. This, however, was not a body of dogma; the worshiper might believe, disbelieve or alter it to his taste.

The Greek religion was for the most part completely free from otherworldliness. It was a religion of everyday life, which sought for temporal blessings such as good crops, deliverance from enemies, health, or peace within the community. In historical times at least it was in its most conspicuous form an affair of the state, although family cult never ceased to exist, and individual religion developed strikingly as the importance of the Greek city-states declined from the 4th century B.C. onward.

Origins.   The people who in historical times called themselves Hellenes (Greeks) came to Greece from an unknown district, perhaps by way of Asia Minor. They brought with them only one deity whose name and native origin are certain, namely Zeus. It is likely that they also had a corn-goddess, whether or not they already called her Demeter, and she may by then have had a daughter, Kore ("the maiden"). The Greeks probably had additional names of deities such as Pluton ("the rich one"), who may well have been the deity of the earth's wealth, *i.e.*, of its crops. Only later, perhaps, was he identified with Hades, the god of the dead, an older form of whose name is Aïdes, perhaps meaning "the unseen." In any case Hades is not a god of the living, who therefore do not worship him. The dead likewise are no longer in the charge of the gods worshiped on earth, and presumably do not worship them. Similarly, the name Helios (Halios, Eëlios) refers not only to the visible sun but also to the sun-god. He had no cult in Greece proper, however, nor had Selene, the moon; gods of the heavens are no concern of people who move on the earth. Zeus is a deity of the weather-sky, that is, of meteorological phenomena such as rain and snow. No other god or goddess of any importance has a name demonstrably Greek. Kronos' name is certainly unHellenic; Apollo's yields no convincing Greek etymology. Athena is a pre-Hellenic goddess, adopted by the incoming Greeks in Mycenaean times as the protectress of their chieftains' castles. Artemis, or Artamis, has a name possibly connected with *artamŏs*. This word, however, means "slaughterer" or "butcher," whereas Artemis is a huntress, a helper in childbirth and on occasion the sender of sudden and painless death to women. The name Hera, if Greek, is the feminine form of *hēros,* a nobleman or gentleman; it thus means "lady"—a title, not a proper name. The name of Hermes (Hermeias) may be etymologically connected with *hĕrma,* stone or rubble; he may have begun as the power haunting cairns put up to mark holy spots or to delimit paths, but this is uncertain. Ares is stated by the Greeks themselves to be Thracian; in any case, the origin of his name is obscure. Aphrodite is certainly oriental. Persephone (her name has several forms) assuredly is not of Greek origin. Hecate comes from Caria, Hephaestus from the volcanic regions of Asia Minor, and Dionysus is a later arrival of Thracian or Thraco-Phrygian origin. There remain only a few minor powers. The Muses (Mousai) are supposed to derive their name from hypothetical Montiai, meaning "prompters" or "reminders." Pan (Pa-on, "feeder") is the little god of Arcadian goatherds. There are also the Nymps ("nymph" means marriageable young woman or bride) and their like. It is not known when the cult of any of these powers began.

Some of the gods composing the classical pantheon were taken from the cults existing in the regions invaded by the Greeks. This occurred through the characteristic Greek power of adapting and naturalizing foreign influences, and there was little or no realization of the different origins of the gods. The great civilization of Minoan Crete had an elaborate religion, an outstanding feature of which was the worship of goddesses. Clear traces are to be found also of gods who are born, grow to maturity and die, probably every year, with the growth and decay of the seasonal vegetation. Both those elements influenced Greek cult and myth. In Greece proper are to be found deities with names that are not Greek and that show the characteristic suffixes (found also in place-names, etc.) of the pre-Greek language. Examples are -*nth*-, as in Hyakinthos, -*na*-, as in Athena, and -*ss*-, as in Phersephassa (Persephone). Also in Greece are fairly clear traces of an ancient cult of one or more goddesses. There is an ingenious modern theory that one of these, probably an earth goddess, was named or nick-named "Da" (a word occurring in classical Greek as an ejaculation). It is contended that this syllable blended with Greek elements to compose two or three divine names, as in Demeter or Damater, "mother Da," and Posei-da-on, "husband of Da." For Poseidon was not originally a sea-god, nor were his earliest worshipers acquainted with the sea. He was a deity of the waters which fertilize the soil, and also, for some obscure reason, a god of horses.

It has been said that these deities are usually anthropomorphic. However, there are traces, probably very early, of their having taken bestial shape. Hera is *boōpis* in Homer; the word probably meant, to the poet, that she had large, cowlike eyes. It could, however, mean "cow-faced," and it is relevant that Hera's priestess Io is said to have been changed into a heifer either by the goddess or by Zeus. Athena is *glaukōpis*, a word used by Homer and other writers to mean "gray-eyed" or "bright-eyed"; but the bird with which Athena is associated, a kind of owl, is called *glaux*, and the epithet may originally have meant "owl-faced." *Poseidon* is said occasionally to have taken the form of a horse, while Zeus and Dionysus appeared under various animal guises. The latter commonly manifested himself as a serpent or a bull; a hymn sung in his honour at Elis actually calls him "noble bull." But such cases as these are comparatively rare and abnormal. In any event they have nothing to do with totemism, a wholly non-European phenomenon, but are examples of theriolatry, which is found in many parts of the world (*see* H. J. Rose, *Primitive Culture in Greece,* p. 47 ff.).

Growing knowledge of the near east gradually reveals the extent to which the early Greeks were influenced by the cults and beliefs of the great oriental civilizations bordering their district. It is justifiable to say, at least, that some Greek myths were related to certain myths current among these peoples, for example, the Hittites. Egyptian and other foreign influences probably entered Greece by way of Crete, but details are still lacking with regard to this and other aspects of the early history of the eastern Mediterranean. The place of origin of the worship of Apollo, for instance, is still unknown, although it is certain that he had connections with Asia (*see* W. K. C. Guthrie, *The Greeks and Their Gods,* p. 74 ff.). A popular and sometimes locally important cult was that of the heroes, literally gentleman; *i.e.,* powerful and worshipful ghosts of real or imaginary men (sometimes women, *heroinai*), the most famous being Heracles. Minor and half-forgotten ("faded") gods were often confused with these beings. (*See* L. R. Farnell, *Greek Hero-Cults.*)

Development.   At some time earlier than the earliest evidence, earlier, that is, than the Homeric poems, the Greeks had combined most of their deities into one divine clan, the head or "house-father" of which was Zeus. Zeus was represented as the begetter of most of the younger deities, and as being himself the son of Kronos and the husband and brother of Hera. His position is that of a chieftain of the heroic age among his relatives and vassals. But this does not mean that he was the chief god in the cult of every community. At Athens, for instance, his festivals, which had increased in number to include some that were not his originally, were dwarfed in importance by those of Athena. Greek worship throughout the Archaic and Classical periods was essentially communal, although nothing prevented an individual from approaching any deity he chose on his own behalf. Every family had its observances, including the worship of the hearth-goddess Hestia, who scarcely achieved the status of a personal deity but always maintained close relations with the sacred fire from which she came. The larger groups, whether supposedly of kin, like the phratries or clans, or merely local, like the demes (townships) into which Attica was divided, had also their own worship; but the most important and impressive rites were naturally those conducted by the state. The nearest approach to a common governing religious body was the oracle of Apollo at Delphi; and even that, though it lent its sanction to innovations on occasion, was often content to tell inquirers that they would be well advised to "worship according to ancestral custom." The oracle had neither a recognized orthodoxy to enforce, nor a disciplined and obedient clergy to support it in any state that might prove recalcitrant. If Apollo were directly and materially concerned, strong measures might indeed be taken. The four "sacred" wars were all fought, nominally at least, in consequence of violation of the god's rights to certain territories; but this was hardly more than vindication of the divine proprietor's lawful claims. In general Delphi confined itself to giving advice. The inquirer, if he rejected this, did so at his own risk, and numerous tales pointed the moral that his consequent peril was real; but the effectiveness of such warnings depended on the degree of respect in which the oracle was held.

Under such a system, the nature of the cults and their distance from savagery varied greatly. In Arcadia and similar backward districts the simple people might perform archaic or grotesque ritual around a shapeless block of stone or a plank of wood, called perhaps only by some such laudatory epithet as "the good god." In a centre of culture, such as Athens, however, the holy places would be marked by stately and beautiful temples, each the dwelling of a deity represented, perhaps, by an ancient cult-statue, but probably also by a masterpiece of sculpture.

The ritual would be orderly and elaborate, comprising hymns, prayers and sacrifices. The hymns were often written by celebrated poets and musicians, although prayer does not seem often to have taken the form of long and invariable liturgical texts. Sacrifice might involve the killing of many beasts before the temple and a general feast on their meat. Normally there would be a procession for the carrying of sacred objects and the leading of victims for sacrifice.

It is evident that the reactions of those present would vary from simple trust that the time-honoured ritual would win the favour of the deity to deep reflection upon the nature of the power addressed, or of divinity itself. From the latter point of view, different deities were very variously adaptable to the growing interest in ethical and theological speculation. After Zeus himself, Apollo, whose title Phoebus, "pure one," represented his concern with purifications, was thought to be sympathetic to a developed and enlightened morality; anecdotes and alleged oracles were current in support of this idea. Artemis, originally in all probability a mother-goddess, developed into a sort of personification of chastity; Athena became wisdom in person. On the other hand, many minor deities such as Pan, the Nymphs, or Hermes showed no moral development, at least in normal Greek thought. The unpopular Ares, too, remained simply a god of violent death and destruction, usually from war, but sometimes from other causes such as plague. The forms of worship were, as usual, conservative, and retained some features obviously dating from early days and comparatively low stages of culture; but even they tended to shed characteristics that advancing morality regarded as objectionable. The practice of human sacrifice, for instance, is attested by numerous legends, by an occasional ritual simulacrum of manslaughter and by the substitution, certain in some cases, merely probable in others, of an animal victim for one originally human. The actual rite was very occasionally revived in historical times; but the idea of human sacrifice became so repugnant to general sentiment that it was practically abandoned from about the 6th century B.C.

The general attitude of the Greek toward his gods was respectful but not servile. Like many Europeans, he would on occasion jest with the objects of his worship. The "Homeric" hymn to Hermes bears witness to this trait, with its humorous tales of Hermes' early rogueries. So does the comic appearance of Dionysus, Heracles and other popular deities on the Attic stage, as in the *Frogs* of Aristophanes.

Personal religion.   The very fact that the great public cults were managed by city-states gave them a certain artificiality. They were in many cases originally connected with the operations of farming, and therefore belonged to those times of the year at which these operations took place.

But the festivals were regulated by the state calendar and this by no means always corresponded with the real seasons. Thus, for example, a ceremony connected with plowing might be held when no farmer was actually plowing his fields. Country dwellers, no doubt, found some compensation for this defect in the worship of their little local powers such as the Nymphs; but, even so, the greatest and most conspicuous forms of worship must have seemed somewhat detached from real life.

In addition to this feeling there was a growing idea that the destiny of the individual was of importance, at least to him, and that the state cults existed rather for the benefit of the community. Hence the immense popularity, from about the end of the 5th century B.C., of the cult of Asclepius, whose powers were exerted on behalf of individuals seeking cure for their diseases rather than to avert some public calamity as was the office, for example, of Apollo. There were also the movements such as Orphism which made eschatological speculations regarding the individual, and the philosophic schools, not least that of Platonism, with their ideas on ethics, the government of the universe and the destiny of the soul. Ethics were not divorced from the conventional worships, but those involved no moral code that might direct conduct in detail. All these tendencies toward regard for the individual were reinforced in Hellenistic times by the passing of the old city-states as important political units. This rendered the ordinary man much more helpless in public affairs than his ancestors had been. The geocentric theory of the universe, too, imperfect though it was, made the earth an insignificantly small place, while astrology, which was generally believed in, represented man as the victim of mechanical and irresistible fate. It is no wonder that in early Hellenistic days the cult of Tyche (Chance, Fortune) was widespread both in public and in private, and that later any system promising relief to man's helplessness was sure of adherents. Broadly speaking, such systems were of two kinds, both depending on knowledge, or *gnosis,* alleged to be supernatural and revealed (though Gnosticism, as such, is the name given to a Christian heresy). The first kind of system was the mystery religion. Mysteries were usually, though not always, of oriental origin, and claimed to secure for their initiates the favour of a particular deity, Isis or Mithra for example, who would care for their well-being, especially after death. Such patrons, being gods, were, according to the generally received theory, exempt from the centripetal influence of the stars, being above and beyond them, and thus beyond the reach of fate. The second system was the higher form of magic, "theurgy," which actually constrained the deities to help their clients. The lower forms of magic were also very popular. These aimed at compelling minor powers, notably the *biaiŏthanatoi* (ghosts of violently and prematurely deceased persons), to help the sorcerer in the desired way, for example, by revealing the future to him, by winning for him the favours of influential persons, by tormenting his enemies or by laming the horses he had bet against. One of the reasons for the ultimate triumph of Christianity over the more respectable of its rivals was the fact that, being unencumbered by fantastic myth and ritual of uncivilized origin, it dealt with the eschatological and other spiritual needs of the time in a more rational manner than did its rivals. What was left of Greek rationality contributed a logical and coherent theology to the new religion. The most stubborn opposition to Christianity came from the simple and unreflective worship of the countryside which had behind it the force of ancestral custom. Compromises were numerous; for example, the cult of Asclepius was replaced by that of miracle-working saints, and the small shrines of the little rustic deities by those of Christian powers. Indeed, traces of the old worship are still found in popular customs in Greece and other countries.

ROME   The earliest Romans were a small community of peasant farmers, probably held together in a loose organization with a king at its head. Under him would be the heads (*patres*) of families or clans, with their retainers (*clientes*). Even in its earliest days the community probably engaged in a certain amount of trade in addition to farming and stock raising, since Rome lies advantageously on the principal natural highway of central Italy, which is the Tiber, and on the border between the Etruscan cities northward and the towns of the Latin league farther south. According to tradition the people were of mixed stock, with some Latin and some Sabine highland blood; various linguistic and other facts tend to confirm this. Threatened by powerful neighbours, they were of necessity warlike.

Like many peoples at a comparable or even at a lower stage of culture, the Romans had developed a few "high gods" by the earliest known period of their history. The names of some of their deities can be recovered, chiefly from surviving festival calendars. None of these was composed earlier than the 1st century B.C., and by that late date many of the oldest feast days and religious seasons had lost their former prominence; but the calendars nevertheless record the gods' names in large letters. Chief among them comes Jupiter (in Latin, Iuppiter), whose name is etymologically equivalent to the Greek Zeus and the Sanskrit Dyaus. It must therefore have come down from immemorial antiquity in the Indo-European family, along with the Latin language. The name Jupiter includes also the stock title *pater; i.e.,* head of the house, hence, person in authority. (Neither *pater* nor its correlative *mater* had originally any physiological meaning.) Like Zeus and Dyaus, Jupiter was a sky- and weather-god, obviously important to farmers.

With him were early associated two other gods, Mars and Quirinus. Mars was a deity of great importance, widely worshiped in Italy, but of doubtful origins—his name is of highly uncertain etymology. His functions were very wide, and included the protection of his worshipers, their cattle and other possessions against all manner of evils, such as disease or the devastation of their property. These evils included the perils of war, and Mars was consequently a warlike god. Quirinus was much less important. He is said to have been Sabine, despite the fact that the sound represented by *qu-* did not exist in the Sabine dialect, and it seems that he was the god of the *quirium,* whatever that may have been. The word would seem to be connected with the name *Quirites* by which Roman citizens were collectively known. Jupiter, Mars and Quirinus formed a triad, but their festivals were separate. Jupiter was worshiped especially on the ides (day of full moon) of each lunar month. Mars was worshiped almost exclusively in his own month, the first of the original Roman year, *Martius* (*i.e.,* March), and in October. Quirinus' feast day was the Quirinalia on Feb. 17.

At least one goddess, Juno, was important in the earliest-known times. She seems to have had no original connection with Jupiter or with any other god save perhaps Janus, one of whose titles was Iunonius. Juno's name may most reasonably be associated with words denoting young maturity, such as *iuuenis,* and so may signify a marriageable woman. Certainly her chief function was to supervise the life of women, and since their sexual life has what may be called a lunar rhythm, Juno has certain lunar associations, under the title of Iuno Couella. The month of June (*Iunius*) is hers, though its name is derived from a stem, *iuni-,* seen in the Etruscan corruption of her name, which is Uni. Her festival, marked by curious and obviously ancient ritual, was the Nonae Caprotinae, or Nones of the Wild Fig, on July 7. A sacrifice was made to her, together with Janus, on the first day (*kalendae*) of every month. On March 1, the dedication day of the temple of Juno Lucina, the birth-goddess, married women held a festival, the Matronalia. This, however, is not one of the oldest holy days. The women swore an oath by this goddess, "Eiuno." There are several examples, too, of a woman speaking of "my Juno," as a man would speak of his "Genius." It has been suggested that there were to begin with many *iunones,* one for each woman, and that the goddess originated from the coalescence of these into the single great figure. But the evidence for an individual *iuno* is late, not earlier than the time of Augustus; while examples of a divine name coupled with a possessive pronoun are fairly common. The locution means no more than, for example: "Such-and-such a divinity, whom I worship"; "this deity in his or her dealings with me." Juno was widely worshiped outside Rome, being sometimes the chief deity of a state, and as such on occasion having warlike functions. Thus at Lanuvium, Juno Sospita Mater Regina was represented clad in a goatskin and bearing a spear and shield.

But the most characteristic deities of this period were vague figures of limited and sharply defined functions. Like the greater gods, they were regarded as possessing superhuman power, known as *numen* from at least the 2nd century B.C. This they could be induced to employ for the benefit of their worshipers if rightly approached. Beyond this, Roman curiosity did not go; the gods have no myths, do not form married pairs (though a masculine and a feminine name are often conjoined) and have no offspring. To name them correctly and to worship them with the proper words and gestures were supremely important; hence there grew up in time elaborate lists of liturgical formulas, the *indigitamenta* (*indigitare* means to address a deity with the appropriate titles, etc.). These are complicated by the intrusion into surviving documents of a host of names of godlings presiding over the most minute details of human life and activity. Some of the names were apparently invented for special occasions, others are due to false etymologies. These numerous godlings appear to be the result of priestly elaboration at a comparatively late period; but it seems true that some such *di minuti* did exist. Thus Janus, who was on his way to develop into a god of beginnings (hence the name, January, of the first month in the reformed calendar and the sacrifice to Janus on all kalends), is almost certain to have been nothing more originally than the personification of an *ianus* or gateway, to pass through which is an act often of magico-religious significance. Vesta, the hearth-goddess, is the sacred hearth itself, the recipient of some cult in every household. Terra or Tellus Mater, the earth-goddess, probably was the holder of that *numen* which was necessary to make the Roman territory productive; certainly she was not goddess of the whole earth. The name of Ceres, the grain-goddess, may have been an adjective, "productive," applied to Terra; she owes her whole personality to her early identification with Demeter. A curious deity is the Genius, a sort of divine double of a man. The name means "begetter," and the Genius was supposed to be pleased if the man was well fed, defrauded if he lived poorly. In classical times every man, bond or free, had a Genius, but it may be that he belonged originally to the head of the house only. Various of these deities form groups. Such are the Indigetes and the Novensides, whose functions remain uncertain; the Lares, originally little gods of the farmland and of the houses standing on it, though their office was enlarged later; and the Penates (singular *penas*), who have an adjectival name, "of the inner rooms," and who particularly looked after the storeroom.

Italian and Etruscan.   At the end of the regal epoch and during the earlier part of the republican, importations of deities from other than purely Etruscan sources took place. The Capitoline cult gave Jupiter as partners Juno and Minerva, the latter not originally a Roman goddess. The grouping is most readily explained by Greek influence coming through Etruria, for the two goddesses were early identified with Hera and Athena, respectively the wife and the daughter of Zeus. Venus, Fortuna and Diana came in during this period from native Italian sources. Very early in the republic, Castor and Pollux were given a temple in the forum, in consequence, according to tradition, of their aid to the Romans at the battle of Lake Regillus (499? B.C.) against the Latin league. (The form Pollux is the Latin corruption of the Greek Polydeuces.) Even among the earliest-known deities are some whose names yield no discoverable Latin etymology, and certain of them are probably Etruscan. Examples are Volcanus, god of destructive fire, at first volcanic fire; Saturnus or Saeturnus, a deity of very uncertain original functions; and Volturnus, apparently a river-god, probably of the Tiber. Almost certainly a very old importation was Hercules. This form of his name is an Italian corruption of the Greek Herakles. His altar stood in the cattle market (*Forum boarium*) near the Palatine, whose traditional boundary swung out to enclose the market. A widely recognized deity, such as Hercules had become, was needed to keep the peace in a market where strangers were dealt with.

Greek (Greco-Roman). As Rome expanded, its relations with the Greek communities of southern Italy and, later, with Greece itself and with the empires of Alexander's successors became more frequent. As a result, Greek cults made their appearance, being sometimes new importations, sometimes modifications of existing worships brought about by identification of Greek with Roman or other Italian deities. A new importation was the cult of Apollo, which steadily grew in importance; he had no generally accepted Italian equivalent. The oracles of the Sibyl of Cumae, supposedly inspired by him, were acquired at an early date, according to tradition by the elder or the younger Tarquin. Apollo, in his capacity as a divine physician, soon followed the oracles of his inspired prophetess. His first Roman temple is said to have been vowed in 433 B.C. "for the public health," which presumably means on the occasion of a plague; he appears, however, to have had some sort of sacred place (*Apollinar*) earlier than this. Evidence of the latter species of cult is the temple (on the Aventine and thus outside the *pomerium*) of Ceres, Liber and Libera, a triad copied from the Eleusinian worship of Demeter, Kore and Iacchus. Iacchus was commonly identified with Dionysus and hence with Liber, the Italian wine-god and associate of Jupiter. The Aventine temple became the central sanctuary of the Roman plebs. It was dated 493 B.C., having been vowed three years earlier; its style was Etruscan, but its decorations were Greek. With Greek cults came Greek art, at least in the form of statues of deities, and Greek mythology also. This the Romans accepted eagerly and apparently at a fairly early date—for, despite their intense national pride, they were remarkably ready to learn from foreign sources anything that struck them as important.

The Romans also developed a Greek attitude toward their own early history. It was hardly respectable for any important place not to have a founder with high, preferably divine, connections and for a barbarian city to be thought something better than barbarous it was well for it to produce some evidence of Greek or, failing that, Trojan origins. As a result of this tendency there grew up various highly artificial legends concerning the foundation of Rome, which finally took their most familiar shape in the tale of Romulus and Remus, sons of Mars and descendants of Aeneas of Troy. The sequel of this particular legend stated that Romulus was transformed into the god Quirinus, this despite the fact that native Roman feeling drew a very sharp line between men and gods. Roman cult had nothing corresponding to Greek hero worship. This embellishment, however, is not known to have been current before the age of Cicero.

The age of Augustus saw a revival of the old cults, fostered and sponsored by his government and reinforced by new splendour of temples. An addition was the development of the worship of the emperor's patron, Apollo. His great temple on the Palatine became the centre of what might not unjustly be called a rival system to that headed by the Capitolian triad. Whatever Augustus' own beliefs may have been, and however much he may have regarded his religious revival as a useful political instrument, it was the beginning of something resembling an age of faith.

Oriental. Although the Roman and the Greco-Roman modes of worship were as a rule decent and originally expressed genuine religious feeling, neither was exciting. Moreover, they were state or family cults concerned with this world, little attention being paid to aspirations for a future life. A dead Roman was thought to join the company of the Good People (*Manes,* a word that has no singular). As a member of a family or of a clan he would be one of the *di parentes*—again, no singular form of this description is known until at earliest the latter part of the 2nd century B.C.—and as such he would share in the respectful attentions of the surviving kin. But little hope was entertained of any effective survival for him, though it was trusted that the memory of a distinguished person would be long kept alive.

During the later years of the republic, however, and still more under the empire, a strong but mostly inarticulate demand for some kind of personal religion was growing. There grew up, chiefly in the east, sundry cults that promised their votaries the personal favour of deities, or even divine rank, if certain conditions were fulfilled. These usually included some form of initiation. The orient first obtained a foothold in Rome in 204 B.C., when by advice of the Sibylline oracles the Great Mother of the Gods (*Mater deum magna Idaea*) was imported from Pessinus in Asia Minor and in 191 B.C. given a temple on the Palatine, in the heart of Rome itself. Her rites, carried out by eunuch-priests, shocked Roman sentiment, and citizens were long forbidden to take part in them; but the goddess was treated with respect, especially as she was associated with Troy and with the legendary ancestry of the Roman people. In 186 B.C. came the affair of the Bacchanalia. A cult of Dionysus was introduced into Italy, comprising rites of initiation and nightly ceremonies that had something of the wildness of the god's original Thracian or Thraco-Phrygian worship. They were alleged to be attended by all manner of sexual and other crimes. Scenting a conspiracy against law and order, the senate took severe and effective measures to suppress the movement, but it was the precursor of numerous Dionysiac mysteries, apparently harmless enough, and varying from serious religious associations to dining and drinking clubs nominally under the patronage of the god. These last characterized the early empire especially. The older mysteries, especially the Eleusinian, retained their prestige and drew many Roman initiates, who seem to have read into them whatever philosophical doctrines they found attractive; but the most marked tendencies of the age were definitely toward the east, to Asia or to Egypt.

Then there were the mysteries of Attis, which were an offshoot of the cult of the Great Mother. Attis, the goddess' young favourite, who had died and been at least partly revived, was their central figure. Lastly came the mysteries of Mithra. They were in some ways the most important of all, and were originally Persian. The worship was for men only, and was popular especially in the army. It centred on the mythical career of Mithra, was divided into grades vaguely reminiscent of those of freemasonry, and carried with it a high and stern morality. It was for a while a formidable rival to Christianity.

ENCYCLOPÆDIA BRITANNICA

Glossary of Selected Foreign Words and Phrases

Avis au lecteur

The English language is richly stocked with foreign words and phrases, borrowed over the centuries from the tongues of those who ruled and interacted with Britain and from the myriad cultures that produced America. Many of these eclectic borrowings are now thoroughly integrated into our daily vocabulary and their foreign origins forgotten. To suggest only a few, such words as *bizarre, catsup, coffee, cookie, dungaree, hazard, magazine, mosquito, pajamas, plaid, tycoon, waffle,* and *zero* are so familiar that we may be unaware that each is borrowed from another language. Yet numerous other foreign words and phrases used in English with varying frequency are recognizably "foreign" and far less familiar to most people. We can nonetheless expect to find such foreign words and phrases punctuating the text of any newspaper, magazine, or book, and our reading is made more enjoyable if we comprehend this special vocabulary.

The following glossary of selected foreign words and phrases is intended as a useful companion to reading. Although not exhaustive, the glossary contains a substantial body of foreign words and phrases likely to be encountered in a variety of general English reading contexts. Present is a wide range of foreign words and phrases drawn from classical as well as contemporary sources. Absent are foreign words and phrases from technical and highly specialized professional vocabularies.

This list is arranged in strict alphabetical order, with entries presented in the form most commonly used in English. This means that some foreign words and phrases correctly introduced by an article drop that article in English usage; this abbreviated form is that which appears in this glossary. Other foreign words and phrases used in English alternatively drop or retain the introductory article. For example, the French phrase *le mot juste* ("just the right word or expression") occasionally appears in an English context simply as *mot juste*. In such cases the

524

entry is alphabetized by its second word, with the article given in parentheses. Thus *(le) mot juste* is alphabetized in this glossary under M. If you are unable to immediately locate a phrase as it occurs in your reading, check the glossary for the second word of the phrase.

Each entry provides both the origin and meaning of the foreign word or phrase and, where appropriate or useful, alternate forms of the phrase. In the case of quotations the source is cited when known. The following abbreviations are used in this glossary:

esp.	especially
fem.	feminine
masc.	masculine
pl.	plural
sing.	singular
usu.	usually
F.	French
G.	German
Gk.	Greek
I.	Italian
L.	Latin
S.	Spanish

ab incunabilis (L.), from the cradle; from childhood—*Livy*

ab initio (L.), from the beginning

à bon chat, bon rat (F.), "to a good cat, a good rat"; tit for tat

à bon marché (F.), at a good price; inexpensive

ab ovo (L.), "from the egg"; from the beginning—*Horace*

ab ovo usque ad mala (L.), "from the egg to the apples"; from the beginning to the end (of a meal); similar to English "from soup to nuts."

à bras ouverts (F.), with open arms

absit invidia (L.), let there be no ill will

ab uno disce omnes (L.), from one learn to know all—*Virgil*

ab urbe condita (L.), from the founding of the city (Rome, founded about 753 B.C.)

à coeur ouvert (F.), with an open heart

à compte (F.), on account

à coup sûr (F.), with a sure stroke; without fail; surely

à demi (F.), half; semi-; in part

ad extremum (L.), to the extreme; to the last

ad hoc (L.), for this (particular occasion *or* purpose)

ad hominem (L.), "to the man"—usu. said of an attack on a person's character rather than a rebuttal to his argument

ad infinitum (L.), to infinity; endlessly

ad initium (L.), at the beginning

ad interim (L.), for the meanwhile; temporary

ad majorem Dei gloriam (L.), to the greater glory of God—motto of the Society of Jesus (Jesuits)

ad nauseam (L.), to the point of nausea or complete disgust

ad patres (L), "(gathered) to his fathers"; dead

à droite (F.), to (or on) the right

æquo animo (L.), with an even mind; calmly

a fortiori (L.), with stronger reason; more conclusively

à gauche (F.), to (or on) the left

Agnus Dei (L.), Lamb of God

à haute voix (F.), in a loud voice; aloud

à huis clos (F.), with closed doors

aide-mémoire (F.), memory aid; summary memorandum used in diplomatic communication

aîné; fem., aînée (F.), elder; senior

à la belle étoile (F.), under the stars; in the open night air

à la fin (F.), in the end

alea jacta est (L.), the die is cast—*Suetonius,* attributed to *Caesar* on his crossing the Rubicon

al fresco (I.), in the open air

aloha (Hawaiian), love to you; greetings; good-bye

alpha kai omega (Gk.), Alpha and Omega (first and last letters of the Greek alphabet); the beginning and the end

alter ego (L.), second self

a maximis ad minima (L.), from the greatest to the least

am Ende (G.), in the end; finally

ami de coeur (F.), "friend of the heart"; bosom friend

ami de cour (F.), "court friend"; false friend

à moitié (F.), half; in part

à mon avis (F.), in my opinion

amor patriae (L.), love of one's country

amor vincit omnia (L.), love conquers all

amour propre (F.), self-love; self-esteem

ancienne noblesse (F.), old-time nobility; the French nobility prior to the Revolution of 1789

ancien régime (F.), old regime; French political and social system prior to the Revolution of 1789; former system

Angst (G.), anxiety

anguis in herba (L.), snake in the grass; unexpected danger

animal bipes implume (L.), "two-legged animal without feathers" (*i.e.,* man)—Latin adaptation of *Plato*

anima mundi (L.), "soul of the world"; vital animating spirit pervading the universe

anno aetatis suae (L.), in the (specified) year of his (*or* her) age

anno Domini (L.), in the year of our Lord

anno mundi (L.), "in the year of the world"; a specified year, reckoned from the supposed year of the world's creation, 4004 B.C., as fixed by James Ussher, or 3761 B.C., as fixed by the Jews

anno urbis conditae (L.), in the year of the founded city (Rome, founded about 753 B.C.)

annos vixit (L.), he (*or* she) lived (a specified number of years)

annuit coeptis (L.), He (God) has smiled on our undertakings—motto on the reverse of the Great Seal of the U.S.—adapted from *Virgil*

annus mirabilis (L.), "marvelous year"; a wonderful year (esp. referring to 1666)

Anschluss (G.), junction; union (esp. referring to Nazi Germany's annexation of Austria in 1938)

ante mortem (L.), before death

ante omnia (L.), before all things; in the first place

à peu près (F.), nearly; approximately

après moi le déluge (F.), after me the deluge—generally attributed to *Louis XV*

à propos de rien (F.), apropos of nothing

à (*or* **au**) **rebours** (F.), the wrong way; against the grain; backwards

ars longa, vita brevis (L.), art is long, life is short

ars poetica (L.), art of poetry

à tort et à travers (F.), at random; haphazardly

à tort ou à raison (F.), rightly or wrongly

à tout prix (F.), at any cost

au bout de son latin (F.), "at the end of one's Latin"; at the end of one's mental resources

au contraire (F.), on the contrary

au courant (F.), up-to-date; in the know; well informed

au fond (F.), fundamentally

au grand sérieux (F.), in all seriousness

au jour le jour (F.), from day to day; from hand to mouth

auld lang syne (Scottish), "old long ago"; good old times

au pied de la lettre (F.), "to the foot of the letter"; literally

au pis aller (F.), if worse comes to worst

aurea mediocritas (L.), the golden mean—adapted from *Horace*

auto-da-fé (Portuguese), "act of faith"; the burning of a heretic

autres temps, autres moeurs (F.), other times, other customs

aux armes (F.), to arms

avant-propos (F.), preface

ave atque vale (L.), hail and farewell!

avis au lecteur (F.), notice, or word, to the reader

à votre santé! (F.), to your health!

à vue (F.), at sight

ayatollah (Arabic), "reflection of Allah"; Shiite Muslim religious leader

ballon d'essai (F.), trial balloon

barrio (S.), a district or neighborhood of a city; village outside a city

beau geste (F.), a magnanimous gesture

(le) beau monde (F.), the fashionable world

(les) beaux-arts (F.), the fine arts

beaux yeux (F.), "beautiful eyes"; good looks

bel esprit (F.), a fine mind; brilliant wit

(la) belle époque (F.), "the fine period"; period at the turn of the 20th century associated with an elegant lifestyle that ended with the onset of World War I

belles-lettres (F.), fiction, including, but not restricted to, light, elegant, and entertaining literature

bête noire (F.), "black beast"; pet aversion

bêtise (F.), silliness; absurdity

bien entendu (F.), well understood; naturally; of course

bienséance (F.), propriety; decorum

bienvenue (F.), welcome

billet-doux; *pl.*, **billets-doux** (F.), love letter

bon bourgeois (F.), respectable citizen

bon gré, mal gré (F.), whether willing or unwilling; willy-nilly

(le) bon mot (F.), clever remark; repartee

bonne chance! (F.), good luck!

bonne foi (F.), "good faith"; honesty; fair play

bon vivant (F.), lover of good living

bracero (S.), Mexican worker admitted to the U.S., esp. for seasonal farm labor

brut (F.), crude; unwrought; unmodified (as in brut champagne)

brutum fulmen; *pl.*, **bruta fulmina** (L.), "a senseless (*i.e.*, harmless) thunderbolt"; an empty threat—*Pliny*

cacoëthes scribendi (L.), mania for writing—*Juvenal*

canard (F.), "duck"; rumor or hoax

carpe diem (L.), seize the day; enjoy the present moment—*Horace*

carte blanche (F.), "blank paper"; full discretionary power

causa sine qua non (L.), an indispensable cause or condition

caveat emptor (L.), let the buyer beware

cave canem (L.), beware of the dog

cela saute aux yeux (F.), "that jumps to the eyes"; self-evident

cela va sans dire (F.), that goes without saying

c'est-à-dire (F.), that is to say

c'est la guerre (F.), that's war; that's life (an expression of resignation to unchangeable situations)

chacun à son goût (F.), each to his own taste

chador (Farsi), traditional head covering worn by Muslim women in Iran

chef d'oeuvre (F.), masterpiece

che sarà, sarà (I.), what will be, will be

chiaroscuro (I.), use or treatment of light and dark areas in a pictorial work of art

cinquecento (I.), "five hundred"; 16th century, esp. referring to Italian art and literature

cogito, ergo sum (L.), I think, therefore I am—*Descartes*

cognoscente; *pl.,* **cognoscenti** (I.), connoisseur(s)

comme il faut (F.), as it should be; fitting; correct

compagnon de voyage (F.), traveling companion

compte rendu (F.), report; an account rendered

con brio (I.), with spirit and force

congé (F.), leave-taking; dismissal

contretemps (F.), mishap

cordon sanitaire (F.), line of guards separating infected and uninfected areas to restrict passage between the two; group of neighboring, essentially neutral states that, by their geographical placement, separate two ideologically hostile or bellicose states

corruptio optimi pessima (L.), the corruption of the best is the worst

coup de foudre (F.), "thunderclap"; love at first sight

coup de maître (F.), masterstroke

coup d'essai (F.), first attempt; trial

coup de théâtre (F.), "stroke of theater"; dramatic turn of events

coup manqué (F.), abortive attempt; failure

crede Deo (L.), trust to God

cum grano salis (L.), with a grain of salt

custos morum (L.), guardian of morals

d'accord (F.), in accord; agreed

dai ichi (Japanese), number one; very good

danse macabre (F.), dance of death

décolletage (F.), low-cut neckline

décolleté (F.), having a low-cut neckline

de facto (L.), in fact; actual

de gustibus non est disputandum (L.), there is no disputing about tastes

Dei gratia (L.), by the grace of God

déjà vu (F.), "already seen"; sense of something previously experienced

de jure (L.), by right; by law

delineavit (L.), he (*or* she) drew (it)

de mal en pis (F.), from bad to worse

demimondaine (F.), a woman of the demimonde

demi-monde *or* **demimonde** (F.), "half-world"; a class of women of questionable reputation

démodé (F.), out of fashion; out-of-date

de mortuis nil nisi bonum (L.), of the dead (say) nothing but good

de nihilo nihilum (L.), from nothing nothing (can come)—*Persius*

Deo gratias (L.), thanks be to God

de palabra (S.), by word of mouth

de pis en pis (F.), worse and worse

de profundis (L.), out of the depths—*Vulgate, Psalms*

de rigueur (F.), obligatory; required by etiquette

détente (F.), relaxation of strained relations, usu. among nations

de trop (F.), in excess; superfluous

deus ex machina (L.), "god from a machine"; person or thing that resolves at the last minute a seemingly impossible dilemma

Deus vult (L.), God wills it

dharma (Sanskrit), natural law; religious duty

Dichtung und Wahrheit (G.), poetry and truth—subtitle of *Goethe*'s autobiography

dies faustus (L.), lucky day

dies infaustus (L.), unlucky day

dies irae (L.), day of wrath; Day of Judgment

divide et impera (L.), divide and rule

docendo discimus (L.), we learn by teaching

dolce far niente (I.), pleasant idleness

Domine, dirige nos (L.), Lord, direct us

Dominus vobiscum (L.), God be with you

Doppelgänger (G.), ghostly counterpart of a living person

dormitat Homerus (L.), "(even) Homer naps" (shortened from *aliquando bonus dormitat Homerus:* sometimes even the good Homer naps)—adapted from *Horace*

ecce agnus Dei (L.), behold the lamb of God

ecce signum (L.), behold the sign; this is the proof

élan vital (F.), vital or creative force of life

embarras de choix (F.), embarrassing variety of choices

embarras de richesse (F.), embarrassing surfeit of wealth

en ami (F.), as a friend

en avant! (F.), forward!; march!

en déshabillé (F.), in a state of undress; casually attired

en effet (F.), in effect; in fact

en famille (F.), with one's family; informally

enfin (F.), finally; in conclusion

en grande tenue (F.), in full dress

en plein air (F.), in the open air

en plein jour (F.), in broad daylight

en principe (F.), in principle

en somme (F.), finally; in short

ensuite (F.), then; next; afterwards

entente (F.), international agreement

entre nous (F.), confidentially

épater les bourgeois (F.), to shock the middle classes

e pluribus unum (L.), one out of many—motto on the obverse of the Great Seal of the U.S.

Ersatz (G.), compensation; substitute; artificial

esprit de l'escalier (F.), "staircase wit"; repartee that comes to mind after the appropriate moment has passed—*Diderot*

et alii; *fem.,* **et aliae** (L.), and others

et cetera (L.), and so forth

et hoc genus omne (L.), and everything of this kind

et sic de ceteris (L.), and so of the rest

et sic de similibus (L.), and so of the like

et tu, Brute (L.), and thou too, Brutus!—attributed to *Julius Caesar* as his last words upon seeing his friend Brutus among his assassins

eureka (Gk.), I have found it!—*Archimedes*

ex animo (L.), from the heart; sincerely

ex cathedra (L.), "from the chair"; authoritatively

excelsior (L.), ever higher

exempli gratia (L.), for example

exeunt omnes (L.), all exit; all leave the stage

ex libris (L.), from the books (*or* library) of

ex more (L.), according to custom

ex necessitate rei (L.), from the necessity of the case

ex nihilo nihil fit (L.), from nothing, nothing is made

ex officio (L.), by virtue of one's office

experto credite (L.), believe those with experience

ex post facto (L.), after the deed is done; retrospectively

ex tempore *or* **extempore** (L.), "from the moment"; without preparation; impromptu

façon de parler (F.), manner of speech; usual way of speaking

factum est (L.), it is done

faire suivre (F.), to have forwarded; please forward

fait accompli (F.), accomplished fact

Fata viam invenient (L.), the Fates will find a way—*Virgil*

faute de mieux (F.), for lack of something better

faux amis (F.), "false friends"; pairs of words with the same or similar form in two languages but with quite distinct meanings; *e.g.*, the English word *sensible* and its French look-alike *sensible,* meaning "sensitive"

faux naïf (F.), falsely naive; pretending to be childlike

felo-de-se (L.), suicide

feu de joie (F.), ceremonial firing of guns into the air as a salute

feux d'artifice (F.), fireworks

fiat experimentum in corpore vili (L.), let the experiment be performed on a worthless body

fiat justitia, ruat caelum (*or* **coelum**) (L.), let justice be done even though the heavens fall

fiat lux (L.), let there be light—*Vulgate, Genesis*

Fidei Defensor (L.), Defender of the Faith—title of English sovereigns

fils (F.), "son"—added to French proper names to distinguish father (*père*) and son; *e.g.*, Dumas *père* and Dumas *fils*

fin de siècle (F.), "end of century"; refers esp. to the end of the 19th century and to its decadence and devotion to aestheticism

(in) flagrante delicto (L.), "while the crime is blazing"; caught in the act; red-handed

force majeure (F.), "superior force"; unforeseeable circumstance beyond one's control

fuit Ilium (L.), "Troy was" (and hence, is no more); its time is past —*Virgil*

furor loquendi (L.), rage for talking

furor poeticus (L.), poetic frenzy

furor scribendi (L.), rage for writing

gaffe (F.), social blunder

garde du corps (F.), bodyguard

gaucherie (F.), awkward, uncouth act

gaudeamus igitur (L.), let us then be joyful

Geist (G.), spirit; essence

Gemeinschaft (G.), communal association; fellowship

Gemütlichkeit (G.), friendliness; cordiality

gens d'affaires (F.), business people

gens d'église (F.), clergy

gens de robe (F.), lawyers; magistrates

gens du monde (F.), fashionable people; high society

Gesellschaft (G.), formal association, usu. characterized by common goals and impersonal relationships

gnóthi seautón (Gk.), know thyself

Götterdämmerung (G.), twilight of the gods; end of the world

grâce à (F.), thanks to (someone *or* something)

grande toilette (F.), ceremonial dress

(le) grand monde (F.), fashionable world; high society

gratia Dei (L.), by God's grace

guerre à outrance (F.), war to the finish (*or* death)

hakīm (Arabic) "wise one"; Muslim physician, judge, or ruler

(la) haute bourgeoisie (F.), upper middle class

(la) haute politique (F.), affairs of state

(le) haut monde (F.), high society

hegira (Arabic) "flight"; Muhammad's flight from Mecca, A.D. 622; a journey, esp. of escape

hic jacet (L.), here lies—inscription preceding name on a tombstone

hic sepultus (L.), here is buried—used in epitaphs

hin und her (G.), here and there

hin und zurück (G.), there and back

hoc age (L.), do this; pay attention to what you are doing

hoc erat in more majorum (L.), this was in the manner of our ancestors

hoi polloi (Gk.), the masses; the common folk

hommage de reconnaissance (F.), token of appreciation

homme d'affaires (F.), businessman

homme d'église (F.), man of the church; clergyman

homme de lettres (F.), man of letters; literary man

homme d'esprit (F.), man of intellect or wit

homme d'état (F.), statesman

honi soit qui mal y pense (F.), shame to him who thinks evil of it

honneur et patrie (F.), honor and fatherland

honoris causa (L.), for the sake of honor; honorary; honorary university degree

horribile dictu (L.), horrible to tell

horribile visu (L.), horrible to see

hors de combat (F.), "out of combat"; disabled

hors de propos (F.), out of place; unfitting; irrelevant

ibidem (L.), in the same place

ici on parle français (F.), French is spoken here

idée fixe (F.), fixed idea; obsession

idem quod (L.), the same as

id est (L.), that is (to say)

ignorantia juris (*or* **legis**) **neminem excusat** (L.), ignorance of the law excuses no one

ignotum per ignotius (L.), "the unknown by the still more unknown"; trying to explain something unknown by reference to something else about which still less is known

il faut cultiver notre jardin (F.), "we must cultivate our garden"; we must tend to our own affairs—*Voltaire*

il va sans dire (F.), it goes without saying

incroyable (F.), unbelievable; also, a French dandy

in futuro (L.), in the future

in hoc signo vinces (L.), by this sign (of the Cross) you shall conquer

in limine (L.), on the threshold; at the beginning

in limine belli (L.), at the outbreak of war

in medias res (L.), in (*or* into) the midst of things

in principio (L.), in the beginning

in rerum natura (L.), in the nature of things

in saecula saeculorum (L.), for ages of ages; forever and ever; world without end

in situ (L.), in its original place

in statu quo (L.), in the same state or condition as before

in statu quo ante bellum (L.), in the same state as before the war

inter alia (L.), among other things

inter nos (L.), between ourselves

intra muros (L.), "within the walls"

in utero (L.), in the womb

in vino veritas (L.), in wine there is truth

invita Minerva (L.), "Minerva being unwilling"; lacking talent or inspiration—*Cicero*

ipse dixit (L.), "he himself said it"; a dogmatic but unproven statement

ipso facto (L.), by the very fact itself

Issei (Japanese), Japanese immigrant to America and esp. to the U.S.

jacta est alea (L.), the die is cast—attributed to *Julius Caesar*

januis clausis (L.), with closed doors; secretly

je pense, donc je suis (F.), I think, therefore I am—*Descartes*

jet d'eau (F.), "water jet"; a decorative fountain

jeu de mots (F.), play on words; pun

jeu d'esprit (F.), witticism

jihad (Arabic), holy war

jinn (Arabic), "demon"; genie

joie de vivre (F.), joy of living

junta (S.), "joined together"; group controlling government after a revolutionary takeover

jus divinum (L.), divine law

(le) juste-milieu (F.), golden mean, or happy medium, referring esp. to political principles

Knesset *or* **Knesseth** (Hebrew), "gathering"; the parliament of Israel

kraal (Afrikaans), a native South African village

ktéma es aeí (Gk.), a possession for all time—*Thucydides*

kudos (Gk.), awards; honors; compliments

Kuomintang (Chinese), "people's national party"; radical Chinese nationalist party founded by Sun Yat-sen in 1912

Kyrie eleison (Gk.), Lord, have mercy upon us

labor omnia vincit (L.), labor conquers all things

laisser-aller (F.), letting go; absence of restraint

laissez-faire (F.), "let (people) do (as they will)"; deliberate abstention from interference

l'appétit vient en mangeant (F.), appetite comes with eating

lapsus calami (L.), slip of the pen

lapsus linguae (L.), slip of the tongue

lapsus memoriae (L.), slip of the memory

la reine le veut (F.), the queen wills it

l'art pour l'art (F.), art for art's sake

lasciate ogni speranza voi ch'entrate (I.), abandon all hope, ye who enter here (through the gates of Hell)—*Dante*

laus Deo (L.), praise be to God

l'chaim (Hebrew), to life!; to your health!

Lebensabend (G.), evening of life

le droit du plus fort (F.), the right of the strongest

le grand oeuvre (F.), the philosopher's stone

le roi est mort, vive le roi (F.), the king is dead, long live the king

le roi le veut (F.), the king wills it

le roi s'avisera (F.), the king will take it under advisement

lèse-majesté (F.), "injured majesty"; high treason

les jeux sont faits (F.), the bets have been placed

le style, c'est l'homme (F.), the style is the man (himself)—adapted from *Buffon*

l'état, c'est moi (F.), the state, it is I—attributed to *Louis XIV*

levée en masse (F.), a mass, or general, uprising

liberté, égalité, fraternité (F.), liberty, equality, fraternity—motto of the French Revolution

Lieb und Leid (G.), joy and sorrow

lingua franca (I.), "Frankish language"; common language used among diverse peoples to communicate

l'oeil du maître (F.), the master's eye

l'usage du monde (F.), the way of the world

magni nominis umbra (L.), the shadow of a great name—*Lucan*

magnum in parvo (L.), a great quantity in a small space

malade imaginaire (F.), imaginary invalid; hypochondriac

maladresse (F.), awkwardness; blunder

mal du pays (F.), homesickness

malheur ne vient jamais seul (F.), misfortune never comes alone (*i.e.,* singly)

manqué; *fem.,* **manquée** (F.), "lacking"; unsuccessful, esp. in the arts

man spricht deutsch (G.), German is spoken (here)

Märchen (G.), folk-tale

mariage de convenance (F.), marriage of convenience; an arranged marriage

materfamilias (L.), mother of a family (*or* household)

mauvaise honte (F.), "false shame"; shyness

mauvais goût (F.), bad taste

mauvais quart d'heure (F.), "bad quarter of an hour"; brief but uncomfortable experience

mélange (F.), mixture

mêlée (F.), skirmish; free-for-all

mens sana in corpore sano (L.), a sound mind in a sound body— *Juvenal*

meum et tuum (L.), "mine and thine"—used in speaking of property rights, *i.e.,* that which is mine and that which belongs to another

mezza voce (I.), "half voice"; with medium volume or tone

mirabile dictu (L.), wondrous to tell

mirabile visu (L.), wondrous to behold

mirabilia (L.), wonders; miracles

(la) mise en scène (F.), stage setting

modus operandi (L.), "method of operating"; mode in which something is or should be done

modus vivendi (L.), "manner of living"; temporary, mutual arrangement or compromise for peaceful coexistence of disputants, pending settlement of conflict

(les) moeurs (F.), customs; mores

(le) monde (F.), "world"; society; fashionable set

(le) monde savant (F.), the learned world

morituri te salutamus (L.), we who are about to die salute you— traditional salutation to the Roman Emperor from gladiators in the arena

(le) mot juste (F.), just the right word or expression

muezzin (Arabic), Muslim crier who calls the faithful to prayer at certain hours

mullah (Arabic), Muslim teacher

multum in parvo (L.), "much in little"; much condensed into a small compass

mutatis mutandis (L.), necessary changes having been made; with appropriate alteration of details

née (F.), "born"—used to indicate a married woman's maiden name; *e.g.,* Jane Wells née Richards

ne plus ultra (L.), "no more beyond"; the ultimate; acme

n'est-ce pas? (F.), isn't it so?

nihil ex nihilo (L.), nothing comes from nothing

nil desperandum (L.), never despair; never say die—*Horace*

nil sine Deo (L.), nothing without God

n'importe (F.), it doesn't matter

Nisei (Japanese), "second generation"; child of immigrant Japanese parents who is born and raised in the U.S.

noblesse oblige (F.), "nobility obligates"; obligations imposed by high rank or birth

nolens volens (L.), willing or unwilling; willy-nilly

nolo contendere (L.), "I do not wish to contend"; a legal plea, tantamount to guilty, by which a defendant offers no defense but refuses to admit guilt

nom de guerre (F.), "war name"; an assumed name

nom de plume (F.), pen name

non compos mentis (L.), not of sound mind

non omnis moriar (L.), I shall not wholly die—*Horace*

non sequitur (L.), "it does not follow"; illogical statement

non sum qualis eram (L.), I am not what I used to be—*Horace*

nosce te ipsum (L.), know thyself

nota bene (L.), note well; take note

nous avons changé tout cela (F.), we have changed all that—*Molière*

novus homo (L.), "new man"; one who has risen from obscurity to prominence; upstart

novus ordo seclorum (L.), a new cycle of the ages—motto on reverse of the Great Seal of the U.S.

nuncio (I.), diplomatic representative of the pope

obiit (L.), he (*or* she) died

obiit sine prole (L.), he (*or* she) died without issue (*i.e.,* offspring)

objets d'occasion (F.), secondhand objects

oblast (Russian), political subdivision of a Soviet republic

obscurum per obscurius (L.), "the obscure by the more obscure"; attempt to explain something obscure by something still more obscure

odalisque (F.), concubine in a harem

omnia mutantur, nos et mutamur in illis (L.), all things are changing, and we are changing with them

omnia vanitas (L.), all is vanity

omnia vincit amor (L.), love conquers all—*Virgil*

on dit (F.), one says; it is said; piece of gossip (as a noun, spelled *on-dit*)

onus probandi (L.), the burden of proof

opéra bouffe (F.), satirical comic opera

ora e sempre (I.), now and always

ore rotundo (L.), "with a round mouth"; with eloquent speech—
Horace

O tempora! O mores! (L.), Oh the times! Oh the customs!—*Cicero*

où sont les neiges d'antan? (F.), where are the snows of yesteryear?
—Villon

(à) outrance (F.), (to) the extreme; (to) the bitter end

outré (F.), exaggerated; eccentric; indecorous

panem et circenses (L.), "bread and circuses"; food and entertainment
necessary to pacify the masses—*Juvenal*

par avance (F.), in advance

par avion (F.), by airplane; airmail

par exemple (F.), for example

par hasard (F.), by chance or accident

parturiunt montes, nascetur ridiculus mus (L.), the mountains are in
labor, and a ridiculous mouse will issue forth—*Horace*

parvenu (F.), "arrived"; upstart

pastiche (F.), imitation of the style of an author or artist; composite
piece with selections drawn from various sources

paterfamilias (L.), father of the family; head of the household

pater patriae (L.), father of (his) country

pax in bello (L.), peace in war

pax vobiscum (L.), peace be with you

perdu (F.), lost

père (F.), "father"—added to French surnames to distinguish father
and son (*fils*); *e.g.,* Dumas *père* and Dumas *fils*

petit bourgeois (F.), "small citizen"; lower middle class

petitio principii (L.), begging the question

peu à peu (F.), little by little

peut-être (F.), perhaps

pièce de résistance (F.), principal dish in a meal; highlight of a collection or program

pièce d'occasion (F.), a work created for a special occasion

pied-à-terre (F.), small apartment for occasional lodging

pinxit (L.), he (*or* she) painted (it)

pis aller (F.), "to go worst"; last resort

pleno jure (L.), with full right

plus ça change, plus c'est la même chose (F.), the more it changes,
the more it is the same

plus royaliste que le roi (F.), more royalist than the king

plus sage que les sages (F.), wiser than the wise

poco a poco (I.), little by little

Politburo (Russian), top policy-making and administrative organ of the Soviet Communist Party

pollice verso (L.), "with the thumb turned down"—Roman spectators' gesture to decree death to a defeated gladiator

post hoc, ergo propter hoc (L.), "after this, therefore because of this"; fallacious argument, illogically reasoning that one event following another must be the result of the first

post mortem (L.), "after death"; usu., an examination of an event just completed

post obitum (L.), "after death"; usu., taking effect after an individual's death

pour acquit (F.), payment received or settled

pour ainsi dire (F.), so to speak

pourboire (F.), tip; gratuity

prima facie (L.), at first view; on the face of it

primus inter pares (L.), first among equals

pro bono publico (L.), for the public good

pro hac vice (L.), for this occasion (only)

pro rege et patria (L.), for king and country

pro re nata (L.), "for a thing born"; for an occasion that arises; when required

pro tempore (L.), for the time being

purdah (Hindi), "screen *or* veil"; Muslim (and in some places, Hindi) practice of secluding women from public view

quae vide (L.), which (things) see

quand même (F.), nonetheless

quantum libet (*or* **placet**) (L.), as much as you please

quantum sufficit (L.), as much as suffices

quattrocento (I.), "four hundred"; 15th century, esp. in Italian art and literature

que sais-je? (F.), what do I know?

quid pro quo (L.), one thing in exchange for another

¿quién sabe? (S.), who knows?

qui sait? (F.), who knows?

quis custodiet ipsos custodes? (L.), who will keep the keepers?—*Juvenal*

quod hoc (L.), in this regard

quod erat demonstrandum (L.), which was to be demonstrated

quod erat faciendum (L.), which was to be done

quod est (L.), which is

quod vide; *pl.,* **quae vide** (L.), which (thing *or* things) see

quot homines, tot sententiae (L.), so many men, so many opinions —*Terence*

quo vadis? (L.), where are you going?

raison d'état (F.), reason of state

raison d'être (F.), reason for being

re (L.), in the matter of; concerning

reductio ad absurdum (L.), reduction to absurdity; disproof of a logical proposition by showing the absurdity of its consequences

re infecta (L.), the business being unfinished

répondez s'il vous plaît (F.), please reply

requiescat in pace (L.), may he (*or* she) rest in peace—used on tombstones

revenons à nos moutons (F.), "let us return to our sheep"; let us get back to the point

roman à clef (F.), "novel with a key"; novel in which real people or events are portrayed as fictional

ruat caelum (*or* **coelum**) (L.), though the heavens fall; come what may

ruse de guerre (F.), war stratagem

rus in urbe (L.), "the country in the city"; urban retreat of pastoral character

sabra (New Hebrew), a native-born Israeli

salaam aleikum (Arabic), peace be with you

sal Atticum (L.), "Attic salt"; example of wit—*Pliny*

salud (S.), **salut** (F.), **salute** (I.), health; to your health; greetings

samizdat (Russian), "self-publishing"; underground Russian literature

sang-froid (F.), "cold blood"; composure; imperturbability

sans doute (F.), without doubt

sans faute (F.), without fail

sans raison (F.), without reason

sans souci (F.), without care or worry

sauvage (F.), "savage"; uncultivated; unsociable; solitary

savoir-faire (F.), instinctive knowledge for doing the right thing

savoir-vivre (F.), knowing how to live; good breeding

scilicet (L.), namely

scripsit (L.), he (*or* she) wrote (it)

sculpsit (L.), he (*or* she) carved (it)

secundum artem (L.), according to the art or accepted practice

secundum naturam (L.), according to nature

secundum usum (L.), according to custom

se habla español (S.), Spanish is spoken (here)

selon (F.), according to

semper fidelis (L.), always faithful

semper idem; *fem.,* **semper eadem** (L.), always the same

seppuku (Japanese), hara-kiri, or suicide by piercing the abdomen with a knife or sword

(et) sequens (*or* **sequentes** *or* **sequentia**) (L.), (and) the following

seriatim (L.), one by one; serially

shalom (Hebrew), peace; greetings; farewell

shibboleth (Hebrew), password; slogan of a particular group

sic (L.), "thus" (shortened from *sic in originali:* thus in the original)— used as a parenthetical insertion in quoted material to indicate that a questionable word or phrase has been faithfully reproduced from the original

sic itur ad astra (L.), thus is the way to the stars (*i.e.,* to immortality) —*Virgil*

sic passim (L.), thus throughout (in the original)

sic transit gloria mundi (L.), so passes away the glory of the world

sile et philosophus esto (L.), be silent and you will pass for a philosopher

silent leges inter arma (L.), laws are silent during war—*Cicero*

s'il vous plaît (F.), if you please; please

sine die (L.), "without a day"; postponed indefinitely

sine prole (L.), without issue; without offspring

sine qua non (L.), "without which not"; a necessity or indispensable condition

si parla italiano (I.), Italian is spoken (here)

sobriquet (F.), nickname; pseudonym

soi-disant (F.), self-styled; would-be

soigné; *fem.,* **soignée** (F.), well cared for; carefully done; well groomed

sotto voce (I.), in a low or subdued voice

soupçon (F.), "suspicion"; minute quantity; a dash

splendide mendax (L.), lying for a noble cause—*Horace*

spolia opima (L.), "rich spoils"; arms stripped from a defeated general by the victor

statim (L.), immediately

status in quo *or* **status quo** (L.), state in which (something is); existing condition

status quo ante bellum (L.), state existing prior to the war

Sturm und Drang (G.), "storm and stress"; name given to the late 18th-century German romantic movement, esp. German literature of the period

sub initio (L.), at the beginning

sub rosa (L.), "under the rose"; in confidence

sub verbo *or* **sub voce** (L.), "under the word"—used for cross-references

sui generis (L.), belonging to a class of its own; unique

suivant (F.), following; next

sunt lacrimae rerum (L.), "there are tears for things"; distress at the inevitability of mortal suffering—*Virgil*

suo jure (L.), in his (*or* her) own right

suo loco (L.), in its proper place

supra (L.), above

sur-le-champ (F.), "on the field"; immediately

surtout (F.), especially

suttee (Sanskrit), "good woman"; obsolete Hindu practice of self-immolation by a widow on her husband's funeral pyre

suum cuique (L.), to each his own

table d'hôte (F.), "host's table"; meal at fixed time and price

tabula rasa (L.), clean slate; the mind in its hypothetical state at birth, not yet affected by experiences, impressions, etc.

tant mieux (F.), so much the better

tant pis (F.), so much the worse

Te Deum Laudamus (L.), We Praise Thee, God—ancient Latin hymn

tempora mutantur, nos et mutamur in illis (L.), the times are changing, and we are changing with them

tempus edax rerum (L.), time, that devours all things—*Ovid*

tempus fugit (L.), time flies—*Virgil*

terra incognita (L.), unknown or unexplored territory

tête-à-tête (F.), "head to head"; private conversation or interview

tous frais faits (F.), all expenses defrayed

tout à coup *or* **tout d'un coup** (F.), suddenly; all at once

tout à fait (F.), completely; quite

tout au contraire (F.), quite the contrary

tout court (F.), quite short; abruptly

tout de même (F.), all the same; even so; nevertheless

tout de suite (F.), immediately

(le) tout ensemble (F.), (the whole thing) taken all together; the general effect

tout est perdu hors l'honneur (F.), all is lost except honor

tout le monde (F.), all the world; everyone

tristesse (F.), sadness

Übermensch (G.), superhuman being; superman

ubi sunt (L.), "where are" (shortened from *ubi sunt qui ante nos fuerunt?:* where are those who lived before us?)

ubi supra (L.), "where above"; in the place mentioned above

ultima ratio regum (L.), "the ultimate argument of kings" (*i.e.,* war)

und so weiter (G.), and so forth

uno animo (L.), with one mind; unanimously

urbi et orbi (L.), to the city (Rome) and to the world

ut infra (L.), as below

ut supra (L.), as above

vade retro me, Satana! (L.), get thee behind me, Satan!—*Vulgate, St. Mark*

vanitas vanitatum, omnia vanitas (L.), vanity of vanities, all is vanity —*Vulgate, Ecclesiastes*

vaquero (S.), herdsman; cowboy

varia lectio; *pl.,* **variae lectiones** (L.), variant reading

veni, vidi, vici (L.), I came, I saw, I conquered—*Julius Caesar*

verbatim et lit(t)eratim (L.), word for word and letter for letter

verbum sat sapienti est (L.), a word to the wise suffices

vide infra (L.), see below

videlicet (L.), namely

vide supra (L.), see above

vis-à-vis (F.), "face to face"; facing; with reference to; in light of

vis medicatrix naturae (L.), the healing power of nature

vive la reine (*or* **le roi**) (F.), long live the queen (*or* king)

vogue la galère (F.), "keep the galley rowing"; keep going, regardless

vox et praeterea nihil (L.), a voice and nothing more; empty words

vox populi (L.), voice of the people

Weltanschauung (G.), world view; philosophy of life

Zeitgeist (G.), spirit of the times

zum Beispiel (G.), for example

LETTER WRITING

Preserving the Art of Letter Writing
List of Honorifics
The History of the Epistle
Forms of Address

Preserving the Art of Letter Writing

Letters are the most direct and personal form of written communication. For centuries, despite shipwreck, waylaid messengers, and exhausted horses, the letter alone preserved communication over distance. Today the telephone has overtaken, if not usurped, this domain. "It's the next best thing to being there," we are told, and indeed the illusion of proximity is alluring. Advancing technology itself has fostered a radically new demand for instantaneousness. The telephone and the jet threaten to alter our perception of time itself. The letter, like the railroad, seems a vestige of a slow-moving past. Yet we know that the telephone will never entirely replace the letter. Our schedules may demand otherwise, but the letter's qualities of permanence, structure, and forethought are not transmissible over wire.

In business the letter performs daily a variety of functions from establishing contact between unknown parties to conveying information too confidential for the telephone. In personal correspondence, also, the letter serves numerous needs, generally sustaining or severing ties and communicating everything from a simple thank-you to an expression of condolence. Whether as a personal memento or a business document, the letter serves as a permanent record. It can capture both the message and its tone and style.

Some people have a natural gift for letter writing, but many feel particularly inept at this endeavor. While their discomfort sometimes stems from a general diffidence at using language, it may be compounded by an inflated or outmoded notion of the formality required for correspondence or by a simple lack of practice in writing letters. In any case nervousness about letter writing quickly reveals itself. On the one hand, many personal letters are excessively informal, suffering from the temporary suspension of the writer's normal concern for correct spelling, gammar, and clear expression; on the other, business letters are frequently stiff and awkward, cloaked in an ill-fitting mantle of formal language and syntax that bears little resemblance to the author's natural

547

writing style. Between these extremes lies the necessary median for successful correspondence: simple, good writing.

Letter writing should be guided by the same principles and concerns as any other form of writing. Organization of thought, clarity of expression, and attention to grammar and spelling are all essential to good writing, whether the product be a novel or a one-paragraph letter. Therefore in a sense this entire book might be construed as a lengthy manual for literate correspondence, with this chapter serving as both a fitting close and apt point of departure. For what better practice is there than letter writing for continuously using the tools offered in this book for the mastery of written English skills?

Letters have structure. They can and should be planned and written with care. Within certain guidelines the form of the letter is flexible. In most cases the degree of formality should reflect the relationship between writer and recipient. Yet not even the most formal or businesslike letter need be devoid of personality and warmth. Offered below are general guidelines for personal and business letters, followed by a List of Honorifics for correctly addressing written correspondence to persons in a variety of public offices and professions.

I. Personal correspondence

The letter we most often have occasion to write is a personal letter to friends or relatives. Because the exact nature and style of each friendly letter is determined by a unique set of circumstances, it is impossible to provide definitive guidelines for writing such letters. Nonetheless, some general suggestions can be offered. First, as always in writing, ideas in any kind of personal correspondence should be clearly presented and spelling and grammar correct. For this reason a simple and direct style is recommended for letter writing, whether for personal or business correspondence. In discussing letter writing as an art form, the *Britannica* notes the counsel of the ancients on composing letters. Although the passage speaks about letters written by masters of the epistolary form, the counsel is helpful for all who are diffident about putting pen to paper.

> . . . The instructions of the ancient grammarians, which were repeated a thousand times afterward in manuals purporting to teach how to write a letter, can be reduced to a few very general platitudes: be natural and appear spontaneous but not garrulous and verbose; avoid dryness and declamatory pomp; appear neither unconcerned

nor effusive; express emotion without lapsing into sentimentality; avoid pedantry on the one hand and banter and levity on the other. Letters vary too much in content, however, for generalizations to be valid to all types. What is moving in a love letter might sound indiscreet in a letter of friendship; an analysis of the self may fascinate some readers, while others prefer anecdotes and scandal. La Bruyère, at the end of the 17th century, remarked that women succeed better than men in the epistolary form. It has also been claimed that a feminine sensibility can be seen in the letters of the most highly acclaimed male masters of this form, such as Voltaire, Mirabeau, Keats, and Baudelaire. Advice to practitioners of the art of letter writing usually can be expressed in the often-quoted line in Shakespeare's *Hamlet:* "To thine own self be true." The English biographer Lytton Strachey (1880–1932), a copious and versatile letter writer himself, wrote: "No good letter was ever written to convey information, or to please its recipient: it may achieve both those results incidentally; but its fundamental purpose is to express the personality of the writer." There are, however, numerous and even contradictory ways of expressing that personality.

A few further points might be added to this sound advice:

• Keep your correspondent in mind. What part of your life or thought is that correspondent interested in? Shape the letter accordingly to fit the recipient.

• Do not be overly concerned with the rules useful for the formal essay—unity, coherence, paragraph structure, etc. *Try* to keep them in the back of your mind, but humor, interest, and personality are far more important in a friendly letter than strict adherence to rhetorical rules.

• Do not make the letter too long. Close it when you have covered all you have to say.

• Above all, make the letter personal. The ideal friendly letter approximates the *voice* of the sender. Avoid efforts to achieve an "epistolary style"; find instead your own writing style.

In addition to regular correspondence with friends and relatives, there is occasional need to write a "formal" social letter. Such letters, however, need not be starched and stilted. Like the friendly letter, the best social letter reflects the personality of its author.

While usually handwritten, social letters can of course be typed but preferably not on letterhead business stationery. A social letter is generally dated in the upper right-hand corner; the name and address of the recipient do not appear; and a comma follows the salutation. If desired, the correspondent's name and address can be placed either above the date or a few lines below the signature, flush with the left margin. If typed, the body of the letter may conform to any of several styles of paragraphing and spacing, but the style chosen should be used consistently.

The discussion below covers the most common types of social letters. While sample letters are included to make the discussion concrete, there is naturally a variety of approaches to each situation.

A. INVITATIONS AND REPLIES   Invitations are nowadays often extended by telephone, but the written invitation is certainly not extinct. It is almost always preferable. Printed or handwritten invitations should include the following information in prominent view: occasion; date and time; location; name of host(ess); R.S.V.P., if desired, or "Regrets Only," meaning that only those unable to attend need reply; and telephone number if replies are to be made by phone. If replies are requested, invitations should be mailed in ample time.

October 10, 1979

Dear Anne and Jack,

Please help us celebrate Dan's 40th birthday at a surprise dinner at our house on Saturday, October 27, at 7:30 P.M. We look forward to seeing you.

Best regards,

Marie Evergreen

R.S.V.P.

If a written reply to an invitation is expected, it should be returned promptly. Whether accepting or refusing an invitation, replies need not be lengthy or formal, only congenial.

October 15, 1979

Dear Marie,

    Thank you for including us in the plans for Dan's birthday celebration. We would love to join you.

Best,

Anne and Jack Simpson

October 15, 1979

Dear Marie,

    I am so sorry that we shall miss Dan's surprise birthday dinner. We had already made plans to be out of town that weekend. Please give Dan our best regards that evening.

Sincerely,

Anne and Jack Simpson

B. CONGRATULATIONS   Certain special occasions warrant congratulations—a marriage, birth, graduation, promotion, award, etc.—and a written note of congratulations is a thoughtful gesture. Whatever the occasion, the note need be only long enough to convey genuine pleasure at the event or achievement.

Dear Dave,

Congratulations on your new job. The library is gaining a talented director. We wish you much success and happiness.

With best regards,

Susan and Peter Framington

Dear Margaret and Henry,

I have just heard about your new baby daughter. Congratulations and all best wishes.

Sincerely,

Helen Winters

Dear Anna,

I read in the newspaper about the prize awarded your photograph. Well-deserved congratulations are in order, and I look forward to seeing the exhibit.

Sincerely,

Chris Reed

A gift sent for a special occasion is usually accompanied by a note of congratulations.

Dear Amy and Ben,

These champagne glasses are to toast your new life together. May it be happy, healthy, and long.

Fondly,

Rachel Easter

C. THANK-YOU'S Thank-you notes should be sent to acknowledge receipt of gifts, hospitality extended, or a special kindness or favor. Like other social notes, thank-you notes can be short. They are best written within a few days of the occasion. In the case of thank-you notes for gifts sent in the mail, courtesy dictates that these be written as soon as possible in order to let the friend know that the gift was received.

Dear Mrs. Easter,

Thank you so much for the lovely champagne glasses. We will long enjoy them and think of you when we use them.

Best regards from us both,

Amy and Ben Horton

Dear Mr. and Mrs. Brown,

Thank you so much for your kind hospitality and marvelous tour of the city. It was wonderful to see you both again. Please call and stop by when you are next in New Haven.

Sincerely,

Kay Roderick

Dear Pat,

    The flowers were beautiful and helped
to brighten my hospital stay. Thank you
so much for thinking of me.

                 With best regards,

                 Alex Massey

D. INQUIRIES ABOUT RECEIPT OF A GIFT If you have sent a gift but
have not received an acknowledgment within a reasonable period, you
may need to inquire if the gift was ever received. This is an awkward letter to write, but it is friendlier to make such an inquiry than to assume
the recipient has ignored writing to thank you. The gift may have been
lost in the mail or not shipped from the store of purchase. In either case,
prior to making appropriate inquiries of the post office or store, you
must determine that the gift never arrived. If *you* receive a letter like
this, a quick reply is called for!

Dear June,

    I sent a hand-knit sweater for your
birthday. Since you didn't mention it in
your last letter, I am wondering if you
ever received the package. If not, let me
know and I will check with the post office.

                 Love,

                 Aunt Hazel

Dear Aunt Hazel,

    I am so glad you wrote. No, I didn't
receive your package. By all means, please
check with the post office. I will be sorry
if one of your beautiful handmade sweaters
is lost.

                 With love,

                 June

Dear Amy,

Since I haven't heard from you, I am
afraid that you might not have received
the wedding gift of crystal champagne glasses
that I sent in the mail some time ago. If
not, please let me know and I will inquire
both at the post office and at the store.

Sincerely,

Rachel Easter

Dear Mrs. Easter,

Your beautiful champagne glasses
did indeed arrive safely, and I am
very embarrassed not to have written
sooner to thank you. I am amazed at
how quickly the time has passed since
our wedding.
Ben and I are very fond of the
glasses and have enjoyed using them
on several occasions. Both of us send
thanks for your thoughtful gift.

With best regards,

Amy and Ben Horton

E. CONDOLENCE LETTERS A letter of condolence expressing sorrow at
someone's death is an important letter to write but the most difficult of
all to compose. In a small, well-written book entitled *Widow,* Lynn
Caine offers succinct, practical, and eminently sound counsel on shaping
this very special kind of correspondence. Do not add to the bereaved's
distress by announcing how inadequate or uncomfortable you feel writing the condolence note. Instead of providing support or comfort, openers such as "I just don't know what to say at a time like this" or "There
are no words to express my feelings" focus indulgently on the *writer's*

discomfort rather than on the family's distress or the shared loss. Condolence letters need not be long or complex. They do not need to be terribly formal or even entirely humorless. Among close friends an appropriate humorous remark can offer a welcome moment of respite and perspective. Above all, a letter of condolence should simply and sincerely convey your feelings and should provide empathy, support, and comfort for the bereaved. If an offer of assistance is made or an invitation extended, it should be followed up by a definite offer or invitation.

```
Dear Mr. Smith,

    Bill and I were terribly sorry to learn
of Mrs. Smith's death.  She has been such a
wonderful and important presence in so many
children's lives and hence in all our lives.
Anne still clearly and very fondly remembers
her days in Mrs. Smith's third-grade class.
    We are all genuinely saddened and share
in your loss.  You and your children are in
our thoughts.

                    Sincerely,

                    Marla and Bill Wagner
```

II. Business correspondence

The guidelines for writing a good business letter are those that apply to any kind of good writing: careful organization and clear expression of the ideas. The structure of a business letter is largely governed by convention. But despite standard format and the special nature of this correspondence, the business letter need not be stiff and devoid of personality. Note the letters used throughout this discussion of business correspondence.

A. MAIN PARTS OF A BUSINESS LETTER   The principal parts of a business letter are briefly discussed below. The different positioning of each part in the various standard business letter formats is covered in the next section.

                                               39 East 79th Street   1.
                                               New York, New York
                                               April 4, 1929   2.

3.   Mr. Walter Pitkin
      Encyclopaedia Britannica
      342 Madison Avenue
      New York, New York

4.   My dear Mr. Pitkin:

5.   This is merely a note of inquiry--having heard nothing from
      you for a year. Does the Art Department still want me to
      get an afternoon tea table picture? Are galleys to be sent
      me? And will you--can you--put the one hundred and fifty
      dollars I am to receive toward a set of the new edition
      of the Encyclopaedia? I don't want to ask for anything
      that is unreasonable--or unusual--but as contributors
      to ordinary books and periodicals may buy at the dealer's
      rates, I wonder if putting my pay check toward the edition
      would give me an author's discount?

      I shall be in town for about six weeks longer and, if there
      is anything you would like me to do, will be very glad to.

6.   Very sincerely yours,

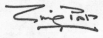

7.   Emily Post

      P.S. My own Britannica is the 9th edition!!

1. *Heading.*   Unless the letter is typed on printed letterhead stationery, a heading is necessary to provide the writer's full address. The heading may be placed at the top right-hand margin (as in the example) or centered at the top of the page. Abbreviations are not traditionally used in the heading.

2. *Date line.*   If a heading is used, the date line is usually typed immediately below. When letterhead stationery is used, the date line is positioned according to the letter format chosen (*see* Section II. B., below). Abbreviations are not traditionally used in the date line.

3. *Inside address.*   The inside address is single-spaced, flush with the left margin. When possible the full address is used. If the street address is unknown, the city is placed on the second line and the state on the third; the ZIP code, optional in the inside address, follows the state.

Keep the inside address to no more than five lines, with none extending past the middle of the page. A line that proves too long can be divided into two, indenting the second line. Abbreviations are not traditionally used for streets, cities, or states unless the official name is abbreviated (*e.g., Ste. Marie Avenue; St. Paul, Minnesota; Washington, D.C.*).

When writing to an individual within a company, the person's name appears above the full name of the company. A title (*Mr., Mrs., Dr., The Rev.,* etc.) precedes the person's name. If a woman's marital status is unknown, it is acceptable to use either *Miss* or *Ms.* as a title. If a person's business title is also used, it is not abbreviated and can be variously placed, with the choice of style obviously influenced by the title's length:

Mr. Walter Pitkin, Assistant to the Editor
Encyclopædia Britannica

Mr. Walter Pitkin
Assistant to the Editor, Encyclopædia Britannica

Mr. Walter Pitkin
Assistant to the Editor
Encyclopædia Britannica

When the person to whom the letter should actually be addressed is unknown, the name of a department within the company can be addressed. The company's name appears on the first line; the department's name on the second.

Encyclopædia Britannica, Inc.
Department of Public Relations
425 N. Michigan Avenue
Chicago, Illinois 60610

(For the correct styling of an inside address for two or more people, *see* 4. *Salutation, below.* For further information on written forms of address for persons in public office or special professions, *see* the List of Honorifics that follows this article.)

4. *Salutation.* The salutation, or greeting, is typed flush with the left margin below the inside address and is followed by a colon. The following guidelines provide appropriate salutations for a variety of situations:

• In general the title and surname are used in the salutation (*Dear Mrs. Bennet:, My dear Dr. Clark:*) unless the writer and addressee are personally acquainted (*Dear Anne:, My Dear Martin:*).

• When addressing two or more persons, the following salutations are correct:

INSIDE ADDRESS STYLING SALUTATION

Two or more men with same surname

Mr. Arthur W. Jones
Mr. John H. Jones Gentlemen:
or *or*
Messrs. A.W. and J.H. Jones Dear Messrs. Jones:
or
The Messrs. Jones

Two or more men with different surnames

Mr. Angus D. Langley Gentlemen: *or* Dear Mr. Langley
Mr. Lionel P. Overton and Mr. Overton:
or *or*
Messrs. A.D. Langley and Dear Messrs. Langley and
L.P. Overton Overton:
or
Messrs. Langley and Overton

Two or more married women with same surname

Mrs. Arthur W. Jones
Mrs. John H. Jones Mesdames:
or *or*
Mesdames A.W. and J.H. Jones Dear Mesdames Jones:
or
The Mesdames Jones

Two or more unmarried women with same surname

Miss Alice H. Danvers
Miss Margaret T. Danvers Ladies:
or *or*
Misses Alice and Margaret Danvers Dear Misses Danvers:
or
The Misses Danvers

Two or more women with same surname but whose marital status is unknown or irrelevant

Ms. Alice H. Danvers Dear Ms. Alice and
Ms. Margaret T. Danvers Margaret Danvers:

INSIDE ADDRESS STYLING   SALUTATION

Two or more married women with different surnames

Mrs. Allen Y. Dow

Mrs. Lawrence R. Frank   Dear Mrs. Dow and Mrs. Frank:
or   *or* Mesdames:
Mesdames Dow and Frank   *or* Dear Mesdames
                                   Dow and Frank:

Two or more unmarried women with different surnames

Miss Elizabeth Dudley   Ladies:
Miss Ann Raymond   *or* Dear Miss Dudley and Miss
or   Raymond:
Misses E. Dudley and A. Raymond   *or*
                                   Dear Misses Dudley and
                                   Raymond:

**Two or more women with different surnames but whose marital status
is unknown or irrelevant**

Ms. Barbara Lee   Dear Ms. Lee and Ms. Key:
Ms. Helen Key

A married couple

Mr. and Mrs. Arthur W. Jones   Dear Mr. and Mrs. Jones:

Several men and women

Ms. Alice H. Danvers   Ladies and Gentlemen:
Mrs. Margaret Jones
Mr. Angus D. Langley
Mr. Lionel P. Overton

• When addressing an all-male group, use *Gentlemen:*

• When addressing an all-female group, use *Ladies:* or *Mesdames:*

• When the gender of the person addressed is not known, the writer can
use either a masculine title (*Dear Mr. Brown:*) or eliminate the title
altogether and repeat the full name (*Dear Lee Brown:*).

• When addressing an unidentified person in a company, the writer can
use the title of the office addressed in the salutation (*Dear Managing
Director of Sales:, Dear Personnel Department Head:*); the conventional salutation *Dear Sir or Madam:;* or the impersonal salutation *To
Whom It May Concern:,* though some people consider this remote and
outdated.

(For further information on correct salutations for persons in public office or special professions, *see* the List of Honorifics that follows this chapter.)

5. *Body.* Most business letters are single-spaced with double spacing between paragraphs. A very short letter may be double-spaced, in which case paragraphs are indented or triple-spaced. The most commonly used formats for a business letter are presented in II.B., below.

6. *Complimentary close.* The complimentary close ends the letter and is typed several lines below the body of the letter. It varies with the degree of formality of the letter and the relationship between writer and recipient. Only the first word of the complimentary close need be capitalized, and a comma usually ends the close. Common complimentary closes include:

Very Formal Letters:	Respectfully, Very respectfully yours,
Less Formal Letters:	Very truly yours, Yours truly,
General Correspondence:	Sincerely (yours), Cordially (yours),
Informal Correspondence:	As ever, Best wishes (*or* regards), Kindest personal regards, Regards, With best wishes (*or* regards),

(For the position of the complimentary close in the various standard letter formats, *see* II.B., below.)

7. *Signature line.* The writer's name should be typed several lines below the complimentary close exactly as the signature will be written. If the writer's full name appears as part of a printed letterhead, no typed signature is necessary. While titles may appear after a name (*e.g., Anne Bennet, M.D.* or *Martin Jones, President*) the only appropriate title to precede the typed signature—though its inclusion is nowadays optional —is *Mrs., Miss,* or *Ms.* No title is included in the written signature. If a woman chooses not to include a title before her typed signature, she is correctly addressed in reply as *Miss* or *Ms.*

B. COMMON BUSINESS LETTER FORMATS   There is a variety of acceptable formats for business letters. The most common are the Full Block, Modified Block, and Modified Semi-block. The letters used to illustrate these formats are taken from the archives of the *Britannica*. These older examples were selected to illustrate how little basic epistolary style has changed over the years. A letter, well written, survives the passage of time.

1. *Full Block.*

January 29, 1936

Mr. F. H. Hooper
Editor
Encyclopaedia Britannica
342 Madison Avenue
New York, New York

My dear Hooper:

I am, as you probably know, a confirmed advocate of
the noble art of forgetting. Not the sort of
indifferent forgetting, born out of sheer carelessness but the scientific forgetting which has become
an absolute necessity in our day and age when
Knowledge is increasing with stellar rapidity.
A hundred years ago, one particularly bright person
might still hope to know everything that was writ
down in the books. Today he stands helpless before
this Niagara of facts and still more facts and still
more facts. The average citizen should therefore
be given a careful training in the art of Forgetting

but at the same time he should be taught where to
find things . . . <u>where</u> <u>to</u> <u>find</u> <u>them</u> <u>for</u> <u>himself</u>.

I have solved this problem for myself by having a
Britannica in every room where debate might rear its
welcome head. I love discussions, but I like them
best when conducted on the basis of established
facts and when we wander away from the firm ground
of actual experience, there is always someone
present who says "wait a moment, before we go any
further . . . let us look it up in the Britannica."

Words, even the best of them, are merely approxima-
tions of ideas and most disputes arise from people
who use the same words and yet mean entirely
different things when they use those identical
words. Being a peaceful sort of person I hate all
unnecessary strife. And I have found the Britannica the best of all possible fire-extinguishers
when an intellectual or spiritual conflagration
threatens the premises. We look it up in the
Britannica first and then when we decide to fight
it out we know at least what we are talking about
for "fighting with the facts in hand" is as good and
fair an indoor sport as playing chess and that I
think is the most sincere compliment ever paid to
your ancient and honorable compendium of human
wisdom.

As ever yours,

Hendrik Willem van Loon

All the parts of the Full Block letter are positioned flush with the left
margin. Paragraphs are double-spaced with no indentation.

2. *Modified Block.*

May 15, 1927

The Editor
Encyclopaedia Britannica
342 Madison Avenue
New York, New York

Dear Sir:

I am sorry to say that as I am on the eve of
departure for a lecture tour in America I cannot
undertake the articles for the E.B. concerning which
you write. I should recommend F.P. Ramsey, King's
College, Cambridge, who would do it much better
than I should.

Even if I had had time, I should have had some
hesitation in accepting your invitation, as I learn
from the pages of the E.B. that I am scarcely a fit
person to be a contributor.

Yours faithfully,

Bertrand Russell

The Modified Block letter differs from the Full Block letter in the positioning of the date line, complimentary close, and signature line. The
date line can be placed just to the right of center or near the right
margin, as above. The complimentary close and signature line are
aligned directly under the date line or between the center point and
right margin, as above.

3. *Modified Semi-block.*

October 14, 1927

Mr. Walter Pitkin
Encyclopaedia Britannica
342 Madison Avenue
New York, New York

Dear Mr. Pitkin:

    I should be willing to write 500 or 600 words on Santayana, and some 800 words on Dewey for the enormous sum of $25.00, provided you put me down for a set of the Britannica. As I am getting $1500 per article in these corrupting days you will see that you are not being cheated. And that set must be a good one--no popular cloth-binding affair--n'est-ce pas?

    I don't like the notion of writing on the subjects of philosophy; my views and mode of presentation would shock the academic world. Also I must stipulate that the two articles referred to above shall be signed articles. And the longer you can give me, the better the articles will be; I am worked to madness just now.

        Sincerely,

        Will Durant

        Will Durant

The Modified Semi-block letter differs from the Modified Block letter in that the paragraphs are indented.

C. SUNDRY PARTS OF A BUSINESS LETTER

```
                              LETTERHEAD


          May 9, 1979

   1.     PERSONAL


          Encyclopaedia Britannica
          425 North Michigan Avenue
          Chicago, Illinois  60611

   2.     Attention:  Mr. P.W. Goetz

          Gentlemen:

   3.     SUBJECT:  PROPOSED ARTICLE ON LANGUAGE

          I am writing to -----------------------------------------
          ----------------------------------------------------------
          ------------------------------------.

          ----------------------------------------------------------
          --------------------.

          Sincerely yours,



          Karl J. Wilson

   4.     KJW:ct
   5.     Enclosures  (3)

   6.     cc:  J. Turner
               B. Jones
```

All of the miscellaneous parts of a business letter are placed flush with the left margin in the letter formats illustrated above.

1. *Special notations.* Capitalized notations are placed between the date and inside address. If used, a PERSONAL or CONFIDENTIAL notation should also be typed on the envelope.

2. *Attention line.* When the writer wishes a letter written to an organization to receive the attention of a particular individual, an attention line is used below the inside address. The traditional salutation following an attention line is *Gentlemen:*, even though the letter is directed to the attention of a single person.

3. *Subject line.* A subject line, announcing the letter's topic, follows the salutation. It is placed either flush with the left margin or centered on the page. It can be introduced by the word SUBJECT: or RE:, or it can be typed in all-capitals and stand alone.

4. *Identification initials.* While there is a trend toward omitting the identification initials, they are traditionally typed flush with the left margin. There is a variety of styles for these initials, but in each case the writer's initials precede those of the typist. If the writer and typist are one, these initials are unnecessary.

5. *Enclosure notation.* If enclosures accompany a business letter, general practice is to indicate this by an enclosure notation. More than one enclosure can be indicated by a parenthetical notation, as above.

6. *Carbon copy notation.* Distribution of carbon copies is noted below the enclosure notation. If the writer wishes the distribution of carbon copies *not* to be indicated on the original letter, a blind carbon copy notation (*bcc:*) is used with the distribution list in this position on the second and subsequent copies of the letter.

D. MISCELLANEOUS MATTERS   When a letter is too lengthy to complete in a single page, the second and subsequent pages are typed on plain stationery. The final sheet should contain at least three message lines—not just the the complimentary close and signature. Each page after the first needs an identifying heading and page number. This can be styled either: stacked, flush with the left (or right) margin, or laid out across the top of the page:

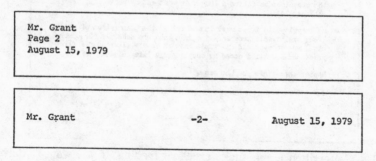

For guidelines on word division at the end of a line, *see* The Spelling Maze. For special problems in business correspondence, including the special format and conventions observed when writing to the military and certain government agencies (*e.g.,* the Department of Defense), consult *Webster's Secretarial Handbook.*

A standard style and format for business correspondence make for ease and efficiency, but they need not confine the human personality. Precisely because these standards generally prevail—and should not be lightly or inappropriately violated—occasional exceptions, such as the following, are refreshing. (The reputation of the writer, it should be noted, weighs heavily in the success of such a letter.)

fred allen:

august third

mr. l.c. schoenewald .
encyclopedia britannica
342 madison avenue
new york city

dear mr. schoenewald...

your records are correct!
i am the owner of a complete set of the encyclopedia what's-this!
you have my permission to so say in one of the forthcoming bulletins!

re my method of using my encyclopedia!

i became an encyclopedia owner through necessity. a well-meaning and erudite acquaintance presented me with two book-ends one xmas. the book-ends were quite far apart, as they were given to me, they kept toppling over and causing the people downstairs to shout up "take off that other shoe!" in self-defense i had to find something to fill in the gap between my book-ends. i shopped around...anthony adverse was too short in width...gone with the wind wouldn't do even lengthwise...even the five foot shelf couldn't quite make it.

"they laughed when i walked into your encyclopedia britannica office with my book-ends". but not for long mr. schoenewald! the encyclopedia filled a long-felt want and my book-ends, mr. schoenewald!

my encyclopedia i use week in and out in the preparation of my "town hall" radio programs. i didn't know who made the first horse shoe, mr. schoenewald. i didn't know where dry cleaning was first practised...until i owned my encyclopedia britannica.

hoping this finds you the same.

sincerely.....

Fred Allen

fred allen
20 reggio ave.
old orchard beach
maine...

P.S.—Well-written letters make excellent reading. If you want to delve into this subject, below are a few suggestion with which to start.

Collected Letters of D. H. Lawrence, edited by Harry T. Moore, 2 vols. (1962).

The First Cuckoo: A Selection of the Most Witty, Amusing, and Memorable Letters to The Times, 1900–1975, edited by Kenneth Gregory (1976).

Letters of E. B. White, edited by Dorothy L. Guth (1976).

The Letters of Katherine Mansfield, edited by J. Middleton Murry (1974, reprint of 1929 edition).

A Treasury of the World's Great Letters from Ancient Days to Our Own Time, edited by M. Lincoln Schuster (1941).

List of Honorifics

POSITION OR TITLE	WRITTEN FORM OF ADDRESS	SALUTATION
Academic Officials		
chancellor (of a university)	Dr. Lee Brown, Chancellor	Sir *or* Madam: Dear Dr. Brown:
dean (of a college or university)	Dr. Lee Brown, Dean *or* Dean Lee Brown	Sir *or* Madam: Dear Dr. Brown: Dear Dean Brown:
president	Dr. Lee Brown, President *or* President Lee Brown	Sir *or* Madam: Dear Dr. Brown: Dear President Brown:
professor, assistant or associate	Mr., Mrs., Miss, Ms., *or* Dr. Lee Brown Assistant *or* Associate Professor of ———	Dear Professor Brown: Dear Mr., Mrs., Miss, Ms., *or* Dr. Brown:
professor, full	Professor Lee Brown *or* Dr. Lee Brown Professor of ———	Dear Professor Brown: Dear Dr. Brown:
Clergy and Religious Orders		
archbishop	The Most Reverend Archbishop of ——— *or* The Most Reverend Lee Brown Archbishop of ———	Your Excellency: *or* Dear Archbishop Brown:

Adapted by permission. From *Webster's Secretarial Handbook* © 1976 by G. & C. Merriam Co., Publishers of Merriam-Webster Dictionaries.

bishop, Catholic	The Most Reverend Lee Brown Bishop of ———	Your Excellency: Dear Bishop Brown:
bishop, Episcopal	The Right Reverend The Bishop of ——— *or* The Right Reverend Lee Brown Bishop of ———	Right Reverend Sir: *or* Dear Bishop Brown:
bishop, other denominations	The Reverend Lee Brown (Denomination) Bishop	Reverend Sir: Dear Bishop Brown:
brotherhood, member of	Brother Lee, S.J.	Dear Brother Lee:
brotherhood, superior of	Brother Lee, S.J. Superior	Dear Brother Lee:
cardinal	His Eminence Lee Cardinal Brown Archbishop of ——— *or* His Eminence Cardinal Brown Archbishop of ———	Your Eminence: My dear Cardinal Brown: Dear Cardinal Brown:
clergyman, Protestant (excluding Episcopal)	The Reverend Lee Brown *or if having doctorate* The Reverend Dr. Lee Brown	Dear Mr. (Mrs., Miss, *or* Ms.) Brown: *or* Dear Dr. Brown:
monsignor	The Right Reverend Monsignor Lee Brown *or* The Rt. Rev. Msgr. Lee Brown	Dear Monsignor Brown:

POSITION OR TITLE	WRITTEN FORM OF ADDRESS	SALUTATION
patriarch (of an Eastern Orthodox Church)	His Beatitude the Patriarch of ——	Most Reverend Lord:
pope	His Holiness the Pope *or* His Holiness Pope ——	Your Holiness: Most Holy Father:
president, Mormon	The President Church of Jesus Christ of Latter-Day Saints	My dear President: Dear President Brown:
priest, Catholic	The Reverend Lee Brown *or if having doctorate* The Reverend Dr. Lee Brown	Dear Father Brown:
priest, Episcopal	The Reverend Lee Brown *or if having doctorate* The Reverend Dr. Lee Brown	Dear Mr. (Mrs., Miss, *or* Ms.) Brown: Dear Father Brown: *or* Dear Dr. Brown:
rabbi	Rabbi Lee Brown *or if having doctorate* Rabbi Lee Brown, D.D.	Dear Rabbi Brown: *or* Dear Dr. Brown:
sisterhood, member of	Sister Mary Theresa, S.C.	Dear Sister: Dear Sister Mary Theresa:
sisterhood, superior of	The Reverend Mother Superior, S.C.	Reverend Mother: Dear Reverend Mother:

Diplomats

ambassador, American	The Honorable Lee Brown American Ambassador *or if in Central or South America* The Ambassador of the United States of America	Sir *or* Madam: Dear Mr.⎫ Ambassador: Madam ⎬
ambassador, foreign	His *or* Her Excellency Lee Brown Ambassador of _____ *or if from Great Britain* His *or* Her Excellency The Right Honorable Lee Brown British Ambassador	Excellency: Dear Mr. ⎫* Ambassador: Madam(e) ⎬
consular officials	*The written form of address to a* *consulate consists of the following:* The (*nationality*) Consulate *or* The Consulate of (*country*) (*city, country, etc.*) *Note: The form of address for the U.S.* *consulate located in Central or* *South America is:* The Consulate of the United States of America	Gentlemen:
	The written form of address to a consul *consists of the following:* The (*nationality*) Consul	Sir *or* Madam(e)*:

---

*Madame is a title used in salutations to distinguish women of non-English-speaking nationality.

POSITION OR TITLE	WRITTEN FORM OF ADDRESS	SALUTATION
	or The Consul of (*country*) (*city, country,* etc.) *Note: Usually correspondence is addressed to the office of the consul rather than to the name of an individual consul. However, if correspondence is addressed to the individual, the name of an American consul is followed by a comma and Esq. The name of a foreign consul is preceded by The Honorable.* *Note: The form of address for the U.S. consul located in Central or South America is:* The Consul of the United States of America	
minister, American	The Honorable Lee Brown American Minister *or if in Central or South America* Minister of the United States of America	Sir *or* Madam: Dear Mr.⎱ Madam⎰Minister:
minister, foreign	The Honorable Lee Brown Minister of ———	Sir *or* Madam(e)*: Dear Mr. ⎱Minister: Madam(e)*⎰

Foreign Heads of State		
premier	His *or* Her Excellency Lee Brown Premier of ———	Excellency: Dear Mr. ⎫ Madam(e)* ⎬ Premier:
president of a republic	His *or* Her Excellency Lee Brown President of ———	Excellency: Dear Mr. ⎫ Madam(e)* ⎬ President:
prime minister	His *or* Her Excellency Lee Brown	Excellency: Dear Mr. ⎫ Madam(e)* ⎬ Prime Minister:
Government Officials—Federal[†]		
attorney general	The Honorable Lee Brown The Attorney General	Sir *or* Madam: Dear Mr. ⎫ Madam ⎬ Attorney General:
cabinet officer addressed as "Secretary"	The Honorable Lee Brown Secretary of ——— *or* The Secretary of ———	Sir *or* Madam: Dear Mr. ⎫ Madam ⎬ Secretary:
director (as of an independent federal agency)	The Honorable Lee Brown Director ——— Agency	Dear Mr., Mrs., Miss, *or* Ms. Brown:
district attorney	The Honorable Lee Brown District Attorney	Dear Mr., Mrs., Miss, *or* Ms. Brown:

[†]Based on historical precedent, some examples are given in the masculine only.

POSITION OR TITLE	WRITTEN FORM OF ADDRESS	SALUTATION
federal judge	The Honorable Lee Brown Judge of the United States District Court for the _____ District of _____	Sir or Madam: My dear Judge Brown: Dear Judge Brown:
former government official	For retired or former, elected public officials the form of address is: The Honorable Lee Brown (local address)	For retired or former national officials of the highest rank (president, supreme court justice, etc.), the salutation Sir or Madam is appropriate, as well as the otherwise standard Dear Mr, Mrs., Miss, or Ms. Brown:
president of the United States	The President The White House or The Honorable Lee Brown President of the United States The White House	Mr. President: My dear Mr. President: Dear Mr. President:†
representative, United States Congress	The Honorable Lee Brown United States House of Representatives	Dear Sir or Dear Madam: Dear Representative Brown: Dear Mr., Mrs., Miss, or Ms. Brown:
senator, United States Senate	The Honorable Lee Brown United States Senate	Sir or Madam: Dear Senator Brown:
speaker, United States House of Representatives	The Honorable Speaker of the House of Representatives or	Sir: Dear Mr. Speaker: Dear Mr. Brown:†

supreme court, associate justice	The Honorable Lee Brown Speaker of the House of Representatives Mr. Justice Brown The Supreme Court of the United States	Sir *or* Mr. Justice: My dear Mr. Justice: Dear Mr. Justice: Dear Mr. Justice Brown:[†]
supreme court, chief justice	The Chief Justice of the United States The Supreme Court of the United States *or* The Chief Justice The Supreme Court	Sir: My dear Mr. Chief Justice: Dear Mr. Chief Justice:[†]
vice-president of the United States	The Vice-President of the United States United States Senate *or* The Honorable Lee Brown Vice-President of the United States	Sir: My dear Mr. Vice-President: Dear Mr. Vice-President:[†]

Government Officials—Local

alderman (councilman, selectman)	The Honorable Lee Brown *or* Alderman (*or* Councilman *or* Selectman) Lee Brown	Dear Mr., Mrs., Miss, *or* Ms. Brown:

POSITION OR TITLE	WRITTEN FORM OF ADDRESS	SALUTATION
judge	The Honorable Lee Brown Judge of the ——— Court of ———	Dear Judge Brown:
mayor	The Honorable Lee Brown Mayor of ———	Sir or Madam: Dear Mayor Brown:
Government Officials—State		
attorney general	The Honorable Lee Brown Attorney General of the State of ———	Sir or Madam: Dear Mr. }Attorney General: Madam }
governor	The Honorable Lee Brown Governor of ———	Sir or Madam: Dear Governor Brown:
judge, state court	The Honorable Lee Brown Judge of the ——— Court	Dear Judge Brown:
lieutenant governor	The Honorable Lee Brown Lieutenant Governor of ———	Sir or Madam: Dear Mr., Mrs., Miss, or Ms. Brown:
representative, state (including assembly- man, delegate)	The Honorable Lee Brown House of Representatives (or The State Assembly or The House of Delegates)	Sir or Madam: Dear Mr., Mrs., Miss, or Ms. Brown:
secretary of state	The Honorable Lee Brown Secretary of State of ———	Sir or Madam: Dear Mr. }Secretary: Madam }

senator, state	The Honorable Lee Brown The Senate of ―――	Sir *or* Madam: Dear Senator Brown:
supreme court, state, associate justice	The Honorable Lee Brown Associate Justice of the Supreme Court of ―――	Sir *or* Madam: Dear Justice Brown:
supreme court, state, chief justice	The Honorable Lee Brown Chief Justice of the Supreme Court of ―――	Sir *or* Madam: Dear Mr. } Madam } Chief Justice:

Military Personnel

The written form of address for all military personnel consists of the full name preceded by full rank (or abbreviation of full rank) and followed by a comma and initials of the branch of service, e.g., Lance Corporal or L/Cpl. Lee Brown, USMC.

The salutation consists of surname preceded by Dear and the basic unit of rank: Dear Corporal Brown:

Miscellaneous Professionals

dentist	Lee Brown, D.D.S. *or* Dr. Lee Brown	Dear Dr. Brown:
lawyer	Mr., Mrs., Miss, or Ms. Lee Brown Attorney-at-Law *or* Lee Brown, Esq.	Dear Mr., Mrs., Miss, or Ms. Brown:
physician	Lee Brown, M.D. *or* Dr. Lee Brown	Dear Dr. Brown:

The History of the Epistle

Epistle, in its original sense a word meaning simply a letter, has come to be used only of formal letters written in ancient times, or of an elaborate kind of literary production, akin to the ode and the elegy, which, while addressed to a particular person, is concerned with public rather than personal affairs or expresses a universal feeling on a particular occasion. The epistle is written for an audience, with a conscious artistry and elaboration of style, to develop an argument or theme.

Even in classical times, the word *epistola* came to have the additional meaning of an imperial decree, and surviving epistles from the ancient world are usually the public utterances of great men, akin to speeches in subject matter and formality. Pseudonymous epistles purporting to set forth the views of men such as Plato, Demosthenes, Aristotle, and Cicero on some topic of moment were numerous under the early Roman empire. The Pauline Epistles of the New Testament are of particular interest, resembling the "imperial edicts and rescripts by which Roman law grew, documents arising out of special circumstances but treating them on general principles." Papal encyclical letters, addressed to the whole church, have carried on this apostolic epistolary tradition.

The epistle in the post-apostolic age was a communication between branches of the church, rather than between individuals. In the following centuries epistles on doctrine and practice were written by the Christian Fathers—Cyprian, Ambrose, Chrysostom, Augustine and Jerome. In the secular world, at the same period, epistles developed increasingly into a branch of literature, and the ten books of Symmachus' *Epistolae,* so highly esteemed in the 4th century, are in the line connecting Cicero's letters with the Renaissance literary epistles, supremely exemplified by Petrarch. The literary epistle developed as a vehicle for satire, as in Swift's *Drapier Letters,* for religious and contemplative ideas, as in Pascal's *Les Provinciales,* and for polemics, as in the epistles of Martin Marprelate.

Poetic epistles of Ovid, Claudian, Ausonius, and other late Latin poets have been preserved, but it is particularly the poetic epistles of Horace, on moral or philosophical subjects, that inspired the epistles in verse that form so very characteristic a section of French poetry. Clément Marot, in the 16th century, first made the epistle popular in France. Nicolas Boileau's 12 epistles (composed 1668–95) are the classic examples. In the 18th century Voltaire enjoyed a supremacy in this species of writing; the *Epître à Uranie* is perhaps the most famous of his verse letters.

In England the verse epistle was first prominently used by Samuel Daniel, whose letter to Lucy, countess of Bristol, is one of the finest examples of this form in English literature. Ben Jonson has some fine Horatian epistles in his *Forests* (1616) and his *Underwoods. Letters to Several Persons of Honour* form an important section in the poetry of John Donne, and Dryden's epistles to Congreve (1694) and to the duchess of Ormond (1700) are among the most graceful and eloquent that we possess. During the age of Queen Anne, John Gay employed the epistle for several exercises in his elegant persiflage. But the great writer of epistles in English is Pope. His "Epistle to Dr. Arbuthnot" has not been surpassed, if equaled, in Latin or French poetry of the same class. After Pope the epistle again fell into desuetude. It revived in the charming naïveté of Cowper's lyrical letters in octosyllabics to his friends, and Samuel Rogers later endeavoured to resuscitate the neglected form in his "Epistle to a Friend." Shelley's "Letter to Maria Gisborne" (1820), Keats's "Epistle to Charles Clarke" (1816), and Landor's "To Julius Hare" (1836), in spite of their romantic coloring, are genuine Horatian epistles.

ENCYCLOPÆDIA BRITANNICA

Forms of Address

United States

SPOKEN FORMS OF ADDRESS In the United States the forms of address emphasize the position occupied by the person addressed. They are concerned with the correct use of the name or the label designating the position. Thus the president of the United States is addressed as "Mr. President" in speaking to him and as "Sir" when in conversation with him. In speaking of or quoting him he is referred to as "The President." In presenting him for an address he is announced as "The President of the United States of America." When the wife of the president is included in the address the speaker says "The President and Mrs. Surname." The vice-president is addressed and referred to in the same manner as the president.

An ambassador is addressed as "Mr. Ambassador" or "Your Excellency," his wife as "Mrs. Surname." The governors of the states are addressed as "Governor." The mayor of a city is addressed as "Your Honor."

In unofficial or private life the trend is away from the use of titles in verbal forms of address. It is not correct, according to distinguished social usage, to make the professional title of major importance in speaking to a person. This is especially true in academic and business circles. Such titles as "Dean," "Doctor" and "Professor" are gradually being dropped from social usage.

When in a strictly business or professional relationship, the title should be used. A student would address a dean as "Dean Surname"; he would probably address a professor with a doctor's degree as "Dr. Surname." It is generally considered antiquated to say "Professor Surname"; the term "Mr." is preferable if he is without a doctor's degree or administrative position. However, some persons, according to local customs, cling to the recognition by title.

582

In the medical profession "Doctor Surname" is always used. The title "Reverend" is seldom used verbally in addressing a clergyman; if he holds a doctor of divinity degree frequently he is addressed as "Dr. Surname." If he holds a position of rank in denominational organizations, such as bishop, he is addressed with a title according to the dictates of the church.

Presentations and introductions. One of the most important forms of address is that used in introductions. An introduction is the form for making easier the beginning of an acquaintanceship between strangers. It must provide a means of identification for the persons being introduced. The form used may also indicate the degree of sponsorship the person making the introduction is assuming for the new relationship.

The simple form of "Miss Smith, Miss Jones" or "Mr. Blank, Mr. Doe," spoken with a genial smile or simple gesture, a glance (never point) or voice inflection, is the easiest form and most generally accepted for all chance meetings, whether in public places, among work associates or on informal occasions.

When respect or additional identification is to be shown, as when the sex, age or position is different, the introduction would be more formal, as "Mrs. Blank, may I present (or may I introduce) (or I would like you to meet my friend Miss Smith) (or Mary Smith) my escort Mr. Doe"; the names would then be repeated: "Miss Smith, Mrs. Blank." The name of the person to whom the greater respect is to be shown is spoken first—in this case Mrs. Blank.

In business introductions, the official title of the person of superior rank is used, as "President Brown, may I present (or introduce) Mr. Newcomer? Mr. Newcomer, Mr. Brown." Then give some identification as the reason for Mr. Newcomer's presence, as "Mr. Newcomer is a new employee in my department; we would like to discuss with you . . ."

SELF-INTRODUCTION Frequently a person must introduce himself. In a business interview he should announce himself by giving his name or presenting a business card, give some identification such as place of residence or business connection, and then state the purpose of his visit, as "I am John Stranger, a senior at New York University. I would like to talk with you about . . ." In answering a telephone a person should always identify the telephone by number and himself by position, as "extension 262, secretary to the president speaking."

Presentation of a speaker. In a presenting a speaker to an audience the person making the introduction should select carefully only such biographical facts about the speaker as have a direct relation to his qualifications to address the audience on the particular subject, or to the occasion for which they are assembled. These remarks should include the name of the person and his present position, and conclude with: "It is my pleasure to present you Mr. Surname (title if preferred)." The person making the introduction should then turn toward the speaker and say "Mr. Surname."

When the speaker is a person of great distinction, such as the president of the United States, no introductory remarks are made about him; the presiding officer simply announces "The President of the United States."

WRITTEN FORMS OF ADDRESS   In all written forms of address the proper use of labels, identity and recognition of position are of paramount importance.

Business forms of address.   Great care should be taken in giving correct identification by title, name and position in the address at the head of a business letter. The salutation should be carefully worded so as to indicate a recognition of the respect due the person because of his position.

The title "The Honorable" should be used in writing to: governors, cabinet officers, United States ambassadors and ministers, judges, senators, members of the house of representatives, the secretary to the president, assistant secretaries of executive departments and the heads of independent boards and commissions.

The title "Esquire" should be used after the names of: chief clerks and chiefs of bureaus of the executive departments, mayors of towns and cities (when the name is used before the title, as "James Burrows, Esquire, Mayor of . . ."); although considered antiquated by some, "Esquire" may be added after the name of any individual gentleman.

Beginnings of formal letters should be as follows: to the president, "The or Mr. President"; to an ambassador, "Sir"; to a minister, "Sir." To the cabinet officers and the justices of the U.S. supreme court, "Sir" is used for formal salutations. To a senator, informally, the salutation would be "My dear Senator Smith"; to a member of the house of representatives, "My dear Mr. Jones." For the U.S. supreme court the informal form is "My dear Mr. Chief Justice" and "My dear Mr. Justice." For the supreme court of a state it is also "My dear Mr. Justice"; for the court of appeals of the state, it is "Chief Judge" and "Judge."

Social forms of address.   The president of the United States, according to social form, should never receive an engraved invitation to dinner from an individual. When his presence is desired the person inviting him should either call at the White House and ask him to select a date or write to him to that effect.

The most formal invitation should read:

> Mr. and Mrs. John Doe
> request the honor of
> the company of
> The American Ambassador to Great Britain and Mrs. Surname
> (occasion, time and place)

The envelope addressed to officials should read:

> The Title of the Position
> and Mrs. Surname

The same form is used for invitations and envelope addresses for all dignitaries. The word "honor" instead of "pleasure" is suggested because of the position of the recipient of the invitation. Between host and guest who are officially equal in rank the word "pleasure" is preferable, but either is correct in all forms of invitations where the name of the guest is to be included.

Acknowledgment of the invitation, either accepting or declining, should be written in the same form as the invitation:

> The Governor of the State of Virginia
> and Mrs. Surname
> regret that they cannot
> accept the invitation of
> Mr. and Mrs. John Doe
> (occasion, time and place)

The place card would read "The President"; his wife's card would read "Mrs. Surname." Similar form for place cards should be used for ambassadors and governors and other ranking dignitaries who are addressed by title of office and not by name. In the case of the American ambassador to Great Britain and his wife, his place card would read "The American Ambassador to Great Britain," his wife's "Mrs. Surname."

The titles "Reverend" and "Honorable" should not precede a surname. The Christian name or title as "Dr." or "Mr." should be used:

The Reverend John Pastor, or the Reverend Dr. Pastor.

Academic degrees and title of position should follow the name: Mr. John Collegian, M.A., or Dr. John Collegian, Director of Admissions.

Great Britain

Forms of address have evolved over many centuries. They are almost all customary and are therefore variable by changes in the same usage which brought them into being.

THE ROYAL FAMILY   A person speaking to the queen should begin "Your Majesty" and continue "Ma'am." Letters, headed "To the Queen's Most Excellent Majesty," should begin "Madam" and end "I remain, with the profoundest veneration, Your Majesty's most faithful subject."

The spoken form of address for the queen mother is the same as for the queen. Letters, headed "To her Gracious Majesty Queen Elizabeth the Queen Mother," should begin "Madam" and end "I remain Your Majesty's most faithful servant."

A person speaking to a prince of the royal family should begin "Your Royal Highness" and continue "Sir." Letters, headed "To H.R.H. the Duke of ____" (or, if not a duke, "To H.R.H. Prince ____"), should begin "Sir" and end "I remain, with the greatest respect, your Royal Highness's most obedient servant." Princesses of the royal family should be addressed *mutatis mutandis* as for princes, "Ma'am" taking the place of "Sir."

Those wishing to address royalty in writing should approach them through the lady or gentleman in waiting.

THE NOBILITY   The peerage in Great Britain has five degrees of rank, namely duke, marquess, earl, viscount and baron. Each of these, their wives and children require a different form of address.

Dukes and duchesses are always dukes and duchesses when addressed either in speech or in writing; the prefixes are "His Grace" for dukes, "Her Grace" for duchesses; *e.g.,* His Grace The Duke of Norfolk. The spoken form of address is "Your Grace." Letters should begin "My Lord Duke" and end "I have the honour to be, my Lord Duke, Your Grace's obedient servant."

The full formal title is not used in addressing any member of the four succeeding grades of peers either in conversation or in the intimacy of a private letter. On envelopes, on invitations, in and on legal documents or tradesmen's communications and bills, they are addressed as marquesses and marchionesses, earls and countesses, vicounts and viscountesses. In conversation, and in letters beginning "Dear . . . ," they must be addressed as "Lord So-and-So" or "Lady So-and-So." In formal correspondence "The Most Honourable" for marquesses and marchionesses and "The Right Honourable" for earls, countesses, viscounts, viscountesses, barons and baronesses may be used.

For a baron, the use of the title is more restricted; it is used only in or on legal documents. On envelopes in nonlegal correspondence, on all invitations or in letters written in the third person, he is styled "Lord." However, a baroness in her own right is always called "Baroness" (*e.g.,* Baroness Ravensdale, Baroness Wentworth) except in speech and in letters beginning "Dear." In invitations, the full title, except in the case of barons, is always used. In letters written in the third person, the full title is used in the first place, but afterward reference is made by means of the colloquial designation; *e.g.,* "The editor presents his compliments to the Marquess of Piccadilly and will be much pleased if Lord Piccadilly . . . ," etc.

In the case of the three higher grades of peers, the eldest son bears a courtesy title; *i.e.,* he is known by one of his father's subsidiary peerages (this, however, does not provide him with a seat in the house of lords).

The eldest son of the eldest son of a duke or of a marquess is also customarily known by one of his grandfather's subsidiary peerages. Never is the bearer of a courtesy title addressed as "The Right Honourable." The younger sons of dukes and marquesses have the prefix "Lord" placed before their Christian names and surnames; the younger sons of earls and all the sons of viscounts and barons have that of "Honourable," generally shortened to "Honble." or "Hon."

The daughters of dukes, marquesses and earls bear the title of "Lady" prefixed to the Christian name and surname. Thus Lady Mary will remain Lady Mary all her life, unless she marries a peer or a younger son whose father has a higher rank than her own father. If she marries a commoner, a knight, a baronet or an Honble., she remains Lady Mary and should always be addressed as such. It is wrong to use only her surname, as "Lady Debrett."

The prefix "Honble." is applied to the unmarried daughters of viscounts and of barons. When a daughter marries, the Christian name is dropped and she becomes The Honble. Mrs. Blank, unless she marries a peer or a man with a courtesy title in the peerage higher than her own. If, for example, she marries a younger son of a duke or a marquess, she becomes Lady (husband's full name), as Lady Edward Jones; she can never become Lady Mary Jones unless her father becomes a marquess or a duke. One great difference between these courtesy titles of Lord and Honourable is that the latter title is not used in conversation, and is never printed on visiting cards.

OTHER RANKS   The wives of baronets and knights are known as "Lady X," but there is nothing in the wife's title to show to which order her husband belongs. The baronet's name is differentiated in writing because the abbreviation "Bt." or "Bart." (preferably the former) follows it on envelopes; the nine different orders of knighthood have their initial letters placed after the name (K.G., knight of the order of the Garter, etc.), but their "ladies" have no right to use these letters. To specify which lady of the same surname is meant, it has become the practice to use the husband's Christian name between parentheses, as Lady (James) Debrett, although this is contrary to tradition and heraldry.

Knights bachelor are knights who do not belong to any of the nine specified orders. They are correctly given the abbreviation, "Kt.," or "Kt. Bach." after their names. They may lay claim, if they possess the necessary qualifications, to such letters as M.D., R.N. or M.P.; the M.P. is always added to the name of any member of the house of commons, no matter what his title may be.

The title of "Right Honourable" (Rt. Hon.; Rt. Honble.) is the prerogative of H.M.'s privy councilors and, as such, is borne by those of them who are not peers. It is used, in the same way as "Honble.," directly in front of the Christian name (e.g., Rt. Hon. R. A. Butler).

Professional designations, such as "Dr." or "Rev.," or naval or military rank precede the prefix of "Honourable," whereas titles of baronetcy and knighthood follow the prefix; e.g., The Rev. The Honble. Jonathan Kenworthy; Colonel The Honble. Edward Wyndham; The Honble. Sir Trevor Bigham, K.B.E., C.B.

Sailors, soldiers and airmen are always addressed by their professional titles—admiral, general, air marshal, captain, colonel, commander, squadron leader and so on, except sublieutenants in the navy, lieutenants and second lieutenants in the army and flying officers in the air force, who in private life remain Thomas Smith, Esq. Captains in the royal navy add R.N. after their names to show that they belong to the senior service.

Judges and doctors may choose tiltes as a matter of personal preference from equally correct forms of title. This can generally be discovered by noticing how they style themselves on their visiting cards; e.g., "Sir Henry Barnard" or "Mr. Justice Barnard"; or "Dr. Drennan."

ENCYCLOPÆDIA BRITANNICA

THE ART OF SPEAKING

The Well-Spoken American
The Craft of Public Speaking
The History of Rhetoric and Oratory

The Well-Spoken American

A funny thing happened to some of us on our way to the 21st century. We started to forget how to talk.

In one way or another most animals—and perhaps plants too—communicate. Some, such as the bees, use a "dance language" of considerable complexity. But only humans talk. Should we not prize highly this most precious gift of nature? Yet, because it is almost impossible *not* to learn to talk, we tend to undervalue the ability. We are all concerned to keep our bodies in good repair but less concerned to develop and improve the marvelous faculty springing from the unique relationship between our vocal cords and our brains.

The way we talk signals to others who and what we are. It declares our identity, "places" us, sets a price tag on our value as human beings. You may object. What we are, you may say, is something larger and deeper than can ever be summed up in what we say and how we say it. True. The fact remains, however, that in today's world, dominated by communication and surface impressions, we are all too often, all too hastily, judged by our talk.

For this reason alone it would seem sensible for us to develop good talk habits. Yet not all of us do. Parents and children use different languages. Teachers despair of breaking through to their students, and the students reverse the complaint. Spoken orders from employers are misunderstood by employees. Heads of government misinterpret each other. Politicians talk more and say less. By the million the words pour out, but all too often there is little connection between speaker and auditor.

The reasons for the decline in our ability to talk well are many. Outstanding is the fact that TV, radio, and film furnish a never-ending supply of poor models. A century or more ago public speakers reached few people. In that sense they were a rarity. But if you *did* happen to listen to a Lincoln, a Douglas, an Emerson, a Robert Ingersoll, you heard language composed and spoken well. The models were few—not avail-

591

able to all—but good. Today the models are many—available to all—
and not so good. Even though TV's Baretta or the Fonz or the "real
folks" who populate the commercials are not necessarily designed for
imitation, we cannot help—especially if we are children—aping them.
As for politicians and other persons in authority, few have any affection
for the language and many are but semiliterate. Talk shows feature hosts
who in another era might have made good backwoods circus barkers;
they also often present guests such as rock stars who are uneasy when
required to use language of words rather than music.

But poor models alone do not account for the worsening of our speech
habits. We should add two other important factors: ignorance and
insecurity.

Our schools are supposed to deal with ignorance. If we are not taught
that "he acts like he was crazy" is not Standard English, the probability is that the "like" of the Winston cigarette ads—as has already
happened—will become part of the language and slightly impoverish it.
Would that the commercial media were better teachers!

Insecurity is a subtler matter. Our age is one in which few of us
feel secure—economically, politically, intellectually, emotionally, or
socially. For this broad statement some evidence may be found in the
proliferation of self-improvement books and cults of instant salvation.
This insecurity inevitably reflects itself in our speech, the index of our
personalities.

Lack of linguistic self-confidence cannot be wholly overcome by
studying grammar textbooks or books like the one you are now reading.
But we can count on a certain amount of improvement once we become
conscious (and yet not *too* conscious) of our faults and then decide to
do something about them. To get us thinking along these lines, I will
list a few common faults, all of which I myself have at one time or
another committed, which is the reason they are so present in my mind.
They are not confined to any single economic group or ethnic minority.
On the contrary they are endemic to most Americans.

A LITTLE MORE SILENCE, PLEASE!   One may be a good speaker and a
poor conversationalist. Conversation is not made up exclusively of uttered words. It is made up of uttered words interspersed with silences
and proper pauses. It is a combination of speaking and listening; and
the listening, if done intelligently, is sometimes more important than
the speaking. We Americans are inclined to interrupt, though this fault
is by no means our unique conversational sin. We are almost as much
inclined to ignore the need for an occasional pause. Insecurity often lies
at the base of babbling. We cover with incessant sound a kind of interior
hollowness. TV, too, is partly responsible, since in the world of the
airwaves the cardinal sin is dead air.

The next time you (or I) engage in conversation, notice how often we fail to let the other person finish a sentence or thought. Also notice *his* conversational etiquette. If *both* interrupt, we get nowhere fast. The virtues—indeed, the power—of appropriate pauses and interludes of silence are not mentioned in books of rhetoric; yet they are part of keeping talk clear and communication unimpeded. Which of us, for example, has not been made furious by the nonstop telephone talker?

THE PERPENDICULAR PRONOUN   We all know the story of the film star who, after talking about himself incessantly for 10 minutes, broke off and said to his interviewer, "Well, enough about me. What did *you* think of my latest picture?" Many of us are that film star. How many of our spoken sentences begin with "I"? How often do we interrupt with "Let me tell you how *I* look at it"? Though it is difficult to keep the ego completely out of conversation, to indulge it too generously makes for a dull, monotonous conversational style. The best talkers are those who give the other person a fair shake and who also try to keep the talk—at least part of the time—on an impersonal plane.

WORD CRUTCHES   I (there I go again) have a bad habit, probably contracted in early childhood and therefore difficult to eradicate, of prefacing statements with the word "well . . ." This bad habit not only fuzzes up what I am saying but also reveals my inner uncertainty. I am using "well" as a crutch. Here are some other crutches: "Right," "um," "uh," "like," "you know," and "OK." To "er-r" is doubtless human, but—like other verbal crutches—it slows down conversation and irritates the listener. Such fillers reflect the fact that we haven't quite thought out what we intend to say. Sometimes in spontaneous talk their use is unavoidable. But just as dependence on real crutches is bound to weaken the leg muscles, so verbal crutches, if excessively used, weaken our conversational powers. We often refer to the "clipped speech" of well-educated English persons. It means that they do not need to use crutches; it is second nature for them to speak as economically as possible.

ALL-PURPOSE WORDS AND PHRASES   One sign of language control is our ability to make distinctions rather than depending on all-purpose tags. The adjective "fantastic," which probably had its origins in the Hollywood film world, may express high, low, or moderate approval of anything from a candy bar to the moon landing. The trouble is not that "fantastic" fails to convey our general meaning but that a constant reliance on such words-of-all-work gradually undermines our capacity for exact expression. The use of "thing" ("it's not her thing"; "she's got a thing for him") as an all-purpose noun has the same effect. Phrases such as "all right!" or "that's for sure" are all-purpose slang terms used for various shadings of assent. Similarly, "no way" and "gross" are overused to express all varieties of negative. The constant use of such phrases renders flabby one's powers of expression. With them we communicate on a minimum basis, when what may be called for is precision and exactness of statement.

VOGUE LINGO   In the film "Saturday Night Fever," one character, a very much "with it" young man, catches the heroine on her use of "super" as an expression of praise. It stamps her, he implies, as out-of-date. But his warning, though well-intentioned, may get the poor girl into difficulties. If we are continually worried about whether we are using the latest fashionable phrase (such as "with it," used above), we will lose sight of our main aim, which is clear communication.

Perhaps all the following familiar examples of vogue lingo are no longer in vogue: *yeah man!, man* (used generally as a form of address), *dig it, hangup, rip off, heavy* (as an intensive), *far out, get the message, blow your mind, neat, hip, with it, bit* ("he gives you the sincere bit"), *up tight, a drag, a bummer, into* ("into yogurt"; "into religion"), *right on, where it's at.* It would be sheer pedantry to censor such expressions completely, for vogue slang can be in certain contexts accurate and appropriate. It is simply their overuse, or rather their use as ready-made counters when we should really use more exact coinage, that gives our speech a dull and unimaginative cast.

CLICHÉS AND EUPHEMISMS   Clichés are difficult to separate from vogue lingo. We may venture a possible distinction: vogue lingo is generally slangy and often originates with outgroups or minorities, whereas clichés are usually drawn from Standard English. A cliché becomes one only by overuse or its use in inappropriate contexts. The first person who used the word "period!" to add extra emphasis at the end of a forceful statement perhaps made a tiny and useful addition to the language. But it is now used routinely when no extra emphasis is needed. Clichés such as "not really" when a simple "no" is in order; "to live with it" as describing the myriad forms of accommodation or acceptance; "relate to," a pompous borrowing from pop psychology; "credibility gap"; "fun" used as an adjective; "the name of the game" as an emphasizer; "gut feeling" for all forms of inner certainty or conviction; and "hopefully," which should be confined to the meaning of "in a hopeful manner"—all these worn or mildly barbarous words and phrases tarnish our speech, dull its sparkle, and in the end reduce the potential of our mental energy.

We have become accustomed to such roundabout words and expressions as "mortician," "realtor," "sanitation engineer," and "pass away." But our tendency to soften certain ideas by couching them in euphemisms can lead to a numbing of the language. At the beauty shop the beautician suggested to my daughter: "You ought to naturalize your hair, dear." It developed that "dear" was being urged simply to dye her hair. Why avoid the most direct verbal route? It is always the most powerful.

THE FASHIONABLE MUMBLE   I think this pitfall began with Marlon Brando and method acting. Since the rise to fame of John Travolta, Sylvester Stallone, and Peter Falk, throwaway enunciation and under-the-breath vocalization have achieved prestige status. Conversely, clear enunciation is "out" or is only accepted when it emanates from highly magnetic and skilled actors such as Richard Burton. Our language derives much of its force and speed from its hard consonants and crisp word endings. To ignore these qualities with modish mumbling or an exaggerated drawl is to insult the magnificence of our English tongue.

A FEW PARTING WORDS   Stop when you are finished. This is not as simple as it may sound. I know, for I am myself a sinner. I make part of my living as a public speaker, often working merely from rough notes. Whenever I have made a point that seems well received by the audience, I make the mistake (insecurity again) of repeating it by un-necessary elaboration. Knowing when to stop is half the secret of good talk. Indeed, two of the sounds most infrequently heard in American conversation are the simple "yes" and "no."

An unfortunate nervous habit some of us have is repeating the last few words of the other person. This curious verbal tic is, once more, the result of insecurity. We reassure ourselves that we are on good terms with the other speaker by mechanically parroting the concluding phrase or even the entire sentence.

Some of us talk in "bunches." Instead of pausing at those places in the sentence that, in writing, would be marked by a comma, semicolon, dash, or parentheses, we stop arbitrarily so that our sentence comes out in a confusing series of little rushes. In many ways President Jimmy Carter is an excellent speaker. His syntax is always correct, and his sentences are economical and intelligible. (This has not always been the case with previous presidents.) But he talks in bunches, and that makes him a less effective speaker than he might be. Tape-record yourself; then listen. If your speech is weakened by this or any of the problems mentioned above, you can begin to cure yourself by an effort of will. But you must think the effort worth making.

Should talk be edited, as writing must be? Obviously not in informal, spontaneous give-and-take. But whenever the situation has some aspect of formality about it—a job interview, a sales pitch, a class recitation, a presentation of any kind—it is not enough to let the words tumble out helter-skelter. It is possible to edit talk by thinking ahead, by forming sentences deliberately, by making use of slight pauses, by hesitating just long enough to permit the choice of the correct word rather than the one that comes first to mind. The aim is to match the words to the thought—obvious enough, but that aim must be constantly remembered.

I have pointed out a few small linguistic lapses of which most of us are occasionally guilty, but this discussion merely scratches the surface. It is a fact that our spoken language in the last two decades has lost some of its accuracy, clarity, economy, and comprehensibility. How the conversion of all of us into well-spoken Americans is accomplished is more than anyone can say. But the first step is to become conscious of our own carelessness. To that end the brief foregoing comments have been directed. Watching ourselves—or rather listening to ourselves— can be overdone, of course. Yet it is worthwhile—especially if we do not seem to be getting through to others—to keep an eye, as it were, on our tongue.

CLIFTON FADIMAN

The Craft of Public Speaking

"Unaccustomed as I am to public speaking," the time-honored phrase runs, "there are some things which I have to say this evening. . . ." Sooner or later most of us face this moment. A political rally, a parent-teachers' meeting, a testimonial dinner for an old friend may call for those traditional "few words" before an audience. Your introduction, polite applause, then silence. The people sitting before you are prepared to be amused, exhorted, aroused, or persuaded in some form or another, depending on what you tell them and how you speak. Nothing can help you now. You are on your own. Start talking.

The task of the public speaker has never been an enviable one, although there are those who find it tolerable, congenial, or even addictive. But in past generations the craft of public speaking was given considerable attention. First rhetoric, later elocution, or public speaking, were taught in the schools, along with spelling, grammar, and composition. Colleges set great store in staging debates and oratorical contests; the lecture became one of America's abiding instructional entertainments. The disciplines of speechmaking were taught and observed.

The television age has changed that in the course of eroding accepted standards of communication, style, and argument. The very word *rhetoric* has become a pejorative among many. Difficult to define by those who use it most, it is too often an excuse for dismissing complex argument, persuasive expression, or attempts to speak with grace and style as somehow lacking in "honesty." Those who talk to us through the magic cathode-ray tube—be they politicians, anchormen, or home economists—pride themselves on giving facts only. This over-communicated generation will not be taken in by carefully crafted words, the new conventional wisdom assures us. So "tell it like it is"—the more unvarnished, the better.

Our national attention span is steadily shortening. We are both picture-conscious and image-conscious. We *watch* the person who is speaking, concentrating our attention on looks and manner as much as on what he is saying. Many of us have lost the auditory patience even to listen to prolonged radio talks (except when we are riding in cars). Still less are we capable of hearing out a politician as he develops his argument on the podium. We prefer question-and-answer sessions or, better yet, confessions wrung out by televised public interrogations. At banquets, conventions, and political meetings, the word goes out: "Keep the speeches short."

And yet we need the stimulus of the spoken word. Despite our protestations of plain speech, bluntness, and anti-rhetoric, we are still swayed by the effective speaker. People who denounce campaign oratory most loudly complain when the guest of honor at the big dinner does nothing but cite statistics or when a president delivers his State of the Union speech in the matter-of-fact style of an engineer confirming specifications for a new widget machine. The lecture tour in the United States still commands big audiences and pays its speakers good money. (For proof we have to look no further than the Watergate scandal tours of the '70s, when just about every conspirator who could speak without an impediment was talking on the chicken-and-peas dining circuit the minute he got out of jail.)

In business oratory the set speech has given way to the "presentation," with films, slides, bar charts, and other audiovisual aids wired into the statements of "your company's" operating officers. Yet for all the detached comment and cold statistics, persuasive speech is still at work among us. Few managers have lost points because they could give a rousing sales talk. The profusion of how-to-do-it books on public speaking, the speech clinics, and the existence of groups like the Toastmasters show how many Americans want to teach themselves how to get on their feet and talk effectively.

The purpose of this essay is to offer some suggestions on how to speak well, how best to say something—as distinguished from merely "speaking," how to handle an audience, and, most important of all, how to organize one's thoughts for speaking in public. In short we are setting forth some revised rules of rhetoric.

The very first edition of the *Britannica* (Vol. 3) in 1771 defined rhetoric as "the art of speaking copiously on any subject, with all the advantage of beauty and force." Our first Scottish editors continued: ". . . every author must invent arguments to make his subject prevail; dispose those arguments, thus found out, in their proper places; and give them the embellishments of language proper to the subject; and, if this discourse be intended to be delivered in public, utter them with that decency and force which may strike the hearer. . . ." The prose is that of a more leisurely age than ours, but their definition is well stated.

There are two ways of speaking in public. One is by reading prepared remarks from a text; the other is by speaking extemporaneously or from a few notes. When you are reading from a text there is not much you can do but read it well. That, however, is no mean accomplishment. After the speech is written, you must study it for a while so that you are truly familiar with it. Nothing kills the spirit of a speech like a mechanical reading. Know your text well enough so that you can raise your eyes from the page and look at your audience occasionally; otherwise you will lose them.

Practice the voice inflections and the pauses. English is not a highly inflected language as is, say, Russian—so speaking effectiveness depends heavily on stress and intonation. If your peroration concludes with the words "we must do something *now*," they must be read with urgency and with the right word stressed. If on the contrary you mumble all the words in exactly the same tone, the whole exercise loses its point, and the listeners do not understand what you are saying. This problem persists even with veteran speakers who read their text. It is surprising how much they could improve communication if they would spend just an hour before the speech going over it and saying it aloud to themselves. There is nothing like practice.

Writing the speech

In preparing a speech on your own, the first thing to do is write an outline. Even a few words will do. Lincoln edited his entire address, it is said, on the back of an old envelope while he was on the train to Gettysburg. To make an outline you have first to know what you want to say—not so easy a thing. If you have a lot to say to an audience and only limited time, pick out one topic and focus on it. If you can make one good point and leave it with an audience, this is far better than thinking of many things to say, trying to cover them all at one sitting, so to speak, and leaving your audience in confusion. An audience's powers of intuition can rarely be presumed.

Once you have isolated your theme, you should organize the presentation. "Every discourse," Socrates told us, "ought to be a living creature, having a body of its own and a head and feet; there should be a middle, beginning, and end, adapted to one another and to the whole." The pattern is familiar, having been used by Cicero and all the great orators since. First you introduce the topic, next produce arguments in favor of it, suggest rebuttals for arguments against it, then conclude the speech with a peroration that sums up your points.

If your first thought is on what you are saying, your second should be on the people to whom you are speaking. The greatest message in the world will fall flat if it is delivered to an audience that does not understand it, is unprepared for it, or is incapable of agreeing with it. In an era when speeches in both the political and the business worlds have become akin to bottled commodities, concocted by anonymous speech writers, and designed often for multiple use, this caution is more important than it ever was. I recall the classic case of an old friend, a speech writer for Democratic politicians in the Northeast during the '30s, who had written a really swinging message for the governor of Pennsylvania about the rights of the union man. He was listening to his radio one evening and by chance tuned in to his own speech. While he thrilled to each ringing declamation, he was disturbed because no answering shouts of applause seemed to be coming from that particular hall. When the speech was over and the radio announcer gave the locale, the appalling truth finally dawned. A speech he had designed for the CIO in Pittsburgh had been mistakenly given to a meeting of the National Association of Manufacturers in Philadelphia.

Since your audience is your most important commodity, it is critical that you find out as much as you can about them beforehand. What are their ages, sex, political persuasions, or religious backgrounds? Why are they coming to hear you? Such questions may be outlawed for the U.S. census takers as smacking of discrimination, but for the speaker who wants to have a strong impact, they are critical. To learn who your audience is helps avoid classic mistakes like telling old World War II stories to a group of young men who are violently against draft registration; talking about the joys of planned parenthood and legalized abortion to the local chapter of the Knights of Columbus; or, indeed, giving a National Association of Manufacturers speech to a convention of militant trade unionists.

Even so crusty an authority as Aristotle was acutely aware of the need for putting one's auditors at ease. As he wrote in the *Rhetoric:* "Of the modes of persuasion furnished by the spoken word there are three kinds. The first kind depends on the personal character of the speaker; the second on putting the audience into a certain frame of mind; the third on the proof, or apparent proof, provided by the words of the speech itself."

The friendly faces

For people who are not hardened speech-givers, the worst thing to overcome is that first moment of terror when they begin to speak. The awesome thought occurs: What am I doing talking to these people? The thought can come to one even in the middle of a speech and even to a veteran speaker. It is enough to demoralize anybody. If savored or indulged at all, it results in a stopped train of thought and about 30 seconds of silence. In a sense anyone who wants to make a public speech of any sort must "psych" himself into thinking that what he has to say is worth saying. He must realize (or at least believe) that the people out there want to hear what he says. It is easy to look at a sea of faces and conclude that they are hostile. They are not. The average audience wants the speech to be a good one, simply because it would like to be entertained. After all, it is there. The people in the audience are generally with you unless you antagonize them.

As a rule of thumb I have always found it useful, looking at any sea of faces, to identify two or three who seem particularly friendly and encouraging. As I go on I keep looking at them, virtually exchanging nods of approval during the whole process. Conversely there might be a couple of dour types who obviously do not like what I am saying; I keep my eyes away from them. There is nothing like one look at an unfriendly and uncompromising face to disrupt a fragile sequence of ideas—unless you are one of those hopelessly polemical people who thrives on sheer conflict. No speech is delivered in a vacuum. When you are communicating you are talking to *someone*. Unless someone is listening you might just as well not be up there on the platform, however lofty the ideas you are expounding.

For almost every speechmaker there is a potential problem of level. An English professor from Vassar College may feel it beneath her to talk about Shakespeare's sonnets to the bunch at the Elks Club. If she shows that she thinks so, she is doomed and her communication useless. If, however, she shares her thoughts with them and puts herself in their position, whatever she says is likely to be a success. Audiences can be talked up to, and audiences can be pulled along with the speaker. They can never be talked down to. The minute an audience feels that a speaker is consciously talking down to it, watch out. At the worst, brickbats. At the best, much coughing and stirring in the seats. Consorted coughing has killed more speakers than any amount of overt heckling.

Sleepers and hecklers

Hecklers, of course, pose another kind of problem. In our day, with protest movements proliferating, it is more fashionable to be against an issue than for it. Curiously enough, some of the most vocal defenders of free speech and civil rights turn out to be the most determinedly militant in their desire to intrude on the rights of speakers.

Hoots, catcalls, obscenities, and thrown objects are thought in some circles quite acceptable as a constitutionally permitted objection to speakers' remarks that do not please.

If you are being heckled you have two choices. You can ignore it, or you can single out one or more of the hecklers and confront them. This is not so hard as it may seem. Most hecklers are powerless when separated from the mob psychology they themselves generate. As long as they are yelling "Throw him out!", "Shut up!", or "Imperialist!", they are effective. Singled out one by one, however, they are only rarely competent to state their case and can be destroyed by any halfway good speaker who knows what he is talking about.

The heckler is basically a coward and generally an incoherent one. Even when he attempts to substantiate his denunciations, it will generally be in a form that is almost incomprehensible to any but a few intimates in his peer group. Thus the wise speaker, by singling out one or two of his tormentors, can turn the tables on them. If there are too many of them, either hire some bodyguards or go home.

Worse than the heckler is the preoccupied or distracted audience, a frequently found phenomenon on the banquet circuit. A steady buzz of conversation can wound a speaker more than violent insult. Audible snoring is the unkindest cut of all. The more convivial the group, the more successful the occasion, the madder the music, and the stronger the wine, the more these dangers concentrate and the rougher it is for the poor body on the lectern to make himself understood. I learned this personally at an early age when I was invited, as a high school orator, to deliver one of the speeches at an annual St. Patrick's Day dinner in New York City. The evening, which began at roughly 6:30, had been a great success. By the time I rose at 9:00, however, to give a very serious speech, the tables of prosperous New York Irish were almost literally awash, and the fumes of varieties of Gaelic malt whiskey gave the room the climate of a Scotch mist. There were no hecklers. But the sounds of die-hard conversationalists and snoring sleepers made even loud microphone talking impossible. In such situations, as I quickly learned, the wise speaker cuts his losses, produces his conclusion about 15 minutes ahead of schedule, and leaves the lectern as quickly as possible, smiling all the way. For months afterward, incidentally, I was congratulated for my "excellent speech" by members of the audience who I knew had not heard a word.

To "keep smiling" despite difficulties is, not so incidentally, a cardinal rule for the speaker. Always remember that anger or petulance does not sit well with an audience. While you have the platform you are master of the situation. You can control the questions. You can pretty well control your audience unless you insult them violently. You should exercise this control but not abuse it. The most bitter question can be disarmed by a good, witty comment or at least a rueful, indulgent smile. You may not convert your questioner, but you will win the others to your side. Conversely an angry retort will only give the questioner more sympathizers and probably achieve very little for you unless your remark is extraordinarily good and pithy.

Wit and funny stories

It is a time-honored convention in this country to relax your audience by beginning the speech with a funny story—generally a piece of recent history, some comment about the occasion, the organization sponsoring you, or some information that you and the audience share. Such openers may vary in length and bite, depending on how well the speaker knows the audience. American audiences are generally programmed for them, however, and really bad is the story which cannot evoke a sympathetic laugh. The best openers are the spontaneous ones, flowing out of the introduction or some very recent happening. The canned story is permissible, its effectiveness inversely proportionate to the number of people in the hall who have heard it before. Gentle digs at the master of ceremonies or other local dignitaries, too, are in the tradition and welcomed, but they should be used with care. "I was wondering whether I'd get a drink here tonight, not having met all of you folks before, but when I took one look at your chairman's red nose and bloodshot eyes, I knew I was among friends. . ." indicates, for example, either a sure feel for the audience or a death wish on the part of the speaker.

Non-Anglo-Saxon countries do not generally enjoy this convention. In Japan, for example, speechmakers will give a 100-percent serious speech on a serious occasion. Humor is something reserved for social conversation—or, on occasion, for a hired comedian. But it is not something to put in your speech. Americans, in fact, are divided themselves on the issue of humor in oratory. One school believes in telling the obligatory joke quickly, then giving a "serious" speech. That was the approach used by politicians like Richard M. Nixon and Dwight D. Eisenhower. Adlai Stevenson, of course, believed in infusing wit into everything he said; in this regard he was much closer to British speechmakers than American. Unfortunately many of his fellow Americans neither got the point of the humor he invoked nor understood the very serious points he made because they thought they were all "jokes."

A little bit of humor goes a long way, however. It can be a most effective tool. Anyone who would like to do a lot of speechmaking should work up a few funny comments about matters known to be shared by the audience and try to inject them in the course of the whole speech—not just at the beginning. Particularly when you are discussing something difficult, which requires considerable thinking and may raise a good deal of opposition, there is nothing like a little bit of humor every few minutes to make people feel sympathetic. The tension you relax thereby will also contribute greatly to audience attentiveness in the next part of your speech.

The best humor of all is the spontaneous wit that arises from the immediate situation. Hence the "in" joke. Nothing gives an audience such a warm, exclusive feeling of good fellowship, as long as they all understand. Gentle *ad hominem* remarks may be hugely successful, but they should be used with care. The chairman of the banquet committee might not mind being publicly reminded of the fact that his law firm charges the most exorbitant fees in town, that he took five years to pass the bar exams himself, and that his fourth wife has just filed suit for divorce. Lecture halls, however, are littered with the bones of speakers who failed to guess right about their chairman's threshold of sensitivity.

The humor of invective will always remain with us, too, and in skillful hands it can be memorable. Denouncing Republican Party scandals during one election campaign, and deftly twisting an old American political slogan, Adlai Stevenson said: "This is the first time I have ever heard of a party going into battle under the slogan 'Throw the rascals in.' " Winston Churchill was a past master of political name-calling. Commenting on the Labour Party leader who succeeded him after World War II, he noted: "[Attlee] is a little modest man with much to be modest about."

Some remarks that would be mundane out of context may be hilarious given the time and place they are spoken. One recalls Stevenson's memorable introduction to a banquet of New York politicians at a Manhattan hotel. He had then been U.S. delegate and ambassador to the United Nations for some years and, as such, was out of the normal run of party politics. He was introduced just after a particularly noisy disturbance had broken out between rival groups of politicians. While feathers were being smoothed, more bottles crashed to the floor, and several groups on the edge of the room started singing. After order had been restored, Stevenson began magisterially: "It is some years since I have had the privilege of addressing a group like this." And then, looking at the chaos in front of him, he added: "I had almost forgotten what I had been missing."

Knowing when to stop

The worst pitfall for the speaker is the impulse to keep talking. Its dangers beckon most seductively when the speech is going well. Just as gout used to be thought the disease of the affluent gourmet who had had his fill of sweetmeats, cheeses, and port, so the temptation to be verbose strikes those who speak best and most fluently. The late Hubert H. Humphrey, as senator and vice president, was one of the great speakers of our day. He possessed that unbeatable combination: brilliance, knowledge of a vast range of subjects, wit and fluency of expression, and superb feel for an audience. Whoever they were—fellow senators, factory workers, union bosses, business leaders, or plain people at a meeting, Americans, Europeans, Japanese, or Koreans—Hubert could reach them. His one failing was a chronic inability to stop at the right time. There was always just that one more thing he wanted to tell them—and peroration would be succeeded by afterthought. His finest speeches, I suspect, were those made when the time limit was absolutely inflexible, and the wisdom, wit, and persuasive power the man possessed had to be contained within 20 precious minutes.

How much worse works the temptation on the amateur speaker who —in the course of what promised to be a 10-minute talk at the PTA, the office meeting, or the local political club—makes the heady discovery that the audience is hanging on every word. Why not take the oratorical ball and run with it? When will he have that big a captive audience in front of him again?

That is precisely the time to settle for a first down and keep your remarks as short as originally intended. You have made your point. You have, like a good actor or singer after an encore, left your audience wishing that you would not leave quite so soon. You will be asked back again.

This holds true for church sermons as well as lay speeches. Many are the souls that have been virtually saved after the first 15 minutes of a sermon, only to lapse back into perdition during the next, less dramatic 20. The only exceptions to this rule, possibly, are political conventions, where the need to whip up some form of group enthusiasm —both for those in the hall and for the TV camera—is felt to be paramount. In such cases reasoned argument gives way to a series of slogans and antiphonal responses. "Shall we permit these rascals to continue plundering the public purse?" "No! No!" comes the answer. But that is a world of its own.

Speaking with style

When speaking from notes it is good to select and repeat some key phrases or slogans. Such phrases serve several purposes. They not only help dramatize your points—the more so if they are well thought out— but also help thread the whole body of remarks together. If you keep referring back, for example, to "government by default," "failed scholars," or "red-ink management," your listeners will probably end up with that one idea embedded in their consciousness.

There is very little new in the art of persuasive speech. The device of the key phrase, for example, goes back through the Wagnerian *Leitmotiv* as far as the Homeric epithet. The epics of Homer were originally told by storytellers and were not committed to manuscript form until a millennium after they were composed. Such phrases as "Apollo the far-darting," "the wine-dark sea," or "deep-browed Odysseus" recur constantly because they were mnemonic devices. They served as aids to recall for both bard and audience.

Cicero, Rome's greatest orator, used many fancy tricks which have gone down in our literature. Their rhetorical definitions have long since been forgotten by most, but they are deeply rooted in our tradition and come instinctively to the speechmaker. Take the figure of speech that the Romans called *praeteritio; i.e.*, a calculated omission. "I will not mention it here," Cicero would say in rhetorical refrain, "that Catiline was a scoundrel, that he murdered his former wife, that he ruined his family fortune. . . . No, I will not mention that here. . . ."* An ancient example, perhaps, but what veteran listener to political speeches has not heard something like it? Beware the debater who denounces his opponent for "vicious *ad hominem*" arguments, then spends the rest of his talk casting sly aspersions on said opponent's record, life-style, ancestry, and thought processes. It happens often enough.

Then there is the device of repetition, using the same words or phrase again and again in different ways to pound home the message. "The Senate knows of these [crimes], the Consul sees them, yet he lives. Lives? He even comes into the Senate chamber. . ." also comes from the first Catilinarian. We have heard this in many a speech. There is nothing so effective as a combination of short vigorous matching statements which mount to a crescendo. This may be dismissed as oratory, but it is good persuasion; and that is really what oratory is all about.

There are different kinds of speaking, of course. If you are making a calm exposition, like a teacher instructing a class or a worker explaining a task, you may not be especially interested in persuading your listeners one way or another. You are explaining. If you are, however, trying to persuade, you will inevitably use as many catchwords as you can—not excepting the so-called "buzzwords" that play on an audiences's fears or prejudices. It is your privilege as an orator to do so. But if you were one of the audience, it would also be your job to try to

---

*Freely translated from the first oration against Catiline, a Roman politician and conspirator (108?–62 B.C.).

ferret out such words and separate intensity of feeling from accurate description.

It is widely held that "oratory" and rich phrasing are unfashionable and should be avoided like the plague. To an extent this is true. Few modern speakers possess the controlled, sustained eloquence of great parliamentarians like Edmund Burke, Daniel Webster, or Lord Macauley. Few modern audiences would have either the patience or the scholarship to understand them. Yet the contrary modern style of plain speaking has been carried to an extreme, often by modern educators whose antecedents fostered oratory and rhetoric among their charges. I remember an experience I had many years ago as a journalist when I was called on to introduce a learned professor of education at a meeting of teachers and press people. I evoked the shades of Plato, Demosthenes, Jefferson, and John Locke, among others, in talking about the tremendous fund of learning that he doubtless possessed. What was my surprise when the scholar rose to announce, with many an "uh" and "um," that he wasn't good at "this here speechifying sort of thing" but that he had "kind of a few things to say," which he "sort of wanted" to put to the audience.

Which brings us to another point. The use of "kind of," "sort of," "I mean," "you know," or "that is to say" is as bad as the use of circumlocutions like "there is a basic feeling here which I think we must not fail to take into account when we are unflinchingly setting our sights on the cherished fundamental goals which lie ahead." There are times when the speaker will need to use clichés and set phrases, particularly when struggling desperately to think fast enough to answer a question. "That's a good question. A very good question. I'm glad you asked that question," uttered by a speaker sweating desperately to field a high ball curving toward the bleachers, is familiar to us all. So at times clichés can be useful. But in most cases they are to be avoided.

There is, finally, nothing so powerful in the speaker's arsenal as a terse expression that can sum up a whole world of meaning. In one of his earlier speeches, Lincoln observed simply that "the ballot is stronger than the bullet." He did not have to elaborate much on that one. Nor was there much need to spin out his meaning after a statement like: "I believe this government cannot endure permanently half slave and half free. I do not expect the Union to be dissolved—I do not expect the house to fall—but I do expect it will cease to be divided."

In modern times John F. Kennedy, with the able assistance of his speech writers, gave us a whole new speaking vocabulary. His trademark was the play on words and word structures. For example, from his inaugural address: "Let us never negotiate out of fear, but let us never fear to negotiate." It was a statement with echoes of Franklin D. Roosevelt's memorable "The only thing we have to fear is fear itself." "If a free society," Kennedy went on to say, "cannot help the many who are poor, it cannot save the few who are rich." And, of course, there was his unforgettable "And so, my fellow Americans, ask not what your country can do for you; ask what you can do for your country."

This is oratory of a good sort, just as eloquent in its modern idiom as Lincoln was in his day or the great populist William Jennings Bryan in his. There is that happy combination of the right thought, the right moment, and the right words which can go down into the history books. One can only imagine the impact of such a moment—or, if lucky, hear or see it on television. Without the drama of a great occasion, we can find ourselves in humbler workaday situations where for a moment or two we may achieve the same kind of perfect communication with an audience, produce a desired reaction, bring home a message that we have traveled far to deliver. Good speaking is within the reach of us all. It just needs sincerity, thought, and a lot of preparation. Start thinking about it now.

". . . and so without further adieu I give you our old friend and colleague, who has a message of considerable importance to tell you tonight. . . ." Take a deep breath, clear your throat, watch for those friendly faces in the crowd, and start talking.

FRANK GIBNEY

The History of Rhetoric and Oratory

Rhetoric

Rhetoric is the name traditionally given to the use of language as an art based on a body of organized knowledge. The study of rhetoric exerted an important formative influence on European culture from ancient times to the 17th century A.D., after which it became less important. Both the nature of its influence and the reason for its decline become apparent from a study of the real character of the so-called art at various stages of its history. The techniques of rhetoric and the knowledge on which they were based were always organized to serve only some specific and limited purpose. Thus, when the purpose changed and new techniques, based on new theories, emerged, the new system was as incomplete as the old had been. The textbooks of rhetoric that men studied never covered more than a small part of the field of linguistic expression; and it was the realization of this that finally led to widespread abandonment of the effort to create an art of discourse.

RHETORIC AS THE ART OF ORATORY: ANCIENT GREECE   In its original form, rhetoric was the systematic study of oratory. It was, as Aristotle later pointed out, the art of persuasion. The first man to teach oratory was the Sicilian Corax during the spate of litigation which followed the establishment of democracy in Agrigentum and Syracuse in the 460s B.C. Another Sicilian, Gorgias of Leontini, introduced the new art—along with the idea that it could be taught by the sophists, rapidly became the favoured form of higher education.

This initial flowering of rhetoric in the 5th and 4th centuries B.C. was marked by important controversies, one of which concerned the use of stylistic devices. Gorgias had employed colourful epithets, antitheses, rhythm and rhyming terminations; the prevalence of antitheses can be clearly seen in Thucydides, both in the speeches and in the historical narrative, and the interest in argument in many of the plays of Euripides.

The next generation saw a reaction, and the plain style of Lysias found many supporters. But the criteria by which each party sought to establish the superiority of its choice—clarity, impressiveness, decorum, beauty, purity of language—depended, except for the last, largely on subjective assessments, and so the problem of mannerism was posed but not solved. The outstanding teacher of the day, Isocrates, and the outstanding orator, Demosthenes, championed a compromise style between the plain and the mannered. But their example was not decisive, and at the close of the 4th century the long battle between the Atticists and the Asian mannerists was still to come.

Another dispute concerned the relationship between rhetoric and morality. It was recognized that scientific proof was not usually possible in oratory. Speeches were concerned with probabiilties. They were often addressed to an uneducated or a potentially inattentive audience, and Gorgias had maintained that an orator therefore could argue the just and the unjust cause with equal force. Regarding rhetoric as an amoral instrument, he was attacked by critics who claimed that oratorical skill had an essentially moral character, since truth and justice provided the best opportunities for persuasion. This view, which Aristotle later endorsed, has much to be said in its favour at the theoretical level, but the fact that an orator's skill could often counterbalance the superior persuasiveness of a just cause remained uncontroverted, and Gorgias continued to find adherents as late as the Renaissance.

A third group of controversies concerned education. The popularity of the rhetorical schools put them in control of the intellectual development of Greece, and rhetoricians who were prepared to accept the consequent responsibility criticized those of their utilitarian colleagues who kept their eyes fixed on the needs of the law courts, and at the same time disagreed among themselves as to what should be added to the rhetorical course. Isocrates recommended political thought.

Plato's *Gorgias* and *Phaedrus*, and the *Antidosis* of Isocrates, deal with these controversies, but the best ancient Greek account of the development of the art is the *Rhetoric* of Aristotle. Aristotle limits his comments on all points to the requirements of oratory for politics, for the law courts, and for a show speech (either on a ceremonial occasion such as a public funeral or as a tour de force for rhetorical public entertainment). This, taken in conjunction with the fact that he composed a separate *Poetics*, suggests that rhetoric at this stage made no claim to be a complete "arts of discourse."

Aristotle's *Rhetoric* begins with the orator's construction of his case. First, he must assemble all the possible arguments, by examining all the "places" (*topoi*, hence "topics") where arguments can be found. Aristotle's spatial metaphor confuses rather than clarifies his meaning, but an example will show what is intended. Suppose that a political speaker is recommending some measure. He must appear to advise what is good. Happiness is universally regarded as good. So are justice, moderation, magnanimity, magnificence. These then are the speaker's "topics." If he examines each in turn, he will see which applies to the case he is handling.

When the arguments have been collected, the orator must decide which to use, and here great stress is laid on understanding the psychology of the audience. Orators must know what provokes anger, admiration, shame, and how different categories of hearers—the young, the old, the well-born—are likely to react. Syllogistic argument is rarely possible in a speech and would in any case appear too cumbersome. Rhetoric must rely on "enthymemes," incomplete syllogisms often based on probable premises ("If you, who are a bad man, admit you would not have taken a bribe, is it likely that I, a good man, would have done so?" and "Dorieus has won a race at Olympia, therefore he has won a crown" [omitting the middle term "the prize at Olympia is a crown"] are both enthymemes) and on "examples," one or more instances which lead to an inductive demonstration (*e.g.*, "Pisistratus asked for a bodyguard and so became dictator; so did Theagenes; therefore Dionysius in asking for a bodyguard is aiming at a dictatorship"). Knowledge of how an audience reacts is important because what is not strictly proof must pass as such. This is the least satisfactory section of the treatise. In stating that truth and justice provide the best arguments, Aristotle would seem to have committed himself to the opinion that the rhetorical substitutes for the syllogism had a certain validity, but he makes no systematic effort to analyze their relation to scientific proof. The work then closes with a discussion of style and the general pattern a speech should follow. Aristotle emphasizes the need for clarity, but admits that metaphors and figures of speech may be used in moderation. Considered as a whole, his survey can be seen to have many gaps which later generations were to fill (see *Traditional Rhetorical Method,* below), but its combination of practical experience with a philosophic breadth of view gave it a lasting importance.

Aristotle's generation saw the passing of the free cities with their active political life; and for the next two centuries the development of rhetoric under the Hellenistic empires was decided by the needs of the courts and the activity of the schools. It was an age of useful but unspectacular advance under the shadow of the noisy controversy between the Atticists and the Asian mannerists. The discussion of general themes, developed in the philosophy schools, proved a handy teaching device and was accepted as a regular branch of oratory. The imitation of well-known orators became a popular exercise. Hermagoras of Temnos (*c.*

150 B.C.) revolutionized the technique of constructing a case when he pointed out that there was always a key point of conflict—which might concern law, fact, or principle—and was the focus round which arguments ought to be grouped.

RHETORIC AS THE ART OF ORATORY: ROME   The discoveries of the Hellenistic age are known through their influence on Latin oratory. The important achievement of Roman rhetoric was the transmission of the Greek tradition to medieval Europe. By the 2nd century B.C. republican Rome was attracting the most adventurous of the Greek teachers. But Greek rhetorical theory was not only restated in such textbooks as the anonymous *Rhetorica ad Herennium* (86–82 B.C.) or Cicero's *De inventione*. It was also applied; and speeches were produced which equaled the best work of the Athenian orators. At the same time, the career and genius of Cicero lent the study of rhetoric a dignity it had previously lacked. In his accusation of Catiline, Cicero portrayed eloquence as wielding real power in great affairs. After his time, the aims of the rhetorical education were linked in men's minds with the urbanity and versatility he had glorified.

With the advent of the empire, political and judicial oratory gradually ceased to be important in the evolution of rhetoric, for Roman autocracy, like its Hellenistic predecessors, extinguished political debate and restricted the scope of the courts. But writers of all kinds had long been using rhetorical devices, and the interest in rhetoric was not sustained by cultivated society's interest in literature. The Greek author Dionysius of Halicarnassus (fl. *c.* 20 B.C.) commented on the orators from the point of view of a literary critic. The 1st century A.D. was still a transitional period in which oratory was brought closer to literature. Quintilian's *Institutio oratoria* (*c.* A.D. 95), in spite of certain contemporary emphases, still looked to the past, giving the most complete account that exists of the art of oratory. It is therefore convenient to take from him the account of rhetorical method that was followed in classical antiquity and continued to be used in the schools.

TRADITIONAL RHETORICAL METHOD   The speaker is concerned with three matters: the art of rhetoric, the speech itself, and the situation that calls it forth. The first of these has five parts: collecting the material (called invenion), arranging it (disposition), putting it into words (style; Latin *elocutio*), memorizing it, and finally delivering it. The second matter, the speech itself, should be divided into five: an introduction (to gain the goodwill of the audience), a statement of the point at issue, arguments to prove it, refutation of contrary arguments (this by some authorities is included under the preceding division), and a conclusion (either a recapitulation or an appeal to the audience's emotions). The third matter, which is the situation, covers the kinds of speech: whether the discussion is general (*e.g.*, "should a man marry?") or particular (*e.g.*, "should Crassus marry?") and whether it is a show speech (called demonstrative), political (called deliberative), or legal.

To return to the five parts of the art of rhetoric, the one dealing with style (the putting of the material into words) received the most space in rhetorical handbooks and is indeed regarded by the modern reader as the chief concern of rhetoric. This is justified insofar as, of the threefold aim of rhetoric, to instruct, to move, and to delight, the thing that contributes almost exclusively to delight is style.

Quintilian and most other ancient authorities teach that the chief virtues of style are four: correctness, clarity, elegance, and appropriateness. Of these, elegance receives most space as it is the easiest to teach, including as it does all the varieties of the figures of thought and of words (or syntax). Among the former are rhetorical questions, impersonation (whereby the speaker invents the actual words of the persons described or even of nonhuman entities such as one's country), and vivid description (whereby an event is not merely stated to have occurred but described in full imaginative detail). Figures of words (or syntax) include antithesis, parallelism of phrases, and repetition of words. Ancient rhetoric was also much concerned with the rhythms of speech, the order of words, and the length and cohesion of sentences.

IMITATION OF THE PAST   When Quintilian wrote, a new kind of rhetoric was beginning to appear. The Roman emperors, in order to win support for the culture their state represented, had begun to subsidize the schools, in which rhetoric provided the syllabus of secondary education. Rhetoricians thus became the high priests of an official cult of the past. The following three centuries produced a mass of historical, critical, and anecdotic writing; and they also saw a determined effort to perpetuate the language and style of the great classics. Imitation, which had hitherto played a subordinate role in rhetorical training, now became its focus, and the popular textbooks of the period, the *Progymnasmata* of Hermogenes (b. *c.* 150) of Tarsus and of Aphthonius (fl. *c.* 400), a pupil of Libanius at Antioch, make it clear that the exercises particularly studied —narrative, description, the expansion of a moral saying, prosopopoeia, and so on—were those that are found not only in oratory but in many other literary genres as well. Rhetorical study now covered a field coextensive with Greek and Latin literature; but, looked at from another point of view, its scope was narrower than before because, within this larger field, only certain writers were thought to deserve imitation.

DECLAMATIONS   The imitation of historians and poets as well as of orators played an important part in rhetorical training, and the vogue for academic declamations showed that oratory itself was admired primarily as a literary genre. Declamations were not normally concerned with contemporary life. A deliberative speech (*suasoria*) would choose a situation from the historical or legendary past: for instance, it might urge the Spartans to hold the pass of Thermopylae against the enemy, or take the part of Agamemnon and argue that he will not sacrifice his daughter Iphigenia at Aulis. Similarly, a legal speech (*controversia*) would deal with a situation that referred to some fictitious "law," such as that the man who kills a tyrant shall be rewarded; the declamation might argue that a man should receive the reward because he was the chief agent in causing the tyrant's death, even though he had not actually killed him with his own hands.

The preparation of declamations as a school exercise gave the pupil practice in getting to the heart of a problem, to the actual issue (Latin *status*) at stake, and had long been used in rhetoric. The method was to ask three questions: Did it happen (*an sit*)? What was it (*quid sit*)? Was it good or bad (*quale sit*)? Thus, in the case of tyrannicide cited above, the pupil would have to discover if the event (a killing) had taken place, how it should be defined (murder, tyrannicide, etc.), and finally, whether it was a praiseworthy or a blameworthy act. Of course in an imaginary case the answer to the first question requires not investigation of fact but plausible conjecture.

EARLY MIDDLE AGES   Christian literature adopted the imaginative approach of the imperial schools. In the Byzantine Empire, schools used the *Progymnasmata* and encouraged imitation. In the west Augustine, who distrusted pagan models, in his *De doctrina Christiana* advised imitating the style of the Bible, though his own writings contain the stylistic devices which came naturally to him after his education in rhetoric. Cassiodorus (6th century) and Isidore of Seville (7th century) both included the traditional rhetorical scheme in their encyclopaedic treatises, counting it among the seven liberal arts as forming one of the trivium together with grammar and dialectic. Bede (d. 735) followed Augustine by showing in his short work *De schematibus ac tropis* how the Bible is not inferior to secular classical literature as a storehouse of figures of speech to imitate. Alcuin (d. 805) continued the traditional rhetorical teaching, but without excessive stress on style, in his dialogue on rhetoric and the virtues.

The disputes of the 11th century provoked a revival of judicial rhetoric which petered out when it was realized that dialectic and law provided better weapons for controversy, and a century later imitation flourished briefly at the school of Chartres. But not until 1150 was education far enough advanced for a unified rhetorical tradition to appear.

MANNERIST RHETORIC IN THE LATER MIDDLE AGES   The 12th century tried to build a new culture based on the theoretical knowledge at its command. In rhetoric, this knowledge was drawn principally from the *Rhetorica ad Herennium* and Cicero's *De inventione*. But the statements in these works concerning the handling of the subject matter were too closely linked with judicial oratory to be useful in an age whose main interest was in epistolary composition, and so attention centred on the sections discussing style. It was assumed that in every genre, in both prose and poetry, two sorts of writing were possible: the one plain, the other "artistic," employing figures of thought and speech. The view that figures were a source of stylistic distinction was a commonplace of classical rhetoric, but their possible functional relation to meaning had not been adequately examined. It is not surprising therefore that the 12th century accepted them as ornamental in character and came to believe that the more figures were used, the better the style. There followed a cult of mannerism, with insistence on particular rhythmic endings, and on etymologies—often fantastic—which gave a richer colour to individual words.

THE RENAISSANCE: THE REVIVAL OF IMITATIVE RHETORIC   The obscurity of manneristic writing provoked a reaction. Petrarch reinstated the cult of the classics and popularized their imitation. Already, as early as the 11th century, Byzantium had seen a recrudescence of the Atticism which had flourished under the late Roman Empire, and its scholars had developed the instructional techniques and compiled the grammars and lexicons required for the exact reproduction of an earlier stage of Greek. The arrival of Byzantine scholars in Italy in the 15th century meant therefore that the systematization of imitative technique spread to the west. Humanist rhetoric was born, with its dictionaries, its handbooks of Latin usage and *exempla* (adages, anecdotes, and other illustrative material), and its memorizing procedures. Ultimately, it accomplished more than its Greco-Roman and Byzantine predecessors; for its imitative purpose was linked with wider ambitions. The humanists were the first to see the literature of a people in its totality as a cultural achievement. They were not content merely to write classical Latin. Desiring to equal the cultural triumphs of antiquity, they attempted every classical genre, thus giving imitation a range it had not had before. And this was also the age when the national literatures of Europe were attaining their maturity, so that imitation was no longer limited to Latin. It was practised in the vernaculars, and with striking success.

THE RENAISSANCE: RAMISM   By 1550, the humanist tradition, embodied in the rhetorical works of Erasmus, had a firm grip on education, but Latin, on which that education rested, was going out of use, and the vernaculars had absorbed all they could absorb through imitation. A new approach to rhetoric was required. As early as the end of the 15th century the Dutch humanist Rodolphus Agricola recommended that writers should develop their subjects with reference to genus, species, causes, effects, similarities, opposites, and suggested 30 such headings, analogous to the "topics" of classical rhetoric. In the 16th century Petrus Ramus (Pierre La Ramée) popularized Agricola's ideas and had an enormous influence. Ramism detached invention and disposition from rhetoric (reckoning them as part of dialectic), leaving it only with style and delivery (memory having fallen into the background). Rhetoric was thus severely limited in scope by losing all concern for content.

THE DECLINE OF RHETORIC   Ramism carried the seeds of its own destruction. The dichotomy it established between thought and the words that formulated thought provoked a search for a plain style which would represent facts without adventitious verbal ornament. Rhetoric fell into discredit. Still an important school subject in the 18th century, it followed rather than led contemporary taste as is evident from the lectures of Hugh Blair, the first professor of rhetoric and belles lettres in Edinburg University, which mirror the period's preoccupation with sensibility and the sublime. But Adam Müller's impressive *Reden über die Beredsamkeit* (1816) and Archbishop Richard Whately's *Principles of Rhetoric* (5th edition revised; 1836) were already, in the main, works of literary history. Convinced of the supreme value of experiment, the 19th century was led eventually to condemn all traditional techniques of style and all organized rhetorical study. Jacob Burckhardt described antiquity's interest in rhetoric as a "monstrous aberration." These extreme views remained popular until the 1930s, when logical positivism drew attention to the importance of studying how language is used. I. A. Richards' *Philosophy of Rhetoric* (1941) emphasized the need for a new art of discourse and substantial attempts were later made, particularly in the United States, to develop such an art in a form suitable for teaching in schools and universities.

Oratory

Oratory may be defined as the art of stirring emotion in the members of an audience by oral exhortation to produce from them an active response of a kind desired by the orator. Originally it was synonymous with rhetoric, defined by Aristotle as the art of persuasion, but after the term rhetoric had been widened to include all forms of literary expression, oral exhortation was more properly described as oratory. It has been of considerable importance in political life, the dissemination of religion by preaching, and the practice of law, chiefly in countries directly influenced by western culture and the literary theory and practice of classical Greece and Rome. In the east, where religion has tended to encourage passivity and quietism, and where mass education has been slow to produce a large literate audience, oratory has not developed as a cultural or political medium, and the leaders of India, for example, have been more likely to encourage passive resistance by example than to attempt to inspire action by oral exhortation.

The importance of oratory in politics, religion and law has differed widely at different times and in different places since its origins in classical times, as have the stylistic conventions which it has followed. In the 18th century, for example, political and forensic oratory derived their form from the fact that they were addressed to a social class extremely limited in composition which shared a background of education in the classics. Thus, it was distinguished, in England especially, by its profusion of allusions to Greek and Latin literature; by the length and complexity of its periods; and, at its best, by strict subordination of style to sense. Its subtlety and complexity of style often obscure the meaning of a particular passage from the modern reader, who also lacks the advantage of judging from the orator's inflection, facial expression and gestures, etc., the sense intended. The classic English exemplar of 18th-century political oratory is Edmund Burke at his best; at its worst, as represented by Lord Chatham's famous grandiloquence, it was turgid and more concerned to create an impression of balance and articulation than to present an argument clearly and accurately.

The style of oratory in England was affected by the rise of Methodism and by the evangelical revival; the deliberate appeal of such great preachers as John Wesley and George Whitefield to a wider audience gave to political and forensic oratory, as well as to preaching, a new forcefulness and emotional appeal. The 18th-century style of oratory in England was thus imperceptibly succeeded in the 19th century (especially after the widening of the franchise by the 1832 Reform bill) by a more popular style addressed to wider audiences without the common bond of a classical education. Biblical allusions and quotations replaced those drawn from the classics, although they were not so generally used as they had been in 17th-century oratory both in England and America, under the influence of Puritanism. By the end of the 19th century a Radical tradition of oratory which made much use of catch phrases was coming into vogue, and in the early 20th century this style became general, being best illustrated in England by the brilliant speeches of David Lloyd George.

The decline of oratory in the 20th century was influenced by the development of broadcasting, which led to abandonment of a grand, declamatory, style in favour of the more personal, intimate, "fireside" approach. The rise of such demagogic orators as Adolf Hitler also influenced its decline, for their frenzied, psychopathological appeal to the baser instincts of their audiences gave political oratory a bad name, and led to distrust of "fine speaking" and all forms of propaganda. Some orators, however, continued to inspire both confidence and action: the speeches of Sir Winston Churchill and Pres. Franklin D. Roosevelt, for example, widely different in style, and blending several traditions of oratory, exemplify modern political oratory at its best.

Among classical orators the two greatest were Demosthenes and Cicero. Modern orators may be divided into three main groups: political, religious and forensic (corresponding to the 18th-century division of oratory as belonging to "the senate, the pulpit and the bar"). Among the most famous political orators are, in Great Britain, Edmund Burke, William Pitt, earl of Chatham, and his son William Pitt the Younger, Charles James Fox, John Wilkes, George Canning, Richard Cobden, Lord Macaulay, John Wilkes, George Canning, Richard Cobden, Lord Macaulay, John Bright, Disraeli, Gladstone, Lord Randolph Churchill, David Lloyd George, and Sir Winston Churchill. Famous British advocates and lawyers include Lord Erskine, Lord Russell of Killowen, Lord Plunket, R. L. Sheil, Lord Birkenhead, Sir Edward Marshall Hall, Patrick Hastings, Lord Carson, and Lord Birkett. The Irish have always shown a particular genius for oratory, and such Irish politicians as Charles Stewart Parnell, Henry Grattan, and Daniel O'Connell were notable for their impassioned eloquence, as were many Irish-born advocates and judges. The United States has produced many great orators, notably Patrick Henry, Daniel Webster, Henry Clay, Rufus Choate, Abraham Lincoln, Wendell Phillips, William Jennings Bryan, Woodrow Wilson, and Franklin D. Roosevelt. In France, the period of the Revolution produced impassioned and effective orators: Mirabeau, Danton, Camille Desmoulins, and almost all the Girondins. Their successors in the 19th century included Benjamin Constant, Lamartine, Guizot, Thiers, Montalembert, Jaurès, Alexandre Ribot, Poincaré, and Briand.

ENCYCLOPÆDIA BRITANNICA

Bibliography

The following bibliography provides the reader interested in further information about our language with a selection of well-known books in the field. This bibliography, however, is by no means exhaustive. For additional references the reader is encouraged to consult the extensive bibliographies in *The Reader's Advisor: A Layman's Guide to Literature,* 12th ed., 3 vols. (1974); Arthur G. Kennedy's *Concise Bibliography for Students of English,* 5th ed. (1972); and Harold B. Allen's *Linguistics and English Linguistics: A Bibliography,* 2nd ed. (1977). A broad listing of dictionaries, including a selection of specialized dictionaries, is found in this volume at the end of Words and Dictionaries: The Basic Tools. Guides to research and use of the library conclude The Library.

I. Looking at language

A. ON LANGUAGE

Bloomfield, Leonard, *Language* (1933).

Bolinger, Dwight, *Aspects of Language,* 2nd ed. (1975).

Burling, Robbins, *Man's Many Voices: Language in Its Cultural Context* (1970).

Farb, Peter, *Word Play: What Happens When People Talk* (1974).

Gleason, Henry A., *Introduction to Descriptive Linguistics,* rev. ed. (1961).

Greenberg, Joseph H., *A New Invitation to Linguistics* (1977).

―――, ed., *Universals of Language,* 2nd ed. (1966).

Hockett, Charles, *A Course in Modern Linguistics* (1958).

Jespersen, Otto, *Language: Its Nature, Development, and Origin* (1922).

Ogden, Charles K., and A. Ivor Richards, *The Meaning of Meaning: A Study of the Influence of Language upon Thought and of the Science of Symbolism* (1959; reprinted 1970).

Potter, Simeon, *Language in the Modern World,* rev. ed. (1975).

————, *Modern Linguistics* (1971).

Pyles, Thomas, and John Algeo, *English: An Introduction to Language* (1970).

Sapir, Edward, *Culture, Language, and Personality,* edited by David G. Mandlebaum (1949).

————, *Language: An Introduction to the Study of Speech* (1921).

Sturtevant, Edgar, *Linguistic Change* (1917; reprinted 1961).

————, *Introduction to Linguistic Science* (1947; reprinted 1976).

B. ON THE ENGLISH LANGUAGE

Allen, Harold B., *Readings in Applied English Linguistics,* 2nd ed. (1964).

Baugh, Albert C., and Thomas A. Cable, *A History of the English Language,* 3rd ed. (1978).

Bradley, Henry, *The Making of English* (1904; rev. by Simeon Potter, 1968).

Brook, George L., *A History of the English Language* (1977).

————, *Varieties of English* (1973).

Gleason, Henry A., *Linguistics and English Grammar* (1965).

Gordon, James, *The English Language: An Historical Introduction* (1922).

Jespersen, Otto, *Growth and Structure of the English Language,* 9th ed. (1948).

Kurath, Hans, *A Phonology and Prosody of Modern English* (1964).

Mitchell, Richard, *Less Than Words Can Say* (1979).

Potter, Simeon, *Changing English,* 2nd rev. ed. (1975).

————, *Our Language* (1976).

Pyles, Thomas, *English Language: A Brief History* (1967).

————, *Origin and Development of the English Language,* 2nd ed. (1971).

Quirk, Randolph, *The Use of English,* 2nd ed. (1968).

Strang, Barbara, *A History of English* (1974).

C. ON THE ENGLISH LANGUAGE IN AMERICA

Allen, Harold B., *The Linguistic Atlas of the Upper Midwest,* 3 vols. (1973–76).

————, and Gary Underwood, eds., *Readings in American Dialectology* (1971).

American Speech (periodical).

Brasch, Ila W., and Walter M. Brasch, *A Comprehensive Annotated Bibliography of American Black English* (1974).

Bronstein, Arthur, *The Pronunciation of American English: An Intro-duction to Phonetics* (1960).

Burling, Robbins, *English in Black and White* (1973).

Fries, Charles, *American English Grammar: The Grammatical Structure of Present-Day American English with Especial Reference to Social Differences or Class Dialects* (1940).

Kenyon, John S., *American Pronunciation*, 10th ed. (1958).

Krapp, George, *The English Language in America*, 2 vols. (1925; re-printed 1960).

Kurath, Hans, *A Word Geography of the Eastern United States* (1949; reprinted 1966).

———, and Raven I. McDavid, Jr., *The Pronunciation of English in the Atlantic States* (1961).

Laird, Charlton, *Language in America* (1972).

McConnell, Ruth E., *Our Own Voices: Canadian English and How It Is Studied* (1979).

McDavid, Raven I., Jr., *Dialects in Culture* (1979).

———, "The Dialects of American English," in *The Structures of American English*, by Winthrop Nelson Francis (1958).

Marckwardt, Albert H., *American English* (1958).

Mathews, Mitford M., *The Beginnings of American English* (1963).

Mencken, Henry L., *The American Language: An Inquiry into the De-velopment of English in the United States,* 4th ed. and two supple-ments, abridged with annotations and new material by Raven I. McDavid, Jr. (1963; reprinted 1977).

Pyles, Thomas, *Words and Ways of American English* (1952).

Reed, Carroll E., *Dialects of American English*, rev. ed. (1977).

Thomas, Charles K., *An Introduction to the Phonetics of American English,* 2nd ed. (1958).

Williamson, Juanita, and Virginia Burke, eds., *A Various Language: Perspectives on American Dialects* (1971).

II. Aids to writing

Barzun, Jacques, *Simple and Direct: A Rhetoric for Writers* (1975).

Bernstein, Theodore M., *The Careful Writer: A Modern Guide to English Usage* (1965).

———, *Dos, Don'ts and Maybes of English Usage* (1977).

———, *Watch Your Language* (1965).

Bryant, Margaret, *Current American Usage: How Americans Say It and Use It* (1962).

Ebbitt, Wilma R., and David R. Ebbitt, *Writer's Guide and Index to English*, 6th ed. (1978).

Evans, Bergen, and Cornelia Evans, *A Dictionary of Contemporary American Usage* (1957).

Flesch, Rudolf, *The Art of Readable Writing*, rev. and enl. ed. (1974).

Follett, Wilson, *Modern American Usage*, edited and completed by Jacques Barzun *et al.* (1966).

Fowler, Henry W., *Dictionary of Modern English Usage*, 2nd ed. by Ernest Gowers (1965).

Graves, Robert, and Alan Hodge, *The Reader over Your Shoulder: A Handbook for Writers of English Prose*, 2nd ed. (1979).

Howard, Philip, *New Words for Old* (1977).

Joos, Martin, *The Five Clocks* (1967).

Lamberts, Jacob J., *A Short Introduction to English Usage* (1972).

Modern Language Association of America, *MLA Handbook for Writers of Research Papers, Theses, and Dissertations*, by Joseph Gibaldi and Walter S. Achert (1977).

Partridge, Eric, *English: A Course for Human Beings*, 4th ed. (1954).

———, *Usage and Abusage: A Guide to Good Usage*, 6th ed. (1965).

Quirk, Randolph, and Sydney Greenbaum, *A Concise Grammar of Contemporary English* (1973).

Roget's International Thesaurus.

Skillin, Marjorie, *Words into Type*, 3rd ed. (1974).

Strunk, William, *Elements of Style*, 3rd ed., with revisions, an introduction, and a chapter on writing by E. B. White (1979).

Turabian, Kate L., *A Manual for Writers of Term Papers, Theses, and Dissertations*, 4th ed. (1973).

University of Chicago Press, *A Manual of Style for Authors, Editors, and Copywriters*, 12th ed. (1969).

Webster's Collegiate Thesaurus (1976).

Zinsser, William, *On Writing Well: An Informal Guide to Writing Nonfiction* (1976).

III. Aids to reading

Abrams, Meyer H., *A Glossary of Literary Terms*, 3rd ed. (1971).

Bartlett, John, *Familiar Quotations*, 14th ed., rev. and enl. (1968).

Beckson, Karl, and Arthur Ganz, *Literary Terms: A Dictionary*, rev. and enl. (1975).

Benét, William Rose, *The Reader's Encyclopedia*, 2nd ed. (1965).

Brewer, Ebenezer C., *Brewer's Dictionary of Phrase and Fable*, rev. by Ivor Evans (1970).

————, *The Reader's Handbook of Famous Names in Fiction, Allusions, References, Proverbs, Plots, Stories and Poems,* new ed., rev. and enl. (1899; reprinted 1966).

Bulfinch, Thomas, *Mythology: The Age of Fable, The Age of Chivalry, Legends of Charlemagne* (1970).

Fulghum, Walter B., *Dictionary of Biblical Allusions in English Literature* (1965).

Gaskell, George, *Dictionary of All Scriptures and Myth* (1960).

Grimal, Pierre, ed., *Larousse World Mythology,* trans. by Patricia Beardsworth (1968).

Harvey, Sir Paul, *The Oxford Companion to English Literature,* 4th ed. (1967).

Holman, Clarence Hugh, *A Handbook to Literature,* 3rd ed. (1972).

Hyamson, Albert M., *A Dictionary of English Phrases* (1922; reprinted 1970).

Magill, Frank N., *Cyclopedia of Literary Characters* (1963).

————, *Magill's Quotations in Context* (1965; second series 1969).

Mawson, Charles O.S., *Dictionary of Foreign Terms,* 2nd ed., rev. and updated by Charles Berlitz (1975).

Mencken, Henry L., *A New Dictionary of Quotations on Historical Principles from Ancient and Modern Sources* (1942; reprinted 1960).

New Century Cyclopedia of Names, edited by Clarence Barnhart, 3 vols. (1954).

New Century Handbook of Leaders of the Classical World, edited by Catherine Avery (1972).

Oxford Dictionary of Quotations, 3rd ed. (1979).

Scott, Arthur F., *Current Literary Terms: A Concise Dictionary of Their Origin and Use* (1965).

Shipley, Joseph, *Dictionary of World Literature,* rev. ed. (1953; reprinted 1966).

Stevenson, Burton, *Home Book of Quotations, Classical and Modern,* 10th ed. (1967).

Webster's Biographical Dictionary (1976).

Zimmerman, John E., *Dictionary of Classical Mythology* (1964).

Index

625

The Abortion
Controversy

The Abortion Controversy

A Documentary History

edited by
Eva R. Rubin

Primary Documents in American History and
Contemporary Issues

Greenwood Press
Westport, Connecticut • London

Library of Congress Cataloging-in-Publication Data

The Abortion controversy : a documentary history / edited by Eva R.
Rubin.
    p.   cm.—(Primary documents in American history and
contemporary issues, ISSN 1069–5605 ; no. 1)
  Includes bibliographical references and index.
  ISBN 0–313–28476–8 (alk. paper)
  1. Abortion—Law and legislation—United States—History—Sources.
2. Abortion—United States—History—Sources.   I. Rubin, Eva R.
II. Series.
KF3771.A7A26   1994
344.73′0546—dc20   93–25068
[347.304546]

British Library Cataloguing in Publication Data is available.

Library of Congress Catalog Card Number: 93–25068
ISBN: 0–313–28476–8
ISSN: 1069–5605

First published in 1994

Greenwood Press, 88 Post Road West, Westport, CT 06881
An imprint of Greenwood Publishing Group, Inc.

Printed in the United States of America

The paper used in this book complies with the
Permanent Paper Standard issued by the National
Information Standards Organization (Z39.48–1984).

10 9 8 7 6 5 4 3 2

Contents

Series Foreword

This series is designed to meet the research needs of high school and college students by making available in one volume the key primary documents on a given historical event or contemporary issue. Documents include speeches and letters, congressional testimony, Supreme Court and lower court decisions, government reports, biographical accounts, position papers, statutes, and news stories.

The purpose of the series is twofold: (1) to provide substantive and background material on an event or issue through the texts of pivotal primary documents that shaped policy or law, raised controversy, or influenced the course of events, and (2) to trace the controversial aspects of the event or issue through documents that represent a variety of viewpoints. Documents for each volume have been selected by a recognized specialist in that subject with the advice of a board of other subject specialists, school librarians, and teachers.

To place the subject in historical perspective, the volume editor has prepared an introductory overview and a chronology of events. Documents are organized either chronologically or topically. The documents are full text or, if unusually long, have been excerpted by the volume editor. To facilitate understanding, each document is accompanied by an explanatory introduction. Suggestions for further reading follow the document or the chapter.

It is the hope of Greenwood Press that this series will enable students and other readers to use primary documents more easily in their research, to exercise critical thinking skills by examining the key documents in American history and public policy, and to critique the variety of viewpoints represented by this selection of documents.

Introduction

ABORTION IS A CONTROVERSIAL SUBJECT ABOUT WHICH PEOPLE ARE DIVIDED

Abortion is a controversial and emotional subject over which people are deeply divided. At this time—the last decade of the twentieth century—compromise between contending factions seems to be impossible because of the passion with which conflicting views are held. Even the terms that partisans of each position use to describe their views bear emotional freight. Anti-abortionists label themselves *pro-life*; they are not just opposed to abortion, they believe that the fetus is a complete, living person, deserving of legal protection. Those in favor of legalized abortion deny that they are *pro* abortion, for indeed most believe that abortion is undesirable, even though it is sometimes necessary. They call themselves *pro-choice*; they believe that women should be able to decide for themselves whether or not they should bear a child, and should not be subjected to the dictates of the government.

In this volume the editor will use the different terms describing each side—anti-abortion and pro-life, or pro-abortion, pro-choice, and pro-abortion rights—interchangeably.

The opinion of the general public, as measured by public opinion polls, appears to be neither wholeheartedly pro-life nor pro-choice. Since the 1970s, public opinion has been fairly constant in supporting legal abortion under some circumstances. But the polls show that the public also agrees that there should be some restrictions on abortion, and does not believe it should be completely unregulated.

In reading public opinion polls it is necessary to look carefully at the questions being asked, as some questions are ambiguously worded and some are designed to produce the answers the pollster wants to hear.

THE ABORTION ISSUE HAS BECOME INVOLVED IN POLITICS

Abortion first became involved in politics in the nineteenth century, when its opponents succeeded in having state legislatures pass laws making abortion a crime. During the 1960s and 1970s reformers went back to the state legislatures in an attempt to have abortion made legal once again. They also filed lawsuits contending that harsh abortion laws were unconstitutional. After the 1973 decision in *Roe v. Wade* had established a constitutional right to choose an abortion during the first three months of pregnancy, the foes of abortion moved into electoral politics. They hoped to be able to elect public officials who would recriminalize abortion and appoint Supreme Court justices who would overturn *Roe v. Wade*.

In the election years 1976 and 1980 abortion even became an issue in the presidential election, although the president does not have much direct authority to deal with the problem. As the *Washington Post* commented at the time, requiring candidates for the presidency to take a stand on abortion is "rather like making a position on Angola the litmus test of someone's fitness to serve on the City Council." Making abortion an issue in electoral politics has had some unfortunate side effects. By turning it into a political issue and forcing public officials to stand and be counted for or against, activists on both sides of the controversy made compromise more difficult and froze people into unyielding positions.

WHAT IS THE STATUS OF ABORTION IN 1993?

The status of abortion in 1993 is as follows. The constitutional right to choose an abortion established in *Roe v. Wade* appears to be secure; a 1992 Supreme Court decision (*Planned Parenthood of Southeastern Pennsylvania v. Casey*) upheld a woman's right to decide whether or not to have a child. However, the Court—with a number of justices who oppose abortion now on board—has held that state legislatures may pass laws imposing a great variety of restrictions on the operation. States now regulate the operation extensively, requiring waiting periods and written consent, requiring minors to notify their parents, and setting many other conditions that must be met. Only a few states still fund abortions for the poor. The availability of abortion has been severely curtailed. Doctors and hospitals are increasingly reluctant to perform abortions. In many states abortion services are available only in a few large cities.

Abortion, then, is still legal, but not always readily available.

AN ONGOING CONTROVERSY

As of this writing, the abortion controversy seems likely to be part of the political and social environment for the rest of the century. So far, attempts to amend the Constitution to give the fetus a right to life have failed, as have endeavors to free abortion of legal restrictions and use government money to pay for the abortions of indigent women. But the political equation is continually changing. Pro-choice forces have learned to use political organizing and direct mail to repel the attacks of their opponents. Frustrated by their failure to make the desired changes by lawful means, some anti-abortion groups have resorted to civil disobedience and even outright violence. What the ultimate outcome may be is entirely unpredictable.

If we look at the abortion laws of other Western nations, we find that there has been a general liberalizing trend over the last several decades. European countries allow abortion but hedge it with restrictions. They also have much better support systems for mothers and babies than we have in the United States. This might also be a good direction for Americans to take.

ALTERNATIVES TO ABORTION

One way of reducing the need for abortion is to improve methods of contraception and convince people to use them. There is, however, a need for more research on effective methods of contraception.

A new drug developed by a French company can be used to avoid some surgical abortions. It is now available in Europe but has not been approved for importation into the United States. The drug, RU-486, acts to prevent the implantation of a fertilized egg. Anti-abortion groups oppose the licensing of this drug because it acts to expel a fertilized egg and can thus be defined as an abortifacient (factor causing abortion). Some abortion opponents also disapprove of contraception.

The best alternative to abortion is to reduce the kinds of situations in which unwanted pregnancies occur.

THE APPROACH OF THIS VOLUME

The documents collected in this volume illustrate some of the crucial moments in the abortion controversy. The focus is on public documents: court cases, congressional committee hearings, presidential speeches, legislative provisions, and the like. Some biographical and autobiograph-

ical materials and a few newspaper accounts are also included. The editor
has tried to find documents that reveal different aspects of the controversy. Hearings before committees of Congress, where experts and advocates of all kinds give their opinions, are especially rich sources of
information.

The volume consists of five parts, each with its own introduction and
a brief explanation of each document. Part I covers historical material
in the pre-1960 period. Part II (1960–1972) focuses on the years when
abortion reform was in the air, and includes accounts of some of the
people and events that were catalysts in the movement for reform. Part
III (1973) reviews the constitutional provisions and court cases that
formed the authority for *Roe v. Wade*, the texts of the abortion cases
themselves, an account of Justice Harry Blackmun's struggle to write a
decision, and some contemporary commentary on the Supreme Court's
opinion. Part IV (1973–1980) deals with the political struggles that followed the decision and some of the key political moves as abortion
became a major issue in national politics. Part V (1980–   ) begins with
the election of President Ronald Reagan in 1980, and describes the controversy as it continues into the 1990s.

Each part concludes with bibliographical suggestions for further reading. Appendix A lists the important Supreme Court decisions that deal
with abortion. Appendix B is a chronology of events in the controversy
over abortion.

Part I

Before 1960

In the 1960s, as the demand for liberalization of old abortion laws escalated, everyone began to ask questions about the history of abortion and its treatment by the law. Had abortion always been a crime? How had Western civilization regarded the matter? Had it been legal in England, in early America when the Constitution was being written, at the time of the ratification of the Fourteenth Amendment? What political and social factors lay behind passage of criminal laws in all but one state of the Union during the last half of the nineteenth century?

Not much information was readily available. As scholars began investigating they found that abortion had been used as a method of population control by all civilizations—along with crude methods of contraception (suppositories of alligator dung!) and infanticide—practically from the beginning of historical time. There had been opposition to these practices; the early Christian Church spoke out against abortion on religious grounds. Law had had very little to say about abortion until the nineteenth century.

In early America, abortion by means of drugs, herbal potions, and various surgical techniques was common but was unregulated. It was considered women's business, family business. Connecticut was the first state to bring abortion into its criminal law. A statute passed in 1821, generally aimed at preventing murder by poisoning, made it a crime to give a poisonous substance to a woman in order to cause miscarriage. Other states gradually followed suit, although the earliest anti-abortion laws seem to have been intended to protect women from the barbarous practices of untrained abortionists.

Laws passed during the last half of the nineteenth century made abortion a crime, and in some cases made the woman who procured one a criminal.

In the eighty years between 1880 and 1960 abortion remained a crime in all states. The criminal law did not stop abortion; abortion went underground. Estimates of the numbers of illegal abortions during these years differ widely because it was impossible to get reliable figures on something that was against the law. There were some estimates of one million illegal abortions a year. Most of the figures were based on the number of women turning up in hospitals after botched abortions.

Some abortions were performed legally. State laws contained exceptions that allowed an abortion when a woman's life was in danger. In some instances doctors were willing to read these exceptions broadly, as covering "therapeutic" abortions (abortions for medical or psychiatric reasons). But the medical profession generally was extremely cautious and conservative, and most doctors were unwilling to risk their safety and their reputations except in extreme cases. The 1950s brought a few stirrings of a demand for change. Conferences were held by physicians and psychiatrists to discuss the problems caused by abortions and by legal restrictions on the practice. Lawyers began to be uneasy about the gap between the law on the books and what was actually occurring in society. But by and large, the years between 1880 and 1960 have been correctly labelled "the silent decades."

Abortion in Historical Context

THE EARLY HISTORY OF ABORTION

In 1974 the Congressional Research Service of the Library of Congress prepared a brief summary of the judicial and legislative aspects of abortion control for members of Congress. A portion of this "issue brief" dealing with the pre-1967 period is printed below.

DOCUMENT 1: An Overview of Judicial History and Legislative History. Congressional Research Service, Library of Congress, Issue Brief on Abortion

---

The moral and legal issues raised by the practice of abortion has tested the philosophers, theologians, and statesmen of every age since the dawn of civilization. The Stoics' belief that abortion should be allowed up to the moment of birth was vigorously opposed by the Pythagoreans who believed that the soul was infused into the body at conception and that to abort a fetus would be to commit murder. Early Roman law was silent as to abortion; and abortion and infanticide was common in Rome, especially among the upper classes. Opposition by scholars and the growing influence of the Christian religion brought about the first prohibition of abortion during the reign of Severus (193–211 A.D.). These laws made abortion a high criminal offense and subjected a woman who violated the provisions to banishment. During the European Middle Ages, major church theologians differentiated between an *embryo informatus* (prior to endowment of a soul) and an *embryo formatus* (after endowment with a soul). The distinction was used to assess punishments for abortion, fines being levied if abortion occurred before animation but death ordered if it [the fetus] was aborted at any time after.

The English common law adopted the doctrine of "quickening," i.e., the first movement of the fetus in the mother's womb, to pinpoint the time when abortion could incur sanctions. Generally, at common law, abortion performed before quickening was not an indictable offense. There is dispute whether abortion of a quick fetus was a felony. The predominant view is that abortion of a quick fetus was, at most, a minor offense. In the United States, the law in all but a few States until the mid-19th Century adopted the pre-existing English common law. Thus, no indictment would occur for aborting a fetus for a consenting female prior to quickening. However, there could be an indictment afterward. Also, as was the case under the common law, a woman herself was not indictable for submitting to an abortion, or for aborting herself, before quickening.

By the time of the Civil War, however, an influential anti-abortion movement began to affect legislation by inducing States to add to or revise their statutes in order to prohibit abortion at all stages of gestation. By 1910 every state had antiabortion laws, except Kentucky whose courts judicially declared abortions to be illegal. In 1967, 49 of the States and the District of Columbia classified the crime of abortion as a felony. The concept of quickening was no longer used to determine criminal liability but was retained in some States to set the punishment. Non-therapeutic abortions were essentially unlawful. The States varied in their exceptions for therapeutic abortions. Forty-two States permitted abortions only if necessary to save the life of the mother. Other States allowed abortion to save a woman from "serious and permanent bodily injury" or [threats to] her "life and health." Three States allowed abortions that were not "unlawfully performed" or that were not "without lawful justification," leaving interpretation of those standards to the courts.

Source: U.S. Library of Congress, Congressional Research Service, "Abortion: Judicial and Legislative Control," Issue Brief # 1B 74019, 1981.

The Hippocratic Oath

One of the earliest mentions of abortion is in the Hippocratic Oath, an oath taken by medical students when they receive their diplomas and become doctors. One phrase in the oath pledges the doctor not to give a woman the means to bring about an abortion.

Hippocrates, an ancient Greek physician who has been described as the Father of Medicine, probably lived sometime between 460 and

377 B.C. Arguing from the prohibition against abortion in the oath, opponents of abortion have concluded that, in Western civilization, abortion has always been considered wrongful. On the other hand, historians point out that abortion was a common practice in both ancient Greece and ancient Rome.

Justice Harry Blackmun discussed the Hippocratic Oath in his opinion in *Roe v. Wade* (1973). His conclusion was that there were a number of competing traditions in the ancient world, and the oath reflects the views of one sect, the Pythagoreans. The oath was an important statement of medical ethics, but its prohibition against abortion was not universally accepted.

DOCUMENT 2: The Hippocratic Oath. Hippocrates of Cos, B.C. c. 460

The regimen I adopt shall be for the benefit of my patients according to my ability and judgment, and not for their hurt or for any wrong. I will give no deadly drug to any, though it be asked of me, and I will counsel such, and especially I will not aid a woman to procure abortion. Whatsoever house I enter, there will I go for the benefit of the sick, refraining from all wrong-doing or corruption, and especially from any act of seduction, of male or female, of bond or free. Whatever things I see or hear concerning the life of men, in my attendance on the sick or even apart therefrom, which ought not to be noised abroad, I will keep silence thereon, counting such things to be as sacred secrets.

Source: *Encyclopaedia Britannica*, 14th ed., s.v. "Medicine, Custom of (Ancient Medicine)," p. 197.

THE COMMON LAW

Historians have also looked to the common law in an attempt to find whether or not our ancestors regarded abortion as a crime. The common law was the body of unwritten law that governed the behavior of men and women in England before the practice of having laws enacted by legislative bodies came into regular usage. The common law was the traditional law that formed the body of legal principles used by judges in deciding cases. It was derived from the traditions of the English people, from ancient legal writers, and from the Bible. One of the best places to find it is in the decisions of courts and the explanations given by judges in deciding actual cases. From time to time, legal scholars attempted to collect these legal principles and reduce them to written form.

One of the early compilations of the criminal law, as it was known in England, was William Hawkins' *A Treatise of the Pleas of the Crown*, first published in 1738. American lawyers were familiar with this book and had it in their libraries. In his discussion of murder, Hawkins considered whether or not abortion should be seen as murder. One of the sources he examined was Chapter 21, verses 22 and 23, of the Book of Exodus in the Bible. This selection seems to say that abortion was not regarded as murder unless the child was born alive and then killed. The biblical quotation appears to be concerned with the mother's well-being.

DOCUMENT 3: The Common Law. Treatise on the Pleas of the Crown. William Hawkins, 1738

Book I. Of Murder. Section 16. And it was anciently holden, That the causing of an Abortion by giving a Potion to, or striking, a Woman big with Child, was Murder: But at this Day, it is said to be a great Misprision [misdemeanor] only, and not Murder, unless the Child be born alive, and die thereof, in which Case it seems clearly to be Murder, notwithstanding some Opinions to the contrary. And in this Respect also, the Common Law seems to be agreeable to the *Mosaical*, which as to the Purpose is thus expressed, *If Men strive and hurt a Woman with Child, so that her Fruit depart from her, and yet no Mischief follows, he shall be surely punished, according as the Woman's Husband will lay upon him, and he shall pay as the Judges determine; And if any Mischief follow, then thou shalt give Life for Life.*

Source: William Hawkins, *A Treatise on the Pleas of the Crown*, 4th ed. Book I, Ch. 31, sec. 16, p. 80 (London: Richardson and Lintot, 1762).

INFANTICIDE AS A MEANS OF POPULATION CONTROL (EUROPE, 1840–1880)

Historian William Langer, in an article entitled "Europe's Initial Population Explosion," described the common practice of sending unwanted infants to "foundling hospitals" or sending them to the country to be nursed. Although these infants were not intentionally killed, there was a general expectation that few of them would survive the infectious diseases prevalent at the time. The practice of giving small children gin or laudanum (an opium derivative) to keep them quiet also had serious medical consequences.

DOCUMENT 4: Disguised Infanticide During Europe's First Population Explosion. William Langer, 1963

For Malthus "the whole train of common diseases and epidemics, wars, plague and famine" were all closely linked to "misery and vice" as positive checks to population growth. But misery and vice also included "extreme poverty, bad nursing of children, excesses of all kinds."

In this context it may be said that in Europe conditions of life among both the rural and urban lower classes—that is, of the vast majority of the population—can rarely have been as bad as they were in the early nineteenth century. Overworked, atrociously housed, undernourished, disease-ridden, the masses lived in a misery that defies the modern imagination. This situation in itself should have drastically influenced the population pattern, but two items in particular must have had a really significant bearing. First, drunkenness: this period must surely have been the golden age of inebriation, especially in the northern countries. The per capita consumption of spirits, on the increase since the sixteenth century, reached unprecedented figures. In Sweden, perhaps the worst-afflicted country, it was estimated at ten gallons of *branvin* and *akvavit* per annum. Everywhere ginshops abounded. London alone counted 447 taverns and 8,659 ginshops in 1836, some of which at least were visited by as many as 5,000–6,000 men, women, and children in a single day.

So grave was the problem of intemperance in 1830 that European rulers welcomed emissaries of the American temperance movement and gave full support to their efforts to organize the fight against the liquor menace. To what extent drunkenness may have affected the life expectancy of its addicts, we can only conjecture. At the very least the excessive use of strong liquor is known to enhance susceptibility to respiratory infections and is often the determining factor in cirrhosis of the liver.

Of even greater and more obvious bearing was what Malthus euphemistically called "bad nursing of children" and what in honesty must be termed disguised infanticide. It was certainly prevalent in the late eighteenth and nineteenth centuries and seems to have been constantly on the increase.

In the cities it was common practice to confide babies to old women nurses or caretakers. The least offense of these "Angelmakers," as they were called in Berlin, was to give the children gin to keep them quiet.

For the rest we have the following testimony from Benjamin Disraeli's novel *Sybil* (1845), for which he drew on a large fund of sociological data: "Laudanum and treacle, administered in the shape of some popular elixir, affords these innocents a brief taste of the sweets of existence and, keeping them quiet, prepares them for the silence of their impending grave." "Infanticide," he adds, "is practised as extensively and as legally in England as it is on the banks of the Ganges; a circumstance which apparently has not yet engaged the attention of the Society for the Propagation of the Gospel in Foreign Parts."

It was also customary in these years to send babies into the country to be nursed by peasant women. The well-to-do made their own arrangements, while the lower classes turned their offspring over to charitable nursing bureaus or left them at the foundling hospitals or orphanages that existed in all large cities. Of the operation of these foundling hospitals a good deal is known, and from this knowledge it is possible to infer the fate of thousands of babies that were sent to the provinces for care.

The middle and late eighteenth century was marked by a startling rise in the rate of illegitimacy, the reasons for which have little bearing on the present argument. But so many of the unwanted babies were being abandoned, smothered, or otherwise disposed of that Napoleon in 1811 decreed that the foundling hospitals should be provided with a turntable device, so that babies could be left at these institutions without the parent being recognized or subjected to embarrassing questions. This convenient arrangement was imitated in many countries and was taken full advantage of by the mothers in question. In many cities the authorities complained that unmarried mothers from far and wide were coming to town to deposit their unwanted babies in the accommodating foundling hospitals. The statistics show that of the thousands of children thus abandoned, more than half were the offspring of married couples.

There is good reason to suppose that those in charge of these institutions did the best they could with what soon became an unmanageable problem. Very few of the children could be cared for in the hospitals themselves. The great majority was sent to peasant nurses in the provinces. In any case, most of these children died within a short time, either of malnutrition or neglect or from the long, rough journey to the country.

The figures for this traffic, available for many cities, are truly shocking. In all of France fully 127,507 children were abandoned in the year 1833. Anywhere from 20 to 30 per cent of all children born were left to their fate. The figures for Paris suggest that in the years 1817–1820 the "foundlings" comprised fully 36 per cent of all births. In some of the Italian hospitals the mortality (under one year of age) ran to 80 or 90 per cent. In Paris the *Maison de la Couche* reported that of 4,779 babies admitted in 1818, 2,370 died in the first three months and another 956 within the first year.

The operation of this system was well known at the time, though largely forgotten in the days of birth control. Many contemporaries denounced it as legalized infanticide, and one at least suggested that the foundling hospitals post a sign reading "Children killed at Government expense." Malthus himself, after visiting the hospitals at St. Petersburg and Moscow, lavishly endowed by the imperial family and the aristocracy, could not refrain from speaking out:

> Considering the extraordinary mortality which occurs in these institutions, and the habits of licentiousness which they have an evident tendency to create, it may perhaps be truly said that, if a person wished to check population, and were not solicitous about the means, he could not propose a more effective measure than the establishment of a sufficient number of foundling hospitals, unlimited as to their reception of children.

In the light of the available data one is almost forced to admit that the proposal, seriously advanced at the time, that unwanted babies be painlessly asphyxiated in small gas chambers, was definitely humanitarian. Certainly the entire problem of infanticide in the days before widespread practice of contraception deserves further attention and study. It was undoubtedly a major factor in holding down the population, strangely enough in the very period when the tide of population was so rapidly rising.

Source: William Langer, "Europe's Initial Population Explosion," *American Historical Review* 69, pp. 7–9 (October 1963).

Contraception and Abortion in America Before 1960

A SHORT HISTORY OF ABORTION POLICY IN THE UNITED STATES; THE HISTORIANS' BRIEF

In 1988 a number of professional historians signed on to an *amicus curiae* brief in a major abortion case (*William Webster v. Reproductive Health Services*) that was scheduled to be heard by the Supreme Court. The Latin term *amicus curiae* means "friend of the court." A "friend of the court" brief is a statement made to a court by persons who are not actual parties to a law case, but who wish to bring additional material to the attention of the judge or judges. Such briefs are filed to support the arguments being made by one of the parties to the lawsuit. The *amici* (friends) here were 281 historians who wanted to give the Court their interpretation of the history of abortion in the United States. Their brief supported the position that, for most of our history, early abortions had not been illegal. It was introduced to strengthen the argument that the traditional law had not interfered with private individuals performing abortions "before quickening"—that is, before the fetus was developed enough to make detectable movements in the womb.

There were seventy-eight *amicus* briefs in the *Webster* case, something of a record. Forty-five briefs were filed to support an anti-abortion position. Abortion rights advocates also filed dozens of briefs.

Although there are some historians who would argue with the interpretation given here, the "historians' brief" represents a mainline view of abortion history. The extensive footnotes to books and articles that appear in the brief are not included in this selection.

DOCUMENT 5: Brief of 281 American Historians as *Amici Curiae* Supporting Appellees in *Webster v. Reproductive Services*, 1988

II. AT THE TIME THE FEDERAL CONSTITUTION WAS ADOPTED, ABORTION WAS KNOWN AND WAS NOT ILLEGAL.

As the Court demonstrated in *Roe v. Wade* [see Document 39], abortion was not illegal at common law. Through the nineteenth century American common law decisions uniformly reaffirmed that women committed no offense in seeking abortions. Both common law and popular American understanding drew distinctions depending upon whether the fetus was "quick," i.e. whether the *woman* perceived signs of independent life. There was some dispute whether a common law misdemeanor occurred when a third party destroyed a fetus, after quickening, without the woman's consent. But early recognition of this particular crime against pregnant women did not diminish the liberty of the woman herself to end a pregnancy in its early stages.

Abortion was not uncommon in colonial America. Herbal abortifacients [things causing abortions] were widely known, and cookbooks and women's diaries of the era contained recipes for medicines. Recent studies of the work of midwives in the 1700s report cases in which the midwives provided women abortifacient compounds. More significantly, these cases are described as routine and are unaccompanied by any particular disapproval.

The absence of legal condemnation of abortion in colonial America is all the more remarkable because both families and society valued children and population growth in a rural economy, with vast unsettled lands, where diseases of infancy claimed many lives. For these reasons, single women more often sought abortions in the Colonial era. The absence of legal condemnation is particularly striking in the New England culture of tight-knit, religiously homogeneous communities in which neighbor observed the private behavior of neighbor and did not hesitate to chastise those who violated pervasive moral norms of the community. In an era characterized by extensive oral and written moral prescripts from community and religious leaders, birth control and abortion were rarely the subject for moralizing. Where abortion is noted, it is not the practice itself that is subject of comment, but rather the violation of other social/sexual norms that gave rise to the perceived need to attempt to abort.

In the late eighteenth century, strictures on sexual behavior loosened considerably. The incidence of premarital pregnancy rose sharply; in the late eighteenth century, one third of all New England brides were pregnant at the time of marriage, compared to less than ten percent in the seventeenth century. Falling birth rates in the 1780s suggest that, at the same time our founders drafted the Constitution, including the Ninth Amendment's guarantee that the enumeration of certain rights "shall not be construed to deny or disparage others retained by the people," the use of birth control and abortion increased.

III. THROUGH THE NINETEENTH CENTURY, ABORTION BECAME EVEN MORE WIDELY ACCEPTED AND HIGHLY VISIBLE.

Through the nineteenth century and well into the twentieth, abortion remained a widely accepted popular practice, despite increasingly vigorous efforts to prohibit it after 1860. Changing patterns of abortion practice and attitudes towards it can only be understood against a more general background of dramatic change in American economic and family life. During the period between ratification of the Constitution and adoption of the Civil War Amendments, Americans moved to cities and increasingly worked for wages. In 1787, the average white American woman bore seven children; by the late 1870s, the average was down to fewer than 5; by 1900 it was 3.56. Carl Degler calls this decline in fertility "the single most important fact about women and the family in American history."

Economic reasons motivated urban couples to limit their family size. Working class married women, faced with the material difficulty of managing a family budget on a single male wage, resorted to abortion as the most effective available means of "conscious fertility control."

But more than economic factors were at work in the restriction of fertility. White middle-class Americans were, in particular, influenced by changing family conceptions and definitions of motherhood. As men's work patterns deviated farther from those of women, "wife" and "home" became powerful symbols of men's economic security and social standing. Nineteenth-century women faced sharply conflicting demands. "The True Woman was domestic, docile, and reproductive. The good bourgeois wife was to limit her fertility, symbolize her husband's affluence, and do good within the world."

To limit the number of children they bore, women adopted a range of strategies, including abortion. Through the 1870s abortion was "common," a "matter of fact" and often "safe and successful." The most common methods of abortion in the nineteenth century involved herbs and devices that women could purchase from pharmacists and use themselves. Nonetheless, in 1871, New York City, with a population of less than one million, supported two hundred full-time abortionists, not including doctors who sometimes performed abortions.

For most of the nineteenth century, abortion was highly visible. "Beginning in the early 1840s abortion became, for all intents and purposes, a business, a service openly traded in the free market. . . . [Pervasive advertising told Americans] not only that many practitioners would provide abortion services, but that some practitioners had made the abortion business their chief livelihood. Indeed, abortions became one of the first specialties in American medical history.

IV. NINETEENTH-CENTURY ABORTION RESTRICTIONS SOUGHT TO PROMOTE OBJECTIVES THAT ARE TODAY PLAINLY INAPPLICABLE OR CONSTITUTIONALLY IMPERMISSIBLE.

Between 1850 and 1880, the newly formed American Medical Association, through some of its vigorously active members, became the "*single most important factor in altering the legal policies toward abortion in this country.*" Nineteenth-century "regular" physicians enlisted state power to limit access to abortion for reasons that are, in retrospect, parochial, and have long since been rejected by organized medicine. The doctors found an audience for their effort to restrict abortion because they appealed to broader concerns: maternal health, consumer protection, a discriminatory idea of the natural subordination of women, nativist fears generated by the fact that elite Protestant women often sought abortions. Some of those seeking these diverse objectives also sought to attribute moral status to the fetus.

A. From 1820-1860, Abortion Regulation in the States Rejected Broader English Restrictions And Sought to Protect Women From Particularly Dangerous Forms Of Abortion.

In 1803, English law made all forms of abortion criminal. Despite this model, for two decades, no American state restricted access to abortion. In 1821, when one state, Connecticut, acted, it prohibited only the administration of a "deadly poison, or other noxious and destructive substance." Moreover, the act applied only after quickening, and punished only the person who administered the poison, not the woman who consumed it. In the late 1820s, three other states followed the Connecticut model, prohibiting the use of dangerous poisons *after quickening*. Most American states did not see abortion as a problem demanding legislative attention.

In 1830, Connecticut became the first state to punish abortion after quickening. In the same year, New York, also animated by a concern for patient safety, considered a law to prohibit *any* surgery, unless two physicians approved it as essential. Prior to scientific understanding of germ theory and antisepsis, any surgical intervention was likely to be fatal. The act finally adopted applied only to surgical abortion and included the first "therapeutic" exception, approving abortion where two physicians agreed that it was "necessary." As the Court recognized in *Roe v. Wade*, until the twentieth century, abortion, particularly when done through surgical intervention, remained significantly more dangerous to the woman than childbirth. Because nineteenth century abortion laws were drafted and justified to protect women, they did not punish women as parties to an abortion.

None of these early laws, restricting forms of abortion thought to be particularly unsafe, were enforced. That absence itself speaks powerfully, particularly since abortion was prevalent. Despite legislative action and medical opposition, common, openly tolerated practice suggests that many Americans did not perceive abortion as morally wrong.

B. From the Mid-Nineteenth Century, A Central Purpose Of Abortion Regulation Was to Define Who Should Be Allowed to Control Medical Practice.

Without exception, physicians were the principal nineteenth-century proponents of laws to restrict abortion. A core purpose of the nineteenth-century laws, and of doctors supporting them, was to "control medical practice in the interest of public safety." This is not to deny that some doctors had moral objections to abortion, as well as moral and social views about women and race. But the most significant explanation for the drive by medical doctors for statutes regulating abortion is the fact that these doctors were undergoing the historical process of professionalization.

Medicine was not then the organized, highly regulated profession we know today. It was an occupation in which conventional and scientifically authoritative modes of practice still contended for stature and authority with more popular modes, such as botanic medicine, homeopathy, herbalists, midwives and abortionists. Allopathic physicians sought to establish and consolidate professional sovereignty. This struggle was not easy, nor was its outcome certain. The professionalizing spirit, illustrated by pressures to require licensure for doctors, was contrary to the egalitarian spirit of public life in Jacksonian America. It was only by mid-century, with the founding of the American Medical Association, that professional sovereignty was tentatively established for "scientific" medicine.

Most nineteenth-century Americans did not seek the help of physicians in dealing with pregnancy, abortion and childbirth. Childbirth remained an affair of family, friends, and midwives until well into the nineteenth century. The process by which childbirth became associated with doctors and hospitals, and with a heightened degree of medical intervention, is a well-documented example of the medical profession's

gradual consolidation of authority. This development was not necessarily coercive or conspiratorial. Women were eager for services and
knowledge that might lessen the risks and pain of childbirth. But the
physician's effort to move childbirth to the hospital involved more than
clinical considerations. Similarly, the deep involvement of doctors in the
early abortion statutes was intimately connected with professional struggles between proponents of "scientific medicine" and those who practiced less conventional modes of healing.

As we have seen, the first anti-abortion laws were "anti-poisoning"
statutes rather than sweeping prohibitions on all abortions. Because
certain abortifacients derived from herbs and purgatives could be fatal
if taken in overly large quantities, it became a crime to "administer"
such remedies. These laws did not express an abhorrence of abortion
any more than current laws banning the unauthorized practice of law
represent an abhorrence of legal representation. Rather, they served the
dual function of protecting the public and solidifying the bounds of
professional authority.

More significant, the nineteenth century movement to regulate abortions was one chapter in a campaign by doctors that reflected a professional conflict between "regulars" (those who ultimately became the
practitioners and proponents of scientific medicine) and "irregulars."
As James Mohr explains:

> Practically, the regular physicians saw in abortion a medical procedure
> that not only gave the competition an edge but also undermined the
> solidarity of their own regular ranks. If a regular doctor refused to perform
> an abortion he knew the woman could go to one of several types of
> irregulars and probably receive one. . . . As more and more irregulars began
> to advertise abortion services openly, especially after 1840, regular phy-
> sicians grew more nervous about losing their practices to healers who
> would provide a service that more and more American women after 1840
> began to want. Yet, if a regular gave in to the temptation to perform an
> occasional discreet abortion, and physicians testified repeatedly that this
> frequently happened among the regulars, he would be compromising his
> own commitment to Hippocratic standards of behavior. *The best way out
> of these dilemmas was to persuade state legislators to make abortion a criminal
> offense. Anti-abortion laws would weaken the appeal of the competition and take
> the pressure off the more marginal members of the regulars' own sect.*

To be sure, some "regulars" were morally troubled by abortion, and
not all "irregulars" were willing to perform them. A variety of reasons
explain why "regular physicians became interested in abortion policy
from an early date and repeatedly dragged it into their prolonged struggle to control the practice of medicine in the United States." In the larger
context, however, public consideration of abortion in antebellum America was more an issue of medical authority and professional sovereignty

than of any particular social or moral attitude toward abortion. Without such an explanation centering on professional imperatives, it is difficult to account for the fact that the American Medical Association and its members became primary proponents of twentieth century statutes legalizing abortion.

C. *Enforcement of Sharply Differentiated Concepts of the Roles And Choices of Men And Women Underlay Regulation of Abortion And Contraception In The Nineteenth Century.*

The American Medical Association's campaign to restrict access to abortion succeeded for many reasons. Concerns over the dangers of surgical abortion to women were well founded. Further, physicians persuaded male political leaders that "abortion constituted a threat to the social order and to male authority." Since the 1840s, a growing movement for women's suffrage and equality had generated popular fears that women were departing from their purely maternal role. These fears were fueled by the fact that family size declined sharply in the nineteenth century.

In 1871, the American Medical Association's Committee on Criminal Abortion described the woman who sought an abortion:

"She becomes unmindful of the course marked out for her by Providence, she overlooks the duties imposed on her by the marriage contract. She yields to the pleasures—but shrinks from the pains and responsibilities of maternity; and, destitute of all delicacy and refinements, resigns herself, body and soul, into the hands of unscrupulous and wicked men. Let not the husband of such a wife flatter himself that he possesses her affection. Nor can she in turn ever merit even the respect of a virtuous husband. She sinks into old age like a withered tree, stripped of its foliage; with the stain of blood upon her soul, she dies without the hand of affection to smooth her pillow."

The nineteenth-century American Medical Association's view of women is strikingly similar to that adopted by this Court in 1872, when women were denied the right to practice law because "divine ordinance," and "the nature of things," prescribed a "family institution [that] is repugnant to the idea of a woman adopting a distinct and independent career from that of her husband." This Court has, of course, now come to see this view as part of our "long and unfortunate history of sex discrimination," and as constitutionally illegitimate.

The women's movement of the nineteenth century affirmed that women should always have the right to decide whether to bear a child and sought to enhance women's control of reproduction through "voluntary motherhood," ideally to be achieved through periodic abstinence. Anxieties about changing family functions and gender roles were critical factors motivating the all-male legislatures that adopted restrictions on abortion.

In contrast to the feminist demand for control of reproduction, the federal government, in 1873, took the lead in banning access to information about both contraception and abortion. The Comstock law restricted not only medical information on abortion and contraception such as a medical text on physiology written by an eminent Harvard scientist, but also literary depictions, such as Leo Tolstoy's disapproving tale of infidelity, *The Kreutzer Sonata*, as well as moral literature, including a pamphlet urging total chastity. An 1876 federal court decision rejected a claim that physicians should have the right to distribute contraceptive information.

In the nineteenth century, opposition to abortion and contraception were closely linked, just as political and doctrinal support for this Court's decisions in *Griswold v. Connecticut* and *Roe v. Wade* are linked in this century. Michael Grossberg observes that "Anthony Comstock had labeled as abortionists everyone who advocated or dealt in family-limitation materials and services."

The core purposes of the Comstock Act were to enforce chastity on the young and unmarried and to preserve the subservient position of women within a "traditional" family structure. Nineteenth-century restrictions on abortion and contraception can only sensibly be understood as a reaction to the uncertainties generated by large shifts in family functions and anxieties generated by women's challenges to their historic roles of silence and subservience.

D. Nineteenth-Century Contraception and Abortion Regulation Also Reflected Ethnocentric Fears About The Relative Birthrates Of Immigrants And Yankee Protestants.

Nativism, notably anti-Catholicism, had been part of American politics and culture as early as the Jacksonian period. The Civil War and Reconstruction Era dramatically raised consciousness about national identity and citizenship. Social conservatives in the 1850s articulated an "organicist" ideal in which social unity would predominate over diversity. By the 1870s social thought was turning the insights of Charles Darwin toward racist ends. The political ideology of "free labor," forged in the nascent Republican Party in the years preceding the Civil War, was severely challenged by an influx of foreign labor in the latter part of the nineteenth century. The discriminatory immigration policies and nativist fears of the late nineteenth and early twentieth centuries had their roots in a far earlier period, when Americans first became concerned about the creation of an urban population of wage workers.

Beginning in the 1890s, and continuing through the first decades of the twentieth century, these nativist fears coalesced into a drive against what was then called "race suicide." The "race suicide" alarmists worried that women of "good stock"—prosperous, white and Protestant—were not having enough children to maintain the political and social supremacy of their group. Anxiety over the falling birth rates of Protestant whites in comparison with other groups helped shape policy governing both birth control and abortion. As James Mohr points out, "The doctors both used and were influenced by blatant nativism. . . . " There can be little doubt that Protestants' fears about not keeping up with the reproductive rates of Catholic immigrants played a greater role in the drive for anti-abortion laws in nineteenth-century America than Catholic opposition to abortion did.

V. ENFORCEMENT OF ABORTION RESTRICTIONS IN THE FIRST HALF OF THE TWENTIETH CENTURY FOLLOWED HISTORIC ETHNIC AND CLASS DIFFERENTIATIONS, AFFIRMED HISTORIC CONCERNS ABOUT ENFORCING GENDER ROLES, AND IMPOSED ENORMOUS COSTS UPON WOMEN, THEIR FAMILIES AND PHYSICIANS.

Statutory restrictions on abortion remained virtually unchanged until the 1960s. Physicians were allowed to perform abortions only "to preserve the mother's life." Nonetheless, the incidence of abortion remained high, ranging from one pregnancy in seven at the turn of the century, to one in three in 1936. Most abortions were performed illegally. Legal restrictions did not stop abortion, but made it furtive, humiliating, and dangerous.

In the first half of the twentieth century, a two-tiered abortion system emerged in which services depended on the class, race, age and residence of the woman. Poor and rural women obtained illegal abortions, performed by people, physicians and others, who were willing to defy the law out of sympathy for the woman or for the fee. More privileged women steadily pressed physicians for legal abortions and many obtained them. Some doctors could be persuaded that deliveries would endanger women's health; the dilation and curettage procedure was indicated for numerous other gynecological health problems.

Shifts in the definition of "therapeutic" abortion responded to larger social forces. Early in the century "race suicide" fears fueled efforts to suppress both abortion and birth control. During the Depression, abortions increased as the medical profession recognized impoverishment as an indication for therapeutic abortion. In the 1940s and 1950s the definition of therapeutic abortion expanded to include psychiatric indications. Physicians were caught in a double bind: abortion was criminal, but the reasons women sought them were so multiple and compelling that they were difficult to resist.

In the 1950s, more restrictive attitudes toward both legal and illegal abortions were part of a conservative response to growing female labor-force participation and independence. The 1960s movement to legalize abortion arose in response to this, rather brief, wave of anti-abortion enforcement. Physicians, particularly those who worked in public hospitals and clinics, saw women who needlessly suffered and died as a consequence of illegal abortions. Others were disturbed that most of those women were poor and black. Many were distressed by the class bias inherent in the psychiatric indications for therapeutic abortions. In the late 1960s, concerned physicians were joined by women who had come to understand that control of reproductive capacity is the *sine qua non* [essential element] of women's self-governance and moral personhood.

As a number of states acted to legalize abortion, additional concerns heightened pressure for recognition of constitutional protection for the basic right of abortion choice. Debate over abortion, now revolving around insoluble metaphysical disputes about the moral status of the fetus, preoccupied state legislatures and often prevented them from addressing other vital issues. Class and regional differentiations were accentuated as it became possible for women with resources to travel to states where abortion was legal. In *Roe v. Wade*, this Court responded to all of these forces in holding that constitutional rights of liberty and privacy protect the right of the woman and her physician to choose abortion.

VI. THE MORAL VALUE ATTACHED TO THE FETUS BECAME A CENTRAL ISSUE IN AMERICAN CULTURE AND LAW ONLY IN THE LATE TWENTIETH CENTURY, WHEN TRADITIONAL JUSTIFICATIONS FOR RESTRICTING ACCESS TO ABORTION BECAME CULTURALLY ANACHRONISTIC OR CONSTITUTIONALLY IMPERMISSIBLE.

Some of those seeking to enlist the power of the state to deny women's liberty to choose abortion have long articulated a concern for the fetus. Yet until the late twentieth century, this concern was always subsidiary to more mundane social visions and anxieties. The mid-nineteenth century physicians' campaign sought to prohibit the practice of botanic medicine and chiropractic, as well as abortion. Protection of fetal life is plainly not the driving concern of such a movement. Those who opposed abortion and birth control to stanch "race suicide," sought to protect the privilege of elite white Anglo-Saxon Protestants, not to protect fetuses.

Religious support for the physicians' campaign to bar abortion was practically non-existent. Physicians vigorously sought to enlist moral authority and organized religion in their campaign to restrict abortion, and "were openly disgusted when the established voices of moral authority refused to speak on their behalf. . . . Medical journals accused the religious journals of valuing abortifacient advertising revenue too highly to risk criticizing the practice."

Further, the small support that physicians found among Protestant religious leaders appeared to be "more worried about falling birth-rates among their adherents than about the morality of abortion itself." The conspicuous absence of religious support for the physicians' anti-abortion crusade is particularly striking compared to extensive religious involvement in other nineteenth-century movements for changing social morality, such as temperance.

Nineteenth-century laws restricting access to abortion were not based on a belief that the fetus is a human being. To the contrary, New Jersey Chief Justice Green expressed the prevailing judicial opinion in 1849 when he asserted that although it was "true, for certain purposes, [that] the law regards an infant as *in being* from the time of conception, yet it seems nowhere to regard it as *in life*, or to have respect to its preservation as a living being." Michael Grossberg summarizes the nineteenth-century cases, saying, "[A] fetus enjoyed rights only in property law and then only if successfully born. It had no standing in criminal law until quickening, and none at all in tort. The law highly prized children, not fetuses."

Judith Walzer Leavitt's analysis of medical decisions about the procedure of craniotomy (a surgical mutilation of the live fetal head to permit vaginal extraction) provides one complex window on the moral status of the fetus, during the period from 1880 to 1920. At this time, most women gave birth at home. When a woman's pelvis was too small to permit delivery, two alternatives were possible. A Caesarean section would ordinarily save the fetus, but posed high risks to the woman's life. A craniotomy killed the fully formed fetus, but with significantly less risk to the woman.

Most physicians thought craniotomy, which could save the life of the woman, the more appropriate choice in this difficult situation. Others based their assessment on their judgment of the social and moral worth of the woman. But the core issue for physicians was the principle that "the obstetrician alone must be the judge of what is to be done." Roman Catholic writers widely condemned craniotomy in popular medical journals, informing obstetricians in 1917 that it was "[b]etter that a million mothers die than that one innocent creature be killed." But continued medical practice and the dialogue demonstrate that neither patients nor physicians attached such high, absolute value to the fetus, even when it was plainly viable.

As this Court observed in *Roe v. Wade*, the pattern of American abortion laws does not seem to support the view that they were designed principally to incorporate a view of the fetus as a person. Both the lesser punishment for abortion than for homicide, and the various exceptions allowing the physician to determine that abortion is justified, rebut the assumption that laws against abortion reflect that belief.

Further, increasing "scientific" understanding does not support attributing enhanced moral value to the fetus. That pregnancy is a biologically continuous process has long been recognized by Americans even when the common law recognized a woman's right to choose abortion. For example, a popular home medical book published in 1817 and dedicated to the *Wives of the Ministers of the Gospel of the United States*, stated: "[T]he contents of the pregnant womb, formed in miniature at conception, are the child, the waters, the membranes holding them, the navel cord, and afterbirth." The book goes on to describe in detail embryonic and fetal development. Historically, claims that startling advances in medical knowledge about pregnancy and fetal development should alter attitudes toward abortion have consistently been highly exaggerated.

Source: Brief of 281 American Historians as Amici Curiae, Supporting Appellees, in *Webster v. Reproductive Health Services*, No. 88-605, Supreme Court of the United States, October Term, 1988.

THE MEDICAL CRUSADE AGAINST ABORTION (1840–1880)

Before the Civil War abortion was used increasingly as a means of controlling family size. Opposition to this practice arose in the medical profession. Many doctors believed that women did not understand the marvelous process of creation that was going on within their bodies, and did not recognize that the fetus was an actual living being. Dr. Hugh L. Hodge, an obstetrician and professor of medicine at the University of Pennsylvania, used his lectures to medical students to impress upon them the importance of opposing the prevalent abortion practices of the era.

Historians, looking back on this period, find that the medical crusade against abortion coincided with a period of professionalization in the practice of medicine. "Regular" physicians (those who had received formal training) were anxious to rid the profession of practitioners that they believed were out on the fringe of proper medical practice— herbalists, chiropractors, and abortionists. Regular physicians were also anxious to replace midwives, who had until this time been the main source of assistance to women giving birth, seeking relief from "women's problems," or wishing abortions.

DOCUMENT 6: Foeticide, or Criminal Abortion: A Lecture Introductory to the Course on Obstetrics and Diseases of Women and Children. Dr. Hugh L. Hodge, University of Pennsylvania, 1869

The history of almost every nation is blackened by the hideous, unnatural crime of *infanticide.*

You have all read of the horrible sacrifices of infants among barbarous nations, to appease or propititate [*sic*] their idol gods. You know that Greeks and Romans, with all their boasted wisdom and refinement, habitually exposed their infants to the most terrible deaths; that this crime is not forgotten in modern times; that among nations, deprived of the light of Christianity, the sacrifices and the wanton destruction of infants still prevail, whether we extend our view to Asia, Africa, or America, or the islands of the sea.

Criminal abortion is almost as prevalent. Hippocrates, the father of medicine, alludes to the potions taken by wicked women, or administered by still more wicked and detestable men, to procure delivery. The females of Rome have their depravity, in this respect, recorded on a monument, *perennius ære*, the Satires of Juvenal.

Would, gentlemen, that we could exonerate the *moderns* from guilt on this subject! It is, however, a mournful fact, which ought to be promulgated, that this crime, this mode of committing murder, is prevalent among the most intelligent, refined, moral, and Christian communities.

We blush, while we record the fact, that in this country, in our cities and towns, in this city, where literature, science, morality, and Christianity are supposed to have so much influence; where all the domestic and social virtues are reported as being in full and delightful exercise; even here individuals, male and female, exist, who are continually imbruing their hands and consciences in the blood of unborn infants; yea, even *medical* men are to be found, who, for some trifling pecuniary recompense, will poison the fountains of life, or forcibly induce labor, to the certain destruction of the fœtus, and not unfrequently of its parent.

So low, gentlemen, is the moral sense of the community on this subject; so ignorant are the greater number of individuals, that even mothers, in many instances, shrink not from the commission of this crime, but will voluntarily destroy their own progeny, in violation of every natural sentiment, and in opposition to the laws of God and man. Perhaps there are few individuals, in extensive practice as obstetricians, who have not had frequent applications made to them by the fathers or mothers of unborn children (respectable and polite in their general appearance and manners), to destroy the fruit of illicit pleasure, under the vain hope of preserving their reputation by this unnatural and guilty sacrifice.

Married women, also, from the fear of labor, from indisposition to have the care, the expense, or the trouble of children, or some other motive equally trifling and degrading, have solicited that the embryo should be destroyed by their medical attendant. And when such individuals are informed of the nature of the transaction, there is an expression of real or pretended surprise that any one should deem the act improper—much more guilty; yea, in spite even of the solemn warning of the physician, they will resort to the debased and murderous charlatan, who, for a piece of silver, will annihilate the life of a fœtus, and endanger even that of its ignorant and guilty mother.

This low estimate of the importance of fœtal life is by no means restricted to the ignorant, or to the lower classes of society. Educated, refined, and fashionable women—yea, in many instances, women whose moral character is, in other respects, without reproach; mothers who are devoted, with an ardent and self-denying affection, to the children who already constitute their family, are perfectly indifferent respecting the fœtus in utero. They seem not to realize that the being within them is indeed *animate*—that it is, in verity, a *human being*—body and spirit; that it is of importance, that its value is inestimable, having reference to this world and the next. Hence, they in every way neglect *its* interest. They eat and drink; they walk and ride; they will practise no self-restraint, but will indulge every caprice, every passion, utterly regardless of the unseen and unloved embryo. They act with as much indifference as if the living, intelligent, immortal existence lodged within their organs, were of no more value than the bread eaten, or the common excretions of the system. Even in cases where mothers have suffered from repeated abortions, where fœtus after fœtus has perished through their neglect or carelessness, and where even their own health is involved in the issue, even in such cases every obstetrician can bear testimony to the great difficulty of inducing our wayward patients to forego certain gratifications, to practise certain self-denials, and to adopt efficient means for the salvation of the child.

This is not all. We can bear testimony, that in some instances, the woman who has been well educated, who occupies high stations in society, whose influence over others is great, and whose character has not been impugned, will deliberately resort to any and every measure which may effectually destroy her unborn offspring. Ashamed, or afraid, to apply to the charlatan, who sustains his existence by the price of blood, dreading it may be publicity, she recklessly and boldly adopts measures, however severe and dangerous, for the accomplishment of her unnatural, her guilty purpose. She will make extra muscular efforts by long fatiguing walks, by dancing, running, jumping, kept up as long as possible; she will swallow the most nauseous, irritating, and poisonous drugs, and in some instances, will actually arm herself with the surgeon's instrument, and operate upon her own body, that she may be delivered of an embryo, for which she has no desire, and whose birth and appearance she dreads.

These facts are horrible, but they are too frequent, and too true. Often, very often, must all the eloquence and all the authority of the practitioner be employed; often he must, as it were, grasp the conscience of his weak and erring patient, and let her know, in language not to be misunderstood, that she is responsible to her Creator for the life of the being within her.

After this exposition, and the details which have been given, and especially in view of the influence which medical science must exert on these questions, it seems hardly necessary to repeat, that physicians, medical men, must be regarded as the guardians of the rights of infants. They alone can rectify public opinion; they alone can present the subject in such a manner that legislators can exercise their powers aright in the preparation of suitable laws; that moralists and theologians can be furnished with facts to enforce the truth on this subject upon the moral sense of the community, so that not only may the crime of infanticide be abolished, but that criminal abortion be properly reprehended, and that women, in every rank and condition of life may be sensible of the value of the embryo and fœtus, and of the high responsibility which rests on the parents of every unborn infant.

While thus advocating, in this place, the importance of Obstetric science, as bearing on the welfare of women and of children, and hence on the best interests of society; while presenting myself, as an advocate, as well as one of the physical guardians of the rights of infants, it is with no ordinary satisfaction that I can survey such an assemblage of intelligent and educated young men as are here collected, who have devoted themselves to the pursuit of a science so exalted, so noble, so useful as that of medicine; who, with an ardent enthusiasm, have determined to wage a war of extermination against any and every opinion and practice which in any degree infringes on the rights of women and their offspring.

In this glorious work I bid you prosper. Your rewards may not be riches and honor, but they will be more valuable and enduring, arising from the smiles of an approving conscience, and the blessing of that Being who has pronounced the severest curse on the crime of murder.

In the above argument addressed, as it was, to students of medicine, my great object was to impress upon their minds the nature and importance of fœtal life, that thus they might be prepared to exert all their talents and influence, for the preservation of the unborn child.

Source: Reprinted in *Abortion in the Nineteenth Century* (New York: Arno Press, 1974), pp. 31–7.

CRIMINAL ABORTION LAWS

State laws prohibiting abortion all differed. The Texas law reproduced here was first enacted in 1857. Note that this law is aimed at the abortionist. Performing an abortion is a felony; if the woman dies, the charge will be murder. An exception allows abortion to save the life of the mother. This law was declared unconstitutional in 1973, in *Roe v. Wade*.

A similar law was enacted in North Carolina in 1881. Using drugs or instruments with the intent to destroy a child becomes a felony. There is an exception if the action is intended to preserve the life of the mother. Using drugs or instruments with the intent to produce a miscarriage is also a felony, although it carries a lesser penalty. The first section of this law appears to apply to an abortion before "quickening" (before the mother can feel the child move). The early statutes did not criminalize abortion until the child was "quick." The second clause could apply to an attempted abortion at any time during pregnancy.

DOCUMENT 7: The Texas Abortion Statute (1857)

Article 1191. Abortion.

If any person shall designedly administer to a pregnant woman or knowingly procure to be administered with her consent any drug or medicine, or shall use towards her any violence or means whatever externally or internally applied, and thereby procure an abortion, he shall be confined in the penitentiary not less than two nor more than five years; if it be done without her consent, the punishment shall be doubled. By 'abortion' is meant that the life of the fetus or embryo shall be destroyed in the woman's womb or that a premature birth thereof be caused.

Article 1192. Furnishing the means.

Whoever furnishes the means for procuring an abortion knowing the purpose intended is guilty as an accomplice.

Article 1193. Attempt at abortion.

If the means used shall fail to produce an abortion, the offender is nevertheless guilty of an attempt to produce an abortion, provided it be shown that such means were calculated to produce that result, and shall be fined not less than one hundred nor more than one thousand dollars.

Article 1194. Murder in producing abortion.

If the death of the mother is occasioned by an abortion so produced or by an attempt to effect the same it is murder.

Article 1196. By medical advice.

Nothing in this chapter applies to an abortion procured or attempted by medical advice for the purpose of saving the life of the mother.

Source: Texas Penal Code, Chap. 9, Title 15.

DOCUMENT 8: North Carolina Statutes Pertaining to Abortion and Kindred Offenses Before the 1967 Law

G.S. 14–44. *Using drugs or instruments to destroy unborn child*. If any person shall willfully administer to any woman, either pregnant or quick with child, or prescribe for any such woman, or advise or procure any such woman to take any medicine, drug or other substance whatever, or shall use or employ any instrument or other means with intent thereby to destroy such child, *unless the same be necessary to preserve the life of the mother*, he shall be guilty of a felony, and shall be imprisoned in the State's prison for not less than one year nor more than ten years, and be fined at the discretion of the court. (1881, c. 351, s. 1; Code, s. 975; Rev., s. 3618; C.S., s. 4226.

G.S. 14–45. *Using drugs or instruments to produce miscarriage or injure pregnant woman*. If any person shall administer to any pregnant woman, or prescribe for any such woman, or advise or procure such woman to take any medicine, drug, or anything whatsoever, with intent thereby to procure the miscarriage of such woman, or to injure or destroy such woman, or shall use any instrument or application for any of the above purposes, he shall be guilty of a felony, and shall be imprisoned in the jail or State's prison for not less than one year nor more than five years and shall be fined, at the discretion of the court.

Source: The General Statutes of North Carolina.

THE LEGAL PROHIBITION OF CONTRACEPTION

Effective use of contraceptives makes abortion unnecessary. But birth control methods have been considered immoral or prohibited by law for much of our history. State and national laws against contraception not only prevented their use as a means of family limitation, but also inhibited research that would lead to safe and effective methods of birth control.

In 1873 the United States Congress passed a law forbidding the use of the U.S. mails for the distribution of obscene literature or anything intended for the prevention of contraception or for abortion. This law, usually referred to as the Comstock Act, was named after Anthony Comstock (1844–1915), who led a nineteenth-century crusade against obscene literature and other items that he thought contributed to vice and crime. The Comstock Act did not forbid contraception directly, but it allowed states with anti-contraception laws to secure their borders against the shipment of contraceptive devices or information from out of state. The bootlegging and sale of these devices—completely unregulated, and often unsafe or ineffective—was common.

The motives that lay behind the passage of anti-contraceptive laws were similar to those that produced anti-abortion legislation. Advocates of both types of laws were concerned about sexual promiscuity and its effect on national virtue, as well as about the declining birthrates. Not only did we need a growing, thriving population to compete in the world, but the use of abortion and contraception by upper- and upper-middle-class families was thought to mean that the poor, immigrants, and African Americans would soon outnumber well-to-do whites of Anglo-Saxon derivation.

In 1934 Congress held hearings on a bill to amend the Comstock Act to allow doctors to prescribe contraceptive devices.

The testimony of Father Charles E. Coughlin before the Judiciary Committee of the House of Representatives during its 1934 hearings illustrates a number of the themes of the anti-contraception forces. Father Coughlin was a well-known and popular political figure and religious leader during the thirties and forties. A forerunner of the televangelists of the 1980s, he taught and preached in a regular radio program, broadcasting from the Shrine of the Little Flower in Dearborn, Michigan. A populist and a demagogue, much criticized for his extreme right-wing views, he had a tremendous following and was a force for politicians of the times to reckon with.

In his testimony Coughlin contends that marriage and sex are for purposes of procreation, not sexual pleasure; the availability of contraceptives will lead to illicit sexual activity. There are also racist themes in his speech. Coughlin believed that immigrants from southern and eastern Europe and African Americans bred faster than people of English and Irish stock, and that the latter had a duty to have children rather than to limit family size by using contraceptives. Population growth, according to Coughlin, is needed for economic reasons.

In his speech Coughlin refers to the theories of Thomas Robert Malthus (1766–1834) that population tends to increase faster than the food and goods necessary to sustain it. He also refers to one of the New Deal programs that was designed to raise farm prices by limiting production; farmers were paid to kill litters of pigs and to destroy crops by plowing them under.

Congress did not pass the amendment. State laws prohibiting contraception lasted well into the 1950s, and the Comstock Act itself was not repealed until 1971.

Margaret Sanger (1883–1966), a dedicated advocate of birth control, also testified before the committee. She believed that physicians should have the right to prescribe contraceptives and that laws forbidding contraception should be repealed. Sanger set up the first birth control clinic in the United States and helped organize international conferences on contraception. In her early experiences as a visiting nurse she had seen the tragic effects on women and families of uncontrolled childbearing. Chapter 7 of her autobiography, published in 1938, has been widely anthologized.

DOCUMENT 9: The Comstock Act (1873). "An act for the suppression of trade in and circulation of obscene literature and articles of immoral use."

That no obscene, lewd, or lascivious book, pamphlet, picture, paper, print, or other publication of an indecent character, or any article or thing designed or intended for the prevention of conception or procuring of abortion, nor any article or thing intended or adapted for any indecent or immoral use or nature, nor any written or printed card, circular, book, pamphlet, advertisement or notice of any kind giving information, directly or indirectly, where, or how, or of whom, or by what means either of the things before mentioned may be obtained or made, nor any letter upon the envelope of which, or postal-card upon which indecent or scurrilous epithets may be written or printed, shall be carried in the mail, and any person who shall knowingly deposit, or cause to be deposited, for mailing or delivery, any of the hereinbefore-mentioned articles or things, or any notice, or paper containing any advertisement relating to the aforesaid articles or things, and any person who, in pursuance of any plan or scheme for disposing of any of the hereinbefore-mentioned articles or things, shall take, or cause to be taken, from the mail any such letter or package, shall be deemed guilty of a misdemeanor, and, on conviction thereof, shall, for every offense, be fined not less than one hundred dollars nor more than five thousand dollars, or imprisoned at hard labor not less than one year nor more than ten years, or both, in the discretion of the judge.

Source: 17 Stat. 599 (1873).

DOCUMENT 10: Proposal to Amend the Comstock Act to Allow Doctors to Prescribe Contraceptives. Testimony Opposing the Amendment by Father Charles E. Coughlin, 1934

Were I on the board of birth control, I imagine I would rather focus my mind on solving not how to eradicate poverty by birth control, but to eradicate poverty by getting rid of *birth control of money*. That is the bet they have overlooked, and their voices have been silent in the face of the greatest catastrophe that ever faced the country, and they have gone back to paste down the pages of Malthusianism. . . .

But today, believing as a Christian, not only as a Catholic but a Presbyterian, a Baptist, a Lutheran, an Episcopalian, and all the other sects of Christianity, believing that marriage was invented by God for what purpose? For the primary purpose of procreation and educating children. I still think there is enough intelligence in the married man and the married woman of our land to consider that matrimony is not simply a legalized bed of prostitution, and consider that matrimony means something more than every man and woman to live like two animals. Surely Christianity has taken that into consideration. They want a man and a woman to be married before there is such a thing as conception, before there is such a thing as birth; and after marriage they want a man to so love his wife that he does not make of her simply his play toy. It was not done before they were married and it is not done after they are married. . . .

I need not go further into that kind of argument. This bill here states, I repeat, that the Criminal Code shall be amended, implicating, gentlemen, that up until this date it has been considered a crime in this country to teach how to propagate, how to commit fornication and get away with it. That is all it means—how to commit adultery and not get caught.

You gentlemen who know something about our modern high schools know it is always a problem of those engaged in them to see that the boys and girls conduct themselves properly. We know how those contraceptives are bootlegged in the corner drug stores surrounding our high schools. Why are they around the high schools? To teach them how to fornicate and not get caught.

There is one more problem which will be brought out in specific manner later on. This is a big country of ours, sometimes referred to as a melting pot. Are you aware of the birth rate of the various elements forming the melting pot?

I happen to be of Anglo-Saxon extraction myself, and most of you gentlemen are all Celtic. From what I know of the figures that are published, we are on our way out. There is no question of it. We who boast of our English, Irish, Scotch, and Irish-Celtic origin are going to be boasters after a while of ancient history and not of modern practice.

It is our race, the Anglo-Saxon and Celtic, I believe, more than others, who are practicing birth control today. Negroes are not practicing it like we are; the Polish people are not practicing it as we are. The Italians are not practicing it as we are. One hundred years from today Washington will be Washington-ski, in the minds of the children to be born. We are being degenerated, and here we are advocating ways and means to uncriminalize the use of contraceptives and to help America forget its Anglo-Saxon origin.

How about the Negroes? The Negroes in one sense are more prolific people than we are.

I heard, I believe it was Dr. Gillis, broadcasting one Sunday some figures on the advance of the Negro in the matter of begetting children. According to his figures, 100 years from now the white man of America will be an oddity. That is shocking to some of you, but go down to Texas, or to New Orleans in Louisiana, and find out for yourself.

Perhaps the Negro deserves to go ahead, perhaps he does, with the advocacy among the whites to curtail the birth of children, and the Negroes' outbegetting us almost 2 to 1.

Some day Congress, a hundred years from now, would look back to the Seventy-third Congress and say, "Yes; they helped all this along."

The half hour that was at my disposal simply to introduce this subject has elapsed. I have not attempted to give one figure; abler people than I are about to follow with that.

The problem is one of, perhaps, economics; but I believe that as we are told, that we in America will reach our apex in production, manpower production, within the next 30 years, and I believe then that we, too, shall be facing the problem of the rise of death over the birth rate, and instead of encouraging the solution of an economic problem by prevention as Malthus advocated, let's turn our minds and our hearts to the greater problem of seeing how the working man gets enough so that he and his wife and a decent family can live.

That is the problem of this Congress, and let us turn our minds upon the solution of the question how we can prevent millions of dollars going into the hands of a few men, and how we can see that at least a few millions can find their way into the hands of our farmers and laborers.

That is the greater problem of the hour. It is to keep poverty, not by committing suicide, it is to meet poverty by putting the wherewithal, in this great land where we have too much to eat, too much to wear, too many houses of shelter, yet have want in the midst of plenty, so that Malthusianism has now become birth control of pigs, birth control of cotton, birth control of wheat. That is not the problem; let us have the wheat, the cotton, the pigs and the rest of it, but let us have more Americans; let us have more Americans to the extent that we can still be Christians, to increase and multiply according to reason, according to nature, according to a regulation that is in the heart of man, and not in a bottle in a drug store.

Source: U.S. Congress, House Committee on the Judiciary, *Hearings on Birth Control*, 73rd Congress, 2d session, January 18, 19, 1934, pp. 126–30.

DOCUMENT 11: "The Turbid Ebb and Flow of Misery." Margaret Sanger's Autobiography, 1938

During these years in New York trained nurses were in great demand. Few people wanted to enter hospitals; they were afraid they might be "practiced" upon, and consented to go only in desperate emergencies. Sentiment was especially vehement in the matter of having babies. A woman's own bedroom, no matter how inconveniently arranged, was the usual place for her lying-in. I was not sufficiently free from domestic duties to be a general nurse, but I could ordinarily manage obstetrical cases because I was notified far enough ahead to plan my schedule. And after serving my two weeks I could get home again.

Sometimes I was summoned to small apartments occupied by young clerks, insurance salesmen, or lawyers, just starting out, most of them under thirty and whose wives were having their first or second baby. They were always eager to know the best and latest method in infant care and feeding. In particular, Jewish patients, whose lives centered around the family, welcomed advice and followed it implicitly.

But more and more my calls began to come from the Lower East Side, as though I were being magnetically drawn there by some force outside my control. I hated the wretchedness and hopelessness of the poor, and never experienced that satisfaction in working among them that so many noble women have found. My concern for my patients was now quite different from my earlier hospital attitude. I could see that much was wrong with them which did not appear in the physiological or medical diagnosis. A woman in childbirth was not merely a woman in childbirth. My expanded outlook included a view of her background, her potentialities as a human being, the kind of children she was bearing, and what was going to happen to them.

The wives of small shopkeepers were my most frequent cases, but I had carpenters, truck drivers, dishwashers, and pushcart vendors. I admired intensely the consideration most of these people had for their own. Money to pay doctor and nurse had been carefully saved months in advance—parents-in-law, grandfathers, grandmothers, all contributing.

As soon as the neighbors learned that a nurse was in the building they came in a friendly way to visit, often carrying fruit, jellies, or gefüllter fish made after a cherished recipe. It was infinitely pathetic to me that they, so poor themselves, should bring me food. Later they drifted in again with the excuse of getting the plate, and sat down for a nice talk; there was no hurry. Always back of the little gift was the question, "I am pregnant (or my daughter, or my sister is). Tell me something to keep from having another baby. We cannot afford another yet."

I tried to explain the only two methods I had ever heard of among the middle classes, both of which were invariably brushed aside as unacceptable. They were of no certain avail to the wife because they placed the burden of responsibility solely upon the husband—a burden which he seldom assumed. What she was seeking was self-protection she could herself use, and there was none.

Below this stratum of society was one in truly desperate circumstances. The men were sullen and unskilled, picking up odd jobs now and then, but more often unemployed, lounging in and out of the house at all hours of the day and night. The women seemed to slink on their way to market and were without neighborliness.

These submerged, untouched classes were beyond the scope of organized charity or religion. No labor union, no church, not even the Salvation Army reached them. They were apprehensive of everyone and rejected help of any kind, ordering all intruders to keep out; both birth and death they considered their own business. Social agents, who were just beginning to appear, were profoundly mistrusted because they pried into homes and lives, asking questions about wages, how many were in the family, had any of them ever been in jail. Often two or three had been there or were now under suspicion of prostitution, shoplifting, purse snatching, petty thievery, and, in consequence, passed furtively by the big blue uniforms on the corner.

The utmost depression came over me as I approached this surreptitious region. Below Fourteenth Street I seemed to be breathing a different air, to be in another world and country where the people had habits and customs alien to anything I had ever heard about.

There were then approximately ten thousand apartments in New York into which no sun ray penetrated directly; such windows as they had opened only on a narrow court from which rose fetid odors. It was seldom cleaned, though garbage and refuse often went down into it. All these dwellings were pervaded by the foul breath of poverty, that moldy, indefinable, indescribable smell which cannot be fumigated out, sickening to me but apparently unnoticed by those who lived there. When I set to work with antiseptics, their pungent sting, at least temporarily, obscured the stench.

I remember one confinement case to which I was called by the doctor of an insurance company. I climbed up the five flights and entered the airless rooms, but the baby had come with too great speed. A boy of ten had been the only assistant. Five flights was a long way; he had wrapped the placenta in a piece of newspaper and dropped it out the window into the court.

Many families took in "boarders," as they were termed, whose small contributions paid the rent. These derelicts, wanderers, alternately working and drinking, were crowded in with the children; a single room sometimes held as many as six sleepers. Little girls were accustomed to dressing and undressing in front of the men, and were often violated, occasionally by their own fathers or brothers, before they reached the age of puberty.

Pregnancy was a chronic condition among the women of this class. Suggestions as to what to do for a girl who was "in trouble" or a married woman who was "caught" passed from mouth to mouth—herb teas, turpentine, steaming, rolling downstairs, inserting slippery elm, knitting needles, shoe-hooks. When they had word of a new remedy they hurried to the drugstore, and if the clerk were inclined to be friendly he might say, "Oh, that won't help you, but here's something that may." The younger druggists usually refused to give advice because, if it were to be known, they would come under the law; midwives were even more fearful. The doomed women implored me to reveal the "secret" rich people had, offering to pay me extra to tell them; many really believed I was holding back information for money. They asked everybody and tried anything, but nothing did them any good. On Saturday nights I have seen groups of from fifty to one hundred with their shawls over their heads waiting outside the office of a five-dollar abortionist.

Each time I returned to this district, which was becoming a recurrent nightmare, I used to hear that Mrs. Cohen "had been carried to a hospital, but had never come back," or that Mrs. Kelly "had sent the children to a neighbor and had put her head into the gas oven." Day after day such tales were poured into my ears—a baby born dead, great relief—the death of an older child, sorrow but again relief of a sort—the story told a thousand times of death from abortion and children going into institutions. I shuddered with horror as I listened to the details and studied the reasons back of them—destitution linked with excessive childbearing. The waste of life seemed utterly senseless. One by one worried, sad, pensive, and aging faces marshaled themselves before me in my dreams, sometimes appealingly, sometimes accusingly.

These were not merely "unfortunate conditions among the poor" such as we read about. I knew the women personally. They were living, breathing, human beings, with hopes, fears, and aspirations like my own, yet their weary, misshapen bodies, "always ailing, never failing," were destined to be thrown on the scrap heap before they were thirty-five. I could not escape from the facts of their wretchedness; neither was I able to see any way out. My own cozy and comfortable family existence was becoming a reproach to me.

Then one stifling mid-July day of 1912 I was summoned to a Grand Street tenement. My patient was a small, slight Russian Jewess, about twenty-eight years old, of the special cast of feature to which suffering lends a madonna-like expression. The cramped three-room apartment was in a sorry state of turmoil. Jake Sachs, a truck driver scarcely older than his wife, had come home to find the three children crying and her unconscious from the effects of a self-induced abortion. He had called the nearest doctor, who in turn had sent for me. Jake's earnings were trifling, and most of them had gone to keep the none-too-strong children clean and properly fed. But his wife's ingenuity had helped them to save a little, and this he was glad to spend on a nurse rather than have her go to a hospital.

The doctor and I settled ourselves to the task of fighting the septicemia. Never had I worked so fast, never so concentratedly. The sultry days and nights were melted into a torpid inferno. It did not seem possible there could be such heat, and every bit of food, ice, and drugs had to be carried up three flights of stairs.

Jake was more kind and thoughtful than many of the husbands I had encountered. He loved his children, and had always helped his wife wash and dress them. He had brought water up and carried garbage down before he left in the morning, and did as much as he could for me while he anxiously watched her progress.

After a fortnight Mrs. Sachs' recovery was in sight. Neighbors, ordinarily fatalistic as to the results of abortion, were genuinely pleased that she had survived. She smiled wanly at all who came to see her and thanked them gently, but she could not respond to their hearty congratulations. She appeared to be more despondent and anxious than she should have been, and spent too much time in meditation.

At the end of three weeks, as I was preparing to leave the fragile patient to take up her difficult life once more, she finally voiced her fears, "Another baby will finish me, I suppose?"

"It's too early to talk about that," I temporized.

But when the doctor came to make his last call, I drew him aside. "Mrs. Sachs is terribly worried about having another baby."

"She well may be," replied the doctor, and then he stood before her and said, "Any more such capers, young woman, and there'll be no need to send for me."

"I know, doctor," she replied timidly, "but," and she hesitated as though it took all her courage to say it, "what can I do to prevent it?"

The doctor was a kindly man, and he had worked hard to save her, but such incidents had become so familiar to him that he had long since lost whatever delicacy he might once have had. He laughed good-naturedly. "You want to have your cake and eat it too, do you? Well, it can't be done."

Then picking up his hat and bag to depart he said, "Tell Jake to sleep on the roof."

I glanced quickly at Mrs. Sachs. Even through my sudden tears I could see stamped on her face an expression of absolute despair. We simply looked at each other, saying no word until the door had closed behind the doctor. Then she lifted her thin, blue-veined hands and clasped them beseechingly. "He can't understand. He's only a man. But you do, don't you? Please tell me the secret, and I'll never breathe it to a soul. *Please!*"

What was I to do? I could not speak the conventionally comforting phrases which would be of no comfort. Instead, I made her as physically easy as I could and promised to come back in a few days to talk with her again. A little later, when she slept, I tiptoed away.

Night after night the wistful image of Mrs. Sachs appeared before me. I made all sorts of excuses to myself for not going back. I was busy on other cases; I really did not know what to say to her or how to convince her of my own ignorance; I was helpless to avert such monstrous atrocities. Time rolled by and I did nothing.

The telephone rang one evening three months later, and Jake Sachs' agitated voice begged me to come at once; his wife was sick again and from the same cause. For a wild moment I thought of sending someone else, but actually, of course, I hurried into my uniform, caught up my bag, and started out. All the way I longed for a subway wreck, an explosion, anything to keep me from having to enter that home again.

But nothing happened, even to delay me. I turned into the dingy doorway and climbed the familiar stairs once more. The children were there, young little things.

Mrs. Sachs was in a coma and died within ten minutes. I folded her still hands across her breast, remembering how they had pleaded with me, begging so humbly for the knowledge which was her right. I drew a sheet over her pallid face. Jake was sobbing, running his hands through his hair and pulling it out like an insane person. Over and over again he wailed, "My God! My God! My God!"

I left him pacing desperately back and forth, and for hours I myself walked and walked and walked through the hushed streets. When I finally arrived home and let myself quietly in, all the household was sleeping. I looked out my window and down upon the dimly lighted city. Its pains and griefs crowded in upon me, a moving picture rolled before my eyes with photographic clearness: women writhing in travail to bring forth little babies; the babies themselves naked and hungry, wrapped in newspapers to keep them from the cold; six-year-old children with pinched, pale, wrinkled faces, old in concentrated wretchedness, pushed into gray and fetid cellars, crouching on stone floors, their small scrawny hands scuttling through rags, making lamp shades, artificial flowers; white coffins, black coffins, coffins, coffins interminably passing in never-ending succession. The scenes piled one upon another on another. I could bear it no longer.

As I stood there the darkness faded. The sun came up and threw its reflection over the house tops. It was the dawn of a new day in my life also. The doubt and questioning, the experimenting and trying, were now to be put behind me. I knew I could not go back merely to keeping people alive.

I went to bed, knowing that no matter what it might cost, I was finished with palliatives and superficial cures; I was resolved to seek out the root of evil, to do something to change the destiny of mothers whose miseries were vast as the sky.

Source: Margaret Sanger, *An Autobiography* (New York: W. W. Norton, 1938).

SIGNS OF CHANGE (1940–1960)

After years of silence, discussions about abortion and related subjects began to take place in the 1940s. Articles appeared in medical and law journals. Doctors, psychiatrists, public health officials and lawyers held conferences on the subject. The National Committee on Maternal Health held a conference at the New York Academy of Medicine in

June, 1942. The subject of the conference was "The Abortion Problem." The American Psychiatric Association had a panel on "Psychiatric Indications and Contra-Indications to the Termination of Pregnancy" at its meeting in Atlantic City in 1952. A symposium, with papers contributed by physicians, psychiatrists, anthropologists, religious leaders and legal experts, was published in 1954 under the title of *Therapeutic Abortion*. In April, 1955 the Planned Parenthood Federation of America held a conference on "Abortion in the United States" at Arden House in New York. Forty-three men and women met for six three-hour sessions, and later reconvened for an additional day's meeting at the New York Academy of Medicine. The proceedings of this meeting were published in 1958 under the title *Abortion in the United States* by the medical book department of Harper Brothers.

One of the major concerns at all of these meetings was the fact that, in spite of laws in all states forbidding abortions, abortions were still being performed. In some cases the provisions in state statutes allowing abortion "to preserve the life of the mother" were being stretched to authorize hospital abortions where the the mother had medical or psychiatric problems. Some doctors were performing abortions illegally in their offices. A few, who disapproved of abortion, sterilized their patients after performing the abortion—a practice that was illegal. And of course there were abortionists without medical training—some competent, some not—who operated on the fringes of society. The worst problems came from self-abortions; women who tried to abort themselves often ended up in the hospital with serious internal injuries. Many of them died. Both the medical and the legal picture were unacceptable.

Dr. Mary S. Calderone, the Medical Director of the Planned Parenthood Federation of America, edited the proceedings of the 1954 conference. She later summed up the work of the conference in a paper given to the Maternal and Child Health Section of the American Public Health Association.

She reported that the conferees had found that there was a need for more reliable information concerning the whole abortion picture, and had urged public health departments to collect such information. They recommended that counseling centers be set up for women seeking abortions—to allow them to discuss their problems, to explore alternatives to abortion, and to determine whether they were actually pregnant. The conferees also believed that abortion should be available on a more equal basis. Well-educated and financially privileged women could find doctors willing to exploit exceptions in the law and authorize hospital abortions, while less-advantaged women went to untrained abortionists or tried to abort themselves. There was a need for better sex information, better information about and access to contraception, and a more responsible approach to pregnancy. The conference also recommended reform of state abortion laws.

DOCUMENT 12: Illegal Abortion as a Public Health Problem. Dr. Mary Steichen Calderone, 1960

In the 22nd edition of the "American Illustrated Medical Dictionary," disease is defined as "any departure from the state of health, an illness or a sickness; most specifically, a definite morbid process having a characteristic train of symptoms. It may affect the whole body or any of its parts, and its etiology, pathology and prognosis may be known or unknown." . . .

Thus in calling illegal abortion a disease of society, I point to the very existence of illegal abortion as a departure from a state of total health of that society. It is a morbid process in the social structure, having a characteristic train of symptoms. It does indeed affect the whole body of society or any of its parts, namely, individuals. As its etiology, pathology, and epidemiology are only partially known, its prognosis, prevention, and treatment can for the most part, therefore, only be guessed at. . . .

However, in 1955 it was exhaustively contemplated by 43 men and women from the various disciplines of obstetrics, psychiatry, public health, sociology, forensic medicine, and law and demography, who were uneasy enough about this dis-ease to sit down for eight, three-hour sessions in an effort to bring it into realistic focus. The proceedings and conclusions of this conference were published in book form in 1958. Here are some of the facts established.

Fact No. 1—In 46 states legal abortion is permitted to preserve the life of the mother; three states allow, in addition, preservation of the health of the mother. Thus in the other states[1] such abortions as are being performed legally, that is, therapeutic abortions, are for the most part being done on the word of psychiatrists that the unwilling mother will otherwise commit suicide. This procedure has developed because medically speaking, that is, from the point of view of diseases of the various systems, cardiac, genitourinary, and so on, it is hardly ever necessary today to consider the life of a mother as threatened by a pregnancy. However, and this is a big however, interpretation of the law varies from city to city within a state.

---

[1]Alaska and Hawaii were not then states.

Fact No. 2—Interpretation of the law also varies between hospitals within a city and between services in the same hospital, because the legal therapeutic abortion rate is higher on private services than on ward services. A public health official put this pointed question at the conference: "Why is there such a difference in the incidence of the therapeutic abortion by hospitals? Is the woman in a public hospital healthier than a woman on a private service in a voluntary hospital or in one voluntary hospital as against another one?" The second fact to be established, therefore, is that the border zone between legal and illegal abortion is narrow and shifts frequently, depending on personnel and locale. Indeed, as one participant bluntly put it: "I would like to call attention to the artifact of distinction between illegal and therapeutic abortion. Actually, according to my definition, in many circumstances the difference between the one and the other is $300 and knowing the right person." So much for fact number two.

From the first two facts it becomes clear that the interpretation of legality is probably in the eye of the beholder. What we have to admit is, as was repeatedly emphasized, that most therapeutic abortions are in the strictest sense of the law actually illegal.

Fact No. 3—Abortion is no longer a dangerous procedure. This applies not just to therapeutic abortions as performed in hospitals but also to so-called illegal abortions as done by physicians. In 1957 there were only 260 deaths in the whole country attributed to abortions of any kind. In New York City in 1921 there were 144 abortion deaths, in 1951 there were only 15; and, while the abortion death rate was going down so strikingly in that 30-year period, we know what happened to the population and the birth rate. Two corollary factors must be mentioned here: first, chemotherapy and antibiotics have come in, benefiting all surgical procedures as well as abortion. Second, and even more important, the conference estimated that 90 per cent of all illegal abortions are presently being done by physicians. Call them what you will, abortionists or anything else, they are still physicians, trained as such; and many of them are in good standing in their communities. They must do a pretty good job if the death rate is as low as it is. Whatever trouble arises usually comes after self-induced abortions, which comprise approximately 8 per cent, or with the very small percentage that go to some kind of nonmedical abortionist. Another corollary fact: physicians of impeccable standing are referring their patients for these illegal abortions to the colleagues whom they know are willing to perform them, or they are sending their patients to certain sources outside of this country where abortion is performed under excellent medical conditions. The acceptance of these facts was such that one outstanding gynecologist at the conference declared: "From the ethical standpoint, I see no difference between recommending an abortion and performing it. The moral responsibility is equal." So remember fact number three; abortion, whether therapeutic or illegal, is in the main no longer dangerous, because it is being done well by physicians.

Fact No. 4—Other countries are having significant experiences with illegal abortion. Take France first, a Catholic country, where no abortions and no contraceptive measures are legal. It is a country, however, whose citizens acting independently have lowered the birth rate by three methods. Two are contraceptive, namely, the use of the condom and withdrawal; the third is abortion. I have no figures on the mortality rate from abortions in France, but various opinions estimate that the ratio of illegal abortions to live births is approximately 1 to 1. Incidentally, France has a law that requires the reporting of all pregnancies to the police!

Next is Japan, a country whose over-population and use of land to the saturation point helped to spark the Second World War. Japan has attacked its high birth rate through a very strong governmental contraceptive program, with contraception available at 900 governmental health centers (the government's budget for family planning in 1958 was $600,000) and also by the legalization of abortion, which can be performed by most physicians at the nominal cost of two or three dollars. It has been estimated that the over-all abortion ratio there is the same as that in France, namely, one abortion for every live birth. In any event, Japan has succeeded in lowering its birth rate by 50 per cent. A young Japanese newspaperman tells me that last year, for the first time in years, there actually were empty seats in the lower grades of schoolrooms in Japan.

Next is Scandinavia: Its three countries have a more or less similar policy on abortion, with boards, carefully set up under governmental auspices, which consider all applications for abortion from the medical, psychiatric, and sociological points of view. In these countries abortion is allowed not only to preserve the life of the mother, but to preserve her health. The legal interpretation of preservation of health is broad, including as its does mental and emotional health and taking into account as it does socioeconomic pressures; eugenic factors, such as hereditary disease; and humanitarian pressures and emotional trauma due to pregnancies resulting from rape, incest, or extreme youth of the mother. Interestingly enough, even with these provisions and with contraception broadly available, Norway, Denmark, and Sweden still admit to some illegal abortions. So fact number four points up that women who are unwillingly pregnant will obtain an abortion, whether legally or illegally as in Scandinavia, or illegally as in a completely closed system, such as in France.

Fact No. 5—Brings us home to the United States, where it is clear that women, unwillingly pregnant women, are also obtaining abortions. These women are as often married as unmarried, more often white than

colored, more often of college level education than of high school education. They are also from all religious groups. Here, as elsewhere, the
difficulty lies in determining the incidence, because the groups for which
we have available statistical data are very restricted. The best statistical
experts we could find would only go so far as to estimate that, on the
basis of present studies, the frequency of illegally induced abortion in
the United States might be as low as 200,000 and as high as 1,200,000
per year. During the course of the conference, however, it was notable
that the figure of 1,000,000 abortions yearly, or one to every four births
in the United States, was advanced again and again by the various
participants. Fact number five, therefore, is that whether the incidence
is as low as 200,000 or as high as 1,200,000, nevertheless, we do have
an illegal abortion problem.

Should public health people look upon it as a problem? Can they
shrug off even 200,000 invasions of pregnant uteri as of no medico-social
importance? But, one can say, only 260 deaths from all types of abortions—that is a low mortality rate. Why should illegal abortion be a
public health problem?

The answer is that we have passed the stage where public health
concerns itself only with death rates. The World Health Organization's
definition of health is that it is "a state of complete physical, mental and
social well-being and not merely the absence of disease." Remember the
French roots of the word dis-ease and the definition, "any departure
from a state of health that can affect the whole body or any of its parts."
As public health people, we are interested in the whole body, that is,
in society. We are also interested in the whole body of the individual
who is a part of society. Here are some of the symptoms of this disease
of society, illegal abortion.

First, medical indecision regarding the interpretation of the law: We
do not have that kind of indecision concerning permissible bacteria
counts above which milk or drinking water are not considered safe. One
can interpret the law in only one way as far as most public health
measures are concerned, but the interpretation of the law regarding
abortion depends upon who is interpreting it and how far he is willing
to go. Indeed, the conference participants recognized that "present laws
and mores have not served to control the practice of illegal abortion"
and they felt that "to keep on the books unchallenged, laws that do not
receive public sanction and observance is of questionable service to our
society."

A second symptom, inequity of application of a medical procedure:
Remember the woman with $300 who knows the right person and is
successful in getting herself legally aborted on the private service of a
voluntary hospital, in contrast to her poorer, less influential sister on
the ward service of the same hospital or in a public hospital in the same

city, a woman in exactly the same physical and mental state as the first one—whose application is turned down?

A third symptom, inconsistency of application: Even with $300 a woman applying at one hospital may be turned down and go to another hospital in the same city where, with the right combination of medical opinions, she may obtain a legal abortion. Is this sound medicine, soundly practiced?

Another symptom, and probably the worst of all, the quasi-legal subterfuges and hypocrisies that must be undertaken by an honest and concerned medical man when he wants to provide his patient with a procedure that in his best medical judgment is indicated.

And last but not least, as a symptom of a disease of our whole social body, the frightening hush-hush, the cold shoulders, the closed doors, the social ostracism and punitive attitude toward those who are greatly in need of concrete help and sympathetic understanding, the unwillingly pregnant women of all ages, both married and unmarried. . . . We should move into this area of concern in several ways.

First, in the prevention of the need for abortions we can do one obvious thing, make sure that means of regulating parenthood are available to every woman in every maternal health service. . . . Making contraceptive advice freely available to all who desire it was one of the recommendations of the conference. The Model Penal Code of the American Law Institute states in its May, 1959, draft that "the restrictions which society places on the distribution of contraceptive . . . information are themselves contributors to the abortion problem."

Another recommendation of the conference: "Encouragement, through early, continued and realistic sex education, of higher standards of sexual conduct and of a greater sense of responsibility toward pregnancy."

A third area, however, could be of real significance. Remembering that a disease that is concealed can never be cured, I would like to enlist public health in an effort to establish better figures on the incidence of illegal abortion. Actually, of course, we know that the nature of this problem is such that one will never get accurate ex post facto figures. We will never find out how many illegal abortions have been performed, but how about trying to find out how many are being asked for? Suppose requests for abortion were made reportable? Why not? Suppose that every time a woman comes to a doctor asking for an abortion, he makes a note of it along with some easily obtained information and sends this note to his health officer. Suppose that after a few such efforts, physicians discovered that the sky did not fall in on them in the person of the law and that the privacy of their patients was being respected. At the end of two or three years we might really know something about this disease of society. . . .

Public health has always risen to the challenge of the unknown, the difficult, the seemingly unconquerable. . . . We should not now hesitate to acknowledge our responsibility even in an area so loaded with emotion and moralistic overtones as illegal abortion and sex education. Here at least we should be brave enough and responsible enough to provide whatever preventive measures are immediately available, while at the same time we should be curious enough to do such fact-finding as might give us a basis for possible additional means of control.

Source: American Journal of Public Health, Vol. 50, no. 7, July 1960, pp. 948–53.

PART I: FOR FURTHER READING

Abortion in Nineteenth Century America. New York: Arno Press, 1974. Reprints of early documents.

Browder, Clifford. *The Wickedest Woman in New York: Madame Restell, the Abortionist.* Hamden, Conn.: Archon Books, 1988.

Degler, Carl. *At Odds: Women and the Family in America from the Revolution to the Present.* New York: Oxford University Press, 1980.

Gordon, Linda. *Woman's Body, Women's Right: A Social History of Birth Control in America.* New York: Penguin Books, 1977.

Kennedy, David. *Birth Control in America: The Career of Margaret Sanger.* New Haven: Yale University Press, 1977.

Mohr, James C. *Abortion in America: The Origins and Evolution of National Policy.* New York: Oxford University Press, 1978.

Noonan, John T., Jr., ed. *The Morality of Abortion.* Cambridge, Mass.: Harvard University Press, 1970.

Reed, James. *The Birth Control Movement and American Society: From Private Vice to Public Virtue.* Princeton: Princeton University Press, 1978.

Shorter, Edward. *A History of Women's Bodies.* New York: Basic Books, 1982.

Tribe, Lawrence. *Abortion and the Clash of Absolutes.* New York: Norton, 1990.

Part II

The Abortion Reform Movement (1960–1972)

It is hard to say precisely what set the abortion reform movement in motion. State abortion laws had remained essentially unchanged since the nineteenth century, but by 1960 pressure for liberalization was building. As the population of the world increased and natural resources were used up, many people thought that it was imperative to limit population growth. Restrictions on birth control and an absolute ban on all abortions seemed to embody unreasonable governmental policies.

Indeed, many illegal abortions were taking place in spite of the prohibitions in state criminal laws. Physicians were dismayed at the toll in injury and death paid by women who went to illegal, unqualified abortionists. Women did not need to die during abortions; with existing medical technology abortion should be safer than childbirth. The medical profession, which had lobbied for strict laws against abortion in the 1870s and 1880s, was now willing to accept the idea that medically necessary abortions should be performed legally, in hospitals. Lawyers were also concerned, disturbed that so many people were willing to flout and disobey the law.

The women's movement emerged in the early 1960s, and abortion rights became one of the issues around which feminists could rally. Feminists contended that it was a woman's right to exercise control over her own body, and that government had no business interfering in private decisions by women and their families. Abortion seemed a necessary, if regrettable, solution to pregnancies where the fetus was likely to be abnormal, where pregnant teenagers were not ready for maternal responsibilities, or where a pregnancy was due to rape, incest, or some other devastating experience.

Public opinion seemed to be changing in ways that would support revisions of state abortion laws. A few bold reformers introduced bills in state legislatures to allow therapeutic abortions (abortions that were deemed necessary for medical reasons). These early reform laws were largely modeled on the American Law Institute's Model State Abortion Statute, which would allow abortions to be performed in hospitals under strictly regulated conditions. A number of European countries had laws of this sort, while the United States still retained one of the most restrictive systems in the world.

While some states were considering new legislation to change their abortion statutes, another type of reform effort began to take place. Women's organizations began to file lawsuits challenging the constitutionality of the older, strict abortion laws. Lawyers arguing these cases in court claimed that the older statutes denied women liberty and equality. The early 1970s saw a wave of reform activity, both in state legislatures and in state and federal courts.

As reform efforts escalated, those opposed to abortion began to organize and speak out. The Roman Catholic Church had a long history of opposition to abortion, and Catholic bishops encouraged the organization of Right-to-Life Leagues across the country. By 1970 Right-to-Life Committees were meeting in thirty-seven states, ready to lobby in state legislatures against bills legalizing abortion.

Abortion laws in the United States were much stricter than in other non-Catholic countries. Japan and some countries in Eastern Europe allowed abortion virtually on demand. Most western European states permitted abortions that were necessary to protect the mother's health. Reformers hoped that the states would move in the direction of the more liberal policies of other Western nations.

The Reformers

THE BAD OLD DAYS (1965)

Testifying before the Senate Committee on the Judiciary in 1975, Pamela Lowry described how counselors at Planned Parenthood of Massachusetts helped women seeking abortions go to Japan and England in the period before abortion was legalized.

DOCUMENT 13: Statements of Ms. Pamela Lowry, Executive Committee Member of NARAL and Director of Constitutional Defense Project, Massachusetts, Before the U.S. Senate. "This is the way things were ... in 1965."

Ms. LOWRY. I am here representing the National Abortion Rights Action League started in 1968. It is a group that is dedicated to protecting the right of choice for all women in the question of the bearing of children. It is a broad coalition group.

I think too often this issue is set up so people assume there are only two sides and both are extremist. But I think there are a large number of people who, while they are not particularly comfortable with abortion and not proabortion, are very strongly prochoice and therefore represent a very strong middle segment of society.

NARAL used to be called the National Association to Repeal Abortion Laws. Its purpose was to repeal restrictive laws across the country. Following the U.S. Supreme Court ruling, it seemed very clear that the name should be changed, that it was no longer necessary to assert any effort in legislative arenas concerning the right to choose; but we were very obviously wrong, and I think that is what brings us all here today.

I have been involved in this field, family planning, sex education, abortion, for about a decade. I started with the Planned Parenthood League of Massachusetts. I can remember on the first official day that I spent there as a staff member, August 1, 1965, the executive director went over and watched the Massachusetts general court defeat a bill which for the first time would have legalized contraception. The legislature voted to make it illegal for a physician to fit a diaphragm or prescribe pills or even give contraceptive advice to a 45-year-old mother. This was the way things were in that time.

Senator BAYH. When was that?

Ms. LOWRY. This was 1965. Just after the *Griswold* decision.

The legislature chose to ignore it, not because they as individuals opposed birth control. We could count the numbers of senators and representatives who voted against birth control whose wives we knew were on the pill. It was very clear this was a vote giving in to a very well organized, very vociferous religious lobby existing in Massachusetts, and known to exist there still.

Planned Parenthood concentrated on changing the contraceptive laws. What was incredible was, at that time, the fact was that it was easier to get a legal abortion in Massachusetts than contraception. Abortion was permitted under a restrictive [condition—] the life of the mother being imperiled. Yet her doctor could go to jail if he prescribed contraception for her. Our concentration was making birth control legal and available by changing the laws. Gradually change they did. People began to be less embarrassed to come forward to legal legitimate sources of information and medical help, and things began to open up.

I think it was inevitable that with this increased honesty and openness, somebody should eventually feel this might apply one step further.

In 1967 a young woman—I think she was about 27 years old—she was married, with one very young child, walked into the Planned Parenthood office and sat down and explained that, for her, it was too late for contraception. They had used a method, it had failed and she was pregnant. She knew that Planned Parenthood dealt with contraception, but could we help her, give her information, tell her where to go to get an abortion? Well, this threw the staff into a bit of a quandary. We did some research and within a week that woman was on a plane going to Japan. The only legal options open to her as a physically healthy person were to either go behind the Iron Curtain or to travel half way around the world.

After this incident we informed our medical advisory committee. They all lifted eyebrows, spoke with concern and felt that because this was an issue of great controversy, we should go very, very slowly on it. As soon as they got back to the offices, however, they went through patient registers and started referring people to us for trips to Japan.

I can appreciate the dilemma on the one hand feeling that it was something nice people weren't involved in, and on the other hand, feeling it was a great relief to have an out—for the patient.

So Planned Parenthood, much against its wishes, found itself involved in referring cases for abortion out of the country and around the world.

In 1968 the British changed their laws. They passed a fairly sweeping reform act. It was a very, very liberal law. The cost of going to London for an abortion was half that of going to Japan. For $800 you could get on the plane and go and get legal medical care. This opened up a tremendous—a flood gate of people who felt that they could somehow manage $800 and who came to Planned Parenthood for help and information.

I can remember some of the cases that came in. Most of them are generally a blur, and I am not sure how valuable it is to start talking about individual case histories. I am sure this committee has been hit with everybody's life story. There are a few who stand out. I don't know if you know Boston, but there was one woman from South Boston who came in. She had five children and was married, and she had never been outside the limits of Metropolitan Boston. The farthest she had gone was on the MTA up to Revere Beach. She had a morbid fear of flying. That woman got together her life sayings and put her five children in the care of her sister and flew off to London. It was an incredible thing to watch this happen. It was an incredible thing to watch these people come in the door and see how they had to pull their lives together and deal with this situation, and on top of it deal with restrictive laws at home. Even more frustrating, the ones who, when you said $800, sat there in utter silence and bewilderment, with tears in their eyes because there was nothing they could do. These were the people who went back out of that office and started the hunt for classic illegal abortions.

I will be honest. There were some half way decent, half way competent illegal practitioners around at that time. There was a licensed physician who was a surgeon and he worked out of Boston about 10 blocks away from a major Catholic maternity hospital. He charged $650. If you wanted an anesthetic it was an additional $100.

There was a man in Newton who I once saw who was also a licensed physician. He was an alcoholic and he drank during procedures in order to steady his hand; and so it went, down the rung of the people who weren't physicians and so on. It was a terrible kind of thing to witness.

People like me who had to sit and counsel them, and people across the country who came in contact with situations like this really felt moved to do something. You either had to get out of it completely and isolate yourself from the reality or do something to change it. This is how groups like NARAL got started with men and women across the country, with somebody who was trapped by the discriminatory laws who felt, "we have to change this, it just isn't fair."

One of the things we did in Boston was to get together a coalition of clergymen, social workers, psychiatrists, family planning experts and physicians and set up a group called Pregnancy Counseling Service which opened its doors the first month in 1970. This was 6 months before the New York law changed. In those months that Pregnancy Counseling Service operated, primarily as an information and referral center, it saw, before the New York law changed, 2,000 women. This was a fledgling operation, a fledgling organization, yet in the first 6 months, we saw 2,000 women from all across Massachusetts; women also came down from Maine, from Vermont, from Connecticut. Forty percent of those women in the pre–New York era went to London and had abortions there. Ten percent decided to continue with their pregnancy or had no option but to continue with their pregnancy. Ten percent got abortions under therapeutic laws that were beginning to loosen up in Massachusetts, California and Washington, D.C., although it cost more to go to California than it did to fly to London. Forty percent of that caseload went illegally or, as people say euphemistically, extra legally. With the advent of the New York law, it was extraordinary what a difference it made. Within 1 month there was not one more illegal case that came through the office. There was not one more trip to London.

Source: U.S. Congress, Senate Committee on the Judiciary, Subcommittee on Constitutional Amendments, *Hearings on Abortion*, Part 3, 1974, pp. 169–72.

THE NATIONAL ORGANIZATION FOR WOMEN

The National Organization for Women (NOW) was founded in 1966, but at first did not take a stand on abortion, fearing that the issue would divide its membership. But in 1967 the organization voted to include abortion in its Women's Bill of Rights. In later years NOW became a strong supporter of abortion rights and was an active participant in state and national political campaigns to keep abortion legal.

DOCUMENT 14: National Organization for Women (NOW) Bill of Rights. The Right of Women to Control Their Reproductive Lives. 1967

WE DEMAND . . .

VIII. The right of women to control their own reproductive lives by removing from the penal code laws limiting access to contraceptive information and devices, and by repealing penal laws governing abortion.

Source: Reprinted in Judith Hole and Ellen Levine, *Rebirth of Feminism* (New York: Quadrangle Books, 1971), Appendix, p. 439.

TWO REFORMERS: LAWRENCE LADER AND PATRICIA MAGINNIS

In 1966 a New York writer, Lawrence Lader, published a book entitled *Abortion*, one of the first accounts of the general abortion situation in the United States. As he continued to write and lecture on the subject he became involved in abortion "referrals"—referring women who appealed to him for help to competent doctors who were willing to perform abortions, even though they were then illegal.

During this period he met and worked with all of the people involved in the abortion reform movement and later wrote several more books on the subject. His 1973 book, *Abortion II: Making the Revolution*, is an insider's account of the campaign to change abortion laws. Lader was a founding member of ASA (Association for the Study of Abortion). He later served as chairman of the board of NARAL (National Abortion Rights Action League) and as president of ARM (Abortion Rights Mobilization).

This selection from his book discusses his own early involvement in the movement and his meeting with West Coast activist Patricia Maginnis, founder of the Society for Humane Abortion.

DOCUMENT 15: Inside the Reform Movement. Lawrence Lader, 1973

Until 1965, I had studied the system through academic research. Now I was to meet this anguish head-on. With the publication of my book and the start of radio and television appearances, the letters and phone calls increased. I was engulfed in misery. "I just don't know how long I can hang on," wrote a 44-year-old Iowa mother, supporting five children and a crippled husband on Social Security. "I am sure if I don't take an overdose of pills, I will lose my sanity."

"My husband got injured, and he can only do light work when he can get it, and I am the main support of my family of five," wrote a black mother from Florida. "Having lost my home, I had to move to a much smaller home, and if I lose this one, my family will be in the street."

A 41-year-old Minnesota mother described her third child, crippled by curvature of the spine, and her fourth, born mentally retarded and physically disabled. She had just started to work and pay off their large medical debts when she became pregnant again. "I feel like I'm drowning and no one will help me."

A 26-year-old New Jersey husband described how his wife "broke down uncontrollably during her fourth pregnancy" and "I was afraid at times to leave her alone with the children." A psychiatrist recommended abortion, but their doctor refused. During the next pregnancy, her husband heard a crash of glass from the bedroom. "My wife was kneeling down, picking up the sharpest pieces of glass. I grabbed them away from her. When I looked at her, tears were streaming down her face. She begged me to let her kill herself. I just held her tight and cried like a baby."

It seemed almost impossible to ignore these appeals. "There are two things that are more important than writing," Erik H. Erikson, the Harvard psychoanalyst, once said. "One is action, and the other is silence." I knew I could go on in no other way but action. Since almost every state law included penalties for helping a woman secure abortion, it implied considerable risk—constant surveillance, tapped telephones, possible arrest.

If my referrals were to have real meaning, they had to produce an open and massive confrontation announced constantly at every interview and broadcast so that women knew the secrecy of the abortion system had been cracked. They would have to become the rallying point of a movement, and give cohesion to women long isolated in lonely, secret compartments. Above all, they would put district attorneys and police officials on notice that the hypocrisy of the old laws was being challenged.

Strangely enough, I found, one becomes quickly immunized to personal risk, and even a phone call from the district attorney with a summons to the grand jury becomes a detail in the daily swarm of technical problems. The real challenge in the first few years was the volume of requests. Each interview or broadcast produced a wave of letters and phone calls. It would take much of the morning writing my answers, and since I refused payment, returning checks and cash that were often enclosed.

To protect my family from intrusion, I insisted on a letter of request, rather than a personal interview. But this could hardly deter women arriving unannounced at my door from Georgia or Indiana, often with no money for hotel or travel to another city, and desperate to find a New York doctor within the day. Nor could it prevent the phone calls in the middle of the night. A woman seeking abortion, understandably, loses all track of time, particularly of the time-gap between East and West Coasts. Somehow, long distance calls always arrived after midnight.

Perhaps the most complex factor was personal involvement. Women would call back to report that the doctor I had suggested was away or that they could not afford the doctor's price. I felt responsible for each case—admittedly dangerous since my own objectivity could be wrecked if each case became a personal torment. Yet I often had to spend hours on the phone, finding another doctor, pleading with a doctor to reduce his price, or simply searching out an inexpensive hotel room for a stranded applicant.

The greatest problem that first year was to find enough qualified physicians to perform in-office abortion. Dr. Spenser had virtually retired, and would only take an occasional case after insistent pleading. The few clues I had for potential doctors came from Paul Krassner, the incisive, satiric editor of *The Realist*, and through his editorial pages, probably the first proponent of open referrals. These clues got me past the first few months. Then a noted Southern physician, a man whose reputation I had known for years through his medical papers and lectures, volunteered to handle a dozen cases a week. Late in 1966, I met Dr. Vuitch, my principal outlet until his arrest.

Finally, I found an excellent medical group, organized by Louis Brown, a physiotherapist, in a New York City apartment. His staff included three or four doctors, each giving a few hours a day apart from their own practices, and thus able to accept more than fifteen cases a day. Brown and his wife developed a unique service. They met all out-of town patients at the airfield with their car, often took them out for lunch or dinner, and if a snow storm delayed their departure, or their cash was low, the Browns would house them without charge in their own apartment.

The top price of the Browns' doctors was $300—the same limit that Dr. Vuitch had accepted. They also agreed to take a reasonable number of indigent cases at half-price or without charge. Naturally, the Browns made money, probably $30 or $40 on each case. Still, these figures— and one must include the risks and legal fees that Vuitch and the Browns' doctors incurred after their indictments—were minimal compared to the standard $1,000 and up charged by many fashionable gynecologists at the time.

There was another factor underlying the strain of those early months— a simple matter of loneliness. I was closed off from everyone except my wife, who bore an immeasurable share of the load. The small New York group, known as the Association for the Study of Abortion, comprised lawyers, doctors, and other professionals who were uninterested in referrals or my confrontation thesis. While the New York Civil Liberties Union had taken a stand against abortion laws, it would be a year until its executive director, Aryeh Neier, telephoned me—a call I would always treasure—to offer any necessary legal defense.

Everything changed at the end of a cross-country trip of radio and television appearances in April 1966. In San Francisco I met Patricia Maginnis, President of the Society for Humane Abortion, the first woman to demand repeal of all abortion laws. It was like coming out of a dark tunnel. We talked for two days—at Fisherman's Wharf where the bay danced with the skimming, white sails of pleasure boats, at the Japanese tea garden in the public park, at her tiny disheveled downtown office where she slept on a blanket roll to save money, amidst mimeograph machines and stacks of pamphlets. We drank and talked, and I took a few hours off to appear on radio shows. . . .

Pat Maginnis was thirty-seven when I met her, a slender, almost frail woman with soft, brown eyes, and a hesitant, high-pitched voice that seemed to disguise the flamboyant campaigner who had already made abortion an issue on the West Coast. There was a hint of toughness, however, in the thrust of her chin. When she talked about abortion, her words rasped and stung. She had gone through three herself, the first by a doctor in Mexico, the last two using risky, self-abortive techniques she had learned during her hospital service with the Women's Army Corps. She had developed an infection and high fever, and put herself into a San Francisco hospital. "That's when you learn how they make terror part of the system," she said. "The hospital staff was more interested in getting me to talk to the police than curing me. The police love to hound women in abortion cases. They kept pounding me with questions—who did it? Where? What did it cost? When I insisted I did it myself, they said I was lying. After the doctors curetted me, they kept talking about a piece of fetal tissue and wanting to have it baptized. They assumed from my name I was Catholic. Of course, I was born one, but outgrew that long ago. When they asked about my religion, I told them I was a Buddhist."

About the same time I started my referrals in New York, Pat Maginnis decided that California abortion laws had to be challenged by direct confrontation. She went to Tijuana on the Mexican border and visited a dozen doctors performing abortions in small clinics—no more legal in Mexico than California, but long tolerated there by authorities. She put the best clinics on a mimeographed sheet with their telephone numbers and addresses, and began standing on the busiest street corners of San Francisco, handing them out to women. Although she insisted she was violating three sections of the Penal Code (Sections 274, 276, and 601 of the State's Business and Professional Code), no one arrested her. She even sent her handbills to the State Attorney General and local police officials, but continued to be ignored.

Finally, after reporters and broadcasters began covering her daily vigils on the street, a policeman stopped her on July 23, 1966, insisting she needed a permit. "Of course I don't need a permit," she told him.

"You're littering the streets," the policeman insisted.

She denied it. "I'm picking up every discarded leaflet, and handing them out again."

Still, she was arrested under Section 188 of the Municipal Police Code (distributing lewd and obscene literature), and released on bail. When the case came to trial on August 17, Municipal Judge Leo Friedman declared that the arrest should have been made under Section 601 of the State Code, which was not within his jurisdiction and Maginnis, therefore, was released. Further, he called Section 188 unconstitutional as a violation of free speech. Jubilantly she announced, "Now I can paper the town with leaflets."

She did nothing in a small way. In a few months, she had become the abortion gadfly of California, provoking arrests, rousing a storm in the papers and broadcasting media, making women aware that the Society for Humane Abortion could become the agent for their demands. She angered many, of course. That was her style: noisy and passionate. It was exactly what was needed from the first woman: to throw off all constraints and take her chances in the furnace of confrontation politics.

Source: Lawrence Lader, *Abortion II: Making the Revolution* (Boston: Beacon Press, 1973), pp. 24-28.

MOUNTING A CONSTITUTIONAL ATTACK ON STATE ABORTION LAWS

Some of the abortion rights partisans thought that court cases challenging the constitutionality of criminal abortion statutes might be a good way to overturn state abortion laws. Could a good case be made? Roy Lucas, a young law professor, thought that state statutes were vulnerable on a number of constitutional grounds. He outlined his argument in a long, technical article in the *North Carolina Law Review*;

an excerpt, printed below, gives a general picture of the case he thought could be made. This article was consulted by lawyers all over the country who were thinking of bringing abortion cases to court.

DOCUMENT 16: A Constitutional Attack on State Abortion Statutes. Roy Lucas, 1968

Existing abortion laws raise significant constitutional issues. The statutes sharply curtail a woman's freedom of choice in (1) planning her family size, (2) risking her physical or mental well-being in carrying a pregnancy to term, (3) avoiding the birth of a deformed child, and (4) bearing a child who is the product of rape or incest. Moreover, present abortion laws are (1) largely unenforced, (2) uncertain in their scope, (3) at odds with accepted medical standards, (4) discriminatory in effect, and (5) based upon the imposition of criminal sanction of subjective religious values of questionable social merit upon persons who do not subscribe to those values.

The constitutional issues implicit in the enactment and application of abortion laws have received scant judicial attention. Research discloses no significant test-case or other litigation attacking the constitutional power of a state to prohibit therapeutic abortion in circumstances not endangering the pregnant woman's life. Moreover, the literature of legal commentary appears to contain no in depth examination of the constitutional issues which might be raised. Numerous reasons can be advanced for the absence of discussion and litigation on this point. Abortion, unlike contraception, remains a subject of intense taboo intertwined in the maze of political silence, religion, life, death, and sex. In the constitutional context it is a problem bearing few factual similarities to any decisions in the 150-year expanse of pre-*Griswold* history. And in theological circles, abortion is hardly a subject for light philosophical speculation—on the contrary, it typically evokes at the outset emotional charges of "murder" and "immorality" which generally are not conducive to a full investigation of underlying issues.

Public attention is more easily directed to contraception as a sociological phenomenon than to abortion. Illegal abortion presently requires surgical apparatus and active physician cooperation. Moreover, it may create serious dangers to a woman's health which do not accompany the use of contraceptives. Also, a surgeon who performs an abortion in order to provoke a constitutional test case may not yet have the organized support which time has given to family planning by contraceptive means. To prescribe contraceptives was, for the physician, a far less active step of civil disobedience than to perform a therapeutic abortion is today.

At the time of ratification of the United States Constitution, a woman's right to abortion within the first 40 days of pregnancy was recognized at the common law. Ratification of the fourteenth amendment, moreover, served to protect the "fundamental rights" of citizens against state encroachment. Thus some foundation exists upon which a historical claim, however weak, might be built. Stronger arguments against the validity of present abortion laws may be found in current constitutional doctrines. A clear constitutional right to marital privacy has been developed recently by the Supreme Court although its exact scope is as yet uncertain [referring to *Griswold v. Connecticut*, 1965; see Document 36]. Also of potential applicability is the constitutional policy of protecting individual liberty from unduly restrictive state legislation. The fourteenth amendment prohibitions against discriminatory or unduly vague laws might also be employed to invalidate state abortion statutes. Within this framework, a constitutional attack can be launched.

Source: Roy Lucas, "Federal Constitutional Limitations on the Enforcement and Administration of State Abortion Statutes," *North Carolina Law Review* 46 (June 1968): 752-55. Footnotes omitted.

TASK FORCE REPORT ON FAMILY LAW AND POLICY:
American Women, 1968

While efforts to reform abortion laws were being pushed in state legislatures, some women were beginning to doubt that reform statutes would do much to improve their lot. Many of the proposed statutes permitted some abortions, but set up a maze of regulations that a woman would have to traverse before an abortion was allowed. Abortions were permitted only for certain conditions—usually if the health of the mother was at stake. Abortions had to be performed in hospitals, and a hospital committee of doctors had to approve the abortion. Well-to-do women might have the money and the know-how to buck the system, but most poor women would find the process too complicated and expensive.

A report issued in 1968 by the Task Force on Family Law and Policy to the Citizens' Advisory Council on the Status of Women—a citizens' group that had been set up by President John F. Kennedy to make recommendations on policies affecting women—came out in favor of the repeal of state abortion laws. Repeal would remove government controls and leave the decision whether or not to have an abortion up to the women involved. Note that the report emphasizes concern

about the population and the environment as well as about women's
rights. It cites the unreliability of contraceptives, and estimates that
only 15 percent of illegal abortions would be legal under the new
laws.

DOCUMENT 17: Personal Rights Relating to Pregnancy

A. LAWS PENALIZING ABORTION

1. Problem definition and context.

The world's population explosion is one of mankind's most crucial
problems.

It took from the beginning of man to 1830 to produce the first billion
people on earth. It took only 100 years (1830–1930) to produce the second
billion; the third billion took only 30 years, from 1930 to 1960; and it is
now estimated by demographers that it will take only 15 years, from
1960 to 1975, to reach a world population of 4 billion. Some demographers estimate that even if all people had only the number of children
they wanted, the population growth rate would be in excess of the needs
or the capability of economic resources to sustain life in an increasingly
industrialized urban world. From this perspective, long range population policy becomes a critical need in all countries in the world, yet few
have done anything toward developing such a national population
policy.

We must face the problem of how to stabilize the world population
growth rate. This necessarily involves the question of what women do
with their lives. Motherhood should not be the exclusive goal of women,
for this encourages the view that the more children, the better the
mother, as well as the view that no marriage is complete without a child.
Praise and social approval for women with large numbers of children
are no longer functionally appropriate to an urban crowded society. This
applies to economically well-to-do women as well as to poor women,
to women in the United States as well as to Latin American and Asian
women, to white women as well as to black women.

Abortion as an alternative to other contraceptive methods is now primarily the pattern in Catholic countries in which chemical and mechanical contraceptive devices have not been available, and in under-
developed countries which have not yet had widespread exposure to
the ideas of birth control. In France, the annual number of abortions
equals the number of live births. In Latin American countries, there is
an average of one abortion for every two live births. In some countries,

like Uruguay, the ratio is as high as three abortions for every live birth. Recent support for family planning has only begun to affect this high rate of abortion, and for many years to come, will serve only a minimal role in stemming the fantastic population growth of the South American continent.

The majority of the women who have been helped with contraceptive advice and devices in Asian countries are women who have already borne five or more children, and hence already have contributed dangerously to the growth rate of their countries.

While it is extremely difficult to assess the incidence of illegal abortions in the United States, estimates range from 250,000 to over a million annually. The vast majority of these cases are married women who have attained the number of children they wish or can afford to care for.

The development of more efficient contraceptives may gradually reduce the incidence of unwanted pregnancies, but we are a long way from this situation, for several reasons.

1. Not all women can use chemical or mechanical contraceptives for a variety of physical and medical reasons.

2. Not all women have access to contraceptive information and devices.

3. Even the pill, the most efficient contraceptive known to date, has a one percent failure rate. There are 25 million women in the United States between the ages of 15 and 44; only about 3 million of these women want to conceive in any given year, leaving 22 million women exposed to the risk of an unwanted pregnancy. Even if all these women could use the pill the failure rate of one percent could still yield as many as 220,000 pregnancies that were not wanted by the women. Research underway now toward the development of "morning after" pills is still a long way from realization.

The central ideology of the family planning movement over the past half-century has been the human right of a woman to determine the number of children she will have. This is also an important foundation for the ability of women to plan their lives to include active and meaningful participation in the world outside the family. In the United States, the family planning ideology has gained widespread acceptance, and most people would state as a corollary of this principle of human rights that every child should be born into a loving environment, a wanted child eagerly awaited by its parents. This is the most fundamental, best "head-start" a child can have, which no ameliorative head-start program, no adoption system for unwed mothers, no community mental health center, can begin to match. We must take the next step to the realization that no woman should be forced to be the unwilling parent of an unwanted child. The task force believes that it is from this perspective that any recommendation for abortion law reform should be viewed.

2. State law reform.

Forty-two States prohibit the performance of an abortion unless it is necessary to save the life of the pregnant woman (or, in the case of Connecticut, the life of the woman or the unborn child). In the remaining eight States (Alabama, California, Colorado, Maryland, Mississippi, New Mexico, North Carolina and Oregon) and the District of Columbia, abortions are permitted in certain other circumstances in addition to cases where abortion is necessary to save the woman's life. For example, Mississippi permits abortions where the pregnancy is the result of rape; California permits abortions where the physical or mental health of the woman is endangered, or in cases of statutory rape of a girl under 15 or where pregnancy is the result of forcible rape or incest. Colorado and North Carolina have recently enacted laws patterned after the American Law Institute's Model Penal Code, which would permit abortions in the following circumstances: continuance of the pregnancy would gravely impair the physical or mental health of the woman; the child would be born with grave physical or mental defect; the pregnancy resulted from rape, incest or other felonious intercourse, including illicit intercourse with a girl below the age of 16.

Bills to make abortion laws less restrictive were introduced in 30 States and were enacted in three (Calif., Colo., N.C.) in 1967. Mississippi amended its law in 1966. In 1968, Maryland amended its law to permit termination of pregnancies by licensed physicians in accredited hospitals, upon written authorization of a hospital abortion review authority, in situations where (1) continuation of the pregnancy is likely to result in the death of the mother, (2) continuation of the pregnancy would gravely impair the physical or mental health of the mother, (3) there is a substantial risk of birth of a child with grave and permanent physical deformity or mental retardation, and (4) the pregnancy resulted from rape. Under the new Maryland law, a licensed physician who performs an abortion in an accredited hospital is not subject to criminal penalty, but if he performs an abortion in violation of the new law, his license may be revoked or suspended under the same procedures for revocation or suspension of licenses provided for unprofessional or dishonorable conduct. (H.B. 88, approved May 7, 1968).

Even if all States enacted the provisions of the Model Penal Code, it is estimated that only about 15% of the illegal abortions would fall within the permitted classes of abortions and the remaining 85% of abortions (170,000 to 850,000 per year) would continue to be subject to criminal sanctions under State abortion laws.

The Task Force on Administration of Justice of the President's Commission on Law Enforcement and Administration of Justice stated in its report (*The Courts*, page 105):

> Abortion laws are another instance in which the criminal law, by its failure to define prohibited conduct carefully, has created high costs for society and has placed obstacles in the path of effective enforcement. The demand for abortions, both by married and unmarried women, is widespread. It is often produced by motives and inclinations that manifest no serious dangerousness or deviation from the normal on the part of the people who seek it. These factors produce the spectacle of pervasive violations but few prosecutions.

That task force concluded that "the time is overdue for realistic reexamination of the abortion laws."

From the experience of other countries it seems clear that what the law permits or does not permit in this area has little effect upon the incidence of abortion. When most abortions are illegal, women either resort to devious, exaggerated claims to obtain a legal abortion, or seek illegal abortions in secret and, for poor women especially, in medically unsafe conditions, or worst of all try to induce the abortion themselves. When abortions are legal, the incidence is about the same, the only difference being the greater health precautions followed in a hospital setting. Criminal abortion laws are generally not enforced and are indeed unenforceable, and when this is the case, it is wise "for the law to withdraw rather than have the majesty of the law brought into disrespect by open disobedience and unpunished defiance" (Robert Drinan, Dean of Boston College Law School, Washington Conference on Abortion, 1967).

Revision of State laws along the lines of the American Law Institute proposal would continue criminal penalties for some abortions while sanctioning others. The repeal of laws penalizing abortion may be more acceptable than the A.L.I. proposal to those who believe that all abortions are doctrinally immoral. As Dean Drinan stated:

> A system of permitting abortion on request has the undeniable virtue of neutralizing the law, so that, while the law does not forbid abortion, it does not on the other hand sanction it, even on a presumably restricted basis.

It may be noted that there is very little difference between Catholics and Protestants on attitudes toward abortion law reform and there is increasing support for liberalizing abortion laws.

Proposals which permit abortions under certain circumstances while penalizing all others deny the right of a woman to control her own reproductive life in light of her own circumstances, intelligence, and conscience. Although governmental agencies and the medical profession may offer service and counsel, they should not exercise the power of decision over the woman's personal right to limit the number of children she will have, and her right to decide whether to terminate a particular pregnancy she does not wish to carry to term.

Convinced that the right of a woman to determine her own reproductive life is a basic human right, the task force recommends that laws penalizing abortion be repealed and urges the Council to encourage the State Commissions on the Status of Women to assume responsibility for educating the public on this issue and in getting State legislatures to repeal criminal abortion laws.

The repeal of criminal abortion laws would mean that abortion would be treated in the same way as other medical procedures. It would mean that abortions could be performed by physicians without penalty and it would virtually eliminate abortions by unauthorized practitioners.

Source: *American Women, 1968*. Report of the Task Force on Family Law and Policy to the Citizen's Advisory Council on the Status of Women, April 1968.

FEMINISTS

Feminists across the nation agreed with the Advisory Council's recommendation (see Document 17). Lucinda Cisler was a co-chairman of the National Organization for Women's Task Force on Abortion. Her 1969 essay, "Unfinished Business: Birth Control and Women's Liberation," presented the case for repeal in much more colorful language than that in the Advisory Council report. It appeared in a collection of feminist essays, poems, manifestos, and other writings from what was called, at the time, "women's lib." The volume was entitled *Sisterhood Is Powerful: An Anthology of Writings from the Women's Liberation Movement.*

In the early days of the women's movement, small discussion groups gathered to exchange views on women's issues and politics. In the course of such discussions medical topics came up, and it became apparent that many women were dissatisfied with the treatment and information they were getting from (mostly male) doctors.

A Boston group, white, middle-class, some married, some single, began reading textbooks and medical journals and discussing their findings with friends who were nurses, doctors, and medical students. They worked the results of their research and discussions into a short course on women and their bodies. The material was later published in book form by a commercial publisher. The introduction to the book states, "Our bodies are the physical bases from which we move out into the world; ignorance, uncertainty,—even, at worst, shame—about our physical selves create in us an alienation from ourselves that keeps us from being the people that we could be."

For women who did not know what medical procedures an abortion involved, the section on abortion described the abortion techniques that were used in 1970. Of course, abortion was illegal in most states when the book was first published. The section on illegal abortions describes the life-endangering practices of unskilled abortionists.

DOCUMENT 18: Reproductive Rights and Women's Liberation. Lucinda Cisler, 1967

Proposals for "reform" are based on the notion that abortions must be regulated, meted out to deserving women under an elaborate set of rules designed to provide "safeguards against abuse." At least the old laws require only the simple, if vague, test of danger to life, whereas the new bills make it quite clear that a woman's own decision is meaningless without the "right" reasons, the concurrence of her family, and the approval of a bunch of strange medical men. Repeal is based on the quaint idea of *justice*: that abortion is a woman's right and that no one can veto her decision and compel her to bear a child against her will. All the excellent supporting reasons—improved health, lower birth and death rates, freer medical practice, the separation of church and state, happier families, sexual privacy, lower welfare expenditures—are only embroidery on the basic fabric: *woman's right to limit her own reproduction....*

Despite all this, the words reform and liberalization and modernization all sound as if they must stand for good things, and many people still confuse them with *repeal*: after all, repeal *is* a kind of reform in the broader sense. The media continue to get the two ideas mixed up and perpetuate the public's confusion. Public opinion polls have repeatedly posed the wrong questions in their samples ("In what circumstances would you allow a woman to have an abortion?") reinforcing the presumptuous notion that someone has a right to disallow a woman to choose, and getting the same tiny percentages "favoring liberalization," again and again. Usually they have not even offered repeal as an alternative choice. This is like asking, "Do you favor freeing a slave when his bondage is (1) injurious to his health, (2) ... ?", instead of asking "Can you justify involuntary servitude under any conditions?"

Source: Lucinda Cisler, "Unfinished Business: Birth Control and Women's Liberation," in *Sisterhood Is Powerful*, edited by Robin Morgan (New York: Vintage Books, 1970), pp. 276–77.

DOCUMENT 19: Having the Abortion

Timing

When the embryo is one month old it is a tiny mass of tissue with no resemblance to a human being. At the end of the first month the embryo is about the size of a small pea. By the end of the second month the growing embryo, by this time called a fetus, is a very fragile one-inch-long mass of differentiated tissue acting as a parasite within the mother's body. When the fetus is three months old it has attained a length of about five inches (Cherniak and Feingold, *Birth Control Handbook*).

The earlier the abortion is done, the safer it is for the woman and the easier it is on the doctor. Even doctors who will perform abortions willingly have some cutoff point, ranging from when the fetus takes clear human shape through the time (near 20 weeks) when the fetus moves (making abortion far more dangerous for the woman), to the time of "viability" (around 28 weeks), when the fetus could survive if born.

Medical Techniques for Abortion

Up to three days after unprotected intercourse. See ... information about the "morning-after pill."

Up to 12 weeks—*vacuum suction*. The suction method is now the most commonly used medical technique for the termination of pregnancy. The procedure involves the dilation, or opening, of the cervix. The cervix is dilated by passing a series of plastic or metal dilators, each slightly larger than the next, into the cervix. When the cervix is dilated, a sterile tube attached to a vacuum aspirator, is inserted into the uterus. The aspirator, working on the same principle as the vacuum cleaner, sucks up the fetal tissue from the uterine wall. The fragments are then drawn out and down the tube by means of the vacuum pump. This whole process rarely takes more than five to seven minutes. Except for the cramping of the uterus, the procedure is painless.

Up to 12 weeks—*dilation and curettage*. The suction method is now much more frequently used than the dilation and curettage, and is considered better because it causes less physical trauma to the uterus. However, some doctors who have been performing the D & C for years prefer to continue using this method. The procedure, which is done on women for various reasons including infertility, involves the dilation of the cervix and the scraping of the womb with a curette. The cervix is dilated by means of graduated dilators starting at 2 mm and proceeding to about 12 mm at 10 weeks' pregnancy and to 14 mm at twelve weeks'. The doctor uses the curette, a metal loop on the end of a long thin handle, to scrape gently the internal uterine wall, removing the fetal tissue with forceps. The patient is totally anesthetized, and requires from six hours to two days of recuperation, during which time there might be some bleeding.

12–16 weeks. In England during this period, doctors use a combination of the vacuum aspiration and D & C with forceps methods; the operation is over a hundred dollars more expensive. In the U.S. a woman should wait until she is 16 weeks' pregnant and can have a saline injection, because after 12 weeks the uterus tilts in such a way that it becomes difficult for the doctor to get all the fetal tissue out. Also, and more important, the uterine lining becomes so soft and spongy that the chance of the curette or aspirator going through the uterus increases, as does the chance of hemorrhage.

After 16 weeks—*saline injection.* With this method, a long needle passed through the locally anesthetized abdomen withdraws some of the amniotic fluid and replaces it with an equal amount of concentrated salt solution. Rarely do patients react unfavorably to the injection of the salt solution. However, if a woman should become hot and have cramps or a burning sensation in the pelvic area the procedure is stopped. The woman's head is raised; she is given water to drink. When the symptoms have subsided the procedure will be continued. Afterward the patient may complain of cramping and nausea. This kind of reaction seems related to minute quantities of salt getting into the abdominal cavity; it is easily treated and has no lasting effects.

Contractions will start some hours later. Generally they will be as strong as those of a full-term pregnancy. No general anesthesia is given, but Demerol or sleeping pills are administered. The salt injection is the simplest part of the procedure. The longest and most difficult part will be the labor. The breathing techniques taught in the childbirth section of this book might help make the contractions more bearable. After eight to fifteen hours of labor the fetus is expelled in a bedpan in the patient's bed.

Unmarried women under twenty are the largest group having saline abortions in New York. The experience may be painful and emotionally harrowing. It is essential that women going through this procedure have good counseling before, during, and after the saline abortion. (The above section is based on an unpublished account by Sonja Hedlund on saline abortions in New York City.)

After 20 weeks—*hysterotomy.* A hysterotomy may be performed if it is 20 weeks or more since LMP [last menstrual period] or if for some reason a woman cannot have a saline abortion or a D & C. In a hysterotomy the fetus is removed through a small abdominal incision, usually below the pubic hairline. This is major surgery, requires several days' hospitalization and convalescence, is therefore more expensive (at least $1,000), and often condemns a woman to Caesarian births thereafter. Although as major surgery the hysterotomy involves more risk, it does not affect a woman's reproductive system at all (unlike the hysterectomy, or removal of the uterus, with which it is often confused).

Methods of the Unskilled Abortionist

The dirty D & C. The D & C in the hands of hurried incompetents, with no anesthetics, no antiseptics, and dirty tools is frightening and dangerous.

The catheter method. Catheters are narrow tubes sold at drugstores for drawing off urine. The catheter is inserted into the uterus through the cervix, a dangerous procedure when attempted by an amateur. Germs introduced into the uterus by the catheter cause an infection. The uterus contracts, thereby "spontaneously" aborting the fetus.

The high douche. Forced douche or injection under pressure of such over-the-counter chemical agents as soap, turpentine, Lysol, vinegar, or lye will produce an abortion if the solution reaches the fetus or sufficiently irritates the uterus. Extremely dangerous.

Both the catheter method and the high douche work on the theory that an infection or dangerous substance will kill the fetus before it kills the woman. They can result in permanent disability or death.

Air pumped into the uterus. This method causes air embolism (air into the bloodstream) *and* sudden and violent death.

Self-induced Abortion

The most unskilled abortionist of all is the woman herself.

External means. Women try extremely hot baths, severe or prolonged exercise, violence to the lower abdomen, and various long sharp tools for self-mutilation. Some of these attempts are very dangerous. None of them work.

Drugstore abortifacients. The woman can also get from her "friendly" druggist a number of abortifacients which, all expensive, endanger her life to varying degrees and almost never work.

1. Soap-base pastes and douche solutions are among the most dangerous. Soap goes directly to the uterine veins to cause blood-vessel blockage, *shock*, and *death*.

2. Desperate women douche with almost any liquid they can think of, running the risk of severe burning of tissues, hemorrhage, shock, and death.

3. Suppository tablets of potassium permanganate, a caustic tissue-destroying agent that damages the vagina walls and can cause

massive hemorrhaging, ulcers, and infection, are sold despite an FDA prohibition.

4. Among the useless folk remedies sold are quinine pills and Humphrey's Eleven pills, which women take in massive, expensive doses (literally hundreds of pills) because once a woman who thought she was pregnant took some around the time when her period was due, and, lo and behold, her period came.

5. Women also take quantities of birth-control pills, which actually support the pregnancy if anything, and when used in this way, are suspected of causing genital deformity in the fetus.

6. Castor oil and other strong purgatives are used to no abortive effect.

Of the many thousand women in the United States who yearly get illegal abortions or try to abort themselves, between two and five thousand actually die. Thousands more spend time in the hospital with septic abortions, peritonitis, gangrene, air embolism, and other acute repercussions. Unknown numbers of them find themselves infertile later on when they want to plan a pregnancy. (At a 1969 abortion conference in Boston, sponsored by the Unitarian Universalist Women's Federation, it was disclosed that 10–20 percent of a local infertility clinic's patients had had previous septic abortions.) And many thousands of women escape from the frightening experience physically whole but with a new cynicism, and rarely acquire any better contraceptive techniques than they were using when they got pregnant.

Source: Boston Women's Health Book Collective, *Our Bodies, Ourselves* (New York: Simon and Schuster, 1973), pp. 144–49.

Catalysts

THE THALIDOMIDE SCARE AND THE GERMAN MEASLES EPIDEMIC

In 1962 a new drug, Thalidomide, was being marketed in Europe and widely prescribed as a tranquilizer. No one knew, at the time, that Thalidomide would cause serious birth defects if taken by pregnant women. The drug caused babies to be born without arms and legs, or with flipper-like appendages. Reports about the births of deformed infants reached Sherri Finkbine, a television actress, in Arizona. She remembered that she had taken doses of Thalidomide, which her husband had brought back from England, for morning sickness. Finkbine's search for an abortion in the United States was futile, and she eventually went to Sweden. Her experience alerted the Food and Drug Administration to the dangers of the drug, and it was banned in the United States. Newspaper accounts of Sherri's travail helped publicize the case for abortion reform.

A German measles epidemic that swept the country from 1962 to 1965 also put pressure on hospitals to allow abortions to prevent the birth of children with severe handicaps. Women who contract German measles during pregnancy run a great risk of having babies with serious birth defects.

DOCUMENT 20: Sherri Finkbine's Story

Three and a half years ago, while pregnant, I discovered that I had inadvertently taken a drug that would force me to give birth to a limbless child, a child as it turned out, that would be just a head and torso. Believe me the thought now years later, still frightens me. Faced with what at that time was an unfortunate choice, my husband and I decided what we considered under the circumstances to be the most humane course of action. We could not knowingly bring a grossly deformed baby into the world to suffer. Also, we had at that time four small children all under the age of seven to consider. What would giving birth to a grossly deformed baby do to their lives? I think any mother knows that the desire to protect her children is a very strong trait in a woman. We had no religious convictions that pre-ordained any answers for it. Newsmen later hounded me with the question: did I think the fetus had a soul? To tell you the honest truth, I had never even thought of it before. . . .

Bob and two other teachers took 63 high school students on a tour through Europe one summer, and at the trip's inception in England he felt the need for something to help him rest. The doctor in England gave him a prescription for some pills which he subsequently barely used as the pressures and responsibilities of the trip lessened. He carried them in his camera case all summer, and when he came home set them on a shelf in a kitchen cupboard. . . . One day I decided that if a tranquilizer could calm you down, why couldn't it calm down the queasiness of a pregnancy? Well, I was wrong. I take every blame for it. I know most doctors kill patients like me, but I took somebody else's prescribed medicine. Never did I ever dream that a little white pill could actually destroy potential life.

Not too many weeks after I started doing this I read on page 11 of our local paper a little, tiny wire-press story on England's desire to practice abortion on mothers who had taken what they called in the article a sleeping pill, or even more horrible, to practice euthanasia on the grotesque babies that were being born because of the drug. Well, I read it, my heart cried out in empathy and I thought no more about it. The next day a similar story appeared, still receiving no real dominance, but this time the drug was called a tranquilizer. Instantly, of course, I thought about those little brown bottles and asked my doctor to check them out. He sent a wire to the pharmacy, and I sat in his office, and he read the wire to me. He said, "Sherri, if you were my own wife I'd tell you the exact same thing. The odds for a normal baby are so against you that I am recommending termination of pregnancy." At that time it seemed very simple to me. He explained that from 16 to 25 therapeutic abortions were done every year in Phoenix. I had only to write a little note to a three-doctor medical board explaining my reasons for wanting the operation. I asked him what we could do if they didn't approve it, and he said "Don't worry, its already approved. I've spoken with them already." . . .

Naturally the thought came to me that if I'd obtained Thalidomide, others had done so. In fact, a contingent of Arizona National Guardsmen had been in Germany the whole past year. The Berlin Wall had just gone up the previous August, and the drug was first manufactured in Germany. It was this concern that made me pick up the telephone the next morning, Sunday, to call Ed Murray, the editor of the Arizona paper. . . .

Well, the paper kept its promise [not to use my name], but rather than merely an article warning of the drug, the front-page, black-bordered story screamed in bold print: "Baby-deforming drug may cost local woman her child here." That did it. . . . Bathed in the merciless glare of national publicity, the doctors cancelled the operation. . . . The surgery, they felt at that point, could be challenged by any citizen. Anyone could have gone to the prosecuting attorney—and the doctor, the hospital, and myself could face criminal prosecution no matter how noble or how right we felt our justification was. So the hospital board and the doctors and lawyers and everyone conferred. They felt the existing laws were so vague—what did "life" mean in the term necessary to save the life of the mother? So they decided that to gain judicial clarity the hospital would petition the State Supreme Court of Arizona for a declaratory judgment prior to doing this. . . . The case was dismissed in court without a hearing. . . .

We had thousands of letters from people giving all sorts of advice and offering an infinite variety of aids, some perhaps new even to doctors here. For instance, a man told me that for thirty cents I could get a dandy abortion—to go out and get a pint of agua ammonia, but dilute it, because, he said, "raw ammonia would loosen a rusty bolt in five minutes." And I can think of a great pun, which I won't give you. But he didn't say whether to drink the ammonia or sit in it, so I thought I'd better not try. A roller coaster ride was prescribed, and smelling turpentine fumes. A hypnotist from Berkeley claimed that he could hypnotize me into an abortion, over the telephone! A skydiver offered me the thrill of my life and a miscarriage as well. And these people were sincere. . . . There was advice of doctors to see in Beaverdam, Milwaukee, Georgia, Chicago, Los Angeles, Juarez, Puerto Rico, in practically every city, and you'd be surprised at some of the places that were recommended. A doctor from New York offered to do the operation for $1,500 in an airplane, thereby out of the state's jurisdiction, he said.

The actual horror of the situation was brutally compounded for me by the thousands of pieces of hate mail I received. . . . From Long Beach somebody told me, "I hope God punishes you for your murderous sin." A Chicago minister warned that it was his duty as God's holy prophet to inform us that God would pour his wrath upon us and our family if we failed to heed him. The letters that sobbed unbridled emotion always got to me. I'm sure you have all read the tragic diary told from the point of view of the unborn child whose mother has an abortion, and I received thousands and thousands of letters like this one from Arkansas. It said: "Mommy, please dear Mommy, let me live. Please, please, I want to live. Let me love you, let me see the light of day, let me smell a rose, let me sing a song, let me look into your face, let me say Mommy." . . .

When we found ourselves unable to get help in the United States we were forced to go overseas. . . . We then remembered a phone call that we had received from the medical journalist of Sweden's largest newspaper offering to arrange an appointment with a Swedish physician. Approval in Sweden is not automatic. They had granted 2,000 out of 4,000 requests the previous year. My husband and I would have two visits each with the social worker, two with a psychiatrist and I would see an obstetrician, and they spared him that interview. . . . Well, after a week's waiting that seemed like an eternity, the board did grant its approval. In retrospect, going through this complex procedure did, as the doctor predicted, prove for me to be a positive thing. I was also comforted by the very realistic attitude of the Swedish people. . . . A typical example of the Swedish attitude was expressed by my doctor after the operation. I made the mistake of asking him, as I had done so often in the past, was the baby a boy or a girl. He decisively stated that it was not a baby but an abnormal growth that would never be a normal child. . . .

If by speaking out against the drug I prevented even one baby from this type of birth and one mother from the heartbreak of seeing it born, then my hurt has been small indeed. Then, too, I hope that our case serves as a catalyst of sorts for abortion reform in our country.

Source: "The Lesser of Two Evils," in *The Case for Legalized Abortion Now*, edited by Alan F. Guttmacher (Berkeley, Calif.: Diablo Press, 1967), pp. 15–25.

CONCERN ABOUT POPULATION PRESSURES

Paul and Ann Ehrlich's *Population Bomb*, published in 1968, and a report sponsored by the Massachusetts Institute of Technology (MIT) entitled *Limits to Growth* expressed the concerns of environmentalists about the rapid growth of population. Both contraception and abortion were seen as playing a role in keeping the earth's population within limits. Organizations such as Planned Parenthood and Zero Population Growth supported the reform of state statutes making abortion a crime. Bob Packwood, Republican senator from Oregon and a strong supporter of reproductive rights, introduced two bills in 1970 that addressed some of the concerns about population growth. One of the bills would have removed tax exemptions from the third child (and subsequent children) born to a family. The other was designed to allow legal abortions in the District of Columbia—a subject over which Congress has the authority to legislate.

While Senator Packwood was worried about overpopulation, other countries were criminalizing abortion in order to spur population growth. In 1966, in Romania Nicolae Ceausescu, a Communist dictator made all abortions a crime.

DOCUMENT 21: Speech by Senator Bob Packwood (Republican, Oregon), Introducing Bills to Provide Tax Incentives for Family Limitation, and to Liberalize Abortion Laws in the District of Columbia, February 24, 1970

S. 3502—INTRODUCTION OF A BILL TO PROVIDE TAX INCENTIVES FOR FAMILY LIMITATION AND S. 3501— INTRODUCTION OF A BILL TO LIBERALIZE THE DISTRICT OF COLUMBIA ABORTION LAWS

Mr. PACKWOOD: Mr. President, in the past 9 months to a year, we have had a substantial amount of discussion about the environmental problems facing this Nation. I think every politician in this country is now on what we might call the environmental bandwagon. By that is commonly meant that we are all against water pollution, and we are all against desecrating our landscapes and ravaging our national forests.

But I think many of us have not faced up to the particular problem that is going to have to be overcome if we are to solve what we call the environmental crisis, and that problem is, basically, people.

Projections indicate that if our numbers continue to grow in this country as they have been growing, by the year 2000 we will have 300 million people in this country—almost 100 million more than the number we have today—and that not too many years thereafter, we can look forward to 400 or 500 million people.

The question is, Are we prepared in this country to face the problems created by 300, 400, or 500 million people?

I shall not contend that it would be impossible to feed 300, 400, or 500 million people in this country. It is not impossible if we do not care whether or not we overutilize the farmland, and if we ignore the effect the pesticides used on the crops to feed that many people may have on the rest of the country. It may not even be impossible to house them, if we do not care that it may be necessary to cut down all of the trees in our national forests and then deplete other natural resources that would have to be found as a substitute for wood to build that many houses. We might even be able to handle the solid waste disposal and the air and water pollution that 300, 400, or 500 million people would cause.

But at some stage, even the United States is finite. At some point we will reach a limit where we cannot handle, we cannot feed, we cannot house all of the people who can be born in this country.

I would rather that we face that problem now, and start to undertake a policy of national population restraint whereby we can look forward to limiting the population of this country by voluntary means, so that we do not have to, in 30, 40, or 50 years, look forward to limiting it by compulsory means.

Last year, the President, in introducing a request for a population commission, indicated that many of the problems that this Nation has faced in the past few years may be due to a rushing population increase, but that what we have had to face in the last 30 years is not by half what we will have to face in the next 30, unless we control our population.

It is for that reason that I have prepared for introduction two bills. One relates to the Nation as a whole, and the other relates to the District of Columbia. I ask unanimous consent that the texts of both of these bills be printed in the RECORD.

The PRESIDING OFFICER. Without objection, it is so ordered.

Mr. PACKWOOD. The first of these bills deals with tax incentives. It provides that, as of January 1, 1973, a family will be allowed a $1,000 deduction for the first child in the family, $750 for the second child, $500 for the third child, and nothing for any children after that. The bill will not apply to children in being prior to January 1, 1973.

The second bill relates to the abortion laws in the District of Columbia. At the moment, the abortion laws in this District are confusing, to say the least. One District judge has said that the abortion law is unconstitutional. Other District judges have not commented on it. The case is on appeal before the U.S. Supreme Court now, and we are left in a situation where no doctor knows whether or not he can legally perform certain types of abortions. If he does perform certain types that might be illegal under the present statute, and the Supreme Court were to reverse the district court case now on appeal before it, such physician might be guilty of a felony.

But be that as it may, if the Supreme Court were to affirm the present abortion decision, all that would do is say that the present law is vague and unconstitutional, and Congress would be faced with the problem, do we want to simply throw the law out, or do we want to try to draw it so specifically and definitely that it would not be vague, and therefore not unconstitutional?

I think Congress should take the lead in this field. I think Congress should pass a law legitimatizing abortions in the District of Columbia, and hold that out as an example to the rest of the country as to what the States should pass. And by legitimatizing, I mean establishing the right of a woman to have an abortion when she wants it, in a licensed hospital, needing only the consent of her physician.

We have seen today the Supreme Court refuse to take jurisdiction of a case on appeal from the California Supreme Court in which the California Supreme Court had ruled that their State's abortion law was unconstitutional.

We have seen the State of Hawaii in the last 2 weeks pass an abortion law that says that any woman, as a matter of right, may have an abortion.

We have seen in the last month the State of Washington place on the ballot, for approval or rejection by its voters next fall, an abortion measure which will allow a woman, as a matter of right, to have an abortion.

It is time that the District of Columbia face up to the problem and that Congress act as it has the power to do for this District, not drag its feet, and hold ourselves out as an example to the rest of this Nation as to what should be allowed.

Mr. President, I have talked about two bills. There is a third leg. The third leg is Senate bill 2108, relating to family planning, and this is the third leg of population restraint. We should, as a goal in this Nation, say that any woman, of any economic circumstance, shall have access to all information concerning birth control, contraception, and all other information that she needs to make a wise choice in the matter of child bearing, and whether or not she wants to give birth to a child.

Second, when contraceptive devices fail, we should have legitimatized abortion, so that that woman, if she does not want the pregnancy, can abort it.

Studies by Dr. Westoff indicate that approximately 22 percent of the pregnancies of married couples in this country are unwanted pregnancies by at least one spouse.

Third, the Government, as a matter of policy, should write into its tax law tax incentives for smaller families. We write into the law tax incentives for oil depletion allowances, tax incentives for charitable giving, tax incentives for all kinds of things; and the most important problem we face in this Nation domestically—I will say it again—the most important problem we face in this Nation domestically, in the next decade, in the next 30 years, is overpopulation. It is not asking too much, if we are willing to write into the tax law gimmicks and incentives for every kind of industry, to write into the tax law an incentive for small families; and that is what I am asking in this bill.

We tie those three things together—family planning, abortion, tax incentives. I think we can control, restrain, and plan the population in this country.

I will say again, in conclusion, that I am convinced that we can probably feed, clothe, and handle the pollution of 300, 400, or 500 million people, if that is all there is to life. But I am hoping that we are willing to pass a policy that makes it possible to restrain our population so that we do not so overcrowd our national forest facilities and recreational campgrounds that those people who want to go someplace to avoid the roar of a Honda can still find the kind of area in this country that has not been crowded out or shouldered aside by the crush of people. It is time we realize that in this country life should be fulfilling and not just a matter of existing.

Source: Congressional Record, February 24, 1970, pp. 54538–39.

THE MEDICAL PROFESSION: NEW MEDICAL TECHNIQUES

Looking back at the period before abortion was decriminalized, a physician testifying before a subcommittee of the House of Representatives argued that new medical techniques developed in the 1960s caused the medical profession to change its attitude toward abortion. Because of new techniques, early abortion was now safer than childbirth if performed by competent physicians. Illegal abortions created a serious public health problem.

The subcommittee was hearing testimony on the effects of abortion on physical and mental health.

DOCUMENT 22: Changes in the Practice of Medicine. Testimony of Dr. Jaroslav Fabian Hulka, Professor of Obstetrics and Gynecology, Before the House Subcommittee on Human Resources, 1989

Good morning. I am Dr. Jerry Hulka, a professor of obstetrics and gynecology at the medical school, and a professor of maternal and child health at the public health school at the University of North Carolina. Before 1967, I was in training and practice in New York City and Pitts-

Figure 1

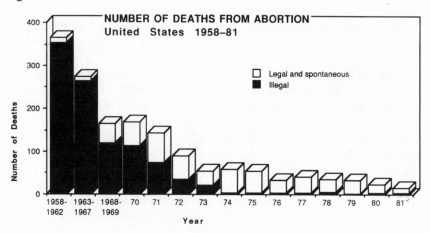

Source: Tietze, C., Henshaw, SK: Induced Abortion: A World Review, 1988 The Alan
Guttmacher Institute, N.Y., 1988

burgh. Complications of illegal abortions were so common that a septic
ward was set aside for the infections. Surgery for hemorrhage was a
common night duty.

When I was asked to present the complications of legal abortion to
the Surgeon General, I organized a literature review around the following question: Why did the United States legalize abortions? A summary
of the 68 reprints I gave him has been provided to you. Briefly, in the
1960's a new, safe method of abortion by vacuum aspiration spread
throughout Europe and England. Dramatic reductions in European mortality and morbidity from legal abortions convinced us American gynecologists, those of us who have to manage these complications, that
legalization would do the same in our country.

For these preventive reasons, obstetricians and gynecologists were
active in making abortions legal in the 1960's. Legalization did have a
dramatic effect on American women's health (see Figure 1). Deaths from
illegal abortion dropped from 300 prior to 1960, to actually no deaths
from illegal abortion in 1979.

Death is the ultimate health disaster, clearly defined and recorded in
our vital statistics. Disasters less defined and recorded are hemorrhages,
infections, and emergency hysterectomies with subsequent infertility
and pelvic pain from the damage caused by septic illegal abortions. These
disasters were deeply heartfelt by every gynecologist who lived through
that era. The relative safety of abortion can be seen by comparing it to
delivery (see Figure 2).

The black bars are delivery and the white are abortion rates in the

Figure 2

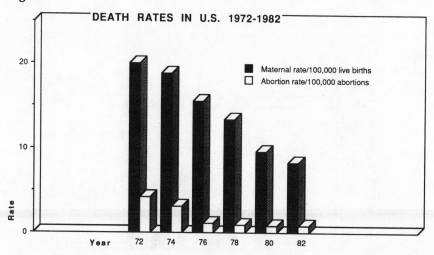

Source: U.S. Centers for Disease Control, Atlanta, Ga., 1989

United States. Having a pregnancy go to term now carries with it 7 to 10 times the risk of death than from having a legal abortion. The medical sequelae [aftermath] of legal abortion was also exhaustively studied. . . .

Although physicians are proud of this major prevention of reproductive damage, I can also tell you that no one, including myself, likes to do abortions. I wish Congress could pass a law that would eliminate abortions, but this is just wishful thinking. Abortions have been universal in human reproducing society since recorded time, regardless of whether they are forbidden by law or religion.

Let me document this for you from my State. In 1968, a unique study documenting illegal abortions in North Carolina was done (see Figure 3). These are compared to legal abortions, the white bars, from our most recent vital health statistics. The total abortions done when they were illegal changed very little when they became legal. One out of four pregnancies ends in induced abortion. This was true before legalization and is true now. . . .

What are the medical consequences of severely restricting abortions? Romania did just that in 1966 (see Figure 4). The birth rate doubled. As illegal abortions were reintroduced, the birth rate declined and maternal mortality rose. The rate of prematurity with accompanying severe birth defects almost doubled when abortions were withheld from high risk pregnancies. . . .

Source: U.S. Congress, House Committee on Government Operations, Human Resources and Intergovernmental Relations Subcommittee, *Hearings*, 101st Congress, 1st session, March 16, 1989, pp. 28–31.

Figure 3

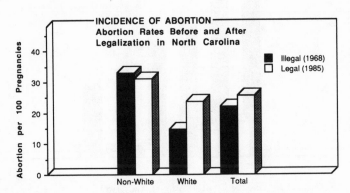

Source: Abernathy, Demography 7:19, 1970 N.C. Center for Health Statistics, 1985

Figure 4
Health Effects of Restricting Legal Abortions in Romania, 1966

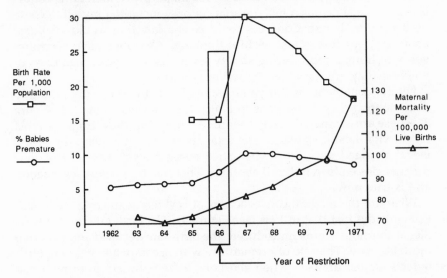

Source: Wright, Am. T. Obstet. Gynecol. 121:146, 1975

Reform Activity in State Legislatures (1967–1972)

Before *Roe v. Wade* was decided in 1973, a number of states either revised their state laws along more liberal lines or, in some cases, repealed their abortion laws altogether.

States interested in revising their laws examined the American Law Institute's Model State Abortion law. The American Law Institute (ALI) is an organization of legal scholars that studies state laws and recommends changes. The organization's draft of an abortion statute was very influential; states considering reform regarded it as a blueprint for their own legislation. A number of states passed laws drafted on this model.

North Carolina was one of the early "reform" states. Its new abortion law, passed in 1967, followed the ALI model closely. Abortion was now to be legal in certain specified situations: where the mother's life or health was in danger, where the pregnancy was the result of rape or incest, or where the child would be born with a grave birth defect. While this type of law legalized abortions under some circumstances, it hedged the operation with a number of restrictions.

By the 1970s reformers were beginning to object to laws that made legal abortions so difficult to obtain. They began to clamor for the outright repeal of abortion statutes, leaving the decision to women and their medical advisors, free from state interference.

DOCUMENT 23: Model Penal Code Abortion Law. American Law Institute, 1962

Section 230.3 Abortion

(1) *Unjustified Abortion.* A person who purposely and unjustifiably terminates the pregnancy of another otherwise than by a live birth commits a felony of the third degree or where the pregnancy has continued beyond the twenty-sixth week, a felony of the second degree.

(2) *Justifiable Abortion.* A licensed physician is justified in terminating a pregnancy if he believes there is substantial risk that continuance of the pregnancy would gravely impair the physical or mental health of the mother or that the child would be born with grave physical or mental defect, or that the pregnancy resulted from rape, incest, or other felonious intercourse. All illicit intercourse with a girl below the age of 16 shall be deemed felonious for purposes of this Subsection. Justifiable abortions shall be performed only in a licensed hospital except in case of emergency when hospital facilities are unavailable.

(3) *Physicians' Certificates; Presumption from Non-Compliance.* No abortion shall be performed unless two physicians, one of whom may be the person performing the abortion, shall have certified in writing the circumstances which they believe to justify the abortion. Such certificate shall be submitted before the abortion to the hospital where it is to be performed and, in the case of abortion following felonious intercourse, to the prosecuting attorney or the police. Failure to comply with any of the requirements of this Subsection gives rise to a presumption that the abortion was unjustified.

Source: American Law Institute, *Model Penal Code: Proposed Official Draft* (Philadelphia: American Law Institute, May 4, 1962).

DOCUMENT 24: The North Carolina Abortion Act of 1967

Section 2. Notwithstanding any of the provisions of [the previous law], it shall not be unlawful to advise, procure, or cause the miscarriage of a pregnant woman or an abortion when the same is performed by a doctor of medicine licensed to practice medicine in North Carolina, if he can reasonably establish that:

- there is substantial risk that continuance of the pregnancy would threaten the life or gravely impair the health of the said woman, or

- there is substantial risk that the child would be born with grave physical or mental defect, or
- the pregnancy resulted from rape or incest and the said alleged rape was reported to a law enforcement agency or court official within seven days after the alleged rape, and
- only after the said woman has given her written consent for said abortion to be performed, and if the said woman shall be a minor or incompetent as adjudicated by any court of competent jurisdiction then only after permission is given in writing by the parents, or if married, her husband, guardian or person or persons standing in loco parentis [in the place of parents] to said minor or incompetent, and
- only when the said woman shall have resided in the State of North Carolina for a period of at least four months immediately preceding the operation being performed except in the case of emergency where the life of the said woman is in danger, and
- only if the abortion is performed in a hospital licensed by the North Carolina Medical Care Commission, and
- only after three doctors of medicine not engaged jointly in private practice, one of whom shall be the person performing the abortion, shall have examined said woman and certified in writing the circumstances which they believe to justify the abortion, and
- only when such certificate shall have been submitted before the abortion to the hospital where it is to be performed; provided, however, that where an emergency exists, and the certificate so states, such certificate may be submitted within twenty-four hours after the abortion.

Source: The General Statutes of North Carolina, G.S. 14–46.

The Politics of State
Legislative Reform
(1967–1973)

NORTH CAROLINA

The political lineup in each state was different. In some states the voters were unalterably opposed to abortion and turned down reform efforts. In states such as New York there were mighty legislative battles. In North Carolina the political complexion of the state, the tactics of legislators interested in abortion reform, the absence of a large bloc of Roman Catholics, and the relative disinterest of the legislature in the abortion issue led to the quick passage of a reform bill.

The North Carolina Population Center published a monograph on the politics behind the bill's passage in 1968.

DOCUMENT 25: *North Carolina Abortion Law 1967: A Study in Legislative Process.* **Sagar C. Jain and Steven W. Sinding, 1968**

Democrat Arthur H. Jones was elected to his first public office—a seat in the 1967 House of Representatives—in North Carolina's regular elections November 1966. Jones was elected from Mecklenburg County, the largest county in the state, where Charlotte, the state's largest city, is located. He had retired as senior vice-president in charge of public relations and personnel matters for North Carolina National Bank, one of the state's three major banks.

To understand Art Jones's motivation to introduce the Abortion Law of 1967, one must go further into his background. A native of Philadelphia, he lived most of his early life in New Jersey. He is, in fact, one of the few "Yankees" in North Carolina's General Assembly. He dropped out of school in the eleventh grade to work. Nine years later he was accepted, without his high school diploma, at Oberlin College in Ohio. Jones was married after his freshman year, and when he returned to Oberlin for his sophomore year he became concerned with the problems of family planning and birth control. This was in 1926 when Ohio had, as did most states, an anti-birth control law. Jones points out several important events that occurred during his sophomore year: he formed on the Oberlin campus what he believes was Ohio's first planned parenthood association; he and other students manufactured contraceptive jelly which was sold at cost to married couples; in a sociology course he began to explore extensively the problems of family planning and social welfare; and he interviewed Margaret Sanger, the noted campaigner for legalized contraception, and wrote several chapters of an undergraduate sociology thesis on family planning, including historical research on abortion. Jones says he made a mental note to "do something" in these areas.

Maintaining interests in family planning, abortion, birth control and social welfare, Jones has been president of the Social Planning Council of Charlotte and the Charlotte Mental Hygiene Association, active in the Mecklenburg County Family Life Council, head of the United Community Services, and a member of the national board of directors of the United Community Fund and Councils of America. In addition, he helped form the first mental health clinic in Charlotte. A factor of importance for this study is Jones's close friendship with Wallace Kuralt, Director of Public Welfare of Mecklenburg County. According to Jones, Kuralt first expressed to him the need for a liberal abortion bill, citing the socio-economic aspects of unwanted pregnancies and deformed children. For several years Kuralt had been accumulating a file of material on abortion. He consulted with the New York based Association for the Study of Abortion and read the Swedish Abortion Law. Kuralt's interest in abortion stemmed from a desire, he said, to control family dependency. He noted that it normally is not the duty of a public welfare department to enter this area, but he added that frequent attacks on the role of welfare in supporting illegitimate children and nonviable dependencies stimulated further thought regarding prevention of these dependencies.

Kuralt has an extensive and highly effective performance in the field of birth control, and his efforts and achievements are widely known. He was also instrumental in drafting North Carolina's voluntary sterilization act. Kuralt has written widely on the use of contraceptive pills to control family size and on distribution of contraceptive devices to reduce dependency. He thinks that these activities legitimately fall within the realm of public welfare.

Jones said his wife's occupation as a counselor in Charlotte and Mecklenburg domestic courts gave her almost daily contact with disruptive family problems stemming from unwanted or deformed children, and her findings played a definite role in his decision to introduce the abortion bill. . . .

[Conclusions]

1. The original initiative for the abortion bill came from a North Carolina county public welfare department. Wallace Kuralt, Director of Mecklenburg County Public Welfare Department, was moved by his professional concern and personal convictions to change the existing legal situation regarding abortions to afford greater legal backing for termination of undesirable pregnancy. In Representative Jones he found a passionate legislative champion. Relying on Jones's sincerity, ability and commitment, Kuralt withdrew from the scene and made no attempt to share the limelight.

2. Under different circumstances, a freshman assemblyman like Representative Jones might be considered foolhardy if he adopted liberalization of abortion as his legislative "cause"—a cause fraught with many potential controversies. But in North Carolina, Jones's decision was justifiable. A small Roman Catholic population, a lack of organized statewide Negro political activity and a weak opposition party in the legislature eliminated many obvious political risks. Also, in view of North Carolina's pronounced concern with building a "progressive" image, advocacy of a socially "liberal" bill, which did not lay hands on any "sacred cows," could hardly be considered politically undesirable.

3. Although a freshman legislator, Jones had several important friends and allies who occupied key legislative positions. . . . Jones drew heavily on these friends for help in winning allies for his bill and for manipulating the time sequence of the various events of his bill. Furthermore, as recently retired senior vice-president of one of the state's foremost banks, Jones had other influential contacts inside and outside the legislature. His professional background and experience commanded respect.

4. No grand strategy was evolved, and no clear course of action was charted for the bill. Indeed, during initial discussions between Kuralt and Jones, only two decisions were made. First, the bill must not be associated with public welfare. Because of negative sentiment toward public welfare in the state, it was feared that the bill might not receive proper consideration if it took on public welfare overtones. Furthermore, any projection of public welfare in the abortion issue might have interjected racial and related controversy into the debate. Second, the bill would supplement existing law through suitable amendments instead of supplanting it with an entirely new law. . . . With the exception of

these decisions, Jones and other proponents of the bill seem to have "played the rest by ear." Initially, Jones was led more by zest for his cause and a consciousness that he had several important legislators as friends rather than by detailed knowledge of the issue involved. No initial consultation with the State Medical Society, and a lack of knowledge regarding the American Law Institute's model abortion law are examples of his naivete, but he learned fast, and functioned most of the time with the facility and ease of a skilled legislative craftsman. . . .

It should be noted that proponents of the bill made mistakes. We have already mentioned that when Jones drafted his original bill he did not consult the State Medical Society, nor did he know about the American Law Institute's model abortion law. These lapses could have hindered passage of the bill. At a later stage the proponents were caught by the testimony of Drs. Easley and Vernon. Their testimony defended the bill on grounds of personal physical comfort of mothers and population control—two arguments the proponents did not want verbalized. Further, although proponents denied that the bill was a "doctor's bill," six of seven pro witnesses were doctors. These failings did not seriously threaten the bill's passage, but several legislators noted inconsistencies which could have proved fatal for the bill in different circumstances.

5. The North Carolina Legislature was embroiled in and deadlocked over several deeply emotional issues—the "brown-bagging" bill, the bill for giving university status to East Carolina College, the "speaker ban" law and the reapportionment bill. As a result, neither legislators nor the public had time and energy to give serious consideration to other issues. . . .

6. North Carolina did not have a recent history on abortion bills, so there was no emotional "backlog" on the subject. . . .

7. Representative Jones's personality, dedication and approach must be given proper credit. Personable, affable, outgoing and "folksy," Jones personified "how to win friends and influence people." His dedication to the bill was unquestionable. An effective orator, he drew heavily on this ability in committee hearings and floor debates. Above all, he was always flexible and reasonable. His willingness to accept all reasonable changes and amendments won him many supporters and often left his opponents without an argument.

Source: Sagar C. Jain and Steven W. Sinding, North Carolina Abortion Law 1967: A Study in Legislative Process, Monograph 2, Carolina Population Center (Chapel Hill, N.C.: University of North Carolina, 1968), pp. 15–16, 48–51.

CALIFORNIA

In California one of the motives behind the reform effort seems to have been concern by lawyers that doctors and hospitals were breaking the law, and the desire by medical personnel to have the law mirror what they believed to be good medical practice. A study done of abortions performed in California hospitals showed that there was little consistency in hospital policies.

A witness who testified in hearings before the Senate Judiciary Committee in 1981 looked back at the California experience.

DOCUMENT 26: The California Abortion Reform Movement Was Led by Doctors, Lawyers and Public Health Experts. Testimony of Herma Hill Kay Before the Senate Committee on the Judiciary, 1981

Twenty years ago, in 1961, the first bill designed to conform California abortion law to existing medical practice was introduced into the California legislature. At that time, California, in common with 41 other states, permitted abortion only to "preserve" the "life" of the mother. But an influential law review article published in 1959* had demonstrated that the law in practice differed from the law on the books. The authors surveyed 26 hospitals in San Francisco and Los Angeles using a questionnaire that included a list of eleven hypothetical cases in which a patient sought hospital approval for the performance of an abortion. These cases presented a variety of maternal, fetal, and psychiatric indications for abortion, and the hospitals were asked to indicate whether the abortion would be approved. Among the eleven cases were the following:

1. A woman with a history of rheumatic fever and resulting heart damage whose medical work-up indicated that her risk of death during or immediately following pregnancy was 30 times greater than if she were not pregnant;

2. A fifteen year old girl, the daughter of a minister, who was raped and impregnated by an escaped inmate of a hospital for mental defectives; and

3. A married woman with five children below the age of thirteen who was forced by her husband's illness to become the primary breadwinner for the family.

---

*Herbert Packer and Ralph Gampell, "Therapeutic Abortion: A Problem in Law and Medicine," *Stanford Law Review* 11 (May 1959).

In only two of these eleven cases was the abortion clearly legal in California in 1959; in two others, the procedure would probably have been legal; while in the remaining seven, an abortion would have been illegal. The results obtained were startling. At least one of the 24 responding hospitals indicated that the abortion could be performed there in all eleven cases; 18 of the hospitals thought their practices were probably not in conformity with the law; and only 6 hospitals believed themselves in strict compliance with legal requirements. In the hypothetical rape case, 15 hospitals would have authorized an abortion that violated legal, but not medical, standards.

The conclusion drawn by the authors was not that existing California law should be rigidly enforced, nor even that the then-prevalent policy of prosecutorial neglect [prosecutors ignoring the violation] be continued. Rather, they argued that the law should be changed to reflect reputable medical practice. They proposed that legal abortion should become a matter for medical judgment, and suggested a statute that would confer immunity from criminal prosecution upon all persons involved in the performance of a therapeutic abortion that had been approved by the hospital's Therapeutic Abortion Committee.

Partly as a result of the influence of this article, the movement for abortion law reform in California was led, not by members of the women's movement, but by doctors, lawyers and public health experts. In 1967, California became one of three states to enact the nation's first therapeutic abortion laws. The California bill, authored by then-State Senator Anthony Beilenson, was shaped more closely to the American Law Institute's Model Penal Code than to the 1959 proposal. It permitted therapeutic abortions when a hospital committee found that there was "substantial risk that continuance of the pregnancy would gravely impair the physical or mental health of the mother," or that "the pregnancy resulted from rape or incest." The dominant themes sounded in the legislative hearings were the need to protect maternal health and to provide guidance for medical practitioners who needed to know the limits within which their medical judgment could legally be exercised.

Mandated reports of practice under the new law were provided by the Department of Health to the California Legislature first on an annual, then a biennial, basis. These reports indicate that the therapeutic abortion law was successful in lowering the number of abortion-related maternal deaths. The 1971 Report indicated that in 1966 and 1967, 35 maternal deaths in California were due to illegal abortion, but that number had declined to 21 such deaths in 1968 and 1969. The number of maternal deaths attributable to therapeutic abortions went from 4 in 1970 to 6 in 1972, but the rate per 100,000 therapeutic abortions during the same period declined from 6.1 in 1970 to 4.3 in 1972, due to the increase in the number of abortions performed. These figures are consistent with national statistics.

Source: U.S. Congress, Senate Committee on the Judiciary, *Hearings on Constitutional Amendments Relating to Abortion*, 97th Congress, 1st session, 1981, pp. 770–72.

Breakthrough in the Courts

When physicians were arrested and prosecuted for performing abortions, reformers saw opportunities that could be used to test the constitutionality of laws making abortion a crime. In 1967 Dr. Leon Belous, a California physician and an advocate of abortion reform, was convicted of referring a woman to an illegal abortionist. He insisted that his case be used to raise a constitutional challenge to California's anti-abortion statute. His appeal was supported by the California Civil Liberties Union and other abortion reform groups. The California Supreme Court declared the state statute unconstitutional, and found, for the first time, a constitutional right to choose an abortion.

Other cases soon began to flow into state and lower federal courts, some of them building on the principles established in *California v. Belous*. *Roe v. Wade*, the case that would later be decided in the United States Supreme Court, was filed in a U.S. district court in Texas. Other abortion cases were decided by courts in Wisconsin and South Dakota. Not all the decisions favored abortion rights. *Rosen v. Louisiana State Board of Medical Examiners* concerned a physician whose license had been taken away for performing an abortion that was not authorized under Louisiana state law. Dr. Rosen went to court to have his license restored, claiming that the Louisiana law was unconstitutional. A U.S. district court in Louisiana ruled in favor of the state, finding that the state had the power to pass legislation protecting the fetus.

In New York, while a battle raged in the legislature over the reform of New York's abortion laws, women's organizations prepared a case attacking the constitutionality of the New York statutes. To start a lawsuit, interested parties file a "complaint," a legal document that identifies the parties, explains why the court has jurisdiction to decide the case, lays out the legal basis for bringing the case, and explains what action the parties wish the court to take. The complaint in *Abramowicz v. Lefkowitz* outlined a broad array of constitutional problems with New York's abortion laws. This case was never decided; before the court could act, the New York legislature passed a liberal law that allowed abortion up until the twenty-fourth week of pregnancy.

The first case to reach the United States Supreme Court came from Washington, D.C. Dr. Milan Vuitch was indicted for performing abortions in violation of the District of Columbia Code. The law in the District allowed abortions that were necessary "for the preservation of the mother's life or health," a rather vague and indefinite standard. The Vuitch case reached the Supreme Court in 1971, and the Court reversed Vuitch's conviction and sent the case back to the trial court for further proceedings. But in doing so, the Court held that the word "health" in the statute included mental health and that prosecutors would have to prove that the abortion was *not* necessary to protect the woman's health in order to convict Dr. Vuitch.

The California case was important because it held that there was a constitutional right to choose an abortion. The New York case set out a range of constitutional questions raised by abortion laws. It also focused on women's rights rather than the rights of doctors. The Vuitch case was important because it seemed to indicate a willingness by the Supreme Court to read federal law in a way that protected doctors. It also suggested that there were votes on the Supreme Court to support a more liberal approach to abortion issues.

DOCUMENT 27: *People v. Belous*. Supreme Court of California, 1969

Opinion of Justice Peters.

Dr. Leon Philip Belous was convicted in January 1967, after a jury trial, of abortion, in violation of section 274 of the Penal Code, and conspiracy to commit an abortion, in violation of section 182 of the Penal Code, both felonies. The court suspended proceedings, imposed a fine of $5,000, and placed Dr. Belous on probation for two years. He appeals from the order granting probation.

Dr. Belous is a physician and surgeon, licensed since 1931 to practice medicine in the State of California, and specializing in obstetrics and gynecology. He has been on the attending staff of the gynecology department of Cedars of Lebanon Hospital in Los Angeles since 1931, is a fellow of the Los Angeles Gynecology and Obstetrical Society, the American College of Obstetrics and Gynecology, the Abdominal Surgical Society, and the Geriatric Society, and a member of the American Board of Obstetrics and Gynecology. He is on the Board of Directors of the California Committee on Therapeutic Abortion, an organization which seeks to liberalize abortion laws. He is considered by his associates to be an eminent physician in his field.

The prosecution's witnesses, a young woman and her husband, Cheryl and Clifton, testified to the following:

In 1966 Cheryl, then unmarried, believed she was pregnant. A family physician gave her pills which would induce menstruation if she were not pregnant, but the pills did not work. She and Clifton had sometime earlier seen Dr. Belous on television, advocating a change in the California abortion laws. They had never heard of Dr. Belous before. Clifton obtained the doctor's phone number from the television station and phoned Dr. Belous; he explained the problem and that they both were "pretty disturbed," and at their "wits' end" and asked for Dr. Belous' help. Dr. Belous told them there was nothing he could do, but Clifton "continued pleading," and threatened that Cheryl would go to Tijuana for an abortion. Finally the doctor agreed to see them at his office.

Dr. Belous examined Cheryl at his Beverly Hills office and confirmed that she was possibly pregnant. Cheryl was otherwise in good health. The visit lasted about 45 minutes and was very emotional. Both Clifton and Cheryl pleaded for help, cried, insisted they were going to have an abortion "one way or another." The doctor lectured them on the dangers of criminal abortions, and Tijuana abortions in particular, and suggested that they get married. He insisted he did not perform abortions. He refused to recommend anyone in Tijuana. Finally, in response to their pleadings, Dr. Belous gave them a piece of paper with a Chula Vista phone number. He told them an abortion would cost about $500. He gave Cheryl a prescription for some antibiotics and instructed her to return for an examination.

Dr. Belous testified that he was very familiar with the abortion business in Tijuana. He had visited the clinics there to learn about conditions and knew that women who went to Tijuana were taking their lives in their hands. He met Kar Lairtus while in Tijuana and knew from personal observation that Lairtus, licensed to practice in Mexico but not in California, was performing skilled and safe abortions in Mexico. Lairtus wanted to obtain a California license, and sought out Belous' help on a number of occasions. When Lairtus moved from Mexico to Chula Vista, he gave the doctor a Hollywood address, and made it known to the doctor that he was performing abortions. It was Lairtus' number that Belous gave to Cheryl and Clifton. Although he had given out Lairtus' number before, in similar situations, where distraught pregnant women insisted they would do anything, Dr. Belous had no idea how many women actually went to Lairtus.

Cheryl and Clifton made arrangements with Lairtus, and went to the address which Lairtus gave them on the phone. After the abortion was performed, while Cheryl was resting, the police, having been advised by another woman that Lairtus was performing abortions at that address, came to his apartment, followed another couple into the apartment and arrested Lairtus. They found two notebooks containing women's names, ages, dates of last menstruation and physicians names, including Dr. Belous' name, which the police interpreted as the referring doctor with whom Lairtus was to split his fees. On the basis of this information, Dr. Belous was arrested at his office. Lairtus pleaded guilty. At Dr. Belous' trial, he testified that although not solicited, he sent Dr. Belous about $100 as a professional courtesy in about half the cases that he had performed abortions on Dr. Belous' patients. Dr. Belous denied receiving any money from Lairtus.

The substance of Dr. Belous' defense was that he gave Lairtus' phone number to Cheryl and Clifton only because he believed that they would, in fact, do anything to terminate the pregnancy, which might involve butchery in Tijuana or self-mutilation; that in face of their pleading and tears, he gave out the phone number of someone whom he knew to be a competent doctor, although unlicensed in the state. The doctor believed that if the young couple carried out their threats, Cheryl's very life was in danger.

Section 274 of the Penal Code, when the conduct herein involved occurred, read:

"Every person who provides, supplies, or administers to any woman, or procures any woman to take any medicine, drug or substance, or uses or employs any instrument or other means whatever, with intent thereby to procure the miscarriage of such woman, unless the same is necessary to preserve her life, is punishable by imprisonment in the State prison not less than two nor more than five years."

The statute was substantially unchanged since it was originally enacted in 1850. . . .

The rights involved in the instant case are the woman's rights to life and to choose whether to bear children. The woman's right to life is involved because childbirth involves risk of death.

The fundamental right of the woman to choose whether to bear children follows from the Supreme Court's and this court's repeated acknowledgment of a "right of privacy" or "liberty" in matters related to marriage, family, and sex . . . (citing cases). That such a right is not enumerated in either the United States or California Constitutions is no impediment to the existence of the right. . . . It is not surprising that none of the parties who have filed briefs in this case have disputed the existence of this fundamental right.

The critical issue is not whether such rights exist, but whether the state has a compelling interest in the regulation of a subject which is within the police powers of the state, whether the regulation is "necessary . . . to the accomplishment of a permissible state policy, and whether legislation impinging on constitutionally protected areas is narrowly drawn. . . . (The Court held the statute unconstitutional and directed the trial court to dismiss the indictment against Dr. Belous.)

Source: 458 Pacific Reporter, 2ᵈ Series, 194 (1969).

DOCUMENT 28: Rosen v. Louisiana State Board of Medical Examiners. U.S. District Court, 1970

In our opinion, the issues in dispute here do not resolve themselves neatly into the questions posed by Dr. Rosen. The issues presented are much more complex, for the current controversy over the wisdom and constitutional validity of existing abortion laws centers upon a problem in which attitudes toward life, being, and sexual activity are in tumultuous disagreement. The specifics of the conflict in courts, legislative halls, and journals have often been the details of statutory language. The root disagreement, however, among men of intelligence and good will on all sides of the controversy has arisen over the evaluation of competing interests affected by abortion and the manner in which these interests are to be protected by law in a democratic society. Nature alone is responsible for the spontaneous abortion, and she needs no justification. But there remains for the determination by society, by whatever means it has chosen for the making of such momentous decisions, the conditions, if any, under which the embryo or fetus of the species homo sapiens may be destroyed within the womb.

The most recent attacks on abortion legislation, like Dr. Rosen's, have focused upon the interests of the pregnant woman as being of primary importance. The interests of the family unit, if any, of which the pregnant woman is a part and the needs of the community have also been advanced as reasons for the relaxation or abolition of laws prohibiting abortions. Little or no importance has been attached by these arguments to whatever interests may be possessed by the embryo or fetus the pregnant woman carries. In at least four instances, arguments such as these have been urged successfully. In all these cases, the right asserted by plaintiffs to be free from unwanted governmental interference—freedom of choice in the matter of abortions—was equated by the court with the "fundamental right to choose whether to have children."

For the purposes of this case we assume, if we are not required to recognize, *e.g.*, Griswold v. Connecticut (1965); Baird v. Eisenstadt, 1970, that as a general matter women possess under our Constitution a "fundamental right" to determine whether they shall bear children before they have become pregnant. A state may interfere with this right of choice only in special circumstances. *E.g.*, Buck v. Bell (1927). We deal in this case, however, not merely with whether a woman has a generalized right to choose whether to bear children, but instead with the more complicated question whether a pregnant woman has the right to cause the abortion of the embryo or fetus she carries in her womb. We do not find that an equation of the generalized right of the woman to determine whether she shall bear children with the asserted right to abort an embryo or fetus is compelled by fact or logic. Exercise of the right to an abortion on request is not essential to an effective exercise of the right not to bear a child, if a child for whatever reason is not wanted. Abstinence, rhythm, contraception, and sterilization are alternative means to this end. The first is, of course, infallible; the latter three are reliable to varying degrees approaching certainty. Before the "moment" of conception has occurred, the choice whether or not to bear children is made in circumstances quite different from those in which such a choice might be made after conception. Apart, the sperm and the unfertilized egg will die; neither has the capacity to grow and develop independently as does the fertilized egg. During fertilization, sperm and egg pool their nucleii and chromosomes. Biologically, a living organism belonging to the species homo sapiens is created out of this organization. Genetically, the adult man was from such a beginning all that he essentially has become in every cell and human attribute. The basic distinction between a decision whether to bear children which is made before conception and one which is made after conception is that the first contemplates the creation of a new human organism, but the latter contemplates the destruction of such an organism already created. To some engaged in the controversy over abortion, this distinction is one without a difference. These men of intelligence and good will do not perceive the human organism in the early part of its life cycle as a human "being" or "person." In their view, the granting to such an organism of the right to survive on a basis of equality with human beings generally should be delayed until a later stage in its development. To others, however, the "moment" of conception or some stage of development very close to this "moment" is the point at which distinctively human life begins. In their view the difference between the decision not to conceive and the decision to abort is of fundamental, determinative importance. Thus the root problem in the controversy over abortion is the one of assigning value to embryonic and fetal life.

In considering the problem of valuing prenatal life, we heed the words of Mr. Justice Holmes:

> It is a misfortune if a judge reads his conscious or unconscious sympathy with one side or the other prematurely into the law, and forgets that what seem to him to be first principles are believed by half his fellow men to be wrong. . . .

Holmes, Collected Legal Papers 295 (1920). When distinctively human life begins is a matter about which reasonable, fair-minded men are in basic disagreement. Thus this case does not concern simply whether the pregnant woman has a fundamental right to be let alone in the control of her body processes, for it is unresolved whether, in the common understanding of the society in which she lives, choice of the destiny of the human organism developing within her is a matter directly affecting only her individual rights. We phrase the question for decision as follows: Can the State of Louisiana, consistent with the Fourteenth Amendment, assign to the human organism in its early prenatal development as embryo and fetus a right to be "born" unless the condition of pregnancy directly and proximately threatens the mother's life? . . .

. . . "[T]he word 'liberty,' in the 14th Amendment, is perverted when it is held to prevent the natural outcome of a dominant opinion, unless it can be said that a rational and fair man necessarily would admit that the statute proposed would infringe fundamental principles as they have been understood by the traditions of our people and our law." Lochner v. New York (1905) (Holmes, J., dissenting). We are not persuaded that the Louisiana abortion laws infringe any fundamental principle as understood by the traditions of our people. As an ethical, moral, or religious matter, a woman's refusal to carry an embryo or fetus to term, both historically and today, has been condemned as wrong by a substantial, if not a dominant, body of opinion, except in very limited circumstances. . . .

Section 37: 1285(6) of the Louisiana Revised Statutes, we conclude, does not offend the due-process clause of the Fourteenth Amendment. We do not recognize the asserted right of a woman to choose to destroy the embryo or fetus she carries as being so rooted in the traditions and collective conscience of our people that it must be ranked as "fundamental." The valuation of embryonic and fetal organisms made by the State of Louisiana is supported by scientific fact. Because we further find that section 37: 1285(6) is necessary to the accomplishment of a permissible state policy, we must decline plaintiff's invitation to void this law.

Judgment will be entered in favor of defendant, dismissing plaintiff's suit.

Source: 318 F.Supp. 1217 (1970).

DOCUMENT 29: Complaint in *Abramowicz v. Lefkowitz* (1970)

---

13. The challenged statutes are unconstitutional on their face and as applied in that they:

(a) invade plaintiffs' right of privacy or liberty in matters related to marriage, family, and sex; the sacred right of every individual to the possession and control of her own person; and the right to be left alone as guaranteed by the First, Fourth, Fifth, Ninth, and Fourteenth Amendments to the Constitution;

(b) chill and deter plaintiffs in the exercise of their rights of association, privacy, and sexual and family relations, as guaranteed by the First, Fourth, Fifth, Ninth, and Fourteenth Amendments;

(c) deprive plaintiffs of the fundamental right of a woman to choose whether to bear children, as guaranteed by the Fourth, Fifth, Eighth, Ninth, and Fourteenth Amendments;

(d) deprive plaintiffs of the right to safe, speedy, and adequate medical care on the basis of wealth in violation of the constitutional guarantee of equal protection of the laws;

(e) deny plaintiffs life and liberty without due process of law, despite a lack of compelling State interest and despite the fact that "Childbirth involves risks of death," *People v. Belous*, in that they force them to expose themselves to the hazards and risks of illegal abortion in order to terminate an unwanted pregnancy;

(f) deprive plaintiffs of safe and adequate medical care on the basis of the religious beliefs of others in violation of the First Amendment guarantee against the establishment of religion;

(g) deny plaintiffs access to information concerning their health, safety, and welfare and the availability of safe, speedy, and adequate medical care in violation of the guarantees of the First Amendment;

(h) deprive plaintiffs of guarantees of due process of law in that the only criterion for a legal abortion is the preservation of the life of the mother which is unconstitutionally vague and without standards;

(i) deprive plaintiffs of what little access they might have to a legal abortion without due process in violation of the Fourteenth Amendment in that they chill and deter doctors and hospitals from performing such medical procedures because of fear of prosecution under the unconstitutionally vague statutes;

(j) constitute cruel and unusual punishment in violation of the Eighth Amendment in that they force plaintiffs to bear and raise unwanted children;

(k) deny plaintiffs their right to pursue a career in violation of their rights of liberty and property as guaranteed by the Fifth and Fourteenth Amendments by forcing them to give birth to a child when they do not wish to;

(l) deprive plaintiffs, most of whom are taxpayers, of equal access to both public and private medical facilities which on information and belief receive substantial Federal and State funding, such equal access guaranteed by the Fifth and Fourteenth Amendments to the Constitution.

Source: Reprinted in D. Schulder and F. Kennedy, *Abortion Rap* (New York: McGraw-Hill, 1971), Appendix, pp. 196–97.

DOCUMENT 30: *United States v. Vuitch* (1971)

II

We turn now to the merits. Appellee Milan Vuitch was indicted for producing and attempting to produce abortions in violation of D.C.Code Ann. § 22–201. That Act provides in part:

> Whoever, by means of any instrument, medicine, drug or other means whatever, procures or produces, or attempts to procure or produce an abortion or miscarriage on any woman, unless the same were done as necessary for the preservation of the mother's life or health and under the direction of a competent licensed practitioner of medicine, shall be imprisoned in the penitentiary not less than one year or not more than ten years. . . .

Without waiting for trial, the District Judge dismissed the indictments on the ground that the abortion statute was unconstitutionally vague. In his view, set out substantially in full below, the statute was vague for two principal reasons:

1. The fact that once an abortion was proved a physician "is presumed guilty and remains so unless a jury can be persuaded that his acts were necessary for the preservation of the woman's life or health."

2. The presence of the "ambivalent and uncertain word 'health.' " . . .

. . . The statute does not outlaw all abortions, but only those which are not performed under the direction of a competent, licensed physician, and those not necessary to preserve the mother's life or health. It is a general guide to the interpretation of criminal statutes that when an exception is incorporated in the enacting clause of a statute, the burden is on the prosecution to plead and prove that the defendant is not within the exception. When Congress passed the District of Columbia abortion law in 1901 and amended it in 1953, it expressly authorized physicians to perform such abortions as are necessary to preserve the mother's "life or health." Because abortions were authorized only in more restrictive circumstances under previous D. C. law, the change must represent a judgment by Congress that it is desirable that women be able to obtain abortions needed for the preservation of their lives or health. It would be highly anomalous for a legislature to authorize abortions necessary for life or health and then to demand that a doctor, upon pain of one to ten years' imprisonment, bear the burden of proving that an abortion he performed fell within that category. Placing such a burden of proof on a doctor would be peculiarly inconsistent with society's notions of the responsibilities of the medical profession. Generally, doctors are encouraged by society's expectations, by the strictures of malpractice law and by their own professional standards to give their patients such treatment as is necessary to preserve their health. We are unable to believe that Congress intended that a physician be required to prove his innocence. We therefore hold that under D.C.Code Ann. § 22–201, the burden is on the prosecution to plead and prove that an abortion was not "necessary for the preservation of the mother's life or health."

. . . There remains the contention that the word "health" is so imprecise and has so uncertain a meaning that it fails to inform a defendant of the charge against him and therefore the statute offends the Due Process Clause of the Constitution. We hold that it does not. The trial court apparently felt that the term was vague because there "is no indication whether it includes varying degrees of mental as well as physical health." It is true that the legislative history of the statute gives no guidance as to whether "health" refers to both a patient's mental and physical state. The term "health" was introduced into the law in 1901 when the statute was enacted in substantially its present form. The House Report on the bill contains no discussion of the term "health" and there was no Senate report. Nor have we found any District of Columbia cases prior to this District Court decision that shed any light on the question. Since that decision, however, the issue has been considered in Doe v. General Hospital of the District of Columbia (1970). There District Judge Waddy construed the statute to permit abortions "for mental health reasons whether or not the patient had a previous history of mental defects." The same construction was followed by the United States Court of Appeals for the District of Columbia Circuit in further proceedings in the same case. We see no reason why this interpretation of the statute should not be followed. Certainly this construction accords with the general usage and modern understanding of the word "health," which includes psychological as well as physical well-being. Indeed Webster's Dictionary, in accord with that common usage, properly defines health as the "[s]tate of being... sound in body [or] mind." Viewed in this light, the term "health" presents no problem of vagueness. Indeed, whether a particular operation is necessary for a patient's physical or mental health is a judgment that physicians are obviously called upon to make routinely whenever surgery is considered.

... We therefore hold that properly construed the District of Columbia abortion law is not unconstitutionally vague, and that the trial court erred in dismissing the indictments on that ground. Appellee has suggested that there are other reasons why the dismissal of the indictments should be affirmed. Essentially, these arguments are based on this Court's decision in Griswold v. Connecticut (1965). Although there was some reference to these arguments in the opinion of the court below, we read it as holding simply that the statute was void for vagueness because it failed in that court's language to "give that certainty which due process of law considers essential in a criminal statute."

Source: 402 *U.S. Reports* 62 (1971).

The Abortion Situation Worldwide

The United States was not the only country being buffeted by the winds of change. Throughout the 1960s and 1970s a number of countries liberalized their abortion laws to some degree. A few countries went in the other direction, making their laws more restrictive. A world review by Christopher Tietze appeared in the 1981 edition of a Fact Book published by the Population Council.

DOCUMENT 31: Abortion Laws and Policies: A World Review. Christopher Tietze, 1981

Among the countries of the world, the legal status of induced abortion ranges from complete prohibition to elective abortion at the request of the pregnant woman. . . . The situation as of mid-1982 can be summarized as follows. Ten percent of the world's 4.5 billion people lived in countries where abortion was prohibited without exception, and 18 percent lived in countries where it was permitted only to save the life of the pregnant woman. Most of the Muslim countries of Asia, almost two-thirds of the countries of Latin America, a majority of the countries of Africa, and five countries in Europe (Belgium, Ireland, Malta, Portugal, and Spain) fell into these two categories. About 8 percent lived under statutes authorizing abortion on broader medical grounds, that is, to avert a threat to the woman's health rather than to her life, and sometimes on eugenic, or fetal, indication (known genetic or other impairment of the fetus or increased risk of such impairment) and/or juridical indication (rape, incest, etc.) as well.

Twenty-five percent of the world's population resided in countries where social factors, such as inadequate income, substandard housing, unmarried status, and the like, could be taken into consideration in the evaluation of the threat to the woman's health (social-medical indication) or where adverse social conditions alone, without reference to health, could justify termination of pregnancy. Important countries in this group were the German Federal Republic, India, Japan, the United Kingdom, and most of the socialist states of eastern Europe.

Countries allowing abortion on request without specifying reasons—generally limited to the first trimester of pregnancy—accounted for 39 percent. Abortions on medical grounds were usually permitted beyond the gestational limit prescribed for abortions on social grounds or for elective abortions. This category included a very heterogeneous list of countries: Austria, the People's Republic of China, Cuba, Denmark, France, the German Democratic Republic, Italy, the Netherlands, Norway, Singapore, Sweden, Tunisia, the United States, the USSR, Vietnam, and Yugoslavia. In some of these countries (e.g., Denmark, France, the German Democratic Republic, India, Italy, Norway) the law regulating abortion requires parental consent if the pregnant woman is a minor, generally defined as under 18 years of age. Elsewhere, statutes governing medical or hospital practice may have the same effect. A few countries (e.g., France, the German Federal Republic, Italy, the Netherlands) require a waiting period of up to one week between application and performance of the procedure. Many countries have "conscience clauses" exempting physicians, nurses, and/or other staff from participating in abortion procedures if they have religious or philosophical objections.

Several of the categories in the preceding paragraphs cover a wide range of situations. A statute authorizing abortion to avert a threat to the pregnant woman's health may define this threat narrowly or broadly, for example, by specifically mentioning mental health. Social indications also may be defined or interpreted narrowly, as in Uruguay, or broadly, as in Japan or Poland.

The abortion statutes of many countries are not strictly enforced and occasional abortions on medical grounds are probably tolerated in most countries. It is well known that in some jurisdictions with restrictive laws abortions can be obtained openly from private physicians, without the interference of authorities, as in Korea or Taiwan, or in nonprofit clinics, as in the Netherlands prior to legalization in 1981; they may even be performed in public health facilities, as in Cuba prior to legalization in 1979 or currently in Bangladesh. Conversely, a statute authorizing abortion on request does not guarantee that the procedure is actually available to all women who may want their pregnancies terminated. Lack of medical personnel and facilities or conservative attitudes among physicians and hospital administrators may effectively curtail access to abortion, especially for economically or socially deprived women, as in parts of Austria, France, the German Federal Republic, India, Italy, and the United States.

Over the past 15 years, a large number of countries have liberalized their abortion laws to various degrees, notably Austria, Canada, the People's Republic of China, Cuba, Denmark, Finland, France, the German Democratic Republic, the German Federal Republic, India, Italy, the Netherlands, Norway, Singapore, Sweden, Tunisia, the United Kingdom, the United States, and Yugoslavia. Four countries in eastern Europe adopted more restrictive legislation than previously in force: Bulgaria, Czechoslovakia, Hungary, and Romania. Four other countries liberalized their abortion policies and later made them more restrictive: Iran, Israel, New Zealand, and the United States.

Major reasons advanced by advocates of less restrictive legislation in matters of abortion, and especially of abortion on request, have been considerations of public health (to combat illegal abortion with its associated morbidity and mortality), social justice (to give poor women access to abortion previously available only to the well-to-do), and women's rights (to secure a postulated right of all women to control their own bodies). A desire to curb population growth, in the interest of economic and social development, has been an explicit reason for the adoption of nonrestrictive abortion policies in only a few countries, such as Singapore and Tunisia, and more recently in China. The majority of countries permitting abortion at the request of the pregnant woman or on broadly interpreted social indications have low birth rates and some of them actively pursue pronatalist population policies.

Opposition to the liberalization of abortion laws has come traditionally from conservative groups, mainly on moral and religious grounds, with the Roman Catholic Church the most vigorous and articulate opponent. Antiabortion policies are also favored by fundamentalist Protestants and Muslims and by Orthodox Jews. Concern about low birth rates has been a major reason for recent restrictive legislation in eastern Europe.

Because of its moral implications, abortion has become one of the most emotional and divisive political issues in a number of countries, including some where restrictive legislation is still in force and others where a liberal policy appeared to be firmly established a few years ago. The International Planned Parenthood Federation addressed the legal issues of abortion in a recent conference.

Source: Christopher Tietze, *Induced Abortion: A World Review, 1981*, 4th ed. (New York: The Population Council, 1981), pp. 7–8.

Public Opinion

As abortion became a topic for decision-making in legislatures and courts, public opinion experts tried to fathom the public's ambivalent and contradictory views on the subject. In an article published in *Science* in 1971, Judith Blake, a demographer at the University of California, undertook a detailed study of public opinion between 1960 and 1970. Her findings were not entirely what people had expected. For one thing, she found that while a majority did not disapprove of abortion when performed to protect the life or health of the mother, there was less support for abortions for other reasons. There was very little support for completely elective abortion, that is, "abortion on demand" for any reason. She also found that there was not a great deal of difference between Catholics and non-Catholics on the matter.

DOCUMENT 32: "Abortion and Public Opinion: The 1960–1970 Decade." Judith Blake, 1971

In Western countries as well as elsewhere the history of population policy has, with few exceptions, been a chronicle of government efforts to repress birth limitation and reward reproduction. The relatively low natality of both continental and overseas Western European peoples is thus a testimony to their powerful motivation to have small-to-moderate size families in the face of strong governmental pressures to prevent them from doing so. In most of the United States, state laws on abortion constitute some of the more repressive of our pronatalist policies. Hence, they are among the many implicit and explicit influences on demographic events that will need revision if population limitation is to be pursued realistically as a national goal. What are the chances of fundamental changes in state laws to remove the legal ban on most kinds of abortion? Whether such modifications will come about primarily through the influence of widespread public opinion, or through the action of particular community groups, is uncertain. However, it is of some importance to know where public opinion stands and the direction in which it is moving.

To answer these questions, I shall analyze the differences and changes in views on abortion among white Americans during the past decade. The data are drawn from five Gallup polls taken during the period 1962 through 1969, and from the National Fertility Study of 1965 conducted by N. B. Ryder and C. F. Westoff. The data on abortion from the last three Gallup polls were gathered at my request. The polls sampled both men and women; the National Fertility Study sampled married women only. As for age, the polls interviewed persons aged 21 and over; the National Fertility Study interviewed those under age 55. All are national samples.

All the Gallup polls posed three identical questions:

Do you think abortion operations should or should not be legal in the following cases:
a. Where the health of the mother is in danger?
b. Where the child may be born deformed?
c. Where the family does not have enough money to support another child?

At my request, the three polls in 1968 and 1969 added a fourth question:

d. Where the parents simply have all the children they want although there would be no major health or financial problems involved in having another child?

The National Fertility Study had a somewhat different introduction to a total of six questions:

I'm going to read to you a list of six possible reasons why a woman might have a pregnancy interrupted. Would you tell me whether you think it would be all right for a woman to do this:
a. If the pregnancy seriously endangered the woman's health?
b. If the woman was not married?
c. If the couple could not afford another child?
d. If they didn't want any more children?
e. If the woman had good reason to believe the child might be deformed?
f. If the woman had been raped?

American Attitudes toward Abortion

In some ways, the public's views on abortion over the past decade accord with what might have been expected; in other ways, they appear surprising and paradoxical. It was to have been expected that, among the reasons for abortion, the justification in terms of the mother's health (already a legal ground in many states) would be more acceptable than the economic ground. In the light of widespread discussion of abortion reform, it was to be anticipated that disapproval would have declined, and that it would have declined most among the highly educated. It also seems understandable that in general non-Catholics would disapprove less than Catholics, but that fundamentalist non-Catholics (located in the South and Midwest) would be on a par with Catholics when it comes to disapproval. What may seem surprising, however, is the above-average disapproval by lower-class non-Catholics throughout the decade (and, in some cases, even an increase in disapproval); the greater feminine than masculine disapproval of financial and discretionary reasons for abortion (even when education is held constant); the above-average disapproval by youthful respondents (except in the case of the mother's health); the fact that respondents widely disapprove economic and discretionary reasons for abortion, in spite of the alleged importance of economic and individualistic motives in American life; and, finally, the rapid increase in tolerance by Catholics regarding all justifications for abortion. . . .

. . . When broken down by age, the data are somewhat surprising. Young women (those under 30) consistently disapprove elective abortion more than older women, although the disapproval of all age groups has lessened over time. Young men, on the other hand, are consistently more in favor of elective abortion, in the three surveys, than older men. It is nonetheless true that, even among young men, two-thirds disapproved. Only among college-educated men (of all ages combined) does disapproval fall to as low as 63 percent.

Non-Catholics and Abortion: Summary and Interpretation

The data presented here enable us to see which reasons for abortion already have strong and relatively stable public support, and which are in the process of gaining adherents. Abortion to preserve the mother's health or prevent child deformity may be said to be publicly well accepted, while abortion for discretionary ("selfish") reasons receives minimal but, nonetheless, rapidly growing support. Legal freedom of elective abortion, however, is rejected by the non-Catholic majority.

Among non-Catholics, the college-educated men are quite clearly the most favorable toward freedom of abortion. I have shown in other papers that for at least 30 years, men of this class have maintained modest family-size goals and have favored widespread distribution of birth-control information. Insofar as any support exists for the distribution of birth-control materials to teen-age girls, it comes from these men. Apparently, many of them desire a limited commitment to reproduction, are ready to see all restrictions on reproductive choice abolished, and are psychologically prepared to take a morally relaxed view of sexual behavior. . . .

When we turn to college-educated women in the non-Catholic population, we see that they do not share an equally positive attitude toward elective abortion. Yet we might have expected the attitude of women to be *more* positive than that of the men, since the inability to terminate an unwanted pregnancy presumably inconveniences women more than men. However, I have shown elsewhere that upper-class women desire somewhat larger families than upper-class men, and are generally less enthusiastic about introducing complete freedom of choice into the reproductive sphere. For example, well-educated women are no more likely to approve contraceptives for unmarried teen-age girls than are poorly educated women, and they are far less likely to approve of them than are well-educated men.

In attempting to account for the seemingly paradoxical views of upper-class women, we must bear in mind their greater involvement than men with reproduction as a career. Motherhood is the principal career for most women, and hence they may well experience ambivalence and uncertainty when confronted by major changes in the conditions of this career. Restrictions on reproductive choice are part of the mystique surrounding the "occupation" of motherhood. Occupational mystiques are, of course, not unique to the feminine sex; their self-serving function has been widely recognized in other spheres. To a very real extent, restrictions on abortion bolster the public sentiment that motherhood is "natural" and inevitable, rather than planned and discretionary. To legalize elective abortion is to drastically undercut women's freedom to create a respected occupational niche for themselves simply by being careless. In a sense, the battle of the sexes at this social level consists precisely in the different vantage points from which men and women approach sexual relations. What is for men a recreation and diversion is for women a potential source of income, social status, and achievement. At the same time, the inconvenience and risk in making reproduction completely discretionary is being passed on to women. Their uncertainty concerning elective abortion is therefore understandable. . . .

My interpretation of why resistance to enhanced availability of abortion is greater among women than among men of the upper class is given credence by the even more pronounced resistance among the lower classes of both sexes. In a sense, the "deviant" attitude is that of the upper-class male, and it is his desire for a small family, his instrumental view of teen-age sexual behavior, and his willingness to approve convenience methods of birth control that require explanation. The remainder of the population holds views that are generally in line with existing traditional and legal norms of sexual behavior and pronatalist constraints. These norms, to an observer, may well appear incompatible with many of the economic and status interests of the individuals they affect. Thus it is easy to see, for example, that many women and poor people would be "better off" with no children, or few children, or fewer children than they have. What is perhaps less apparent is that the norms supporting such reproductive behavior are in line with, and, indeed, a part of the many *non*economic goals and interests of most of the population—in particular, a commitment to family roles and rewards. . . .

Views Held by Catholics on Abortion

Let us now examine the views held by Catholics. In general, they disapprove of legalizing abortion more than non-Catholics, but the difference is less than might be expected when one considers that the Catholic Church unconditionally bans the induced termination of pregnancy. The largest differences between Catholics and non-Catholics occur with regard to justifications that are least disapproved by both religious groups—the mother's health and child deformity—because non-Catholics are so close to unanimous in their approval of these reasons for abortion. However, although not equaling the views of non-Catholics, the amount of disapproval by Catholics has decreased rapidly since the beginning of the decade. . . .

Conclusion

Our examination in this article of the opinions of various groups in the population on the legalization of abortion contradicts the conclusions usually drawn by those who argue on a priori ideological grounds that certain groups *should* support legalized abortion in the United States. According to the latter, abortion should be supported most strongly by the less advantaged and by women. Clearly, this is not the case. Legalized abortion is supported most strongly by the non-Catholic, male, well-educated "establishment." I have explained this finding in terms of the occupational and familial roles that such men play, in contrast with the roles performed by women in their own class, and by men and women in classes beneath them.

We may conclude, therefore, that changes in abortion laws, like most social changes, will not come about by agitation at the grass roots level, or by the activity of righteously indignant individuals who cannot currently circumvent existing statutes. Rather, it is to the educated and influential that we must look for effecting rapid legislative change in spite of conservative opinions among important subgroups such as the lower classes and women. These subgroups would probably avail themselves of the enhanced freedom to have abortions once it was secured for them by those whose social investment in traditional family norms and statuses is more limited. But these subgroups will not necessarily accord widespread approval to the practice of discretionary abortion, nor is it clear that the population generally will do more than tolerate abortion as a necessary evil—even if it is relied on extensively as a stopgap measure. This popular ambivalence, plus the cumbersomeness of state-by-state change in abortion laws, suggest that a Supreme Court ruling concerning the constitutionality of existing state restrictions is the only road to rapid change in the grounds for abortion. Interestingly, such a ruling would be no more at variance with public opinion than some other famous judicial decisions have been. Hence, if we heeded only the fact that 80 percent of our white population disapproves elective abortion, our expectations concerning major reform would be too modest. We must also take into account the more positive views of a powerful minority; and we must bear in mind that changes far more radical than this one have been effected lawfully by such minorities, even when the issues enjoyed no more public support than currently exists for elective abortion.

Source: Judith Blake, "Abortion and Public Opinion: The 1960–1970 Decade," *Science* 171 (1971): 540–48. Copyright 1971 by the AAAS.

Philosophical Arguments For and Against the Liberalization of Abortion Laws

As the controversy over reform of abortion laws became more heated, different arguments were advanced for and against the liberalization of abortion laws. Many of the arguments were based on social considerations—the toll in death and serious injury from illegal abortions, the tragedy of unwanted children, the burdens on families. Underlying these arguments were religious and philosophical concerns. The following questions were among those frequently asked: Is the fetus a person? Does abortion involve the killing of a human being? When does an embryo become a person? When does life begin? When, if ever, is the killing of the unborn justifiable? If a choice must be made between mother and child, when do the mother's interests prevail?

Opinions on these matters differed wildly. Extreme conservatives, a group that included the Roman Catholic clergy, believed that abortion was only justifiable when the life of the mother would be at risk in childbirth. Liberals, reformers, and feminists emphasized the individual's right to control her own body, and believed that the interests of fully formed, adult women overrode those of the fertilized egg, the zygote, the embryo, or the fetus. Moderates tried to split the difference and supported abortion rights under some circumstances but rejected the idea of abortion on demand, believing that some restrictions on abortion were desirable.

Interestingly enough, these general religious and philosophical issues were not fully argued in *Roe v. Wade*, the Supreme Court's decision about the constitutionality of state criminal abortion laws. Lawyers and judges emphasized legal and constitutional rather than moral questions. But these underlying issues continued to fuel the debate over abortion long after 1973.

In a paper published in 1971 in the journal *Philosophy and Public*

Affairs, Roger Wertheimer, a professional philosopher, tried to sort out the different strands of argument over the morality of abortion. The themes and arguments that he discussed surfaced over and over again in the continuing controversy; they are restated in the testimony over proposed constitutional amendments before the Senate Judiciary Committee in 1974 and 1975. Professor Wertheimer's analysis shows us why the different positions were unreconcilable and why it was so difficult to find a consensus on the issue of abortion.

DOCUMENT 33: "Understanding the Abortion Argument." Roger Wertheimer, 1971

[When is abortion justifiable?]

At what stage of fetal development, if any, and for what reasons, if any, is abortion justifiable? Each part of the question has received diverse answers, which in turn have been combined in various ways.

According to the liberal, the fetus should be disposable upon the mother's request until it is viable; thereafter it may be destroyed only to save the mother's life. To an extreme liberal the fetus is like an appendix, and may be destroyed upon demand anytime before its birth. A moderate view is that until viability the fetus should be disposable if it is the result of felonious intercourse [rape], or if the mother's or child's physical or mental health would be gravely impaired. This position is susceptible to wide variations. The conservative position is that the fetus may be aborted before quickening but not after, unless the mother's life is at stake. For the extreme conservative, the fetus, once conceived, may not be destroyed for any reason short of saving the mother's life.)

This last might be called the Catholic view, but note that it, or some close variant of it, is shared by numerous Christian sects, and is or was maintained by Jews, by Indians of both hemispheres, by a variety of tribes of diverse geographical location and cultural level, and even by some contemporary atheistical biochemists who are political liberals. Much the same can be said of any of the listed positions. I call attention to such facts for two reasons. First, they suggest that the abortion issue is in some way special, since, given any position on abortion and any position on any other issue, you can probably find a substantial group of people who have simultaneously held both. Second, these facts are regularly denied or distorted by the disputants. Thus, liberals habitually argue as though extreme conservatism were an invention of contemporary scholasticism [Catholic thought] with a mere century of popish heritage behind it. This in the face of the fact that the position has had the force of law in most American states for more than a century, and continues to be law even in states where Catholicism is without influence. We shall see that these two points are not unrelated. . . .

[When does a human life begin?]

First off I should note that the expressions "a human life," "a human being," "a person" are virtually interchangeable in this context. As I use these expressions, except for monstrosities, every member of our species is indubitably a person, a human being at the very latest at birth. Virtually everyone, at least every party to the current controversy, *actually* does agree to this. However, we should be aware that in this area both agreement and disagreement are often merely verbal and therefore only apparent. For example, many people will say that it takes a month or even more after birth for the infant to become a person, and they will explain themselves by saying that a human being must have self-consciousness, or a personality. But upon investigation this disagreement normally turns out to be almost wholly semantic, for we can agree on all the facts about child development, and furthermore we can agree, at least in a general way, in our moral judgments on the care to be accorded the child at various stages. Thus, though they deny that a day-old infant is a person, they admit that its life cannot be forfeited for any reason that would not equally apply to a two-year-old. . . .

Implicit in my remarks is the suggestion that one way to find out how someone uses the expression "human being" and related ones is by looking at his moral judgments. . . .

[The defense of the conservative position]

The defense of the extreme conservative position runs as follows. The key premise is that a human fetus is a human being, not a partial or potential one, but a full-fledged, actualized human life. Given that premise, the entire conservative position unfolds with a simple, relentless logic, every principle of which would be endorsed by any sensible liberal. Suppose human embryos are human beings. Their innocence is beyond question, so nothing could justify our destroying them except, perhaps, the necessity of saving some other innocent human life. That is, since similar cases must be treated in similar ways, some consideration would justify the abortion of a prenatal child if and only if a comparable consideration would justify the killing of a postnatal child.

This is a serious and troubling argument positing an objection in principle to abortion. It is the *only* such argument. Nothing else could possibly justify the staggering social costs of the present abortion laws. . . .

The Catholic defense of the status quo is left unfazed, even untouched by the standard liberal critique that consists of an inventory of the calamitous effects of our abortion laws on mother and child, on family, and on society in general. Of course, were it not for those effects we would feel no press to be rid of the laws—nor any *need* to retain them. That inventory does present a conclusive rebuttal of any of the piddling objections conservatives often toss in for good measure. But still, the precise, scientific tabulations of grief do not add up to an argument here, for sometimes pain, no matter how undesirable, may not be avoidable, may not stem from some injustice. I do not intend to understate that pain; the tragedies brought on by unwanted children are plentiful and serious—but so too are those brought on by unwanted parents, yet few liberals would legalize parricide [parent-killing] as the final solution to the massive social problem of the permanently visiting parent who drains his children's financial and emotional resources. In the Church's view, these cases are fully analogous; the fetus is as much a human life as is the parent; they share the same moral status. Either can be a source of abiding anguish and hardship for the other—and sometimes there may be no escape. In this, our world, some people get stuck with the care of others, and sometimes there may be no way of getting unstuck, at least no just and decent way. Taking the other person's life is not such a way. . . .

There is a subsidiary approach, a peculiarly liberal one, which seeks to disarm the Catholic position not by disputing it, but by conceding the Catholic's right to believe it and act accordingly. The liberal asks only that Catholics concede him the same freedom, and thus abandon support of abortion laws. The Catholic must retort that the issue is not, as the liberal supposes, one of religious ritual and self-regarding behavior, but of minority rights, the minority being not Catholics but the fetuses of all faiths, and the right being the right of an innocent human being to life itself. The liberal's proposal is predicated on abortion being a crime without a victim, but in the Catholic view the fetus is a full-scale victim and is so independent of the liberal's recognition of that fact. Catholics can no more think it is wrong for themselves but permissible for Protestants to destroy a fetus than liberals can think it wrong for themselves but permissible for racists to victimize blacks. Given his premise, the Catholic is as justified in employing the power of the state to protect embryos as the liberal is to protect blacks. . . .

[Liberals can't accept the Catholics' first premise.]

Now, why do liberals, even the cleverest ones, so consistently fail to make contact with the Catholic challenge? After all, as I have made plain, once premised that the fetus is a person, the entire conservative position recites the common sense of any moral man. The liberal's failure is, I suggest, due to that premise. To him, it is not simply false, but

wildly, madly false, it is nonsense, totally unintelligible, literally unbelievable. Just look at an embryo. It is an amorphous speck of apparently coagulated protoplasm. It has no eyes or ears, no head at all. It
can't walk or talk; you can't dress it or wash it. Why, it doesn't even
qualify as a Barbie doll, and yet millions of people call it a human being,
just like one of us. It's as though someone were to look at an acorn and
call it an oak tree, or, better, it's as though someone squirted a paint
tube at a canvas and called the outcome a painting, a work of art—and
people believed him. . . .

The Catholic claim would be a joke were it not that millions of people
take it seriously, and millions more suffer for their solemnity. Liberals
need an explanation of how it is possible for the conservatives to believe
what they say, for after all, conservatives are not ignorant or misin-
formed about the facts here—I mean, for example, the facts of embryol-
ogy. So the liberal asks, "How *can* they believe what they say? How *can*
they even make sense of it?" The question is forced upon the liberal
because his conception of rationality is jeopardized by the possibility
that a normal, unbiased observer of the relevant facts could really accept
the conservative claim. It is this question, I think, that drives the liberal
to attribute the whole antiabortion movement to Catholicism and to the
Roman clergy in particular. . . .

[Is the personhood of the fetus simply a matter of terminology?]

At this juncture of the argument, a liberal with a positivistic background will announce that it's just a matter of definition whether the
fetus is a person. If by this the liberal means that the question "Is a fetus
a person?" is equivalent to "Is it proper to call a fetus a person?"—that
is, "Is it true to say of a fetus, 'it is a person'?"—then the liberal is quite
right and quite unhelpful. But he is likely to add that we can define
words any way we like. . . .

A more sophisticated liberal may suggest that fetuses are borderline
cases. Asking whether fetuses are persons is like asking whether viruses
are living creatures; the proper answer is that they are like them in some
ways but not in others; the rules of the language don't dictate one way
or the other, so you can say what you will. . . . And finally, precisely
because with the virus you can say what you will, it is unlike the fetus.
As regards the virus, scientists can manage nicely while totally ignoring
the issue. Not so with the fetus, because deciding what to call it is
tantamount to a serious and unavoidable moral decision.

This last remark suggests that the fetus' humanity is really a moral
issue, not a factual issue at all. . . .

The liberal dates hominization [personhood] from birth or viability.
The choice of either stage is explicable by reference to some obvious
considerations. At birth the child leaves its own private space and enters

the public world. And he can be looked at and acted upon and interacted with. And so on. On the other hand, someone may say viability is the crucial point, because it is then that the child has the capacity to do all those things it does at birth; the sole difference is a quite inessential one of geography. . . .

[Does life begin at conception?]

Liberals always misplace the attractions of fertilization as the critical date when they try to argue that if you go back that far, you could just as well call the sperm or the egg a human being. But people call the zygote [fertilized egg] a human life not just because it contains the DNA blueprint which determines the physical development of the organism from then on, and not just because of the potential inherent in it, but also because it and it alone can claim to be the beginning of the spatio-temporal-causal chain of the physical object that is a human body. And though I think the abortion controversy throws doubt on the claim that bodily continuity is the *sole* criterion of personal identity, I think the attractions of that philosophical thesis are of a piece with the attractions of fertilization as the point marking the start of a person. Given our conceptual framework, one can't go back further. Neither the sperm nor the egg could be, by itself, a human being, any more than an atom of sodium or an atom of chlorine could by itself properly be called salt. One proof of this is that *no one* is in the least inclined to call a sperm or an egg a human life. . . .

These are some of the considerations, but how are they actually presented? What, for example, does the liberal say and do? Note that his arguments are usually formulated as a series of rhetorical questions. He points to certain facts, and then, quite understandably, he expects his listeners to respond in a particular way—and when they don't, he finds their behavior incomprehensible. First he will point to an infant and say, "Look at it! Aren't you inclined to say that it is one of us?" And then he will describe an embryo as I did earlier, and say, "Look at the difference between it and us! Could you call that a human being?" All this is quite legitimate, but notice what the liberal is doing. First, he has us focus our attention on the *earliest stages* of the fetus, where the contrast with us is greatest. He does not have us look at the fetus shortly before viability or birth, where the differences between it and what he is willing to call a human being are quite minimal. Still, this is not an unfair tactic when combating the view that the fertilized egg is a human life. . . .

We seem to be stuck with the indeterminateness of the fetus' humanity. This does not mean that, whatever you believe, it is true or true for you if you believe it. Quite the contrary, it means that, whatever you believe, it's not true—but neither is it false. You believe it, and that's the end of the matter.

[What is the moderate position?]

But obviously that's not the end of the matter; the same urgent moral and political decisions still confront us. But before we run off to make our existential leaps over the liberal-conservative impasse, we might meander through the moderate position. I'll shorten the trip by speaking only of features found throughout the spectrum of moderate views. For the moderate, the fetus is not a human being, but it's not a mere maternal appendage either; it's a human fetus, and it has a separate moral status just as animals do. A fetus is not an object that we can treat however we wish, neither is it a person whom we must treat as we would wish to be treated in return. Thus, *some* legal prohibitions on abortion *might* be justified in the name of the fetus *qua* human fetus, just as we accord some legal protection to animals, not for the sake of the owners, but for the benefit of animals themselves.

Ultimately, most liberals and conservatives are, in a sense, only extreme moderates. Few liberals really regard abortion, at least in the later stages, as a bit of elective surgery. Suppose a woman had her fifth-month fetus aborted purely out of curiosity as to what it looked like, and perhaps then had it bronzed. Who among us would not deem both her and her actions reprehensible? One might refuse to outlaw the behavior, but still, clearly we do not respond to this case as we would to the removal of an appendix or a tooth. Similarly, in my experience few of even the staunchest conservatives consistently regard the fetus, at least in the earlier stages, in the same way as they do a fellow adult. When the cause of grief is a miscarriage, the object of grief is the mother; rarely does anyone feel pity or sorrow for the embryo itself. . . .

The moderate position is as problematic as it is popular. The moderate is driven in two directions, liberalism and conservatism, by the same question: Why do you make these exceptions and not those?

The difficulty here is comparable to that regarding animals. There are dogs, pigs, mosquitoes, worms, bacteria, etc., and we kill them for food, clothing, ornamentation, sport, convenience, and out of simple irritation or unblinking inadvertence. We allow different animals to be killed for different reasons, and there are enormous differences between people on all of this. In general, for most of us, the higher the evolutionary stage of the species or the later the developmental stage of the fetus, the more restricted our permission to kill. But it is far more complicated than that, and anyone with a fully consistent, let alone principled, system of beliefs on these matters is usually thought fanatical by the rest of us. . . .

I am suggesting that what our natural response to a thing is, and how we naturally react to it cognitively, affectively, and behaviorally, is partly definitive of that thing, and is therefore partly definitive of how we ought to respond to that thing. Often only an actual confrontation will tell us what we need to know, and sometimes we may respond differently, and thus have differing understandings.

Source: Roger Wertheimer, "Understanding the Abortion Argument," *Philosophy and Public Affairs* 1, no. 1 (1971): 67–95. [A shortened version.]

PART II: FOR FURTHER READING

Boston Women's Health Book Collective. *Our Bodies, Ourselves: Updated and Expanded for the 90's*, New York: Simon and Schuster, 1992.

Callahan, Daniel. *Abortion: Law, Choice and Morality*. London: Macmillan, 1970.

Davis, Nanette. *From Crime to Choice: The Transformation of Abortion in America*. Westport, Conn.: Greenwood Press, 1985.

Feinberg, Joel, ed. *The Problem of Abortion*. Belmont, Calif.: Wadsworth, 1973.

Gallup, George H. *The Gallup Polls: Public Opinion 1935–1971*. 3 vols. New York: Random House, 1973.

Hole, Judith, and Ellen Levine. *Rebirth of Feminism*. New York: Quadrangle Books, 1971.

Irons, Peter. *The Courage of Their Convictions*. New York: Free Press, 1988.

Lader, Lawrence. *Abortion II: Making the Revolution*. Boston: Beacon Press, 1973.

Luker, Kristin. *Abortion and the Politics of Motherhood*. Berkeley: University of California Press, 1984.

Nathanson, Bernard N. *Aborting America*. Garden City, N.Y.: Doubleday, 1979.

Westoff, Charles F., and N. B. Ryder. *The Contraceptive Revolution*. Princeton: Princeton University Press, 1977.

Part III

The 1973 Abortion Cases

By 1971 fourteen states had revised their abortion laws to permit abortions under certain circumstances, and four states had repealed their abortion statutes, but in a majority of the states abortion remained a crime. Change was coming through state legislative activity, but it was coming slowly, one state at a time. And it was also true that voters in some of the states were determined to keep abortion illegal.

Perhaps the courts could provide a shortcut. A Supreme Court decision declaring that laws restricting abortion were unconstitutional would bring change much more quickly, overturning all state laws at a single blow. Under Chief Justice Earl Warren (1953–1969) the Supreme Court had made a number of decisions that had worked similar revolutionary changes in the law and politics of the country. The Court had overturned state laws requiring racial segregation in public schools. It had made a number of important changes in the way the criminal justice system was administered. And it had announced a "one-man, one-vote" ruling that was forcing the states to give voters equal representation in voting for members of Congress and state legislatures. Advocates of abortion reform hoped that they could use the judicial system to bring about changes in abortion laws as well.

Throughout 1970 and 1971 a number of abortion cases were filed in state and federal courts, but only one of these cases reached the Supreme Court. That case, *United States v. Vuitch* (1971) (see Document 30), was decided on a technical point of law and did not really address the general question of the constitutionality of laws limiting a woman's decision to have an abortion. If the Court accepted another abortion case, it would have to decide some difficult questions. Did a woman have a constitutional right to decide for herself whether or not to have an abortion? What part of the Constitution protected such a right? Were the reasons for state laws forbidding abortions sufficiently strong to outweigh a woman's right (if she had one)? And what about the fetus—did it have rights that were constitutionally protected? If the proper case were presented to it, the Supreme Court would face these questions.

Cases do not reach the Supreme Court simply because there are important constitutional questions that need to be decided. The Court will only act if there is an actual case before it.

Sarah Weddington and Linda Coffee, two young lawyers practicing in Dallas, Texas, considered bringing such a case. They thought they could present winning arguments against the constitutionality of Texas' old (1857) abortion statute, a law that forbade abortions except to save the life of a mother. But they needed a plaintiff, a client who could claim that *her* constitutional rights were being violated. Persons and groups wishing to test the constitutionality of statutes must do so by bringing a real lawsuit that seeks to resolve a real conflict between real parties. Weddington and Coffee were put in touch with a young, pregnant woman who had been denied an abortion, and she agreed to let them represent her in court. Her case, filed in a United States district court in Dallas, would eventually reach the Supreme Court.

In the Supreme Court, the case was argued twice, once in 1971 and again in 1972. After the first argument, the Court decided to put off final decision until after two new justices, selected by President Nixon, could take part in the decision. Almost everyone expected the Court to take a conservative stand and hold that abortion was a matter for the states to decide for themselves. Almost no one, including those in favor of abortion reform, expected the Court to decide that the right to choose an abortion was protected by the Constitution. People were also surprised by the strong vote in favor of abortion rights: seven justices voted for, two voted against.

If proponents of change thought that a Supreme Court decision could settle such an explosive issue decisively, they were sadly mistaken. The decision was hardly announced before opponents vowed to reverse it—in the courts, in the legislatures, on the election trail, using whatever means it would take. *Roe v. Wade* lit a political flash fire that divided the nation and was still sizzling and burning twenty years later.

The Law and the Cases

THE CONSTITUTIONAL PROVISIONS: LIBERTY, PRIVACY, AND THE NINTH AMENDMENT

Did the Constitution provide a basis for a ruling in favor of abortion rights?

Constitutional provisions that are relevant to a woman's claim to a protected constitutional right to choose an abortion are to be found in the Ninth Amendment and the Fourteenth Amendment to the Constitution, and in a right to privacy that is not explicitly written into the Constitution, but has been established in several court decisions.

The Ninth Amendment has never received a definitive interpretation by the Supreme Court. It appears to grant rights to the people in addition to those that have been spelled out specifically in the Bill of Rights. Some constitutional scholars believe that the Congress that proposed the amendment intended these "unenumerated rights" to cover customary, traditional, and time-honored rights, those freedoms that Americans have always believed that they have, whether they are listed or not. The men who drafted the Bill of Rights did not think that it was possible to specify all such rights and included the Ninth Amendment as an instruction to the courts that the rights of the people were to be protected generously.

Some justices have argued that the right to privacy might be one of these traditional unenumerated rights. Certainly there is a strong national conviction that the personal affairs of individuals should be free from government regulation. It is also possible to argue that the Founding Fathers would have considered the reproductive lives of men and women a private area that was none of government's business.

DOCUMENT 34: The Ninth Amendment (1791)

The enumeration in the Constitution of certain rights shall not be construed to deny or disparage others retained by the people.

interpret   *misosprileia,*

Source: Constitution of the United States.

THE FOURTEENTH AMENDMENT

The Fourteenth Amendment was adopted (in 1868) to ensure that the decisions hammered out by the Civil War would be respected by future generations. Before the Civil War state governments could hold people in slavery and could decide what rights they did and did not have. For protection from arbitrary action by the states, people had to look to their state constitutions or to the power of the vote. The United States Constitution did not protect them against their own states.

The Bill of Rights protects us against the national government, the government in Washington. The Fourteenth Amendment added protections against the tyranny of state governments. Section 1 has three clauses: (1) the privileges and immunities clause, (2) the due process clause, and (3) the equal protection clause. These clauses proclaim that "no state" shall interfere with the privileges and immunities, the liberty, or the equality of the people.

The abortion rights reformers argued that the "liberty" protected by the due process clause included the freedom of women to decide on abortions without interference by the state. Some of the women's groups thought that the equal protection clause was also relevant since laws prohibiting abortion affected the equality of women.

The state of Texas had a different view of the Fourteenth Amendment's applicability. It claimed that the section protecting the "life, liberty, and property" of all persons protected the lives of fetuses, and that fetuses should be recognized as "persons" within the meaning of this clause.

In *Roe v. Wade* the Supreme Court held that the term *liberty* in the Fourteenth Amendment covered a woman's right to choose an abortion (at least early in pregnancy). It held that the right to privacy gives women a right to choose whether or not to bear a child, free from interference by the state. It held that a fetus is not a person within the meaning of the Fourteenth Amendment, since the framers of the amendment thought that "persons" were people who were already born. The Court did not discuss the issue of equality.

DOCUMENT 35: The Fourteenth Amendment, Section 1 (1868)

All persons born or naturalized in the United States, and subject to the jurisdiction thereof, are citizens of the United States and of the State wherein they reside. No state shall make or enforce any law which shall abridge the privileges or immunities of citizens of the United States; nor shall any State deprive any person of life, liberty, or property, without the due process of law; nor deny to any person within its jurisdiction the equal protection of the laws.

Source: Constitution of the United States.

GRISWOLD V. CONNECTICUT AND THE RIGHT TO PRIVACY

The right to privacy is not set forth in the Constitution in so many words. In 1965, however, in an opinion written by Justice William O. Douglas, the Supreme Court found that a constitutional right to privacy stems from various provisions in the Bill of Rights (First, Third, Fourth, Fifth, and Ninth Amendments) that protect privacy interests.

The case that established the right to privacy in constitutional law, *Griswold v. Connecticut*, grew out of a controversy over laws prohibiting the manufacture, sale, or use of contraceptives. By 1965 most states had long since repealed such laws, but Connecticut still retained an antique statute on its books that made it a crime to teach the use of contraceptives or to *use* contraceptives. This law made it difficult for family planning groups like Planned Parenthood to teach contraceptive methods in their clinics.

Estelle Griswold, executive director of the Planned Parenthood League of Connecticut, and Dr. C. Lee Buxton, the medical director of the league and a professor at Yale Medical School, were convicted of giving information on contraception to married couples in violation of the law. They appealed, and their case came before the Supreme Court. Although not all nine justices were in total agreement on the reasoning behind the decision, six justices held that the Constitution does protect the right of private persons to use birth control methods.

The "right to privacy" precedent established in this decision was one of the constitutional bases for the *Roe* decision, eight years later.

DOCUMENT 36: *Griswold v. Connecticut* (1965)

Mr. Justice DOUGLAS delivered the opinion of the Court. . . .

. . . We are met with a wide range of questions that implicate the Due Process Clause of the Fourteenth Amendment. Overtones of some arguments suggest that *Lochner v. State of New York* [1905] . . . should be our guide. But we decline that invitation as we did in *West Coast Hotel Co. v. Parrish* [1937]. . . . We do not sit as a super-legislature to determine the wisdom, need, and propriety of laws that touch economic problems, business affairs, or social conditions. This law, however, operates directly on an intimate relation of husband and wife and their physician's role in one aspect of that relation.

The association of people is not mentioned in the Constitution nor in the Bill of Rights. The right to educate a child in a school of the parents' choice—whether public or private or parochial—is also not mentioned. Nor is the right to study any particular subject or any foreign language. Yet the First Amendment has been construed to include certain of those rights. . . .

[Previous] cases suggest that specific guarantees in the Bill of Rights have penumbras, formed by emanations from those guarantees that help give them life and substance. . . . Various guarantees create zones of privacy. The right of association contained in the penumbra of the First Amendment is one. . . . The Third Amendment in its prohibition against the quartering of soldiers "in any house" in time of peace without the consent of the owner is another facet of that privacy. The Fourth Amendment explicitly affirms the "right of the people to be secure in their persons, houses, papers, and effects, against unreasonable searches and seizures." The Fifth Amendment in its Self-Incrimination Clause enables the citizen to create a zone of privacy which government may not force him to surrender to his detriment. The Ninth Amendment provides: "The enumeration in the Constitution, of certain rights, shall not be construed to deny or disparage others retained by the people. . . .

The Fourth and Fifth Amendments were described in *Boyd v. United States* [1886] . . . as protection against all governmental invasions "of the sanctity of a man's home and the privacies of life." We recently referred in *Mapp v. Ohio* [1961] . . . to the Fourth Amendment as creating a "right to privacy, no less important than any other right carefully and particularly reserved to the people." . . .

We have had many controversies over these penumbral rights of "privacy and repose." . . . These cases bear witness that the right of privacy which presses for recognition here is a legitimate one.

The present case, then, concerns a relationship lying within the zone of privacy created by several fundamental constitutional guarantees. And it concerns a law which, in forbidding the *use* of contraceptives rather than regulating their manufacture or sale, seeks to achieve its goals by means having a maximum destructive impact upon that relationship. Such a law cannot stand in light of the familiar principle, so often applied by this Court, that a "governmental purpose to control or prevent activities constitutionally subject to state regulation may not be achieved by means which sweep unnecessarily broadly and thereby invade the area of protected freedoms." . . . Would we allow the police to search the sacred precincts of marital bedrooms for telltale signs of the use of contraceptives? The very idea is repulsive to the notions of privacy surrounding the marriage relationship.

We deal with a right of privacy older than the Bill of Rights—older than our political parties, older than our school system. Marriage is a coming together for better or worse, hopefully enduring, and intimate to the degree of being sacred. It is an association that promotes a way of life, not causes; a harmony in living, not political faiths; a bilateral loyalty, not commercial or social projects. Yet it is an association for as noble a purpose as any involved in our prior decisions.

Source: 381 *U.S. Reports* 479 (1965).

HOW THE CASES GOT STARTED

In 1975, testifying before the Senate Committee on the Judiciary, which was holding hearings on whether an amendment restricting abortions should be added to the Constitution, Sarah Weddington, the attorney who argued the *Roe* case before the Supreme Court, explained how she got involved in the case.

DOCUMENT 37: Testimony of Sarah Weddington, Attorney, Before the Senate Committee on the Judiciary, 1975

Senator Birch Bayh (Democrat, Indiana) Chairman of the Subcommittee on Constitutional Amendments of the Senate Committee on the Judiciary. Could you give us a 1-minute response or a 2-minute response to the question of deep down why you felt strongly enough to get involved in this *Roe v. Wade* situation and carry it all the way to the Supreme Court?

Ms. Weddington. By accident. I had a group of friends in Austin who wanted to do abortion counseling. They came to me and said they were afraid if they did that they would be prosecuted for it.

I was a young lawyer. The *Roe v. Wade* case was my first contested case. I had been taught in law school that where there was a wrong, there was a remedy. I decided after doing some research that to deny women that alternative, that choice, was wrong, and so there ought to be a remedy. And we filed the lawsuit.

Quite frankly, if I had known when I filed the case all that it would entail and that I would end up before the Supreme Court, I would probably have been so frightened of it, I would not have done it.

Senator Bayh. Let me define it. Why did you think if there is a wrong, there is a remedy? Why did you think there was a wrong involved?

Ms. Weddington. I think it is because when you analyze the whole situation that you are in essence putting the right of the woman involved against the interest of the fetus. It seemed to me that in law, we have always recognized that full legal rights attach at birth. When I look at the women who are involved and the impact of pregnancy on them, from all of the different ramifications there are, I cannot help but believe that a woman ought to have the ability to determine the course of her life. She ought to be able to determine what things will happen to her, how they will happen, and what her life will be about. She cannot make those decisions if there is a complete prohibition against abortion because at this time, we do not have total means of avoiding pregnancy.

Methods fail. Sometimes people are not informed about methods. Sometimes they do not use them well. However, when a woman is faced with an unwanted pregnancy, I see all of the questions that are involved from her life. When I look at the interest of the life of the fetus compared to the interests of the woman I simply—after looking at everything I know, and for all the years I have been in this discussion—have to say that the basic underlying principle to me is that the women should have the right to make a choice. We should not force a choice on those who do not wish an abortion. Any choice should be an informed choice, but the woman, in the last analysis, should have that choice of how her life will go.

Senator Bayh. Were you satisfied with the distinctions that the Court made between the trimesters? Or, were you satisfied with those limitations on the position that you argue very strongly, the right of the woman to have choice to do what she wants to with her life?

Ms. Weddington. It is probably not the decision I would have written, because there had been no prior precedents in law for the trimester approach. I think that Justice Blackmun might have been acting in the role of a moderator.

Senator Bayh. How would you have written the decision? I mean, just briefly?

Ms. Weddington. I think, briefly, had I simply been looking at prior legal precedent I would have had to have written that all prior precedent has been to the extent that life begins at birth; and that, therefore, the law was unconstitutional because it went against the principle that life begins at birth.

I think Blackmun was subject to some of the same concerns that you have expressed today, and he was trying to find a way to do two things. One, to resolve the balancing between the interest of the woman and the interest of the fetus, particularly in later pregnancy.

And second, I think the Court felt that there might be numerous States that might attempt to write different kinds of statutes. Therefore, the Court attempted to set up some sort of guidelines for the States to have an indication of the kinds of restrictions that they could constitutionally pass and that the Court would uphold.

In that sense, I am satisfied with the decision and feel that it was a very good one on the Court's part. The Court has been accused of legislating, and I suppose in a sense it did. And yet I think, given considerations for what would happen otherwise, that it was a good thing for them to have done.

Source: U.S. Congress, Senate Committee on the Judiciary, *Hearings on Constitutional Amendments*, 94th Congress, 1st session, 1975, v. 4, pp. 514–15.

INSIDE THE COURT

A book published in 1979 entitled *The Brethren* went behind the scenes to describe the making of the abortion decisions. Written by two investigative reporters, the book gives a picture of the maneuvering and bargaining that takes place as the nine justices try to come to an agreement on how to decide a difficult case. Because the reporters relied on gossip from law clerks and other court personnel in collecting their information, there has been some criticism of the accuracy of parts of the book. But it is well known from other accounts that the process by which nine highly individualistic thinkers reach a consensus often involves a certain amount of give and take.

The justices who took part in the decision were as follows. The name of the president who appointed each justice appears in parentheses.

Chief Justice Warren E. Burger (Republican. President Nixon)

Justice William O. Douglas (Democrat. President Roosevelt)

Justice Potter Stewart (Republican. President Eisenhower)

Justice William J. Brennan (Democrat. President Eisenhower)

Justice Byron R. White (Democrat. President Kennedy)

Justice Thurgood Marshall (Democrat. President Johnson)

Justice Harry Blackmun (Republican. President Nixon)

Justice William H. Rehnquist (Republican. President Nixon)

Justice Lewis O. Powell (Democrat. President Nixon)

DOCUMENT 38: Deciding the Abortion Cases: *The Brethren.* Bob Woodward and Scott Armstrong, 1979

Harry Blackmun returned to Rochester, Minnesota, for the summer of 1972 and immersed himself in research at the huge Mayo Clinic medical library. Rochester and the clinic were home to Blackmun, a safe harbor after a stormy term. He worked in a corner of the assistant librarian's office for two weeks without saying a word to anyone on the Mayo staff about the nature of his inquiry.

In his summer office in a Rochester high-rise, Blackmun began to organize the research that would bolster his abortion opinion. He talked by phone nearly every day with one of his clerks who had agreed to stay in Washington for the summer.

Blackmun pondered the relevance of the Hippocratic oath, which prohibits doctors from performing abortions. He also wanted to understand the positions of the medical organizations and to learn more about the advances in sustaining the life of a fetus outside the womb.

One by one, new elements found their way into his draft. His clerk worked each change into the text back in Washington. The language remained Blackmun's; the more rigorous analysis was the work of the clerk. For the first time, the right to privacy emerged explicitly. It was not absolute. It was limited by the state's interest in protecting the pregnant woman's health and the potential life of the fetus.

As they developed their analytic basis, Blackmun and his clerk tried to answer the crucial question: when did the state's interest in protecting the life of the fetus become overriding and outweigh the woman's right to privacy? Clearly there was such a point. The state's interest increased with time. But no definite answer could be derived from the Constitution.

Blackmun turned to medicine. Doctors often divided pregnancies into three equal stages, or trimesters, each of roughly three months. Abortions were generally safe in the first trimester and, under proper medical conditions, could be performed safely in the second. It was at about this time, at the end of the second trimester, that the fetus became *viable*, or capable of living outside the womb. That was at about twenty-four to twenty-eight weeks, six months for all practical purposes. Therefore, the two medical interests—protecting both the health of the mother and the potential life of the fetus—seemed to converge and become overriding at about this six-month point. Abortions during the first two trimesters could and should be permitted. The draft gradually emerged as a strong, liberal prescription. It would prohibit states from interfering until the third trimester.

The clerk who was working on the opinion began to worry that one of the other clerks, strongly opposed to abortions, might try to change their boss's mind. He took no chances. Each night he carefully locked up the work he had been doing for Blackmun. At the end of the summer, he carefully sealed the latest draft in an envelope, put his initials across the tape, and had it locked in Blackmun's desk. Only Blackmun's personal secretary knew where it was.

[Justice] Powell also made abortion his summer research project. As a young lawyer in Richmond in the 1930s, Powell had heard tales of girls who would "go away" to Switzerland and New York, where safe abortions were available. If someone were willing to pay for it, it was possible to have an abortion.

Powell understood how doctors viewed abortion. His father-in-law had been a leading obstetrician in Richmond, and his two brothers-in-law were obstetricians. Powell had heard all the horrifying stories of unsanitary butchers and coat-hanger abortions.

Nevertheless, Powell came quickly to the conclusion that the Constitution did not provide meaningful guidance. The right to privacy was tenuous; at best it was implied. If there was no way to find an answer in the Constitution, Powell felt he would just have to vote his "gut." He had been critical of Justices for doing exactly that; but in abortion, there seemed no choice.

When he returned to Washington, he took one of his law clerks to lunch at the Monocle Restaurant on Capitol Hill. The abortion laws, Powell confided, were "atrocious." His would be a strong and unshakable vote to strike them. He needed only a rationale for his vote.

In a recent lower court case, a federal judge had struck down the Connecticut abortion law.* This opinion impressed Powell. The judge had said that moral positions on abortion "about which each side was so sure must remain a personal judgment, one that [people] may follow

---

Markle v. Abele.

in their personal lives and seek to persuade others to follow, but a
judgment they may not impose upon others by force of law." That was
all the rationale Powell needed.

Brennan and Douglas worried that votes might have shifted since the
previous spring. Blackmun remained a question mark, Stewart might
defect, and they were not sure what Powell would do.

At conference on October 12, Blackmun made a long, eloquent and
strongly emotional case for striking down the laws. Stewart too seemed
ready to join. But the big surprise was Powell. He made it 6 to 3.

Immediately after conference, Douglas called Blackmun to tell him
that his presentation had been the finest he had heard at conference in
more than thirty years. He hoped the call would sustain Blackmun for
the duration.

Before the end of October, Blackmun's new draft in the abortion case
was circulated to the various chambers.

Brennan read it carefully. He waded through the positions of the
medical professional organizations, the expanded historical section, the
long-winded digest of the medical state of the art. Despite all this, Blackmun's bottom line was acceptable. The states would be prohibited from
regulating abortions until "viability." That meant state regulation only
during the third trimester. But Brennan spotted a weakness in the argument. Connecting the state's interest in the fetus to the point of viability was risky. Blackmun himself had noted that medical advances
made fetuses viable increasingly early. Scientists might one day be capable of sustaining a two-week-old fetus outside the womb. Advances
in medicine could undermine the thrust of the opinion.

Brennan had other concerns. Blackmun had focused on the rights of
the doctor and the rights of the state. The most important party, the
woman, had been largely neglected. Her rights were the ones that
needed to be upheld.

Brennan found yet another analytical fault in the draft. Blackmun had
discussed at length the state's dual interests in protecting the pregnant
woman's health and the potential life of the fetus. Both interests were
closely intertwined in Blackmun's draft. Brennan thought they were
quite distinct. He handed Blackmun's draft to one of his clerks. "It
doesn't do it," he said.

Brennan's clerks worked up a long memorandum. The delicate question, however, was how to communicate Brennan's thoughts to Blackmun. If Brennan phoned and said, "Harry, here are my ideas,"
Blackmun might be intimidated or fumble for months and still not change
the draft adequately. On the other hand, if Brennan sent a printed
opinion to the conference, Blackmun might think he was trying to steal
the majority. The last thing Brennan wanted was to author the Court's

abortion decision. He could imagine too vividly what the Catholic bishops would say.

In mid-November, Brennan took his clerk's memo and recast it as a series of casual thoughts and suggestions. It was important that it not appear to be an alternative draft. Brennan addressed a cover memo to Blackmun saying he fully agreed with his draft, but wanted to pass along some ideas. Brennan's thoughts ran forty-eight pages. Copies were sent to all the Justices.

Blackmun liked some of Brennan's suggestions. He quickly sent a memo to the Justices saying that he was incorporating them. Before he revised his draft, however, he decided that there was another set of views to be taken into account.

The Chief had made it clear to Blackmun that he would "never" join the draft as it stood, permitting unrestricted abortions up to viability, or the end of the second trimester. Blackmun wanted the Chief's vote, and he thought he saw a way to get it while still taking into account Brennan's suggestions. Instead of the one demarcation line, viability, Blackmun would create two. This would also be more medically sophisticated; it would show that the two state interests—protecting the pregnant woman's health and protecting potential life of the fetus—arose at different times. He settled on a formula.

1. First 12 weeks (first trimester); no state interest at all; abortions unrestricted and left up to the medical judgment of the doctor.

2. 12 to 24 weeks (second trimester); state interest arises and abortions can be regulated only to protect the woman's health.

3. After 24 weeks (third trimester); state interest arises to protect the potential life of the fetus.

This formula had the effect of somewhat limiting abortions in the second trimester. But eliminating viability as the dividing point, Brennan's worry, guaranteed that medical science could not keep reducing the time period during which abortions would be legally available.

Marshall was not happy with Blackmun's proposal. It was too rigid. Many women, particularly the poor and undereducated, would probably not get in touch with a doctor until some time after the first 12 weeks. A woman in a rural town might not have access to a doctor until later in pregnancy. And according to the Blackmun proposal, the states could effectively ban abortions in the 12-to-24-week period under the guise of protecting the woman's health. Marshall preferred Blackmun's original linkage to viability. If viability were the cut-off point, it would better protect the rural poor. Clearly, viability meant one thing in Boston, where there were fancy doctors and hospitals. There, a fetus might be sustained only a few months. But in rural areas with no hospitals and few, if any, doctors, viability was probably close to full-term, or late in the third trimester.

Marshall presented all this to Blackmun in a memo.

Blackmun respected Marshall's point of view. Marshall clearly knew a lot about many real world problems that Blackmun would never see. He incorporated all of Marshall's suggestions. His new draft specified:

1. For the stage up to "approximately" the end of the first trimester, abortions would be left to the medical judgment of the doctor.

2. For the stage after "approximately" the end of the first trimester, abortion procedures could be regulated to protect the woman's health.

3. For the stage after "viability," abortions could be regulated or even prohibited, to protect the fetus.

The clerks in most chambers were surprised to see the Justices, particularly Blackmun, so openly brokering their decision like a group of legislators. There was a certain reasonableness to the draft, some of them thought, but it derived more from medical and social policy than from constitutional law. There was something embarrassing and dishonest about this whole process. It left the Court claiming that the Constitution drew certain lines at trimesters and viability. The Court was going to make a medical policy and force it on the states. As a practical matter, it was not a bad solution. As a constitutional matter, it was absurd. The draft was referred to by some clerks as "Harry's abortion."

Stewart had one more change that he insisted on before he would join the opinion. It was imperative that they say more clearly that a fetus was not—as far as the Fourteenth Amendment was concerned—a person. If the fetus were a person, it had rights protected by the Constitution, including "life, liberty and property." Then the Court would be saying that a woman's rights outweighed those of the fetus. Weighing two sets of rights would be dangerous. The Court would be far better off with only one set of rights to protect. Stewart was certain that in legal terms a fetus was not a person. No previous case had held so. States conceded that, where the mother's life was at stake, a fetus had no rights. When the Fourteenth Amendment was passed in 1868, abortions were common enough to suggest that the state legislatures that had ratified the Amendment did not consider fetuses to have rights.

Blackmun did not disagree, but he felt the point was implicit in the opinion. Why expand it and stir up trouble?

Stewart was insistent, and Blackmun finally agreed to say clearly that a fetus was not a person.

Source: Bob Woodward and Scott Armstrong, *The Brethren* (New York: Simon and Shuster, 1979).

THE CASES: *ROE V. WADE* AND *DOE V. BOLTON*

By 1972 a number of abortion cases were in the pipeline to the Supreme Court. *Roe v. Wade*, the first case that was accepted for decision, tested the constitutionality of a Texas statute that made it a felony for anyone to destroy an embryo or fetus, except "on medical advice for the purpose of saving the life of the mother." This law, passed originally in 1854 and revised in 1857, was typical of older abortion laws in many states.

Jane Roe was the pseudonym for an unmarried pregnant woman who wanted an abortion and could not have one because of the Texas statute. She claimed that she had been gang raped and had been unable to obtain an abortion in Texas. She challenged the statute on a number of constitutional grounds, including equal protection of the laws, due process of law, and the right to privacy.

The case was a class action suit, that is, it was brought to determine not only Jane Roe's rights, but the rights of all women in the same or similar situations. There were several plaintiffs in addition to Jane—a married couple and a physician—who also gave reasons why the Texas law interfered with their rights.

Justice Blackmun wrote the opinion of the Court. Seven justices voted in favor of a right to abortion under limited circumstances. Two justices dissented.

DOCUMENT 39: *Roe v. Wade* (1973)

Mr. Justice BLACKMUN delivered the opinion of the Court. . . .

We forthwith acknowledge our awareness of the sensitive and emotional nature of the abortion controversy, of the vigorous opposing views, even among physicians, and of the deep and seemingly absolute convictions that the subject inspires. One's philosophy, one's experiences, one's exposure to the raw edges of human existence, one's religious training, one's attitudes toward life and family and their values, and the moral standards one establishes and seeks to observe, are all likely to influence and to color one's thinking and conclusions about abortion.

In addition, population growth, pollution, poverty and racial overtones tend to complicate and not to simplify the problem.

Our task, of course, is to resolve the issue by constitutional measurement, free of emotion and predilection. We seek earnestly to do this, and, because we do, we have inquired into, and in this opinion place some emphasis upon, medical and medical-legal history and what history reveals about man's attitudes toward the abortion procedure over the centuries. We bear in mind, too, Mr. Justice Holmes' admonition in his now-vindicated dissent in *Lochner v. New York* . . . (1905): "[The Constitution] is made for people of fundamentally differing views, and the accident of our finding certain opinions natural and familiar or novel and even shocking ought not to conclude our judgment upon the question whether statutes embodying them conflict with the Constitution of the United States." . . .

[The constitutional attack on the Texas statutes.]

The principal thrust of appellant's attack on the Texas statutes is that they improperly invade a right, said to be possessed by the pregnant woman, to choose to terminate her pregnancy. Appellant would discover this right in the concept of personal "liberty" embodied in the Fourteenth Amendment's Due Process Clause, or in personal marital, familial, and sexual privacy said to be protected by the Bill of Rights or its penumbras [shadows] . . . or among those rights reserved to the people by the Ninth Amendment. . . . Before addressing this claim, we feel it is desirable briefly to survey, in several aspects, the history of abortion, for such insight as that history may afford us, and then to examine the state purposes and interests behind the criminal abortion laws. . . .

[The history of state abortion laws.]

It perhaps is not generally appreciated that the restrictive criminal abortion laws in effect in a majority of States today are of relatively recent vintage. Those laws, generally proscribing [forbidding] abortion or its attempt at any time during pregnancy except when necessary to preserve the pregnant woman's life, are not of ancient or even of common-law origin. Instead, they derive from statutory changes effected, for the most part, in the latter half of the 19th century. . . .

Three reasons have been advanced to explain historically the enactment of criminal abortion laws in the 19th century and to justify their continued existence.

[1. To protect morality.]

It has been argued occasionally that these laws were the product of a Victorian social concern to discourage illicit sexual conduct. Texas, however, does not advance this justification in the present case, and it appears that no court or commentator has taken the argument seriously. . . .

[2. To protect women against dangerous operations.]

A second reason is concerned with abortion as a medical procedure. When most criminal abortion laws were first enacted, the procedure was a hazardous one for the woman. . . . Thus it has been argued that a State's real concern in enacting a criminal abortion law was to protect the pregnant woman, that is, to restrain her from submitting to a procedure that placed her life in serious jeopardy.

Modern medical techniques have altered this situation. . . .

[3. To protect new human life.]

The third reason is the State's interest—some phrase it in terms of duty—in protecting prenatal life. Some of the argument for this justification rests on the theory that a new human life is present from the moment of conception. The State's interest and general obligation to protect life then extends, it is argued, to prenatal life. Only when the life of the pregnant mother herself is at stake, balanced against the life she carries within her, should the interest of the embryo or fetus not prevail. Logically of course, a legitimate state interest in this area need not stand or fall on the acceptance of the belief that life begins at conception or at some other point prior to live birth. In assessing the State's interest, recognition may be given to the less rigid claim that as long as at least *potential* life is involved, the State may assert interests beyond the protection of the pregnant woman alone. . . .

It is with these interests, and the weight to be attached to them, that this case is concerned.

[A right to privacy allows a woman to make private decisions about her own welfare.]

The Constitution does not explicitly mention any right of privacy. In a line of decisions, however, going back perhaps as far as . . . 1891, the Court has recognized that a right of personal privacy, or a guarantee of certain areas or zones of privacy, does exist under the Constitution. . . .

This right of privacy, whether it be founded in the Fourteenth Amendment's concept of personal liberty and restrictions upon state action, as we feel it is, or, as the District Court determined, in the Ninth Amendment's reservation of rights to the people, is broad enough to encompass a woman's decision whether or not to terminate her pregnancy. The detriment that the State would impose upon the pregnant woman by denying this choice altogether is apparent. Specific and direct harm medically diagnosable even in early pregnancy may be involved. Maternity, or additional offspring, may force upon the woman a distressful life and future. Psychological harm may be imminent. Mental and physical health may be taxed by child care. There is also the distress, for all concerned, associated with the unwanted child, and there is the problem of bringing a child into a family already unable, psychologically and otherwise, to care for it. In other cases, as in this one, the additional difficulties and continuing stigma of unwed motherhood may be involved. All these are factors the woman and her responsible physician necessarily will consider in consultation.

[The state has a valid interest in regulating health.]

On the basis of elements such as these, appellant and some *amici* argue that the woman's right is absolute and that she is entitled to terminate her pregnancy for whatever reason she alone chooses. With this we do not agree.... As noted above, a State may properly assert important interests in safeguarding health, in maintaining medical standards, and in protecting potential life. At some point in pregnancy, these respective interests become sufficiently compelling to sustain regulation of the factors that govern the abortion decision. The privacy right involved, therefore, cannot be said to be absolute. In fact, it is not clear to us that the claim asserted by some *amici* that one has an unlimited right to do with one's body as one pleases bears a close relationship to the right of privacy previously articulated in the Court's decisions. The Court has refused to recognize an unlimited right of this kind in the past....

We, therefore, conclude that the right of personal privacy includes the abortion decision, but that this right is not unqualified and must be considered against important state interests in regulation....

[A state must have compelling reason to limit a fundamental right.]

Where certain "fundamental rights" are involved, the Court has held that a regulation limiting these rights may be justified only by a "compelling state interest" ... and that legislative enactments must be narrowly drawn to express only the legitimate state interests at stake.... Appellant [Jane Roe], as has been indicated, claims an absolute right that bars any state imposition of criminal penalties in this area. Appellee [Texas] argues that the State's determination to recognize and protect prenatal life from and after conception constitutes a compelling state interest.... We do not agree fully with either formulation....

[Personhood of the fetus.]

A. The appellee and certain *amici* argue that the fetus is a 'person' within the language and meaning of the Fourteenth Amendment. In support of this, they outline at length and in detail the well-known facts of fetal development. If this suggestion of personhood is established, the appellant's case, of course, collapses, for the fetus' right to life is then guaranteed specifically by the Amendment. The appellant con-

ceded as much on reargument. On the other hand, the appellee conceded on reargument that no case could be cited that holds that a fetus
is a person within the meaning of the Fourteenth Amendment.

The Constitution does not define "person" in so many words. . . . [In
nearly all instances in which the word "person" is used] the use of the
word is such that it has application only postnatally. None indicates,
with any assurance, that it has any possible pre-natal application.

All this, together with our observation . . . that throughout the major
portion of the 19th century prevailing legal abortion practices were far
freer than they are today, persuades us that the word "person," as used
in the Fourteenth Amendment, does not include the unborn. . . .

This conclusion, however, does not of itself fully answer the contentions raised by Texas, and we pass on to other considerations.

[The woman's right to privacy is not absolute throughout pregnancy.]

B. The pregnant woman cannot be isolated in her privacy. She carries
an embryo and, later, a fetus, if one accepts the medical definitions of
the developing young in the human uterus. . . . The situation therefore
is inherently different from marital intimacy, or bedroom possession of
obscene material, or marriage, or procreation, or education. . . . As we
have intimated above, it is reasonable and appropriate for a State to
decide that at some point in time another interest, that of health of the
mother or that of potential human life, become[s] significantly involved.
The woman's privacy is no longer sole and any right of privacy she
possesses must be measured accordingly.

[When does life begin?]

Texas urges that, apart from the Fourteenth Amendment, life begins
at conception and is present throughout pregnancy, and that, therefore,
the State has a compelling interest in protecting that life from and after
conception. We need not resolve the difficult question of when life begins. When those trained in the respective disciplines of medicine, philosophy, and theology are unable to arrive at any consensus, the
judiciary, at this point in the development of man's knowledge, is not
in a position to speculate as to the answer. . . .

In view of . . . this, we do not agree that, by adopting one theory of
life, Texas may override the rights of the pregnant woman that are at
stake. We repeat, however, that the State does have an important and
legitimate interest in preserving and protecting the health of the pregnant woman, whether she be resident of the State or a nonresident who
seeks medical consultation and treatment there, and that it has still
another important and legitimate interest in protecting the potentiality
of human life. These interests are separate and distinct. Each grows in

substantiality as the woman approaches term and at a point during pregnancy, each becomes "compelling."

[How the competing interests are to be balanced.]

[The state's interest.] With respect to the State's important and legitimate interest in the health of the mother, the "compelling" point, in the light of present medical knowledge, is at approximately the end of the first trimester [first 3 months]. This is so because of the now-established medical fact . . . that until the end of the first trimester mortality in abortion may be less than mortality in normal childbirth. It follows that, from and after this point, a State may regulate the abortion procedure to the extent that the regulation reasonably relates to the preservation and protection of maternal health. . . .

[The woman's interest.] This means, on the other hand, that for the period of pregnancy prior to this "compelling" point, the attending physician, in consultation with his patient, is free to determine, without regulation by the State, that in his medical judgment, the patient's pregnancy should be terminated.

[The interest of the fetus.] With respect to the State's important and legitimate interest in potential life, the "compelling" point is viability. This is so because the fetus then presumably has the capability of meaningful life outside the mother's womb. . . . If the State is interested in protecting fetal life after viability, it may go so far as to proscribe [forbid] abortion during that period, except when it is necessary to preserve the life or health of the mother.

[The Texas statute is unconstitutional.]

Measured against these standards, Art. 1196 of the Texas Penal Code, in restricting legal abortions to those "procured or attempted by medical advice for the purpose of saving the life of the mother," sweeps too broadly. The statute makes no distinction between abortions performed early in pregnancy and those performed later, and it limits to a single reason, "saving" the mother's life, the legal justification for the procedure. The statute, therefore, cannot survive the constitutional attack made upon it here. . . .

[A summary of what has been decided.]

To summarize and to repeat:
1. A state criminal abortion statute of the current Texas type, that excepts from criminality only a *lifesaving* procedure on behalf of the mother, without regard to pregnancy stage and without recognition of the other interests involved, is violative of the Due Process Clause of the Fourteenth Amendment.
(a) For the stage prior to approximately the end of the first trimester,

the abortion decision and its effectuation must be left to the medical judgment of the pregnant woman's attending physician.

(b) For the stage subsequent to approximately the end of the first trimester, the State, in promoting its interest in the health of the mother, may, if it chooses, regulate the abortion procedure in ways that are reasonably related to maternal health.

(c) For the stage subsequent to viability, the State in promoting its interest in the potentiality of human life may, if it chooses, regulate, and even proscribe, abortion except where it is necessary, in appropriate medical judgment, for the preservation of the life or health of the mother. . . .

This holding, we feel, is consistent with the relative weights of the respective interests involved, with the lessons and examples of medical and legal history, with the lenity of the common law, and with the demands of the profound problems of the present day. . . .

Source: 410 U.S. Reports 113 (1973).

DOCUMENT 40: *Roe v. Wade* (1973). Dissenting Opinions

Mr. Justice WHITE with whom Mr. Justice REHNQUIST joins, dissenting.

With all due respect, I dissent. I find nothing in the language or history of the Constitution to support the Court's judgments. The Court simply fashions and announces a new constitutional right for pregnant women. . . . The upshot is that the people and the legislatures of the 50 States are constitutionally disentitled to weigh the relative importance of the continued existence and development of the fetus, on the one hand, against a spectrum of possible impacts on the mother, on the other. As an exercise of raw judicial power, the Court perhaps has authority to do what it does today; but in my view its judgment is an improvident and extravagant exercise of the power of judicial review that the Constitution extends to this Court.

Mr. Justice REHNQUIST dissenting.

The fact that a majority of the States reflecting, after all, the majority sentiment in those States, have had restrictions on abortions for at least a century is a strong indication, it seems to me, that the asserted right to an abortion is not "so rooted in the traditions and conscience of our people as to be ranked as fundamental." . . . There apparently was no question concerning the validity of this [the Texas] provision or of any of the other state statutes when the Fourteenth Amendment was adopted. The only conclusion possible from this history is that the drafters did not intend to have the Fourteenth Amendment withdraw from the States the power to legislate with respect to this matter.

Source: 410 *U.S. Reports* 172, 222 (1973).

DOE V. BOLTON: THE COMPANION CASE

Another abortion case was decided the same day that *Roe v. Wade* was decided. While the *Roe* case tested the constitutionality of a law that was over 100 years old, the *Doe* case looked at one of the so-called reform statutes that had been passed in the 1960s. Georgia's law did not prohibit abortion altogether, but allowed the operation under certain circumstances: when the woman's life was in danger, when the child would be born with a serious and permanent defect, or when pregnancy resulted from rape. However, the law hedged permission to have an abortion with a number of tight restrictions:

1. The operation had to be performed in a hospital accredited by the Georgia Commission on Accreditation of Hospitals (JCAH).
2. A hospital abortion committee had to approve the operation.
3. Two doctors, in addition to the woman's own doctor, had to sign off on the abortion.
4. The woman had to be a resident of Georgia.

It was not easy to meet these conditions. Hospital abortion committees approved very few abortions.

The Supreme Court overturned the law, stating that it restricted the abortion right that had been recognized in *Roe v. Wade* too severely. Justice Douglas' concurring opinion illustrates the restrictive nature of the Georgia law. His special concern was that the law interferes with the doctor-patient relationship.

DOCUMENT 41: *Doe v. Bolton* (1973). Concurring Opinion of Justice William O. Douglas

---

Under the Georgia Act, the mother's physician is not the sole judge as to whether the abortion should be performed. Two other licensed physicians must concur in his judgment. Moreover the abortion must be performed in a licensed hospital; and the abortion must be approved in advance by a committee of the medical staff of that hospital. . . .

The right of privacy has no more conspicuous place than in the physician-patient relationship, unless it be in the priest-penitent relationship.

It is one thing for a patient to agree that her physician may consult with another physician about her case. It is quite a different matter for the State compulsorily to impose on that physician-patient relationship another layer or, as in this case, still a third layer of physicians. The right of privacy—the right to care for one's health and person and to seek out a physician of one's own choice protected by the Fourteenth Amendment—becomes only a matter of theory, not a reality, when a multiple-physician-approval system is mandated by the State. . . .

The imposition by the State of group controls over the physician-patient relationship is not made on any medical procedure apart from abortion, no matter how dangerous the medical step may be. The oversight imposed on the physician and patient in abortion cases denies them their 'liberty,' *viz.*, their right of privacy, without any compelling, discernible state interest. . . .

The protection of the fetus when it has acquired life is a legitimate concern of the State. Georgia's law makes no rational, discernible decision on that score. For under the Code, the developmental stage of the fetus is irrelevant when pregnancy is the result of rape, when the fetus will very likely be born with a permanent defect, or when a continuation of the pregnancy will endanger the life of the mother or permanently injure her health. When life is present is a question we do not try to resolve. While basically a question for medical experts . . . it is, of course, caught up in matters of religion and morality.

Source: 410 U.S. Reports 179, 219–221 (1973).

The Immediate Reaction to the Abortion Decisions

The immediate reaction to the decisions was mixed. Former President Lyndon B. Johnson had died of a heart attack on January 22, and news of his death drew some of the attention away from the Supreme Court's action. Liberal newspapers like the *Washington Post* praised the decision. Conservative papers, opposed to abortion, were surprised and dismayed. Anti-abortion forces had expected the decision to go in their favor. They were also surprised at the seven-to-two vote against them.

News stories reported a variety of responses in different parts of the country and some confusion about the practical implications of the decision.

The Catholic Church was outraged, and its bishops immediately called for resistance to the ruling. Roman Catholics were urged to disobey any laws requiring abortion, and the National Conference of Catholic Bishops announced that the Church would excommunicate Catholics who performed abortions or who agreed to undergo the operation.

In those states where anti-abortion sentiment was strong, the state legislatures that were in session passed resolutions and introduced legislation designed to discourage abortions. Congressmen made speeches condemning the Supreme Court and introduced constitutional amendments to rescind or modify the Court's decision.

PUBLIC REACTION

The Supreme Court's decision in *Roe v. Wade* "came like a thunderbolt," wrote Lawrence Lader, the writer and abortion reform advocate whose new book, *Abortion II*, had just gone to press when the decision was announced. The reaction of the general public to this bolt from the blue was, at first, mixed and uncertain.

The Roman Catholic Church, however, was quick to voice its disapproval. The National Conference of Catholic Bishops denounced the decision in a statement made on January 24, 1973. Cardinal Krol, President of the National Conference, told the press that the Court had opened the doors to the greatest slaughter of innocent life in the history of mankind.

Women's groups, especially those that had been involved in reform work in the legislatures or litigation in the courts, were ecstatic. They could not believe that the Court had accomplished with one constitutional ruling what they had been trying to do, with only moderate success, during years of struggle in the legislative process. They would find, however, that the battle was not to be won so easily and painlessly. One of the worst predictions of all time was made by Lee Giddings, the executive director of the National Association for Repeal of Abortion Laws (the name for NARAL before 1973). She was quoted as saying that "before you know it this will be past history and abortion will be just another medical procedure. People will forget about this whole thing" (see Document 44). Twenty years after this statement was made, the abortion controversy was still boiling away on the front political burner.

Initially, editorial writers and columnists were not sure what to make of the decision. Columnists in some papers predicted a furious political conflict between "right-to-life" groups and abortion reformers. Others denounced the Supreme Court for taking the lead in trying to settle, by judicial fiat, an issue of public policy that should have been left to the state legislatures and the voters.

DOCUMENT 42: Statement of the Committee for Pro-Life Affairs, National Conference of Catholic Bishops, January 24, 1973

The sweeping judgment of the U.S. Supreme Court in the Texas and Georgia abortion cases is a flagrant rejection of the unborn child's right to life. The Court has chosen to ignore the scientific evidence regarding the unborn child's human growth and development during the first six months of life in the womb of its mother. No consideration has been given to the parental rights of the child's father.

In effect, the opinion of the Court has established that abortion-on-request is the public policy of this nation.

Despite attempts to do so, the Court has failed to justify its opinion on theological, historical or scientific grounds. Nonetheless, during the first six months of the child's life, the Court has made the doctor the final judge as to who will live and who will die. This seems to reverse the history of American jurisprudence that prohibits the deprivation of the right to life without due process of law. Never before has a humane society placed such absolute and unrestricted power in the hands of an individual.

Although as a result of the Court decision abortion may be legally permissible, it is still morally wrong, and no Court opinion can change the law of God prohibiting the taking of innocent human life. Therefore, as religious leaders, we cannot accept the Court's judgment and we urge people not to follow its reasoning or conclusions.

Meeting as the Bishops' Committee on Pro-Life Affairs, we have formulated the following recommendations:

1. Every legal possibility must be explored to challenge the opinion of the United States Supreme Court decision that withdraws all legal safeguards for the right to life of the unborn child.

2. We urge all State legislatures to protect the unborn child to the fullest extent possible under this decision and to restrict the practice of abortion as much as they can.

3. The Catholic Church pledges all its educational and informational resources to a program that will present the case for the sanctity of the child's life from conception to birth. This will include the scientific information on the humanity of the unborn child and the progress of human growth and development of the unborn child, the responsibility and necessity for society to safeguard the life of the child at every stage of its existence, the problems that may exist for a woman during pregnancy and more humane and morally acceptable solutions to these problems.

4. Hospitals and health facilities under Catholic auspices will not find this judgment of the Court compatible with their faith and moral convictions. We feel confident that the hospitals will do all in their power to be the type of institution where good morals and good medicine will be practiced. We are also confident that our hospitals and health care personnel will be identified by a dedication to the sanctity of life, and by an acceptance of their conscientious responsibility to protect the lives of both mother and child. We strongly urge our doctors, nurses and health care personnel to stand fast in refusing to provide abortion on request, and in refusing to accept easily available abortion as justifiable medical care.

In conclusion, we are saying that the Court has written a charter for abortion on request, and has thereby deprived the unborn child of his or her human rights. This is bad morality, bad medicine and bad public policy, and it cannot be harmonized with basic moral principles. We also believe that millions of our fellow Americans will share our reactions to this opinion. We have no choice but to urge that the Court's judgment be opposed and rejected.

Source: United States Catholic Conference, Documentation on the Right to Life and Abortion, Washington, D.C., 1974, pp. 59–60.

DOCUMENT 43: "Abortion: Out of the 19th Century." *Washington Post*, 1973

The Supreme Court has gone a long way toward resolving the large and thorny issue of the extent to which a state may intervene in decisions a woman may make during pregnancy about whether or not to bear her child. In a 7-2 decision the Court decided that the constitutional right to privacy is broad enough to limit the power of the states to regulate abortion decisions and the conditions under which they may be carried out, but that the right is not absolute.

After assessing the best medical opinion available to it, the Court divided pregnancy into three stages and balanced the woman's right of privacy against the state's interests in maternal health and in potential life. During the first three months of pregnancy, the right of privacy is found to be virtually absolute because during that period "mortality in abortion is less than that in normal childbirth." During the next four months, when the risks to the mother's life are higher, the Court held that a state "may regulate the abortion procedure to the extent that the regulation reasonably relates to the preservation and protection of maternal health." During the final stages of pregnancy, when the fetus has the capability of "meaningful life outside the mother's womb," the Court held that the state had "an important and legitimate interest in potential life" which might permit it to "go so far as to proscribe abortion during that period except when it is necessary to preserve the life or health of the mother."

The decision delighted proponents of abortion reform because it loosened the rules considerably as it nullified the abortion laws of more than 40 states which have laws similar to those involved in the decision, although it did not satisfy those who argued unsuccessfully that the right to privacy is absolute. It dismayed opponents of abortion, who see it as part of a larger moral decay and as a step toward a lessening of the general reverences for life.

In our view, the Court's decision was both wise and sound. The decision points out that the majority of the criminal abortion laws in effect in the states today derive from statutory changes enacted in the latter half of the 19th century and that prior to that time, "a woman enjoyed a substantially broader right to terminate a pregnancy than she does in most states today." In moving the law out of the 19th century, the Court wisely chose to ground its decision on the individual's right of privacy as balanced against the state's interest in regulating her conduct. In recognizing limits on the right, the Court took cognizance of what seems to us to be entirely legitimate state interests, but it did it in a balanced and graduated way.

The essence of the decision seems to be that individual liberties of citizens are to be protected unless a compelling showing of state interest is made by the government. Thus, even though it revolved about the hotly debated issue of abortion, it represented an enlargement of individual freedom. We welcome it.

Source: Editorial, *Washington Post*, January 31, 1973.

DOCUMENT 44: "Despite Court's Ruling Abortion Fight Goes On." Michael T. Malloy, 1973

Their victory was so complete that even veteran campaigners for liberal abortion laws seemed stunned when the U.S. Supreme Court last week handed down rulings that will make abortions cheap, common, and readily available in every state.

"We really haven't gotten over it," says Lee Gidding, executive director of the National Association for Repeal of Abortion Laws. "It was such a shock. We didn't expect it to be so sweeping. It's just superb."

The High Court ruled 7 to 2 that the states may not forbid women to have abortions during the first six months of pregnancy. It knocked down so many restrictions that only four "abortion-on-demand" states— New York, Washington, Hawaii, and Alaska—seem to have laws liberal enough to meet the Court's new standards.

White's Angry Dissent

"My impression is that it wipes out every law in this country that restricts a woman's access and right to medical care," says Dr. Jack Stack, a Michigan physician who has worked to liberalize his state's abortion law.

Opponents of abortion, many bitter about the Court's ruling, seemed to agree. "The Court apparently values the convenience of the pregnant mother more than the continued existence and development of the life or potential life which she carries . . . by investing mothers and doctors with the Constitutionally protected right to exterminate it," said Justice Byron R. White in an angry dissenting opinion.

The Roman Catholic archbishop of New York, Terence Cardinal Cooke, asked: "How many millions of children . . . will never live to see the light of day because of the shocking action of the majority of the U.S. Supreme Court?"

Effect on Population

About 400,000 to 500,000 more abortions a year may result from the ruling, says Dr. Christopher Tietze, associate director of the Population Council. Legal abortions, now totaling about 600,000 a year nationwide, may increase by 1 million or more, he says. But Tietze adds that if the New York abortion pattern, which he has analyzed, emerges elsewhere, then about 70 per cent of the legal abortions will be performed on women who would have had illegal abortions anyway.

If other aspects of New York's experience are repeated nationally, the Court's decision could also have important effects on problems such as illegitimacy, poverty, welfare, health, and the ultimate size and composition of the American population.

Tietze says New York City's birth rate dropped 25 per cent in the first two years of the liberal law, and he attributes half of that decline to abortions.

New York City's soaring illegitimacy rate had doubled since 1963. It began to drop within a year after the new law took effect.

Almost half of the New York City women who seek legal abortions are black. They have 6 abortions for every 10 normal births; the ratio is 4 to 10 for white women.

"It will certainly help people stay off welfare and get out of this substandard economic condition," Tietze says of the Court's decision. "It might reduce the [national] birth rate by as much as half a million, out of 3.5 million live births per year. I think it would come pretty close to a population which would stabilize in the early part of the Twenty-first Century."

Other expected effects include a sharp drop in the cost of an abortion. It fell in New York City to an average of $150 to $200 from $500 to $600 in 1970.

Another result may be an improvement in the health of new mothers and of newborn babies. Death rates for both dropped to record lows in New York City after abortion was legalized. Tietze says this is because "high-risk mothers . . . older women, very young women, black women with problems having to do with poverty, have taken more advantage of the abortion law than middle-class white women, who are more likely to use contraception."

"There is a lot of evidence some people prefer an abortion every year to a pill every day," says Dr. Andre Hellegers, a Washington, D.C., foe of abortion. He sees a switch from contraception to abortion as one of several dismaying results that could come from the Court's decision. He also cites promiscuity.

"This is likely to make people take risks they otherwise wouldn't," he says. "If someone gets steamed up and doesn't have a diaphragm, one may now think of an abortion being available and go ahead anyway.

"It may mean one can do any experiments one wishes on a live-born fetus," Hellegers adds. "A live born fetus can be obtained through hysterectomy. There should be appearing under this law a number of live fetuses. And it should lead to a fair amount of experimenting with them."

The Court held that unborn children are not "persons" and therefore do not have Constitutional rights, not even the "right to life," on which antiabortion groups have based their campaigns against liberalization. The ruling falls especially hard on them now because they seemed to be gaining ground in recent months.

Nixon Intervention

Voters in Michigan and North Dakota defeated efforts to liberalize their abortion laws in referendums last November. The legislatures of Connecticut, New York, and Pennsylvania voted for tougher laws last year, although laws enacted in the latter two states received gubernatorial vetoes. President Nixon personally intervened to support repeal of the liberal New York law.

"We were worried because abortion was being used as a political football," says Ms. Gidding. "The opposition was well-organized, well-financed, and the hierarchy of the Catholic Church was making a real last-ditch fight."

All "right-to-life" lawmaking efforts appear dead now. The Court's combined decisions overturning Georgia and Texas abortion laws mean that all similar state laws are unconstitutional. To be Constitutional, new laws would have to leave abortion entirely to the decision of the mother and her doctor during the first three months of pregnancy, and could regulate abortions only in ways that promote maternal health during the second three months, such as by licensing abortion clinics. The Court allowed but did not require the states to protect the "potential life" of a fetus only during the last three months of pregnancy. Because the issue did not come up in the Georgia or Texas cases, the Court did not determine what rights, if any, a father has regarding his unborn child.

Battle Continues

Supporters of abortion aren't taking their gloves off yet, despite their overwhelming victory. "The emphasis now has got to be on implementation," says Ms. Gidding. "We are concerned to see that referral services are nonprofit, that there are high-standard clinics all around the country, and to see there is good education about contraception so people don't have to get an abortion in the first place.

"I don't feel these fanatics on the other side will just sit back and take this," she continues. "I think they'll press for whatever legislation they can get away with, and they'll be pushing for a Constitutional amendment. We would just as soon not have abortion laws replaced by any new laws, but to have the new regulations written by state boards of health or whatever agency normally governs medical practice."

The foes of abortion haven't given up, but they are talking now about long-range hopes for a Constitutional amendment or a change in the make-up of the High Court. "I feel this opinion will be reversed," says Monsignor James McHugh, director of the Family Life Division of the U.S. Catholic Conference. "It may take a quarter of a century. It may take 50 years. But I think it will happen."

Lee Gidding disagrees: "Before you know it this will be past history and abortion will be just another medical procedure. People will forget about this whole thing."

Source: Michael T. Malloy, "Despite Court's Ruling Abortion Fight Goes On," *National Observer*, February 3, 1973.

DOCUMENT 45: "High Court's Abortion Legislation." Edwin A. Roberts, Jr., 1973

The U.S. Supreme Court, we are frequently reminded, is not in the business of affirming the views of the American majority. Rather, it is the Court's responsibility to interpret the Constitution according to the Justices' best lights.

Unlike congressmen, the Justices do not represent the people even nominally. Nevertheless it sometimes seems that the jurists suffer from cabin fever, that they look wistfully now and then at the Capitol just across the road.

The Court's 7-to-2 decision in favor of legalized abortion is puzzling both in substance, for what it allows, and in style, for the way it allows it. Reading Justice Harry A. Blackmun's majority opinion, one is struck by its legislative tone. It sounds more like a Senate bill than a judicial decision, and there is good reason to believe history will one day mark it a hideous error.

Justice Blackmun writes: "With respect to the state's important and legitimate interest in the health of the mother, the 'compelling' point, in the light of present medical knowledge, is at approximately the end of the first trimester [12-week period]. This is so because of the now established medical fact that until the end of the first trimester mortality in abortion is less than in normal childbirth.

"It follows that, from and after this point, a state may regulate the abortion procedure to the extent that the regulation reasonably relates to the preservation and protection of maternal health. . . .

"If the state is interested in protecting fetal life after viability, it may go so far as to proscribe abortion during that period except when it is necessary to preserve the life or health of the mother."

Expect to Be Disappointed

Now all of us are free to agree or disagree with the Supreme Court, and we must expect to be disappointed from time to time when the wisdom of the Court runs counter to our own interests or convictions. If we don't like a decision we have four choices: resign ourselves to the fact, work for a Constitutional amendment, move to Australia, or start a revolution.

And so it is with a profound sense of futility that once again I file a brief in support of the 1.6 million babies who will be killed this year before they are born.

In this opinion, Justice Blackmun dismisses the central question with these words: "We need not resolve the difficult question of when life begins. When those trained in the respective disciplines of medicine, philosophy, and theology are unable to arrive at any consensus, the judiciary, at this point in the development of man's knowledge, is not in a position to speculate as to the answer."

A Duty to 'Speculate'

I suggest the Court is too modest. The Court had a duty to "speculate" about when life begins because it is certain when life begins. In a recent letter to the editor of the New York Times, Dr. Landrum B. Shettles, a physician at New York's Presbyterian Hospital with "20 years' work in this field," makes these telling observations based on his expertise and not on "any known religious influence":

"Concerning when life begins, a particular aggregate of hereditary tendencies (genes and chromosomes) is first assembled at the moment of fertilization when an ovum (egg) is invaded by a sperm cell. This restores the normal number of required chromosomes (46) for survival, growth, and reproduction of a new composite individual.

When Life Begins

"By this definition a new composite individual is started at the moment of fertilization. However, to survive, this individual needs a very specialized environment for nine months, just as it requires sustained care for an indefinite period after birth. But from the moment of union of the germ cells, there is under normal development a living, definite, going concern. To interrupt a pregnancy at any stage is like cutting the link of a chain; the chain is broken no matter where the link is cut. Naturally, the earlier a pregnancy is interrupted, the easier it is technically, the less the physical, objective encounter. To deny a truth should not be made a basis for legalizing abortion."

To deny a truth should not be made a basis for legalizing abortion.

Right there Dr. Shettles has put his finger on the outrageous and unquestionably immoral fault in the Court's decision. Human life begins at conception—that is a fact. Medical men know it's a fact. High-school biology students know it's a fact. And the Supreme Court of the United States knows it's a fact.

An Inconvenient Fact

But it's an inconvenient fact. To recognize it would have made impossible the result the Court legislators wanted. So in their concern for unmarried pregnant women, for the miserable mothers of very large, very poor families, and for the simple convenience of housewives who want to escape the domestic routine, the Justices have declared what is known with certainty to be unknowable.

The Court then goes on to muddy the waters with references to a woman's right to privacy, even though privacy is not the issue. Women can be as private about their bodies as they choose. But if they have sexual intercourse, it is their responsibility to prevent conception if no baby is wanted. If they are fearful of the pill or if the 95 per cent effectiveness of mechanical contraceptives worries them, let both partners use a device. That should do it.

But once conception occurs, let's let the new life live. Nobody should kill an unborn baby, even though the Supreme Court says it's all a matter of size.

Source: Edwin A. Roberts, Jr., "High Court's Abortion Legislation," *National Observer*, March 10, 1973.

DOCUMENT 46: "The State Houses: Anti-Abortion Forces Fight Court Decision." Judith Randal, 1973

WASHINGTON—Almost 20 years after Brown vs. Board of Education committed the nation to desegregation of the public schools, the principle is still being fought on various fronts and by various means.

Already, it is apparent that a similar scenario of delay, if not worse, is in store for the Supreme Court's January decision making abortion in the first 13 weeks of pregnancy a private matter between a woman and her physician.

Item: Since the court's decision, more than 50 resolutions have been introduced in more than 20 states, and in some cases have passed either one or both houses of the legislature, to permit hospitals to refuse to perform abortions or otherwise throw obstacles in the way of women wishing to terminate a pregnancy. Some of these also would place limitations on contraception and sterilization.

Item: In the same interval, more than a dozen proposed constitutional amendments have been offered in Congress to abrogate the court's decision and leave to the states the right to decide whether abortion would be permitted. One proposal—that of Rep. Lawrence J. Hogan, R-Md.— is the prototype of several others and would flatly prohibit abortion "from the moment of conception."

The House, at least, may well pass one or more of these proposed amendments in the hope that this troublesome topic pitting the women's rights movement against anti-abortion forces will be turned over to state legislatures and so not be an issue in the 1974 congressional election races.

Item: A measure of dubious constitutionality introduced by Sen. Frank Church, D-Idaho, has passed the Senate, 92 to 1. It would protect hospitals refusing to perform abortions on moral or religious grounds from loss of federal payments for the support of such services as Medicare.

A similar measure is pending in the House and also is likely to pass— the more so because the chairman of the health subcommittee, Rep. Paul Rogers, from Palm Beach, Fla., represents a constituency most of which presumably would not be affected by such a statute, since much of it is elderly or able to afford an out-of-state abortion if none was available locally.

All of this controversy has created an ideal climate for influence to be brought to bear, and the "anti" forces are better organized and better funded than the "pro." Chief among those opposing abortion is the Right-To-Life movement, which likes to claim that its point of view is not being heard. Actually, it is not only well-financed by sources that are predominantly identified with Roman Catholicism, but also very adept at getting its message across.

Two of many examples of its effectiveness: (1) The Catholic bishop and several R.T.L. members from the home districts of many representatives on the House Health Subcommittee have visited those members to lobby for Church's proposal, while at the same time pro-abortion women arriving to hear the sub-committee discuss the measure have repeatedly found scheduled hearings abruptly terminated, rescheduled or closed. (2) R.T.L. has picketed the San Jose office of Rep. Don Edwards, D-Calif., who heads the House Judiciary subcommittee concerned with constitutional amendments and has pressured him to endorse their position even before the hearings he has promised have taken place.

The R.T.L. and associated organizations would have the public and legislators believe that they alone endorse such alternatives to abortion as maternity benefits for unmarried women, research to develop better contraceptives and eased adoption laws. The record shows that opponent groups like the National Women's Political Caucus, the Women's Lobby and the National Organization for Women—not to mention the National Commission on Population and the American Future—also favor such measures and in many cases endorsed them before R.T.L.

Since about half of R.T.L.'s 300 member groups enjoy tax-exempt status, there is at least the suspicion from all of this activity that, in trying to influence legislation, R.T.L. may be violating Internal Revenue laws. And that in seeking to impose Catholic doctrine on a predominantly Protestant population, it would deprive all women who become pregnant of the choice of whether to bear a child—this despite the fact that where abortions have been legal, Catholic as well as non-Catholic women have taken substantial advantage of the opportunity.

What is happening is, of course, reminiscent of the fight that sent Margaret Sanger to jail in the early days of the struggle to legalize birth control and, as late as the 1950's, saw non-Catholic doctors dismissed from the staffs of Catholic hospitals for their participation in family planning activities. And again it is the poor and indigent who stand to suffer while the more affluent always will be able to find a way.

Ironically, it was to protect women against then-dangerous procedures that the abortion laws were passed in the 19th century. However, in those states where they remained in effect until the Supreme Court decision, complications after illegal abortion became a leading cause of maternal death.

Unless the Supreme Court ruling is translated into actual services over the length and breadth of this country—as now seems unlikely—any change in that situation is improbable.

Source: Judith Randal, "The State Houses: Anti-Abortion Forces Fight Court Decision," *Washington Star News*, May 13, 1973. © *The Washington Post*.

REACTION IN CONGRESS

Congress was slow to react to the Supreme Court's decision. It wasn't until after Good Friday, when sermons had been preached in Catholic parishes across the nation, that letters began to pour into congressional offices.

There was no immediate burst of oratory in the House or Senate. Senator James B. Allen, a conservative Democrat from Alabama, filed a speech in the *Congressional Record* on January 23 criticizing the decision and asking permission to file statements from two cardinals that expressed the shock and dismay of the Catholic Church.

On January 30 Representative Lawrence J. Hogan, a Maryland Republican, printed a speech in the *Record* that ripped into the Court's decision. Hogan introduced an amendment to the Constitution that would extend the Fourteenth Amendment's guarantee of life to the unborn, the aged, the ill, and the incapacitated.

In May, Senator James L. Buckley introduced an amendment to the Constitution that would protect unborn children at every stage in their development. Buckley, who had been elected from New York with the support of both the Republican and the Conservative parties, would become a leader of the right-to-life forces in the Senate. His amendment, with some variations, used a basic formula that would be found in many subsequent proposals.

In the congressional elections in the fall of 1974 anti-abortion forces tried to identify and defeat congressmen who supported abortion rights. This tactic, only moderately successful in 1974, was used more effectively in succeeding elections, frightening members of Congress who might otherwise have agreed with the Court's decision.

But the state legislatures, not Congress, were the arenas in which the major battles over abortion were to be fought. Except for its ability to cut off funding for abortions in federal spending programs and federal projects, Congress has little authority to regulate abortion.

Congress *can* propose amendments to the Constitution. Over fifty proposals to amend the Constitution were introduced during the first session of the 94th Congress (1974–75); a number of such amendments would be introduced in each Congress thereafter. As of 1993 none of the amendments had succeeded in winning the two-thirds vote necessary to send them to the states for ratification.

DOCUMENT 47: Remarks in the Senate by Senator James B. Allen (Alabama) on the Abortion Ruling, January 23, 1973

Mr. President, I am shocked at the ruling of the Supreme Court legalizing abortions, and I believe this decision is bad logic, bad law, and bad morals. It strikes down the laws in some 31 States and will require the rewriting of the laws of all States except Alaska, Hawaii, New York, and Washington to conform to the decision. The Supreme Court is up to its old falling of permissiveness and of taking over the legislative functions of the Congress and of the State legislatures. First, it outlaws the death penalty for criminals and then it permits it to be imposed on unborn babies. I deplore this decision and believe it will have an unwholesome effect on the quality of life of our civilized society.

I ask unanimous consent that statements of Cardinals Cooke and Krol, and the table showing the effect on State laws, published in the New York Times on January 23, 1973, be printed in the *Record*.

There being no objection, the statements and table were ordered to be printed in the *Record*, as follows:

Cardinals' Statements on Court Ruling

(Following are statements issued by Cardinal Cooke and John Cardinal Krol, Archbishop of Philadelphia and president of the National Conference of Catholic Bishops, in reaction to the Supreme Court decision on abortions.)

How many millions of children prior to their birth will never live to see the light of day because of the shocking action of the majority of the United States Supreme Court today?

Whatever their legal rationale, seven men have made a tragic utilitarian judgment regarding who shall live and who shall die. They have made themselves a "super legislature." They have gone against the will of those American people who spoke their minds in favor of life as recently as last November in referendums in Michigan and North Dakota. They have usurped the powers and responsibilities of the legislatures of 50 states to protect human life.

I remind all Americans, however, that judicial decisions are not necessarily sound moral decisions.

In spite of this horrifying decision, the American people must rededicate themselves to the protection of the sacredness of all human life. I hope and pray that our citizens will do all in their power to reverse this injustice to the rights of the unborn child.

Cardinal Krol

The Supreme Court's decision today is an unspeakable tragedy for this nation. It is hard to think of any decision in the 200 years of our history which has made more disastrous implications for our stability as a civilized society. The ruling drastically diminishes the constitutional guaranty of the right to life and in doing so sets in motion developments which are terrifying to contemplate.

The ruling represents bad logic and bad law. There is no rational justification for allowing unrestricted abortion up to the third month of pregnancy. The development of life before and after birth is a continuous process and in making the three-month point the cutoff for unrestricted abortion, the Court seems more impressed by magic than by scientific evidence regarding fetal development. The child in the womb has the right to life, to the life he already possesses, and this is a right no court has the authority to deny.

Apparently the Court was trying to straddle the fence and give something to everybody—abortion on demand before three months for those who want that, somewhat more restrictive abortion regulations after three months for those who want that. But in its straddling act, the Court has done a monstrous injustice to the thousands of unborn children whose lives may be destroyed as a result of this decision.

No court and no legislature in the land can make something evil become something good. Abortion at any stage of pregnancy is evil. This is not a question of sectarian morality but instead concerns the law of God and the basis of civilized society. One trusts in the decency and good sense of the American people not to let an illogical court decision dictate to them on the subject of morality and human life.

Affect on States of Abortion Vote

Washington, Jan. 22.—Following is a table showing how each state is affected by the Supreme Court's decision today on abortion.

States with legalized abortion laws not affected by today's decision:

Alaska	New York
Hawaii	Washington

States with relatively modern abortion laws that will require considerable rewriting to conform:

Alabama	Maryland
Arkansas	Mississippi
California	New Mexico
Colorado	North Carolina
Delaware	Oregon

Florida	South Carolina
Georgia	Virginia
Kansas	

States with older anti-abortion laws that have been entirely invalidated and that must write new laws:

Arizona	Nevada
Connecticut	New Hampshire
Idaho	New Jersey
Illinois	North Dakota
Indiana	Ohio
Iowa	Oklahoma
Kentucky	Pennsylvania
Louisiana	Rhode Island
Maine	South Dakota
Massachusetts	Tennessee
Michigan	Texas
Minnesota	Utah
Missouri	Vermont
Montana	West Virginia
Nebraska	Wyoming

Source: S 1862, *Congressional Record*, January 23, 1973, S 1,862.

DOCUMENT 48: Remarks in the House of Representatives by Representative Lawrence J. Hogan (Maryland), January 30, 1973

Mr. Speaker, I address the House today still badly shaken following the decision of the U.S. Supreme Court on January 22 legalizing abortion.

I have been a foe of abortion because I cannot accept that it can be right—that it can be legal—to end one human life for the personal convenience of another human being.

I must stand up and protest this gross disregard for human life which is now the official law of the United States of America. I have lived 44 years, and I have always deeply loved my country. This is the first time in all those years that I have been in deep despair over the future of my country.

Mr. Speaker, I have introduced today a constitutional amendment—

House Joint Resolution 261—which would offset the recent Supreme Court decision on abortion.

If I had been alive in Nazi Germany, I like to think that I would have had the courage to stand up and protest the inhumane actions of my government. I feel very much the same today. My initial reaction to the Supreme Court's decision was that I did not want to be a part of a government which abandoned all respect for life. I seriously considered resigning from Congress. But then I decided that the preferable course would be to stay and do whatever I can to remedy the Court's action. The vehicle I have chosen in order to turn around this shocking new policy of our Government, of which I am so deeply ashamed, is to stay and fight for adoption of the constitutional amendment—House Joint Resolution 261—which I introduced today.

I am speaking today for those who cannot speak. I am speaking on behalf of our unborn children. Those who are concerned with equality of rights should not forget a group who are now in more need of constitutional protection than any other in our society—our most helpless minority, our unborn children.

The fundamental right of life itself is being neglected and denied to many of our fellow humans. To remedy this grave situation, I have introduced today a constitutional amendment—House Joint Resolution 261—that will insure that the unborn, the aged, the ill, and the incapacitated have a right to life that is every bit as valid as that guaranteed all of us under the 14th amendment.

Because of the Supreme Court's decisions in Roe against Wade and Doe against Bolton both decided January 22, 1973, the necessity for this amendment is now clearly evident. It is the only effective recourse open to those of us who value every human being's right to life.

Source: H 2574, Congressional Record, January 30, 1973, H 2,574.

DOCUMENT 49: "Protection of the Unborn"—Introduction of a Joint Resolution to Amend the Constitution by Senator James L. Buckley (New York), May 31, 1973

Mr. President, about 4 months ago, the Supreme Court, in a pair of highly controversial, precedent-shattering decisions, Roe against Wade and Doe against Bolton, ruled that a pregnant woman has a constitutional right to destroy the life of her unborn child. In so doing, the Court not only contravened the express will of every State legislature in the country; it not only removed every vestige of legal protection hitherto enjoyed by the child in the mother's womb; but it reached its result through a curious and confusing chain of reasoning that, logically extended, could apply with equal force to the genetically deficient infant, the retarded child, or the insane or senile adult.

After reviewing these decisions, I concluded that, given the gravity of the issues at stake and the way in which the Court had carefully closed off alternative means of redress, a constitutional amendment was the only way to remedy the damage wrought by the Court. My decision was not lightly taken for I believe that only matters of permanent and fundamental interest are properly the subject for constitutional amendment. I regret the necessity for having to take this serious step, but the Court's decisions, unfortunately, leave those who respect human life in all its stages from inception to death with no other recourse. . . .

Mr. President, the full import of the Court's action is as yet incompletely understood by large segments of the public and by many legislators and commentators. It seems to be rather widely held, for example, that the Court authorized abortion on request in the first 6 months of pregnancy, leaving the States free to proscribe the act thereafter. But such is far from the truth. The truth of the matter is that, under these decisions, a woman may at any time during pregnancy exercise a constitutional right to have an abortion provided only that she can find a physician willing to certify that her "health" requires it; and as the word "health" is defined, that in essence means abortion on demand.

The [Court] attempts to distinguish three stages of pregnancy, but upon examination this attempt yields, in practical effect, distinctions without a difference. In the first 3 months, in the words of the Court, "the abortion decision and its effectuation must be left to the medical judgment of the pregnant woman's attending physician." This means, for all intents and purposes, abortion on request. During the second trimester of pregnancy, the State may—but it need not—regulate the abortion procedure in ways that are reasonably related to maternal health. The power of the State's regulation here is effectively limited to matters of time, place and perhaps manner.

Thus, through approximately the first 6 months of pregnancy, the woman has a constitutionally protected right to take the life of her unborn child, and the State has no "compelling interest" that would justify prohibiting abortion if a woman insists on one.

After the period of "viability", which the Court marks at 6, or alternatively 7, months of pregnancy, the State "may"—but, again, it need not—proscribe abortion except "where it is necessary for the preservation of the life or health of the mother." This provision, which appears at first glance to be an important restriction, turns out to be none at all, as the Court defines health to include "psychological as well as physical well-being," and states that the necessary "medical judgment may be exercised in the light of all factors—physical, emotional, psychological, familial, and the woman's age—relevant to the well-being" of the mother. The Court, in short, has included under the umbrella of "health" just about every conceivable reason a woman might want to advance for having an abortion.

It is clear, then, that at no time prior to natural delivery is the unborn child considered a legal person entitled to constitutional protections; at no time may the unborn child's life take precedence over the mother's subjectively-based assertion that her well-being is at stake.

In reaching these findings, the Court in effect wrote a statute governing abortion for the entire country, a statute more permissive than that enacted by the hitherto most permissive jurisdiction in the country; namely, my own State of New York. Nor is that all. In the course of its deliberations, the Court found it necessary to concede a series of premises that can lead to conclusions far beyond the immediate question of abortion itself. These premises have to do with the conditions under which human beings, born or unborn, may be said to possess fundamental rights.

I shall have a good deal to say about these extended implications of the Court's decisions in the months ahead, but for the moment, I would like to touch briefly on one or two basic points:

First, it would now appear that the question of who is or is not a "person" entitled to the full protection of the law is a question of legal definition as opposed to practical determination. Thus, contrary to the meaning of the Declaration of Independence, contrary to the intent of the framers of the 14th amendment, and contrary to previous holdings of the Court, to be created human is no longer a guarantee that one will be possessed of inalienable rights in the sight of the law. The Court has extended to government, it would seem, the power to decide the terms and conditions under which membership in good standing in the human race is determined. This statement of the decisions' effect may strike many as overwrought, but it will not appear as such to those who have followed the abortion debate carefully or to those who have read the Court's decisions in full. When, for example, the Court states that the unborn are not recognized by the law as "persons in the whole sense," and when, further, it uses as a precondition for legal protection the test whether one has a "capability of meaningful life," a thoughtful man is necessarily invited to speculate on what the logical extension of such arguments might be.

If constitutional rights are deemed to hinge on one's being a "person in the whole sense", where does one draw the line between "whole" and something less than "whole"? [Is it] simply a question of physical or mental development? If so, how does one distinguish between the child in his 23d week of gestation who is lifted alive from his mother's womb and allowed to die in the process of abortion by hysterotomy, and the one that is prematurely born and rushed to an incubator? It is a well known scientific fact that the greater part of a child's cerebral cortex is not formed, that a child does not become a "cognitive person", until some months after normal delivery. Might we not someday determine that a child does not become a "whole" person until sometime after birth, or never become "whole" if born with serious defects? And what about those who, having been born healthy, later lose their mental or physical capacity? Will it one day be found that a person, by virtue of mental illness, or serious accident, or senility, ceases to be a "person in the whole sense", or ceases to have the "capability for meaningful life," and as such is no longer entitled to the full protection of the law?

Mr. President, the list of such questions is virtually endless.

Source: S 17538–39, Congressional Record, May 31, 1973, S 17538–39.

THE LAW PROFESSORS

Law reviews and scholarly journals brought out some classic commentaries on the case. Professors of law found a number of problems with the decision and serious flaws with Justice Blackmun's opinion. Justice Blackmun had written that there was no evidence that the Fourteenth Amendment was intended to include the unborn as "persons." Professor Robert M. Byrn of Fordham University found this to be a fundamental error. Byrn's position, however, is extremely controversial.

One of the most quoted of the critiques was that of John Hart Ely, a professor at Yale Law School. His article, which appeared in the Yale Law Journal, contends that there was no sound basis in constitutional law for the decision. He compared the decision to that in Lochner v. New York, a decision handed down in 1905. In that case the Supreme Court held that state laws setting a limit on the hours a week a worker could be required to labor violated the worker's "freedom of contract." The Supreme Court seemed to be writing its own views about free market economics into the Constitution. Was it doing the same thing in Roe v. Wade?

A third article on Roe argued that the Court should not have rested its decision on the Constitution's protection of liberty and privacy. Professor Donald Regan saw the legal and philosophical problem in the abortion cases to be one of "samaritanism." In American law persons have never been legally required to give aid to others (although they may have a moral duty to come to another's aid). Regan thinks that laws requiring a woman to carry a fetus to term violate this legal principle.

A final selection, this one from an article written in 1983, takes the position that the Supreme Court's decision in *Roe* was not out of the ordinary. Professor Lawrence Friedman pokes fun at law professors (he is one himself) for getting hung up on legal doctrine, and finds the decision a moderate and cautious attempt to solve a social problem by translating it into legal language and taking it to court.

The critical comment on the Supreme Court's decisions in these cases was extensive and came from a variety of different directions. Was the decision good constitutional law? Good history? Did it reflect the views of the American public? Was it morally acceptable? Was it good politics? Should defenders of abortion have worked through the state legislatures rather than going to the courts? Many of these questions ran through the debate that continued for the next twenty years.

DOCUMENT 50: "An American Tragedy: The Supreme Court on Abortion." Robert M. Byrn, 1973

"[I]f the deliberate extinguishment of human life has any effect at all, it more likely tends to lower our respect for life and brutalize our values."

"New York courts have already acknowledged that, in the contemporary medical view, the child begins a separate life from the moment of conception."

I. Introduction

On January 22, 1973, in the companion cases of *Roe v. Wade* and *Doe v. Bolton*, the Supreme Court of the United States declared that unborn children are not persons under section one of the fourteenth amendment. Basing its decision on a right of personal privacy to choose whether or not to abort, the Court held further that a state may not enact abortion legislation protecting unborn children for the period of gestation prior to the time the children are said to be " 'viable,' that is, potentially able to live outside the mother's womb, albeit with artificial aid. Viability is usually placed at about seven months (28 weeks) but may occur earlier, even at 24 weeks." . . .

The writer has long maintained that unborn children are in all respects live human beings protected by section one of the fourteenth amendment, particularly the equal protection clause. In an opinion replete with error and fraught with dangerous implications, the Supreme Court in *Wade* found to the contrary. It is with these issues that this article is concerned.

Roe v. Wade is in the worst tradition of a tragic judicial aberration that periodically wounds American jurisprudence and, in the process, irreparably harms untold numbers of human beings. Three generations of Americans have witnessed decisions by the United States Supreme Court which explicitly degrade fellow human beings to something less in law than "persons in the whole sense." One generation was present at *Scott v. Sandford*, another at *Buck v. Bell* and now a third at *Roe v. Wade*. Are not three generations of error enough?*

With respect to unborn children, the *Wade* decision means at a minimum: that an unborn child is neither a fourteenth amendment person nor a live human being at any stage of gestation; an unborn child has no right to live or to the law's protection at any stage of gestation; a state may not protect an unborn child from abortion until viability; after viability, a state may, if it chooses, protect the unborn child from abortion, but an exception must be made for an abortion necessary to preserve the life or health of the mother; and finally, health having been defined in *Doe v. Bolton* to include "all factors—physical, emotional, psychological, familial, and the woman's age—relevant to the well-being of the patient," it follows that a physician may with impunity equate the unwantedness of a pregnancy with a danger to the pregnant woman's health—emotional, psychological or otherwise. Thus, even after viability, there is little that a state can do to protect the unborn child.

III. The Fundamental Errors in *Wade*: In General

Upon analysis, it becomes evident that the structure of the Court's opinion in *Wade* is defective. The Court agreed that if the fourteenth amendment personhood of the unborn child were established, "the appellant's case, of course, collapses, for the fetus' right to life is then guaranteed specifically by the Amendment." Hence, the approach of the Court should have been to decide: (a) whether the unborn child, as a matter of fact, is a live human being, (b) whether all live human beings are "persons" within the fourteenth amendment, and (c) whether, in the light of the answers to (a) and (b), the state has a compelling interest in the protection of the unborn child, or to put it another way, whether there are any other interests of the state which would justify denying to the unborn child the law's protection of his life. Instead, the Court reversed the inquiry, deciding first that the right of privacy includes a right to abort, then deciding that the unborn child is not a person within the meaning of the fourteenth amendment, and finally, refusing to re-

---

*The Dred Scott decision held that Negroes were not citizens and slaves were property; *Buck v. Bell* upheld a state law allowing the sterilization of mental defectives.

solve the factual question of whether an abortion kills a live human being. . . .

C. The Fourteenth Amendment

The early American abortion statutes were a continuum of the striving of the common law to protect human life from its very beginning. When, with the discovery of the ovum in 1827, science clearly identified conception as the beginning of life, the law began to move its protection back to the earliest stages of gestation, and penalize abortional acts prior to quickening without, in some cases, even requiring proof of pregnancy. Quickening began to disappear, first as a practical norm for initial criminality and then as a factor calling for increased punishment.

The Supreme Court in *Wade* admitted that "[t]he anti-abortion mood prevalent in this country in the late 19th century was shared by the medical profession. Indeed, the attitude of the profession may have played a significant role in the enactment of stringent criminal abortion legislation during that period." In 1859, an American Medical Association Committee on Criminal Abortion, appointed to investigate criminal abortion with a view to its suppression, criticized the quickening criterion of criminality and "the grave defects of our laws, both common and statute, as regards the independent and actual existence of the child before birth, as a living being." On the basis of the report, the Association adopted resolutions protesting " 'against such unwarrantable destruction of human life,' calling upon state legislatures to revise their abortion laws, and requesting the cooperation of state medical societies in pressing the subject.' " . . .

Whatever may be said of the common law and the early nineteenth century, it is evident that in the period from 1859 to 1871, spanning a war fought to vindicate the essential dignity of every human being and the subsequent ratification of the fourteenth amendment in 1868, the anti-abortion mood prevalent in the United States can be explained only by a desire to protect live human beings in the womb from the beginning of their existence. When the fourteenth amendment was ratified in 1868, the law of at least twenty-eight of the thirty-seven states of the United States incriminated abortional acts prior to quickening—two by common law, and the remainder by statute. In the next fifteen years one additional state (Colorado) entered the United States and at least seven more states incriminated pre-quickening abortional acts.

As previously indicated, the overwhelming weight of authority is to the effect that at least one of the purposes of these statutes was the protection of unborn children at all gestational stages. The fourteenth amendment era, which finally saw the extension of the equal protection clause to aliens and corporations in the 1880's and, during the same period, witnessed the expression of a new liberality in interpretation of basic constitutional guarantees, was an era of solicitude for the basic right of the unborn child to live no matter what his gestational age might be, and without regard to "quickening."

Given the background of the fourteenth amendment, this solicitude should come as no surprise. The evil, for which the due process and equal protection clauses were designed as a remedy, is typified in the arguments of counsel in *Bailey v. Poindexter's Executor*, wherein a provision in a will that testator's slaves could choose between emancipation and sale was held void on the ground that slaves had no legal capacity to choose. In support of the position, counsel argued:

These decisions are legal conclusions flowing ... from the one clear, simple, fundamental idea of chattel slavery. That fundamental idea is, that, in the eye of the law, so far certainly as civil rights and relations are concerned, the slave is not a person, but a thing. The investiture of a chattel with civil rights or legal capacity is indeed a legal solecism and absurdity. The attribution of legal personality to a chattel slave,—legal conscience, legal intellect, legal freedom, or liberty and power of free choice and action, and corresponding legal obligations growing out of such qualities, faculties and action—implies a palpable contradiction in terms.

The court agreed with the arguments of counsel that the slave is property and "has no civil rights or privileges," and the court, in dictum, went on to observe that the social right of "protection from injury" is limited to free persons.

This, then, was the evil: human beings were degraded to the status of property, without civil rights—without even the right to the law's protection of their lives—unless the legislature, by policy decision, should grant it to them.

Slavery typified the evil, but the remedy was not limited to slaves alone. It was the intent of the framers of the fourteenth amendment that never again would *any* human being be deprived of fundamental rights by an irrational and arbitrary classification as a non-person. Thus, Congressman John A. Bingham, who sponsored the amendment in the House of Representatives, noted that it was "universal" and applied to "any human being." Congressman Bingham's counterpart in the Senate, Senator Jacob Howard, emphasized that the amendment applied to every member of the human race:

It establishes equality before the law, and it gives to the humblest, the poorest, the most despised of the race the same rights and the same protection before the law as it gives to the most powerful, the most wealthy, or the most haughty.

The Court in *Wade* made no reference to the intent of the framers. Had it done so, in the context of a proper understanding of what had originally motivated the enactment of state abortion legislation, how could it have excluded unborn children from personhood under the due process and equal protection clauses? . . .

VIII. Conclusion

Every decision to abort is a decision to kill a "live human being," a child [with] a separate life," a "human" who is "unquestionably alive" and has "an autonomy of development and character." This is the stark, overwhelming reality about abortion.

In *Wade*, the Supreme Court, with full knowledge of the mortal consequences that would ensue, removed a whole class of live human beings from the law's protection, and left their continued existence to the unfettered discretion of others. But "[h]uman beings are not merely creatures of the State, and by reason of that fact, our laws should protect the unborn from those who would take his life for purposes of comfort, convenience, property or peace of mind rather than sanction his demise."

Perhaps it is a measure of the extent to which the quality-of-life philosophy dominates our jurisprudence that a justice of the Supreme Court can write in the "environmental context" of the destruction of trees and animals, "any man's death diminishes me, because I am involved in Mankinde," while in the human context of the destruction of unborn children, he can opine, contrary to fact, that "the fetus, at most, represents only the potentiality of life;" and proceed to exile the unborn beyond the pale. But unborn children are also a part of mankind and, aware of it or not, his opinion did diminish the Court and all the rest of us.

First, *Dred Scott*, then *Buck v. Bell* and now the most tragic of them all—*Roe v. Wade*. Three generations of error are three too many—and the last of them shall be called the worst.

Source: *Fordham Law Review*, May 1973, vol. 41, pp. 807, 809, 812–13, 835–38, 861–62.

DOCUMENT 51: "The Wages of Crying Wolf: A Comment on *Roe v. Wade*." John Hart Ely, 1973

Of course a woman's freedom to choose an abortion is part of the "liberty" the Fourteenth Amendment says shall not be denied without due process of law, as indeed is anyone's freedom to do what he wants. But "due process" generally guarantees only that the inhibition be procedurally fair and that it have some "rational" connection—though plausible is probably a better word—with a permissible governmental goal.

What is unusual about *Roe* is that the liberty involved is accorded a far more stringent protection, so stringent that a desire to preserve the fetus's existence is unable to overcome it—a protection more stringent, I think it fair to say, than that the present Court accords the freedom of the press explicitly guaranteed by the First Amendment. What is frightening about *Roe* is that this super-protected right is not inferable from the language of the Constitution, the framers' thinking respecting the specific problem in issue, any general value derivable from the provisions they included, or the nation's governmental structure. Nor is it explainable in terms of the unusual political impotence of the group judicially protected vis-à-vis the interest that legislatively prevailed over it. And that, I believe—the predictable early reaction to *Roe* notwithstanding ("more of the same Warren-type activism")—is a charge that can responsibly be leveled at no other decision of the past twenty years. At times the inferences the Court has drawn from the values the Constitution marks for special protection have been controversial, even shaky, but never before has its sense of an obligation to draw one been so obviously lacking.

IV

Not in the last thirty-five years at any rate. For, as the received learning has it, this sort of thing did happen before, repeatedly. From its 1905 decision in *Lochner v. New York* into the 1930's the Court, frequently though not always under the rubric of "liberty of contract," employed the Due Process Clauses of the Fourteenth and Fifth Amendments to invalidate a good deal of legislation. According to the dissenters at the time and virtually all the commentators since, the Court had simply manufactured a constitutional right out of whole cloth and used it to superimpose its own view of wise social policy on those of the legislatures.

. . . The problem with *Roe* is not so much that it bungles the question it sets itself, but rather that it sets itself a question the Constitution has not made the Court's business. It *looks* different from *Lochner*—it has the shape if not the substance of a judgment that is very much the Court's business, one vindicating an interest the Constitution marks as special— and it is for that reason perhaps more dangerous. Of course in a sense it is more candid than *Lochner*. But the employment of a higher standard of judicial review, no matter how candid the recognition that it is indeed higher, loses some of its admirability when it is accompanied by neither a coherent account of why such a standard is appropriate nor any indication of why it has not been satisfied.

V

I do wish "Wolf!" hadn't been cried so often. When I suggest to my students that *Roe* lacks even colorable support in the constitutional text, history, or any other appropriate source of constitutional doctrine, they tell me they've heard all that before. When I point out they haven't heard it before from *me*, I can't really blame them for smiling.

But at least crying "Wolf!" doesn't influence the wolves; crying "Lochner!" may. Of course the Warren Court was aggressive in enforcing its ideals of liberty and equality. *But by and large, it attempted to defend its decisions in terms of inferences from values the Constitution marks as special.* Its inferences were often controversial, but just as often our profession's prominent criticism deigned not to address them on their terms and contented itself with assertions that the Court was indulging in sheer acts of will, ramming its personal preferences down the country's throat—that it was, in a word, Lochnering.

Source: Yale Law Journal, vol. 82, pp. 920, 935–36, 943–44 (1973).

DOCUMENT 52: "Rewriting *Roe v. Wade*." Donald H. Regan, 1979

II. Abortion as Self-Defense

I have already mentioned that for those who cannot bring themselves to view removing a fetus from a woman's body as an omission for purposes of the bad-samaritan principle, there is another possibility. We can concede that the woman who has an abortion actively kills the fetus but argue that she acts in self-defense. We can view the woman who secures an abortion as merely resisting the fetus's unjustified attack on her person.

Obviously the fetus is not like a willful attacker knowingly bent on murder or mayhem. But, despite the absence of much authority, it seems clear that the privilege of self-defense extends beyond a privilege to resist willful attacks. Surely we would recognize a privilege to defend oneself against an assailant one knew to be insane, even though such an assailant would be free of any criminal liability. Indeed, I have no doubt that we would recognize a privilege to defend oneself against an attacker whose conduct could not even be regarded as volitional. Suppose, for example, one found oneself cabined in a very small space with someone who was seized by wild convulsions while holding a sharp cleaver.

There are limits, of course, to the situations in which one can harm an innocent person to avoid harm to oneself. If someone begins to shoot at me, I cannot seize a completely uninvolved bystander and use him as a shield. If I find myself and another non-swimmer on a boat that is foundering, I cannot throw him off to save myself. The question is, where does abortion fall on this spectrum?

It may help to recall some facts about the early stages of fetal life. The fetus begins as a zygote, inside the woman but unattached. It is not until days later that it adheres to the uterine wall, then burrows into the endometrium, sprouts chorionic villi, and grapples onto the woman's insides. Once attached, it sends out its own hormone signals, which trigger the enormous changes pregnancy works on the woman's body. The woman simply is not pregnant until the blastocyst latches on and commandeers the woman's metabolism. On this account, the fetus may seem less "active" than the violent insane attacker or even than the person in convulsions brandishing a cleaver, but the fetus is not at all like an uninvolved bystander. The fetus is involved with the woman carrying it, and it is the fetus's presence and nothing else that threatens harm to the woman. Nor does the fetus seem like the second occupant of a foundering boat. The difference, of course, is that the woman *is* the boat. Perhaps the closest analogue of abortion would be a case where two persons are in an ocean together without any boat at all, swimming or treading water. One tires first and begins in a delirium to cling to the other. Surely the one being clung to may disentangle himself and save himself if he can.

There may be some special wrinkles to self-defense against innocent attackers. First, the *Restatement (Second) of Torts* suggests that there may be a duty to retreat before using force against an innocent attacker in cases where retreat would not be required if the attack were willful. But there is never a duty to retreat except where the harm threatened can be avoided by retreating. There is no escape from the burdens of pregnancy save abortion.

Source: Michigan Law Review, vol. 77, pp. 1,569, 1,611–12 (August 1979).

DOCUMENT 53: "The Conflict over Constitutional Legitimacy." Lawrence M. Friedman, 1983

What *Roe* did, in essence, was to take a social problem and reduce it to a legal problem, at least in form. The technique does not always work. It failed in *Dred Scott*, for example. But there the Court failed because it came out on the wrong side of the issue, not because of form or technique. The solution was unacceptable to a large, passionate, committed group of people. The Court can do a lot, but it cannot control passions that run deep enough to bring on war. The abortion decision may be of this type, but there is good reason to doubt it.

I have argued that the abortion case did not come out of the blue. It rested on a base of prior law. The prior law was rather porous and spongy, but it was there, at least from *Griswold* on. The Court did not jump into the abortion decision feet first. It went slowly and carefully, did considerable soul-searching, and came out with a decision that in form was highly legalistic. The Court acted, as it always does, in the classic common-law way, building on the base of the past.

The abortion issue, however, turned out to be more difficult than the Court expected. The decision provoked enormous controversy. The reaction was volcanic—a slow rumble, followed by eruptions. No one predicted so strong a response. Yet after a decade, the controversy is still essentially legal and electoral. Nobody has taken to the street. Compared to the aftermath of *Brown v. Board of Education*, for example, the reaction to *Roe v. Wade*—for all its sound and fury—has been relatively toothless. There has been no special, thorough attack on the Court— not, at any rate, because of this case alone. There are some proposals to tinker with its jurisdiction. But the Court has not been a lightning rod for accumulated furies, as was true of the race cases. The reaction, in short, although loud and continuous, has also been solidly normal and well within the ground rules of debate. There is no reason to doubt it will continue to be so.

Most constitutional experts are doctrinalists. Their strength is their grasp of the Court's legal language. But constitutional discourse is more a barrier than a help to discussion. Judges and scholars speak a kind of foreign language. It is a conventional language, and has a certain hypnotic charm. It has little to do with the actual thoughts of actors in the system. Many scholars believe that the power, prestige, and legitimacy of the Court depend on the grammar of this language—that if the Court departs from convention, in word or deed, and begins speaking English, it is inevitably doomed.

There is no hard evidence to support this view. My own notion is the opposite. The power, prestige, and legitimacy of the Court depend mostly on what it does. If the Court sits high, it is because it has staked out a position of bold moral authority. The public thinks better of its motives than those of politicians. And the public is not wholly wrong. The Court may not be "bound" in the naive sense some people think it is. It is bound by its very freedom and power—bound to move carefully, bound to consider the consequences of its acts. In some curious way, the public may understand this. And in some curious way, the Court may command the most respect precisely when it is most dramatically "countermajoritarian." As I have argued, the "majority" here may be, in part, an illusion. A large silent group feels that *Roe v. Wade* is wise and just. The Court is its outlet, its spokesman. The Court has been, on the whole, rather moderate and cautious. But the future course of the abortion dispute is likely to be troubled. Neither the Constitution nor the Court can accommodate all sides.

Source: Lawrence M. Friedman, "The Conflict over Constitutional Legitimacy," in *The Abortion Dispute and the American System*, edited by Gilbert Y. Steiner (Washington, D.C.: Congressional Quarterly Press, 1983), pp. 22–23, 27–28.

PART III: FOR FURTHER READING

Cox, Archibald. *The Court and the Constitution*. Boston: Houghton Mifflin, 1989.

Faux, Marion. *Roe v. Wade*. New York: New American Library, 1988.

Friendly, Fred W., and Martha J.H. Elliott. *The Constitution: That Delicate Balance*. New York: Random House, 1984.

O'Brien, David. *Storm Center: The Supreme Court in American Politics*. New York: W. W. Norton, 1986.

Rubin, Eva R. *Abortion, Politics and the Courts*. Rev. ed. Westport, Conn.: Greenwood Press, 1987.

Sarvis, Betty, and Hyman Rodman. *The Abortion Controversy*. 2nd ed. New York: Columbia University Press, 1974.

"A Stunning Approval for Abortion." *Time*, February 5, 1973.

Tribe, Lawrence. *Abortion: The Clash of Absolutes*. New York: W. W. Norton, 1990.

Weddington, Sarah. *A Question of Choice*. New York: Grosset/Putnam, 1992.

Woodward, Bob, and Scott Armstrong. *The Brethren*. New York: Simon and Schuster, 1979.

Part IV

The Battle Lines Are Drawn (1974–1980)

In the years following the 1973 abortion decision, there was political maneuvering on many different levels. State legislatures went back to the drawing board to revise state abortion laws in line with the new legal rules. In those states where there was strong political opposition to abortion, the legislators tried to find ways to restrict abortion within the framework set out in *Roe*. As they tested the limits of the decision, some states passed laws that later would be found unconstitutional.

This was a time of massive organization by anti-abortion forces. The Roman Catholic Church had begun organizing efforts during the "reform" period, and could build on the state organizations that were already in place. In 1975 the National Conference of Catholic Bishops decided to get into politics in earnest to fight against abortion and launched a political action campaign that called for the organizing of right-to-life units in all of the thousands of Catholic parishes across the country. One of their objectives would be the defeat of pro-abortion officials in the next round of elections. A number of new right-to-life organizations sprang into being across the country; these organizations did not have formal ties to the Catholic Church, although most of their members were Roman Catholic laymen. During the 1970s right-to-life organizations began to form alliances with other groups, especially conservative (New Right) Republicans and fundamentalist religious figures. Popular fundamentalist preachers like Jerry Falwell of the Moral Majority and West Coast preacher-activist Tim LaHaye began to give their flocks the anti-abortion message.

In the decade after *Roe* the anti-abortion cause began to have an impact on politics. In 1976 Ellen McCormack, a New York housewife, formed a Right to Life Party and entered her name in the race for the presidency. Abortion became a political issue in dozens of local, state, and congressional elections. It was widely thought that Ronald Reagan owed his election to the presidency to the firm support and high-tech fund-raising of groups that represented fundamentalists, Roman Catholics, New Right Republicans, and opponents of abortion.

Abortion rights supporters also sought to strengthen their organizations and make them more effective. During the reform period many of these groups had been amateurishly organized. During the 1970s they formed national political organizations and learned professional public relations skills.

New national organizations on both sides put pressure on members of Congress to advance their interests. Right-to-life groups were successful in getting Congress to block the funding of abortions under Medicaid. They also introduced amendments to the Constitution that would return the regulation of abortion to the states or extend constitutional protection to the lives of the unborn. Although Congress held hearings on a number of these amendments between 1974 and 1976, none of them received a sufficient number of votes to send them out to the states for ratification.

The Supreme Court did not take a new abortion case until 1976. After that date it held several state laws that restricted abortion rights unconstitutional. Support on the Court for abortion rights seemed, however, to be slipping. The seven-to-two majority of 1973 had become a five-to-four majority by 1980. And the Republican presidential campaign of 1980 promised that a Republican president would appoint justices to the Supreme Court who would try to reverse *Roe v. Wade.*

State Legislative Action and Judicial Response (1974–1980)

MISSOURI PASSES A RESTRICTIVE STATUTE

Beginning in 1973, state legislatures in those states where there was strong anti-abortion sentiment began to pass laws placing restrictions on abortions. Some of these laws were designed to discourage women from having abortions and doctors from performing them. The Supreme Court would eventually have to pass on the constitutionality of such statutes, and some provisions would be upheld, others overturned.

Missouri was one of the states with a legion of strong, vocal opponents of abortion. In 1974 the Missouri state legislature enacted a bill into law that contained a number of provisions restricting abortion. Other states would soon use the Missouri law as a model as they began to write restrictive statutes of their own.

Provisions in the Missouri law that became standard parts of legislative proposals in other states included:

1. *written consent provisions* (see section 3). A woman was required to give her consent in writing before having an abortion.

2. *spousal consent provisions* (section 3). Written consent of the husband (spouse) was required.

3. *parental consent* (section 3). Unmarried minors under 18 were required to get the consent of a parent or guardian.

4. *hospital requirements* (section 4). Abortions after the twelfth week had to be performed in hospitals.

5. *physician certification that the fetus was not viable* (section 5).

6. *criminal penalties* for physicians who did not comply with these provisions (section 6).

7. *fetal research prohibited* (section 6 (3)).

8. *informed consent* (section 8). A requirement that the woman be informed of certain facts.

9. *record keeping and reporting* of abortions (sections 10, 11).

See Documents 87 and 88 for other state regulations.

DOCUMENT 54: The Missouri Abortion Statute (1974)

H. C. S. House Bill No. 1211

An Act relating to abortion with penalty provisions and emergency clause.

Be it enacted by the General Assembly of the State of Missouri, as follows:

SECTION 1. It is the intention of the general assembly of the state of Missouri to reasonably regulate abortion in conformance with the decisions of the supreme court of the United States.

SECTION 2. Unless the language or context clearly indicates a different meaning is intended, the following words or phrases for the purpose of this act shall be given the meaning ascribed to them:

(1) "Abortion," the intentional destruction of the life of an embryo or fetus in his or her mother's womb or the intentional termination of the pregnancy of a mother with an intention other than to increase the probability of a live birth or to remove a dead or dying unborn child;

(2) "Viability," that stage of fetal development when the life of the unborn child may be continued indefinitely outside the womb by natural or artificial life-supportive systems;

(3) "Physician," any person licensed to practice medicine in this state by the state board of registration of the healing arts.

SECTION 3. No abortion shall be performed prior to the end of the first twelve weeks of pregnancy except:

(1) By a duly licensed, consenting physician in the exercise of his best clinical medical judgment.

(2) After the woman, prior to submitting to the abortion, certifies in writing her consent to the abortion and that her consent is informed and freely given and is not the result of coercion.

(3) With the written consent of the woman's spouse, unless the abortion is certified by a licensed physician to be necessary in order to preserve the life of the mother.

(4) With the written consent of one parent or person in loco parentis of the woman if the woman is unmarried and under the age of eighteen

years, unless the abortion is certified by a licensed physician as necessary in order to preserve the life of the mother.

SECTION 4. No abortion performed subsequent to the first twelve weeks of pregnancy shall be performed except where the provisions of section 3 of this act are satisfied and in a hospital.

SECTION 5. No abortion not necessary to preserve the life or health of the mother shall be performed unless the attending physician first certifies with reasonable medical certainty that the fetus is not viable.

SECTION 6. (1) No person who performs or induces an abortion shall fail to exercise that degree of professional skill, care and diligence to preserve the life and health of the fetus which such person would be required to exercise in order to preserve the life and health of any fetus intended to be born and not aborted. Any physician or person assisting in the abortion who shall fail to take such measures to encourage or to sustain the life of the child, and the death of the child results, shall be deemed guilty of manslaughter and upon conviction shall be punished as provided in Section 559.140, RSMo. Further, such physician or other person shall be liable in an action for damages as provided in Section 537.080, RSMo.

(2) Whoever, with intent to do so, shall take the life of a premature infant aborted alive, shall be guilty of murder of the second degree.

(3) No person shall use any fetus or premature infant aborted alive for any type of scientific, research, laboratory or other kind of experimentation either prior to or subsequent to any abortion procedure except as necessary to protect or preserve the life and health of such premature infant aborted alive.

SECTION 7. In every case where a live-born infant results from an attempted abortion which was not performed to save the life or health of the mother, such infant shall be an abandoned ward of the state under the jurisdiction of the juvenile court wherein the abortion occurred, and the mother and father, if he consented to the abortion, of such infant shall have no parental rights or obligations whatsoever relating to such infant, as if the parental rights had been terminated pursuant to section 211.411, RSMo. The attending physician shall forthwith notify said juvenile court of the existence of such live-born infant.

SECTION 8. Any woman seeking an abortion in the state of Missouri shall be verbally informed of the provisions of section 7 of this act by the attending physician and the woman shall certify in writing that she has been so informed.

SECTION 9. The general assembly finds that the method or technique of abortion known as saline amniocentesis whereby the amniotic fluid is withdrawn and a saline or other fluid is inserted into the amniotic sac for the purpose of killing the fetus and artificially inducing labor is deleterious to maternal health and is hereby prohibited after the first twelve weeks of pregnancy.

SECTION 10. 1. Every health facility and physician shall be supplied with forms promulgated by the division of health, the purpose and function of which shall be the preservation of maternal health and life by adding to the sum of medical knowledge through the compilation of relevant maternal health and life data and to monitor all abortions performed to assure that they are done only under and in accordance with the provisions of the law.

2. The forms shall be provided by the state division of health.

3. All information obtained by physician, hospital, clinic or other health facility from a patient for the purpose of preparing reports to the division of health under this section or reports received by the division of health shall be confidential and shall be used only for statistical purposes. Such records, however, may be inspected and health data acquired by local, state, or national public health officers.

SECTION 11. All medical records and other documents required to be kept shall be maintained in the permanent files of the health facility in which the abortion was performed for a period of seven years.

SECTION 12. Any practitioner of medicine, surgery, or nursing, or other health personnel who shall willfully and knowingly do or assist any actions made unlawful by this act shall be subject to having his license, application for license, or authority to practice his profession as a physician, surgeon, or nurse in the state of Missouri rejected or revoked by the appropriate state licensing board.

SECTION 13. Any physician or other person who fails to maintain the confidentiality of any records or reports required under this act is guilty of a misdemeanor and, upon conviction, shall be punished as provided by law.

SECTION 14. Any person who contrary to the provisions of this act knowingly performs or aids in the performance of any abortion or knowingly fails to perform any action required by this act shall be guilty of a misdemeanor and, upon conviction, shall be punished as provided by law.

SECTION 15. Any person who is not a licensed physician as defined in section 2 of this act who performs or attempts to perform an abortion on another as defined in subdivision (1) of section 2 of this act, is guilty of a felony, and upon conviction, shall be imprisoned by the department of corrections for a term of not less than two years nor more than seventeen years.

SECTION 16. Nothing in this act shall be construed to exempt any person, firm, or corporation from civil liability for medical malpractice for negligent acts or certification under this act.

SECTION A. Because of the necessity for immediate state action to regulate abortions to protect the lives and health of citizens of this state, this act is deemed necessary for the immediate preservation of the public health, welfare, peace and safety, and is hereby declared to be an emergency act within the meaning of the constitution, and this act shall be in full force and effect upon its passage and approval.

SECTION B. If any provision of this Act or the application thereof to any person or circumstance shall be held invalid, such invalidity does not affect the provisions or application of this Act which can be given effect without the invalid provision or application, and to this end the provisions of this Act are declared to be severable.

Approved June 14, 1974.

Effective June 14, 1974.

Source: Appendix to Opinion of the Court: *Planned Parenthood of Central Missouri v. Danforth*, 428 *U.S. Reports* 85 (1976).

PARENTAL CONSENT AND THE RIGHTS OF MINORS

The Missouri law came before the Supreme Court in 1976 in a case entitled *Planned Parenthood of Central Missouri v. Danforth*. The Court upheld most of its provisions but declared several unconstitutional. Spousal consent, parental consent for *all* minors, and a section that prohibited a specific abortion method (section 9) were overturned. The Court also held that parts of the section placing criminal penalties on physicians were too vague and unclear.

The vote in this case was five to four. Justice Blackmun again wrote for the majority. Justices White, Rehnquist, and Stevens and Chief Justice Burger dissented in part.

One of the provisions of the state law that was overturned (section 3) required that unmarried women under the age of eighteen get the consent of one parent (or a person acting as a parent, such as a guardian) before an abortion could be performed.

The idea that minors could get abortions without consulting their parents was deeply disturbing to many adults. The Missouri law addressed that concern. The Supreme Court, however, held that by giving a parent (or parental substitute) an absolute veto over a minor's decision, the law opened the door to arbitrary decisions by parents that could block abortions which were in the best interests of the minor. Many minors were, in addition, responsible enough to make decisions for themselves. A decision to have a child has such serious consequences for a young woman that it should not be made arbitrarily or without some evaluation of what her best interests might be. Holding that minors have constitutional rights that must not be arbitrarily overridden, the Court rejected the parental consent provision. Critics of the decision thought that it was destructive of parental authority and the traditional structure of family life.

The *Danforth* decision did not end the controversy about parental consent. A second decision, involving a Massachusetts law, later led to a compromise between minors' rights and parental authority.

In 1974 Massachusetts had passed a law requiring parental consent for abortions for all unmarried women under eighteen. The Court rejected the provision, but was badly split as to why the law was unconstitutional. Four justices objected to the law because it allowed a parent an absolute right to veto a child's abortion. Four other justices thought there should be distinctions for minors who were mature enough to make their own decisions. An opinion by Justice Powell offered a compromise, suggesting to Massachusetts that it set up a procedure that allowed mature minors to override a parental veto by going to a state court. If the judge agreed that the minor was responsible enough to make her own decision, or that the abortion was in her best interests, the abortion could be performed.

After the decision was handed down the Massachusetts legislature revised its law to incorporate the procedure suggested by Justice Powell.

Critics found a number of problems with the law and with the compromise. Minors could avoid the whole problem by going to New York or another state for an abortion. The Massachusetts judiciary resented having abortion decisions dumped in their laps. And many minors were incapable of going through the intricate procedures required by the law, even when an abortion might be in their best interests.

The problem of abortions for minors did not go away with these decisions. Many states continued to include some form of parental consent or parental notification provision in their state abortion laws.

Two 1990 Supreme Court decisions upheld notification requirements, requirements that parents be notified before a doctor performed an abortion. Minnesota's requirement that both parents be notified was rejected (*Hodgson v. Minnesota*, 1990). An Ohio law required the notification of one parent and was found constitutional (*Ohio v. Akron Center for Reproductive Health*, 1990). Both state laws contained "judicial by-pass" provisions that allowed a minor to have an abortion if her best interests required it.

DOCUMENT 55: *Planned Parenthood of Central Missouri v. Danforth* (1976)

Mr. Justice BLACKMUN delivered the opinion of the Court.

We agree with appellants and with the courts whose decisions have just been cited that the State may not impose a blanket provision, such as § 3(4), requiring the consent of a parent or person *in loco parentis* as a condition for abortion of an unmarried minor during the first 12 weeks of her pregnancy. Just as with the requirement of consent from the spouse, so here, the State does not have the constitutional authority to give a third party an absolute, and possibly arbitrary, veto over the decision of the physician and his patient to terminate the patient's pregnancy, regardless of the reason for withholding the consent.

[6] Constitutional rights do not mature and come into being magically only when one attains the state-defined age of majority. Minors, as well as adults, are protected by the Constitution and possess constitutional rights. See, e. g., *Breed v. Jones* (1975); *Goss v. Lopez* (1975); *Tinker v. Des Moines School Dist.* (1969); *In re Gault* (1967). The Court indeed, however, long has recognized that the State has somewhat broader authority to regulate the activities of children than of adults. It remains, then, to examine whether there is any significant state interest in conditioning an abortion on the consent of a parent or person *in loco parentis* that is not present in the case of an adult.

One suggested interest is the safeguarding of the family unit and of parental authority. It is difficult, however, to conclude that providing a parent with absolute power to overrule a determination, made by the physician and his minor patient, to terminate the patient's pregnancy will serve to strengthen the family unit. Neither is it likely that such veto power will enhance parental authority or control where the minor and the nonconsenting parent are so fundamentally in conflict and the very existence of the pregnancy already has fractured the family structure. Any independent interest the parent may have in the termination of the minor daughter's pregnancy is no more weighty than the right of privacy of the competent minor mature enough to have become pregnant.

We emphasize that our holding that § 3(4) is invalid does not suggest that every minor, regardless of age or maturity, may give effective consent for termination of her pregnancy. The fault with § 3(4) is that it imposes a special-consent provision, exercisable by a person other than the woman and her physician, as a prerequisite to a minor's termination of her pregnancy and does so without a sufficient justification for the restriction. It violates the strictures of *Roe* and *Doe*.

Source: 428 *U.S. Reports* 52 (1976).

DOCUMENT 56: *Bellotti v. Baird* (1979)

Mr. Justice POWELL: Section 12S provides in part:
"If the mother is less than eighteen years of age and has not married,

the consent of both the mother and her parents [to an abortion to be performed on the mother] is required. If one or both of the mother's parents refuse such consent, consent may be obtained by order of a judge of the superior court for good cause shown, after such hearing as he deems necessary. Such a hearing will not require the appointment of a guardian for the mother. If one of the parents has died or has deserted his or her family, consent by the remaining parent is sufficient. If both parents have died or have deserted their family, consent of the mother's guardian or other person having duties similar to a guardian, or any person who had assumed the care and custody of the mother is sufficient. The commissioner of public health shall prescribe a written form for such consent. Such form shall be signed by the proper person or persons and given to the physician performing the abortion who shall maintain it in his permanent files." . . .

C

Third, the guiding role of parents in the upbringing of their children justifies limitations on the freedoms of minors. The State commonly protects its youth from adverse governmental action and from their own immaturity by requiring parental consent to or involvement in important decisions by minors. But an additional and more important justification for state deference to parental control over children is that "[t]he child is not the mere creature of the state; those who nurture him and direct his destiny have the right, coupled with the high duty, to recognize and prepare him for additional obligations." "The duty to prepare the child for 'additional obligations' must be read to include the inculcation of moral standards, religious beliefs, and elements of good citizenship." This affirmative process of teaching, guiding, and inspiring by precept and example is essential to the growth of young people into mature, socially responsible citizens.

We have believed in this country that this process, in large part, is beyond the competence of impersonal political institutions. Indeed, affirmative sponsorship of particular ethical, religious, or political beliefs is something we expect the State not to attempt in a society constitutionally committed to the ideal of individual liberty and freedom of choice. Thus, "[i]t is cardinal with us that the custody, care and nurture of the child reside first in the parents, whose primary function and freedom include *preparation for obligations the state can neither supply nor hinder.*"

Unquestionably, there are many competing theories about the most effective way for parents to fulfill their central role in assisting their children on the way to responsible adulthood. While we do not pretend any special wisdom on this subject, we cannot ignore that central to many of these theories, and deeply rooted in our Nation's history and tradition, is the belief that the parental role implies a substantial measure of authority over one's children. Indeed, "constitutional interpretation has consistently recognized that the parents' claim to authority in their own household to direct the rearing of their children is basic in the structure of our society."

Properly understood, then, the tradition of parental authority is not inconsistent with our tradition of individual liberty; rather, the former is one of the basic presuppositions of the latter. Legal restrictions on minors, especially those supportive of the parental role, may be important to the child's chances for the full growth and maturity that make eventual participation in a free society meaningful and rewarding. Under the Constitution, the State can "properly conclude that parents and others, teachers for example, who have [the] primary responsibility for children's well-being are entitled to the support of laws designed to aid discharge of that responsibility." . . .

III . . .

A

The pregnant minor's options are much different from those facing a minor in other situations, such as deciding whether to marry. A minor not permitted to marry before the age of majority is required simply to postpone her decision. She and her intended spouse may preserve the opportunity for later marriage should they continue to desire it. A pregnant adolescent, however, cannot preserve for long the possibility of aborting, which effectively expires in a matter of weeks from the onset of pregnancy.

Moreover, the potentially severe detriment facing a pregnant woman is not mitigated by her minority. Indeed, considering her probable education, employment skills, financial resources, and emotional maturity, unwanted motherhood may be exceptionally burdensome for a minor. In addition, the fact of having a child brings with it adult legal responsibility, for parenthood, like attainment of the age of majority, is one of the traditional criteria for the termination of the legal disabilities of minority. In sum, there are few situations in which denying a minor the right to make an important decision will have consequences so grave and indelible.

Yet, an abortion may not be the best choice for the minor. The circumstances in which this issue arises will vary widely. In a given case, alternatives to abortion, such as marriage to the father of the child, arranging for its adoption, or assuming the responsibilities of motherhood with the assured support of family, may be feasible and relevant to the minor's best interests. Nonetheless, the abortion decision is one that simply cannot be postponed, or it will be made by default with far-reaching consequences.

[5, 6] For these reasons, as we held in *Planned Parenthood of Central*

Missouri v. Danforth, "the State may not impose a blanket provision ...
requiring the consent of a parent or person *in loco parentis* as a condition
for abortion of an unmarried minor during the first 12 weeks of her
pregnancy." Although, as stated in Part II, *supra*, such deference to
parents may be permissible with respect to other choices facing a minor,
the unique nature and consequences of the abortion decision make it
inappropriate "to give a third party an absolute, and possibly arbitrary,
veto over the decision of the physician and his patient to terminate the
patient's pregnancy, regardless of the reason for withholding the consent." We therefore conclude that if the State decides to require a pregnant minor to obtain one or both parents' consent to an abortion, it also
must provide an alternative procedure whereby authorization for the
abortion can be obtained.

A pregnant minor is entitled in such a proceeding to show either: (1)
that she is mature enough and well enough informed to make her abortion decision, in consultation with her physician, independently of her
parents' wishes; or (2) that even if she is not able to make this decision
independently, the desired abortion would be in her best interests. The
proceeding in which this showing is made must assure that a resolution
of the issue, and any appeals that may follow, will be completed with
anonymity and sufficient expedition to provide an effective opportunity
for an abortion to be obtained. In sum, the procedure must ensure that
the provision requiring parental consent does not in fact amount to the
"absolute, and possibly arbitrary, veto" that was found impermissible
in *Danforth*. . . .

. . . As the District Court recognized, "there are parents who would
obstruct, and perhaps altogether prevent, the minor's right to go to
court." There is no reason to believe that this would be so in the majority
of cases where consent is withheld. But many parents hold strong views
on the subject of abortion, and young pregnant minors, especially those
living at home, are particularly vulnerable to their parents' efforts to
obstruct both an abortion and their access to court. It would be unreal-
istic, therefore, to assume that the mere existence of a legal right to seek
relief in superior court provides an effective avenue of relief for some
of those who need it the most.

[10] We conclude, therefore, that under state regulation such as that
undertaken by Massachusetts, every minor must have the opportunity—
if she so desires—to go directly to a court without first consulting or
notifying her parents. If she satisfies the court that she is mature and
well enough informed to make intelligently the abortion decision on her
own, the court must authorize her to act without parental consultation
or consent. If she fails to satisfy the court that she is competent to make
this decision independently, she must be permitted to show that an
abortion nevertheless would be in her best interests. If the court is

persuaded that it is, the court must authorize the abortion. If, however, the court is not persuaded by the minor that she is mature or that the abortion would be in her best interests, it may decline to sanction the operation.

[11] There is, however, an important state interest in encouraging a family rather than a judicial resolution of a minor's abortion decision. Also, as we have observed above, parents naturally take an interest in the welfare of their children—an interest that is particularly strong where a normal family relationship exists and where the child is living with one or both parents. These factors properly may be taken into account by a court called upon to determine whether an abortion in fact is in a minor's best interests. If, all things considered, the court determines that an abortion is in the minor's best interests, she is entitled to court authorization without any parental involvement. On the other hand, the court may deny the abortion request of an immature minor in the absence of parental consultation if it concludes that her best interests would be served thereby, or the court may in such a case defer decision until there is parental consultation in which the court may participate. But this is the full extent to which parental involvement may be required. For the reasons stated above, the constitutional right to seek an abortion may not be unduly burdened by state-imposed conditions upon initial access to court.

Source: 443 U.S. Reports 622 (1979).

STATES CUT OFF FUNDING FOR ELECTIVE ABORTIONS

Another move taken by anti-abortion states was to cut off public funding of abortions under the Medicaid plan, a health program financed in part by the states, in part by Washington, under the federal Social Security Act.

In the period between 1973 and 1977, forty-five states and the District of Columbia allowed Medicaid coverage of all legal abortions. Three states (Indiana, Ohio, and Louisiana) refused to pay any money for elective abortions (those not necessary for health reasons). Nine other states wanted to deny funding to such abortions, but had been ordered to fund them by federal district courts.

In 1977 the Supreme Court was asked to decide whether states were required to pay for elective abortions either by the Medicaid statutes or by the Constitution. The answer the Court gave was no.

After these decisions a number of states withdrew all funding for abortions that were not medically necessary. By the end of 1978 only sixteen states paid for all or most abortions.

In the following selection from a case coming from Connecticut, the Court answered the following question: If Connecticut pays for childbirth, does the equal protection clause of the Constitution require that it also fund abortions for women who do not want to bear children?

DOCUMENT 57: The Abortion Funding Case: *Maher v. Roe* (1977)

Mr. Justice POWELL. The Constitution imposes no obligation on the States to pay the pregnancy-related medical expenses of indigent women, or indeed to pay any of the medical expenses of indigents. But when a State decides to alleviate some of the hardships of poverty by providing medical care, the manner in which it dispenses benefits is subject to constitutional limitations. Appellees' [those parties challenging the Connecticut rule] claim is that Connecticut must accord equal treatment to both abortion and childbirth, and may not evidence a policy preference by funding only the medical expenses incident to childbirth. . . .

At issue in *Roe* was the constitutionality of a Texas law making it a crime to procure or attempt to procure an abortion, except on medical advice for the purpose of saving the life of the mother. . . .

The Texas law in *Roe* was a stark example of impermissible interference with the pregnant woman's decision to terminate her pregnancy. . . .

The Connecticut regulation before us is different in kind from the laws invalidated in our previous abortion decisions. The Connecticut regulation places no obstacles—absolute or otherwise—in the pregnant woman's path to an abortion. An indigent woman who desires an abortion suffers no disadvantage as a consequence of Connecticut's decision to fund childbirth; she continues as before to be dependent on private sources for the service she desires. The State may have made childbirth a more attractive alternative, thereby influencing the woman's decision, but it has imposed no restriction on access to abortion that was not already there. The indigency that may make it difficult—and in some cases, perhaps, impossible—for some women to have abortions is neither created nor in any way affected by the Connecticut regulation. We conclude that the Connecticut regulation does not impinge upon the fundamental right recognized in *Roe*.

Our conclusion signals no retreat from *Roe* or the cases applying it. There is a basic difference between direct state interference with a protected activity and state encouragement of an alternative activity consonant with legislative policy. Constitutional concerns are greatest when the State attempts to impose its will by force of law; the State's power to encourage actions deemed to be in the public interest is necessarily far broader. . . .

Source: 432 U.S. Reports 469–476 (1977).

LEGISLATIVE ATTEMPTS BY CONGRESS TO LIMIT ABORTION

Congress did not have constitutional authority to legislate directly on abortion. But it did have authority to prohibit the use of federal tax money for abortion and to forbid the financing of any federal programs that included abortion. Opponents of abortion in Congress were quick to attach "riders" (amendments) to appropriations bills forbidding the expenditure of any tax money for abortions.

Medicaid was the main source of money for abortions for people on welfare. The fact that the government not only permitted abortion but was actually financing over 300,000 abortions a year, at a cost of $50 million, scandalized pro-lifers. Every year after 1973 amendments were attached to the giant appropriations bill for the Department of Health, Education and Welfare to stop the use of any federal funds to pay for abortions or promote or encourage abortions. In 1976 and thereafter these amendments were sponsored by a Republican member of Congress from Illinois, Henry Hyde, and were nicknamed "Hyde Amendments." Each year supporters of abortion lobbied to include exceptions to the amendment to allow abortions where rape or incest had occurred or where the mother's "health" was involved; in later years these exceptions were included.

DOCUMENT 58: Amendment to the Department of Health, Education and Welfare Appropriations Bill (Hyde Amendment). 1976

None of the funds provided by this joint resolution shall be used to perform abortions except where the life of the mother would be endangered if the fetus were carried to term.

Source: Public Law 94-439, sec. 209. 90 Stat. 1434.

THE EDELIN CASE (1975)

The manslaughter prosecution of a physician who had performed an abortion helped raise the political temperature on the abortion issue. After *Roe v. Wade*, Massachusetts' law forbidding abortion was no longer valid. However, sentiment against abortion was strong, especially in the Roman Catholic sections of Boston.

In October 1973, Dr. Kenneth Edelin performed a second trimester abortion on an unmarried teenager in a city hospital. He was charged not with abortion, which was legal, but with manslaughter under the theory that the baby had been born alive and had either been killed or allowed to die by the physician. Dr. Edelin's supporters claimed that the prosecution was politically motivated and that opponents of abortion were trying to use the manslaughter charge to punish the doctor and publicize the issue.

In the trial judge's charge to the jury, part of which is reprinted below, Judge McGuire explains to the jurors what manslaughter is and what they must find if they decide to convict Dr. Edelin on that charge. Had the baby actually been alive when it was aborted? If not, it was not a "person." Had Dr. Edelin caused its death by extremely careless behavior? If not, even if the baby had been born, he was not guilty of manslaughter. If the baby was not alive when it was removed from its mother, the operation was an abortion and was not subject to criminal prosecution.

The jury found Dr. Edelin guilty of manslaughter. His conviction, however, was overturned by an appeals court on the grounds that there was no evidence to support a conviction for manslaughter.

The question of the "personhood" of the fetus was to become a major point of controversy in the abortion debate. Not only was it necessary, in a prosecution for manslaughter, to find that a "person" had been killed, but the claim of a constitutional right to life for the fetus also depends on its status as a person. The Fourteenth Amendment to the Constitution protects persons. It reads, "No State shall . . . deprive any person of life, liberty or property, without due process of law." For this reason, one of the goals of the right-to-life movement has been to have the legal definition of personhood extended to the unborn.

Although abortion has been legal since *Roe v. Wade*, some states have created a crime of "feticide" (the killing of a fetus) that includes fatal assaults on women in which a fetus is also killed. In general, however, the law has not recognized the unborn as legal persons, though in some states it is possible to sue for the wrongful death of a fetus, and unborn children may inherit property.

Lawyers often contend that the inclusion of fetuses as persons would require drastic changes in a number of legal rules and raise some perplexing legal questions. Would unborn persons be counted for purposes of representation in the legislature, for example, or for the census? After one state (Missouri) declared that life begins at the moment of conception, a high school student raised an interesting question. When carded for a drinking offense because he was under eighteen, he claimed that since his life had begun at conception he was nine months older than his driver's license indicated.

DOCUMENT 59: The Trial of Dr. Edelin: The Judge's Charge to the Jury. 1974

... Let me first discuss the word "Person." I do this at the very beginning because if there had been no "person" as such in this case there could not be any conviction of the crime of manslaughter. That is so because one of the essential elements of the crime of manslaughter, of course, is the death of a person. So we come to the very beginning to define the word "person."

The Constitution of the United States does not define "person" in so many words. There are several references in this regard in the Constitution. . . . In nearly all of these instances, the use of the word is such that it has applicability only postnatally. That means after birth. None of the definitions indicates with any assurance that it has any possible prenatal application.

I have read to you previously the three subdivisions of that decision which are binding. The State may not interfere in this decision except in the latter stages of pregnancy, and at that time only, as I have said, to insure that a qualified person will perform the abortion, or to proscribe in the latter stages after viability the performance of an abortion. At the time the facts in this case took place, the Commonwealth of Massachusetts had no statute or laws in effect to regulate abortion. Therefore it follows that abortion in Massachusetts at that time was protected by the decision in Roe vs. Wade.

If in your consideration of the facts of this case—and I go back saying "if," because as I have said so often, you are the sole judges of the facts—but if in your consideration of the facts of this case you determine that the terms "viability" and "potential for life" have any applicability, they are to be taken as meaning first as to viability, the ability to live postnatally, that is, after birth, and second a child's potential for life means the power to live outside its mother, and independent only on its own systems.

A fetus is not a person, and not the subject of an indictment for manslaughter. In order for a person to exist, he or she must be born. Unborn persons, as I said, are not the subject of the crime of manslaughter. Birth is the process which causes the emergence of a new individual from the body of its mother. Once outside the body of its mother, the child has been born within the commonly accepted meaning of that word.

Killing or causing the death of a person who is born alive and is outside the body of his or her mother may be the subject of manslaughter. In order for the defendant to be found guilty in this case, you must be satisfied beyond a reasonable doubt, as I have defined that term for you, that the defendant caused the death of a person who had been alive outside the body of his or her mother.

If you believe beyond a reasonable doubt that the defendant, by his conduct caused the death of a person, once that person became such as I have defined the word for you, you may find the defendant guilty of the crime of manslaughter, if that death was caused by wanton or reckless conduct on the part of the defendant. If, on the other hand, you do not find beyond a reasonable doubt that the defendant by his conduct caused the death of a person, then you must acquit him of the crime charged.

And if you find that even though death occurred, it was not due beyond a reasonable doubt to any wanton or reckless conduct on the part of the defendant, then likewise you must acquit.

Source: 93rd Congress, 2nd Session. *Commonwealth of Mass. v. Kenneth Edelin.* No. 81823 (Mass. Super. Ct. 1974). Reprinted in U.S. Congress, Senate Committee on the Judiciary, *Hearings*, 1974, pp. 305–16.

Amending the Constitution

A HUMAN LIFE AMENDMENT

Immediately after the *Roe* decision was handed down, a number of proposals for constitutional amendments that would reverse the decision were introduced in Congress. Amending the Constitution is a difficult process. Congress may propose amendments by a joint resolution passed by a two-thirds vote in each House. Once the amendment is approved by Congress it goes to the states for ratification. The usual method of ratification requires three-fourths of the state legislatures (thirty-eight states) to vote in favor of the amendment. The Founding Fathers intentionally made the amending process difficult, so that people would have to think carefully about changing the Constitution.

Two proposed "human life" amendments were considered by Congress during 1974 and 1975. One, sponsored by Senator James Buckley, a Conservative/Republican from New York, would have defined the term *person* in the Fourteenth Amendment to include unborn persons. The Fourteenth Amendment states that "No state . . . shall deprive any person of life, liberty, or property, without due process of law." In *Roe* the Supreme Court had held that persons were those who had already been born. Senator Buckley's amendment would define persons more broadly.

Senator Jesse Helms, a Republican from North Carolina, introduced a proposal that would go even further, specifically stating that the unborn were human beings from the moment of conception.

DOCUMENT 60: Senate Joint Resolution 119 (The Buckley Amendment). 1974

Section 1. With respect to the right to life, the word "person", as used in this article and in the fifth and fourteenth articles of amendment to the Constitution of the United States, applies to all human beings, including their unborn offspring at every stage of their biological development, irrespective of age, health, function, or condition of dependency.

Sec. 2. This article shall not apply in an emergency when a reasonable medical certainty exists that continuation of the pregnancy will cause the death of the mother.

Sec. 3. Congress and the several States shall have power to enforce this article by appropriate legislation within their respective jurisdictions.

Source: U.S. Congress, Senate Committee on the Judiciary, Subcommittee on Constitutional Amendments, *Hearings on Constitutional Amendments*, 93rd Congress, 1st session, March 4, 1974, Part 1, p. 1.

DOCUMENT 61: Senate Joint Resolution 130 (The Helms Amendment). 1974

Section 1. Neither the United States nor any State shall deprive any human being from the moment of conception, of life without due process of law; nor deny to any human being, from the moment of conception, within its jurisdiction, the equal protection of the laws.

Sec. 2. Neither the United States nor any State shall deprive any human being of life on account of illness, age, or incapacity.

Sec. 3. Congress and the several States shall have the power to enforce this article by appropriate legislation.

Source: U.S. Congress, Senate Committee on the Judiciary, Subcommittee on Constitutional Amendments, *Hearings on Constitutional Amendments*, 93rd Congress, 1st session, March 4, 1974, Part 1, pp. 1–2.

HEARINGS ON TWO CONSTITUTIONAL AMENDMENTS BEFORE THE SUBCOMMITTEE ON CONSTITUTIONAL AMENDMENTS OF THE SENATE COMMITTEE ON THE JUDICIARY, 1974–1975

The Senate committee that considers all proposed constitutional amendments held public hearings on the two above proposed amendments at a number of different dates throughout 1974 and 1975. People representing all points of view were invited to testify in favor of, or against, the amendments. A wide array of witnesses appeared, and they discussed a number of controversial points. Religious leaders and scientists stated their views about when life begins. It was clear that the Supreme Court had been right in saying that there was no general agreement on the answer to this question; members of different religions held differing views. Many scientists believed that the question was essentially a religious or moral question, not one that science could answer.

A number of other issues were explored, including the public health benefits of safe, legal abortions, and the use of abortion as a method of birth control or to prevent the birth of children conceived during rape or incest. Some of the testimony was highly emotional.

The record of the hearings fills four very large volumes in the public documents section of the library. A few selections, representing different points of view on different topics, are reproduced below.

DOCUMENTS 62 A-M: Selections from the Hearings Before the Senate Committee on the Judiciary on Two Proposed Human Life Amendments to the Constitution

DOCUMENT 62-A: Position of the Roman Catholic Church

"We do not propose to advocate sectarian doctrine, but to defend human rights."—John Cardinal Krol, Archbishop of Philadelphia.

Last month Mr. Justice Blackmun was quoted as saying that the court's abortion ruling "will be regarded as one of the worst mistakes in the Court's history or one of its great decisions, a turning point." I agree with Justice Blackmun at least to this extent, that the abortion decisions will be viewed as a tragic mistake. But I am convinced that they will ultimately be seen as *the* worst mistake in the Court's history. Only a constitutional amendment can correct this mistake.

At the same time, we are aware that amending our Constitution is not a step to be taken lightly. Congress and the states are obliged to reflect seriously on such an action. In this process of reflection it is essential to consider the views of many concerned Americans. It is precisely as concerned Americans who are moral leaders that we appear here today.

We do not propose to advocate sectarian doctrine but to defend human rights, and specifically, the most fundamental of all rights, the right to life itself. While we are leaders of the Catholic Church in the United States, we believe that what we say expresses the convictions of many Americans who are members of other faiths and of no faith.

I do not intend to dwell at length on this point, but I believe it is important at least to raise it, in order to dispose of a facile but misleading slogan often directed against those who speak against abortion. We reject any suggestion that we are attempting to impose "our" morality on others. First, it is not true. The right to life is not an invention of the Catholic Church or any other church. It is a basic human right which must undergird any civilized society. Second, either we all have the same right to speak out on public policy or no one does. We do not have to check our consciences at the door before we argue for what we think is best for society. We speak as American citizens who are free to express our views and whose freedom, under our system of government, carries with it a corresponding obligation to advocate positions which we believe will best serve the good of our nation. Third, in our free country, decisions concerning issues such as the one before this Subcommittee are made by legislators who themselves are free to act according to their own best judgment. We dare not forget, however, that to separate political judgment from moral judgment leads to disorder and disaster.

In order to grasp what is at stake in the issue before us, it is essential to understand the nature of the being whom an abortion kills. There is an impression in some quarters that the child before birth is simply a lump of tissue, an undifferentiated part of its mother's body, rather like an appendix. Nothing could be farther from the truth.

What comes into existence at the moment of conception is nothing less than a human being in the earliest stages of development. As our detailed statement shows, medical science has amply documented the humanity of the fetus. There would be no question about the humanity of the unborn except that some wish to kill them.

Source: U.S. Congress, Senate Committee on the Judiciary, Subcommittee on Constitutional Amendments, *Hearings on Constitutional Amendments*, 93rd Congress, 1st session, March 4, 1974, Part 1, pp. 1, 874–75.

DOCUMENT 62-B: Statement by an Elder of the Presbyterian Church

"Human life begins with the creation of man and is a continuous process."—Jane Stitt, Task Force to Study Abortion, Presbyterian Church.

. . . I am an elder in the Presbyterian Church of the United States and was invited to join this panel this morning because this particular church has done some serious study on the subject of abortion over a period of the last 4 years. The general assembly of our church, which is an elected body of about 450 people, endorsed a statement on the subject of abortion in 1970, and if I may I would like to introduce this complete statement into the record.

Senator BAYH: Glad to introduce it, without objection.

Ms. STITT: Following that statement, there was a feeling that the church needed not only a pronouncement but also an exhaustive study on the subject of abortion, and so a subsequent general assembly asked that a committee be appointed to do a comprehensive study on the subject of abortion relative to what the Bible taught, to the morality of it and the safety of it, the legality of it and so on. It was interesting that this committee was made up of five women and four men, which I think said something about our church's recognition of the fact that they needed a broad base of input when they were studying the subject of abortion.

I served on that committee. Senator Bayh said yesterday, he felt a little reluctant about his position, and I felt very reluctant about mine. I was born knowing that abortion was wrong and so was everybody in this room. I didn't want anybody forcing me to think about it. It was, you know, a felony, and I didn't want to rethink the question of abortion.

But our church was wise enough to know that it is possible as times change for the church to need to rethink its position. This happened even in New Testament times when the church had to rethink its position on the subject of circumcision. There comes a time every now and then when we are forced to look at subjects that we would rather not think about.

Now, in the time I have left me today, I would like to refer to two very basic questions relative to the issues that were brought out in the statements by our church.

The first is the question that you have heard reiterated and that you will hear reiterated: When does human life begin? I would say from our findings that this is an improper question. The question, rather than when does human life begin is: When did human life begin? Human life began with the creation of man and is a continuous process. We have the adult man and woman. We have the egg and the sperm. We have the fertilized egg. We have the embryo. We have the fetus. We have the new born child. We have the growing child and then the adult, then the egg and the sperm and on and on.

Just because we have not participated in abortion does not mean that we have not interfered with the process of life. It does not mean that we have not denied the right to life.

If I opt for not having children at all, if I take a vow of celibacy, I have interfered with the life process. If I choose a homosexual way, I have interfered with the life process. This is borne out by the fact that some religious groups have opposed pharmaceutical and mechanical contraception; they have known that human life is precious at all stages.

. . .

Source: U.S. Congress, Senate Committee on the Judiciary, Subcommittee on Constitutional Amendments, *Hearings on Constitutional Amendments*, 93rd Congress, 1st session, March 4, 1974, Part 1, pp. 264–65.

DOCUMENT 62-C: Statement by a Rabbi of the New York Federation of Reformed Synagogues

"Judaism . . . does not equate abortion with murder. To the contrary, in Judaism, a fetus is not considered a full human being."—Rabbi Balfour Brickner.

. . . If it is true, that religious views play an inordinately important role in determining our value judgments on the subject of abortion, then how much the more should the view of Justice Oliver Wendell Holmes be heeded when he said that "moral predilections must not be allowed to influence our minds in setting legal distinctions." The coercive powers of the state must not be employed in the service of sectarian moral views. To do otherwise would be to violate the establishment clause of the first amendment: "Congress shall make no law respecting an establishment of religion. . . . " The presentation of that right of individual conscience was essentially what the Supreme Court sought to support in its historic decision. Just as the state must never say—and has not said—that a person not wishing an abortion must have one, so too the state must never be allowed so to legislate as to prevent a woman wishing an abortion from having one. The right of individual conscience must be maintained.

That right is now being challenged again. There are those who maintain that a fetus is a full, human being from the moment of conception.

Senate Joint Resolution 119 (Senator Buckley's proposed resolution) makes that equation when it suggests that the word "person" as used in the 5th and 14th articles of amendment to the Constitution be construed as "human being" and applied also to the unborn in every stage of their biological development. Senate Joint Resolution 130 (Senator Helms' proposal) in essence makes the same equation. Were either of these resolutions to become law it would follow that anyone electing to have an abortion would be guilty of murder; that is, taking a human life. The thrust of these resolutions is clearly to make abortion illegal and therefore impossible, frustrating the effect of last year's Supreme Court decision. We in Reform Judaism must therefore oppose these amendments and any similar efforts and we do so on the basis of our understanding of our tradition of Jewish law.

Judaism does not believe that the word "person" connotes a full human being. It does not equate abortion with murder. To the contrary, in Judaism, a fetus is not considered a full human being and for this reason has no "juridical personality" of its own. Jewish law is quite clear in its statement that an embryo is not reckoned a viable living thing (in Hebrew, a bar kayyama) until 30 days after its birth. One is not obliged to observe the laws of mourning for an expelled fetus. As a matter of fact, the laws of mourning, et cetera, are not applicable for a child who does not survive until his 30th day.

In Judaism the fetus in the womb is not a person (lav nefesh hu) until it is born (Rashi, Yad Ramah, and Me'iri, all to Sanhedrin 72b). According to Jewish law, a child is considered a "person" only when it is "come into the world." Thus, there is no capital liability for feticide. By the reckoning, abortion cannot be considered murder. The basis for this decision is scriptural. . . .

Source: U.S. Congress, Senate Committee on the Judiciary, Subcommittee on Constitutional Amendments, *Hearings on Constitutional Amendments*, 93rd Congress, 1st session, March 4, 1974, Part 1, p. 268.

DOCUMENT 62-D: Statement by a Biologist on the Question of When Life Begins

---

(" . . . from the scientific point of view, this question is unanswerable, because it is not formulated in terms that can be dealt with operationally."—Dr. Gerald M. Edelman, Professor, Rockefeller University.

I speak as a scientist with some experience in cell biology and in molecular biology, and also as a concerned citizen. My main fields of scientific inquiry are immunology—or how the body distinguishes self from not-self—and various areas of cell biology, particularly cell growth and division, and the analysis of the structure of spermatozoa, including those from human beings.

I was first educated as a physician and after a year of medical training at the Massachusetts General Hospital, spent 2 years in general practice, including obstetrics, as a Captain in the United States Army. Subsequent to that, I obtained a doctoral degree in protein physical chemistry. For the last 14 years, I have spent most of my time doing medical research. In 1972, I was the recipient of the Nobel Prize in Physiology or Medicine for work on the chemical structure of antibodies.

As I understand it, one of the main questions before this committee is whether we can tell when life, particularly human life, begins. I hope to show that, from the scientific point of view, this question is unanswerable, because it is not formulated in terms that can be dealt with operationally. It is important, I believe, to make this remark before getting to any substantive matters, in order to avoid large amounts of useless rhetoric. I should add that it is equally useless to comment on tautologies represented by statements that, for example, "the union of the sperm and the egg represents the first occasion in which the full genetic potential exists for the growth of an animal", a statement which is undeniable by logic alone.

The detailed comments I shall make about the role of science in such matters may sound negative to this subcommittee, but I believe that there are many questions that cannot be answered by scientific experimentation that are nonetheless important and obviously need to be answered. It seems to me that this in no way restricts the value of expert testimony by scientists. Indeed, one of the tasks before this committee is to determine whether the main question can be answered by scientists. I believe it cannot, but also believe that my obligation is to explain why it cannot. If you know what you cannot do, you are way ahead, even in fields outside of the law.

It may seem to this committee, which has heard the strong statements of previous testimony, that this is a weaker position. But I believe that the statements made in that testimony represent a straw man, consisting of a mixture of scientific fact, philosophic conjecture and personal opinion, all represented as scientific.

In rebuttal to this position, I can only say that I know of no scientific paper in any reputable journal that has proven when life indeed begins. If such a paper exists, I would certainly be glad to know of it and to know whether its claims have been verified.

The great advances in modern biology at the level of both living cells and the molecules of which they are made reveal that there is no scientifically sound way of distinguishing the living from the nonliving.

For example, viruses have all the properties of living cells except the capacity for independent existence: they contain genetic information and they evolve, they reproduce themselves and they grow. Yet, they have a completely definable molecular structure and they crystallize just as molecules crystallize and may therefore seem to be dead. At a higher level, it is clear that there is a continuum of properties possessed by cells, tissues, organs and individuals.

If one asserts that a fertilized egg contains a full complement of genes from the father and the mother, and is therefore privileged as "more alive", then counter examples can easily be brought to mind. Biologists have produced complete frogs from eggs alone without sperm and have even produced frogs from the nuclei of skin cells, which contain just as much genetic information as a fertilized egg.

Such complete genetic information is, in fact, in every cell of the body except sperm and eggs, yet no one raises issues about the loss of skin cells or even brain cells for that matter. Losing a sperm, or millions of them, or losing an egg each month would on this basis be a horrendous loss, for they too are "alive", yet it occurs normally to everyone....

... Well, from this point of view, I believe that a zygote needs no more protection from the law than an egg.

If one somehow attempts to glorify a fertilized egg or even an early embryo, one must confront questions that are not capable of scientific answers. At what step of development does a living, individual human being appear? This is essentially a religious and moral question and is therefore open to sectarian interpretations and prejudices.

Science can assert that people are not cells or just collections of cells. It is the set of capacities of a whole person, for example, the capacity to be conscious, self-aware, develop and absorb culture that defines an individual. Although a fetus may have the potential for these, it has no more than any other collection of cells and certainly has not these capacities.

Source: U.S. Congress, Senate Committee on the Judiciary, Subcommittee on Constitutional Amendments, *Hearings on Constitutional Amendments*, 93rd Congress, 1st session, March 4, 1974, Part 2, pp. 248–49.

DOCUMENT 62-E: The Position of the National Right to Life Committee

---

"Our organization . . . will work unceasingly until all such life is adequately protected."—Kenneth D. Vanderhoef, President, National Right to Life Committee, Inc.

By way of introduction, I also would like to outline what the National Right to Life Committee is. The National Right to Life Committee is an affiliation of State right to life organizations throughout the United States. Each of the 50 States has a member on our board of directors, and the 50-member board are the actual managers of the corporation. While every State of the Union is represented, they vary rather substantially from State to State, both in their organization and membership. In such States as California, we have over 120 right to life groups, all of them affiliated, however, under a State affiliation and coalition represented by one member on our board of directors. Various States, as I mentioned, vary in both their membership and the structures that they have.

Over the past several years, the National Right to Life Committee has been able to draw upon these individual State organizations for assistance and guidance, such organizations as the Human Life Organization of the State of Washington, which is the first group to be involved in a State referendum vote in 1970 on the question of abortion. The background and expertise gained in that election was called upon as a resource by the States of Michigan and North Dakota that were likewise faced with an abortion referendum in 1972.

Additionally, we have as one of our most active organizations the New York State right to life organization, which successfully repeal[ed] the law in the State of New York, but because of the veto of Governor Rockefeller over the legislature and the people of the State of New York, their actions were nullified.

We are basically a volunteer, nondenominational, nonsectarian organization. The actual membership and numbers reflected we feel represent the majority of the people of this country. The effect of over 60 percent of the people of the State of Michigan rejecting an abortion statute proposed to them on their referendum ballot, the statute being far narrower than the Supreme Court decision of 1972, would indicate that such States as Michigan have collectively a conscience which rejects the basic principle that we can in fact take life, including the life of the unborn. This is likewise reflected by some 70 percent of the people of the State of North Dakota, and certainly the substantial majority of the legislators representing the people of New York.

The National Right to Life Committee has outlined three basic purposes. One is to promote respect for the worth and dignity of all human life, including the life of the unborn from the moment of conception; second, to promote, encourage, and sponsor such amendatory and statutory measures which will provide protection for human life before and after birth, particularly for the defenseless, the incompetent, the impaired and the incapacitated; and third, we intend to engage in such activities as will assist in the accomplishment of those purposes outlined above.

To place your deliberations on the human life amendment in context, some historical evidence should be reviewed. The majority of the people of this country have rejected the abortion mentality as a solution to any problems that are facing this Nation. The National Right to Life Committee is a coalition of these people whose one basic effort is to demonstrate to this legislative body and to other people of this country that the destruction of any life is not an acceptable alternative in our constant quest to solve the human problems of this Nation. It is the position of the National Right to Life Committee to coordinate on a national level a movement that will properly reflect the genuine and sincere concern of the people of this Nation. Our organization likewise will not accept the ultimate rejection of this basic value judgment to protect all human life and will work unceasingly until all such life is adequately protected.

Source: U.S. Congress, Senate Committee on the Judiciary, Subcommittee on Constitutional Amendments, *Hearings on Constitutional Amendments*, 93rd Congress, 1st session, March 4, 1974, Part 2, pp. 2–3.

DOCUMENT 62-F: Statement by an African-American Physician and Anti-Abortion Activist, Chairman of the Board of Directors, National Right to Life Committee

"The doctor and pregnant woman were elevated to the rank of super-citizens with the private right to kill by contract."—Dr. Mildred Jefferson.

Although it is a privilege for me to be here, I am somewhat saddened that we must take the strong measures that we must to prevent the destruction of lives of those who cannot defend themselves. Most immediately, there are those unborn who would be considered social embarrassment or economic burdens. The jeopardy already extends to the newly born with severe mental or physical defects. The elderly are being invited to die with dignity, and those who accept the invitation may soon find themselves invited or perhaps urged to choose to die. If a society can develop tolerance for destroying lives at the beginning and the end, why not apply the methods to eliminate the deformed, defective, incapable, the incompetent, or the inconvenient anywhere along the scale? If the destruction of life is permissible for social and economic reasons, why not for political reasons?

It is reasonable to apply the extermination principle of social change to that segment of the population that cannot fight back, cannot riot in the streets and of course, cannot vote. Getting rid of babies before they can be born in their own time can be arranged so very readily with our modern medical technology. Separating the word "abortion" from the fact of what abortion does allows it to be promoted as a welcome escape from a problem without considering the threat of harm in the promise of the relief.

The act of killing an unborn child involves complex medical, moral, and legal issues. On January 22, 1973, the majority of the Supreme Court of the United States undertook to reduce them to a simple medical problem by handing down decisions on abortion which left the abortion decision to be a private matter between a woman and a doctor, subject to the doctor's medical judgment. The Court acted in the tradition of the 19th century Court that decided to settle the problem of slavery by declaring one enslaved Dred Scott to be "property" therefore not a person and not entitled to the protection of citizenship. The 20th century Court may have intended to create social revolution with its abortion rulings. If so, the Court succeeded in turning the wheel of social progress a full turn backward.

By joining the strong team of the woman and the doctor against the unborn child, the High Court destroyed a principle of justice in our legal system which guaranteed some balance for the weak in conflict with the strong by joining with the weak against the strong. By requiring the unborn child to escape an extermination team of the mother and doctor for 6 months before having [a] chance of protection by the State, the High Court destroyed fairness in the application of our laws. By allowing the State to protect the life that Mr. Justice Blackmun called potential in the last 3 months before birth only if it chooses, means that the Court did not guarantee protection for the life of that child at any point before birth or after if the State should choose not to protect that life. And that opens the jeopardy to us all.

The Supreme Court destroyed the foundations of democracy in the abortion decisions by creating three categories of citizenship. The doctor and pregnant woman were elevated to the rank of super-citizens with the private right to kill by contract. Man, the father of the child, was reduced to the level of subcitizen with no defined right to protect the life of his unborn child. The unborn child was declared nonperson in the eyes of the law, and therefore, noncitizen only to allow his or her life to be taken.

Source: U.S. Congress, Senate Committee on the Judiciary, Subcommittee on Constitutional Amendments, *Hearings on Constitutional Amendments*, 93rd Congress, 1st session, March 4, 1974, Part 3, pp. 7–8.

DOCUMENT 62-G: Statement by Feminists Against Abortion

"Each time a woman resorts to abortion . . . she allows some part of the male power structure to force her into a destructive act."—Pat Goltz, Feminists for Life.

We are for the legal and social equality of women and men. We are here in support of the human life amendment to the Constitution of the United States, which would protect human life from conception until natural death.

Our primary reason is a feminist one. The only consistent philosophy a feminist can have about other instances of human life is one of granting dignity to all of them. We are demanding an end to class stereotyping for women; we cannot and dare not introduce a new class stereotype based on age, mental and physical condition, or degree of unwanted-ness. We who were once defined as less than human cannot, in claiming our rights, deny rights to others based on a subjective judgment that they are less than human.

Our Government and our society exists to protect the rights of each individual, and the most basic right is that of life itself.

Abortion has been presented as the solution to the problems faced by women with untimely pregnancies. The vast majority of these problems can be put into one category: discrimination. We are unilaterally opposed to discrimination based on either sex or maternal status. We reserve the right to be treated as equals and to be mothers at the same time.

Abortion is a nonsolution. Each time a woman resorts to abortion, she entrenches discrimination. She allows some part of the male power structure to force her into a destructive act, in order to be treated with the dignity which is inherent in her.

Many women who promote abortion do not do so out of zeal. They are driven to it. They have allowed their bodies to be raped by the abortionist's knife and like the victim of sexual assault it is a traumatic experience. It interrupts physical, hormonal, and physical life streams. It is no wonder that in every poll, more men favor abortion than women. It is no wonder that women who have been subjected the longest to the male education establishment are most likely to support abortion.

Women are in tune with the earth, the ecology. We do not destroy: we create. Women recognize that human personhood begins biologically at conception. We insist on the right to exist in our full sexuality which includes the reproductive function. . . .

Rape is the only case in which a women [sic] does not willingly consent to intercourse. The solution to the rape problem is not abortion, but the creation of a society in which rape is unknown.

The immediate solution is to teach women to report their rapes immediately so that pregnancy can be prevented. Failure to do so is implied consent to provide life support to the unborn child who may result. The immediate solution also consists of forcing changes in attitude toward raped women so that they are not treated as common criminals if they report their rapes.

In rape with pregnancy resulting there are actually two victims: the mother and her baby. It is not just, to kill one of the victims for the father's crime.

A comment must also be made about the term "compulsory pregnancy" which the other side uses. It is an emotion-laden term, and its purpose is emotional. Its result is to take the discussion out of the realm of the rational. In actual fact, even accidental pregnancies cannot be called compulsory since the woman consented to intercourse. Completing a pregnancy does not, however, require a woman to raise a child. The "compulsory pregnancy" crowd claims adoption is inhumane. They further deny that there is any implied agreement on the part of the woman to supply life support systems to a child who otherwise would not live. But many of them get violently angry if it is suggested that the father has not given implied agreement by his intercourse, to support the mother financially, even though anybody or any group could substitute.

Source: U.S. Congress, Senate Committee on the Judiciary, Subcommittee on Constitutional Amendments, *Hearings on Constitutional Amendments*, 93rd Congress, 1st session, March 4, 1974, Part 3, pp. 108–9.

DOCUMENT 62-H: Statement by a Member of Congress and Women's Rights Advocate

(" . . . the fate of women is once again to be decided by men."—Hon. Bella S. Abzug, Representative in Congress from the State of New York.)

I appreciate the opportunity to testify against approval of abortion prohibition amendments to the Constitution, which potentially could affect every woman of childbearing age in the United States.

I appear before you as a Member of Congress, but also as a woman who is aware that in the consideration of this proposal, the fate of women is once again to be decided by men. I recognize that views both for and against the right to abortion are found in both sexes. The fact remains, however, that these are amendments aimed exclusively at women, which have been introduced by men and submitted to a legislative body consisting entirely of men.

In the other body, women number only 16 out of 435 Members, and if an abortion prohibition should be approved by the Congress, which I certainly hope will never happen, it would then be submitted to legislatures that are now roughly 93-percent male in composition.

Women are at your mercy, as they were during their 100-year struggle to win suffrage. I remind you of the inequities in the present legislative situation, not to make any sweeping prejudgments as to where individual Members of the Senate may stand on this issue, but so that you may be conscious of your particular responsibility also to represent women, who in this setting regrettably have no franchise. . . .

Man and woman are equal in the act of conception, but after that single act has occurred, it is the woman's body that carries and nurtures the embryo and the fetus.

It is the woman who experiences the physical and psychological changes of pregnancy.

It is the woman who has the discomforts and sometimes the medical complications that accompany pregnancy.

It is the woman who feels the pain of childbirth. It is the woman who may have the post partum depression. . . .

And in our society, it is still the woman who bears the major responsibility of caring for and raising the child and who often must leave school or her work to do so.

Childbearing and childraising is a great experience for most women. For some it is not. For some it is sometimes. The point is that it is a totally individual experience, the most highly personal process in a woman's life.

And yet the Buckley and Helms amendments might mobilize the full power and authority of the state and its legal apparatus to interfere in this private process, to dictate to the individual citizen who is a woman what she is to do with her body and with her life.

I oppose these amendments because I believe they might create insoluble conflicts within the Constitution. They could inflict upon us arbitrary legal definitions of physical processes for which there is no universally agreed upon medical definition. They would produce legal chaos. And they would not work.

Let us start with the last point first. This Nation has already had the bitter experience of another kind of national prohibition as mandated by the 18th amendment to the Constitution. We know that not only did that Prohibition fail to accomplish its avowed highly moral purpose, but was responsible for the lawless and violent era of the bootlegger and gangster, and the rise of organized crime which still plagues our society.

We don't have to speculate about whether a similar failure would result from the adoption of a constitutional prohibition of abortion, because we already have the answer.

Until the U.S. Supreme Court issued its decision last year, most States had antiabortion laws. Prior to 1830, there were no statutes in the U.S. prohibiting abortion. Between 1830 and 1956, however, virtually every State adopted laws which prohibited abortion unless necessary to preserve the life of the woman.

The main reason for enactment of these laws was that under 19th Century conditions, before aseptic surgical techniques were developed, abortions were extremely dangerous and sometimes fatal, even when performed by physicians. Protection of the health of the woman was the major concern behind the enactment of these laws. Today, however, with a variety of techniques available and with abortions more available to women in the early stages of their pregnancy, an abortion can be safer than childbirth.

Even though abortion was outlawed in most of the States, at least until 5 or 6 years ago, abortions were performed, and they will continue to be performed whether the Constitution is amended or not, whether we follow Buckley, Helms, Hogan, Whitehurst or not. This is a fact that no amount of moral wishing can overcome.

It has been generally estimated that all throughout the period when antiabortion laws were on the books, about 1 million American women were having abortions each year. The rarified atmosphere in which the present amendments are projected really strains credulity. Illegal abortions were so common and profitable they were said to be the third largest source of criminal revenue, following only narcotics and gambling.

Source: U.S. Congress, Senate Committee on the Judiciary, Subcommittee on Constitutional Amendments, *Hearings on Constitutional Amendments*, 93rd Congress, 2nd session, March 4, 1974, Part I, pp. 100–102.

DOCUMENT 62-I: Statement by an African-American Civic Leader, Washington, D.C.

"Those blacks who oppose legalized abortion must reflect upon black history and see the paradox for the present."—Mary Treadwell Barry, Youth Pride Inc., Washington, D.C.

Chairman Bayh, and members of the committee. Senator, my name is Mary Treadwell Barry, and I welcome this opportunity to share my views with you on the issue of abortion. I believe it important for you to understand the experience and personal base from which I speak.

Some of my statement I have deleted for purposes of time. For 5 years I was coexecutive director of Youth Pride, Inc., and also one of Pride's three founders. During the last 2 1/2 years I have served as executive director of Pride.

Briefly, my positions have allowed me to share the lives of primarily inner city males—street dudes—ages 14 to 25. Over 80 percent of Pride's trainee population are juvenile or adult law offenders, with the peripheral problems which this status breeds. Naturally I have become involved in the dude's domestic problems, since on the average, a 15-year-old trainee has at least one dependent.

I have also simultaneously served in other community positions such as chairman of the board of the National Capital Head Start Program, a preschool early childhood education program, for 1 1/2 years and a board member for 2 1/2 years. I have kept my feet to the ground in the quest to understand and not rhetorize the folk with whom I struggle. I do not work for any organized abortion cause or counseling group; nor do I often speak on this issue. I don't speak on this problem because of the possible ultimate effect to me which the legislation may cause, for I've made my decisions on this subject, and had occasion to implement them.

There are four segments of the abortion issue which I believe are of importance for me to deal with, not as a technical expert in medicine, law, or psychology but as an experienced observer and sharer of abortion-related problems. The first segment is best put before you in a statement which I prepared in 1971 during the fight to change this country's laws.

I am happy to join in the campaign in support of the Women's National Abortion Act Coalition. As a black woman, I support the abortion campaign for reasons inherent in being a member of the black minority in racist America. I want to talk about rights and choices. Every woman should have the right to control her body and its usage, as she so chooses. Every woman should have the right to conceive, when she so chooses. Every woman should have the right to sexual fulfillment without fear of conception, if she so chooses. Women must secure these rights by liberating the minds of those legislators opposed to the personal freedoms of any of America's second-class citizens; women, being 53 percent of the population, are America's largest number of second-class citizens.

The legislators of this country are overwhelmingly male and overwhelmingly white. While rejecting legalized abortion, these very men sit in hypocritical splendor and refuse to provide an adequate guaranteed annual income for those children born to women without financial and social access to safe abortion.

While rejecting legalized abortion, these very men refuse to fund quality, inexpensive prenatal and postnatal care to women without access to abortion. While rejecting legalized abortion, these very men refuse to fund quality education and training for the children of the women without access to abortion.

These men have never been faced with a knitting needle or coat-hanger in the greasy backroom of an urban garage, nor have they swallowed masses of quinine tablets or turpentine only to permanently endanger physical well-being. Yet their wives, mistresses, and girlfriends have ready access to (and have always had ready access to) psychiatrists and therapeutic abortions.

While the wealthy, the elite, and the powerful have always had this access, the masses—both black and white—have always been penalized for being the masses.

Black women have been economically and socially denied access to legal abortion or therapeutic abortion. Black women do not have more babies than white women; they have simply had fewer abortions. Very few black women have had $500 or more for illegal abortions. Very few black women have had access to the white psychiatric community granting therapeutic abortions.

At this point, a few members of my community will tell me that legalized abortion is simply another white man's trick to foster racial genocide. They will say that we need to reproduce as many black children as possible, which only adds numbers.

The fight for black self-determination needs expertise, not numbers. There is no magic in a home where someone has reproduced five or more black babies and can manage neither economically, educationally, spiritually, nor socially to see that these five black babies become five highly trained black minds.

Those blacks who oppose legalized abortion must reflect upon black history and see the paradox for the present: that under slavery, blacks were encouraged to reproduce to assure an adequate supply of muscle energy people. Wake up, brothers and sisters, America no longer needs muscle energy people.

We have no shortage of black babies. Thousands of black babies live in the public agencies and foster homes across this country.

It is our responsibility to adopt these children and provide the parental, financial, and moral support necessary to mold their futures. These are our children, and the numbers of these homeless black babies is so severe that adoption agencies are now placing these children in nonblack homes. Black people cannot afford pregnancy as an ego trip.

Black women particularly need this personal freedom to be able to fulfill themselves sexually without fear of conception. The outside pressures of this society wreak enough havoc within the black home and the black unit. It is unspeakable that legislated, racist pressures should accompany the black woman to her bedroom and creep insidiously into the center of her bed. I will stay out of the legislature, if the legislature will stay out of my bed.

Nor can black people afford to have their personal freedoms imposed upon by religious tenets or rhetoric. Let no church dare to define womb life to me when every day I see black life defiled, maimed, and killed both physically and psychologically.

Let no preacher ask me to religiously consider unborn life when I question the wisdom of introducing yet another black baby into life in white America. I question this wisdom in the name of all our unborn George Jacksons. I'll stay out of church, if the church will stay out of my bed.

Finally, a word to men: this society has encouraged men to view fatherhood as proof of their masculinity. Some men, in turn, have put this trip on women to conceive, to the benefit of no one concerned. Tremendous value is placed on the male heir and the continuance of the family name.

We as black people have no time for these misconceptions and perversions of values. We cannot get caught up in the misconception that fatherhood proves masculinity and motherhood reinforces femininity.

I hope I have clearly stated my position and what is at stake for black women in reform abortion legislation; in both economic and social terms, the black women have much to gain from the laws regarding this most personal of personal freedoms.

Black women must consider the larger consequences in a society which is not only unwilling to provide a quality life for black children, but tries to destroy life for all black people.

Source: U.S. Congress, Senate Committee on the Judiciary, Subcommittee on Constitutional Amendments, *Hearings on Constitutional Amendments*, 93rd Congress, 1st session, March 4, 1974, Part 4, pp. 683–85.

DOCUMENT 62-J: Statement by an Attending Physician in a New York Hospital, 1965–1972

"I have seen women die from illegal abortions."—Dr. Michael M. Levi, Medical Director of OB/Gyn Associates, New York City.

Senator Bayh, I thank you for allowing me to testify before this committee, and I think it is a privilege, and I would like to discharge that responsibility which I think, as a physician, to the best I know how. I would like to tell you something about me.

I am Dr. Michael M. Levi, a fellow of the American College of Obstetricians and Gynecologists, and I have served as an assistant professor at Columbia University School of Medicine from, actually from 1962 as a research fellow, up to 1971, 1972, as an assistant clinical professor. This was my last rank. During that period—namely 1965 to 1972—I was an attending physician at Harlem Hospital, a municipal hospital in New York City, and from responsibility and by choice, I perform abortions.

May I interject that up to 1971 I did not perform one legal or illegal abortion.

During my years at Harlem Hospital, prior to the liberalization of the New York abortion law, I have seen women die from illegal abortions; many women die.

I have watched a 21-year-old die of an infection incurred during a criminal abortion. I, as a physician, could not reconcile her death with my oath to preserve lives.

I have seen a mother of four die, leaving her children without her love and guidance, because she could not afford another child. Her act of love for her children led to her death from a self-induced abortion.

I have seen a desperate 27-year-old threaten suicide if she was not given an abortion. This was in 1967, and being forbidden to help her, we denied her the abortion. She committed suicide.

For these three and the many, many more I remember, I cannot reconcile my conscience and the hippocratic oath with the tragedies that have taken place.

Since morality cannot be legislated and since the Constitution is committed to a separation of church and state, I am here not to discuss the moral issues, but to testify about the medical issues confronting this committee.

The interruption of pregnancy is an old and worldwide procedure. No matter what the laws, no matter what the availability of services, the decision to terminate a pregnancy belongs to the individual woman. It did, it does, and it will belong to the individual woman.

John Robbins, chief executive officer of Planned Parenthood Federation of America reported in "Family Planning Perspectives" that there are 55 million abortions performed each year in this world, four abortions for each live birth. This is compared to 48 million women who used the contraceptive pill or intrauterine device and 24 million who have sterilizations. This makes abortion the most common form of birth control in this world.

That, I submit, is a fact, not a moral argument. This is the fact that we are here today to deal with. It would be absurd to imagine that women wishing to terminate an unwanted pregnancy will not find the means to do so, even if abortion is prohibited by law.

Source: U.S. Congress, Senate Committee on the Judiciary, Subcommittee on Constitutional Amendments, *Hearings on Constitutional Amendments*, 93rd Congress, 1st session, March 4, 1974, Part 2, p. 570.

DOCUMENT 62-K: Statement by a Woman Born with Congenital Defects Due to German Measles

"It is said that those who may be deformed should be aborted so they do not have to lead an unhappy life. . . . I wholeheartedly disagree."—Mary Hartle, Volunteer, Women's Center, Minneapolis, Minn.

Mr. Chairman and members of the committee, my name is Mary Hartle. I come before you today to support the Buckley and Helms amendments. My remarks will center on two main reasons for arguing against women being allowed to have abortions—German measles and rape. When the move to legalize abortion started heavily a decade ago, the proponents originally argued that abortion should be legalized for women who had had German measles during pregnancy and for women and young girls who had been raped.

I would first like to address myself to the German measles question. During the first trimester of pregnancy, with me, my mother contracted German measles. The first trimester is the most dangerous time to contract German measles for the baby has the greatest chance of being affected by the German measles during this time.

I was born in 1952 with a heart defect and cataracts in my eyes. Heart and eye defects are two of the three major handicaps occurring from German measles. My first year of life was in a very precarious state. I underwent heart surgery in December 1952 and eye surgery in October 1952 and again in June 1953. After the operations my health improved immensely.

My heart condition has been corrected such that my heart is now normal. My vision was improved to the point where I can see at 20/200 with correction. Thus, I can see objects clearly and read regular size print at a close distance.

It is said that those who may be deformed should be aborted so they do not have to lead an unhappy life and so as to not cause a great hardship on their families. I wholeheartedly disagree with this argument for several reasons. First of all, many unborn babies whose mothers are exposed to German measles are not born with birth defects [and] do not live unhappy, lonely, unproductive lives. Thirdly, I know my parents would carry me to term again, if they had to do it all over again, and I am sure this is true for most other parents of disabled children.

It is thought by most people that a handicap incapacitates a person so completely that they are rendered unemployable persons who are dependent on their relatives and society at large. However, this is a falsehood. Most physical handicaps can be reduced to a mere physical nuisance if the individual receives medical treatment, the proper training in the use of alternative techniques, and the proper opportunity to use his skills. Because of the medical treatment I received, and the alternative techniques to sight which I use, my blindness has been reduced to a physical inconvenience for me.

The real problem of blindness, and all other handicaps, is not the occasional physical limitation it imposes, but rather societal attitudes toward blindness. Misconceptions and misinformation about blindness which give rise toward prejudice and discrimination against the blind are the real problems of blindness. Thus, I consider blindness to be a social handicap, not a physical handicap.

Source: U.S. Congress, Senate Committee on the Judiciary, Subcommittee on Constitutional Amendments, *Hearings on Constitutional Amendments*, 93rd Congress, 1st session, March 4, 1974, Part 2, p. 327.

DOCUMENT 62-L: Statement by a Woman Who Lost a Child to a Congenital Disease

" . . . the need to preserve the right to abortion when a fetus is known to have Tay-Sachs disease or a comparable disorder."—Mrs. Kay Jacobs, National Capitol Tay-Sachs Foundation.

Statistically, one in every 900 Jewish marriages is between two carriers who are therefore capable of producing a child with Tay-Sachs disease. One child in every 3,600 births to Jewish couples will be afflicted with Tay-Sachs disease, and every child born with this disease will die by the age of 4.

I am not here to speak about every facet of the abortion question, but to help develop an understanding of the need to preserve the right to abortion when a fetus is known to have Tay-Sachs disease or a comparable disorder. There are a great many people who wish to deny potential parents of infants with fatal genetic disorders the option to terminate affected pregnancies.

However, once a doomed baby is born, these same people who insist on his birth disappear, leaving total responsibility to his parents. Besides the heartbreak, mental anguish, and, quite frankly, physical burden that the parents must endure, there is the problem of finding people willing or qualified to help in caring for such a child.

In most cases the families seek out institutionalization at some point because of increasing medical problems or simply overwhelming demands on the parents' time. Most retardation centers are inappropriate, and hospital care costs are prohibitive. Most insurance companies refuse to cover prolonged hospital care on the basis that it is custodial care—even though the medical profession disagrees. Even those insurance companies that do cover a prolonged hospital stay will not cover the cost of a nurse at home, which for many families would be a more acceptable form of help. . . .

It all started for us 4 1/2 years ago when we had our first baby. She was beautiful and, we were assured, healthy and normal. She grew and developed very normally for several months, or so we were told. There were a few little problems such as a pronounced startle response which she never outgrew, but the doctor reassured us that she was normal.

By 10 months of age, she had begun to grow weak and to lose some of the skills she had learned, and once again I pleaded with the pediatrician to tell me what was wrong. Again, as before, I was put off. Finally, a couple of weeks prior to her 1st birthday, he admitted that her development was not progressing normally, and we were referred to a specialist at Children's Hospital here in Washington. We brought Joann home the day before her 1st birthday with the knowledge that she had Tay-Sachs disease, that the birthday cake placed in front of her the next day would be the only one she would ever see, and that she would no doubt be dead before her 4th birthday.

Source: U.S. Congress, Senate Committee on the Judiciary, Subcommittee on Constitutional Amendments, *Hearings on Constitutional Amendments*, 93rd Congress, 1st session, March 4, 1974, Part 2, p. 319.

DOCUMENT 62-M: Statement by a Developmental Neuropsychologist, National Institutes of Health

"These data . . . support the view of those who support legalized abortion [as] a moral, humanitarian act."—James Prescott, National Institutes of Health.

I have recently completed a cross-cultural study of societies characterized by a high degree of physical affection with those characterized by low degrees of physical affection to determine whether the amount of body contact was related to warfare and violence. This data was derived from a book, "A Cross Cultural Summary," by R. B. Textor which consists of computer printouts of relationships among various variables. This was the data resource which I used to test some of these relationships. I found that societies rated high on the physical affection scale were less violent than those that do not give their children a great deal of physical affection. These societies rarely engaged in warfare, and when they did, they tended to assimilate captured enemies rather than torture and kill them. Those societies that were not affectionate tended to be warlike and to enslave or torture and kill the captured enemy. . . .

From all of the above, it can hardly be contested that the experience of unwantedness is harmful, sometimes fatally harmful, to the child. The question remains of whether it is preferable for society to allow abortion as a legal method of preventing the birth of an unwanted child rather than face the consequences for the child and the society. If abortion represents a disrespect for human life and constitutes an act of murder, as is sometimes contended, then it would be expected that societies which permit and practice abortion should also be characterized by a disrespect for the quality of human life and physical violence.

Simply stated, cultures which punish abortion can be summarized as follows—the overall relationship is in the tables in my summary statement.

Fifty-five percent of cultures which punish abortion practice slavery.

One hundred percent of cultures which punish abortion practice polygyny.*

Seventy percent of cultures which punish abortion have a high desire for children.

Seventy percent of cultures which punish abortion place high pressure upon the child to develop self-reliant behavior.

Seventy-eight percent of cultures which punish abortion restrict youth sexual experience.

Eighty-eight percent of cultures which punish abortion punish extra-marital sex.

Seventy-six percent of cultures which punish abortion kill, torture and mutilate the enemy captured in warfare.

Some of these relationships are self-evident. Certainly if a society forces a woman to carry a pregnancy which she does not want, [she] is a woman in bondage, is a woman in slavery. And so it is not surprising to find such cultures practicing human slavery.

The above data . . . do not support the antiabortionists' point of view, but rather provide support for the opposite point of view; namely, that

*Polygyny = a husband may take more than one wife.

societies which prevent and punish abortion also show disrespect of human life, practice slavery, are physically violent, [allowing] killing, torturing and mutilation of the enemy, and repress the expression of physical affection, that is, sexual repression.

These data, in turn, support the view of those who support legalized abortion that it is a moral, humanitarian act which is characterized by a concern for the quality of human life, its integrity and dignity, and that these objectives are obtained by not permitting the birth of unwanted children. Our goal should be one of wanted children, well cared for and loved. The right of the woman to be pregnant by choice and to be a mother by choice is essential for a humane and compassionate society.

I strongly oppose any effort to prohibit abortion and I urge you to do likewise.

Source: U.S. Congress, Senate Committee on the Judiciary, Subcommittee on Constitutional Amendments, *Hearings on Constitutional Amendments*, 93rd Congress, 1st session, March 4, 1974, Part 2, pp. 437–38.

THE REPORT OF THE UNITED STATES COMMISSION ON CIVIL RIGHTS ON THE HUMAN LIFE AMENDMENTS (1975)

The Civil Rights Commission was established by the Civil Rights Act of 1957 as a bipartisan agency to study civil rights problems and report to the president and Congress. A 1975 report, *Constitutional Aspects of the Right to Limit Childbearing*, discussed some of the problems the commission thought might follow from the adoption of constitutional amendments on abortion. A majority on the commission thought that an abortion amendment would reflect essentially religious views, and so might conflict with the First Amendment. They also believed an abortion amendment would cause turmoil in other parts of the law.

Opponents of abortion considered the report to be a biased, partisan document.

DOCUMENT 63: Report of the United States Civil Rights Commission on Constitutional Aspects of the Right to Limit Childbearing. 1975

[Undermining the First Amendment]

"Congress shall make no law respecting an establishment of religion, or prohibiting the free exercise thereof; or abridging the freedom of speech, or of the press; or the right of the people peaceably to assemble, and to petition the Government for a redress of grievances."

Whether a proposed constitutional amendment outlaws abortion or declares that a State may outlaw abortion without regard to any other amendments to the Constitution, those who propose such amendments should be fully aware of the extent to which such measures would infringe upon the First Amendment, applied to the States through the Fourteenth Amendment. Whereas a constitutional amendment outlawing abortion creates a direct and immediate conflict with the free exercise and establishment of religion clauses of the First Amendment, a constitutional amendment permitting a State to outlaw abortion indirectly subverts the same clauses of the First Amendment. Outlawing abortion is a constraint on the First Amendment when the restriction flows from wholly or partially nonsecular, or religious, motives. When no wholly secular reason can be advanced for the prohibition, then to outlaw abortion is a direct assault on the freedom of conscience protected by the First Amendment.

Those who advocate such an amendment should clearly understand that they would be compelling every woman to accept the view that a constitutionally protected person exists from the "moment of conception," even when such a view conflicts with an individual woman's religious views, and that they would be, in effect, amending the First Amendment. The Supreme Court in *Roe* and *Doe* did not put the governmental stamp of approval on abortion or on any view of when life begins. Instead, the Court decided that no governmental intervention on either side of an issue of morality and religion, at least in the first trimester, was consistent with American legal tradition. . . .

[In *Roe v Wade* the Court did not decide when life begins.]

The intrinsic aspect of the abortion issue is the question of when life begins. On this question, the Court said in *Roe*, "we need not resolve the difficult question of when life begins. When those trained in the respective disciplines of medicine, philosophy, and theology are unable to arrive at any consensus, the Judiciary, at this point in the development of man's knowledge, is not in a position to speculate as to the answer." Of course, Congress and State legislatures, having no more or different information available to them, are in no better position to speculate on the subject than the Court. After the majority Justices discussed "the wide divergence of thinking on this most sensitive and difficult question," they concluded that, "In view of all this, we do not agree that, by adopting one theory of life, Texas may override the rights of the pregnant women that are at stake." . . .

[The Court left individuals free to decide for themselves whether the fetus has life.]

The majority in *Roe* did not legalize the philosophical position that a fetus has no life and can, therefore, be aborted; instead, they adopted the view that whether a fetus has life or not is up to each individual to decide, unfettered by the State. If members of Congress and the people succeed in amending the Constitution to make the philosophical view that life begins at conception a matter of fundamental law, then they would be consciously abridging the First Amendment. . . .

[There were secular (nonreligious) reasons behind early abortion laws.]

To take the last point first, there were wholly secular medical reasons for outlawing abortion in the 19th century. As the Court said in *Roe*, "Antiseptic techniques, of course, were based on discoveries by Lister, Pasteur and others, first announced in 1867, but were not generally accepted and employed until about the turn of the century." On the first point, at a time when all surgical procedures including abortion were particularly dangerous, anti-abortion statutes would satisfy the compelling State interest test or the valid State objective test on a purely secular ground. Furthermore, given the circumstance of medical knowledge and common understanding, in 1868, there was no reason for the framers of the Fourteenth Amendment to intend that anti-abortion laws based on unsafe medical procedures would violate the amendment, or that they would even consider the issue. A better question to put is that asked by the *Roe* majority, namely, does "person" in the Fourteenth Amendment include fetuses? In any case, even adopting the position of the dissenters in *Roe* and *Doe*, the question of when life begins still seems to involve excessive entanglement of government and religion.

[The original intent of the First Amendment was that no particular religious view should have government endorsement.]

In the First Congress, James Madison introduced a series of amendments to the Constitution, part of which became the Bill of Rights. The original language of the First Amendment read, "The civil rights of none shall be abridged on account of religious belief or worship, nor shall any national religion be established, nor shall the full and equal rights of conscience be in any manner, or on any pretense infringed." After alteration by the House and Senate, the present language of the amendment, "Congress shall make no law respecting an establishment of religion, or prohibiting the free exercise thereof . . . ," was agreed upon. In replacing the original language with the present language, some early commentators, including Joseph Story, in his *Commentaries on the Con-*

stitution, explain that the intent was not to interfere with any State establishments of religion but "to exclude from the national government all power to act on the subject." Therefore, those who favor a constitutional amendment outlawing abortion in every State would be assaulting directly the original intent not to give national recognition to any particular religious views or persuasion. This same intent is seen in the free exercise clause, according to Story. The whole power over religion was left to "state governments to be acted upon according to their own sense of justice and the state constitution; and the Catholic and the Protestant, the Calvinist and the Armenian, the Jew and the Infidel, may sit down at the common table of the national councils without any inquisition into their faith or mode of worship." Story asserted that the purpose of the establishment clause was to prevent Congress from giving preference to any denomination of the Christian faith, and not to withdraw the Christian religion as a whole from the protection of Congress. Christianity was the dominant religion and to encourage Christianity was acceptable so long as it was not incompatible with private rights of conscience and freedom of religious worship. . . .

[An amendment prohibiting abortion would force people to accept one set of religious views on the subject.]

If the people should decide to adopt an amendment prohibiting abortion, they would be compelling a definition of personhood and life which may conflict with an individual woman's religious views and that would be, in effect, amending the First Amendment. Even if the people should decide to adopt an amendment permitting States to enact legislation prohibiting abortions, without regard to any other section of the Constitution, they would be permitting amendment of the First Amendment indirectly. Additionally, they would be inviting the people within each State to amend the freedom of religion clause contained in each State constitution.

[The Fourteenth Amendment states that "no State shall deprive any person of life, liberty or property without due process of law."
     Is the fetus a person under the Fourteenth Amendment?]

FETAL RIGHTS BEFORE AND AFTER THE PROPOSED CONSTITUTIONAL AMENDMENTS

One purpose of the proposed anti-abortion constitutional amendments is to accord a right to life to "unborn offspring at every stage of their biological development" or "from the moment of conception." The Supreme Court in *Roe* explained that if a fetus is a person within the language of the Fourteenth Amendment, then the fetus' right to life is guaranteed specifically by the amendment. But after examining every instance in which "person" is used in the Constitution, the Court concluded that the word has no prenatal application. In short, "the word 'person' as used in the Fourteenth Amendment does not include the unborn." . . .

[Even if they are not constitutional "persons," embryos and fetuses have some rights.]

This does not mean that embryos and fetuses have no rights. In fact, at or after viability (when a fetus is capable of living outside the mother's womb), a State may proscribe abortions altogether, out of its interest in fetal life "except where it is necessary, in appropriate medical judgment, for the preservation of the life or health of the mother." Those who oppose establishing viability as the point when fetal rights take precedence over the mother's right to end a pregnancy often argue that, even though a small child is dependent on others for its care, this does not make a small child's rights subservient to the rights of everyone else; therefore, previability dependence on the pregnant woman should not make the fetus' interest subservient to hers. This analysis is misleading. A small child can be cared for by anyone, including its mother, without injury to the caretaker's own life or well-being; thus, no conflict of the right to existence or well-being is necessary. A fetus inside a woman is dependent on her life-support system, alone, often to the detriment of her life or well-being. If a woman chooses to carry the child until viability, it makes logical and biological sense to either compel her to forego abortion at that point or to deliver the fetus so that it can be artificially sustained to full term. At or after viability, the risk to her life is greatest in an abortion, and the potential for fetal life is also greatest.

[Torts are wrongful acts (but not necessarily crimes). Individuals can go to court to get remedies for wrongful acts, sometimes money damages.

If a fetus should become a legal person from the moment of conception, there would be some consequences for tort law.]

TORTS

Consistent with the analysis in *Roe*, traditionally, "In areas other than criminal abortion, the law has been reluctant to endorse any theory that life, as we recognize it, begins before birth or to accord legal rights to the unborn except in narrowly defined situations and except when the rights are contingent upon live birth." In traditional tort law, recovery was denied for prenatal injury even though a child was born alive. This rule, announced in a decision of Justice Oliver Wendell Holmes in 1884 when he was on the Supreme Judicial Court of Massachusetts, was followed by every American court until about 1946. . . .

The key to the wrongful death cases is that they do not involve balancing the rights of a mother against the right to recover for the wrongful death of the fetus. They do involve efforts by prospective parents to collect damages for injury done to the fetus *in utero* which results in impairment of the born alive child's physical or mental facilities. Enactment of the proposed constitutional amendments would create chaos in this area of the law of torts. From the moment of conception, suit could be had against allegedly negligent actors, including the mother, for injury against the fetus.

If a pregnant woman were in an automobile or airplane accident, a suit could be brought on behalf of the fetus as well as its mother. Someone as guardian might, on behalf of the fetus, sue its mother for negligence if she contracted a disease, smoked, took a harmful drug, or had an accident. Medical malpractice suits, not only on behalf of the woman but also on behalf of a supposedly miscarried fetus, could be another object of litigation. Such litigation would probably be characterized by disputes over whether the woman was pregnant, when the moment of conception occurred, what the potential value of the fetus was, based on its stage of development, and such other matters which are not easily determined. . . .

[The amendment would also require unforeseen changes in tax law, property law, and criminal law.]

Source: U.S. Commission on Civil Rights, Report, *The Constitutional Aspects of the Right to Limit Childbearing*, April 1975.

Politics and Elections

From 1974 on, political maneuvering was intense, and abortion became a political issue in election campaigns at local, state, and national levels of government. By 1976 it had even become a campaign issue in the presidential election. The political parties took stands on abortion in their platforms. The Right to Life Party fielded a candidate in the 1976 presidential campaign—Ellen McCormack, a New York housewife. She ran in seventeen states and received over 200,000 votes.

The issue energized groups that had been on the fringes of politics. In 1975 the Roman Catholic Church announced a major political campaign that would take the Church into the political arena, conducting a public information campaign and encouraging its parishioners to support candidates opposed to abortion. Political action committees were to be set up in congressional districts and directed to be nonsectarian and bipartisan. In theory, the Church itself would not be directly involved in politics, thus endangering its tax-exempt status.

RELIGIOUS GROUPS ENTER THE POLITICAL FRAY

DOCUMENT 64: Pastoral Plan for Pro-Life Activities. National Conference of Catholic Bishops, 1975

III. Legislative/Public Policy Effort

26. In recent years there has been a growing realization throughout the world that protecting and promoting the inviolable rights of

persons are essential duties of civil authority, and that the maintenance and protection of human rights are primary purposes of
law. As Americans, and as religious leaders, we have been committed to governance by a system of law that protects the rights
of individuals and maintains the common good. As our founding
fathers believed, we hold that all law is ultimately based on Divine
Law, and that a just system of law cannot be in conflict with the
law of God.

27. Abortion is a specific issue that highlights the relationship between morality and law. As a human mechanism, law may not
be able fully to articulate the moral imperative, but neither can
legal philosophy ignore the moral order. The abortion decisions
of the United States Supreme Court (January 22, 1973) violate the
moral order, and have disrupted the legal process which previously attempted to safeguard the rights of unborn children. A
comprehensive pro-life legislative program must therefore include the following elements:

a. Passage of a constitutional amendment providing protection for
the unborn child to the maximum degree possible.

b. Passage of federal and state laws and adoption of administrative
policies that will restrict the practice of abortion as much as
possible.

c. Continual research into and refinement and precise interpretation
of *Roe* and *Doe* and subsequent court decisions.

d. Support for legislation that provides alternatives to abortion.

28. Accomplishment of this aspect of this Pastoral Plan will undoubtedly require well-planned and coordinated political action by citizens at the national, state, and local levels. This activity is not
simply the responsibility of Catholics, nor should it be limited to
Catholic groups or agencies. It calls for widespread cooperation
and collaboration. As citizens of this democracy, we encourage
the appropriate political action to achieve these legislative goals.
As leaders of a religious institution in this society, we see a moral
imperative for such political activity.

Means of Implementation of Program

29. The challenge to restore respect for human life in our society is
a task of the Church that reaches out through all institutions,
agencies, and organizations. Diverse tasks and various goals are
to be achieved. The following represents a systematic organization and allocation of the Church's resources of people, institutions, and finances which can be activated at various levels to

restore respect for human life and insure protection of the right to life of the unborn.

1. State Coordinating Committee

30. A. It is assumed that overall coordination in each state will be the responsibility of the State Catholic Conference or its equivalent. Where a State Catholic Conference is in process of formation or does not exist, bishops' representatives from each diocese might be appointed as the core members of the State Coordinating Committee. . . .

2. The Diocesan Pro-life Committee

33. a) *General Purpose*
The purpose of the committee is to coordinate groups and activities within the diocese (to restore respect for human life), particularly efforts to effect passage of a constitutional amendment to protect the unborn child. In its coordinating role, the committee will rely on information and direction from the Bishops' Pro-life Office and the National Committee for a Human Life Amendment. The committee will act through the Diocesan Pro-life Director, who is appointed by the bishop to direct pro-life efforts in the diocese. . . .

3. The Parish Pro-life Committee

36. The Parish Pro-life Committee should include a delegate from the Parish Council, representatives of various adult and youth parish organizations, members of local Knights of Columbus Councils, Catholic Daughters of America Chapters, and other similar organizations.

Objectives

37. (a) Sponsor and conduct intensive education programs touching all groups within the parish, including schools and religious education efforts.

38. (b) Promote and sponsor pregnancy counseling units and other alternatives to abortion.

39. (c) Through ongoing public information programs, generate public awareness of the continuing effort to obtain a constitutional amendment. The NCCB, the National Committee for a Human Life Amendment, and the State and Diocesan Coordinating Committees should have access to every congressional district for information, consultation, and coordination of action. A chairperson should be designated in each district who will co-

ordinate the efforts of parish pro-life groups, K of C groups, etc., and seek ways of cooperating with nonsectarian pro-life groups, including right-to-life organizations. In each district, the parishes will provide one basic resource, and the clergy will have an active role in the overall effort.

40. (d) Prudently convince others—Catholics and non-Catholics—of the reasons for the necessity of a constitutional amendment to provide a base for legal protection for the unborn.

4. The Pro-life Effort in the Congressional District

41. Passage of a constitutional amendment depends ultimately on persuading members of Congress to vote in favor of such a proposal. This effort at persuasion is part of the democratic process, and is carried on most effectively in the congressional district or state from which the representative is elected. Essentially, this effort demands ongoing public information activity and careful and detailed organization. Thus it is absolutely necessary to encourage the development in each congressional district of an identifiable, tightly-knit, and well-organized pro-life unit. This unit can be described as a public interest group or a citizen's lobby. No matter what it is called:

a. its task is essentially political, that is, to *organize people* to help persuade the elected representatives; and

b. its range of action is limited, that is, it is focused on passing a constitutional amendment.

42. As such, the congressional district pro-life group differs from the diocesan, regional, or parish pro-life coordinator or committee, whose task is pedagogic and motivational, not simply political, and whose range of action includes a variety of efforts calculated to reverse the present atmosphere of permissiveness with respect to abortion. Moreover, it is an agency of citizens, operated, controlled, and financed by these same citizens. *It is not an agency of the Church, nor is it operated, controlled, or financed by the Church.*

43. The congressional district pro-life action group should be bipartisan, nonsectarian, inclined toward political action. It is complementary to denominational efforts, to professional groups, to pregnancy counseling and assistance groups.

44. Each congressional district should have a chairperson who may serve as liaison with the Diocesan Coordinating Committee. In dioceses with many congressional districts, this may be arranged through a regional representation structure.

5. Objectives of the Congressional District Pro-life Group

45. (1) To conduct a continuing public information effort to persuade all elected officials and potential candidates that abortion must be legally restricted.

46. (2) To counterbalance propaganda efforts opposed to a constitutional amendment.

47. (3) To persuade all residents in the congressional district that permissive abortion is harmful to society and that some restriction is necessary.

48. (4) To persuade all residents that a constitutional amendment is necessary as a first step toward legally restricting abortion.

49. (5) To convince all elected officials and potential candidates that "the abortion issue" will not go away and that their position on it will be subject to continuing public scrutiny.

50. (6) To enlist sympathetic supporters who will collaborate in persuading others.

51. (7) To enlist those who are generally supportive so that they may be called upon when needed to communicate to the elected officials.

52. (8) To elect members of their own group or active sympathizers to specific posts in all local party organizations.

53. (9) To set up a telephone network that will enable the committee to take immediate action when necessary.

54. (10) To maintain an informational file on the pro-life position of every elected official and potential candidate.

55. (11) To work for qualified candidates who will vote for a constitutional amendment, and other pro-life issues.

56. (12) To maintain liaison with all denominational leaders (pastors) and all other pro-life groups in the district.

57. This type of activity can be generated and coordinated by a small, dedicated, and politically alert group. It will need some financial support, but its greatest need is the commitment of other groups who realize the importance of its purposes, its potential for achieving those purposes, and the absolute necessity of working with the group to attain the desired goals.

Conclusion

58. The challenges facing American society as a result of the legislative and judicial endorsement of permissive abortion are enormous. But the Church and the individual Catholics must not avoid the

challenge. Although the process of restoring respect for human life at every stage of existence may be demanding and prolonged, it is an effort which both requires and merits courage, patience, and determination. In every age the Church has faced unique challenges calling forth faith and courage. In our time and society, restoring respect for human life and establishing a system of justice which protects the most basic human rights are both a challenge and an opportunity whereby the Church proclaims her commitment to Christ's teaching on human dignity and the sanctity of the human person.

Source: National Conference of Catholic Bishops, Washington, D.C., 1975.

FUNDAMENTALIST CHURCHES BECOME INVOLVED IN POLITICS

Protestant churches have been involved in politics sporadically, concerned with particular issues, but in the 1970s there were attempts to involve them more directly in partisan politics. This involvement was encouraged by pro-life organizations. The Republican Party also saw an opportunity to appeal to church groups, especially conservative and fundamentalist sects, by invoking old-fashioned morality and basic American values. Abortion was one of the issues that began to energize religious voters.

An article in the Raleigh, North Carolina, *News and Observer* reported on growing interest by fundamentalist churches in the South in the late seventies.

DOCUMENT 65: "Churches Step Up Political Efforts." Johanna Seltz, 1978

Church groups, especially conservative Christian groups, are openly jumping into politics.

Some recent developments:

- Candidates for the state legislature take the pulpit in Raleigh's Tabernacle Baptist Church in April 1978 for cross-examination by the Wake County Christians for Good Government.

- Busloads of Bible-carrying citizens intent on defeat of the Equal Rights Amendment crowd the legislature's halls during the 1977 General Assembly.

- Christians for Morality call a press conference in April 1977 on the steps of the Legislative Building to announce introduction of a bill to combat pornography.

- The Baptist State Convention hires a lawyer to lobby and teach Baptists how to lobby.

- Thousands of picketing Christians from fundamentalist church schools picket the Wake County Courthouse in April 1978, singing hymns and giving speeches about freedom of religion.

- Clergymen face legislative committees June 1, 1978, to testify against abortion.

- Baptists by the thousands swamp their legislators this spring with petitions and letters demanding a vote against liquor-by-the-drink.

WCTU, civil rights

Church involvement in politics is not new—witness the Women's Christian Temperance Union and its fight for prohibition. The civil rights movement of the 1950s and 1960s was championed by the black churches.

(Whites exercise influence through "the chamber of commerce and the Rotary; we have the church," said the Rev. Joy J. Johnson, president of the predominantly black General Baptist State Convention and first chairman of its Political Action Committee.)

But the activity comes in peaks, usually spurred by a "negative issue that seems to evoke the wrath," according to Bernard Cochran, religion professor at Meredith College. And though it is difficult to identify a peak until it's past, Cochran said we seem to be in one now.

"Used to be they tried to keep it hid under a bushel," said Secretary of State Thad Eure. Today church involvement in politics is more open, he said.

'A little more open'

"Everything now is a little more open than it used to be, even women's bathing suits," Eure said.

"I like to think of it as Christianity in life, not religion in politics," said D. P. McFarland, executive director of the liquor-fighting Christian Action League.

"I think it's a trend of the times," McFarland added. "If we are not concerned about those laws under which we live, what else can we be concerned about? I hear so many times that you can't legislate morality. I say the only thing you can legislate is morality."

The trend toward increased political activity by religious groups and increased visibility can be seen outside the state, too.

Anita Bryant's crusade

The defeat of parimutuel betting in Texas was credited to the Southern Baptists. Anita Bryant's crusade against homosexual rights is biblically based.

Some of the most vocal opponents of a proposed lobbyists' disclosure bill—that would require many church groups to register as lobbyists— are churches. The tuition tax credit bill now before Congress has heavy support from the Catholic church and strong opposition from the Baptists.

Times have changed since the Rev. S. Collins Kilburn, director of social ministries for the N.C. Council of Churches, drew astonished stares in 1971 when he tried to discuss tax and prison reform with the legislators. No longer do lawmakers assume, as they did then, that a church person at the office door means a sermon against the demon alcohol.

"I think nationwide there is an increase in the number of citizens' groups trying to influence legislation," Kilburn said.

"You could make an argument that it's a refinement of the activities of the 1960s, (the civil rights and peace movement)," said George Reed, director of Christian citizenship education for the Baptist State Convention of North Carolina.

"Or you could make the argument that it's a reaction to the activities in the 1960s," Reed said.

The Rev. J. Malloy Owen, pastor of St. Mark's United Methodist Church of Raleigh, has his name on the letterheads of N.C Coalition for Decency, Wake County Christians for Good Government and Christians for Morality. He sees the increase in activity as a reaction to "the new morality, which is nothing but the old immorality."

"People are shocked into this," Owen said. "For instance, why do so many Christians rally to Anita Bryant when her image comes across as so brash? It's to be expected that Christians committed to the long-accepted American concept of the family would resent the idea of two men marrying each other or adopting children.

"It would be alarming if the majority let a militant minority sweep away our heritage," he said.

J. Marse Grant, editor of the Baptist State Convention newspaper the Biblical Recorder, pointed a finger at Watergate. Citizens, including Christians, are demanding accountability from government, he said.

"You don't want to blame everything on Watergate," Grant said, "but it might be people in the church are saying, 'Hey, I'm going to have a part in these decisions.'

"They're determined to be involved and this is healthy in a democracy," he said.

Broader media coverage of politics increases involvement because people "have more to react to," said the Rev. Charles V. Petty, director of the Christian Life Council of the Baptist State Convention in Raleigh.

Government growth

The growth of government has also kicked Christian groups into politics, Petty said.

"Frankly, we Christian people have done what we wanted to and now we're being told you have to conform to certain regulations and requirements . . . We can't ignore it."

The Rev. W.W. Finlator of Raleigh, a long-time fighter for civil liberties, sees the increase in religious groups active on conservative issues as a direct outgrowth of the burgeoning conservative charismatic, evangelical movement.

Said Meredith's Professor Cochran, "Right wing theology and right wing politics can be demonstrated as walking hand-in-hand."

Cochran said he supports church involvement in politics but fears "the vigilante mentality that wages crusades against minorities of any kind."

"I fear much of the activity (now) is in that narrow range," he said.

'Saturday night sins'

Cochran, Finlator, Kilburn and others are also disappointed that church activity is more likely to be around an issue they consider peripheral, such as liquor. But Southern churches are traditionally "harder on the Saturday night sins than Sunday morning sins," Kilburn said.

The Southern church grew out of the revival movement that concentrated on personal salvation and has only recently become touched by the social gospel movement of the North, which believed salvation included changing social conditions, not just individual hearts, Kilburn said.

Churches are also "largely influenced by the middle-upper class people who do not want the social structure changed because they're comfortable," he said. "It's easier to preach against booze, bingo and burlesque than an inequitable tax system."

"The first thing you have to learn when you get into the political process is to establish priorities," said Petty of the Baptist Christian Life Council, which has lobbied against liquor and for the Equal Rights Amendent. "The real practical dilemma for a church is that some of these issues are extremely volatile, which means they can literally blow a church sky high."

Separation question

The vision of church groups tackling politics raises the question of how involved the church can get before it violates the separation of church and state.

Sen. William G. Smith, D-New Hanover, contends the churches have "contributed to the obliteration of the line between church and state.

"Churches are always the first groups to assert separation, but they are also the first in line when it comes to subsidies—exemptions on their property, whether it's for the church or the gambling casino next door where they have their bingo games. And they want special rules for their private schools," Smith said.

Said Cochran, "I think it's erroneous that church state separation means there may be no church involvement in the political arena. The problem arises when such involvement comes out of a vested interest.

"Political involvement is most valid when it involves working for the causes of humanity, not, for example, a campaign against taxation of church properties," he said.

Called shaky ground

When the churches try to institutionalize their beliefs through law they are also on shaky ground, Cochran said.

In Massachusetts, where the Catholic Church has vast influence, laws prohibiting the sale of contraceptives or dissemination of birth control information were struck down by the Supreme Court as violations of the separation of church and state, Cochran said.

"I have a hard time seeing how church people exerting their influence and expressing their opinions is a violation of separation of church and state," said Reed of the Baptist State Convention. "How is it different from any other crowd with a position on an issue?"

Of religious groups active at the General Assembly, only the liberal N.C. Council of Churches has a registered lobbyist, according to the Secretary of State's Office.

The other groups rely on building up pressure at the grassroots.

"Quite frankly most legislators couldn't care less what someone from out of their district thinks. We go to the home folks," said Petty.

His office contacts ministers who get the word out on "when to pack the people in" or keep the letters coming, Petty said.

Christians for Morality used this approach to lobby successfully for an anti-pornography bill sponsored by Sen. I. Beverly Lake Jr., D-Wake.

"We wrote to every pastor of every denomination in the state encouraging them to get letters and petitions to Senator Lake," said Owen. "And then we sent a second letter."

In a relatively new approach, the Wake County Christians for Good Government grilled legislative candidates on key "moral" positions.

'Helping people'

"We were not endorsing candidates but helping people ... vote knowledgeably," Owen said.

Source: News and Observer, Raleigh, North Carolina, July 9, 1978.

ABORTION BECOMES AN ISSUE IN PRESIDENTIAL POLITICS, 1976–1977

In the 1976 election, for the first time, abortion became an issue in presidential politics. Republican President Gerald L. Ford, who, as vice president, had succeeded Richard Nixon, hoped to win a second term in 1976. Ford was a moderate on abortion and believed that the issue should be left to the state legislatures. But he also wanted the support of the Catholic Church and hoped his position would appeal to conservatives and right-to-life groups. His moderate position was not acceptable to the more militant right-to-lifers, and they did not flock to his banner in 1976. It was not until 1980 that the abortion issue would have an important impact on the election for president.

Betty Ford, the president's wife, did not agree with her husband. Speaking to reporters, she said, "I am glad to see that abortion has been taken out of the backwoods and been put in the hospital where it belongs."

Jimmy Carter, the Democratic nominee for president and a born-again Christian, won the 1976 election. Although the Democrats included a pro-abortion plank in their platform, Carter expressed disagreement with it. As president he generally supported congressional attempts to stop federal tax money from going to pay for abortions. Carter agreed with the Supreme Court's holding, in 1977, that government was not required to pay for abortions under the Medicaid program. In a news conference in July 1977, Carter made a comment about abortion funding that made headlines across the country and infuriated pro-choice partisans.

DOCUMENT 66: President Ford on Abortion. Public Forum, West Bend High School (Indiana), April 2, 1976

Question: Mr. President, you expressed some concern that the Supreme Court went too far in its decision legalizing abortion and allowing abortion on demand, for any reason, by the mother. Yet, you have been reluctant to support a human life—or to call for a human life amendment. Mr. Ford, does it not concern you that over a million human beings are being killed each year in the United States by abortion?

The President: The facts are that I do think that the Supreme Court decision went much too far. I also happen to believe that all or most of the amendments that I have seen introduced in either the House or the Senate likewise are too inflexible and also go too far. And furthermore, as I am sure that others who are familiar with the legislative process know, as a practical matter you won't get two-thirds of the Members of the House of Representatives and 75 percent of the Senate to pass it anyhow.

But the more important point—and this is the point that I make—I think we can get reasonable remedies in this area that reflect the moral conviction of the individual, that protect the mother in case of rape, in case of any health problem. In my judgment, there is an area between the two extremes that will protect a good share of those that you are talking about—the one million. I don't think you can get it by a constitutional amendment, and I think the Supreme Court went too far. But in my judgment, this is a very personal moral decision, and I think working in the legislative way and working with the Court we can come up with a better solution than the one we have at the present time.

Source: Weekly Compilation of Presidential Documents, Vol. 12, no. 15, p. 552, April 2, 1976.

DOCUMENT 67: President Carter's "Life Is Not Fair" Comments. News Conference. July 12, 1977

Question: Mr. President, how comfortable are you with the recent Supreme Court decision that says the Federal Government is not obligated to provide money for abortions for women who cannot afford to pay for them themselves?

The President: I do not think that the Federal Government should finance abortions except when a woman's life is threatened or when the pregnancy was a result of rape or incest. I think it ought to be interpreted very strictly.

In my opinion, the Federal Government being willing to finance abortions, as it has been in recent months, is an encouragement of abortion and its acceptance as a routine contraceptive means. And I think within that strict definition that I've given you, I would like to prevent the Federal Government financing abortions.

I think it's accurate to say that Secretary of HEW Califano [Secretary Joseph Califano, Department of Health, Education and Welfare] agrees with me completely. And we are trying to make it possible for the people of this Nation to understand how to prevent unwanted pregnancies with educational programs and with the availability of contraceptives and other devices, when they believe in their use, as an alternative to abortion. But I don't believe that either the States or the Federal Government should be required to finance abortions.

Question: Mr. President, how fair do you believe it is then, that women who can afford to get an abortion can go ahead and have one, and women who cannot afford to are precluded?

The President: Well, as you know, there are many things in life that are not fair, that wealthy people can afford and poor people can't. But I don't believe that the federal Government should take action to try to make these opportunities exactly equal, particularly when there is a moral factor involved. . . .

Source: Weekly Compilation of Presidential Documents, Vol. 13, no. 29, pp. 990–1, July 12, 1977.

PART IV: FOR FURTHER READING

Callahan, Sidney, and Daniel Callahan, eds. *Abortion: Understanding Differences.* New York: Plenum Press, 1984.

Crawford, Alan. *Thunder on the Right.* New York: Pantheon Books, 1980.

Deckard, Barbara. *The Women's Movement.* New York: Harper and Row, 1975.

Ehrlich, Paul R. *The Population Bomb.* New York: Ballantine Books, 1968.

Frohock, Fred. *Abortion: A Case Study in Law and Morals.* Westport, Conn.: Greenwood Press, 1983.

Garfield, Jay L., and Patricia Hennessey, eds. *Abortion: Moral and Legal Perspectives.* Amherst: University of Massachusetts Press, 1983.

Rubin, Eva R. *Abortion, Politics and the Courts.* Rev. ed. Westport, Conn.: Greenwood Press, 1987.

Wardle, Lyn D., and Mary A. Wood. *A Lawyer Looks at Abortion.* Provo, Utah: Brigham Young University Press, 1982.

Weber, Paul J. "Bishops in Politics: The Big Plunge." *America,* May 22, 1976, pp. 220–23.

Weisbrod, Robert G. *Black Genocide? Birth Control and the Black American.* Westport, Conn.: Greenwood Press, 1975.

Part V

The Reagan and Bush Administrations and Beyond (1980–   )

Following the election of President Ronald Reagan in 1980 there was an increase in political activity on the abortion issue on both state and national levels. The "Religious Right" (evangelical Christians, Roman Catholics, and other groups with a strong religious and moral approach to politics) had formed an important component in the coalition that brought the Republicans into office. This segment of the Republican Party pushed for governmental action to outlaw abortion.

The Republican platform adopted by the party's national convention in the summer of 1980 contained a plank supporting a constitutional amendment that would extend constitutional protection to the unborn and prohibit abortion. The platform also came out against the public funding of abortion, and promised that the party would work for the appointment of conservative judges who would protect "the sanctity of innocent human life."

In the years that followed, abortion was an issue in political campaigns in both national and state elections. Pro-life and pro-choice organizations lobbied for and against restrictions on abortion. A number of state legislatures passed laws restricting access to abortions. Pro-choice organizations challenged the constitutionality of these restrictive state statutes in the courts.

Congress was also called on to support the pro-life cause. It continued to refuse to pay for government programs that included provisions that promoted abortion and contraception. A number of proposals for constitutional amendments banning abortions were introduced in the House and Senate; although hearings were held by the Senate Judiciary Committee on a number of these amendments, none was passed. Anti-abortion activists also attempted to have Congress pass a "human life" bill that defined the term *person* in the

Constitution to include human embryos from the moment of conception onward. Such a bill, it was hoped, would bypass the need for a constitutional amendment. Pro-abortion forces later countered this strategy by introducing a "freedom of choice" bill that protected the right of a woman to choose an abortion; it was hoped that such a statute would protect abortion rights even if the Supreme Court acted to overturn *Roe v. Wade.*

State and federal courts were deeply involved in lawsuits related to the abortion issue. A number of cases reached the Supreme Court, which found a wide array of restrictions on abortion to be constitutional. By 1992 the promises of Republican presidents to name to the Supreme Court new justices who would oppose abortion rights had resulted in the selection of five new conservative members of the Court, all personally opposed to abortion. But in spite of Republican efforts to pack the Court with opponents of abortion, three of the new justices showed themselves unwilling to overrule *Roe v. Wade,* a decision that had been accepted law for nineteen years. After all the political maneuvering, there were still only four votes on the Court for overturning the 1973 decision. But although *Roe* was not directly overturned, the Reagan–Bush Supreme Court showed itself to be sympathetic to state laws restricting abortion, as long as they did not make access to abortion unreasonably difficult.

A number of new problems, issues, and strategies were on the front burner during the 1980s and 1990s. Pro-life partisans mounted a public relations campaign to convince the public that fetuses being aborted feel pain; using a sonogram of an actual abortion, they produced a film, *The Silent Scream,* that seemed to support their contention. The Senate held hearings on this issue in 1985, but the results were inconclusive. In an effort to substantiate another pro-life claim, the president directed the surgeon general of the United States to undertake a study to determine whether abortions had harmful after-effects on women. In 1989 a subcommittee of the House of Representatives investigated this proposition, but did not find much evidence to support it.

In another new development, anti-abortionists who were frustrated by the failure of the political system to outlaw abortion began to use direct action tactics and civil disobedience to demonstrate their impatience and outrage. There was some outright violence, and the Department of Justice, the FBI, and the Bureau of Alcohol, Tobacco and Firearms (BATF) were called in to investigate kidnappings of abortionists and the bombings and arson of abortion clinics. Operation Rescue and other direct action groups mounted campaigns to blockade abortion clinics and discourage women from having abortions. Fake abortion clinics, set up in some areas, lured pregnant women into their offices with promises of free abortions, and then attempted to persuade the women to forego the operations.

The Food and Drug Administration, an agency of the federal government, banned the importation into the United States of a new French drug, RU-486. The drug acts to induce abortion by preventing embryonic development in the early stages of pregnancy. Abortion rights organizations charged that the ban was politically motivated and sought to have it reversed.

Throughout the last years of the 1980s, pro-choice groups, increasingly well-organized and well-financed, used sophisticated campaign techniques to target anti-abortion officials running for public office. The political advantage that pro-life organizations had enjoyed during the early part of the decade was no longer unchallenged.

Between 1980 and 1992 public opinion remained relatively unchanged on the main issue—whether abortion should remain legal. Although polling results differed according to the way questions were worded, they seemed to show that the public generally favored legal abortions, but was opposed to public funding of abortion-related services and wanted laws requiring minors to consult with their parents before having abortions. The public rejected the idea of using abortion as a substitute for contraception or allowing it for frivolous reasons like the selection of a baby of a particular sex.

Yet despite public support for legalized abortion, abortions became increasingly hard to get. In many states doctors and hospitals refused to perform the operation, and places actually offering abortion services were few and far between—usually only in the big cities.

All in all, the years following the 1980 election were full of turmoil and contention over the abortion issue. In the election year of 1992 the question was as controversial as ever, and there were no signs of consensus or compromise by the extremists on either side.

The election of President Bill Clinton in November 1992 did promise some changes in public policies related to abortion. The new president was expected to take executive action to end the ban on abortions in military hospitals, to rescind the "gag rule" (see Document 86) that forbade abortion counseling in federally subsidized family planning clinics, and to approve the French morning-after abortion pill, RU-486 (see Document 91), for use in the United States. It was also likely that a Democratic president would appoint justices more supportive of abortion rights to the Supreme Court.

National Politics

In 1980 and in the years thereafter abortion became an important issue on the national political scene. Both parties adopted planks in their platforms at the national nominating conventions. The Republicans came out in favor of a right-to-life amendment and the appointment of justices to the Supreme Court who would reverse *Roe v. Wade.* The Democratic Party supported the proposed Equal Rights Amendment to the Constitution, which stated that equal rights should not be denied to any person because of sex. The Democrats also supported a right to choose an abortion.

The Republican victory in the 1980 elections has been attributed to the enthusiastic support of the ticket by voters opposed to the decline in "family values," who hoped that the Republicans would promote morality in national life. Many of these voters believed that abortion was immoral and should be prohibited. In the election years 1984, 1988, and 1992, the parties continued to take opposite positions on the abortion issue. By 1992 some Republicans had begun to believe that opposition to abortion hurt the party, driving pro-choice voters over to the Democrats, but a move at the 1992 Republican National Convention in Houston, Texas, to modify the party's position on abortion was strongly rejected by the convention delegates.

REPUBLICAN AND DEMOCRATIC PLATFORM STATEMENTS ON ABORTION AND THE SELECTION OF JUDGES (1980–1992)

DOCUMENT 68: Republican Party Platform, 1980

Abortion. There can be no doubt that the question of abortion, despite the complex nature of its various issues, is ultimately concerned with equality of rights under the law. While we recognize differing views on this question among Americans in general—and in our own Party—we affirm our support of a constitutional amendment to restore protection of the right to life for unborn children. We also support the Congressional efforts to restrict the use of taxpayers' dollars for abortion.

We protest the Supreme Court's intrusion into the family structure through its denial of the parents' obligation and right to guide their minor children.

The judiciary. We will work for the appointment of judges at all levels of the judiciary who respect traditional family values and the sanctity of innocent human life.

Source: CQ Almanac, 1980, p. 63-B. Congressional Quarterly Inc., Washington, D.C., 1981.

DOCUMENT 69: Democratic Party Platform, 1980

The Democratic Party recognizes reproductive freedom as a fundamental human right. We therefore oppose government interference in the reproductive decisions of Americans, especially those government programs that deny poor Americans their right to privacy by funding or advocating one or a limited number of reproductive choices only.

Source: CQ Almanac, 1980, p. 97-B. Congressional Quarterly Inc., Washington, D.C., 1981.

DOCUMENT 70: President Carter's August 1, 1980, Statement on the Platform's Section on Abortion

Since the beginning of my administration, I have personally opposed federal funding of abortion. I am sworn to uphold the laws passed by Congress, and the Constitution of the United States as interpreted by the federal courts, but my personal view remains unchanged.

Source: CQ Almanac, 1980, p. 122-B. Congressional Quarterly, Inc., Washington, D.C., 1981.

DOCUMENT 71: Republican Party Platform, 1984

[Abortion]. The unborn child has a fundamental individual right to life which cannot be infringed. We therefore reaffirm our support for a human life amendment to the Constitution, and we endorse legislation to make clear that the Fourteenth Amendment's protections apply to unborn children. We oppose the use of public revenues for abortion and will eliminate funding for organizations which advocate or support abortions. We commend the efforts of those individuals and religious and private organizations that are providing positive alternatives to abortion by meeting the physical, emotional, and financial needs of pregnant women and offering adoption services where needed.

We applaud President Reagan's fine record of judicial appointments, and we reaffirm our support for the appointment of judges at all levels of the judiciary who respect traditional family values and the sanctity of innocent human life.

Source: CQ Almanac, 1984, p. 55-B. Congressional Quarterly, Inc., Washington, D.C., 1985.

DOCUMENT 72: Democratic Party Platform, 1984

[Reproductive Freedom]. The Democratic Party recognizes reproductive freedom as a fundamental human right. We therefore oppose government interference in the reproductive decisions of Americans, especially government interference which denies poor Americans their right to privacy by funding or advocating one or a limited number of reproductive choices only. We fully recognize the religious and ethical concerns which many Americans have about abortion. But we also recognize the belief of many Americans that a woman has a right to choose whether and when to have a child. The Democratic Party supports the 1973 Supreme Court decision on abortion rights as the law of the land and opposes any constitutional amendment to restrict or overturn that decision. We deplore violence and harassment against health providers and women seeking services and will work to end such acts. We support a continuing federal interest in developing strong local family planning and family life education programs and medical research aimed at reducing the need for abortion.

Source: CQ *Almanac*, 1984, p. 93-B. Congressional Quarterly, Inc., Washington D.C., 1985. (The Democrats did not have a separate abortion plank in their 1988 platform, but the Democratic candidate, Michael Dukakis, supported the right of women to make their own decisions based on their own beliefs.)

DOCUMENT 73: Transcript of Debate Between Walter Mondale and President Reagan on Domestic Policy, October 7, 1984

[Discussion of the abortion issue. This debate was sponsored by the League of Women Voters and was televised. Diane Sawyer, a newswoman, asks the questions.]

MS. SAWYER: I'd like to turn to an area that I think few people enjoy discussing, but that we probably should tonight, because the positions of the two candidates are so clearly different and lead to very different policy consequences—and that is abortion and right to life. I'm exploring for your personal views of abortion, and specifically how you would want them applied as public policy.

First, Mr. President, do you consider abortion murder or a sin? And second, how hard would you work, what kind of priority would you give in your second term legislation to make abortion illegal? And specifically, would you make certain, as your party platform urges, that Federal Justices that you appoint be pro-life?

MR. REAGAN: I believe that in the appointment of judges that all that was specified in the party platform was that they observe . . . have a . . . they respect the sanctity of human life. Now that I would want to see in any judge, and with regard to any issue having to do with human life.

But with regard to abortion—and I have a feeling that this is . . . there's been some reference without naming it here, in remarks of Mr. Mondale, tied to injecting religion into government. With me, abortion is not a problem of religion; it's a problem of the Constitution. I believe that until and unless someone can establish that the unborn child is not a living human being, then that child is already protected by the Constitution which guarantees life, liberty, and the pursuit of happiness to all of us. And I think that this is what we should concentrate on, [Applause] is trying. . . .

I know there was weeks and weeks of testimony before a Senate committee. There were medical authorities, there were religious . . . there were clerics there, everyone talking about this matter of pro-life. And at the end of all of that, not one shred of evidence was introduced that the unborn child was not alive. We have seen premature births that are now grown-up, happy people going around.

Also, there is a strange dichotomy in this whole position about our courts ruling that abortion is not the taking of a human life. In California some time ago, a man beat a woman so savagely that her unborn child was born dead with a 'fractured skull. And the California state legislature unanimously passed a law that was signed by the then Democratic governor—signed a law that said that any man who so abuses a pregnant woman that he causes the death of her unborn child shall be charged with murder. Now, isn't it strange that that same woman could have taken the life of her unborn child and it was abortion, not murder, but if somebody else does it, that's murder? And it recognizes—it used the term "death of the unborn child."

So this has been my feeling about abortion, that we have a problem now to determine. And all evidence so far comes down on the side of the unborn child being a living human being.

MS. SAWYER: A two-part follow-up—do I take it from what you said about the platform, then, that you don't regard the language, and don't regard in your own appointments, abortion position a test of any kind for justices that it should be? And also, if abortion is made illegal, how would you want it enforced? Who would be the policing units that would investigate, and would you want the women who have abortions to be prosecuted?

MR. REAGAN: The laws regarding that always were state laws. It was only when the Supreme Court handed down a decision that the Federal Government intervened in what had always been a state policy. Our laws against murder are state laws. So, I would think that this would be the—the point of enforcement on this.

I . . . as I say, I feel that we have a problem here to resolve, and no one has approached it from that matter. It is . . . it does not happen that the church that I belong to had that as part of its dogma. I know that some churches do. Now, it is a sin if you're taking a human life. At the same time, in our Judeo-Christian tradition, we recognize the right of taking human life in self-defense, and therefore I've always believed that a mother—if medically, it is determined that her life is at risk if she goes through with the pregnancy—she has a right then to take the life of even her own unborn child in defense of her own.

MS. SAWYER: Mr. Mondale, to turn to you, do you consider abortion a murder or a sin? And, bridging from what President Reagan said, he has written that if society doesn't know whether life—does human life, in fact, does begin at conception—as long as there is a doubt, that the unborn child should at least be given the benefit of the doubt, and that there should be protection for that unborn child?

MR. MONDALE: This is one of the most emotional and difficult issues that could possibly be debated. I think your questions, however, underscore the fact: there is probably no way that government should or could answer this question in every individual case and in the private lives of the American people.

The Constitutional amendment proposed by President Reagan would make it a crime for a woman to have an abortion if she had been raped or suffered from incest. Is it really the view of the American people, however you feel on the question of abortion, that government ought to be reaching into your living rooms and making choices like this? I think it cannot work, won't work, and will lead to all kinds of cynical evasions of the law. Those who can afford to have them will continue to have them. The disadvantaged will go out in the back alley, as they used to do. I think these questions are inherently personal and moral, and every individual instance is different. Every American should beware . . . be aware of the seriousness of the step. But there are some things that government can do, and some things they cannot do.

Now, the example that the President cites has nothing to do with abortion. Somebody went to a woman and nearly killed her. That's always been a serious crime, and always should be a serious crime. But how does that compare with the problem of a woman who's raped? Do we really want those decisions made by judges who've been picked because they will agree to find the person guilty? I don't think so, and I think it's going in exactly the wrong direction. In America, on basic moral questions, we have always let the people decide in their own personal lives. We haven't felt so insecure that we've reached for the club of state to have our point of view. It's been a good instinct, and we're the most religious people on earth.

One final point. President Reagan, as Governor of California, signed a bill which is perhaps the most liberal pro-abortion bill of any state in the union.

Source: *CQ Almanac*, 1984, pp. 112–13. Congressional Quarterly, Inc., Washington, D.C., 1985.

DOCUMENT 74: Republican Party Platform, 1988

Deep in our hearts we do believe . . . that the unborn child has a fundamental right to life which cannot be infringed. We therefore reaffirm our support for a human life amendment to the Constitution, and we endorse legislation to make clear that the Fourteenth Amendment's protections apply to unborn children. We oppose the use of public revenues for abortion and will eliminate funding for organizations which advocate or support abortion. We commend the efforts of those individuals and private organizations that are providing positive alternatives to abortion by meeting the physical, emotional, and financial needs of pregnant women and offering adoption services where needed.

We applaud President Reagan's fine record of judicial appointments, and we reaffirm our support for the appointment of judges at all levels of the judiciary who respect traditional family values and the sanctity of human life.

Source: CQ Almanac, 1988, p. 54-A. Congressional Quarterly Inc., Washington D.C., 1989.

DOCUMENT 75: Republican Party Platform, 1992

We believe the unborn child has a fundamental independent right to life that cannot be infringed. We therefore reaffirm our support for a human life amendment to the Constitution, and we endorse legislation to make clear that the Fourteenth Amendment's protections apply to unborn children. We oppose using public revenues for abortion and will not fund organizations that advocate it. We commend those who provide alternatives to abortion by meeting the needs of mothers and offering adoption services. We reaffirm our support for appointment of judges who respect traditional family values and the sanctity of human life.

Source: CQ Almanac, 1992, p. 85-A. Congressional Quarterly Inc., Washington D.C., 1993.

DOCUMENT 76: Democratic Party Platform, 1992

Choice. Democrats stand behind the right of every woman to choose, consistent with Roe v. Wade, regardless of ability to pay, and support a national law to protect that right. It is a fundamental constitutional liberty that individual Americans—not government—can best take responsibility for making the most difficult and intensely personal decisions regarding reproduction. The goal of our nation must be to make abortion less necessary, not more difficult or more dangerous. We pledge to support contraceptive research, family planning, comprehensive family life education, and policies that support healthy child-bearing and enable parents to care most effectively for their children.

Source: *CQ Almanac*, 1992, p. 59-A. Congressional Quarterly Inc., Washington D.C., 1993.

CONGRESS DELIBERATES

Congress does not have constitutional authority to regulate the subject of abortion directly. However, after a Republican administration was re-elected in 1984 with strong pro-life support, pro-life Senators and Representatives were eager to take action to promote their cause. Since Congress does have the power to prevent federal funding of abortions, it continued to amend appropriations bills (see Documents 57 and 58) to forbid the use of taxpayers' funds for abortions performed under Medicaid and other federally funded public health programs. Members of Congress also continued to introduce resolutions that would initiate the process of constitutional amendment.

The states' rights amendment

None of the constitutional amendments on which the Committee on the Judiciary had held hearings in 1974 and 1975 reached the floor of the Senate for a vote. In 1981 the Committee again considered a group of constitutional amendments—and again took no further action. It was not until 1983 that one of the amendments was successfully reported out of committee. This amendment, nicknamed the "states' rights" amendment, was introduced by Senator Orrin Hatch, a Republican from Utah. It provided that the regulation of abortion be returned to the states. Political observers thought that the amendment would pass easily. But after ten hours of debate in the Senate, the proposed amendment was rejected by a close vote. Forty-nine Senators voted in favor of the amendment, fifty-one were opposed. Since constitutional amendments require a two-thirds vote in each house of Congress, eighteen more votes would have been required to send the amendment out to the states for ratification.

DOCUMENT 77: The Proposed Hatch Amendment to the Constitution. 1983

A JOINT RESOLUTION. To amend the Constitution and establish legislative authority in Congress and the States with respect to abortion.

Resolved by the Senate and House of Representatives in Congress assembled (two-thirds of each House concurring therein), That the following article is proposed as an amendment to the Constitution of the United States which shall be valid to all intents and purposes as part of the Constitution when ratified by the legislatures of three-fourths of the several states within seven years from the date of its submission by the Congress:

ARTICLE—

"A right to abortion is not secured by this Constitution. The Congress and the several States shall have the concurrent power to restrict and prohibit abortions."

Source: Senate Joint Resolution 3, 98th Congress, 1st session, 1983.

THE HUMAN LIFE BILL (1981)

Because passage of a constitutional amendment was so difficult, pro-life politicians looked for another way to get federal protection for the lives of the unborn. A lawyer named Stephen H. Galebach had an interesting proposal; he thought there was a way to use the ordinary legislative process to protect fetal rights. He suggested the introduction of a two part "human life" bill. The first section of the bill would declare that fetuses are "persons" within the meaning of the Fourteenth Amendment (see Document 35) and that life begins at conception. Then, drawing on congressional power to regulate the jurisdiction of the federal courts, the bill would prohibit federal courts from hearing any challenge to state laws protecting life. If courts could not hear abortion cases, they would not have the power to rule such state statutes unconstitutional. Republican Senator Jesse Helms of North Carolina thought that Galebach's plan would allow Congress to accomplish by ordinary legislation what it was finding it difficult to do by the more rigorous procedure required for amending the Constitution. Congress did not, however, pass this bill.

DOCUMENT 78: The Proposed Human Life Statute. Senate Bill 158. 1981

Section 1. The Congress finds that present day scientific evidence indicates a significant likelihood that actual human life exists from conception.

The Congress further finds that the 14th Amendment to the Constitution of the United States was intended to protect all human beings.

Upon the basis of these findings, and in the exercise of the powers of

Congress, including its power under Section 5 of the Fourteenth Amendment to the Constitution of the United States, the Congress hereby declares that for the purpose of enforcing the obligation of the States under the 14th Amendment not to deprive persons of life without due process of law, human life shall be deemed to exist from conception, without regard to race, sex, age, health, defect, or condition of dependency; and for this purpose "person" shall include all human life as defined therein.

Section 2. Notwithstanding any other provision of law no inferior federal court . . . shall have jurisdiction . . . in any case . . . arising from any State law . . . that (1) protects the rights of human persons between conception and birth, or (2) prohibits, limits or regulates . . . the performance of abortions.

Source: Congressional Record, January 19, 1981, pp. 5287–88.

THE FREEDOM OF CHOICE BILL (1992)

Abortion rights supporters, afraid that the Supreme Court would overturn the right to choose an abortion, tried to get Congress to pass a Freedom of Choice Act. Such a law would attempt to guarantee the right to abortion by writing it into federal statutory law. At first, anticipating a hostile decision in *Planned Parenthood of Southeastern Pennsylvania v. Casey*, Democrats in Congress fought to get such a bill passed before the 1992 election, sure that President Bush would veto it. The abortion rights issue could then be used against him in the campaign. But when the Supreme Court did not overrule *Roe v. Wade* in the *Casey* case (see Document 85), the steam went out of the move to get the bill through Congress. Its supporters decided to wait until after the election to push for its passage.

DOCUMENT 79: The Proposed Freedom of Choice Act. H.R. 25. 1992

A Bill: to protect the reproductive rights of women, and for other purposes,—

Section 1. Short title.

This Act may be cited as the Freedom of Choice Act of 1991.

Section 2. Right to Choose.

(a) In General—Except as provided in subsection (b), a State may not restrict the right of a woman to choose to terminate a pregnancy—

(1) before fetal viability; or

(2) at any time, if such termination is necessary to protect the life or health of the woman.

(b) Medically Necessary Requirements. A State may impose requirements medically necessary to protect the life or health of women referred to in subsection (a).

(c) Rules of construction—Nothing in this Act shall be construed to:

(1) prevent a State from protecting unwilling individuals from having to participate in the performance of abortions to which they are conscientiously opposed;

(2) prevent a State from requiring a minor to involve a parent, guardian, or other responsible adult before terminating a pregnancy.

Section 3. Definition of a State.

As used in this Act, the term "State" includes the District of Columbia, the Commonwealth of Puerto Rico, and each other territory and possession of the United States.

Source: Congressional Quarterly Weekly Report, July 4, 1992, p. 1952.

PACKING THE SUPREME COURT

One of the promises made by the Republicans during the election campaigns of 1980–1992 was that a Republican president would appoint justices to the Supreme Court who could be counted on to overturn *Roe v. Wade.* However, the president alone does not make Supreme Court appointments. The President nominates, but the United States Senate must confirm the nominees. During President Reagan's first term Republicans controlled the Senate. But by 1986 the situation had changed, and control returned to the Democrats. The Democrats were not, however, willing or able to keep Republican presidents from filling Supreme Court vacancies with extremely conservative justices.

During President Carter's term in office (1977–1981), there were no vacancies on the Supreme Court, and Carter had no opportunity to choose a justice. During President Reagan's two terms in office, several aging justices retired, and the president had the opportunity to make significant changes in the composition of the Court. He appointed a new chief justice and three associate justices. Following through on the promises in the Republican Party platforms, he sought justices with a clear record of opposition to abortion. In his campaign speeches he had also promised to appoint a woman (the first woman ever to serve) to the Court.

In 1981, on the retirement of Justice Potter Stewart, the president nominated Sandra Day O'Connor, a Republican who was serving as a state court judge in Arizona. O'Connor was a conservative lawyer and judge with a good record, and had also served in the Arizona legislature. The Senate Committee on the Judiciary, which oversees judicial appointments, quizzed her on her judicial philosophy, including her views on abortion.

Judicial nominees often have a problem answering questions about their views on specific subjects. They do not want to commit themselves on issues that may come before them for judgment. Judge O'Connor stated that she was personally opposed to abortion but did not want to say whether or not she would vote to overturn *Roe v. Wade*.

President Reagan's other Supreme Court selections were all chosen with an eye to their views on abortion, but like Judge O'Connor, none of them wished to make a definite commitment to rule as the president wished. Antonin Scalia, Reagan's second nominee, was not questioned extensively. A third nominee, Judge Robert Bork, was rejected by the Senate because an extensive record in writings and speeches of his conservative views made him an easy target for civil rights organizations that were afraid he would vote for drastic changes in the area of constitutional rights. A subsequent nominee, Judge Anthony Kennedy, who was later confirmed, was not willing reveal his views on abortion.

In filling the two vacancies on the Court that occurred during his administration, President Bush attempted to avoid controversy by choosing men who did not have a public record on the abortion issue (or on many other public issues). His nominees, David H. Souter and Clarence Thomas, were both confirmed.

When he appeared before members of the Senate Committee on the Judiciary during his confirmation hearings, Souter responded evasively to questions about abortion.

Faye Wattleton, president of Planned Parenthood, and Senator Alan Simpson, Republican from Wyoming, exchanged words about Souter's refusal to reveal his views.

DOCUMENT 80: Testimony of Sandra Day O'Connor Before the Senate Judiciary Committee. Hearings on Her Nomination to Be an Associate Justice of the Supreme Court, 1981

PERSONAL AND JUDICIAL PHILOSOPHY ON ABORTION

The CHAIRMAN. Judge O'Connor, there has been much discussion regarding your views on the subject of abortion. Would you discuss your philosophy on abortion, both personal and judicial, and explain your actions as a State senator in Arizona on certain specific matters: First, your 1970 committee vote in favor of House bill No. 20, which would have repealed Arizona's felony statutes on abortion. Then I have three other instances I will inquire about.

Judge O'CONNOR. Very well. May I preface my response by saying that the personal views and philosophies, in my view, of a Supreme Court Justice and indeed any judge should be set aside insofar as it is possible to do that in resolving matters that come before the Court.

Issues that come before the Court should be resolved based on the facts of that particular case or matter and on the law applicable to those facts, and any constitutional principles applicable to those facts. They should not be based on the personal views and ideology of the judge with regard to that particular matter or issue.

Now, having explained that, I would like to say that my own view in the area of abortion is that I am opposed to it as a matter of birth control or otherwise. The subject of abortion is a valid one, in my view, for legislative action subject to any constitutional restraints or limitations.

I think a great deal has been written about my vote in a Senate Judiciary Committee in 1970 on a bill called House bill No. 20, which would have repealed Arizona's abortion statutes. . . .

. . . The bill did not go to the floor of the Senate for a vote; it was held in the Senate Caucus and the committee vote was a vote which would have taken it out of that committee with a recommendation to the full Senate.

The bill is one which concerned a repeal of Arizona's then statutes which made it a felony, punishable by from 2 to 5 years in prison, for anyone providing any substance or means to procure a miscarriage unless it was necessary to save the life of the mother. It would have, for example, subjected anyone who assisted a young woman who, for instance, was a rape victim in securing a D. & C. procedure within hours or even days of that rape.

At that time I believed that some change in Arizona statutes was appropriate, and had a bill been presented to me that was less sweeping than House bill No. 20, I would have supported that. It was not, and the news accounts reflect that I supported the committee action in putting the bill out of committee, where it then died in the caucus.

I would say that my own knowledge and awareness of the issues and concerns that many people have about the question of abortion has increased since those days. It was not the subject of a great deal of public attention or concern at the time it came before the committee in 1970. I would not have voted, I think, Mr. Chairman, for a simple repealer thereafter.

The CHAIRMAN. Now the second instance was your cosponsorship in 1973 of Senate bill No. 1190, which would have provided family planning services, including surgical procedures, even for minors without parental consent.

Judge O'CONNOR. Senate bill No. 1190 in 1973 was a bill in which the prime sponsor was from the city of Tucson, and it had nine other cosigners on the bill. I was one of those cosigners.

I viewed the bill as a bill which did not deal with abortion but which would have established as a State policy in Arizona, a policy of encouraging the availability of contraceptive information to people generally. . . .

It did not provide for any surgical procedure for an abortion, as has been reported inaccurately by some. The only reference in the bill to a surgical procedure was the following. It was one that said:

> A physician may perform appropriate surgical procedures for the prevention of conception upon any adult who requests such procedure in writing.

That particular provision, I believe, was subsequently amended out in committee but, be that as it may, it was in the bill on introduction.

Mr. Chairman, I supported the availability of contraceptive information to the public generally. Arizona had a statute or statutes on the books at that time, in 1973, which did restrict rather dramatically the availability of information about contraception to the public generally. It seemed to me that perhaps the best way to avoid having people who were seeking abortions was to enable people not to become pregnant unwittingly or without the intention of doing so.

The CHAIRMAN. The third instance, your 1974 vote against House Concurrent Memorial No. 2002, which urged Congress to pass a constitutional amendment against abortion.

Judge O'CONNOR. Mr. Chairman, as you perhaps recall, the *Roe* v. *Wade* decision was handed down in 1973. I would like to mention that in that year following that decision, when concerns began to be expressed, I requested the preparation in 1973 of Senate bill No. 1333 which gave hospitals and physicians and employees the right not to participate in or contribute to any abortion proceeding if they chose not to do so and objected, notwithstanding their employment. That bill did pass the State Senate and became law.

The following year, in 1974, less than a year following the *Roe* v. *Wade* decision, a House Memorial was introduced in the Arizona House of Representatives. It would have urged Congress to amend the Constitution to provide that the word person in the 5th and 14th amendments applies to the unborn at every stage of development, except in an emergency when there is a reasonable medical certainty that continuation of the pregnancy would cause the death of the mother. The amendment was further amended in the Senate Judiciary Committee.

I did not support the memorial at that time, either in committee or in the caucus.

The CHAIRMAN. Excuse me. My time is up, but you are right in the midst of your question. We will finish abortion, one more instance, and we will give the other members the same additional time, if you will proceed.

Judge O'CONNOR. I voted against it, Mr. Chairman, because I was not sure at that time that we had given the proper amount of reflection or consideration to what action, if any, was appropriate by way of a constitutional amendment in connection with the *Roe* v. *Wade* decision.

It seems to me, at least, that amendments to the Constitution are very serious matters and should be undertaken after a great deal of study and thought, and not hastily. I think a tremendous amount of work needs to go into the text and the concept being expressed in any proposed amendment. I did not feel at that time that that kind of consideration had been given to the measure. I understand that the Congress is still wrestling with that issue after some years from that date, which was in 1974.

Thank you, Mr. Chairman.

The CHAIRMAN. Now the last instance is concerning a vote in 1974 against a successful amendment to a stadium construction bill which limited the availability of abortions.

Judge O'CONNOR. Also in 1974, which was an active year in the Arizona Legislature with regard to the issue of abortion, the Senate had originated a bill that allowed the University of Arizona to issue bonds to expand its football stadium. That bill passed the State Senate and went to the House of Representatives.

In the House it was amended to add a nongermane rider which would have prohibited the performance of abortions in any facility under the jurisdiction of the Arizona Board of Regents. When the measure returned to the Senate, at that time I was the Senate majority leader and I was very concerned because the whole subject had become one that was controversial within our own membership.

I was concerned as majority leader that we not encourage a practice of the addition of nongername riders to Senate bills which we had passed without that kind of a provision. Indeed, Arizona's constitution has a provision which prohibits the putting together of bills or measures or riders dealing with more than one subject. I did oppose the addition by the House of the nongermane rider when it came back.

It might be of interest, though, to know, Mr. Chairman, that also in 1974 there was another Senate bill which would have provided for a medical assistance program for the medically needy. That was Senate bill No. 1165. It contained a provision that no benefits would be provided for abortions except when deemed medically necessary to save the life of the mother, or where the pregnancy had resulted from rape, incest, or criminal action. I supported that bill together with that provision and the measure did pass and become law.

The CHAIRMAN. Thank you. My time is up. We will now call upon Senator Biden.

Senator BIDEN. Thank you, Mr. Chairman.

Source: U.S. Congress, Senate Committee on the Judiciary, *Hearings on the Nomination of Sandra Day O'Connor of Arizona to Serve as an Associate Justice of the Supreme Court of the United States*, 97th Congress, 1st session, 1981, pp. 60–63.

Excerpts from Hearings Before the Senate Committee on the Judiciary, on the Nomination of David H. Souter to Be an Associate Justice of the Supreme Court, 1990

DOCUMENT 81: Testimony of Faye Wattleton, President of Planned Parenthood Federation of America, before the Senate Committee on the Judiciary. Nomination of David H. Souter to Be an Associate Justice of the Supreme Court, 1990

Thank you, Mr. Chairman, and to the committee. It is also my pleasure to speak before you this morning.

I speak as the president of the Planned Parenthood Action Fund, which is the political advocacy arm of the Planned Parenthood Federation of America [PPFA]. PPFA is the Nation's oldest and largest nonprofit, private provider of reproductive health care in this country. For 75 years, we have given men and women access to the information and medical care that enable them to decide when and if they will be parents. Every year, nearly 2 million Americans—many of them young and poor—come to our 879 medical centers. We are not a special interest group, as some have implied. Our views represent those of millions of Americans—as a matter of fact, the majority of Americans—who want to preserve their right to make their most fundamental private reproductive decisions.

Last week, David Souter told us that the responsibility of a Supreme Court Justice, and I quote, "is to make the promises of the Constitution a reality for our time and to preserve that Constitution for generations that will follow us." We agree completely. We also believe that one of the promises of our Constitution is the protection of our fundamental right of privacy and reproductive freedom.

Until these hearing, Judge Souter's views on these constitutional promises were virtually unknown, and Planned Parenthood did not oppose his nomination. Instead, supported by 87 percent of the electorate, we asserted that Americans have the right to know Judge Souter's views on fundamental issues such as the rights of privacy and reproductive freedom.

But after days of evasive answers and filibusters, we know little more about his views on these issues than we did before the hearings began, and what we do know is profoundly disturbing. It is clear that Judge Souter sees reproductive freedom as an unsettled issue. He does not accept reproductive rights as an established constitutionally protected right, one of the promises of our Constitution.

Judge Souter acknowledged the existence of a right to marital privacy but would not acknowledge the right of married people to use contraception as outlined in *Griswold*. He also refused to comment on the later *Eisenstadt* decision that extended this right to unmarried people.

In fact, he said in regard to *Griswold*, and I quote, "If there were a successful attack on *Roe*, that would call into question prior privacy cases." This is a contention that Planned Parenthood has made all along.

In other words, Americans may not have the fundamental right to prevent unwanted pregnancy, much less the safety to terminate a problem pregnancy.

Judge Souter steadfastly refused to answer questions about a woman's right to abortion, saying that it would be inappropriate for him to comment because it is likely that *Roe* v. *Wade* would be coming back to the Supreme Court. And yet he was willing to comment extensively on the appropriate standard of review for cases including gender discrimination, the free exercise clause, racial discrimination, all of which are likely, like *Roe*, to come before the Court.

He refused to tell Senator Kennedy if he considered abortion moral or immoral, even in cases of rape or incest, saying it would, and I quote again, "dispel the promise of impartiality in approaching this issue" if it came before him. Yet Judge Souter has no qualms about expressing his own moral views about the death penalty and white-collar crime, issues on which the Supreme Court is repeatedly asked to rule.

The resignation of Justice Brennan has left the Supreme Court precariously balanced. Last year, and again this year, the Court issued decisions that seriously weakened *Roe* and unleashed wholesale assaults on reproductive rights in State legislatures nationwide. Indeed, when asked what the practical consequences of overturning *Roe* would be, Judge Souter reduced the issue to a Federal-State squabble.

Twenty-four years ago, when David Souter was counseling a young woman in Boston facing an unwanted pregnancy, Planned Parenthood was doing similar work, working with trained counselors, nurses and volunteers all over the United States. The one experience that Judge Souter claims as his sole source of sensitivity on this critical issue of private life is an experience that Planned Parenthood clinics cope with every day. We know, as do most Americans, that *Roe* v. *Wade* liberated American women and saved our lives like no other recent Supreme Court decision. Its real life consequences have been matched by few judicial acts in the history of our republic.

For women and their families, the right to reproductive choice creates a foundation for exercising many of the other constitutional privileges we enjoy as Americans. Clearly, the health and well-being of American women and of future generations that David Souter expressed concern about will rest in the hands of the next Supreme Court Justice. What choices will my daughter, your daughters, our granddaughters have? Will the promises of our Constitution remain a reality for them? It depends largely on the views of the next Supreme Court Justice on privacy and reproductive freedom.

Any Supreme Court nominee who rejects the fundamental nature of these privacy rights in a democracy must likewise be rejected by the citizens of that democracy. American women, quite frankly, are quite tired of having our rights placed up for grabs. We urge you to keep the faith of the American people and American women, women who will not forget who nominated the next Justice and who confirmed him. We urge you to reject the nomination of David Hackett Souter to the U.S. Supreme Court, and thereby send a message that the period of tolerance for political gamesmanship around our fundamental reproductive rights has ended.

Source: U.S. Congress, Senate Committee on the Judiciary, *Hearings on the Nomination of David Souter to be Associate Justice of the Supreme Court*, 101st Congress, 1st session, 1990, pp. 382–83.

DOCUMENT 82: Comments by Senator Alan Simpson (Republican, Wyoming) before the Senate Committee on the Judiciary. Nomination of David H. Souter to Be an Associate Justice of the Supreme Court, 1990

Senator SIMPSON. Thank you, Mr. Chairman.

How do you do, ladies? Nice to see you today.

I want both of you [Faye Wattleton and Kate Michelman, Director of the National Abortion Rights Action League] to know and I think you are aware of my position on this terribly anguishing matter. I think you know that I am in favor of a woman's right to choose. I have held that view, formed within 2 years after *Roe* v. *Wade* through a legislative debate.

I am also very supportive of most of the objectives of Planned Parenthood. I have stated those things and have provided some of my own personal funds for dues over the years to some of those groups.

But I really believe you are making a big mistake on this one. That's too bad. You know, it's perfectly all right, but I think these things are going to come up again. There are going to be other Supreme Court choices when you are really going to need to be in the trenches. This is not one of those cases. This is my view.

I believe you are seriously in error in demanding that Judge Souter answer specific questions on this issue, because he is a sitting judge. And since we have heard a remarkable array of extremely technical discussions over the last few days, which are like going to law school again, let's not forget Canon 3(a)(6) of the ABA Code of Judicial Ethics. It prohibits a sitting judge, and that is Judge Souter, from comment on a "pending or impending matter" likely to come before the Court. He is prohibited from doing that, absolutely prohibited under the ethics of the ABA, who have given him a rating that is the highest they can give.

Nearly everyone has conceded that abortion will be before the Supreme Court again, and thus, that subject is covered by the ABA Code. You are really asking Judge Souter to violate the rule of judicial ethics in order that your organizations, both of them, can have advance knowledge of his position on the particular issue of abortion.

Why are you asking of Judge Souter that which he is forbidden to answer by the Code of Judicial Conduct?

Ms. WATTLETON. Well, Senator Simpson, I would seriously object to your characterization of our asking Judge Souter to comment on the constitutional protection of reproductive privacy for the basis of our organization's foreknowledge of how he might rule.

As I spoke earlier in my comments, our views represent the overwhelming majority of the American people and I sit here, not only as head of an organization but also as an American, the American people have a right to know.

Yes, there are judicial ethics. As a matter of fact, I think that there is a law that forbids the judge to answer questions about specific cases, but virtually every aspect of American life at some time comes into question and must be adjudicated. We believe that this is an important aspect of American constitutional law that deserves to be probed very thoroughly. Perhaps it should be seen as something that is integrally important to the integrity of women in this country. We do not consider it an issue that we want to take a chance on. We may have a difference of opinion, but such is the democratic process. It is our opinion without a clear understanding of his judicial philosophy in this area, not how he will rule on *Roe* v. *Wade*, that Mr. Souter should not sit on the Supreme Court.

Ms. MICHELMAN. I would like to share that. I don't think any member of this committee asked Judge Souter specific questions about specific cases, or specific facts that may come before a case, or may be involved in a case.

What the attempt was to get at how he would, what kind of legal reasoning, legal approach he would use to evaluating whether there is a fundamental constitutional right to privacy. He did, as I said earlier and as Faye has said, he was more forthcoming in other areas of law where, in fact, the Court will have to rule in the future. He singled this one out and we think it is not acceptable that he should be able to single this out and raises too great a risk.

Senator SIMPSON. I see. You know, we talked about the issue of gender discrimination, first amendment free exercise, and those issues, critical issues. Those are much broader in scope than the question, do you support a constitutional basis for abortion rights?

You know that and I know that. Judge Souter was granted latitude on those broader issues, but he simply is not granted this kind of latitude on this specific issue of abortion.

Ms. WATTLETON. I might point out that Mr. Souter chose not to answer the question do you believe that the Constitution protects the right not to procreate. He declined to answer that after having established that he believed that it protected marital privacy.

Senator SIMPSON. I know that. I guess I can only judge that you wish Judge Souter to advise all political litigants that he is not impartial and not using the tools of a judge if he were to hear an abortion case. I think that is what you are asking him to do.

Source: U.S. Congress, Senate Committee on the Judiciary, *Hearings on the Nomination of David H. Souter to be Associate Justice of the Supreme Court*, 101st Congress, 1st session, 1990, pp. 396–97.

ABORTION DECISIONS BY THE REAGAN–BUSH SUPREME COURT, 1983–1992

Should *Roe v. Wade* be overruled?

Appointments made to the Supreme Court by President Reagan and President Bush caused a modification of the constitutional principles that had been laid down in *Roe v. Wade*, but to the surprise of many observers did not result in a Court willing to overrule the decision itself. Pro-life activists had been hoping for a conservative majority that would turn the regulation of abortion back to the state legislatures and that some states would then respond by recriminalizing abortion.

In 1973 only two justices had dissented from the Court's decision giving constitutional status to a woman's right to choose an abortion. By 1992 five new justices had been added to the Court, all by presidents who were critical of the abortion ruling. If all five of the new justices had voted with the original dissenters, Roe would have been doomed. What happened?

The first of President Reagan's justices, Sandra Day O'Connor, joined the Court in 1981, the only woman ever to serve on that body. Her appointment was praised by liberal women's organizations, even though O'Connor, a conservative Republican, had stated that she was personally opposed to abortion. Her first chance to vote in a case involving this issue came in 1983, in a case entitled City of Akron v. Akron Center for Reproductive Health, better known as the Akron Ordinance Case.

The Akron ordinance was a regulation drafted with the help of right-to-life organizations and enacted by the city council of Akron, Ohio. It was intended to put a number of powerful restrictions on the performance of abortions—waiting periods, parental consent, hospitalization requirements, and many others. Until this time, such restrictive provisions had been rejected by the Supreme Court as unconstitutional burdens on the right of women to choose abortions. The Court, as expected, overturned many of the ordinance's provisions. Justice O'Connor now cast her first vote in an abortion case. She voted to uphold the ordinance and wrote a dissent that was joined by Justices White and Rehnquist. Her dissent not only revealed that she thought some state regulation of abortion was acceptable, but put forward several new ideas. She criticized Justice Blackmun's division of pregnancy into three trimesters, or three-month periods, as artificial and unworkable. Justice O'Connor thought that new medical technology was pushing back the date at which a fetus was viable, that is, the date when a fetus could be separated from its mother and still be kept alive. Roe's dating of viability at the end of the second trimester was obsolete. Furthermore, second trimester abortions were becoming safer, so state regulation in this period was less justified. The Roe framework was thus "on a collision course with itself." As medical technology changed, the Court would find itself reviewing state legislative decisions on medical questions—an unsuitable task for courts.

Justice O'Connor also stated that while abortion is a constitutional right in some senses, it is a partial right. She thought the proper question for the Court to ask in deciding whether state laws were too restrictive was whether they were "unduly burdensome." Since the state has a valid interest in protecting life, not just in the third trimester but throughout pregnancy, state regulations should be upheld unless they unduly burden a woman's right to choose.

Her vote in this case told us that Justice O'Connor, the only woman justice, was unwilling to vote to overturn a decision that has been called the most concretely important thing the Supreme Court has ever done for women.

Six years later, in 1989, the composition of the Supreme Court had been drastically changed; it was well on its way to becoming the "Rehnquist Court." Chief Justice Burger had retired and Justice Rehnquist had replaced him. Another conservative, Antonin Scalia, had been chosen to fill the vacant associate justiceship. President Reagan had appointed a third conservative judge, Anthony Kennedy, to fill the place left by the retirement of moderate justice Lewis O. Powell. Opponents of abortion now saw a possible five-vote majority for the overruling of *Roe.* The advocates of abortion rights were afraid that the Court would use a new case, *Webster v. Reproductive Health Services*, to do just that. But again, Justice O'Connor refused to take the final step and vote to overrule *Roe.* In a case that brought another restrictive state statute before the Court, she voted to uphold sections of the Missouri statute but stated that it was unnecessary to reexamine the *Roe* precedent. There were still only four votes to repudiate Justice Blackmun's earlier opinion.

Justice Scalia wrote a venomous opinion attacking O'Connor for her middle-of-the-road position (see Document 84).

In *Planned Parenthood of Southeastern Pennsylvania v. Casey*, the Court was again faced with a state statute designed to discourage abortions and another opportunity to overturn *Roe v. Wade*. By 1992, when this case was decided, there were five new faces on the Supreme Court. Justice David Souter had taken office in 1990 and Justice Clarence Thomas in 1991. Interest groups on both sides of the abortion question were sure that the *Casey* decision would bring a definitive ruling on abortion. Either a constitutional right to choose would be retained, or *Roe* would be jettisoned and the whole subject turned back to the states to regulate as they wished.

To the dismay of anti-abortion activists, three of the new justices combined to support a compromise. The Court upheld some parts of the Pennsylvania law and rejected others. But Justices O'Connor, Souter, and Kennedy jointly wrote an opinion saying that they believed an important precedent like *Roe v. Wade* should be supported unless there were compelling reasons for repudiating it. They stated that it was a watershed decision that should be retained.

Roe v. Wade had thus survived twenty years of strife to remain a part of settled constitutional law. And since President Clinton had taken a position supporting choice, it was probable that his nominees to the Supreme Court would be selected with their support for that position in mind.

DOCUMENT 83: *City of Akron v. Akron Center for Reproductive Health* (1983). Excerpts from the O'Connor Dissent

---

[The decision in this case was six to three against the constitutionality of the Akron ordinance.]

Our recent cases indicate that a regulation imposed on "a lawful abortion 'is not unconstitutional unless it unduly burdens the right to seek an abortion.' " *Maher v. Roe*. In my view, this "unduly burdensome" standard should be applied to the challenged regulations throughout the entire pregnancy without reference to the particular "stage" of pregnancy involved. If the particular regulation does not "unduly burden" the fundamental right, then our evaluation of that regulation is limited to our determination that the regulation rationally relates to a legitimate state purpose. . . .

The trimester or "three stage" approach adopted by the Court in *Roe* . . . is a completely unworkable method of accommodating the conflicting personal rights and compelling state interests that are involved in the abortion context. . . .

Just as improvements in medical technology inevitably will move *forward* the point at which the State may regulate for reasons of maternal health, different technological improvements will move *backward* the point of viability at which the State may proscribe abortions except when necessary to preserve the life and health of the mother. . . .

The *Roe* framework, then, is clearly on a collision course with itself. As the medical risks of various abortion procedures decrease, the point at which the State may regulate for reasons of maternal health is moved further forward to actual childbirth. As medical science becomes better able to provide for the separate existence of the fetus, the point of viability is moved further back toward conception. . . . The *Roe* framework is inherently tied to the state of medical technology that exists whenever particular litigation ensues. Although legislatures are better suited to make the necessary factual judgments in this area, the Court's framework forces legislatures, as a matter of constitutional law, to speculate about what constitutes "accepted medical practice" at any given time. Without the necessary expertise or ability, courts must pretend to act as science review boards and examine those legislative judgments. . . .

The state interest in potential human life is . . . extant throughout pregnancy. In *Roe* the Court held that . . . that interest could not become compelling until the point at which the fetus was viable. The difficulty with this analysis is clear: *potential* life is no less potential in the first weeks of pregnancy than it is at viability or afterward. At any stage in pregnancy, there is the *potential* for human life. . . . Accordingly, I believe that the State's interest in protecting potential human life exists throughout pregnancy. . . .

The "undue burden" required in the abortion cases represents the required threshold inquiry that must be conducted before this Court can require a State to justify its legislative actions under the exacting "compelling state interest" standard. . . .

The abortion cases demonstrate that an "undue burden" has been found for the most part in situations involving absolute obstacles or severe limitations on the abortion decision. . . .

In determining whether the State imposes an "undue burden," we must keep in mind that when we are concerned with extremely sensitive issues, such as the one involved here, "the appropriate forum for their resolution in a democracy is the legislature. We should not forget that 'legislatures are ultimate guardians of the liberties and welfare of the people in quite as great a degree as the courts.' "

Source: 462 U.S. Reports 454–466 (1983).

DOCUMENT 84: *Webster v. Reproductive Health Services* (1989). Excerpts from the Concurring Opinion of Justice Antonin Scalia

---

[The decision in this case was five to four to uphold the Missouri law.]

The outcome of today's case will doubtless be heralded as a triumph of judicial statesmanship. It is not that, unless it is statesmanlike needlessly to prolong this Court's self-awarded sovereignty over a field where it has little proper business since the answers to most of the cruel questions posed are political and not juridical—a sovereignty which therefore quite properly, but to the great damage of the Court, makes it the object of the sort of organized public pressure that political institutions in a democracy ought to receive.

Justice O'CONNOR's assertion that a " 'fundamental rule of judicial restraint' " requires us to avoid reconsidering *Roe* cannot be taken seriously. . . .

The real question, then, is whether there are valid reasons to go beyond the most stingy possible holding today. . . . Ordinarily, speaking no more broadly than is absolutely required avoids throwing settled law into confusion; doing so today preserves a chaos that is evident to anyone who can read and count. Alone sufficient to justify a broad holding is the fact that our retaining control, through *Roe*, of what I believe to be, and many of our citizens recognize to be, a political issue, continuously distorts the public perception of the role of this Court. We can now look forward to at least another Term with carts full of mail from the public, and streets full of demonstrators, urging us—their unelected and life-tenured judges who have been awarded those extraordinary, undemocratic characteristics precisely in order that we might follow the law despite the popular will—to follow the popular will. . . .

It thus appears that the mansion of constitutionalized abortion law, constructed overnight in *Roe v. Wade*, must be disassembled door-jamb by door-jamb, and never entirely brought down, no matter how wrong it may be.

Source: 109 *Supreme Court Reporter* 3064–67 (1989).

DOCUMENT 85: *Planned Parenthood of Southeastern Pennsylvania v. Casey* (1992). Joint Concurring Opinion by Justices David H. Souter, Sandra D. O'Connor, and Anthony M. Kennedy

[In this decision the Court split into different groups. Four justices wanted to overrule *Roe v. Wade*. Three justices voted to uphold the Pennsylvania law, but did not believe that it was necessary to abandon *Roe*. Two justices dissented. Justice Stevens found parts of the law unconstitutional; Justice Blackmun would have invalidated the entire statute.

The excerpt here is from the Souter, O'Connor, Kennedy opinion that reworks but does not abandon *Roe v. Wade*.]

At issue in these cases are five provisions of the Pennsylvania Abortion Control Act of 1982 as amended in 1988 and 1989. The Act requires that a woman seeking an abortion give her informed consent prior to the abortion procedure, and specifies that she be provided with certain information at least 24 hours before the abortion is performed. For a minor to obtain an abortion, the Act requires the informed consent of one of her parents, but provides for a judicial bypass option if the minor does not wish or cannot obtain a parent's consent. Another provision of the Act requires that, unless certain exceptions apply, a married woman seeking an abortion must sign a statement indicating that she has notified her husband of her intended abortion. The Act exempts compliance with these three requirements in the event of a 'medical emergency,' which is defined in Section 3203 of the Act. In addition to the above provisions regulating the performance of abortions, the Act imposes certain reporting requirements on facilities that provide abortion services. . . .

After considering the fundamental constitutional questions resolved by Roe, principles of institutional integrity, and the rule of stare decisis, we are led to conclude this: the essential holding of Roe v. Wade should be retained and once again reaffirmed.

It must be stated at the outset and with clarity that Roe's essential holding, the holding we reaffirm, has three parts. First is a recognition of the right of the woman to choose to have an abortion before viability and to obtain it without undue interference from the State. Before viability, the state's interests are not strong enough to support a prohibition of abortion or the imposition of a substantial obstacle to the woman's effective right to elect the procedure. Second is a confirmation of the state's power to restrict abortions after fetal viability, if the law contains exceptions for pregnancies which endanger a woman's life or health. And third is the principle that the state has legitimate interests from the outset of the pregnancy in protecting the health of the woman and the life of the fetus that may become a child. These principles do not contradict one another; and we adhere to each. . . .

Men and women of good conscience can disagree, and we suppose some always shall disagree, about the profound moral and spiritual implications of terminating a pregnancy, even in its earliest stage. Some of us as individuals find abortion offensive to our most basic principles of morality, but that cannot control our decision. Our obligation is to define the liberty of all, not to mandate our own moral code. The underlying constitutional issue is whether the state can resolve these philosophic questions in such a definitive way that a woman lacks all choice in the matter, except perhaps in those rare circumstances in which the pregnancy is itself a danger to her own life or health, or is the result of rape or incest. . . .

Our cases recognize 'the right of the individual, married or single, to be free from unwarranted governmental intrusion into matters so fundamentally affecting a person as the decision whether to bear or beget a child.' Our precedents 'have respected the private realm of family life which the state cannot enter.' These matters, involving the most intimate and personal choices a person may make in a lifetime, choices central to personal dignity and autonomy, are central to the liberty protected by the Fourteenth Amendment. At the heart of liberty is the right to define one's own concept of existence, of meaning, of the universe, and of the mystery of human life. Beliefs about these matters could not define the attributes of personhood were they formed under compulsion of the State. . . .

Although Roe has engendered opposition, it has in no sense proven 'unworkable,' representing as it does a simple limitation beyond which a state law is unenforceable. . . .

We have seen how time has overtaken some of Roe's factual assumptions: advances in maternal health care allow for abortions safe to the mother later in pregnancy than was true in 1973, and advances in neonatal care have advanced viability to a point somewhat earlier. But these facts go only to the scheme of time limits on the realization of competing interests, and the divergences from the factual premises of 1973 have no bearing on the validity of Roe's central holding, that viability marks the earliest point at which the state's interest in fetal life is constitutionally adequate to justify a legislative ban on nontherapeutic abortions. . . .

An entire generation has come of age free to assume Roe's concept of liberty in defining the capacity of women to act in society and to make reproductive decisions. . . .

The Court must take care to speak and act in ways that allow people to accept its decisions on the terms the Court claims for them, as grounded truly in principle, not as compromises with social and political pressures having, as such, no bearing on the principled choices that the Court is obliged to make. Thus the Court's legitimacy depends on making legally principled decisions under circumstances in which their principled character is sufficiently plausible to be accepted by the Nation. . . .

So to overrule under fire in the absence of the most compelling reason to reexamine a watershed decision would subvert the Court's legitimacy beyond any serious question. . . .

We conclude that the basic decision in Roe was based on a constitutional analysis which we cannot now repudiate. The woman's liberty is not so unlimited, however, that from the outset the State cannot show its concern for the life of the unborn, and at a later point in fetal development the state's interest in life has sufficient force so that the right of the woman to terminate the pregnancy can be restricted.

Source: 112 *Supreme Court Reporter* 2791 (1992).

Freedom of speech and the abortion controversy

In May 1991, in a case entitled *Rust v. Sullivan* (the "gag rule case"), the Supreme Court upheld administrative rules issued by the Department of Health and Human Services that prohibited health workers in clinics subsidized by government funds from giving patients information about abortion. About 4,000 clinics receive federal funding under the Public Health Service Act of 1970, and millions of poor women go to these clinics for health care and family planning information.

The Supreme Court voted five to four to uphold. It had to decide two questions. The first was whether the withholding of information about abortion was authorized by the Public Health Service Act. The second was whether the First Amendment was violated—whether the rules abridged freedom of speech.

Congress had passed the Public Health Service Act in order to encourage family planning. The clinics give advice on contraception to their clients. The act specifically forbids the expenditure of funds for abortion; but does this mean that doctors and nurses cannot *tell* their patients about abortion, cannot even *mention* that abortion is an available option if contraception fails?

Critics of the Health Service rules cried "censorship." They contended that the government was restricting freedom of speech. They also claimed that the regulations violated a woman's right to choose an abortion.

The Supreme Court rejected these contentions. Chief Justice Rehnquist wrote the Court's opinion. The central idea in his opinion was that when government pays for a program, it can make rules governing the program. There is an old adage, "He who pays the piper calls the tune," that seems to represent the chief justice's position.

Justice Rehnquist agreed that under *Roe v. Wade* there was a constitutionally protected right to choose an abortion. But that did not mean, the chief justice wrote, that the government had to subsidize the right.

Justice Blackmun's dissenting opinion disagreed with the chief justice's argument. He did not think that government could make suppression of free speech a condition for getting federal funds. He also thought government was using its muscle to keep women from making a decision that the constitution protected, namely, the decision to choose an abortion.

Justice Stevens also dissented. His argument was that the Public Health Service Act did not authorize the government to forbid abortion counseling, but only said that it could not pay for abortion services.

DOCUMENT 86: *Rust v. Sullivan* (1991)

Chief Justice REHNQUIST delivered the opinion of the Court.
The challenged regulations implement the statutory prohibition by

prohibiting counseling, referral, and the provision of information regarding abortion as a method of family planning. They are designed to ensure that the limits of the federal program are observed. The Title X program is designed not for prenatal care, but to encourage family planning. A doctor who wished to offer prenatal care to a project patient who became pregnant could properly be prohibited from doing so because such service is outside the scope of the federally funded program. The regulations prohibiting abortion counseling and referral are of the same ilk; "no funds appropriated for the project may be used in programs where abortion is a method of family planning," and a doctor employed by the project may be prohibited in the course of his project duties from counseling abortion or referring for abortion. This is not a case of the Government "suppressing a dangerous idea," but of a prohibition on a project grantee or its employees from engaging in activities outside of its scope.

To hold that the Government unconstitutionally discriminates on the basis of viewpoint when it chooses to fund a program dedicated to advance certain permissible goals, because the program in advancing those goals necessarily discourages alternate goals, would render numerous government programs constitutionally suspect. When Congress established a National Endowment for Democracy to encourage other countries to adopt democratic principles, it was not constitutionally required to fund a program to encourage competing lines of political philosophy such as Communism and Fascism. Petitioners' assertions ultimately boil down to the position that if the government chooses to subsidize one protected right, it must subsidize analogous counterpart rights. But the Court has soundly rejected that proposition. Within far broader limits than petitioners are willing to concede, when the government appropriates public funds to establish a program it is entitled to define the limits of that program. . . .

Justice BLACKMUN, dissenting.

Until today, the Court never has upheld viewpoint-based suppression of speech simply because that suppression was a condition upon the acceptance of public funds. Whatever may be the Government's power to condition the receipt of its largess upon the relinquishment of constitutional rights, it surely does not extend to a condition that suppresses the recipient's cherished freedom of speech based solely upon the content or viewpoint of that speech. . . .

. . . "[A]bove all else, the First Amendment means that government has no power to restrict expression because of its message, its ideas, its subject matter, or its content."

Justice STEVENS, dissenting.

In my opinion, the Court has not paid sufficient attention to the language of the controlling statute or to the consistent interpretation accorded the statute by the responsible cabinet officers during four different Presidencies and 18 years.

The relevant text of the "Family Planning Services and Population Research Act of 1970" has remained unchanged since its enactment. 84 Stat. 1504. The preamble to the Act states that it was passed:

> "To promote public health and welfare by expanding, improving, and better coordinating the family planning services and population research activities of the Federal Government, and for other purposes." *Ibid.*

The declaration of congressional purposes emphasizes the importance of educating the public about family planning services. Thus, § 2 of the Act states, in part, that the purpose of the Act is:

> "(1) to assist in making comprehensive voluntary family planning services readily available to all persons desiring such services;
>
> . . .
>
> "(5) to develop and make readily available information (including educational materials) on family planning and population growth to all persons desiring such information." 42 U.S.C. § 300 (Congressional Declaration of Purpose).

In contrast to the statutory emphasis on making relevant information readily available to the public, the statute contains no suggestion that Congress intended to authorize the suppression or censorship of any information by any Government employee or by any grant recipient.

Source: 111 *Supreme Court Reporter* 1759 (1991).

State Legislation During the 1980s

With a Republican right-to-life president in the White House and new judicial appointments to the Supreme Court, state legislatures in those states that had pro-life majorities began to pass new laws restricting abortions. They hoped that, in the new political climate, some of these state laws would be upheld.

The kinds of state laws passed fell into several categories:

1. *Bans.* Laws that prohibit virtually all abortions.
2. *Counseling bans.* Laws preventing health care providers from suggesting abortion or referring patients to abortion providers.
3. *Husband notification.* Laws requiring a woman to notify her husband or get his consent to an abortion.
4. *Parental notification.* Laws requiring minors to notify one or both parents, or to get the consent of their parents.
5. *Informed consent.* Laws requiring women to receive abortion counseling.
6. *Waiting periods.* Twenty-four-hour waiting periods before having an abortion.
7. *Public facilities, employees.* No public facilities or public employees to be involved in abortions.
8. *Public funding.* No public funds to be used for abortions. Medicaid funds not to be used unless a woman's life was in danger.

State legislatures passing these laws did not expect the courts to uphold them all, but hoped that some provisions would be upheld. After 1986 the Supreme Court was more sympathetic to restrictive abortion laws.

Pictorial representations of the spread of state restrictions on abortion appeared in a number of newspapers and magazines in the summer of 1992.

The newspaper of the National Organization for Women, the *National NOW Times*, printed an article that expressed the views of many women that these restrictive state laws are not simply reasonable restrictions that do not "unduly burden" the right to abortion. The author calls them "Back Alley Laws" with dangerous and harmful restrictions that are intended to lead to a complete ban on abortion.

DOCUMENT 87: A Look at State Abortion Laws

Bans
Laws that prohibit virtually all abortions. Most date from before *Roe.*

Counseling Bans
Laws that prevent certain health-care providers from giving advice or referrals regarding abortion.

Notification of Husband
A requirement that a woman must gain consent from or notify her husband.

Notification of Parent
Laws that require minors seeking abortions to notify one or both parents or obtain consent.

Informed Consent/Delay
Laws that require women be counseled and/or given state-prepared materials. Often they must wait up to 24 hours or more before proceeding.

Public Facilities/Employees
States that prohibit the use of public facilities for abortion, or that prohibit public employees from participating in an abortion.

Public Funds
States that will not provide Medicaid funding for abortions unless the woman's life is in danger.

Alabama ✖ ● ■ $	Michigan ✖ ● $
Alaska ■	Minnesota ●
Arizona ✖ ◆ $	Mississippi ✖ ■ $
Arkansas ✖ ● $	Missouri ○ ● ■ ◆ $
California ✖	Montana ▲ ■ $
Colorado ✖ ▲ $	Nebraska ● ■ $
Connecticut	Nevada ■ $
Delaware ✖ ■ $	New Hampshire ✖ $
D.C. ✖ $	New Jersey
Florida ▲ ■ $	New Mexico ✖ $
Georgia ● $	New York
Hawaii	N. Carolina
Idaho ■	N. Dakota ○ ▲ ● ■ ◆ $
Illinois ▲ $	Ohio ● ■ $
Indiana ● ■ $	Oklahoma ✖ $
Iowa	Oregon
Kansas ✖ ● ■ $	Pennsylvania ▲ ■ ◆
Kentucky ▲ ■ ◆ $	Rhode Island ▲ ● ■ $
Louisiana ✖ ○ ● ■ ◆ $	S. Carolina ▲ ● $
Maine ■ $	S. Dakota ■ $
Maryland ✖ ■	Tennessee ■ $
Massachusetts ✖ ● ■	

Texas ✖ $

Utah ✖ ▲ ● ■ $

Vermont ✖

Virginia ■

Washington

W. Virginia ✖ ●

Wisconsin ✖ ■

Wyoming ●

Source: NARAL.

DOCUMENT 88: A Pro-Choice View of Abortion Laws. *National NOW Times*, 1991

Following the Supreme Court decision in *Webster v. Reproductive Health Services*, state lawmakers have been crafting legislation designed to restrict women's access to abortion. In some states, anti-abortion legislators have proposed a complete ban on abortion, using language that clearly states that abortion is illegal, even in the cases of rape, incest or when the life or health of the woman is in danger.

The extreme language used in bills proposing an outright ban on abortion often makes lawmakers wary. In states where such overtures to ban abortion have gained little support from other representatives, anti-abortion lawmakers have softened their approach. They have also crafted legislation to restrict clinics, and laws to make medical records non-confidential. Introduced as "protection" measures, these bills are more acceptable to some legislators—even pro-choice lawmakers—than a complete ban on abortion.

In order to effectively stop such legislation, we must understand these ambiguous terms used by abortion opponents and refer to these bills as Back Alley Abortion Laws—dangerous and harmful restrictions on women's access to abortion, used as stepping stones to a complete ban on abortion.

Abortion opponents have concentrated heavily on restricting young women's right to abortion by mandating parental involvement. **Teen Endangerment** is one term abortion rights supporters have used to decode so-called "parental consent" laws, which require one or both parents to give written permission before their daughter can obtain an abortion. In cases where the young woman cannot obtain her parents' consent, she must apply for a judicial bypass, an overwhelming obstacle for a girl who is unable to negotiate the legal maze that confronts her at the courthouse.

Parental notification laws require that one or both parents be notified before their daughter can obtain an abortion. Although notification laws technically do not permit parents to veto their daughter's decision, some states either require that one parent sign a form or impose a waiting period between the notification and abortion. While consent and notification requirements differ, the results are the same—young women's access to abortion is delayed or obstructed because of government attempts to legislate family communication.

Informed consent laws, or more accurately termed **Anti-Abortion Counseling**, require physicians to subject every woman seeking an abortion to explicitly anti-abortion material that professionals know to be misleading or contrary to medical knowledge. As with any medical procedure, physicians have a professional, legal and ethical obligation to supply their patients with all relevant medical information, including risks involved and options available. There is no evidence to suggest that physicians are not complying with this obligation in the case of abortions. These **Back Alley Laws** leave the door open for the use of shocking and deceptive literature and films to deter a woman from making an objective choice.

Waiting period[s], which is an innocuous term for **Mandatory Delays**, are being proposed by anti-abortion legislators. This means the woman receives "counseling" on one day and must return after the waiting period for the actual procedure. For a rural woman who must travel to the city, such a delay may make a real choice impossible.

Spousal consent or more appropriately, **Husbands' Consent** laws forbid an adult woman from having an abortion unless she first notifies or obtains the consent of her husband or male partner. The Supreme Court ruled in 1976 that it is unconstitutional to force a woman to secure her husband's approval before having an abortion, but some states are still attempting to pass these laws.

Statistical reporting laws, or more appropriately termed **Breach of Confidentiality,** laws make confidential medical records, including the patient's name, length of pregnancy, reason for obtaining abortion, race and age of woman, name of doctor performing abortion, and how much it will cost, available to the public. Anti-abortion politicians have proposed these laws with the excuse that accurate statistics about abortion are necessary to ensure that clinics are operating safely and legally. However, clinics have always kept this vital information about individual patients confidential, and released summary data to the Department of Health. Removing the confidential status is just another way to terrorize and intimidate women who get abortions, and the doctors who perform them, making them potential targets for harassment.

Clinic regulation laws attempt to regulate abortion facilities to a greater extent than other medical facilities in which procedures of comparable risk are performed. Because abortion is a surgical procedure, anti-abortion legislators attempt to run private clinics out of business by mandating unnecessary and excessive equipment and procedural requirements. Some proposed laws would require that a clinic have facilities more on the scale of a hospital.

Restrictions on the use of public facilities for abortions are an attempt to ban the performance of abortion at hospitals which receive any public funding, even when the woman would pay for the full cost of the procedure and no public funds would be used. In areas where a public hospital is the only abortion provider, these laws have a devastating effect, forcing women to travel to other areas—even other states—to receive care. This is costly, if not impossible, for many women.

These laws, supposedly designed to protect women, are actually burdensome and redundant. They intimidate women and attempt to obstruct their access to reproductive health care. By defining these restrictions in such ambiguous terms, anti-abortion state lawmakers have found a way to chip away at abortion rights without appearing to be fundamentalist extremists. We must publicize the real repercussions of these restrictive laws, and stand firm in our belief that access to abortion must be equal.

Source: Kristin Thomson, "Back Alley Laws: Redefining Anti-Abortion Legislation," National Organization for Women, The *National NOW Times*, May–June 1991, pp. 9–10.

New Issues and Problems

ABORTION CLINIC VIOLENCE

Frustrated by their failure to outlaw abortion by legal and political means, some pro-life (anti-abortion) organizations turned to physical violence—arson, bombing, harassment of patients and doctors at clinics, and other criminal or marginally legal tactics. Direct action techniques dramatized the opposition to abortion and attracted media attention to the pro-life cause.

In March 1985 a subcommittee of the Committee on the Judiciary of the House of Representatives held hearings on abortion clinic violence. Representative Don Edwards of California, chair of the subcommittee, opened the proceedings by stating that the purpose of the hearings was not to argue the pros and cons of abortion but to investigate reports about threats, the disruption of activities at abortion clinics, intimidation of patients and staff, as well as instances of bombing, arson, and kidnapping. Representatives of the Federal Bureau of Investigation and the Bureau of Alcohol, Tobacco and Firearms were called before the subcommittee to explain what action the federal government was taking to stop illegal behavior.

Excerpts from testimony before the subcommittee illustrate the range of problems of concern to members of Congress. One of the interesting questions raised by the hearings was whether anti-abortion activities were protected by the First Amendment, since they were expressions of opinion on public issues. Organized civil disobedience to the law has frequently been a tactic of people who believe their access to other means of change is blocked. One of the members of the subcommittee compared anti-abortion protests to the civil rights protests of the 1960s. The testimony also raised a philosophical question: When individuals believe that a law is wrong, immoral, and unjust, do they have the right to break that law? Is there a higher law that demands obedience when human law appears to be immoral?

Witnesses before the committee included people who had complaints about harassment and fraudulent behavior. Anti-abortion activists were also represented. Joseph M. Scheidler, executive director of the Pro-Life Action League, appeared to defend the use of disruptive tactics. Other pro-life groups besides Scheidler's indulge in similar activities. The best known is probably Randall Terry's Operation Rescue, which received nationwide publicity when it blocked access to an abortion clinic in Atlanta, Georgia, during the Democratic Party's national convention in the summer of 1988.

DOCUMENT 89: Abortion Clinic Violence. Hearings Before a Subcommittee of the House of Representatives, 1985 and 1986

Mr. Edwards [Representative Don Edwards of California, Democrat, Chairman of the subcommittee]. We have received reports about clinic entrances being blocked, clinics being invaded to disrupt activities, telephone threats, property damage and so on. We strongly condemn all forms of violence that infringe the exercise of constitutional rights. The purpose of these hearings is to explore the scope and impact of this problem. We also want to ask whether the Federal Government, and particularly the Department of Justice, should be involved in investigating such violence under the civil rights laws. . . .

To date the role of the Federal Government in prosecuting clinic violence has been limited or nonexistent. The Justice Department has available to it a statute making it a Federal crime to interfere with the exercise of a constitutional right. Reproductive freedoms are constitutionally protected, yet the Justice Department has not intervened here. . . .

[Is this disruptive behavior a form of civil disobedience? Freedom of speech?]

Mr. Sensenbrenner [James Sensenbrenner, Jr., Representative from Wisconsin, Republican]. What is, really, the difference between somebody expressing their opposition to abortion in front of an abortion clinic with a garbage can full of baby bottles and one expressing their support for the equal rights amendment in the Illinois State Capitol by pouring pig's blood on the floor?

Both of those are legitimate expressions of political issues, and yet, we hear condemnations of the other type of activity. . . .

I went to school at the University of Wisconsin during the war in Vietnam, and those who were legitimately opposed to the war picketed various activities at the university with signs stating that they did so out of a moral opposition, which was their right, to the war in Vietnam. At the same time we see many of the pro-Life pickets using some of the same words of the antiwar movement of 15 and 20 years ago, and I see a similarity. . . .

Mrs. Schroeder [Patricia Schroeder, Representative from Colorado, Democrat]. Thank you very much, Mr. Chairman. And thanks to the witnesses. Because I think what we've clearly seen here is laying out of the facts and showing that this has gone beyond mere speech.

Freedom of speech is one thing, but freedom of speech does not allow breaking and entering, invasion of privacy, bomb threats, and vandalism and every other thing. That's way beyond freedom of speech. And I think you've laid that out very, very clearly. . . .

Mr. DeWine [Michael DeWine, Representative from Ohio, Republican]. I would just make one final comment, that I find this situation very similar to the 1960's, early 1960's, the civil rights movement. I find it more similar to the civil rights movement than, maybe, to the Vietnam experience. I think maybe the same issues that we were dealing with at the time we're dealing with now. And I, personally, have observed a lot of it myself, as I'm sure everybody in the room has. . . .

[Does a higher moral law justify the breaking of laws for a good purpose?

One of the organizations sponsoring direct action to deter abortions is the Pro-Life Action League of Chicago, Illinois. Its executive director, Joseph M. Scheidler, testified before the subcommittee on March 6, 1985. Mr. Scheidler is the author of a booklet entitled "Closed: 99 Ways to Stop Abortion," which sets out a number of strategies for disrupting the activities of abortion clinics.

In the following selection two Democrats, John Conyers, Representative from Michigan, and Patricia Schroeder, Representative from Colorado, question Mr. Scheidler.]

Mr. Conyers. But what we are here today about is to discuss the violations of law, criminal violations of laws that are not being prosecuted. And it seems to me that you have advocated that there are some violations of the law that you would support, apparently based on your notion of a higher law. And that is why we are here, I think, to try to draw the line a little bit more carefully on.

Mr. Scheidler. I understand that.

Mr. Conyers. How we protect the first amendment, which I happen to be a great supporter of, but how we give everybody the right to be free from assault, intimidation, threats, harassment and violence.

Mr. Scheidler. I don't believe in any of those things: assault, intimidation, threats, harassment, or violence. . . .

Mrs. Schroeder. Thank you for being here, sir. I have some questions. My understanding is, and maybe it's wrong, but that you have advocated followers to go into clinics, posing as patients, and then begin shouting slogans, linking arms to block off labs and procedure rooms. Now, do you think that is legal?

Mr. Scheidler. That is some kind of a mutation. We do go into the clinics. We do pose as patients and we talk to the patients inside the clinic. If we have a sit-in we will go into the clinic, obviously for a sit-in. We don't mix the two.

Mrs. Schroeder. You don't see that as conspiracy or trespass?

Mr. Scheidler. It's trespass if you think that an abortion clinic is a dentist office. But they are killing people inside that room. We'd like to get that point across. When we go in to save a human life—and I have a letter from Becky's mother—

Mrs. Schroeder. Now wait just a second. Let me ask the question. The Human Life Amendment has not passed. My understanding is we're operating under a constitutional decision that says—

Mr. Scheidler. Well, let's get a human life amendment, then, out of this committee.

Mrs. Schroeder. Well, I think that it is now legal for people to go into those clinics.

Mr. Scheidler. It's still immoral.

Mrs. Schroeder. That is your decision.

Mr. Scheidler. No, that's God's decision. "Thou shalt not kill" is not my decision.

Mrs. Schroeder. Again, this is a country that Jefferson said was big enough for more than one opinion, sir. I respect your opinion, but I ask you to respect my opinion and—

Mr. Scheidler. Not when it's killing my brothers and sisters.

Mrs. Schroeder. But what I hear you saying is that you are going to define what the law is, then. You nodded your head "yes."

Mr. Scheidler. Yes.

Mrs. Schroeder. Is that correct?

Mr. Scheidler. Yes.

Mrs. Schroeder. Well, the way I read this, the chapter headings here in your book are kind of amazing: "Taking Information from License Plates, Using Private Detectives. Using Threats, Pressure. Graffiti. Get the Dirt on Them. Night Telephone Messages. Use of Inflammatory Rhetoric, How to Rattle Your Opponent. Don't Let the Garbage Men Collect the Garbage. How to Deal with Goon Squads." And I could read all 99.

You don't think that those are illegal because you think your cause is higher than the law?

Mr. Scheidler. We are trying to save human lives, and sometimes to—

Mrs. Schroeder. But do you think your cause, then, is higher than the law?

Mr. Scheidler. Yes.

Source: U.S. Congress, House Committee on the Judiciary, *Oversight Hearings before the Subcommittee on Civil and Constitutional Rights*, 99th Congress, 1st and 2nd sessions, March 6, 12, and April 3, 1985, and December 17, 1986, pp. 1–2, 39–40, 41, 45, 60–65.

HEALTH EFFECTS OF ABORTION ON WOMEN; THE KOOP REPORT, 1989

One of the principal arguments against abortion was that it had serious after-effects on women's health. In 1987 President Reagan, responding to the concerns of pro-life organizations, directed Surgeon General C. Everett Koop to assemble evidence on the physical and psychological impact of abortion on women.

The Department of Health and Human Services set aside $200,000 for the project, and the surgeon general and his staff met with experts and spent a year and a half compiling the report. It was completed in 1989 but not released to the public.

Administration critics claimed that it was not released because it concluded that abortions did not have harmful effects on women, but were, in most cases, less dangerous than childbirth. Surgeon General Koop wrote a letter to the president saying that he was not releasing the report because he was dissatisfied with the quality of the research available on the subject. (The report was never released, but Congress printed it in the *Congressional Record*.)

A committee of Congress held hearings on the medical and psychological impact of abortion in March 1989. The surgeon general was asked to testify before the committee about his report and why it was not released.

DOCUMENT 90: Statement of Surgeon General C. Everett Koop, Public Health Service, Before the Subcommittee on Human Resources and Governmental Relations of the House Committee on Government Operations, March 16, 1989

On July 30, 1987, President Reagan stated that he thought women were not being informed about the health effects of abortion on women, and the President directed the Surgeon General to assemble a body of information on the health effects of abortion on women. . . .

Review of published studies on the psychological sequelae [consequences] of abortion by statisticians at NCHS and CDC indicated that the methodology in virtually all of those studies was seriously flawed. Our studies regarding the psychological outcomes of abortion could not be conclusive for several reasons: One, the lack of consensus regarding the symptoms, the severity, and duration of adverse mental reactions post-abortion; two, the lack of controls for psychologic symptoms or disorders associated with life events experienced before or after the abortion; three, the methodological difficulties related to sampling to form an appropriate study group; four, finding a technique to surmount the fact that as many as half the women who have had abortions are likely to deny it on a questionnaire; and finally, the paucity of long-term followup on post-abortion women.

Because the reports of studies of psychological effects would not permit it, we could not prepare a report that could withstand scientific and statistical scrutiny. It was decided that I would so inform the President with an explanatory letter rather than with a report. . . .

My letter to the President focused on psychological effects of abortion, because obstetricians and gynecologists had long since concluded that the physical sequelae of abortion were no different than those found in women who carried pregnancy to term or who had never been pregnant.

I had nothing further to add to that subject in my letter to the President. I have personally counseled women post-abortion, who have had serious reactions to abortion, so I know that they do exist. I also have known women who claim positive health effects, so I know that they exist.

However, the data from the literature at this time are insufficient, scientifically and statistically, with adequate controls to support the premise that abortion does or does not produce a specific post-abortion syndrome. There has never been a statistically viable prospective study on a cohort of women of childbearing age that would yield information on the effects of abortion on women.

To do such a study which would be credible to both sides of the abortion argument would consume a great deal of time and would be very expensive.

You asked for comments, Mr. Chairman, on a prevention strategy. Simply put, the only way to prevent adverse health effects of abortion is to prevent the abortions themselves. Most abortions would not take place if pregnancies were not unplanned and unwanted. Therefore, it seems that efforts should be directed toward whatever means would minimize the number of unwanted and unplanned pregnancies.

First of all, young people should be told very explicitly that sexual activity carries with it risks, not only of pregnancy but also of sexually transmitted disease.

Further information would include the understanding of contraception. It is significant that the median age of women having an abortion is about 23.4 years, with a median education of 12.7 years. There is no doubt that they would understand what we are talking about.

Obviously, expansion of research into reproduction and male and female contraception would complement such an endeavor. It would be important to classify methods of birth control that are truly contraceptive and not abortifacient, because a large segment of the population has no compunction about using true contraception, but would be opposed to birth control if the method is abortifacient.

It is worth mentioning, sir, that the first press release by a wire service after my visit to the White House completely misinterpreted my letter to the President. The release implied that there was no evidence of health effects post-abortion, rather than saying there was insufficient scientific and statistical evidence on which to base an unimpeachable report. That erroneous news release was picked up by all three major networks and repeated verbatim.

Source: U.S. Congress, House Committee on Government Operations, Human Resources and Intergovernmental Relations Subcommittee, *Medical and Psychological Impact of Abortion*, 101st Congress, 1st session, 1989, pp. 193–96.

THE IMPORT BAN ON A NEW ABORTIFACIENT DRUG, RU-486

For those anxious to decrease the number of abortions being performed each year, the discovery by a French scientist of a drug that would cause the body to reject a fertilized egg seemed to be an important breakthrough.

RU-486, developed and tested in France in the 1980s, is a synthetic steroid. One of its effects is to block the hormones that allow a fertilized egg to develop in the lining of the uterus. Thus, it has an "abortifacient" (abortion causing) or "contragestational" (preventing development of the fetus) effect.

The new drug had a wide variety of other possible uses. Medical researchers wanted it allowed into the United States for use in treating a variety of medical conditions and for use in research on cancer, AIDS, and other diseases. The Food and Drug Administration (FDA), an agency of the United States government, prevented its importation, citing a policy allowing it to block the importation of unapproved drugs.

Many people believed that the FDA acted because of pressures from anti-abortion groups, to which the Republican administration was sensitive.

A subcommittee of Congress decided to investigate these charges. Congressman Ron Wyden, Democrat from Oregon, brought together doctors, researchers, and government officials to try to get to the bottom of the holdup on licensing the drug for distribution in the United States. Feminist groups mounted a political campaign to get the drug approved for use in this country.

The election of President Clinton in 1992 was expected to change government policy on importation of the drug.

DOCUMENT 91: Hearings Before a Subcommittee of the House of Representatives on the Import Ban of RU-486, 1990

Chairman WYDEN: Few recent drugs have generated as much interest as RU 486. The drug is considered a success in France as an alternative to surgical abortion. Many scientists now believe that the drug can successfully treat debilitating and life-threatening illnesses such as breast cancer, brain cancer, diabetes, and Cushing's Syndrome. According to published reports, both western industrialized nations and the Third World are now testing RU 486 in various trials and, in some cases, to distribute the drug.

But the response of United States health authorities to RU 486 has been markedly different and resistant. The FDA has banned the importation of the drug for personal use on the grounds that RU 486 is a health hazard threatening the safety of the user.

What proof does the agency have to back up its conclusions about RU 486? To answer this question, subcommittee staff spent almost a year investigating the FDA's documentary evidence. FDA files—the legal foundation for the import ban—are notable for what they contain and for what they lack.

The subcommittee asked, for example, if the FDA believed there was an active black market in this drug—a good reason for imposing a ban. But apparently there is nothing in the file which remotely justifies this concern. In fact, RU 486 is sold by prescription only, and then administered only in a tightly controlled, precertified clinical environment. This is simply not like buying a bottle of aspirin. . . .

The subcommittee asked if the FDA had done any research regarding the drug's safety. There is nothing in the file. But in France, where more than 65,000 women have taken the drug during the last few years, the RU 486 safety record is very strong. Let me summarize.

According to the FDA files there are: One, no records of injuries due to the drug; two, no records of a black market, foreign or domestic; and three, no record that there has been any attempt to import the drug into the United States. Nevertheless, the FDA has concluded that this drug is a health hazard. Why or how, we don't know.

Let us turn to what is in the FDA file. For the most part, it is filled with letters and correspondence from antiabortion activists and their allies in Congress. These communications are remarkable both for their character and their timing. It would seem when certain folks pressed FDA's button, the FDA was only too happy to respond quickly. For example, only 19 days elapse between one particular high-level, congressional demand on FDA to stop personal importation of the drug and the RU 486 import ban. This certainly has to be a new land-speed record for an agency response to congressional inquiries.

But the reality is we are losing the chance to do cutting-edge medical research because the company that makes RU 486 is boycotting the United States for two reasons: The arbitrary, political, and unscientific RU 486 policies of the FDA, and the protests that have been promised from antiabortion groups. The fact is the drug's manufacturer has made a business decision to use its supplies only in countries where government regulators will give them a fair shake. . . .

As a result of FDA's RU 486 policies, antiabortion politics, and the manufacturer's business decisions, Americans now suffering from horrible illnesses will not have the hope of cures they had before the import ban was imposed.

Americans with breast cancer and other dread diseases have become the innocent victims of this administration's political brinkmanship with the pro-choice movement on abortion, and there will be needless suffering.

Nonabortion research with RU 486 will be done outside the United States where the manufacturer, their licensees, and affiliated scientists have their work evaluated for its scientific merit, not its ability to meet a political litmus test.

Until the United States Government signals the world that RU 486 will be treated like any other drug, many of our citizens will have to wait to secure the multiple benefits scientists will describe today.

Source: U.S. Congress, House Committee on Small Business, Subcommittee on Regulation, Business Opportunities and Energy, Hearings, 101st Congress, 2nd session, 1990, pp. 1–3.

PUBLIC OPINION IN THE 1990s

By the 1990s public opinion about abortion appeared to have stabilized, with a majority in favor of keeping abortion legal, but not in favor of allowing abortion under all circumstances. The public seemed generally content with the compromise that had been offered in *Roe v. Wade*; only 36 percent of respondents in one Gallup poll favored overturning the ruling (Gallup polls, August and September 1991, *The Gallup Report, 1991*).

Another poll tested identification of the public with the pro-life and pro-choice positions. Fifty-eight percent of the adults polled were in favor of choice. In spite of the Republican pro-life stand, a greater number of Republicans than Democrats said they were pro-choice. Only 17 percent of the people polled were in favor of outlawing abortion altogether (Louis Harris and Associates, 1992, CBS News-New York Times poll, 1992; reprinted in the *National Journal*).

In its limited and conditional support of abortion rights in the *Casey* decision, the Supreme Court seemed, surprisingly, closer to the public than either of the major political parties. While a majority of those polled favored keeping abortion legal, there was strong support for several kinds of restrictive state laws.

DOCUMENT 92: Public Opinion Polls Showing Support for Legal Abortion, 1975–1992

Gallup polls showing changing support for and opposition to legal abortions, 1975–1992

Should abortion be legal under all circumstances, legal only under some circumstances, or illegal in all circumstances?

Date	Always Legal	Certain Circumstances	Always Illegal
Jan 1992	31	53	14
May 1991	32	50	17
1990	31	53	12
1989	29	51	17
1988	24	57	17
1983	23	58	16
1981	23	52	21
1980	25	53	18
1979	22	54	19

Date	Always Legal	Certain Circumstances	Always Illegal
1977	22	55	19
1975	21	54	22

What types of laws restricting abortion are favored by the public?

Type of Restriction	% Favor	% Oppose	% No Opinion
1. A law requiring doctors to inform patients about alternatives to abortion before performing the procedure.	86	12	2
2. A law requiring women seeking abortions to wait 24 hours before having the procedure done.	73	23	4
3. A law requiring that the husband of a married woman be notified if she decides to have an abortion.	73	25	2
4. A law requiring women under 18 to get parental consent for any abortion.	70	27	3

Source: *Gallup Poll Monthly*, January 1992, pp. 6–7.

PART V: FOR FURTHER READING

Blank, Robert H. *Mother and Fetus: Changing Notions of Maternal Responsibility.* Westport, Conn.: Greenwood Press, 1992.

Costa, Marie, ed. *Abortion: A Reference Handbook.* Santa Barbara, Calif.: ABC-Clio, 1991.

Glendon, Mary Ann. *Abortion and Western Law.* Cambridge, Mass.: Harvard University Press, 1987.

Lader, Lawrence. *RU 486: The Pill that Could End the Abortion Wars and Why American Women Don't Have It.* Reading, Mass.: Addison-Wesley, 1991.

Luker, Kristin. *Abortion and the Politics of Motherhood.* Berkeley: University of California Press, 1984.

Paige, Connie. *The Right to Lifers: Who They Are, How They Operate, Where They Get Their Money.* New York: Summit Books, 1983.

Reagan, Ronald. *Abortion and the Conscience of the Nation.* New York: Thomas Nelson, 1984.

Staggenborg, Suzanne. *The Pro-Choice Movement.* New York: Oxford University Press, 1991.

Steiner, Gilbert Y., ed. *The Abortion Dispute and the American System.* Washington, D.C.: Brookings Institution, 1983.

Tietze, Christopher. *Induced Abortion: A World Review*. 5th ed. New York: Population Council, 1983.
Vinovskis, M. A. *An "Epidemic" of Adolescent Pregnancy: Some Historical and Policy Considerations*. New York: Oxford University Press, 1988.

Epilogue: 1993 and After

A NEW PRESIDENT ACTS

William Jefferson Clinton was inaugurated as President of the United States on January 20, 1993. A few days later, on January 22, the eve of the twentieth anniversary of *Roe v. Wade*, he signed executive orders overturning five of the restrictions on abortion established during the Reagan administration.

The first of these eliminated the gag rule, the administrative regulation that banned anyone except doctors from discussing abortions at clinics receiving federal funding. The gag rule had made it illegal for nurses and other personnel in family planning clinics to let patients know that abortion was an alternative option to childbirth. The Supreme Court had held in *Rust v. Sullivan* (Document 86) that these restrictions were constitutional and did not limit freedom of speech. In 1992 Congress passed a law overturning the regulation, but President Bush vetoed the legislation.

A second Clinton order lifted restrictions on the use of fetal tissue in medical research—again, where the research received federal funds. This ban had also been imposed by President Reagan and was supported by President Bush, who vetoed a 1992 bill that would have lifted the prohibition. President Clinton said that the ban had "significantly hampered the development of possible treatments for individuals afflicted with serious diseases and disorders, such as Parkinson's disease, Alzheimer's disease, diabetes and leukemia."

A third order directed the Secretary of Health and Human Services to review prohibitions against the importation of RU-486 (mifepristone), the so-called abortion drug (see Document 91). Women's organizations had been pressing the government to allow the drug to be marketed in the United States, since it would provide an alternative to surgical abortions. The drug induces abortions during the early stages of pregnancy. Importation had been forbidden by the Food and Drug Administration as part of an anti-abortion policy promoted by the Reagan and Bush administrations. Clinton's order urged the lifting of the ban unless there were clear medical reasons not to do so.

A ban on abortions in overseas military hospitals was also ordered cancelled. President Bush had blocked a 1992 attempt by Congress to eliminate the ban. President Clinton's order would allow such hospitals to perform abortions, as long as they were paid for from private funds and not by the government.

The final executive order replaced a Reagan-Bush administration policy that barred U.S. aid to international family planning programs that included abortion counseling. President Clinton believed that United States support of international programs designed to control rapid population growth was in the national interest.

All five of these actions fulfilled promises the president had made during the 1992 election campaign; the new administration pledged that it would follow a pro-choice policy. Clinton announced that his intention was to promote policies that kept abortion safe, but decreased the need for it.

AN ASSASSINATION IN FLORIDA

Changes in administration policy did not mean that the forces opposing abortion would capitulate without a fight. On January 23, the twentieth anniversary of the Supreme Court's decision in *Roe v. Wade*, the annual anti-abortion protest took place in Washington, D.C., with over 75,000 marchers demonstrating that the pro-life movement intended to continue its campaign to outlaw abortion. On March 10, in Pensacola, Florida, there was an even more dramatic illustration of the passion and intensity generated by the anti-abortion cause. A Florida doctor who performed abortions at a local clinic was shot and killed during an anti-abortion protest by a group called Rescue America. The shock over the doctor's assassination brought demands for action by law enforcement authorities. Up until this time, protests had merely probed the edges of violence (see Document 89). Although clinics had been bombed and set on fire and abortion providers threatened with death, until now no one had been killed.

THE SUPREME COURT LIMITS FEDERAL ENFORCEMENT AUTHORITY

Action to protect abortion providers and restrain anti-abortion protesters is largely in the hands of state and local police. But an old civil rights law, dating from the Reconstruction Era, had been used in a number of cases to stop the blockading of abortion clinics. The law, passed in 1871, was originally intended for use against the Ku Klux Klan. Under this statute abortion rights organizations could go to federal courts to apply for court orders to stop trespassing on clinic grounds, the impeding of access to the medical facilities, or interference with the provision of abortion services. In 1992 the Supreme Court had been asked for a definitive interpretation of this old law; anti-abortionists claimed that it was improper to use it in abortion-related situations. On January 13, 1993, the Supreme Court agreed (*Bray v. Alexandria Women's Health Clinic*). By a vote of five to four the Court held that the 1871 law could not be used to protect citizens against lawless activities related to abortion.

A new clinic blockade case, scheduled for decision in 1994, may bring another federal statute to bear on the activities of anti-abortion protesters. The Racketeer Influenced and Corrupt Organizations Act (RICO), originally aimed at organized crime, has been invoked in lawsuits accusing Operation Rescue and other anti-abortion groups of unlawful activities. The Supreme Court will decide whether this statute can be used in abortion-related cases.

LEGISLATION IN CONGRESS

Both the Supreme Court's decision in *Bray v. Alexandria Women's Health Clinic* and the killing of the doctor in Pensacola led lawmakers in Washington to believe that it was time to introduce new legislation tailored to fit contemporary problems. Attorney General Janet Reno has stated that she and the Department of Justice will promote legislation making it a federal felony to obstruct access to an abortion clinic. A bill has already been introduced in Congress by Representatives Charles Schumer (D, N.Y.) and Constance Morella (R, Md.) making it a federal crime for anyone to physically obstruct, impede, or hinder access to a clinic. A similar bill has been introduced in the Senate. By April, 1993, Justice Department aides were consulting with members of Congress to broaden the bill to bar any interference with or threats to doctors or other medical personnel. The bill, called the Freedom of Access to Clinic Entrances

Act, was expected to get serious consideration by Congress during 1993. Anti-abortion advocates believed that such a bill would be unconstitutional and would interfere with legitimate protests and demonstrations.

Congress was already considering other legislation dealing with the abortion dispute. A Freedom of Choice Act has been before Congress since 1989, but has not been passed (see Document 79), in part because of a threatened veto. The bill was reintroduced in both houses of Congress in 1993 and was expected to pass eventually, in some form, although abortion opponents hoped to dilute it by adding a number of restrictions on its basic guarantee. Congress was also interested in making President Clinton's order allowing abortion to be discussed at federally funded clinics a permanent part of the law. A Family Planning Act, authorizing an expenditure of $500 million, was expected to make it impossible for a future president to ban abortion counseling by executive order. The Clinton administration also asked Congress to fund family planning programs abroad. With the world's population moving rapidly toward nine or ten billion people, many lawmakers were frightened about the effect of such a population explosion on the United States.

But the refusal, on June 31, 1993, of the House of Representatives to remove the Hyde Amendment (see Document 58) from the federal spending bill, seemed to indicate that abortion rights legislation might not be guaranteed easy or automatic passage in the legislative branch. The House voted 255 to 158 to refuse Medicaid funding for abortions for poor women—unless the pregnancy was the result of rape or incest, or unless the woman's life was in danger. Senate action on the bill has yet to come.

CHANGES IN THE SUPREME COURT

On March 19, 1993, Justice Byron R. White announced that he would retire at the end of the current term of the Supreme Court. White's retirement gave President Clinton his first opportunity to add a new member to that high tribunal. Predictions had been that he would look for someone who was not overly controversial but was generally supportive of abortion rights. Clinton had stated that he would "try to pick a person who has a fine mind, good judgment, wide experience in the law and in the problems of real people and somebody with a big heart." On a television talk show during the campaign, Clinton outlined the criteria he would use in picking a nominee. "I'd be looking for someone, first of all, who was unquestionably qualified by reason of training, experience, judgment... Then I would look for someone who has an expansive view of the Constitution and the Bill of Rights, someone who believed in the constitutional right to privacy." He also said that he would want people on the Supreme Court who were pro-choice (*Washington Post*, March 20, 1993, p. A1).

In June, after floating the names of a number of candidates in the press, the president nominated Ruth Bader Ginsburg, a judge on the United States Court of Appeals for the District of Columbia, to fill the vacancy. Although she had been a cautious and moderate judge on the Court of Appeals, Judge Ginsburg had a strong record on women's rights issues and was expected, if confirmed by the Senate, to vote with other justices favoring abortion rights.

As the United States moved into the 1990s, abortion was still an enormously controversial subject. The controversy over its morality, its constitutionality, and its place in public policy-making was likely to continue throughout the decade.

APPENDIX A

Major Supreme Court Decisions Related to Abortion, 1973–1993

MAJOR CASES DECIDED IN THE SUPREME COURT OF THE UNITED STATES, 1973–1993, ON STATE AND FEDERAL LAWS REGULATING ABORTION

This list gives the date the case was decided, name of case, citation to the case in *U.S. Supreme Court Reports*, the vote of the justices, a note indicating whether the decision was pro-abortion (PA) or anti-abortion (AA), and a generalization about the holding. A glossary of terms used in state and federal legislation follows the list.

1973. *Roe v. Wade* (410 U.S. 113). Vote 7-2. PA
    A Texas law making abortion a crime was found to be unconstitutional. The Constitution was interpreted to protect a woman's right to choose to have an abortion during the first three months of pregnancy. State regulation of abortion was acceptable, in some circumstances, in the last six months of pregnancy.

1973. *Doe v. Bolton* (410 U.S. 179). Vote 7-2. PA
    This was a companion case to *Roe v. Wade*. A Georgia law requiring that abortions be performed in hospitals, with two doctors present, and be approved by a hospital committee was found to limit the constitutional right too strictly and was held unconstitutional.

1976. *Planned Parenthood of Central Missouri v. Danforth* (428 U.S. 552). Vote 5-4. PA
    The first major case decided since *Roe*. The Court overturned a Missouri law that required a woman to obtain the consent of her parents or husband before an abortion, required a lecture on fetal development, and required record keeping and reporting of all abortions by physicians.

1976. *Bellotti v. Baird* (428 U.S. 132). Vote 5-4. PA
The Court sent a state law requiring parental consent for minors seeking abortions back to the state for clarification.

1977. *Beal v. Doe* (432 U.S. 438). Vote 6-3. AA
The Court held that the Social Security Act (Medicaid) did not require the federal government to fund elective abortions.

1977. *Maher v. Roe* (432 U.S. 464). Vote 6-3. AA
A state can refuse to fund abortions under Medicaid—except where the operation is medically necessary.

1977. *Poelker v. Doe* (432 U.S. 59). Vote 6-3. AA
A city hospital could refuse to perform nontherapeutic abortions at public expense.

1979. *Colautti v. Franklin* (439 U.S. 379). Vote 6-3. PA
A state statute designed to protect viable fetuses was held to be too vague and unclear.

1979. *Bellotti v. Baird* (443 U.S. 622). Vote 8-1. PA
A state statute requiring parental notification and consent for minors wanting abortions did not provide a means for overriding parental refusal when the best interests of the minor were at stake.

1980. *Harris v. McRae* (448 U.S. 297). Vote 5-4. AA
Congress can forbid federal funding of abortions without violating the Constitution. States need not fund abortions unless they are medically necessary.

1981. *H.L. v. Matheson* (450 U.S. 398). Vote 6-3. AA
A state can require that parents of dependent minors be *notified* before abortions are performed.

1983. *City of Akron v. Akron Center for Reproductive Health* (462 U.S. 416). Vote 6-3. PA
A very restrictive city ordinance was held to impose too many conditions on abortion rights. It required parental consent and notification, written consent by the patient, a fetal development lecture, waiting periods, hospitalization, and special procedures for disposing of fetal remains.

1983. *Planned Parenthood of America of Kansas City v. Ashcroft* (462 U.S. 476). Vote 6-3 on part, 5-4 on part. PA/AA
Some provisions of a Missouri law were upheld, others overturned. Upheld were hospitalization for second trimester abortions, pathological reports, the presence of a second doctor, and parental consent or permission of a court for abortions for minors.

1983. *Simopoulous v. Virginia* (462 U.S. 506). Vote 8-1. AA
Hospitalization for second trimester abortions was upheld.

1986. *Thornburgh v. American College of Obstetricians and Gynecologists* (476 U.S. 747). Vote 5-4. PA
A Pennsylvania law was held to be too restrictive. It required informed con-

sent, reporting, protection of viable fetuses, and the presence of a second physician.

1989. *Webster v. Reproductive Health Services* (109 S.Ct. 3040). Vote 5-4. AA

Upheld restrictive provisions of a Missouri law, including viability testing and prohibition of use of public facilities or public funds for abortions.

1990. *Hodgson v. Minnesota* (497 U.S. 417). Vote 5–4. AA

The Supreme Court struck down part of a Minnesota law that required notification of both parents for a minor's abortion. But another section of the law requiring notification of both parents was upheld because it included a judicial bypass provision.

1990. *Ohio v. Akron Center for Reproductive Health* (497 U.S. 502). Vote 6–3. AA

Ohio parental notification requirement for minors was upheld. Judicial bypass procedure was included.

1991. *Rust v. Sullivan* (111 S.Ct. 1759). Vote 5–4. AA

The so-called gag rule was upheld. Department of Health and Human Services rules prohibited recipients of federal funds from counseling women about abortions.

1992. *Planned Parenthood of Southeastern Pennsylvania v. Casey* (112 S.Ct. 2791). Vote 7-2. PA/AA

The Supreme Court did not overrule *Roe v. Wade*, but upheld a number of restrictions on abortion in a Pennsylvania statute. The new test to be used in abortion cases is: Does the state law place an undue burden on the right to choose an abortion?

1993. *Bray v. Alexandria Women's Health Clinic* (113 S.Ct. 753). Vote 5–4. AA

A 122-year-old Reconstruction statute forbidding the deprivation of civil rights by private organizations was held *not* to apply to protesters who block abortion clinics.

TERMS USED IN STATUTES REGULATING ABORTION

criminal penalties. Criminal penalties imposed on physicians who do not abide by regulations imposed on the abortion process.

fetal development lecture. A lecture describing the different stages of fetal development in the womb, often with pictures of the developing fetus.

fetal protection. Regulations designed to protect any viable fetuses that survive an abortion.

gag rule. A rule forbidding counselors to recommend abortions.

hospitalization. Requirement that abortions be performed in hospitals.

informed consent. Requiring written permission from the woman before an abortion can be performed. Some laws also require that the woman be given information, often a lecture on fetal development.

judicial bypass. A procedure that allows a minor to go to court if her parents refuse consent to an abortion.

medical necessity. Abortions (therapeutic) that are medically necessary.

nontherapeutic abortions. Abortions not required for health or psychiatric reasons.

parental consent. Requiring consent of parents.

parental notification. Requiring notification of the parents of minors before an abortion.

reporting and record keeping. Doctors and hospitals required to keep records of abortions.

saline amniocentesis. A commonly used abortion procedure that was prohibited by some state laws.

spousal consent. Requiring consent of husbands.

spousal notification. Requiring notification of husbands.

two physician requirement. Requiring that two doctors be present at an abortion.

unemancipated minor. A minor living with her parents who is not married or has not borne a child.

viability. The point at which a fetus can survive outside the womb.

viability testing. Tests to see whether a fetus is old enough to be viable.

waiting period. A period between a request for an abortion and the performance of an abortion. Often 24 hours.

APPENDIX B
Chronology of Events in the Abortion Controversy

1803 (England) Lord Ellenborough's Act. Part of a comprehensive crime act, this act of Parliament made attempts to induce an abortion, after quickening, a felony.

1821 First state statute addressing the abortion issue. Connecticut enacted a statute forbidding murder by poisoning that included using poisonous substances to induce miscarriage.

1825–41 First wave of state laws criminalizing abortion. Ten states enact criminal statutes punishing persons who perform abortions or administer harmful substances that cause abortions.

1868 The Fourteenth Amendment to the United States Constitution is ratified. This amendment has been the basis for constitutional claims that reproductive choice is protected by rights to liberty and privacy.

1860–80 Second wave of state laws criminalizing abortion. Forty or more states enact anti-abortion laws.

1954 Conference on abortion held in New York by Planned Parenthood and the New York Academy of Medicine.

1959 The American Law Institute, a professional think-tank of lawyers and judges, drafts a Model State Abortion Law proposing reforms that would make legal abortions more available.

1961 An abortion reform law, based on the American Law Institute model, is introduced in the California state legislature.

1963–65 A German measles (Rubella) epidemic sweeps the United States. German measles can cause birth defects. Women contracting German measles seek abortions.

1967–70 Twelve states pass laws liberalizing abortion.

1967   The British Parliament passes the Abortion Act of 1967, permitting abortion until viability for mental or physical health reasons.

1967   Colorado, North Carolina, and California are the first three states to pass reform laws that make legal abortions available under some circumstances.

The National Organization for Women includes a "Right of Women to Control Their Reproductive Lives" in its NOW Bill of Rights.

1968   NARAL (National Association for the Reform of Abortion Laws) is formed. NARAL later changed its name to National Abortion Rights Action League.

President Johnson's Advisory Committee on the Status of Women recommends the repeal of all abortion laws.

1969   California Supreme Court decides a case holding that the right to abortion is protected by the Constitution (*California v. Belous*).

1970   Hawaii, New York, Alaska, and Washington repeal their abortion laws, leaving the decision in private hands.

1973   Supreme Court decides *Roe v. Wade* and *Doe v. Bolton*.

1974   For the first time abortion becomes an issue in congressional elections.

1975   Catholic bishops initiate a political action plan, organized in the parishes, to combat abortion.

1976   The Republican and Democratic parties adopt abortion planks in their platforms for the presidential election.

A right-to-life candidate, Ellen McCormack, enters the presidential race.

First major abortion case since *Roe v. Wade* decided by the Supreme Court (*Planned Parenthood of Central Missouri v. Danforth*).

1977   Medicaid decisions. The Supreme Court holds that neither the Constitution nor the Social Security Act requires states or the federal government to fund nonmedical abortions.

1978   Pregnancy Disability Act of 1978. Forbids discrimination in pay or benefits on the basis of pregnancy.

1980   Republican and Democratic platforms adopt opposing positions on abortion in the presidential campaign.

President Carter states that he is personally opposed to abortion and does not support the pro-abortion plank in the Democratic platform.

President Reagan elected with strong support by opponents of abortion. Promises to appoint justices to the Supreme Court who oppose abortion.

1981   President Reagan appoints the first woman justice, Sandra Day O'Connor, to the Supreme Court. She is opposed by anti-abortionists who are afraid her views on abortion are too liberal.

Proposed Human Life Statute introduced in Congress (Senator Helms, Republican, North Carolina).

Congressional hearings held on the proposed Human Life Statute and on proposed amendments to the Constitution that would return the control of abortion to the states.

1982   "Army of God," an anti-abortion group, firebombs an abortion clinic in Illinois and kidnaps the doctor and his wife.

An AP-NBC News poll shows that 75 percent of Americans oppose a proposed constitutional amendment to ban abortions.

The Senate Judiciary Committee, voting ten to seven, approves a proposed constitutional amendment that would return the abortion issue to the states.

The Justice Department files a brief in a Supreme Court case that implies that *Roe v. Wade* was wrongly decided and urges the Court to defer to state laws restricting abortion rights.

1983   On the tenth anniversary of *Roe v. Wade* about 26,000 people march on the Capitol to protest the ruling.

President Reagan announces his continued support of legislation to restrict abortion.

A Roman Catholic archbishop demands the resignation of a nun, the director of the Michigan State Department of Social Services, because of her refusal to oppose state payments for abortions.

Margaret M. Heckler, nominated to be secretary of Health and Human Services by President Reagan, testifies to her long-standing opposition to abortion.

The Senate Judiciary Committee sends a proposed constitutional amendment on abortion to the full Senate. The Senate rejects the amendment 50–59 (approval requires a two-thirds vote).

Five Democratic candidates for president assert their support for abortion rights.

A Texas doctor is found guilty of murdering a fetus in a 1979 abortion.

The National Conference of Bishops announces that it will renew its anti-abortion campaign.

Congress passes an appropriations bill that bars the use of federal funds for abortions unless the life of the mother is endangered.

1984   President Reagan, in his State of the Union Address, urges that abortion be banned.

The FBI investigates the bombing of abortion clinics in different parts of the country.

Archbishop John J. O'Connor of New York urges Catholics to vote against political candidates who approve abortion.

Planned Parenthood announces a survey showing that the number of abortions declined in 1982, the first such change since 1973.

The Republican Party platform endorses a human life amendment to the Constitution.

Walter Mondale, Democratic candidate for president, reiterates his support of abortion rights and opposes a constitutional amendment banning abortion.

Justice Blackmun receives a death threat, and Supreme Court proceedings are interrupted by an anti-abortion demonstrator.

Voters in Colorado ban state funding of abortion.

1985 In his State of the Union Address, President Reagan asks Congress for legislation to protect the unborn.

The film "The Silent Scream" is shown on Jerry Falwell's television show. The film contends that fetuses feel pain during abortions.

A shot is fired into Justice Blackmun's apartment.

Death threats are received by Justice Lewis Powell and Senator Alphonse D'Amato (Republican, New York).

The Alan Guttmacher Institute reports that the rate of teenage pregnancies in the United States is twice that of other industrialized countries.

Attorney General Edwin Meese III states that the Justice Department will appoint federal judges who believe in "the sanctity of life."

The National Abortion Rights Action League (NARAL) announces a "Silent No More" campaign, urging women to speak out about abortion experiences.

Acting Solicitor General of the United States Charles Fried files a brief for the United States in *Thornburgh v. American College of Obstetricians and Gynecologists* asking the Supreme Court to overrule *Roe v. Wade*.

NARAL and other pro-choice groups and eighty-one members of Congress file a brief opposing the government's position.

President Reagan withdraws funding for the UN Fund for Population Activities to protest coercive abortion policies in China.

Bomb and arson attacks on abortion clinics occur in five states.

Clinic bombers are sentenced to prison in Maryland.

Anti-abortion proposals are turned down in referenda on the ballots in three New England towns.

The Supreme Court hears arguments in two new abortion cases. It denies a request of the U.S. government to participate in the oral arguments.

1986 President Reagan proclaims January 19 National Sanctity of Life Day. He addresses the annual March for Life.

President Reagan's State of the Union Address includes a statement supporting a right to life for the unborn.

The National Organization for Women (NOW) stages a pro-choice March for Women's Lives in Washington, D.C. An estimated 85,000–125,000 attend.

The House Select Committee on Children, Youth and Families releases a report on teenage pregnancy predicting (annually) 1 million pregnancies, 400,000 abortions, and 500,000 births. The report says that 55 percent of the births will be to unmarried mothers.

The Supreme Court ruling in *Thornburgh v. American College of Obstetricians and Gynecologists* reaffirms *Roe v. Wade* by a vote of 5–4.

NOW files a lawsuit against Joseph Scheidler and the Pro-Life Action League seeking a court order that would stop harassment of abortion clinics.

President Reagan nominates William Rehnquist to be chief justice of the United States, replacing Chief Justice Warren E. Burger. Antonin Scalia is nominated as associate justice. The Senate confirms both appointments.

The French announce successful tests of RU–486, a drug that could cause safe and simple abortions within ten days of a missed menstrual period.

1987 Justice Lewis F. Powell retires and Robert Bork is nominated as his replacement. The Senate rejects his nomination. Judge Anthony Kennedy is nominated and confirmed.

The Department of Health and Human Services rules that family planning clinics that receive federal funds may not offer abortion counseling (the so-called gag rule).

During his confirmation hearings for the post of attorney general, Richard Thornburgh states that the 1973 Supreme Court decision on abortion was wrong.

1988 Police arrest anti-abortion protesters in Atlanta. Operation Rescue stages a massive assault on abortion clinics during the Republican National Convention.

The Democratic Party platform includes a plank advocating freedom of reproductive choice.

The Republican Party platform supports a right to life for the unborn child.

Democratic presidential nominee Michael Dukakis states that the abortion decision must be left to individual women.

George Bush is elected on a right-to-life platform.

1989 President Bush addresses an anti-abortion rally in the District of Columbia. He states that *Roe v. Wade* was wrong.

Rumania rescinds an absolute ban on abortions.

The Food and Drug Administration bans the importation of RU-486, a drug that induces early abortions by preventing the implantation of a fertilized egg.

The Supreme Court hands down a decision in *Webster v. Reproductive Services* that does not explicitly overrule *Roe v. Wade*, but gives a signal that the Court will defer to state legislation limiting abortions.

The convention of the National Organization for Women promises a political fight to reverse the *Webster* decision.

Governors in Virginia and New Jersey win elections on platforms favoring abortion rights. Local abortion rights candidates win in California.

Pennsylvania enacts a new law severely restricting abortion.

A freedom of reproductive choice bill is introduced in Congress; it attempts to secure reproductive rights with a federal statute.

Rally for Safe and Legal Abortions in the District of Columbia has an estimated 300,000–600,000 participants.

Norma McCorvey (aka Jane Roe) has her house blasted by shotgun fire.

1990   Republican Party National Chairman Lee Atwater asks the Republican Party to soften its stance on abortion to attract voters.

Guam enacts a law barring all abortions except where a woman's life is threatened.

A Washington, D.C., anti-abortion rally draws 200,000 pro-life demonstrators.

Justice William Brennan retires. President Bush nominates David Souter as an associate justice, and Souter is confirmed by the Senate.

The National Conference of Roman Catholic Bishops hires a public relations firm to mount an anti-abortion campaign.

Cardinal John O'Connor of New York warns Roman Catholics that they risk excommunication for supporting legal abortion.

Connecticut passes a statute guaranteeing abortion rights under state law.

The Supreme Court upholds two state laws requiring notification of parents when minors seek abortions (*Hodgson v. Minnesota; Ohio v. Akron Center for Reproductive Health*).

1991   Utah enacts a strict anti-abortion statute.

Maryland enacts a bill liberalizing access to abortion.

Louisiana enacts stringent restrictions on abortion.

A federal judge orders U.S. marshalls to Wichita, Kansas, to protect abortion clinics against violence.

Candidates running for president in 1992 mark out their positions on abortion.

The Supreme Court upholds a gag rule forbidding clinics receiving federal funds from giving patients information on abortions (*Rust v. Sullivan*).

Justice Thurgood Marshall retires. President Bush nominates Clarence Thomas as associate justice. Thomas is confirmed by the Senate by a narrow margin.

1992   New York revokes the medical licenses of two doctors for botched abortions.

The Irish Supreme Court allows a pregnant fourteen-year-old girl to go to England for an abortion, overruling the Irish attorney general.

Operation Rescue blocks abortion clinics in Buffalo, N.Y.

Virginia passes a parental notification bill. It is vetoed by the governor.

A restrictive abortion law in Guam is struck down by a federal court.

Kansas passes a restrictive abortion law. It also increases penalties for persons blockading abortion clinics.

The German parliament passes a law easing restrictions on abortion. The law is later blocked by the German Federal Constitutional Court.

The presidential candidates take stands on abortion. Clinton and Perot support, President Bush opposes, abortion rights.

Congress passes legislation to allow tissue from aborted fetuses to be used for medical research. Vetoed by President Bush.

Congress passes a law nullifying the gag rule. Vetoed by President Bush.

The Supreme Court upholds a Pennsylvania law limiting abortions, but refuses to overturn *Roe v. Wade* (*Planned Parenthood of Southeastern Pennsylvania v. Casey*).

1993 Governor Bill Clinton of Arkansas is elected President of the United States. He promises to seek areas of compromise on the abortion issue.

Bill Clinton takes office as President of the United States. Remove four federal restrictions on abortion by executive order.

The Supreme Court refuses to allow use of a provision of the Civil Rights Act of 1871 to enjoin anti-abortion demonstrations that block abortion clinics. (*Bray v. Alexandria Women's Health Clinic*).

The Supreme Court lets stand court decisions overturning restrictive abortion laws in Guam and Louisiana. Restrictive North Dakota law goes into effect while awaiting appellate court review.

Dr. David Gunn, who performed abortions, is shot and killed in Pensacola, Florida.

Roussel-Uclef S.A. of France, maker of the abortion pill RU-486, agrees to license the drug in the United States.

Dr. Milan M. Vuitch, a doctor involved in the early abortion reform movement, dies in Washington, D.C.

The German Federal Constitutional Court finds that life begins at conception and strikes down laws easing restrictions on abortion in western Germany.

The House of Representatives passes a spending bill for the District of Columbia that allows the District to use local funding to pay for abortions for poor women.

The House of Representatives retains the Hyde Amendment, restricting federal funding for abortions except for victims of rape and incest.

The Freedom of Choice bill stalls in Congress because of disputes over wording.

The Treasury funding bill drops ban on including coverage of abortions in health insurance plans of federal employees.

A doctor providing abortion services is shot and wounded outside an abortion clinic in Wichita, Kansas. A doctor and owner of abortion clinics is shot to death in Alabama.

Gallup poll finds that 58% of Roman Catholics do not believe all abortions should be banned; 84% disagree with Catholic Church ban on artificial birth control.

Ruth Bader Ginsburg takes oath as Associate Justice of the Supreme Court, replacing Byron R. White.

Joycelyn Elders is confirmed as Surgeon General of the United States, in spite of outspoken views on abortion.

The Supreme Court opens new term. New case, *National Organization for Women v. Scheidler*, will decide whether anti-racketeering statute (RICO) can be used against groups that block abortion clinics.

George F. Allen (Republican) is elected Governor of Virginia, with strong backing by opponents of abortion.

Index

ABA, Code of Judicial Ethics, 255

Abortion: access to, 183–85, 206, 235; alternatives to, 230–31, 239, 243; as birth control method, 58–59, 145; conferences on, 37–42; costs of, 145; as crime, 1, 2, 4, 6–7, 25–26; dangers of, 204, 206, 208, 215; death rate from, 39, 67, 76–78, 87–88; in early America, 11, 12; in early twentieth century, 18, 40–41; government policies toward, 45, 57–62, 74–75, 103–4; illegal, 2, 18, 19, 22–25, 25–26, 37–42, 45, 49, 50, 53, 54, 55, 56, 57, 59, 60–62, 75, 76–78, 90–96, 127, 145, 151, 208; legalization of, 19, 76–78; morality of, 22–25, 39–40, 56, 109–16, 141–43, 220, 237; in nineteenth century, 12–26; philosophical arguments about, 110–16; physical and psychological impact, 234, 276–78; procedures and technology, 18, 45, 64–67, 75–78, 204, 257; public funding, 183–85, 230–31, 239, 244, 288; and public opinion, 103–8; and racial arguments, 27–31, 206–7; self, 23–24, 33, 37, 61, 66–67, 208; statistics, 41–42, 75–78, 208; therapeutic, 2, 4, 14, 18, 38, 39, 46, 50, 56, 69, 87, 90–96, 206

abortion clinics, 263–66; false, 234–35; regulation of, 271–72; violence against, 234, 273–77, 287

abortion counseling, 235, 265–66, 267–69

Abortion in the United States, 37

abortion law reform, 42, 46, 50–58, 60–62, 71, 74–75, 79–90, 117

abortion law repeal, 57–62, 63, 79

abortion laws (state) before 1973, 4, 13, 25–26, 38, 46, 55–57, 60–62, 73–74, 131–39, 162; constitutional challenges, 46

abortion referrals, 51–55, 90–93, 264–65; services, 147

Abortion Rights Mobilization (ARM), 51

abortion rights organizations, 171–72

abortionists, 12, 14, 16, 21, 33, 37, 39, 45, 49, 53, 63, 66–67, 97–99, 208; prosecutions of, 90–96

Abramowicz v. Lefkowitz, 90

Abzug, Bella S., 202–4

adoption, 151, 202, 206

Africa, 100

African Americans, 27, 28, 199–200, 204–7

Akron, Ohio, city ordinance, 178, 259–60

Alabama, 154

About the Editor

EVA R. RUBIN is Professor of Political Science and Public Administration at North Carolina State University. She is the author of *Abortion, Politics and the Courts* (Greenwood Press, 1987, rev. edition) and *The Supreme Court and the American Family* (Greenwood Press, 1986).